Karl Marx

The International Library of Essays in Classical Sociology
Series Editors: Alan Sica and David Chalcraft

Titles in the Series:

Charlotte Perkins Gilman
Patricia Lengermann and
Gillian Niebrugge-Brantley

Talcott Parsons
Victor Lidz

Karl Marx
Bertell Ollman and Kevin B. Anderson

W.E.B. Du Bois
Reiland Rabaka

Max Weber
Alan Sica

Emile Durkheim
Ivan Strenski

Karl Marx

Edited by

Bertell Ollman

New York University, USA

Kevin B. Anderson

University of California, Santa Barbara, USA

ASHGATE

© Bertell Ollman and Kevin B. Anderson 2012. For copyright of individual articles please refer to the Acknowledgements.

All rights reserved. No part of this publication may be reproduced, stored in a retrieval system or transmitted in any form or by any means, electronic, mechanical, photocopying, recording or otherwise without the prior permission of the publisher.

Wherever possible, these reprints are made from a copy of the original printing, but these can themselves be of very variable quality. Whilst the publisher has made every effort to ensure the quality of the reprint, some variability may inevitably remain.

Published by
Ashgate Publishing Limited
Wey Court East
Union Road
Farnham
Surrey GU9 7PT
England

Ashgate Publishing Company
Suite 420
101 Cherry Street
Burlington
VT 05401-4405
USA

www.ashgate.com

British Library Cataloguing in Publication Data
Karl Marx. – (The international library of essays in
  classical sociology)
  1. Marx, Karl, 1818–1883. 2. Communism and society.
  3. Philosophy, Marxist.
  I. Series II. Ollman, Bertell. III. Anderson, Kevin, 1948–
  335.4–dc22

Library of Congress Control Number: 2011934979

ISBN 9780754677574

Printed and bound in Great Britain by the
MPG Books Group, UK

Contents

Acknowledgements	ix
Series Preface	xiii
Introduction	xv

PART I THEORY AND METHOD

1 Georg Lukács (1972), 'Reification and the Consciousness of the
Proletariat', in *History and Class Consciousness*, Cambridge, MA:
MIT Press, pp. 83–103.   3

2 Raya Dunayevskaya (2000), 'The Age of Revolutions: Industrial,
Social-Political, Intellectual', in *Marxism and Freedom: From 1776
until Today*, New York: Humanity Books, pp. 27–37.   27

3 Bertell Ollman (1990), 'Putting Dialectics to Work: The Process of
Abstraction in Marx's Method', *Rethinking Marxism*, **3**, pp. 26–74.   41

4 Peter G. Stillman (1983), 'The Unity of Science and Revolution:
Marxism as Critique' (also appeared as 'Marx's Enterprise of Critique'),
in Roland Pennock (ed.), *Marxism*, New York: New York University Press,
pp. 252–76.   91

5 Hilde Weiss (and Karl Marx) (1979), 'Karl Marx's "Enquête Ouvrière"',
in Tom Bottomore (ed.), *Karl Marx*, Oxford: Basil Blackwell, pp. 172–84.   117

PART II POLITICAL ECONOMY

6 David McNally (2008), 'From Financial Crisis to World Slump:
Accumulation, Financialization, and the Global Slowdown', presented at
Historical Materialism Conference, London, 8 November 2008, pp. 133–54.   133

7 Martha E. Gimenez (2007), 'Self-Sourcing: How Corporations Get Us To
Work Without Pay!', *Monthly Review*, **59**, pp. 37–41.   155

8 Fredy Perlman (1972), *The Reproduction of Daily Life*, Detroit, MI: Black
and Red Books, pp. 1–24.   161

9 Immanuel Wallerstein (1974), 'The Rise and Future Demise of the World
Capitalist System: Concepts for Comparative Analysis', *Comparative Studies
in Society and History*, **16**, pp. 387–415.   183

10 David Harvey (2004), 'The "New" Imperialism: Accumulation by
Dispossession', *Socialist Register*, **40**, pp. 62–87.   213

vi   *Karl Marx*

PART III STATE AND POLITICS

11 Michael Parenti (1990), 'The Constitution as an Elitist Document',
in Bertell Ollman and Jonathan Birnbaum (eds), *The United States
Constitution: 200 Years of Anti-federalist, Abolitionist, Feminist,
Muckraking, Progressive, and Especially Socialist Criticism*, New York:
New York University Press, pp. 141–62.   241
12 Franz Neumann (1973), 'The Monopolistic Economy: Property and
Contract', a selection from *Behemoth: The Structure and Practice of
National Socialism, 1933–1944*, as reprinted in Jeffry Kaplow (ed.),
Western Civilization: Mainstream Readings and Radical Critiques,
New York: Knopf, pp. 353–62.   263
13 Vincent Navarro (2006), 'The Worldwide Class Struggle', *Monthly Review*,
58, pp. 18–33.   273
14 Karl Renner (1979), 'The Economic and Social Functions of the Legal
Institutions', in Tom Bottomore (ed.), *Karl Marx*, Oxford: Basil Blackwell,
pp. 123–7.   289
15 Nicos Poulantzas (1969), 'The Problem of the Capitalist State', *New Left
Review*, **58**, pp. 67–87, and Ralph Miliband (1970), 'The Capitalist State:
Reply to Nicos Poulantzas', *New Left Review*, **59**, pp. 53–60.   295
16 Ernest Mandel (1994), 'The Marxist Case for Revolution Today', in
Steve Bloom (ed.), *Revolutionary Marxism and Social Reality in the
20th Century: Collected Essays of Ernest Mandel*, Atlantic Highlands, NJ:
Humanities Press, pp. 179–206 (originally appeared in *Socialist Register*,
25, [1989], pp. 159–84).   315

PART IV THE INDIVIDUAL AND SOCIETY

17 Erich Fromm (1989), 'Psychoanalysis and Sociology', in Stephen Eric
Bronner and Douglas MacKay Kellner (eds), *Critical Theory and Society:
A Reader*, New York: Routledge, pp. 37–9.   345
18 Ellen Meiksins Wood (1990), 'The Uses and Abuses of "Civil Society"',
Socialist Register, **26**, pp. 60–84.   349
19 Georg Rusche (1978), 'Labor Market and Penal Sanction: Thoughts on the
Sociology of Criminal Justice', *Crime and Social Justice*, **10**, pp. 1–8. 375
20 Michael D. Yates (2008), 'The Injuries of Class', *Monthly Review*, **59**,
pp. 1–10.   385
21 Sut Jhally and Bill Livant (1991), 'Sports and Cultural Politics: The
Attraction of Modern Spectator Sports', *Rethinking Marxism*, **4**, pp. 121–7. 395

PART V CULTURE AND RELIGION

22 Max Horkheimer and Theodor W. Adorno, trans. Edmund Jephcott (2002),
    excerpt from 'The Culture Industry: Enlightenment as Mass Deception',
    in *Dialectic of Enlightenment: Philosophical Fragments*, Stanford, CA:
    Stanford University Press, pp. 94–111, 268–9.   405
23 Paul Werner (2012), 'Museum, Inc.: Inside the Global Art World
    (Over-the-Cliff Notes)', pp. 1–11.   425
24 Fredric Jameson (1991), excerpt from 'The Cultural Logic of Late
    Capitalism', in *Postmodernism, or the Cultural Logic of Late Capitalism*,
    Durham, NC: Duke University Press, pp. 1–16 (originally appeared in
    New Left Review, **146** (1984), pp. 53–64).   437
25 Ishay Landa (2005), 'Aroma and Shadow: Marx vs. Nietzsche on Religion',
    Nature, Society, and Thought, **18**, pp. 461–99.   455

PART VI HISTORY

26 E.P. Thompson (1963), 'Exploitation', in *The Making of the English
    Working Class*, London: Victor Gollancz, pp. 189–212.   497
27 Perry Anderson (1974), 'The Feudal Mode of Production', in *Passages
    from Antiquity to Feudalism*, London: New Left Books, pp. 147–54.   521
28 G.E.M. de Ste. Croix (1981), 'The Decline and Fall of Rome', excerpts
    from *Class Struggle in the Ancient Greek World: From the Archaic Age
    to the Arab Conquest*, London: Duckworth, pp. 453, 497–503.   529

PART VII COLONIALISM, RACE AND GENDER

29 C.L.R. James (writing under the name J.R. Johnson) (1943), 'Negroes in
    the Civil War: Their Role in the Second American Revolution', *New
    International*, **9**, pp. 338–41.   541
30 Oliver C. Cox (1948), excerpts from 'Race Relations – Its Meaning,
    Beginning, and Progress', in *Caste, Class, and Race: A Study in Social
    Dynamics*, New York: Monthly Review Press, pp. 321–35.   549
31 Nancy C.M. Hartsock (1983), 'The Feminist Standpoint: Developing the
    Ground for a Specifically Feminist Historical Materialism', in Sandra
    Harding and Merrill B. Hintikka (eds), *Discovering Reality: Feminist
    Perspectives on Epistemology, Metaphysics, Methodology, and Philosophy
    of Science*, Boston: D. Reidel, pp. 283–310.   565
32 Kevin B. Anderson (2002), 'Marx's Late Writings on Non-Western and
    Precapitalist Societies and Gender', *Rethinking Marxism*, **14**, pp. 84–96.   593

PART VIII ECOLOGY

33 John Bellamy Foster (2002), 'Marx's Ecology in Historical Perspective',
    International Socialism Journal, **96**, pp. 71–86.   609
34 Paul Burkett (2005), 'Marx's Vision of Sustainable Human Development',
    Monthly Review, **57**, pp. 34–62.   623

Name Index   653

Acknowledgements

Ashgate would like to thank our researchers and the contributing authors who provided copies, along with the following for their permission to reprint copyright material:-

American Enterprise Institute for Public Research for the essay: Michael Parenti (1990), 'The Constitution as an Elitist Document', in Bertell Ollman and Jonathan Birnbaum (eds), *The United States Constitution: 200 Years of Anti-federalist, Abolitionist, Feminist, Muckraking, Progressive, and Especially Socialist Criticism*, New York: New York University Press, pp. 141–62.

Cambridge University Press for the essay: Immanuel Wallerstein (1974), 'The Rise and Future Demise of the World Capitalist System: Concepts for Comparative Analysis', *Comparative Studies in Society and History*, **16**, pp. 387–415.

David McNally for his essay: David McNally (2008), 'From Financial Crisis to World Slump: Accumulation, Financialization, and the Global Slowdown', presented at Historical Materialism Conference, London, 8 November 2008.

John Bellamy Foster for his essay: John Bellamy Foster (2002), 'Marx's Ecology in Historical Perspective', *International Socialism Journal*, **96**, pp. 71–86.

MEP Publications for the essay: Ishay Landa (2005), 'Aroma and Shadow: Marx vs. Nietzsche on Religion', *Nature, Society, and Thought*, **18**, pp. 461–99.

Merlin Press for the essays: David Harvey (2004), 'The "New" Imperialism: Accumulation by Dispossession', *Socialist Register*, **40**, pp. 62–87; Ernest Mandel (1994), 'The Marxist Case for Revolution Today', in Steve Bloom (ed.), *Revolutionary Marxism and Social Reality in the 20th Century: Collected Essays of Ernest Mandel*, Atlantic Highlands, NJ: Humanities Press, pp. 179–206 (originally appeared in *Socialist Register*, **25**, [1989], pp. 159–84).; Ellen Meiksins Wood (1990), 'The Uses and Abuses of "Civil Society"', *Socialist Register*, **26**, pp. 60–84.

MIT Press for the essay: Georg Lukács (1972), 'Reification and the Consciousness of the Proletariat', in *History and Class Consciousness*, Cambridge, MA: MIT Press, pp. 83–103.

Monthly Review Foundation for the essays: Martha E. Gimenez (2007), 'Self-Sourcing: How Corporations Get Us To Work Without Pay!', *Monthly Review*, **59**, pp. 37–41; Vincent Navarro (2006), 'The Worldwide Class Struggle', *Monthly Review*, **58**, pp. 18–33; Michael D. Yates (2008), 'The Injuries of Class', *Monthly Review*, **59**, pp. 1–10; Paul Burkett (2005), 'Marx's Vision of Sustainable Human Development', *Monthly Review*, **57**, pp. 34–62.

New Left Review for the essays: Nicos Poulantzas (1969), 'The Problem of the Capitalist State', *New Left Review*, **58**, pp. 67–78, and Ralph Miliband (1970), 'The Capitalist State: Reply to Nicos Poulantzas', *New Left Review*, **59**, pp. 53–60; Fredric Jameson (1991), excerpt from 'The Cultural Logic of Late Capitalism', in *Postmodernism, or the Cultural Logic of Late Capitalism*, Durham, NC: Duke University Press, pp. 1–16 (originally appeared in *New Left Review*, **146** (1984), pp. 53–64).

New York University Press for the essay: Peter G. Stillman (1983), 'The Unity of Science and Revolution: Marxism as Critique' (also appeared as 'Marx's Enterprise of Critique'), in Roland Pennock (ed.), *Marxism*, New York: New York University Press, pp. 252–76. Copyright © 1983 by New York University.

Paul Werner for his essay: Paul Werner (2012), 'Museum, Inc.: Inside the Global Art World (Over-the-Cliff Notes)', pp. 1–11.

Random House, Inc. for the essay: E.P. Thompson (1963), 'Exploitation', in *The Making of the English Working Class*, London: Victor Gollancz, pp. 189–212. Copyright © 1963 by E.P. Thompson. Used by permission of Pantheon Books, a division of Random House, Inc.

Social Justice for the essay: Georg Rusche (1978), 'Labor Market and Penal Sanction: Thoughts on the Sociology of Criminal Justice', *Crime and Social Justice*, **10**, pp 1–8.

Springer for the essay: Nancy C.M. Hartsock (1983), 'The Feminist Standpoint: Developing the Ground for a Specifically Feminist Historical Materialism', in Sandra Harding and Merrill B. Hintikka (eds), *Discovering Reality: Feminist Perspectives on Epistemology, Metaphysics, Methodology, and Philosophy of Science*, Boston: D. Reidel, pp. 283–310. Copyright © 1983 by D. Reidel Publishing Company.

Stanford University Press for the essay: Max Horkheimer and Theodor W. Adorno, trans. Edmund Jephcott (2002), excerpt from 'The Culture Industry: Enlightenment as Mass Deception', in *Dialectic of Enlightenment: Philosophical Fragments*, Stanford, CA: Stanford University Press, pp. 94–111, 268–69. Copyright © 1944 by Social Studies Association, NY. New edition Copyright © S. Fisher Verlag GmbH, Frankfurt am Main, 1969; English trans. Copyright © 2002 Board of Trustees of Leland Stanford Jr. University.

Taylor & Francis for the essays: Bertell Ollman (1990), 'Putting Dialectics to Work: The Process of Abstraction in Marx's Method', *Rethinking Marxism*, **3**, pp. 26–74. Copyright © 1990 Association for Economic and Social Analysis; Sut Jhally and Bill Livant (1991), 'Sports and Cultural Politics: The Attraction of Modern Spectator Sports', *Rethinking Marxism*, **4**, pp. 121–7. Copyright © 1991 Association for Economic and Social Analysis; Kevin B. Anderson (2002), 'Marx's Late Writings on Non-Western and Precapitalist Societies and Gender', *Rethinking Marxism*, **14**, pp. 84–96. Copyright © 2002 Association for Economic and Social Analysis.

Taylor & Francis Group LLC - Books for the essay: Erich Fromm (1989), 'Psychoanalysis and Sociology', in Stephen Eric Bronner and Douglas MacKay Kellner (eds), *Critical Theory and Society: A Reader*, New York: Routledge, pp. 37–9.

The Oliver Cromwell Cox Institute for the essay: Oliver C. Cox (1948), excerpts from 'Race Relations – Its Meaning, Beginning, and Progress', in *Caste, Class, and Race: A Study in Social Dynamics*, New York: Monthly Review Press, pp. 321–35.

Verso for the essay: Perry Anderson (1974), 'The Feudal Mode of Production', in *Passages from Antiquity to Feudalism*, London: New Left Books, pp. 147–54.

Wiley for the essays: Hilde Weiss (and Karl Marx) (1979), 'Karl Marx's "Enquête Ouvrière"', in Tom Bottomore (ed.), *Karl Marx*, Oxford: Basil Blackwell, pp. 172–84. Reproduced with permission of Blackwell Publishing Ltd; Karl Renner (1979), 'The Economic and Social Functions of the Legal Institutions', in Tom Bottomore (ed.), *Karl Marx*, Oxford: Basil Blackwell, pp. 123–7. Reproduced with permission of Blackwell Publishing Ltd.

Every effort has been made to trace all the copyright holders, but if any have been inadvertently overlooked the publishers will be pleased to make the necessary arrangement at the first opportunity.

Publisher's Note:

The material in this volume has been reproduced using the facsimile method. This means we can retain the original pagination to facilitate easy and correct citation of the original essays. It also explains the variety of typefaces, page layouts and numbering.

Series Preface

Twenty years ago the so-called canon wars raged throughout the social sciences in Europe and the anglophone sphere. The argument was then heard in all quarters that deconstruction, globalization, post-colonialism, computerization, queer theory, and other similar forces had rendered 19th century social theory impotent and irrelevant to the analysis of the new cultural environment. Whereas between 1920 and about 1985, serious engagement with Marx, Durkheim, Weber, Simmel, and other members of the classical pantheon were required components of theorizing, the backlash against this tradition threatened to relegate this astonishing body of scholarship to a poorly imagined, unnecessary past. Recognizing that this storm is passing, and that younger scholars are rediscovering just how pertinent to contemporary issues the classics have remained, this new series will put at their disposal a set of volumes which aim to provide handy, expert guidance in the search for useable materials from the classical tradition. Volumes treating Marx, Durkheim, Weber, Gilmore, Du Bois, Spencer, Simmel, and Parsons will appear first, to be followed by others covering theorists of similar rank. Each volume will be prepared by a recognized authority, whose task is to locate the best and most useful articles from the scholarly journal literature in English, assemble them in a meaningful pattern which best illuminates a given theorist's lasting importance, and write an introduction by means of which novices, in particular, can confidently discover for themselves why 'the classics' remain vital and necessary to their work. Whereas multi-volume sets with similar intentions appeared some time ago, this series has the virtue of being less cumbersome and more up-to-date, featuring a propitious mix of classic statements in the secondary literature, as well as the newest contributions to the ongoing reappropriation of 'the canon'. Our goal is to provide serious scholars, from novice to senior, with enough material to become conversant with a classic theorist's work, all within the covers of a single volume.

ALAN SICA and DAVID CHALCRAFT
Series Editors

Introduction

I

What makes for a good Marxist article? What kind of problems do Marxists tend to study? What do they highlight ... call into question ... try to explain ... and to change? And how do they do this ... coming from what assumptions, with what aims ... and privileging which social divisions, vantage points and categories? None of these questions are put to rest in this book. Ours is the more modest effort of obtaining partial answers by providing examples of outstanding work on a wide variety of topics by some of the leading Marxist scholars of the last hundred years. We also wish to show some of what the broad Marxist tradition has already achieved and to offer a selection of these essays as possible models for emulation by others interested in these matters. It should be clear that there is no Marxist orthodoxy on display here, but rather a family of approaches inspired by the writings of Marx and, to a lesser extent, his lifetime collaborator, Frederick Engels.

The current economic crisis has sparked a renewed interest among all manner of people in Marx's thinking on crisis and on economics more generally. But just as the latter provides the indispensable context in which to grasp the former, all of Marx's writings on sociology, politics, culture, history, alienation, revolution, communism, dialectics and much else are directly or indirectly related to his systematic analysis of capitalist political economy, one part of which is his theory of crisis. Given the prevailing division of knowledge into the separate subject matters of competing academic disciplines (sociology is probably least guilty here), it is not surprising that most people restrict their study of Marxism to one or two isolated patterns in what is a complex tapestry of intersecting and overlapping ideas. But if none of the parts – no matter how large – can be adequately understood closed off from its essential connections to the rest, what can we expect from this approach? At a time when the personal and political stakes involved in grasping Marx's analysis of our worsening economic plight have never been higher, the need to acquire a more rounded knowledge of Marx's ideas has become more important than ever.

Thus, while any of the essays in this volume can be read with profit on its own, this also means that the more one reads into the book – even from sections that seem to have little to do with each other – the better one will be able to grasp what came before. Ideally – though we dare not insist on it – to receive the full benefit, one should consider reading the entire book, though it is probably a good idea to start with the section that is of greatest interest.

There is, of course, no real replacement for Marx's own writings as a privileged source for understanding his ideas, but, as we know, Marx never got to do his planned books on the state, or on dialectics, or on several other crucial topics. Nor did he ever finish his major work on political economy. For the most part, we are limited in our effort to understand Marx's system to the handful of books he did publish (including several works co-authored by Engels), books based on his drafts that were heavily edited by Engels and later by Karl Kautsky, and published by them, an extensive collection of unfinished writings and notes, and a wide assortment of articles, manifestos, speeches and letters. Not only is the bulk of this work in various states of undress, but several areas that Marx himself recognized as especially important to complete his system never got the attention he wanted to give them. Now if we add to this the need to take account of what has occurred in capitalism since Marx's death (what some have referred to as 'bringing Marxism up to date'), then one can see why a collective work – like ours – that builds on what Marx said but also only suggested, and uses both to analyse more recent developments, including some in spheres that Marx neglected, is not only justified but necessary if we are to make effective use of all that Marxism has to contribute to the construction of a better world.

II

The best way to approach what is most distinctive about Marxist scholarship may be to contrast it to a couple of its main competitors within the American academy. Positivism is the belief, particularly widespread in the social sciences, that knowledge accumulates through empirical study of one or more easily separable features in the world before us. After hypothesizing a causal relationship between two or more of these features, case studies are undertaken to determine whether what was expected actually occurs. The result is then presented in quantitative terms to allow for generalizations that are referred to as 'theories'. In attempting to reproduce a method that has been so successful in the natural sciences, however, those who practise this approach have to make the following assumptions:

1. That the object(s) of study can be easily separated from its larger context (neither the system(s) in which it exists nor its history is given much if any attention).
2. That whatever is studied can be found elsewhere or is repeated often enough to permit the instances in which it occurs to be counted (unique conditions and events are declared off limits for scientific investigation with the proviso 'All things being equal' that accompanies each of the features chosen).
3. That the qualities found in the subject of study are likely to persist, since nothing is known or looked for that has any bearing on what might bring on a change (stasis, equilibrium and, in human terms, harmony are taken as given so that whatever disrupts this situation generally produces surprise).
4. That the beliefs and practices of individuals (even when the subject of study is a group) offer the best opportunity for research that meets the conditions laid down by our first three assumptions (hence, the prevalence of 'methodological individualism').
5. That the class structure of society plays no role in determining which questions get studied (but treating this structure as irrelevant is not the same as showing it is unimportant or that ignoring it in this way does not itself play a role in the class struggle).
6. That any evaluation of the facts studied can only be based on values derived from sources – whether philosophical, religious or psychological – that stand outside the world of facts and have no necessary relations with them ('objectivity' becomes 'neutrality', and neutrality becomes easy).

7. That the sum of what is done here as well as what is assumed in order to do it represents the best of science.

The second approach to knowledge is not nearly as widespread in the academy as positivism or as different as the latter is from Marxism, but it is because of its combination of similarities and differences with Marxism that 'radicalism' (our name for it) can help us bring out what is special about Marxist scholarship. As is evident from the name, radicalism is an approach to knowledge shared by most non-Marxist political, social and cultural radicals. Its chief defining feature is its rejection – particularly for the social sciences and the humanities – of all the assumptions associated with positivism. The members of this otherwise highly diverse group believe that the effort to separate any subject from its own history and larger social context has left the social sciences and to a lesser extent the humanities resembling nothing so much as a zoo, where each animal is kept in a separate cage and deprived of all the conditions and routines needed to show what it really is and can be. What can be learned about an animal, or a human being, or a class of people, or even one of the conditions that shape them when treated in this way? Limited to a relatively small piece of a much more complex whole, the findings of any such study are likely to be partial, one-sided and distorted, or at best trivial. Radical scholars also criticize their positivist opponents for what they view as an obsession with quantification that rules out studying phenomena, no matter how important, that are unique or do not allow easy dissection into numbered parts. But their major complaint is that by its commitment to studying what is precise, quantifiable, a-systemic, a-historical and, at least for the moment, apparently unchanging, the positivist approach is biased on behalf of the status quo and, therefore, if only by implication, of the classes and other groups that benefit from it.

Believing that no one can be neutral 'on a moving train' (Howard Zinn's metaphor for the evolving clashes that characterize our society), most radicals will present their values at the outset of a study, while insisting that their commitments have no bearing on their objectivity, understood as some combination of openness, honesty and the desire to investigate all sides to an issue. Their values will also determine most of the problems they treat, the oppressed group or groups they want to help, and a lot of how they try to help them, including adopting the point of view and occasionally the 'voice' of the victims. Throughout, the facts that are emphasized, the version of the larger system and of history that is introduced as well as the tone and language used all serve the dual purpose of expounding what the study has found and securing a ringing condemnation of the injustices it describes. An alternative vision of a world that is more compatible with the values by which the existing state of affairs has been found wanting generally rounds out a typical work of radical scholarship.

A lot of what we have characterized as radical scholarship can be found in most Marxist works, just as many non-Marxist radicals make use of some of the elements that come out of the Marxist tradition. Like the radicals, Marxists reject the whole set of positivist assumptions listed above, but, rather than simply rail against them, Marxists are usually more interested in uncovering what in the real world these distortions reflect and why – other than through frequent repetition by biased schools and media – so many people have come to accept them. Similarly, the radical insight into the systematic bias that lies behind positivist claims to neutrality is extended by Marxists into an inquiry of how exactly this works and the role it plays in the class struggle.

But the main difference between radical and Marxist scholarship lies in the nature of the system to which most of the subjects they study belong. Radicals can be interested in many systems, political, social, cultural, economic and so on, large and small, of short or long duration, including the whole of society or the whole of nature, and even capitalism, but as a rule no one of these is given absolute priority of place and importance in accounting for the development of the others. Marxists, on the other hand, view capitalism, the system dominated by capital accumulation and whatever that both requires and reproduces, in exactly this way. It is through their place and function in the capitalist totality that all other systems acquire an order, influence, meaning and worth for the range of problems with which Marxists are concerned. While allowing a relative autonomy of various subsystems like family, religion or the state, everything that falls within the capitalist system is affected by it in one way or another, directly or indirectly, more or less (usually more), sooner or later (usually sooner), all the while contributing to the reproduction and development of the very whole that is shaping them. This doesn't prohibit some Marxists from taking culture, politics or other non-economic issues as the starting point for the multifaceted analysis of social forces that places them in the overall context of capital, and we have included a number of these contributions on such subjects as ecology, race, gender, and psychology in this volume.

Singling out capitalism in the above manner, Marxists go on to prioritize its mode of production (the interconnection between production, distribution, exchange and consumption) as the best vantage point from which to view and study the workings and development of the entire system. The same perspective leads one to conclude that the most important social division in this society is between capitalists (as embodiments of the impersonal power of capital), with their chief interest in maximizing profits, and workers who operate their enterprises, with their chief interest in securing higher wages, shorter hours, job security and safe conditions (and indirectly, therefore, in structural change that would secure all this over the long term), all of which would eat into and then eliminate altogether both capitalist profits and the alienated labor on which it depends. The struggle between capital and labour over their incompatible interests extends beyond the enterprise to all the areas of society – politics, education, media, culture, religion and so forth – anywhere that an advantage can be gained for the non-stop battle going on in the economy. Without denying the importance of other divisions of society at particular moments of time and for certain kinds of problems, the success of the economic class struggle in remaking society in its image (which includes the ways this is hidden and denied in ideology) secures for class and the working class in particular a special position in both Marxist analysis and the kind of politics it gives rise to.

With capital accumulation, the mode of production, the division of society into classes, class interests (emerging from the situation of each class but only partly and intermittently present in their thinking) and the class struggle between workers and capitalists as the main focal points of study, Marxists' well-known concern with history is usually directed to locating the preconditions in the past for the development of just these features in the present. It is in this way, and through this form, that the past is viewed as internally related to the present. Similarly, Marx's projection of our likely future is also derived from what he found in his study of capitalism, where both its most impressive achievements and its worst problems are found to contain the 'germs of communism'. It is in this way, and through the form of an as yet unrealized potential, that the probable future is viewed as internally related to the present, and our real past and likely future become essential ingredients of any in-depth Marxist study of capitalism.

Progress on the path that carries capitalism through its various stages to a socialist transformation and on to communism is neither steady nor certain. Marx said 'capitalism is full of contradictions', of mutually dependent processes that are simultaneously supporting and undermining one another, and a good deal of his work involved tracing the relations and evolution of these contradictions throughout society. Consisting of both objective and subjective dimensions, of conditions that pull in more than one direction and people who have to decide which way to go, Marx's contradictions always allow for more than one resolution. Which is not to say that the development of capitalist conditions over time – through a combination of removing some alternatives from the choices that are on offer and making others much more attractive (or unattractive) – do not exert an increasing pressure on workers, through their objective class interests, to resolve the contradictions in which they find themselves by moving in a socialist direction. They do. But communism is not inevitable, and Marx concedes the possibility of a retrogression to barbarism should our efforts to overcome capitalism in a positive manner fail. More recently, we have learned that attempts to build socialism without the basic material and other conditions ('germs of communism') provided by capitalism can also produce tragic results.

Today, however, a worsening economic crisis, the extremes of exploitation and alienation, rapid climate change, spreading pollution, disease, hunger and corruption across the globe, the rise of totalitarian governments, multiple wars and the constant threat of nuclear war are all connected one way or another to a global capitalist system that gives top priority to maximizing profits and treats all its destructive social and natural costs as necessary means or 'externalities' (collateral damage), or both. It is for this sorry plight that Marxism – and only Marxism – offers us an indispensable analysis and class-based political strategy that is adequate to the scale, complexity and urgency of our problems. But it still remains for us to put it into practice.

Do all or even most Marxists fit comfortably in the garment we have just laid out for them? Of course not – and this also applies to the editors of this volume – but it is our belief that, taken together, the outstanding writings we have assembled will fill out its contours remarkably well.

III

Theory and Method

We begin the volume with a section on theory and method. In recent decades, Marx's dialectical method has achieved greater and greater prominence in treatments of his work. Recall that in his 1883 speech at Marx's graveside his comrade Friedrich Engels pronounced Marx's theory of value and surplus value to have been his key theoretical contribution.

By the 1920s, however, the ground was shifting toward the primacy of dialectics: The philosopher Georg Lukács maintained in the opening pages of his influential *History and Class Consciousness* (1923) that the dialectical method was in fact the key to Marxism. We therefore begin Part I – and this book – with Lukács's germinal discussion of reification or fetishism. The first writer to place commodity fetishism at the centre of Marxist theory, Lukács elaborates, in Chapter 1, a concept of capitalism that emphasizes the fragmentation of the worker as characteristic of the most advanced, mechanized capitalist production. He argues further that this reification, wherein human relations in the factory come to resemble those between things, is not limited to the factory, but shapes all human relations under capitalism. In carrying out this analysis, Lukács re-Hegelianizes Marxism.

This pathway is continued in Chapter 2, which is from Raya Dunayevskaya's discussion of the French revolution and Hegelian dialectics in her *Marxism & Freedom* (1958). After sketching the French revolution from a grassroots sans-culotte perspective, Dunayevskaya concludes that where Kant and other Enlightenment philosophers anticipated the revolution philosophically, it was their successor Hegel whose philosophy summed up that period of revolution – and the concomitant creation of the new capitalist order – in all of its contradictions. Dunayevskaya elaborates a number of Hegel's core concepts, from alienation and contradiction to a radical notion of subjectivity. She grounds her discussion in the young Marx's characterization in the *1844 Manuscripts* – a text unavailable to Lukács in 1923 – of Hegel's concept of negativity as a moving and creative principle.

Chapter 3 is Bertell Ollman's 'Putting Dialectics to Work', which he does by emphasizing the oft-missed relational character of all the processes Marx examines ('the philosophy of internal relations') along with the process of abstraction, with which Marx brings any part of these intersecting relations into focus so he can deal with it separately. Together they allow Marx to control the extension (both spatial and temporal) and the degree of generality of all the relations that come into his studies as well as the vantage points from which they are viewed.

We follow this with Peter Stillman's essay on Marx's concept of critique (Chapter 4). Stillman shows how Marx uses – and supersedes – the German idealist category of critique. For Stillman, Marx's critique of political economy involves not only the traditional idealist immanent or internal critique, but also the reformulation on that basis of the way capitalism actually works, here dropping some hints about a new society beyond capitalism. In this way, Marx criticizes and reconstructs both theory and our concept of reality.

We end Part I with a piece on Marx's own empirical research. Chapter 5, Hilde Weiss's essay on Marx's 'Enquête Ouvrière', takes up the lengthy questionnaire that Marx had distributed to French workers via a socialist journal in 1880. The questionnaire was composed with great exactitude in order to focus on the lived experience of factory workers. Moreover, as Weiss shows, the ordering and structure of Marx's questions were designed to encourage workers to develop a more generalized consciousness about capitalism and its exploitative social relations.

Political Economy

Part II centres on political economy, or rather the Marxist critique of political economy. We open with David McNally's essay on the 2008 Great Recession (Chapter 6). McNally examines the crisis and its roots not only in the collapse of fictitious or speculative capital based upon derivatives and other forms of financialization, but also in the global downward restructuring of the living conditions of working people that preceded the crisis and which has deepened in its wake. He also critiques calls for greater regulation of capital rather than a more fundamental change in the system.

As Chapter 7 by Martha Gimenez shows, one aspect of the restructuring of capitalism in the neoliberal era is the phenomenon of 'self-sourcing', whereby formerly paid work becomes unpaid labour performed by the consumer in what is usually referred to as self-service, whether in restaurants, stores or white collar work in which computerization has eliminated clerical jobs.

This is followed by Fredy Perlman's accessible and clear exposition of Marx's concepts of commodity fetishism and surplus value, in language that reflects the experiences of late twentieth-century factory workers (Chapter 8). Issues like indirectly social labour, alienation and exploitation are elaborated in succinct form.

We close this section on political economy with two essays on the international dimensions of capitalist accumulation, particularly with regard to the Global South. In Chapter 9, his now classic 1974 essay, Immanuel Wallerstein sets out an early version of his world-system theory, in which areas peripheral to early capitalism – Latin America, Asia, Africa – were not underdeveloped, but rather developed as dependent forms of agricultural capitalism. Moreover, these peripheral areas were and are crucial not only to the origins of capitalism in the European 'core', but also to its continuing existence.

Chapter 10, David Harvey's contribution on the new imperialism, takes up changes since 1970, arguing that the US has become weakened in both the political and economic spheres. From this standpoint, the US's resort to numerous and protracted wars in the twenty-first century represents a desperate strategy to shore up a fading global hegemony in the face of other rising powers.

State and Politics

Part III, on the state and politics, begins with Michael Parenti's historical analysis of a founding document of the modern capitalist political order, the US Constitution (Chapter 11). Parenti finds that the Constitution was written by propertied men suspicious of democracy in any form. For example, he holds that its famous checks and balances were designed more to check popular power than to limit central government. Nor was the Constitution ever ratified by anything approaching universal suffrage, even for adult white males. At the same time, however, certain concessions were made to democratic pressures, especially in the Bill of Rights.

In Chapter 12 Franz Neumann theorizes another case of the relationship of the political power and the economic sphere, that of Nazi Germany. If one allows that twentieth-century capitalism had assumed monopolistic and bureaucratic features, then the Nazi regime is quintessentially capitalist, Neumann writes. Moreover, the Nazi regime allowed capital to overcome some of the obstacles besetting it in liberal society, such as challenges from trade unions or incomplete monopolization. Nazism did so by taking to an extreme a key feature of modern capitalist society, bureaucratization.

Vicente Navarro's contribution (Chapter 13) takes these issues to the present, to the neoliberal phase of capitalism. Navarro holds that the anti-statist side of neoliberal ideology masks the strengthening of the state, especially in the military, prison and security spheres. He also sketches a global class struggle during this same period. As against the common perception of North–South conflict, Navarro argues that the real conflict today is between international dominant and subordinate classes, usually organized at the regional level, as, for example, in the Western hemisphere. In these conflicts, the working people of both the wealthier and the poorer lands have generally been losing ground.

Operating at a more general level, Karl Renner's essay (Chapter 14) reflects on the relationship of legal to economic institutions in Marx's thought. Renner challenges both those who see Marx as a reductionist for whom law is a mere reflection of economic forces and those who have attempted to refute Marx by claiming that law sometimes influences the economy. Instead, he sketches the complex relation Marx develops between law and economy, especially during periods of transition from one historical mode of production to another.

At a still more general level, the sophisticated debate between Nicos Poulantzas and Ralph Miliband in Chapter 15 seeks to elucidate the form that the connections between the ruling classes and the capitalist system as a whole take in the most modern forms of capitalism. Their debate concerns these kinds of questions: Is the state apparatus relatively autonomous with regard to capital, or does it have a more instrumentalist relation to it? To what degree are state functions part of an objective system of relations that includes capital and to what degree are they altered by the particular ideologies – and even personalities – of leaders or groups that take control of the state?

Our final selection in Part III is Ernest Mandel's essay on revolution and the social reality of the twentieth century. In Chapter 16 Mandel not only examines revolutionary movements in the Global South and what was then the USSR-dominated Eastern European bloc, but also assesses carefully the possibility of revolutionary movements inside the developed capitalist societies of Western Europe, North America and Japan. In so doing, Mandel argues that revolutionary possibilities are more real than is usually supposed.

The Individual and Society

Part IV begins with Erich Fromm's brief 1929 essay on Marx and Freud (Chapter 17), a foundational text for the Frankfurt School of critical theory. Fromm argues that psychology can deepen its understanding of human behaviour by embracing Marx's critique of capital. This would help it to see, for example, that the family exists within and is conditioned by the overall capitalist system. Fromm also poses the question of a broader form of social psychology that would look at the psychic characteristics of both modern bourgeois society and its specific social classes.

Our next selection also deals with the individual and society at a broad theoretical level, albeit not through psychology. Chapter 18, Ellen Wood's essay on the history and present status – as of 1990 – of the concept of civil society, traces this concept within Marxism to Antonio Gramsci's elaboration of a socialist strategy that would challenge not only the capitalist economic system, but also the cultural and ideological forms that reinforce that system. However, Wood argues, recent uses of the term civil society – popularized by ex-Marxists – have taken the form of a radical liberalism that emphasizes democracy, pluralism and difference. The new civil society discourse does so at the cost of virtually eliminating class and capitalist domination from political discourse, even on the left.

Our other selections for Part IV take up more specific aspects. In Chapter 19 Fromm's Frankfurt School colleague Georg Rusche examines crime and punishment, issues not often associated with changes in the capitalist mode of production. In his 1933 essay, Rusche suggests that the tremendous historical variation in punishment – from physical mutilation, to slavery and penal servitude, to large-scale capital punishment and, finally, to the modern penitentiary – can be connected to overall capitalist development. Punishment has varied in severity and pervasiveness not so much because of the changing nature of crime as because of changes in the type and quantity of the labour force required by capital, he concludes: in times of labour shortage, physical punishment or forced labour predominate; in times of labour surplus, as in modern industrial capitalism, punishment turns toward executions and the penitentiary.

Moving us closer to the present, to the eve of the Great Recession, Chapter 20 by Michael Yates focuses on the psychosocial situation of working people in the pre-2008 'boom' times. Yates surveys the conditions of life and labour of the US working class, portraying a life of insecurity and fear for the vast majority. The occupations he samples include not only autoworkers, but also those toiling in restaurants, as office staff, as custodians, as security guards and in healthcare.

Our final selection for the section on the individual and society is Sut Jhally and Bill Livant's essay on sports, competition and capitalism (Chapter 21). Contrary to other Marxists who have seen competitive sports as a pernicious mirror of capitalist competition, Jhally and Livant contrast the openness of competitive sports, where the criteria and results are clear, to normal competition under capitalism, where the criteria and the results are mystified and uncertain.

Culture and Religion

Part V, on culture and religion, begins with Frankfurt School theorists Max Horkheimer and Theodor Adorno's classic critique of the culture industry, which they define as composed of Hollywood movies, mainstream popular music, cartoons and other corporate capitalist products in the sphere of popular culture (Chapter 22). The culture industry not only introduces the methods of capitalist manufacture into cultural production, but also flattens out the critical content of traditional popular culture in a pro-capitalist and conformist direction. In this way, the culture industry helps create a more affirmative stance towards capitalism within the working class.

In Chapter 23 Paul Werner critiques an institution of 'high culture', New York's Guggenheim Museum. Werner writes that the early twenty-first-century management of the Guggenheim helped to link the art world more closely to neoliberal capitalism, as seen in the speculative bubble in the price of art and in the equally pronounced commodification of the museum and its audience.

This is followed by Fredric Jameson's discussion of postmodernism, a still more contemporary moment in the development of culture under capitalism (Chapter 24). He devotes particular attention to postmodern art and architecture in the work of Andy Warhol, Frank Gehry and other representative figures. Jameson holds that the commodification, the depthlessness and the lack of affect in these newer cultural forms express, in his celebrated formulation, the 'cultural logic of late capitalism'.

We conclude Part V with Ishay Landa's discussion of Marx and Nietzsche on religion (Chapter 25). Landa critiques contemporary attempts to view these two thinkers as sharing a common atheistic attack on bourgeois morality, arguing instead that they approached the critique of Christianity from diametrically opposite points of view. Nietzsche's critique is fundamentally elitist, conservative and anti-humanist, whereas Marx's is egalitarian and emancipatory, Landa concludes.

History

Part VI on history comprises three contributions, each by distinguished British historians, who discuss the modern capitalist, feudal and ancient Greco-Roman modes of production. In Chapter 26 E.P. Thompson takes up the levels of exploitation and the standard of living of the English working class from 1789 through the 1840s. As a whole, he argues, the emergent working class experienced the early industrial revolution as a catastrophe. Sifting through the work of leading economic historians, some of them relatively conservative, Thompson argues that the economic catastrophe was accompanied by a wave of political repression in response to the French revolution and by the self-constitution of the working class through its life experience, its organizations and its development of a distinctive culture.

Chapter 27, Perry Anderson's contribution, takes us back to the birth of the feudal mode of production in Western Europe in the aftermath of the Roman Empire. He discusses the distinctive features of Western European feudalism, including the decentralization of political power, the serf–lord relation and the growth of semi-independent towns.

Finally, in Chapter 28 G.E.M. de Ste. Croix examines late Rome's decline. Surveying the harsh system of tax collection, which involved physical punishment, imprisonment and torture, de Ste. Croix argues that the upper classes drained society in a 'vampire-like' process of extraction that ruined the peasantry during the Empire's last two centuries. At the same time, the wealthy senatorial class often managed to avoid taxes. In ruining the peasantry, the upper classes dried up both their tax base and the major source of recruits for the army.

Colonialism, Race and Gender

Part VIII focuses on colonialism, race and gender and begins with the Afro-Caribbean philosopher C.L.R. James's early essay on Blacks and the Civil War in the US (Chapter 29). James surveys the Abolitionist movement, including its Black component, both in terms of leaders like Frederick Douglass and masses who never ceased their freedom struggle. He also analyses the class composition of the US in this period, with particular attention to the free farmers of the Midwest, who came to support Abolition. He concludes with a brief examination of Marx's writings on the Civil War as a second American revolution.

In Chapter 30 Oliver C. Cox examines capitalism, slavery and racism in broad socio-historical terms. Cox argues that racism in the form of colour prejudice was not a widely held feature of pre-modern European civilization, whether Greco-Roman or medieval. Racism in its modern form arose in the aftermath of the enslavement of millions of Africans in the early capitalist period, as ideologists of the system gradually settled upon a rationalization of slavery that would justify the perpetual enslavement of people of African descent.

Chapter 31 by Nancy Hartsock develops a feminist historical materialism, critically appropriating many categories developed by Marx, who she argues paid scant attention to gender. She develops a materialist theory of reproduction and the sexual division of labour.

Just as Marx attempts to theorize from a proletarian standpoint, Hartsock attempts to do so from a feminist standpoint.

The final contribution in this section is Kevin Anderson's survey of Marx's late writings (Chapter 32). Anderson argues that the 1872–75 French edition of *Capital*, the 1877–81 writings on village communism in Russia and, most importantly, the still partially unpublished 1879–82 notebooks on non-Western and pre-capitalist societies and gender show us a Marx who has placed gender, colonialism and multilinear perspectives of social development at the centre of his theorizing.

Ecology

The last part of this volume is devoted to ecology. In Chapter 33 John Bellamy Foster argues that ecology was a centrally important if subsequently neglected issue in Marx's writings. He devotes particular attention to what he terms Marx's concept of a 'metabolic rift' (p. 611), according to which capitalist agricultural production has destroyed the basis for a healthy interaction between human beings and the earth. While this aspect of Marx received some attention during the first years after his death, this discussion was cut short by the rise of Stalinism, which strove for industrial development at all costs, shunting aside the ecological dimensions of Marx's critique of capitalism.

In Chapter 34 Paul Burkett examines Marx's concept of communism. Burkett refutes commonly held notions to the effect that Marx's stress on production excluded sustainability. He argues that the type of communal production advocated by Marx's escapes the 'tragedy of the commons' because it is rationally planned and does not assume an inherent human right to exploit nature.

Now let the adventure in Marxism – for this is what we are inviting you to – begin!

Part I
Theory and Method

[1]

Reification and the Consciousness of the Proletariat

> To be radical is to go to the root of the
> matter. For man, however, the root is man
> himself.
>
> Marx: *Critique of Hegel's*
> *Philosophy of Right.*

Georg Lukács

IT is no accident that Marx should have begun with an analysis of
commodities when, in the two great works of his mature period,
he set out to portray capitalist society in its totality and to lay
bare its fundamental nature. For at this stage in the history of
mankind there is no problem that does not ultimately lead back
to that question and there is no solution that could not be found
in the solution to the riddle of commodity-*structure*. Of course the
problem can only be discussed with this degree of generality if it
achieves the depth and breadth to be found in Marx's own analyses. That is to say, the problem of commodities must not be considered in isolation or even regarded as the central problem in
economics, but as the central, structural problem of capitalist
society in all its aspects. Only in this case can the structure of
commodity-relations be made to yield a model of all the objective
forms of bourgeois society together with all the subjective forms
corresponding to them.

I

The Phenomenon of Reification

1

The essence of commodity-structure has often been pointed out.
Its basis is that a relation between people takes on the character
of a thing and thus acquires a 'phantom objectivity', an autonomy
that seems so strictly rational and all-embracing as to conceal
every trace of its fundamental nature: the relation between
people. It is beyond the scope of this essay to discuss the central

HISTORY AND CLASS CONSCIOUSNESS

importance of this problem for economics itself. Nor shall we consider its implications for the economic doctrines of the vulgar Marxists which follow from their abandonment of this starting-point.

Our intention here is to *base* ourselves on Marx's economic analyses and to proceed from there to a discusssion of the problems growing out of the fetish character of commodities, both as an objective form and also as a subjective stance corresponding to it. Only by understanding this can we obtain a clear insight into the ideological problems of capitalism and its downfall.

Before tackling the problem itself we must be quite clear in our minds that commodity fetishism is a *specific* problem of our age, the age of modern capitalism. Commodity exchange and the corresponding subjective and objective commodity relations existed, as we know, when society was still very primitive. What is at issue *here*, however, is the question: how far is commodity exchange together with its structural consequences able to influence the *total* outer and inner life of society? Thus the extent to which such exchange is the dominant form of metabolic change in a society cannot simply be treated in quantitative terms—as would harmonise with the modern modes of thought already eroded by the reifying effects of the dominant commodity form. The distinction between a society where this form is dominant, permeating every expression of life, and a society where it only makes an episodic appearance is essentially one of quality. For depending on which is the case, all the subjective and objective phenomena in the societies concerned are objectified in qualitatively different ways.

Marx lays great stress on the essentially episodic appearance of the commodity form in primitive societies: "Direct barter, the original natural form of exchange, represents rather the beginning of the transformation of use-values into commodities, than that of commodities into money. Exchange value has as yet no form of its own, but is still directly bound up with use-value. This is manifested in two ways. Production, in its entire organisation, aims at the creation of use-values and not of exchange values, and it is only when their supply exceeds the measure of consumption that use-values cease to be use-values, and become means of exchange, i.e. commodities. At the same time, they become commodities only within the limits of being direct use-values distributed at opposite poles, so that the commodities to be exchanged

REIFICATION AND THE CONSCIOUSNESS OF THE PROLETARIAT 85

by their possessors must be use-values to both—each commodity to its non-possessor. As a matter of fact, the exchange of commodities originates not within the primitive communities, but where they end, on their borders at the few points where they come in contact with other communities. That is where barter begins, and from here it strikes back into the interior of the community, decomposing it."[1] We note that the observation about the disintegrating effect of a commodity exchange directed in upon itself clearly shows the qualitative change engendered by the dominance of commodities.

However, even when commodities have this impact on the internal structure of a society, this does not suffice to make them constitutive of that society. To achieve that it would be necessary —as we emphasized above—for the commodity structure to penetrate society in all its aspects and to remould it in its own image. It is not enough merely to establish an external link with independent processes concerned with the production of exchange values. The qualitative difference between the commodity as one form among many regulating the metabolism of human society and the commodity as the universal structuring principle has effects over and above the fact that the commodity relation as an isolated phenomenon exerts a negative influence at best on the structure and organisation of society. The distinction also has repercussions upon the nature and validity of the category itself. Where the commodity is universal it manifests itself differently from the commodity as a particular, isolated, non-dominant phenomenon.

The fact that the boundaries lack sharp definition must not be allowed to blur the qualitative nature of the decisive distinction. The situation where commodity exchange is not dominant has been defined by Marx as follows: "The quantitative ratio in which products are exchanged is at first quite arbitrary. They assume the form of commodities inasmuch as they are exchangeables, i.e. expressions of one and the same third. Continued exchange and more regular reproduction for exchange reduces this arbitrariness more and more. But at first not for the producer and consumer, but for their go-between, the merchant, who compares money-prices and pockets the difference. It is through his own movements that he establishes equivalence. Merchant's capital is originally merely the intervening movement between extremes which it does not control and between premises which it does not create."[2]

86 HISTORY AND CLASS CONSCIOUSNESS

And *this* development of the commodity to the point where it becomes the dominant form in society did not take place until the advent of modern capitalism. Hence it is not to be wondered at that the personal nature of economic relations was still understood clearly on occasion at the start of capitalist development, but that as the process advanced and forms became more complex and less direct, it became increasingly difficult and rare to find anyone penetrating the veil of reification. Marx sees the matter in this way: "In preceding forms of society this economic mystification arose principally with respect to money and interest-bearing capital. In the nature of things it is excluded, in the first place, where production for the use-value, for immediate personal requirements, predominates; and secondly, where slavery or serfdom form the broad foundation of social production, as in antiquity and during the Middle Ages. Here, the domination of the producers by the conditions of production is concealed by the relations of dominion and servitude which appear and are evident as the direct motive power of the process of production."[3]

The commodity can only be understood in its undistorted essence when it becomes the universal category of society as a whole. Only in this context does the reification produced by commodity relations assume decisive importance both for the objective evolution of society and for the stance adopted by men towards it. Only then does the commodity become crucial for the subjugation of men's consciousness to the forms in which this reification finds expression and for their attempts to comprehend the process or to rebel against its disastrous effects and liberate themselves from servitude to the 'second nature' so created.

Marx describes the basic phenomenon of reification as follows: "A commodity is therefore a mysterious thing, simply because in it the social character of men's labour appears to them as an objective character stamped upon the product of that labour; because the relation of the producers to the sum total of their own labour is presented to them as a social relation, existing not between themselves, but between the products of their labour. This is the reason why the products of labour become commodities, social things whose qualities are at the same time perceptible and imperceptible by the senses. . . . It is only a definite social relation between men that assumes, in their eyes, the fantastic form of a relation between things."[4]

What is of central importance here is that because of this

REIFICATION AND THE CONSCIOUSNESS OF THE PROLETARIAT   **87**

situation a man's own activity, his own labour becomes something objective and independent of him, something that controls him by virtue of an autonomy alien to man. There is both an objective and a subjective side to this phenomenon. *Objectively* a world of objects and relations between things springs into being (the world of commodities and their movements on the market). The laws governing these objects are indeed gradually discovered by man, but even so they confront him as invisible forces that generate their own power. The individual can use his knowledge of these laws to his own advantage, but he is not able to modify the process by his own activity. *Subjectively*—where the market economy has been fully developed—a man's activity becomes estranged from himself, it turns into a commodity which, subject to the non-human objectivity of the natural laws of society, must go its own way independently of man just like any consumer article. "What is characteristic of the capitalist age," says Marx, "is that in the eyes of the labourer himself labour-power assumes the form of a commodity belonging to him. On the other hand it is only at this moment that the commodity form of the products of labour becomes general."[5]

Thus the universality of the commodity form is responsible both objectively and subjectively for the abstraction of the human labour incorporated in commodities. (On the other hand, this universality becomes historically possible because this process of abstraction has been completed.) *Objectively*, in so far as the commodity form facilitates the equal exchange of qualitatively different objects, it can only exist if that formal equality is in fact recognised—at any rate in *this* relation, which indeed confers upon them their commodity nature. *Subjectively*, this formal equality of human labour in the abstract is not only the common factor to which the various commodities are reduced; it also becomes the real principle governing the actual production of commodities.

Clearly, it cannot be our aim here to describe even in outline the growth of the modern process of labour, of the isolated, 'free' labourer and of the division of labour. Here we need only establish that labour, abstract, equal, comparable labour, measurable with increasing precision according to the time socially necessary for its accomplishment, the labour of the capitalist division of labour existing both as the presupposition and the product of capitalist production, is born only in the course of the develop-

HISTORY AND CLASS CONSCIOUSNESS

ment of the capitalist system. Only then does it become a category of society influencing decisively the objective form of things and people in the society thus emerging, their relation to nature and the possible relations of men to each other.[6]

If we follow the path taken by labour in its development from the handicraft via co-operation and manufacture to machine industry we can see a continuous trend towards greater rationalisation, the progressive elimination of the qualitative, human and individual attributes of the worker. On the one hand, the process of labour is progressively broken down into abstract, rational, specialised operations so that the worker loses contact with the finished product and his work is reduced to the mechanical repetition of a specialised set of actions. On the other hand, the period of time necessary for work to be accomplished (which forms the basis of rational calculation) is converted, as mechanisation and rationalisation are intensified, from a merely empirical average figure to an objectively calculable work-stint that confronts the worker as a fixed and established reality. With the modern 'psychological' analysis of the work-process (in Taylorism) this rational mechanisation extends right into the worker's 'soul': even his psychological attributes are separated from his total personality and placed in opposition to it so as to facilitate their integration into specialised rational systems and their reduction to statistically viable concepts.[7]

We are concerned above all with the *principle* at work here: the principle of rationalisation based on what is and *can be calculated*. The chief changes undergone by the subject and object of the economic process are as follows: (1) in the first place, the mathematical analysis of work-processes denotes a break with the organic, irrational and qualitatively determined unity of the product. Rationalisation in the sense of being able to predict with ever greater precision all the results to be achieved is only to be acquired by the exact breakdown of every complex into its elements and by the study of the special laws governing production. Accordingly it must declare war on the organic manufacture of whole products based on the *traditional amalgam of empirical experiences of work*: rationalisation is unthinkable without specialisation.[8]

The finished article ceases to be the object of the work-process. The latter turns into the objective synthesis of rationalised special systems whose unity is determined by pure calculation and which must therefore seem to be arbitrarily connected with each other.

REIFICATION AND THE CONSCIOUSNESS OF THE PROLETARIAT   89

This destroys the organic necessity with which inter-related special operations are unified in the end-product. The unity of a product as a *commodity* no longer coincides with its unity as a use-value: as society becomes more radically capitalistic the increasing technical autonomy of the special operations involved in production is expressed also, as an economic autonomy, as the growing relativisation of the commodity character of a product at the various stages of production.[9] It is thus possible to separate forcibly the production of a use-value in time and space. This goes hand in hand with the union in time and space of special operations that are related to a set of heterogeneous use-values.

(2) In the second place, this fragmentation of the object of production necessarily entails the fragmentation of its subject. In consequence of the rationalisation of the work-process the human qualities and idiosyncrasies of the worker appear increasingly as *mere sources of error* when contrasted with these abstract special laws functioning according to rational predictions. Neither objectively nor in his relation to his work does man appear as the authentic master of the process; on the contrary, he is a mechanical part incorporated into a mechanical system. He finds it already pre-existing and self-sufficient, it functions independently of him and he has to conform to its laws whether he likes it or not.[10] As labour is progressively rationalised and mechanised his lack of will is reinforced by the way in which his activity becomes less and less active and more and more *contemplative*.[11] The contemplative stance adopted towards a process mechanically conforming to fixed laws and enacted independently of man's consciousness and impervious to human intervention, i.e. a perfectly closed system, must likewise transform the basic categories of man's immediate attitude to the world: it reduces space and time to a common denominator and degrades time to the dimension of space.

Marx puts it thus: "Through the subordination of man to the machine the situation arises in which men are effaced by their labour; in which the pendulum of the clock has become as accurate a measure of the relative activity of two workers as it is of the speed of two locomotives. Therefore, we should not say that one man's hour is worth another man's hour, but rather that one man during an hour is worth just as much as another man during an hour. Time is everything, man is nothing; he is at the most the incarnation of time. Quality no longer matters. Quantity

90 HISTORY AND CLASS CONSCIOUSNESS

alone decides everything: hour for hour, day for day. . . ."[12]

Thus time sheds its qualitative, variable, flowing nature; it freezes into an exactly delimited, quantifiable continuum filled with quantifiable 'things' (the reified, mechanically objectified 'performance' of the worker, wholly separated from his total human personality): in short, it becomes space.[13] In this environment where time is transformed into abstract, exactly measurable, physical space, an environment at once the cause and effect of the scientifically and mechanically fragmented and specialised production of the object of labour, the subjects of labour must likewise be rationally fragmented. On the one hand, the objectification of their labour-power into something opposed to their total personality (a process already accomplished with the sale of that labour-power as a commodity) is now made into the permanent ineluctable reality of their daily life. Here, too, the personality can do no more than look on helplessly while its own existence is reduced to an isolated particle and fed into an alien system. On the other hand, the mechanical disintegration of the process of production into its components also destroys those bonds that had bound individuals to a community in the days when production was still 'organic'. In this respect, too, mechanisation makes of them isolated abstract atoms whose work no longer brings them together directly and organically; it becomes mediated to an increasing extent exclusively by the abstract laws of the mechanism which imprisons them.

The internal organisation of a factory could not possibly have such an effect—even within the factory itself—were it not for the fact that it contained in concentrated form the whole structure of capitalist society. Oppression and an exploitation that knows no bounds and scorns every human dignity were known even to pre-capitalist ages. So too was mass production with mechanical, standardised labour, as we can see, for instance, with canal construction in Egypt and Asia Minor and the mines in Rome.[14] But mass projects of this type could never be *rationally mechanised*; they remained isolated phenomena within a community that organised its production on a different ('natural') basis and which therefore lived a different life. The slaves subjected to this exploitation, therefore, stood outside what was thought of as 'human' society and even the greatest and noblest thinkers of the time were unable to consider their fate as that of human beings.

As the commodity becomes universally dominant, this situa-

REIFICATION AND THE CONSCIOUSNESS OF THE PROLETARIAT   91

tion changes radically and qualitatively. The fate of the worker becomes the fate of society as a whole; indeed, this fate must become universal as otherwise industrialisation could not develop in this direction. For it depends on the emergence of the 'free' worker who is freely able to take his labour-power to market and offer it for sale as a commodity 'belonging' to him, a thing that he 'possesses'.

While this process is still incomplete the methods used to extract surplus labour are, it is true, more obviously brutal than in the later, more highly developed phase, but the process of reification of work and hence also of the consciousness of the worker is much less advanced. Reification **requires** that a society should learn to satisfy all its needs in terms of commodity exchange. The separation of the producer from his means of production, the dissolution and destruction of all 'natural' production units, etc., and all the social and economic conditions necessary for the emergence of modern capitalism tend to replace 'natural' relations which exhibit human relations more plainly by rationally reified relations. "The social relations between individuals in the performance of their labour," Marx observes with reference to pre-capitalist societies, "appear at all events as their own personal relations, and are not disguised under the shape of social relations between the products of labour."[15]

But this implies that the principle of rational mechanisation and calculability must embrace every aspect of life. Consumer articles no longer appear as the products of an organic process within a community (as for example in a village community). They now appear, on the one hand, as abstract members of a species identical by definition with its other members and, on the other hand, as isolated objects the possession or non-possession of which depends on rational calculations. Only when the whole life of society is thus fragmented into the isolated acts of commodity exchange can the 'free' worker come into being; at the same time his fate becomes the typical fate of the whole society.

Of course, this isolation and fragmentation is only apparent. The movement of commodities on the market, the birth of their value, in a word, the real framework of every rational calculation is not merely subject to strict laws but also presupposes the strict ordering of all that happens. The atomisation of the individual is, then, only the reflex in consciousness of the fact that the 'natural

92   HISTORY AND CLASS CONSCIOUSNESS

laws' of capitalist production have been extended to cover every manifestation of life in society; that—for the first time in history—the whole of society is subjected, or tends to be subjected, to a unified economic process, and that the fate of every member of society is determined by unified laws. (By contrast, the organic unities of pre-capitalist societies organised their metabolism largely in independence of each other).

However, if this atomisation is only an illusion it is a necessary one. That is to say, the immediate, practical as well as intellectual confrontation of the individual with society, the immediate production and reproduction of life—in which for the individual the commodity structure of all 'things' and their obedience to 'natural laws' is found to exist already in a finished form, as something immutably given—could only take place in the form of rational and isolated acts of exchange between isolated commodity owners. As emphasised above, the worker, too, must present himself as the 'owner' of his labour-power, as if it were a commodity. His specific situation is defined by the fact that his labour-power is his only possession. His fate is typical of society as a whole in that this self-objectification, this transformation of a human function into a commodity reveals in all its starkness the dehumanised and dehumanising function of the commodity relation.

2

This rational objectification conceals above all the immediate—qualitative and material—character of things as things. When use-values appear universally as commodities they acquire a new objectivity, a new substantiality which they did not possess in an age of episodic exchange and which destroys their original and authentic substantiality. As Marx observes: "Private property *alienates* not only the individuality of men, but also of things. The ground and the earth have nothing to do with ground-rent, machines have nothing to do with profit. For the landowner ground and earth mean nothing but ground-rent; he lets his land to tenants and receives the rent—a quality which the ground can lose without losing any of its inherent qualities such as its fertility; it is a quality whose magnitude and indeed existence depends on social relations that are created and abolished without any intervention by the landowner. Likewise with the machine."[16]

REIFICATION AND THE CONSCIOUSNESS OF THE PROLETARIAT   93

Thus even the individual object which man confronts directly, either as producer or consumer, is distorted in its objectivity by its commodity character. If that can happen then it is evident that this process will be intensified in proportion as the relations which man establishes with objects as objects of the life process are mediated in the course of his social activity. It is obviously not possible here to give an analysis of the whole economic structure of capitalism. It must suffice to point out that modern capitalism does not content itself with transforming the relations of production in accordance with its own needs. It also integrates into its own system those forms of primitive capitalism that led an isolated existence in pre-capitalist times, divorced from production; it converts them into members of the henceforth unified process of radical capitalism. (Cf. merchant capital, the role of money as a hoard or as finance capital, etc.)

These forms of capital are objectively subordinated, it is true, to the real life-process of capitalism, the extraction of surplus value in the course of production. They are, therefore, only to be explained in terms of the nature of industrial capitalism itself. But in the minds of people in bourgeois society they constitute the pure, authentic, unadulterated forms of capital. In them the relations between men that lie hidden in the immediate commodity relation, as well as the relations between men and the objects that should really gratify their needs, have faded to the point where they can be neither recognised nor even perceived.

For that very reason the reified mind has come to regard them as the true representatives of his societal existence. The commodity character of the commodity, the abstract, quantitative mode of calculability shows itself here in its purest form: the reified mind necessarily sees it as the form in which its own authentic immediacy becomes manifest and—as reified consciousness—does not even attempt to transcend it. On the contrary, it is concerned to make it permanent by 'scientifically deepening' the laws at work. Just as the capitalist system continuously produces and reproduces itself economically on higher and higher levels, the structure of reification progressively sinks more deeply, more fatefully and more definitively into the consciousness of man. Marx often describes this potentiation of reification in incisive fashion. One example must suffice here: "In interest-bearing capital, therefore, this automatic fetish, self-expanding value, money generating money, is brought out in its pure state and in this form it no longer bears the birth-marks of its origin. The social relation is consummated in the relation of a thing, of money, to itself. Instead of the actual transformation of money into capital, we see here only form without content. . . . It becomes a property of money to generate value and yield interest, much as it is an attribute of pear trees to bear pears. And the money-lender sells his money as just such an interest-bearing thing. But that is not all. The actually functioning capital, as we have seen, presents itself in such a light that it seems to yield interest not as functioning capital, but as capital in itself, as money-capital. This, too, becomes distorted. While interest is only a portion of the profit, i.e. of the surplus value, which the functioning capitalist squeezes out of the labourer, it appears now, on the contrary, as though interest were the typical product of capital, the primary matter, and profit, in the shape of profit of enterprise, were a mere accessory and by-product of the process of reproduction. Thus we get a fetish form of capital, and the conception of fetish capital. In M-M' we have the meaningless form of capital, the perversion and objectification of production relations in their highest degree, the interest-bearing form, the simple form of capital, in which it antecedes its own process of reproduction. It is the capacity of money, or of a commodity, to expand its own value independently of reproduction—which is a mystification of capital in its most flagrant form. For vulgar political economy, which seeks to represent capital as an independent source of value, of value creation, this form is naturally a veritable find, a form in which the source of profit is no longer discernible, and in which the result of the capitalist process of production—divorced from the process—acquires an independent existence."[17]

Just as the economic theory of capitalism remains stuck fast in its self-created immediacy, the same thing happens to bourgeois attempts to comprehend the ideological phenomenon of reification. Even thinkers who have no desire to deny or obscure its existence and who are more or less clear in their own minds about its humanly destructive consequences remain on the surface and make no attempt to advance beyond its objectively most derivative forms, the forms furthest from the real life-process of capitalism, i.e. the most external and vacuous forms, to the basic phenomenon of reification itself.

Indeed, they divorce these empty manifestations from their

REIFICATION AND THE CONSCIOUSNESS OF THE PROLETARIAT   95

real capitalist foundation and make them independent and permanent by regarding them as the timeless model of human relations in general. (This can be seen most clearly in Simmel's book, *The Philosophy of Money*, a very interesting and perceptive work in matters of detail.) They offer no more than a description of this "enchanted, perverted, topsy-turvy world, in which Monsieur Le Capital and Madame La Terre do their ghost-walking as social characters and at the same time as mere things."[18] But they do not go further than a description and their 'deepening' of the problem runs in circles around the eternal manifestations of reification.

The divorce of the phenomena of reification from their economic bases and from the vantage point from which alone they can be understood, is facilitated by the fact that the [capitalist] process of transformation must embrace every manifestation of the life of society if the preconditions for the complete self-realisation of capitalist production are to be fulfilled.

Thus capitalism has created a form for the state and a system of law corresponding to its needs and harmonising with its own structure. The structural similarity is so great that no truly perceptive historian of modern capitalism could fail to notice it. Max Weber, for instance, gives this description of the basic lines of this development: "Both are, rather, quite similar in their fundamental nature. Viewed sociologically, a 'business-concern' is the modern state; the same holds good for a factory: and this, precisely, is what is specific to it historically. And, likewise, the power relations in a business are also of the same kind. The relative independence of the artisan (or cottage craftsman), of the landowning peasant, the owner of a benefice, the knight and vassal was based on the fact that he himself owned the tools, supplies, financial resources or weapons with the aid of which he fulfilled his economic, political or military function and from which he lived while this duty was being discharged. Similarly, the hierarchic dependence of the worker, the clerk, the technical assistant, the assistant in an academic institute *and* the civil servant and soldier has a comparable basis: namely that the tools, supplies and financial resources essential both for the business-concern and for economic survival are in the hands, in the one case, of the entrepreneur and, in the other case, of the political master."[19]

He rounds off this account—very pertinently—with an analysis of the cause and the social implications of this phenomenon:

96 HISTORY AND CLASS CONSCIOUSNESS

"The modern capitalist concern is based inwardly above all on *calculation*. It requires for its survival a system of justice and an administration whose workings can be *rationally calculated*, at least in principle, according to fixed general laws, just as the probable performance of *a machine* can be calculated. It is as little able to tolerate the dispensing of justice according to the judge's sense of fair play *in individual cases* or any other irrational means or principles of administering the law . . . as it is able to endure a patriarchal administration that obeys the dictates of its own caprice, or sense of mercy and, for the rest, proceeds in accordance with an inviolable and sacrosanct, but irrational tradition. . . . What is specific to modern capitalism as distinct from the age-old capitalist forms of acquisition is that the strictly rational *organisation of work* on the basis of *rational technology* did not come into being *anywhere* within such irrationally constituted political systems nor could it have done so. For these modern businesses with their fixed capital and their exact calculations are much too sensitive to legal and administrative irrationalities. They could only come into being in the bureaucratic state with its rational laws where . . . the judge is more or less an automatic statute-dispensing machine in which you insert the files together with the necessary costs and dues at the top, whereupon he will eject the judgment together with the more or less cogent reasons for it at the bottom: that is to say, where the judge's behaviour is on the whole *predictable*."

The process we see here is closely related both in its motivation and in its effects to the economic process outlined above. Here, too, there is a breach with the empirical and irrational methods of administration and dispensing justice based on traditions tailored, subjectively, to the requirements of men in action, and, objectively, to those of the concrete matter in hand. There arises a rational systematisation of all statutes regulating life, which represents, or at least tends towards a closed system applicable to all possible and imaginable cases. Whether this system is arrived at in a purely logical manner, as an exercise in pure legal dogma or interpretation of the law, or whether the judge is given the task of filling the 'gaps' left in the laws, is immaterial for our attempt to understand the *structure* of modern legal reality. In either case the legal system is formally capable of being generalised so as to relate to every possible situation in life and it is susceptible to prediction and calculation. Even Roman Law, which comes

REIFICATION AND THE CONSCIOUSNESS OF THE PROLETARIAT   97

closest to these developments while remaining, in modern terms, within the framework of pre-capitalist legal patterns, does not in this respect go beyond the empirical, the concrete and the traditional. The purely systematic categories which were necessary before a judicial system could become universally applicable arose only in modern times.[20]

It requires no further explanation to realise that the need to systematise and to abandon empiricism, tradition and material dependence was the need for exact calculation.[21] However, this same need requires that the legal system should confront the individual events of social existence as something permanently established and exactly defined, i.e. as a rigid system. Of course, this produces an uninterrupted series of conflicts between the unceasingly revolutionary forces of the capitalist economy and the rigid legal system. But this only results in new codifications; and despite these the new system is forced to preserve the fixed, change-resistant structure of the old system.

This is the source of the—apparently—paradoxical situation whereby the 'law' of primitive societies, which has scarcely altered in hundreds or sometimes even thousands of years, can be flexible and irrational in character, renewing itself with every new legal decision, while modern law, caught up in the continuous turmoil of change, should appear rigid, static and fixed. But the paradox dissolves when we realise that it arises only because the same situation has been regarded from two different points of view: on the one hand, from that of the historian (who stands 'outside' the actual process) and, on the other, from that of someone who experiences the effects of the social order in question upon his consciousness.

With the aid of this insight we can see clearly how the antagonism between the traditional and empirical craftsmanship and the scientific and rational factory is repeated in another sphere of activity. At every single stage of its development, the ceaselessly revolutionary techniques of modern production turn a rigid and immobile face towards the individual producer. Whereas the objectively relatively stable, traditional craft production preserves in the minds of its individual practitioners the appearance of something flexible, something constantly renewing itself, something produced by the producers.

In the process we witness, illuminatingly, how here, too, the *contemplative* nature of man under capitalism makes its appearance.

98 HISTORY AND CLASS CONSCIOUSNESS

For the essence of rational calculation is based ultimately upon the recognition and the inclusion in one's calculations of the inevitable chain of cause and effect in certain events—independently of individual 'caprice'. In consequence, man's activity does not go beyond the correct calculation of the possible outcome of the sequence of events (the 'laws' of which he finds 'ready-made'), and beyond the adroit evasion of disruptive 'accidents' by means of protective devices and preventive measures (which are based in their turn on the recognition and application of similar laws). Very often it will confine itself to working out the probable effects of such 'laws' without making the attempt to intervene in the process by bringing other 'laws' to bear. (As in insurance schemes, etc.)

The more closely we scrutinise this situation and the better we are able to close our minds to the bourgeois legends of the 'creativity' of the exponents of the capitalist age, the more obvious it becomes that we are witnessing in all behaviour of this sort the structural analogue to the behaviour of the worker *vis-à-vis* the machine he serves and observes, and whose functions he controls while he contemplates it. The 'creative' element can be seen to depend at best on whether these 'laws' are applied in a—relatively—independent way or in a wholly subservient one. That is to say, it depends on the degree to which the contemplative stance is repudiated. The distinction between a worker faced with a particular machine, the entrepreneur faced with a given type of mechanical development, the technologist faced with the state of science and the profitability of its application to technology, is purely quantitative; it does not directly entail *any qualitative difference in the structure of consciousness.*

Only in this context can the problem of modern bureaucracy be properly understood. Bureaucracy implies the adjustment of one's way of life, mode of work and hence of consciousness, to the general socio-economic premises of the capitalist economy, similar to that which we have observed in the case of the worker in particular business concerns. The formal standardisation of justice, the state, the civil service, etc., signifies objectively and factually a comparable reduction of all social functions to their elements, a comparable search for the rational formal laws of these carefully segregated partial systems. Subjectively, the divorce between work and the individual capacities and needs of the worker produces comparable effects upon consciousness. This results

REIFICATION AND THE CONSCIOUSNESS OF THE PROLETARIAT   99

in an inhuman, standardised division of labour analogous to that which we have found in industry on the technological and mechanical plane.[22]

It is not only a question of the completely mechanical, 'mindless' work of the lower echelons of the bureaucracy which bears such an extraordinarily close resemblance to operating a machine and which indeed often surpasses it in sterility and uniformity. It is also a question, on the one hand, of the way in which objectively all issues are subjected to an increasingly *formal* and standardised treatment and in which there is an ever-increasing remoteness from the qualitative and material essence of the 'things' to which bureaucratic activity pertains. On the other hand, there is an even more monstrous intensification of the one-sided specialisation which represents such a violation of man's humanity. Marx's comment on factory work that "the individual, himself divided, is transformed into the automatic mechanism of a partial labour" and is thus "crippled to the point of abnormality" is relevant here too. And it becomes all the more clear, the more elevated, advanced and 'intellectual' is the attainment exacted by the division of labour.

The split between the worker's labour-power and his personality, its metamorphosis into a thing, an object that he sells on the market is repeated here too. But with the difference that not every mental faculty is suppressed by mechanisation; only one faculty (or complex of faculties) is detached from the whole personality and placed in opposition to it, becoming a thing, a commodity. But the basic phenomenon remains the same even though both the means by which society instills such abilities and their material and 'moral' exchange value are fundamentally different from labour-power (not forgetting, of course, the many connecting links and nuances).

The specific type of bureaucratic 'conscientiousness' and impartiality, the individual bureaucrat's inevitable total subjection to a system of relations between the things to which he is exposed, the idea that it is precisely his 'honour' and his 'sense of responsibility' that exact this total submission,[23] all this points to the fact that the division of labour which in the case of Taylorism invaded the psyche, here invades the realm of ethics. Far from weakening the reified structure of consciousness, this actually strengthens it. For as long as the fate of the worker still appears to be an individual fate (as in the case of the slave in antiquity),

HISTORY AND CLASS CONSCIOUSNESS

the life of the ruling classes is still free to assume quite different forms. Not until the rise of capitalism was a unified economic structure, and hence a—formally—unified structure of consciousness that embraced the whole society, brought into being. This unity expressed itself in the fact that the problems of consciousness arising from wage-labour were repeated in the ruling class in a refined and spiritualised, but, for that very reason, more intensified form. The specialised 'virtuoso', the vendor of his objectified and reified faculties does not just become the [passive] observer of society; he also lapses into a contemplative attitude *vis-à-vis* the workings of his own objectified and reified faculties. (It is not possible here even to outline the way in which modern administration and law assume the characteristics of the factory as we noted above rather than those of the handicrafts.) This phenomenon can be seen at its most grotesque in journalism. Here it is precisely subjectivity itself, knowledge, temperament and powers of expression that are reduced to an abstract mechanism functioning autonomously and divorced both from the personality of their 'owner' and from the material and concrete nature of the subject matter in hand. The journalist's 'lack of convictions', the prostitution of his experiences and beliefs is comprehensible only as the apogee of capitalist reification.[24]

The transformation of the commodity relation into a thing of 'ghostly objectivity' cannot therefore content itself with the reduction of all objects for the gratification of human needs to commodities. It stamps its imprint upon the whole consciousness of man; his qualities and abilities are no longer an organic part of his personality, they are things which he can 'own' or 'dispose of' like the various objects of the external world. And there is no natural form in which human relations can be cast, no way in which man can bring his physical and psychic 'qualities' into play without their being subjected increasingly to this reifying process. We need only think of marriage, and without troubling to point to the developments of the nineteenth century we can remind ourselves of the way in which Kant, for example, described the situation with the naïvely cynical frankness peculiar to great thinkers.

"Sexual community", he says, "is the reciprocal use made by one person of the sexual organs and faculties of another . . . marriage . . . is the union of two people of different sexes with a view to the mutual possession of each other's sexual attributes for the duration of their lives."[25]

REIFICATION AND THE CONSCIOUSNESS OF THE PROLETARIAT 101

This rationalisation of the world appears to be complete, it seems to penetrate the very depths of man's physical and psychic nature. It is limited, however, by its own formalism. That is to say, the rationalisation of isolated aspects of life results in the creation of—formal—laws. All these things do join together into what seems to the superficial observer to constitute a unified system of general 'laws'. But the disregard of the concrete aspects of the subject matter of these laws, upon which disregard their authority as laws is based, makes itself felt in the incoherence of the system in fact. This incoherence becomes particularly egregious in periods of crisis. At such times we can see how the immediate continuity between two partial systems is disrupted and their independence from and adventitious connection with each other is suddenly forced into the consciousness of everyone. It is for this reason that Engels is able to define the 'natural laws' of capitalist society as the laws of chance.[26]

On closer examination the structure of a crisis is seen to be no more than a heightening of the degree and intensity of the daily life of bourgeois society. In its unthinking, mundane reality *that* life seems firmly held together by 'natural laws'; yet it can experience a sudden dislocation because the bonds uniting its various elements and partial systems are a chance affair even at their most normal. So that the pretence that society is regulated by 'eternal, iron' laws which branch off into the different special laws applying to particular areas is finally revealed for what it is: a pretence. The true structure of society appears rather in the independent, rationalised and formal partial laws whose links with each other are of necessity purely formal (i.e. their formal interdependence can be formally systematised), while as far as concrete realities are concerned they can only establish fortuitous connections.

On closer inspection this kind of connection can be discovered even in purely economic phenomena. Thus Marx points out— and the cases referred to here are intended only as an indication of the methodological factors involved, not as a substantive treatment of the problems themselves—that "the conditions of direct exploitation [of the labourer], and those of realising surplus-value, are not identical. They diverge not only in place and time, but also logically."[27] Thus there exists "an accidental rather than a necessary connection between the total amount of social labour applied to a social article" and "the volume whereby society seeks to satisfy the want gratified by the article in question."[28]

102 HISTORY AND CLASS CONSCIOUSNESS

These are no more than random instances. It is evident that the whole structure of capitalist production rests on the interaction between a necessity subject to strict laws in all isolated phenomena and the relative irrationality of the total process. "Division of labour within the workshop implies the undisputed authority of the capitalist over men, who are but parts of a mechanism that belongs to him. The division of labour within society brings into contact independent commodity-producers who acknowledge no other authority than that of competition, of the coercion exerted by the pressure of their mutual interests."[29]

The capitalist process of rationalisation based on private economic calculation requires that every manifestation of life shall exhibit this very interaction between details which are subject to laws and a totality ruled by chance. It presupposes a society so structured. It produces and reproduces this structure in so far as it takes possession of society. This has its foundation already in the nature of speculative calculation, i.e. the economic practice of commodity owners at the stage where the exchange of commodities has become universal. Competition between the different owners of commodities would not be feasible if there were an exact, rational, systematic mode of functioning for the whole of society to correspond to the rationality of isolated phenomena. If a rational calculation is to be possible the commodity owner must be in possession of the laws regulating every detail of his production. The chances of exploitation, the laws of the 'market' must likewise be rational in the sense that they must be calculable according to the laws of probability. But they must not be governed by a law in the sense in which 'laws' govern individual phenomena; they must not under any circumstances be rationally organised through and through. This does not mean, of course, that there can be no 'law' governing the whole. But such a 'law' would have to be the 'unconscious' product of the activity of the different commodity owners acting independently of one another, i.e. a law of mutually interacting 'coincidences' rather than one of truly rational organisation. Furthermore, such a law must not merely impose itself despite the wishes of individuals, it may *not even be fully and adequately knowable*. For the complete knowledge of the whole would vouchsafe the knower a monopoly that would amount to the virtual abolition of the capitalist economy.

This irrationality, this—highly problematic—'systematisation' of the whole which diverges *qualitatively and in principle* from the

REIFICATION AND THE CONSCIOUSNESS OF THE PROLETARIAT 103

laws regulating the parts, is more than just a postulate, a pre-supposition essential to the workings of a capitalist economy. It is at the same time the product of the capitalist division of labour. It has already been pointed out that the division of labour disrupts every organically unified process of work and life and breaks it down into its components. This enables the artificially isolated partial functions to be performed in the most rational manner by 'specialists' who are specially adapted mentally and physically for the purpose. This has the effect of making these partial functions autonomous and so they tend to develop through their own momentum and in accordance with their own special laws independently of the other partial functions of society (or that part of the society to which they belong).

As the division of labour becomes more pronounced and more rational, this tendency naturally increases in proportion. For the more highly developed it is, the more powerful become the claims to status and the professional interests of the 'specialists' who are the living embodiments of such tendencies. And this centrifugal movement is not confined to aspects of a particular sector. It is even more in evidence when we consider the great spheres of activity created by the division of labour. Engels describes this process with regard to the relation between economics and laws: "Similarly with law. As soon as the new division of labour which creates *professional lawyers* becomes necessary, another new and independent sphere is opened up which, for all its essential dependence on production and trade, still has also a special capacity for reacting upon these spheres. In a modern state, law must not only correspond to the general economic condition and be its expression, but must also be an *internally coherent expression* which does not, owing to inner contradictions, reduce itself to nought. And in order to achieve this, the faithful reflection of economic conditions suffers increasingly. . . ."[30] It is hardly necessary to supplement this with examples of the inbreeding and the interdepartmental conflicts of the civil service (consider the independence of the military apparatus from the civil administration), or of the academic faculties, etc.

REIFICATION AND THE CONSCIOUSNESS OF THE PROLETARIAT   209

Notes

1 *A Contribution to the Critique of Political Economy*, p. 53.
2 *Capital* III, p. 324.
3 *Capital* III, p. 810.
4 *Capital* I, p. 72. On this antagonism cf. the purely economic distinction between the exchange of goods in terms of their value and the exchange in terms of their cost of production. *Capital* III, p. 174.
5 *Capital* I, p. 170.
6 Cf. *Capital* I, pp. 322, 345.
7 This whole process is described systematically and historically in *Capital* I. The facts themselves can also be found in the writings of bourgeois economists like Bücher, Sombart, A. Weber and Gottl among others—although for the most part they are not seen in connection with the problem of reification.
8 *Capital* I, p. 384.
9 *Capital* I, p. 355 (note).
10 That this should appear so is fully justified from the point of view of the *individual* consciousness. As far as class is concerned we would point out that this subjugation is the product of a lengthy struggle which enters upon a new stage with the organisation of the proletariat into a class—but on a higher plane and with different weapons.
11 *Capital* I, pp. 374–6, 423–4, 460, etc. It goes without saying that this 'contemplation' can be more demanding and demoralizing than 'active' labour. But we cannot discuss this further here.
12 *The Poverty of Philosophy*, pp. 58–9.
13 *Capital* I, p. 344.
14 Cf. Gottl: *Wirtschaft und Technik*, Grundriss der Sozialökonomik II, 234 et seq.
15 *Capital* I, p. 77.
16 This refers above all to capitalist private property. *Der heilige Max. Dokumente des Sozialismus* III, 363. Marx goes on to make a number of very fine observations about the effects of reification upon language. A philological study from the standpoint of historical materialism could profitably begin here.
17 *Capital* III, pp. 384–5.
18 Ibid., p. 809.
19 *Gesammelte politische Schriften*, Munich, 1921, pp. 140–2. Weber's reference to the development of English law has no bearing on our problem. On the gradual ascendancy of the principle of economic calculation, see also A. Weber, *Standort der Industrien*, especially p. 216.

210   HISTORY AND CLASS CONSCIOUSNESS

20 Max Weber, *Wirtschaft und Gesellschaft*, p. 491.
21 Ibid., p. 129.
22 If we do not emphasise the class character of the state in *this* context, this is because our aim is to understand reification as a *general* phenomenon constitutive of the *whole* of bourgeois society. But for this the question of class would have to begin with the machine. On this point see Section III.
23 Cf. Max Weber, *Politische Schriften*, p. 154.
24 Cf. the essay by A. Fogarasi in *Kommunismus*, Jg. II, No. 25/26.
25 *Die Metaphysik der Sitten*, Pt. I, § 24.
26 *The Origin of the Family*, in S. W. II, p. 293.
27 *Capital* III, p. 239.
28 Ibid., p. 183.
29 *Capital* I, p. 356.
30 Letter to Conrad Schmidt in S.W. II, pp. 447–8.

References

A Contribution to a Critique of Political Economy, trans. by N. I. Stone, New York and London, 1904.

Capital (3 vols.), Foreign Language Publishing House, Moscow, 1961, 1962.

S.W. = Marx/Engels, *Selected Works* (2 vols.), Lawrence and Wishart, London, 1950.

The Poverty of Philosophy, Foreign Languages Publishing House, Moscow, n.d.

[2]

THE AGE OF REVOLUTIONS: INDUSTRIAL, SOCIAL-POLITICAL, INTELLECTUAL

Raya Dunayevskaya

Our modern machine age was born of three eighteenth century revolutions—the Industrial Revolution, the American Revolution and the French Revolution. In embryo, every major question of the modern crisis was posed then. Indeed, we are first now living through the ultimate development of the contradictions that arose with the creation of industrialism. The proof that our age has not resolved the contradictions it faced at birth is as big as life. The One-Party Totalitarian State is the supreme embodiment of these contradictions. The central problem remains: *Can* man be free?

The totality of the world crisis today, and the need for a total change, compels philosophy, a total outlook. We today can better understand the revolutions in thought of that era than any previous period in history. The Industrial Revolution had undermined the old feudal order. The labor of men—under the discipline of the yarn-making and spinning machines, coke-smelted iron and the steam engine—conjured up for the capitalist greater wealth than the discovery of gold and the opening of a virgin American continent to trade. Not even the loss of "the colonies in the new world" could halt the development of industrial capitalism in England. Not so in backward France where royalty and the vested interests of the old feudal order kept the fledgling bourgeoisie in check.

1776 saw the birth of America as a nation. It was the year of publication of Adam Smith's, *The Wealth of Nations,* which

MARXISM AND FREEDOM

marked the birth of classical political economy. The impact that the Industrial Revolution exerted on English political economy, the French Revolution exerted on German idealist philosophy. Under this impact, the greatest of the German idealist philosophers, Georg Wilhelm Friedrich Hegel, reorganized all hitherto existing philosophy. These revolutions in thought can be fully understood only in the light of the revolutions in action, particularly the development of the great French Revolution. There is nothing in thought—not even in the thought of a genius—that has not previously been in the activity of the common man.

1) The French Revolution in Books and in Life

Despite the mountain of books on the French Revolution, there is not, to this day, a full account of the depth and breadth of the activity of the French masses. It is only recently that Daniel Guérin has written a truly pioneering work, *The Class Struggles in the First French Republic*,[1] but this has yet to be translated into English. In 1947 there was published in America the translation of *The Coming of the French Revolution* by Georges Lefebvre, Professor Emeritus of the History of the French Revolution at the University of Paris, but that analysis limits itself to the beginnings of the Revolution.[2]

The French Revolution was marked at once by great daring, continuity and permanence of its revolutionary actions. There were great mass mobilizations not only against the royalists, but against the right wing of the rising bourgeoisie (the Girondists), and *also* against the left wing (the Mountain or the Jacobins) led by that best known of all revolutionary leaders, Robespierre.

It is a popular pastime of liberal historians to say that 1789, which brought the middle class into power, was "a child of eighteenth century philosophy." And they add that 1793 was "only" a "work of circumstance and necessity." The inference seems to be that because the masses had no "theory," they left no real imprint on "history." The truth is that precisely the spontaneity of 1789 and of 1793, *especially 1793*, bears both the stamp and the seal of the demands of the mass movement and the *method* by

THE AGE OF REVOLUTIONS

which the masses meant to construct a new society in place of the old.

It is true that prior to the Revolution the *sans-culottes*, that is, the deepest layers of the mass movement, had no *theory* of direct democracy. Neither did anyone else, least of all the philosophers. It is true that the town poor did not organize themselves as a conscious substitute for parliament. But they spontaneously infused the old institutions, such as the Commune, with a new content. At the same time entirely new forms of association—clubs, societies, committees—sprung up everywhere. By the simple act of not going home after voting but remaining at the polls and talking, the electoral assemblies were transformed into genuine communal assemblies of deliberation and action. The Sections of Paris seethed with life. They remained in *permanent* session. First, they met daily (opening at five or six in the evening). Second, they elected a *bureau of correspondence* to assure contact among the various Sections of the capital, thereby keeping constantly informed of developments and *coordinating* their actions. Third, they watched and tracked down suspects and saw to it that the revolutionary spirit was not controverted.

Thus, on January 1790, they opposed the arrest of Marat and made their views known through actions to *consolidate* the gains of the Revolution. On June 18, 1791, they adopted Robespierre's suggestion for the abolition of all distinctions between "active" citizens, that is, those who could pay the tax for voting, and "passive" citizens or those who could not. Indeed, some Sections had already taken matters into their own hands and had already abolished this distinction. The mass movement thus taught the new bourgeoisie its first lesson in democracy. By July 1792, the Assembly sessions became public: women and young people, who were not eligible to vote, were admitted to the galleries.

In his work, Guérin shows how the *sans-culottes* instinctively felt the necessity to oppose their own direct, supple and clear forms of representation to the indirect, cumbersome and abstract representation of parliamentary democracy. The Sections, Communes and popular societies, day after day, immediately expressed the will of the masses, of the revolutionary vanguard. The feeling that they were the most effective instruments and the most authen-

MARXISM AND FREEDOM

tic interpreters of the Revolution gave them the boldness to dispute power with the sacrosanct Convention. The people were so little enmeshed in a lifeless, preconceived idea, they were so far removed from all abstract formalism, that the concrete forms of their dual power varied at each instant. But let us begin from the beginning.

2) *The Parisian Masses and the Great French Revolution*

July 14, 1789, signalled the most thoroughgoing bourgeois revolution. In distinction from the American Revolution which had preceded it, the French people were not struggling against a foreign enemy. Their suffering came from their own anointed rulers. The enemy was within. The monarchy, corrupt to the marrow of its royal bones and blue blood, kept the masses in poverty and restricted the movements of the young burghers. The nobility, landlords and clergy lived in wanton luxury on the bent backs of the peasants held in bondage.

At the very time that science had been set free by the rising commercial and industrial class in England, the regime in France tried to maintain serfdom in thought by prohibiting scientists from overstepping the limits set by superstitious faith.

These contradictions and antagonisms reached a point of explosion and of unity with the storming of the Bastille. Classes fused into a new nation to rid themselves of the old order. On the countryside the peasants refused to pay tithes, sacked chateaux, burned deeds and repossessed the commons. In the cities workers and free burghers organized themselves into committees, clubs, societies and Communes to assure the destruction of the old and the creation of the new social order.

The Revolution began with the storming of the Bastille in 1789, but the feudal monarchy was not finally and completely overthrown until the working masses in the Sections of Paris carried through the insurrection of August 10, 1792. Only then did the legislature decide that the new assembly, the Convention, would be elected by universal suffrage. *Democracy, thus, was not invented by philosophic theory nor by the bourgeois leadership. It was discovered by the masses in their method of action. There*

THE AGE OF REVOLUTIONS

is a double rhythm in destroying the old and creating the new which bears the unmistakable stamp of the *self-activity which is the truly working class way of knowing*. This, in fact, was the greatest of all the achievements of the great French Revolution— the workers' discovery of their own way of knowing.

The masses *did* something. They fought concretely for bread and clothes; for arms to fight the enemy at home and abroad; for price controls. The established leaders opposed. The masses then used the committees they had themselves created to impose their will on the Assembly. They linked their demand for bread and work with their demand for political freedom and full citizenship. Necessity, not theory, forced them to act directly in the shaping of the new society. Their actions not only gained them their demands but taught them who truly represented them. By 1793, it was not Robespierre and the Jacobins, but the *enragés* Jacques Roux, Theophile Leclerc and Jean Varlet. They were the true spokesmen for the mass revolutionary movement.[3]

"Deputies of the Mountain," said Jacques Roux, "it is a pity that you have not climbed from the third to the ninth floor of the houses of this revolutionary town; you would have been softened by the tears and groans of the vast masses, lacking bread and without clothes, reduced to this state of distress and misfortune by the gambling on the Stock Exchange and speculation in food."

Theophile Leclerc invited the legislators to rise at three in the morning and to take their place among the citizens who besieged the doors of the bakers: "Three hours of his time passed at the door of a bakery would do more to train a legislator than four years spent on the benches of the Convention."

To Robespierre, Reason was the "Supreme Being." But Reason, said Jean Varlet, lived among the masses: "During four years, constantly on the public square among groups of the people, among the *sans-culottes*, among the people whom I love, I have learned how naively, and just by saying what they think, the poor devils of the garrets reasoned more surely, more boldly than the fine gentlemen, the great talkers, the bumbling men of learning; if they wish to gain scientific knowledge let them go and move about like me among the people."[4]

The working class of France, in 1789, was numerically weak. Yet these approximately six hundred thousand, out of a population of some twenty-five million, had accomplished miracles in the thorough destruction of the old order. They did not, and could not, at this birth-stage of capitalist development, separate themselves completely from the revolutionary bourgeois leadership. They had learned that only by their own mass mobilizations and constant activity could they obtain their demands. Robespierre, who had learned so effectively to mobilize those enormous energies against feudal and royal reaction, worked to confine the Revolution. In the material and historic circumstances of the time, the Revolution could not, in any case, have realized the equalitarian principles for which the true representatives of the Parisian masses fought. We cannot follow Robespierre in the course he charted. For our purpose it is sufficient to note that he opened the door to the White Terror which took his life as it prepared the ground for Napoleon.

The great French Revolution, begun for "Liberty, Equality and Fraternity" emblazoned on its Declaration of the Rights of Man —even as the American Revolution, fought under the banner of the Declaration of Independence—ended in the consolidation of power by a new ruling class. This was a new exploitative class which, nevertheless, had a wider popular support than the feudal predecessor it so thoroughly destroyed: (1) Without temporizing, the new ruling class gave legal sanction to, and participated in, the extermination of feudal tithes without indemnification. (2) Where the peasants had seized the land to which they were formerly bound as serfs, this property of Church and emigré nobility was nationalized. (3) The King was deposed and universal male suffrage was established for the first time in the first modern Republic in Europe.

The Industrial Revolution *and* the definitive taking of the land by the peasants formed the solid economic foundation of the new ruling class.[5] This foundation assured the capitalists of remaining the ruling class, whether the form of political power was Republic or Empire.

Half a century later, the young Marx drew from the French Revolution, from the *mass* movement, the principles of revolu-

THE AGE OF REVOLUTIONS

tionary socialism. Before Marx's birth, however, Hegel had already met the challenge of the French Revolution to reorganize completely the premises of philosophy.

3) The Philosophers and the Revolution: Freedom and the Hegelian Dialectic

Hegel did not examine the French Revolution directly. He criticized the philosophers. All of philosophy before Hegel—from Bacon and Descartes through the Encyclopaedists, Rousseau, and Kant—was certain that it had worked out all fundamental problems, and that, unencumbered by the feudal order and the authority of the Church which trespassed the rights of science, the millennium would bring itself.

Rousseau and Kant did doubt that happiness would automatically result from the progress of science (industry). They sensed inherent contradiction and appealed to *human* emotions and powers. But they could go no further than an attempt to reconcile opposites through an *outside* force, that is, the practical reason of men behaving according to a universal law—"the general will."

Kant had written his *Critique of Practical Reason* the year *before* the French Revolution. Though his enthusiasm for the Revolution never wavered, he could not meet the new, unprecedented, living challenge to his philosophical premises. Hegel alone met the challenge.

There can be no question of the impact of the French Revolution upon Hegel. Nor can there be any question of the impact upon him of the division of labor and the subjugation of the worker to the machine which had been given such an impetus by the industrial development following the Revolution.

In his First System (1801) Hegel *himself* boldly faced this great new negative phenomenon—alienated labor: "The more mechanized labor becomes, the less value it has and the more the individual must toil." "The value of labor decreases in the same proportion as the productivity of labor increases . . . The faculties of the individual are infinitely restricted, and the consciousness of the factory worker is degraded to the lowest level of dullness."[6]

Hegel's description here is reminiscent of Marx's works, but he did not see the positive elements of alienated labor. Nor could he have seen them. It was to be some forty years before the factory worker would reveal all his great creative energies and be ready to challenge the new order of capitalism. All Hegel saw was a wild animal. There is no more dramatic moment in the history of thought, than when the young Hegel, describing the conditions of workers in capitalist production, breaks off the manuscript of his First System, which forever remained unfinished.

As he retired to his ivory tower, away from the realities of the day, his central theme of alienation was abstracted from the productive system. So profound, however, was the impact of what he himself called a "birth-time and a period of organization," that labor remained integral to his philosophy. We can see this in "Lordship and Bondage," that section in the *Phenomenology* where Hegel shows that the bondsman gains "a mind of his own"[7] and stands higher than the lord who lives in luxury, does not labor, and therefore cannot really gain true freedom.

Marx did not know Hegel's early writings, which were not published until the twentieth century, but he caught the critical impact from the *Phenomenology*, which he summed up as follows: "Thus the greatness of the Hegelian philosophy of its final result —the dialectic of negativity as the moving and creative principle— lies in the first place in the circumstances that Hegel . . . grasps the essence of labor . . . the true active relating of man to himself . . . as human essence is only possible . . . through the collective action of man, only as a result of history."[8]

Marx pointed out that insofar as the Hegelian philosophy "holds fast the alienation of man, even if man appears only in the form of spirit, all elements of criticism lie hidden in it and are often already prepared and worked out in a manner extending far beyond the Hegelian standpoint."[8]

What remained integral to the older, as to the younger, Hegel was the French Revolution. It had revealed that the overcoming of opposites is not a single act but a constantly developing process, a development through contradiction. He called it dialectics. It is through the struggle of opposites that the movement of humanity is propelled forward. As Hegel formulated it, in his

THE AGE OF REVOLUTIONS

Philosophy of History, it was not so much *from* as *through* slavery that man acquired freedom. Hegel was not content merely to affirm the dialectical principle of self-movement and self-activity through opposition. He examined all of human history in this light. His patient tracing of the specific forms of the creating and overcoming of opposites is a landmark that has never been equalled.

"In my view," Hegel wrote, "everything depends on grasping and expressing the ultimate truth not as Substance but as Subject as well."[9] Freedom is the animating spirit, the "Subject" of Hegel's greatest works. All of history, to Hegel, is a series of historical stages in the development of freedom. This is what makes him so contemporary. *Phenomenology of Mind, Science of Logic,* and *Philosophy of Mind* have to be considered *as a whole*. Freedom is not only Hegel's point of departure. It is his point of return: "When individuals and nations have once got in their heads the abstract concept of full-blown liberty, there is nothing like it in its uncontrollable strength, just because it is the very essence of mind, and that as its very actuality. Whole continents, Africa and the East, have never had this idea, and are without it still. The Greeks and Romans, Plato and Aristotle, even the Stoics, did not have it. On the contrary, they saw that it is only by birth (as e.g. an Athenian or Spartan citizen), or by strength of character, education or philosophy (—the sage is free even as a slave and in chains) that the human being is actually free. It was through Christianity that this idea came into the world."[10]

The young Hegel may or may not have had reservations on the point that it was through Christianity that the idea of freedom was born. But whether Christianity is taken as the point of departure, or whether—as with Marx—the point of departure is the *material* condition for freedom created by the Industrial Revolution, the essential element is this: man has *to fight* to gain freedom; thereby is revealed "the negative character" of modern society. As Marx's collaborator, Frederick Engels, pointed out: IF man were in fact free, there would be no problem, no *Phenomenology*, no *Logic*. What is crucial to both Hegel and Marx is that there are barriers in contemporary society, which prevent the full development of man's potentialities, of man's "universality."

MARXISM AND FREEDOM

Hegel was tracing the development of philosophic thought and used some head-cracking terms, abstractions, but the applicability of his method and his ideas go beyond his own use of them. Brought out of their abstractions, Hegel's "Absolutes" have applicability and meaning for every epoch, ours most of all. Despite the fact that Hegel is tracing the dialectic of "pure thought," the dialectic of "Absolute Knowledge," "the Absolute Idea" and "Absolute Mind" are not confined to thought processes alone, and Hegel did not separate his philosophy from actual history. For every stage of development of thought there is a corresponding stage in the development of the world.[11]

This genius achieved the seemingly impossible. Because to him there was one Reason, and one Reason only—whether he *called* it "World Spirit" or "Absolute Mind," it was the *actuality of freedom*—he succeeded in breaking down the division between the finite and infinite, the human and divine. His LOGIC *moves*. Each of the previously inseparable divisions between opposites—between thought and reality—is in constant process of change, disappearance and reappearance, coming into head-on collision with its opposite and developing thereby. It is thus, and thus alone, that man finally achieves true freedom, not as a possession, but as a dimension of his being: "If to be aware of the idea—to be aware, i.e., that men are aware of freedom as their essence, aim, and object—is matter of *speculation,* still this very idea itself is the actuality of men—not something which they *have,* as men, but which they *are.*"[12]

Hegel's *presupposition,* that human capacity has infinite possibility of expansion, enabled him to present, even if only in thought, the stages of development of mankind as stages in the struggle for freedom. Thus, he could present the past and the present as a continuous development to the future, from lower to ever higher stages. This bond of continuity with the past is the lifeblood of the dialectic. Hegel envisions a society where man realizes all of his human potentialities and thus achieves consciously what the realm of nature achieves through blind necessity. "The Truth," that is, freedom as part of man's very nature, is not something "added" by Hegel. It is of the grandeur of his vision and flows from the very nature of the *Absolute Method,* dialectical philoso-

THE AGE OF REVOLUTIONS

phy: "To hold fast the positive in its negative, and the content of the presupposition in the result, is the most important part of rational cognition."[18]

When Marx said that the Ideal is nothing but the reflection of the real, translated into thought, he was not departing either from Hegel's dialectic *method or* from his Absolutes. We shall see this when we come to Marx's CAPITAL and *his* Absolute—the "new passions and forces" for a new society.

"To hold fast the positive in the negative," meant for Marx to hold fast to the concept of the self-activity of the proletariat creating a new social order out of the old, miserable, negative capitalist society which is in existence.

Hegel did not see the creativity of the factory worker—nor could he have at that infant stage of development. He worked out all the contradictions *in thought alone.* In life all contradictions remained, multiplied, intensified. It would however be a complete misreading of his philosophy were we to think that because he resolved the contradictions of life in thought alone that, therefore, his Absolute is either a mere reflection of the separation between the intellectual world and the world of material production, *or* that he thereby remained sealed off from the world in a closed, ontological system. Quite the reverse. Hegel broke with the whole tendency of introversion which characterized German idealist philosophy. Where all other philosophers put the realization of truth and freedom in the soul, or in heaven, Hegel drew history into philosophy.

NOTES

1. Daniel Guérin, *La Lutte de Classes Sous La Première République*, two volumes, Paris 1946.

2. The reader should also consult *The French Revolution* and *After Robespierre: Thermidorian Reaction* by Albert Mathiez.

3. Cf. Marx: "The revolutionary movement which began in 1789 in *Cercle social*, which in the middle of its course had as its chief representatives *Leclerc* and *Roux* and which was temporarily defeated with *Baboef's* conspiracy, brought forth the *communist* idea which Baboeuf's friend *Buonarroti* reintroduced into France after the Revolution of 1830." (*The Holy Family*, pp. 160-1.)

4. The quotations of Varlet, Roux, and Leclerc are from Daniel Guérin, *op. cit.*

5. Frederick Engels, in his *Peasant Wars in Germany*, has pointed out that the sixteenth century German Reformation betrayed the peasant revolts by not giving them the land and, as a result, the country itself "disappeared for three centuries from the ranks of countries playing an independent part in history." The question of land and the peasant as the prerequisite for a successful revolution was brought home to us in the Civil War. We suffer still from this incomplete revolution in the South where the Negro did not get his "40 acres and a mule." To deal with it here, however, is out of the scope of the present work.

6. Quoted by Herbert Marcuse, *Reason and Revolution*, p. 79.

7. In his penetrating introduction to Hegel's *Early Theological Writings*, Richard Kroner, who, it need hardly be stressed, is no Marxist, has this to say: "Perhaps young Marx, reading this, found the germ of his future program. In any case, foreshadowed in the words ('mind of his own') is the pattern of the labor movement which was to make the proletarian conscious of his existence and to grant him the knowledge of having a mind of his own."

8. See Appendix A, "Critique of the Hegelian Dialectic."

9. *Phenomenology of Mind*, p. 80.

10. *Philosophy of Mind*, paragraph 482, pages 401-02.

11. Anyone who gets a headache grappling with the metaphysical struggles of consciousness and self-consciousness leading to the "Absolute," has the difficulty primarily because of one failing—the failure to hold firmly to the actual historic periods Hegel had in mind when he described the development of "pure thought" from the rise of the ancient Greek city-state through the French Revolution. Once he does hold firmly to the historical development, he can see in the *Phenomenology of Mind* not only the past but the present as well, the daily life experiences common to all of us. Who hasn't seen the "Alienated Soul" or "Unhappy Consciousness" among his restless friends— the tired radicals who cannot find a place for themselves in or out of the bourgeois fold, fall into "a giddy whirl of self-perpetuating disorder," and

MARXISM AND FREEDOM

land on the green couch? Who hasn't seen "the true and virtuous" among the labor bureaucrats turning away from reality "in a frenzy of self-conceit" because they have given their "all" for the workers only to be repaid in wildcats? Indeed the *Phenomenology* contains both the tragedy of our times and its comedy.

12. *Philosophy of Mind*, par. 482, p. 101.
13. *Science of Logic*, Vol. II, page 476.

References

Guérin, Daniel, *La Lutte de Classes Sous La Première République;* 2 Vols; Paris, 1946.

Hegel, Georg Wilhelm Friedrich, *Phenomenology of Mind, The;* translated by J. B. Baillie;

————, *Philosophy of Mind;* translated from The *Encyclopaedia of the Philosophical Sciences*, by William Wallace; Oxford University Press, Oxford, 1894.

————, *Science of Logic;* 2 Vols.; translated by W. H. Johnston and L. G. Struthers; The Macmillan Co., New York, 1951.

Marcuse, Herbert, *Reason and Revolution: Hegel and the Rise of Social Theory;* 2nd edition; Humanities Press, New York, 1954.

Marx, Karl and Frederick Engels, *History of Economic Theories from the Physiocrats to Adam Smith;* The Langland Press, New York, 1952.

————, *Holy Family, The;* Foreign Languages Publishing House, Moscow, 1956.

Mathiez, Albert, *After Robespierre: Thermidorian Reaction;* A. A. Knopf, New York, 1931.

————, *French Revolution, The;* A. A. Knopf, New York, 1928.

[3]

Putting Dialectics to Work: The Process of Abstraction in Marx's Method

Bertell Ollman

The Problem:
How to Think Adequately About Change and Interaction

Is there any part of Marxism that has received more abuse than his dialectical method? I am not just thinking about enemies of Marxism and socialism, but also about scholars who are friendly to both. It is not Karl Popper but George Sorel in his Marxist incarnation who refers to dialectics as "the art of reconciling opposites through hocus pocus" (1950, 171), and the English socialist economist, Joan Robinson, who on reading *Capital* objects to the constant intrusion of "Hegel's nose" between her and Ricardo (1953, 23). But perhaps the classic complaint is fashioned by the American philosopher, William James, who compares reading about dialectics in Hegel—it could just as well have been Marx—to getting sucked into a whirlpool (1978, 174).

Yet, other thinkers have considered Marx's dialectical method among his most important contributions to socialist theory, and Lukács goes so far as to claim that orthodox Marxism relies solely upon adherence to his method (1971, 1). Though Lukács may be exaggerating to make his point, it is not, in my view, by very much. The reasons for such widespread disagreement on the meaning and value of dialectics are many, but what stands out is the inadequate attention given to the nature of its subject matter. What, in other words, is dialectics about? What questions does it deal with and why are they important? Until there is more clarity, if not consensus, on its basic task, treatises on dialectics will only succeed in piling one layer of obscurity upon another. So this is where we must begin.

First and foremost, and stripped of all qualifications added by this or that dialectician, the subject of dialectics is change, all change, and interaction, all kinds and degrees of interaction. This is not to say that dialectical thinkers recognize the existence of change and interaction while nondialectical thinkers do not. That would be foolish. Everyone recognizes that everything in the world changes, somehow and to some degree, and that the same holds true for interaction. The problem is how to think adequately about them, how to capture them in thought. How, in other words, can we think about change and interaction so as not to miss or distort the real changes and interactions that we know, in a general way at least, are there (with all the implications this has for how to study them and to communicate what we find to others)? This is the key problem addressed by dialectics; this is what all dialectics is about, and it is in helping to resolve *this* problem that Marx turns to the process of abstraction.

The Solution Lies in the Process of Abstraction

In his most explicit statement on the subject, Marx claims that his method starts from the "real concrete" (the world as it presents itself to us) and proceeds through "abstraction" (the intellectual activity of breaking this whole down into the mental units with which we think about it) to the "thought concrete" (the reconstituted and now understood whole present in the mind) (1904, 293-94). The real concrete is simply the world in which we live, in all its complexity. The thought concrete is Marx's reconstruction of that world in the theories of what has come to be called "Marxism." The royal road to understanding is said to pass from the one to the other through the process of abstraction.

In one sense, the role Marx gives to abstraction is simple recognition of the fact that all thinking about reality begins by breaking it down into manageable parts. Reality may be in one piece when lived, but to be thought about and communicated it must be parcelled out. Our minds can no more swallow the world whole at one sitting than can our stomachs. Everyone then, and not just Marx and Marxists, begins the task of trying to make sense of their surroundings by distinguishing certain features, and focusing on and organizing them in ways deemed appropriate. "Abstract" comes from the Latin, "abstrahere," which means "to pull from." In effect, a piece had been pulled from or taken out of the whole and is temporarily perceived as standing apart.

We "see" only some of what lies in front of us, "hear" only part of the noises in our vicinity, "feel" only a small part of what our body is in contact with, and so on through the rest of our senses. In each case, a focus is established and a kind of boundary set within our perceptions distinguishing what is relevant from what is not. It should be clear that "What did you see?" (What caught your eye?) is a different question from "What did you *actually* see?" (What came into your line of vision?). Likewise, in thinking about any subject we focus on only some of its qualities and relations. Much that could be included—that may in fact be included in another person's view or thought, and may on another occasion be included in our own—is left out. The mental activity involved in establishing such boundaries, whether conscious or unconscious—though it is usually an amalgam of both—is the process of abstraction.

Responding to a mixture of influences that include the material world and our experiences in it as well as to personal wishes and social constraints, it is the process of abstraction that establishes the specificity of the objects with which we interact. In setting boundaries, in ruling so far and no further, it is what makes something one (or two or more) of a kind, and lets us know where that kind begins and ends. With this decision as to units, we also become, as we shall see, committed to a particular set of relations between them—relations made possible and even necessary by the qualities that we have included in each—a register for classifying them, and a mode for explaining them.

From what has been said so far, it is clear that "abstraction" is itself an abstraction. I have abstracted it from Marx's dialectical method, which in turn was abstracted from his broad theories, which in turn were abstracted from his life and work. The mental activities that we have collected and brought into focus as "abstraction" are more often associated with the processes of perception, conception, defining, reasoning, and even thinking. It is not surprising, therefore, if the process of abstraction strikes many people as both foreign and familiar at the same time. Each of these more familiar processes operates in part by separating out, focusing on, and emphasizing only some aspects of that reality with which they come into contact. In "abstraction," we have simply separated out, focused on, and emphasized certain common features of these other processes. Abstracting "abstraction" in this way is neither easy nor obvious, and therefore few people have done it. Consequently, though everyone abstracts, of necessity, only a few are aware of it as such. This philosophical impoverishment is reinforced by the fact that most people are lazy abstractors, simply and uncritically accepting the mental units with which they think as part of their cultural inheritance.

A further complication in grasping "abstraction" arises from the fact that Marx uses the term in three different, though closely related, senses. First, and most important, it refers to the mental activity of subdividing the world into the mental constructs with which we think about it, which is the process that we have been describing. Second, it refers to the results of this process, the actual parts into which reality has been apportioned. That is to say, for Marx, as for Hegel before him, "abstraction" functions as a noun as well as a verb, the noun referring to what the verb has brought into being. In these senses, everyone can be said to abstract (verb) and to think with abstractions (noun). But Marx also uses "abstraction" in a third sense, where it refers to a suborder of particularly ill-fitting mental constructs. Whether because they are too narrow, take in too little, focus too exclusively on appearances, or are otherwise badly composed, these constructs do not allow an adequate grasp of their subject matter.

Taken in this third sense, abstractions are the basic unit of ideology, the inescapable ideational result of living and working in alienated society. "Freedom," for example, is said to be such an abstraction whenever we remove the real individual from "the conditions of existence within which these individuals enter into contact" (Marx 1973, 164). Omitting from the meaning of "freedom" the conditions that make freedom possible (or impossible)—including the real alternatives available, the role of money, the socialization of the person choosing, and so on—leaves a notion that can only distort and obfuscate even that part of reality which it sets out to convey. A lot of Marx's criticism of ideology makes use of this sense of "abstraction," as when he says that people in capitalist society are "ruled by abstractions" (1973, 164). Such remarks, of which there are a great many in his writings, must not keep us from seeing that Marx also abstracts in the first sense given above and, like everyone else, thinks with abstractions in the second sense, and that the particular way in which he does both goes a long way in accounting for the distinctive character of Marxism.

Despite several explicit remarks on the centrality of abstraction in Marx's work, the process of abstraction has received relatively little attention in the literature on Marxism. Serious work on Marx's dialectical method can usually be distinguished on the basis of which of the categories belonging to the vocabulary of dialectics is treated as pivotal. For Lukács (1971), it was the concept of totality that played this role; for Mao (1968), it was contradiction; for Raya Dunayevskaya (1982), it was the negation of the negation;

for Scott Meikle (1985), it was essence; for the Ollman of *Alienation* (1976), it was internal relations; and so on. Even when abstraction is discussed—and no serious work dismisses it altogether—the main emphasis is generally on what it is in the world or in history or in Marx's research into one or the other that is responsible for the particular abstractions made, and not on the process of abstraction as such, on what exactly he does and how he does it.[1] Consequently, the implications of Marx's abstracting practice for the theories of Marxism remain clouded, and those wishing to develop these theories, and where necessary revise them, receive little help in their efforts to abstract in the manner of Marx. In what follows, it is just this process of abstraction, how it works and particularly how Marx works it, that serves as the centerpiece for our discussion of dialectics.

How Marx's Abstractions Differ

What then is distinctive about Marx's abstractions? To begin with, it should be clear that Marx's abstractions do not and cannot diverge completely from the abstractions of other thinkers both then and now. There has to be a lot of overlap. Otherwise, he would have constructed what philosophers call a "private language," and any communication between him and the rest of us would be impossible. How close Marx came to falling into such an abyss and what can be done to repair some of the damage already done are discussed in the longer work of which this essay is a part. Second, in depicting Marx's process of abstraction as a predominantly conscious and rational activity, I do not mean to deny the enormous degree to which what results from this activity accurately reflects the real world. However, the materialist foundations of Marx's thinking are sufficiently (though by no means "adequately") understood to be taken for granted here while we concentrate on the process of abstraction as such.

Keeping these two qualifications clearly in mind, we can now say that what is most distinctive about Marx's abstractions, taken as a group, is that they focus on and incorporate both change and interaction (or system) in the

1. Possible exceptions to this relative neglect of abstractions in discussions of Marx's method include E. V. Ilyenkov (1982), where the emphasis is on the relation of abstract to concrete in *Capital;* A. Sohn-Rethel (1978), which shows how commodity exchange produces abstractions; D. Sayer (1987), which concentrates on the ideological products of the process of abstraction; and L. Nowak (1980), which presents a neo-Weberian reconstruction of some aspects of this process. Insightful, though limited, treatments of abstraction can also be found in articles by A. Sayers (1981), J. Allen (1983), and R. J. Horvath and K. D. Gibson (1984). An early philosophical account of abstraction, which Marx himself had a chance to read and admire, is found in the work of Joseph Dietzgen (1928).

Dialectics and Abstraction

particular forms in which these occur in the capitalist era. It is important to underline from the start that Marx's main concern was capitalism. He sought to discover what it is and how it works, as well as how it emerged and where it is tending. We shall call the organic and historical processes involved here the double movement of the capitalist mode of production. Each movement affects the other, and how one grasps either affects one's understanding of both. But how does one study the history of a system, or the systemic functioning of evolving processes, where the main determinants of change lie within the system itself? For Marx, the first and most important step was to incorporate the general form of what he was looking for—to wit, change and interaction—into all the abstractions he constructed as part of his research. Marx's understanding of capitalism, therefore, is not restricted to the theories of Marxism, which relate the components of the capitalist system, but some large part of it is found within the very abstractions with which these theories have been constructed.

Beginning with historical movement, Marx's preoccupation with change and development is undisputed. What is less well known, chiefly because it is less clear, is how he thought about change, how he abstracted it, and how he integrated these abstractions into his study of a changing world. The underlying problem is as old as philosophy itself. The ancient Greek philosopher, Heraclitus, provides us with its classic statement when he asserts that a person cannot step into the same river twice. Enough water has flowed between the two occasions so that the river we step into the second time is not the same river that we walked into earlier. Yet our common sense tells us that it is, and our speech practice reflects this view. Heraclitus, of course, was not interested in rivers but in change. His point is that change goes on everywhere and all the time but that our manner of thinking about it is sadly inadequate. The flow, the constant alteration of movement away from something and toward something else, is generally missing. Usually, where change takes place very slowly or in very small increments, its impact can be safely neglected. On the other hand, depending on the context and on our purpose in it, even such change, because it occurs outside our attention, may occasionally startle us and have grave consequences for our lives.

Even today few are able to think about the changes they know to be happening in ways that do not distort, usually by underplaying, what is actually happening. From the titles of so many works in the social sciences, it would appear that a good deal of effort is being directed toward studying change of one kind or another. But what is actually taken as "change" in most of these works? It is not the continuous evolution and alteration that goes on in their subject matter, the social equivalent of the flowing water in

Heraclitus's river. Rather, almost invariably, it is a comparison of two or more differentiated states in the development of the object or condition or group under examination. As the sociologist, James Coleman, who defends this approach, admits, "the concept of change in science is a rather special one, for it does not immediately follow from our sense impressions...It is based on a comparison, or difference between two sense impressions, and simultaneously a comparison of the times at which the sense impressions occurred." Why? Because, according to Coleman, "the concept of change must, as any concept, itself reflect a state of an object at a point in time" (1968, 428-29). Consequently, a study of the changes in the political thinking of the American electorate, for example, gets translated into an account of how people voted (or responded to opinion polls) in 1956, 1960, 1964, and so on, and the differences found in a comparison of these static moments is what is called "change." It is not simply, and legitimately, that the one, the difference between the moments, gets taken as an indication of or evidence for the other, the process; rather, it stands in for the process itself.

In contrast to this approach, Marx set out to abstract things, in his words, "as they really are and happen," making how they happen part of what they are (Marx and Engels 1964, 57). Hence, capital (or labor, money, etc.) is not only how capital appears and functions but also how it develops; or rather, how it develops, its real history, is also part of what it is. It is also in this sense that Marx could deny that nature and history "are two separate things" (Marx and Engels 1964, 57). In the view which currently dominates the social sciences, things exist *and* undergo change. The two are logically distinct. History is something that happens to things; it is not part of their nature. Hence the difficulty of examining change in subjects from which it has been removed at the start. Whereas Marx, as he tells us, abstracts "every historical social form as in fluid movement, and therefore takes into account its transient nature *not less* than its momentary existence" (1958, 20, emphasis added).

But history for Marx refers not only to time past but to future time. Whatever something is becoming—whether we know what that will be or not—is in some important respects part of what it is along with what it once was. For example, capital, for Marx, is not simply the material means of production used to produce wealth, which is how it is abstracted in the work of most economists. Rather, it includes the early stages in the development of these particular means of production, or "primitive accumulation," indeed whatever has made it possible for it to produce the kind of wealth it produces in just the way it does (namely, permits wealth to take the form of value, something produced not because it is useful but for purposes of exchange).

Dialectics and Abstraction

Furthermore, as part of its becoming, capital incorporates the accumulation of capital that is occurring now, together with its tendency toward concentration and centralization, and the effect of this tendency on both the development of a world market and an eventual transition to socialism. According to Marx, the tendency to expand surplus-value and with it production, and therefore to create a world market, is "directly given in the concept of capital itself" (1973, 408).

That capital contains the seeds of a future socialist society is also apparent in its increasingly socialized character and in the growing separation of the material means of production from the direct control of capitalists, making the latter ever more superfluous. This "history" of capital is part of capital, contained within the abstraction that Marx makes of capital, and part of what he wants to convey with its covering concept. All of Marx's main abstractions—labor, value, commodity, money, and so on—incorporate process, becoming, history in just this way. Our purpose here is not to explain Marx's economics but simply to use some of his claims in this area to illustrate how he integrates what most readers would take to be externally related phenomena—in this case, its real past and likely future—into his abstraction of its present form.

Marx often uses the qualifying phrase "in itself" to indicate the necessary and internal ties between the future development of anything and how it presents itself at this moment. Money and commodity, for example, are referred to as "in themselves" capital (1963, 396). Given the independent form in which they confront the worker in capitalist society, something separate from him but something he must acquire in order to survive, money and commodity ensure the exchange of labor-power and their own transformation into means of production used to produce new value. Capital is part of what they are becoming, part of their future, and hence part of them, just as money and commodity are parts of what capital was, parts of its past, and hence parts of it. Elsewhere, Marx refers to money and commodity as "potential capital," as capital "only in intention, in their essence, in what they were destined to be" (1971, 465; 1963, 399-400). Similarly, all labor is abstracted as wage labor, and all means of production as capital, because this is the direction in which they are evolving in capitalist society (1963, 409-10).

To consider the past and likely future development of anything as integral to what it is, to grasp this whole as a single process, does not keep Marx from abstracting some part or instant of this process for a particular purpose and from treating it as relatively autonomous. Aware that the units into which he has subdivided reality are the results of his abstractions, Marx is able to re-abstract this reality, restricting the area brought into focus in line with the requirements of his current study. But when he does this, he often underlines its character as a temporally stable part of a larger and ongoing process by referring to it as a "moment." In this way, commodity is spoken of as a "moment in exchange," money (in its aspect as capital) as a "moment" in the process of production, and circulation in general as a "moment in the system of production" (1973, 145, 217). Marx's naming practice here reflects the epistemological priority he gives to movement over stability, so that stability, whenever it is found, is viewed as temporary and/or only apparent, or as he says on one occasion, as a "paralysis" of movement (1971, 212). With stability used to qualify change rather than the reverse, Marx, unlike most modern social scientists, did not and could not study why things change (with the implication that change is external to what they are, something that happens to them). Given that change is always a part of what things are, his research problem could only be *how, when,* and *into what* they change and why they sometimes appear not to change (ideology).

Before concluding our discussion of the place of change in Marx's abstractions, it is worth noting that thinking in terms of processes is not altogether alien to common sense. It occurs in abstractions of actions, such as eating, walking, fighting, and so on, indeed whenever the gerund form of the verb is used. Likewise, event words, such as "war" and "strike," indicate that, to some degree at least, the processes involved have been abstracted as such. On the other hand, it is also possible to think of war and strike as a state or condition, more like a photograph than a motion picture, or if the latter, then a single scene that gets shown again and again, which removes or seriously underplays whatever changes are taking place. And unfortunately, the same is true of most action verbs. They become action "things." In such cases, the real processes that go on do not get reflected, certainly not to any adequate degree, in our thinking about them. It is my impression that, in the absence of any commitment to bring change itself into focus in the manner of Marx, this is the more typical outcome.

Earlier we said that what distinguishes Marx's abstractions is that they contain not only change or history but also some portion of the system in which it occurs. Since change in anything only takes place in and through a complex interaction between closely related elements, treating change as intrinsic to what anything is requires that we treat the interaction through which it occurs in the same way. With a static notion of anything, it is easy to conceive of it as also discrete, logically independent of, and easily separable from its surrounding conditions. They do not enter directly into what it is. Viewing the same thing as a process makes it necessary to extend the

Dialectics and Abstraction

boundaries of what it is to include at least some part of the surrounding conditions that enter into this process. In sum, as far as abstractions are concerned, change brings mutual dependence in its wake. Instead of a mere sequence of events isolated from their context, a kind of one-note development, Marx's abstractions become phases of an evolving and interactive system.

Capital, which we examined earlier as a process, is also a complex relation encompassing the interaction among the material means of production, capitalists, workers, value, commodity, money, and more—and all this over time. Marx says, "the concept of capital contains the capitalist"; he refers to workers as "variable capital" and says capital is "nothing without wage labor, value, money, price, etc." (1973, 512; 1958, 209; 1904, 292). Elsewhere, the processual character of these aspects of the capital relation is emphasized in referring to them as "value in process" and "money in process" (1971, 137). If capital, like all other important abstractions in Marxism, is both a process and a relation, viewing it as primarily one or the other could only be a way of emphasizing either its historical or systemic character for a particular purpose.

As in his abstractions of capital as a process, so too in his abstractions of capital as a relation, Marx can focus on but part of what capital contains. While the temporally isolated part of a process is generally referred to as a "moment," the spatially isolated aspect of a relation is generally referred to as a "form" or "determination." With "form," Marx usually brings into focus the appearance and/or function of any relation, that by which we recognize it, and most often it is its form that is responsible for the concept by which we know and communicate it. Hence, value (a relation) in its exchangeable form is called "money"; while in the form in which it facilitates the production of more value, it is called "capital"; and so on. "Determination," on the other hand, enables Marx to focus on the transformational character of any relational part, on what best brings out its mutual dependence and changeability within the interactive system. Upon analysis, moments, forms, and determinations all turn out to be relations. So that after referring to the commodity as a moment in wealth, Marx immediately proceeds to pick it apart as a relation (1973, 218). Elsewhere, Marx refers to interest, profit, and rent as forms which through analysis lose their "apparent independence" and are seen to be relations (1971, 429).

Earlier, we saw that some abstractions that contain processes could also be found in what we called common sense. The same is true of abstractions that focus on relations. Father, which contains the relation between a man and a child, is one. Buyer, which contains the relations between a person and something sold or available for sale, is another. But compared to the number and scope of relations in the world, such relations are few and meager in their import. Within the common sense of our time and place, most social ties are thought about in abstractions that focus on the parts one at a time, separately as well as statically. Marx, however, believed that in order to adequately grasp the systemic connections that constitute such an important part of reality one has to incorporate them, along with the ways in which they change, into the very abstractions in and with which one thinks about them. All else is make-do patchwork, a one-sided, lopsided way of thinking that invites the neglect of essential connections together with the distortion of whatever influence they exert on the overall system.

Where have we arrived? Marx's abstractions are not things but processes. These processes are also, of necessity, systemic relations in which the main processes with which Marx deals are all implicated. Consequently, each process serves as an aspect, or subordinate part, of other processes grasped as clusters of relations, just as they do with respect to that process. In this way, Marx brings together what we have called the double movement of the capitalist mode of production (its history and organic movement) in the same abstractions, uniting in his thinking what is united in reality. And whenever he needs to focus on but part of this complex, he does so as a moment, a form or a determination.

Marx's abstractions seem to be very different, especially as regards the treatment of change and interaction, from those in which most people think about society. But if Marx's abstractions stand out as much as our evidence suggests they do, it is not enough to display them. We also need to know what gives Marx the philosophical license to abstract as he does. Whence comes his apparent facility in making and changing abstractions? And what is the relation between his abstractions and those of common sense? It is because most readers cannot see how Marx could possibly abstract as he does that they continue to deny, and perhaps not even notice, the widespread evidence of his practice. Therefore, before making a more detailed analysis of Marx's process of abstraction and its place and role in his dialectical method and broader theories, a brief detour through his philosophical presuppositions is in order.

The Philosophy of Internal Relations

According to Marx, "the economists do not conceive of capital as a relation. They cannot do so without at the same time conceiving of it as a historically transitory, i.e., a relative—not an absolute—form of produc-

Dialectics and Abstraction

tion" (1971, 274). This is not a comment about the content of capital, about what it is, but about the *kind* of thing it is, to wit, a relation. To grasp capital, as Marx does, as a complex relation that has at its core internal ties between the material means of production and those who own them, those who work on them, their special product, value, and the conditions in which owning and working go on, is to know capital as a historical event, as something that emerged as a result of specific conditions in the lifetime of real people and that will disappear when these conditions do. Viewing such connections as external to what capital is—which, for them, is simply the material means of production or money used to buy the means of production—the economists fall into treating capital as an ahistorical variable. Without saying so explicitly and certainly without ever explicitly defending this position, capital becomes something that has always been and will always be.

The view held by most people, scholars and others, in what we have been calling the common-sense view, maintains that there are things and there are relations, and that neither can be subsumed in the other. This position is summed up in Bishop Butler's statement that G. E. Moore adopts as a motto, "Everything is what it is, and not another thing," taken in conjunction with Hume's claim, "All events seem entirely loose and separate" (1903, title page; 1955, 85). On this view, capital may be found to have relations with labor, value, and so on, and it may even be that accounting for such relations plays an important role in explaining what capital is. But capital is one thing and its relations quite another. Marx, on the other hand, following Hegel's lead in this matter, rejects what is, in essence, a logical dichotomy. For him, as we saw, capital is itself a relation, in which the ties of the material means of production to labor, value, commodity, and so on are interiorized as parts of what capital is. Marx refers to "things themselves" as "their interconnections" (Marx and Engels 1950, 488). Moreover, these relations extend backward and forward in time, so that capital's conditions of existence as they have evolved over the years and its potential for future development are also viewed as parts of what it is.

On the common-sense view, any element related to capital can change without capital itself changing. Workers, for example, instead of selling their labor-power to capitalists as occurs in capitalism could become slaves or serfs or owners of their own means of production, and in every case their instruments of work would still be capital. The tie between workers and the means of production here is contingent, a matter of chance, and therefore external to what each really is. In Marx's view, a change of this sort would mean a change in the character of capital itself, in its appearance and/or functioning no matter how far extended. The tie is a necessary and essential one; it is an internal relation. Hence, where its specific relationship to workers has changed, the means of production become something else, and something that is best captured by a concept other than "capital." Every element that comes into Marx's analysis of capitalism is a relation of this sort. It is this view that underlies and helps to explain his practice of abstraction and the particular abstractions that result, along with all the theories raised on them.

It appears that the problem non-Marxists have in understanding Marx is much more profound than is ordinarily thought. It is not simply that they do not grasp what Marx is saying about capital (or labor or value, etc.) because his account is unclear or confused or that the evidence for his claims is weak or undeveloped. Rather, the basic form, the relation, in which Marx thinks about each of the major elements that come into his analysis is unavailable, and therefore its ideational content is necessarily misrepresented, if only a little (though usually it is much more). As an attempt to reflect the relations in capitalist society by incorporating them into its core abstractions, Marxism suffers the same distorting fate as these relations themselves.

In the history of ideas, the view that we have been developing is known as the philosophy of internal relations. Marx's immediate philosophical influences in this regard were Leibniz, Spinoza, and Hegel, particularly Hegel. What all had in common is the belief that the relations that come together to make up the whole get expressed in what are taken to be its parts. Each part is viewed as incorporating in what it is all its relations with other parts up to and including everything that comes into the whole. To be sure, each of these thinkers had a distinctive view of what the parts are. For Leibniz, it was monads; for Spinoza, modes of nature or God; and for Hegel, ideas. But the logical form in which they construed the relation between parts and whole was the same.

Some writers on Marx have argued for a restricted form of internal relations that would apply only to society and not to the natural world (Rader 1979, chap. 3). But reality does not allow such absolute distinctions. People have bodies as well as minds and social roles. Alienation, for example, affects all three, and in their alienated forms each is internally related to the others. Likewise, capital, commodities, money, and the forces of production all have material as well as social aspects. To maintain that the philosophy of internal relations does not respect the usual boundaries between nature and society does not mean that Marx cannot for certain purposes abstract units that fall primarily or even wholly on one or the other side of this divide. Whenever he speaks of "thing" or, as is more frequent, of "social relations," this is what occurs, but in every case what has been momentarily put aside is internally related to what has been brought into focus. Consequently, he is unlikely to minimize or dismiss, as many operating with external relations do, the influences of either natural or social phenomena on the other.

What is the place of such notions as "cause" and "determine" within a philosophy of internal relations? Given the mutual interaction Marx assumes between everything in reality, now and forever, there can be no cause that is logically prior to and independent of that to which it is said to give rise and no determining factor that is itself not effected by that which it is said to determine. In short, the common-sense notions of "cause" and "determine" that are founded on such logical independence and absolute priority do not and cannot apply. In their stead we find frequent claims of the following kind: the propensity to exchange is the "cause or reciprocal effect" of the division of labor; and interest and rent "determine" market prices and "are determined" by it (1959a, 134; 1971, 512). In any organic system viewed over time, each process can be said to determine and be determined by all others. However, it is also the case that one part often has a greater effect on others than they do on it; and Marx also uses "cause" and especially "determine" to register this asymmetry. Thus, in the interaction among production, distribution, exchange, and consumption—particularly though not exclusively in capitalism—production is held to be more determining (1904, 274ff.). A good deal of Marx's research is devoted to locating and mapping whatever exercises a greater or special impact on other parts of the capitalist system, but, whether made explicit or not, this always takes place on a backdrop of reciprocal effect (another complementary sense of "cause" and "determine" will be presented later).

Returning to the process of abstraction, it is the philosophy of internal relations that gives Marx both license and opportunity to abstract as freely as he does, to decide how far into its internal relations any particular will extend. Making him aware of the need to abstract—since boundaries are never given and when established never absolute—it also allows and even encourages re-abstraction, makes a variety of abstractions possible, and helps to develop his mental skills and flexibility in making abstractions. If "a relation," as Marx maintains, "can obtain a particular embodiment and become individualized only by means of abstraction," then learning how to abstract is an absolutely indispensable step in learning how to think (1973, 142).

Operating with a philosophy of external relations does not absolve others from the need to abstract. The units in and with which one thinks are still abstractions and products of the process of abstraction as it occurs during socialization, particularly in the acquisition of language. Only, in this case, one takes boundaries as given in the nature of reality as such, as if they have the same ontological stature as the qualities perceived. The role played by the process of abstraction is neither known nor appreciated. Consequently, there is no awareness that one can, and often should, re-abstract, and the ability and flexibility for doing so is never acquired. Whatever re-abstraction occurs, of necessity, as part of learning new languages or new schools of thought, or as a result of important new experiences, takes place in the dark, usually unconsciously, certainly unsystematically, with little understanding of either assumptions or implications. Marx, on the other hand, is fully aware that he abstracts and of its assumptions and implications both for his own thinking and that of others—hence the frequent equation of ideology in those he criticizes with their inadequate abstractions.[2]

Three Modes of Abstraction: Extension

Once we recognize the crucial role abstraction plays in Marx's method, how different his own abstractions are, and how often and easily he re-abstracts, it becomes clear that Marx constructs his subject matter as much as he finds it. This is not to belittle the influence of natural and social conditions on Marx's thinking, but rather to stress how, given this influence, the results of Marx's investigations are prescribed to a large degree by the preliminary organization of his subject matter. Nothing is made up of whole cloth, but at the same time Marx only finds what his abstractions have placed in his way. These abstractions do not substitute for the facts, but give them a form, an order, and a relative value; just as frequently changing his abstractions does not take the place of empirical research, but does determine, albeit in a weak sense, what he will look for, even see, and of course emphasize. What counts

2.   In order to forestall possible misunderstandings, it may be useful to assert that the philosophy of internal relations is not an attempt to reify "what lies between." It is simply that the particular ways in which things cohere become essential attributes of what they are. The philosophy of internal relations also does not mean, as some of its critics have charged, that investigating any problem can go on forever (to say that boundaries are artificial is not to deny them an existence, and, practically speaking, it is simply not necessary to understand everything in order to understand anything); or that the boundaries which are established are arbitrary (what actually influences the character of Marx's or anyone else's abstractions is another question); or that we cannot mark or work with some of the important objective distinctions found in reality (on the contrary such distinctions are a major influence on the abstractions we do make); or finally, that the vocabulary associated with the philosophy of internal relations—particularly "totality," "relation," and "identity"—cannot also be used in subsidiary senses to refer to the world that comes into being after the process of abstraction has done its work. For a more detailed discussion of the philosophy of internal relations, see Ollman (1976, 12-40, 256-96).

Dialectics and Abstraction   *41*

as an explanation is likewise determined by the framework of possible relationships imposed by Marx's initial abstractions.

So far we have been discussing the process of abstraction in general, our main aim being to distinguish it from other mental activities. Marx's own abstractions were said to stand out insofar as they invariably included elements of change and interaction, while his practice of abstracting was found to include more or less of each as suited his immediate purpose. Taking note of the importance Marx gave to abstractions in his critique of ideology, we proceeded to its underpinnings in the philosophy of internal relations, emphasizing that it is not a matter of this philosophy's making such moves possible—since everybody abstracts—but of making them easier and enabling Marx to acquire greater control over the process. What remains is to analyze in greater detail what actually occurs when Marx abstracts and to trace its results and implications for some of his major theories.

The process of abstraction, which we have been treating as an undifferentiated mental act, has three main aspects or modes, which are also its functions vis-à-vis the part abstracted on one hand, and the system to which the part belongs and which it in turn helps to shape on the other. That is, the boundary setting and bringing into focus that lie at the core of this process occur simultaneously in three different, though closely related, senses. These senses have to do with extension, level of generality, and vantage point. First, each abstraction can be said to achieve a certain extension in the part abstracted, and this applies both spatially and temporally. In abstracting boundaries in space, limits are set in the mutual interaction that occurs at a given point of time. While in abstracting boundaries in time, limits are set in the distinctive history and potential development of any part, in what it once was and is yet to become. Most of our examples of abstractions so far have been drawn from what we shall now call "abstraction of extension."

Second, at the same time that every abstraction establishes an extension, it also sets a boundary around and brings into focus a particular level of generality for treating not only the part but the whole system to which it belongs. Operating rather like a microscope that can be set at different degrees of magnification, this mode of abstraction enables us to see the unique qualities of any part or the qualities associated with its function in capitalism or the qualities that belong to it as part of the human condition (to give only the most important of these levels of generality). In abstracting capital, for example, Marx gives it an extension in both space and time, as well as a level of generality such that only those qualities associated with its appearance and functioning as a phenomenon of capitalism are highlighted (i.e., its production of value, its ownership by capitalists, its exploitation of workers, etc.). The qualities a given capital may also possess as a Ford Motor Company assembly line for making cars or as a tool in general, that is, qualities that it has as a unique object or as an instance of something human beings have always used, are not brought into the picture. They are abstracted out. This aspect of the process of abstraction has received the least attention, not only in our own discussion but in other accounts of dialectics. In what follows, we shall refer to it as "abstraction of level of generality."

Third, at the same time that abstraction establishes an extension and a level of generality, it also sets up a vantage point or place within the relationship from which to view, think about, and piece together the other components in the relationship; meanwhile, the sum of their ties (as determined by the abstraction of extension) also becomes a vantage point for comprehending the larger system of which it is part, providing both a beginning for research and analysis and a perspective in which to carry it out. With each new perspective, there are differences in what can be perceived, a different ordering of the parts, and a different sense of what is important and how much. Thus, in abstracting capital, Marx not only gives it an extension and a level of generality (that of capitalism); he also views the interrelated elements that compose it from the side of the material means of production and simultaneously transforms this configuration itself into a vantage point for viewing the larger system in which it is an internally related part, providing himself with a perspective in which all other parts will appear (one that gives to capital the central role). We shall refer to this aspect of abstraction as "abstraction of vantage point." By manipulating extension, level of generality, and vantage point, Marx puts things into and out of focus, into better focus, and into different kinds of focus, enabling himself to see more clearly, investigate more accurately, and understand more fully and more dynamically his chosen subject.

As regards the abstraction of extension, Marx's general stand in favor of large units is evident from such statements as, "In each historical epoch, property has developed differently and under a set of entirely different social relations. Thus, to define bourgeois property is nothing else than to give an exposition of all these social relations of bourgeois productions...To try to give a definition of property an independent relation, a category apart, an abstraction and eternal idea, can be nothing but an illusion of metaphysics and jurisprudence" (n.d., 154). Obviously, large abstractions are needed to think adequately about a complex, internally related world.

The specifics of Marx's position emerge from his frequent criticisms of the political economists for offering too narrow abstractions (narrow in the double sense of including too few connections and too short a time period) of one or another economic form. Ricardo, for example, is reproached for abstracting too short a period in his notions of money and rent, and for omitting social relations in his abstraction of value (1968, 125; 1971, 131). One of the most serious distortions is said to arise from the tendency among political economists to abstract processes solely in terms of their end results. Commodity exchange, for example, gets substituted for the whole of the process by which a product becomes a commodity and eventually available for exchange (1973, 198). As Amiri Baraka so colorfully points out: "Hunting is not those heads on the wall" (1966, 173). By thinking otherwise for the range of problems with which they are concerned, the political economists avoid seeing the contradictions in the specific capitalist processes that give rise to these results.

The same narrowing of abstractions obtains a similar ideological result in thinking about human beings. In order to maximize individual freedom, Max Stirner sought to abstract an "I" without any messy presuppositions. Marx's response is that by excluding all that brought it into existence and the full context in which it acts, this "I" is not a particularly helpful abstraction for understanding anything about the individual, least of all his or her freedom (Marx and Engels 1964, 477-82). Yet, something like Stirner's "I," in the person of the isolated individual, has become the standard way of thinking about human nature in capitalist society. It is the preferred abstraction of extension in which bourgeois ideology treats human beings.

Granted the unusually large extensions Marx gives to his abstractions, we now want to examine the effects and implications of this practice for his work. What do such abstractions make possible, perhaps even necessary, and what do they make impossible? Consider all that a wide-angle photograph does in giving value to what is included, to what crowds the edges as well as to what appears at the center. Notice the relations it establishes as important, or at least relevant, and even the explanations that are implicit in what is included and what is left out. Something very similar occurs through the extension given to units of thinking in the process of abstraction. It is by placing so much in his abstractions, and by altering them as often as he does, that Marx greatly facilitates his analysis of what we have called the double motion of the capitalist mode of production. In particular, Marx's practice in abstracting extension serves as the basis for his theory of identity; it underlies his criticism of existing systems of classification and their replacement by the various classificatory schemes that distinguish his theories, for example, the class division of society, forces/relations of production, appearance/essence, and so on; and it enables him to capture in thinking the real movements going on in both nature and society.

As regards identity, Marx claims,

> It is characteristic of the entire crudeness of "common sense," which takes its rise from the "full life" and does not cripple its natural features by philosophy or other studies, that where it succeeds in seeing a distinction it fails to see a unity, and where it sees a unity it fails to see a distinction. If "common sense" establishes distinction determinations, they immediately petrify surrepticiously and it is considered the most reprehensible sophistry to rub together these conceptual blocks in such a way that they catch fire (Marx and Engels 1961, 339).

According to the common-sense approach, things are either the same (the sense in which Marx uses "unity" here) or different. A frequent criticism that Marx makes of the political economists is that they see only identity or difference in the relations they examine (1971, 168, 497, and 527). Marx has it both ways—he is forever rubbing these blocks together to make fire. Most striking are his numerous references to what most people take to be different subjects as identical. Such is his claim that "the social reality of nature and human natural science, or natural science about man are identical terms" (1959a, 111). Demand and supply (and in a "wider sense" production and consumption) are also said to be identical (1968, 505). The list of such claims, both with and without the term "identity," is very long. An example of the latter is his reference to "bourgeoisie, i.e. capital" (Marx and Engels 1945, 21).

In one place, Marx says that by "identity" he means a "different expression of the same fact" (1968, 410). This appears straightforward enough, but in Marx's case this "fact" is relational, composed of a system of mutually dependent parts. Viewing this mutual dependence within each of the interacting parts, viewing the parts as necessary aspects of each other, they become identical in expressing the same extended whole. Consequently, Marx can claim that labor and capital are "expressions of the same relation, only seen from opposite poles" (1971, 491). Underlying all such claims are abstractions of extension that are large enough to contain whatever is held to be identical.

If Marx often expands the size of an abstraction to bring out identity, he is equally capable of reducing it, generally by omitting qualities that emphasize its interdependence, in order to mark some difference. The complex relations of identity and difference that Marx attributes to production, distribution, exchange, and consumption in his Introduction to the *Critique*

Dialectics and Abstraction

of Political Economy is based on just such manipulation of these abstractions (1904, 274-92).

Besides its effect on the relation of identity, Marx's practice in abstracting extension also has major implications, as I have indicated, for the various classificatory schemes that frame his theories. Every school of thought stands out in large measure by the distinctions it makes and does not make, and by those it singles out as being in some respect the most important. Marxism is no exception. Among the better known classifications found in Marx's work are the juxtapositions of forces and relations of production, base and super-structure, materialism and idealism, nature and society, objective and subjective conditions, essence and appearance, the periodization of history based on different modes of production, and the class division of society (particularly the split between workers and capitalists).

Most accounts of Marxism try very hard to establish where one element in each of these classifications ends and the next one begins, to define neatly and permanently the boundaries that subdivide the structures into which Marx organizes human existence. However, given Marx's practice of abstracting extension based on his philosophy of internal relations, it should be clear that this is a fruitless exercise. It is only because they assume that Marx is operating with a philosophy of external relations in which the boundaries between things are taken to be of the same order as their other sense-perceptible qualities (hence determined and discoverable once and for all) that these critics can so consistently dismiss the overwhelming evidence of Marx's practice. Not only does Marx often redraw the boundaries of each of these units, but with every classification there are instances where his abstractions of individual units are large enough to contain most or even all of the qualities that seemed to fall into other contrasting units.

Marx's materialist conception of history, for example, is characterized by a set of overlapping contrasts between mode of production and "social, political and intellectual life processes," base and superstructure, forces and relations of production, economic structures (or foundations) and the rest of society, and material and social existence (1904, 11-12). Since Marx did not take much care to distinguish these different formulations, there is a great deal of dispute over which one to stress in giving an account of his views. But on two points there is widespread agreement: (1) that the first term in each pairing is in some sense determinant of the latter; and (2) that the boundaries between the terms in each case are more or less set and relatively easy to establish. But how clear-cut can such boundaries be if Marx can refer to "religion, family, state, law, morality, science, art, etc." as "particular modes of production," community and the "revolutionary class" as forces of production (which also has "the qualities of individuals" as its subjective side), theory "insofar as it gets ahold of people" as a "material force," and can treat laws regarding private property (which would seem to be part of the superstructure) as part of the base and class struggle (which would seem to be part of political life) as part of the economic structure (1959, 103; 1973, 495; n.d., 196; 1970, 137; Acton 1962, 164)? It is worth noting, too, that Engels could even refer to race as an economic factor (Marx and Engels 1951, 517).

To be sure, these are not the main uses to which Marx put these categories, but they do indicate something of their elasticity, something about how encompassing he could make his abstractions if he wanted to do so. And it does show how futile it is to try to interpret the sense in which one part is said to determine the other before coming to grips with the practice that rearranges the boundaries between them.

Perhaps the classification that has suffered the greatest misunderstanding as a result of readers' efforts to arrive at permanent boundaries is Marx's class division of society. Marx's abstraction of extension for class brings together many people but not everything about them. Its main focus is on whatever it is that both enables and requires them to perform a particular function in the prevailing mode of production. As a complex relation, class contains other aspects such as distinguishing social and economic conditions (ones that generally accompany their position in the mode of production), a group's opposition to other similarly constituted groups, its cultural level, its state of mind (encompassing both ideology and degree of consciousness of themselves as a class), and forms of intra-class communication and of inter-class political struggle. But how many of these aspects Marx actually includes in abstracting the extension of class or of any one of the classes into which he divides society varies with his problem and purpose at the time. Likewise, since all of these aspects in their peculiar configuration have evolved over time, there is also a decision to make regarding temporal extension, over how much of this evolution to include in the abstraction. How widely Marx's decisions on these matters may differ can be seen from such apparently contradictory claims as "all history is the history of class struggle" (where class contains a bare minimum of its aspects) and "class is the product of the bourgeoisie" (where class is abstracted as a sum of all these aspects) (Marx and Engels 1945, 11; Marx and Engels 1964, 93).

What class any person belongs to and even the number of classes in society are also affected by where exactly Marx draws his boundaries. Thus, "working class," for example, can refer to everyone who is employed by capitalists or to all the people who work for capitalists but also produce value (a smaller group) or to all the people who not only work for capitalists and

Dialectics and Abstraction

produce value but are also organized politically as a class (a smaller group still). As regards temporal extension, Marx can also abstract a particular group to include where they seem to be heading, together with the new set of relations that await them but which they have not yet fully acquired. In the case of peasants who are rapidly losing their land and of small businessmen who are being driven into bankruptcy, this translates into becoming wage laborers (Marx and Engels 1945, 16). Hence, the class of workers is sometimes abstracted broadly enough to include them as well, that is, people in the process of becoming workers along with those who function as workers at this moment. Marx's well-known reference to capitalism as a two-class society is based on his abstracting all groups into either workers or capitalists depending on where they seem to be heading, the landlords being the major group that is moving toward becoming capitalists. Abstracting such large spatial and temporal extensions for class is considered helpful for analyzing a society that is rapidly developing toward a situation where everyone either buys labor-power or sells it.

At the same time, Marx could abstract much more restricted extensions, which allowed him to refer to a variety of classes (and fragments of classes) based on as many social and economic differences between these groups. In this way, bankers, who are usually treated as a fragment of the capitalist class, are sometimes abstracted as a separate monied or financial class (1968, 123). This helps explain why Marx occasionally speaks of "ruling classes" (plural), a designation that also usually includes landlords, narrowly abstracted (Marx and Engels 1964, 39).

Obviously for Marx, arriving at a clear-cut, once-and-for-all classification of capitalist society into classes is not the aim, which is not to deny that one such classification (that of capitalists/landlords/workers) enjoys a larger role in his work, or that one criterion for determining class (a group's relationship to the prevailing mode of production) is more important. Much to the annoyance of his critics, Marx never defines "class" or provides a full account of the classes in capitalist society. *Capital* (vol. 3) contains a few pages where Marx appears to have begun such an account, but it was never completed (1959b, 862-63). In my view, had he finished these pages most of the problems raised by his theory of class would remain, for the evidence of his many shifting abstractions of class is clear and unambiguous. Thus, rather than looking for which class a person or group belongs to or how many classes Marx sees in capitalist society—the obsession of most critics and of not a few of his followers—the relevant question is, do we know on any given occasion when Marx uses "class," or the label associated with any particular class, to whom he is referring and why he refers to them as a class? Only then can the discussion of class advance our understanding, not of anything or of everything, but of what it is Marx is trying to explain. It cannot be repeated too often that Marx is chiefly concerned with the double movement of the capitalist mode of production, and arranging people into classes based on different though interrelated criteria is a major means for uncovering this movement. Rather than simply a way of registering social stratification as part of a flat description or as a prelude to rendering a moral judgment, which would require a stable unit, class helps Marx to analyze a changing situation of which it is an integral and changing part (Ollman 1978, chap. 2).

Besides making possible his theory of identity and the various classifications that mark his theories, Marx's practice of abstracting broad extensions for his units also enables him to capture in thought the various real movements he sets out to investigate in reality. In order to grasp things "as they really are and happen," Marx's stated aim, in order to trace their happening accurately and to give it the right weight in the interactive system to which it belongs, Marx extends his abstractions to include how things happen as part of what they are (Marx and Engels 1964, 35). Until now, change has been considered in a very general way. What I have labeled the double movement (organic and historical) of the capitalist mode of production, however, can only be fully understood by breaking it down into a number of submovements, the most important of which are quantity/quality, metamorphosis, and contradiction.[3] These are some of the main ways in which things move or happen; they are forms of change. Organizing becoming and time itself into sequences, they are the main pathways that bring order to the flow of events. As such, they help structure all of Marx's theories, and are indispensable to his account of how capitalism works, how it developed, and where it is tending.

Quantity/quality change is a historical movement containing moments of before and after, encompassing both build-up (or build-down) and what it leads to. Initially, the movement is one of quantitative change: one or more of the aspects that constitute any process-cum-relation gets larger (or smaller), or increases (or decreases) in number. Then, at a certain point with the attainment of a critical mass—which is different for each entity studied—a qualitative transformation occurs, understood as a change in appearance

---

3. Other important dialectical movements are mediation, interpenetration of polar opposites, negation of the negation, precondition and result, and unity and separation. These are all treated in the longer work of which this essay is a part, and the role that abstraction plays in constructing and helping to make visible the movements of quantity/quality, metamorphosis, and contradiction applies equally to them.

Dialectics and Abstraction

and/or function, while the entity overall remains essentially the same. In this way, Marx notes, money becomes capital, that is, acquires the ability to buy labor-power and produce value only when it reaches a certain amount (1958, 307-8). In order for such change to appear as an instance of the transformation of quantity into quality, Marx's abstractions have to contain the main aspects whose quantitative change is destined to trigger the coming qualitative change, as well as the new appearances and/or functions embodied in the latter, and all this for the time it takes for this to occur. Abstracting anything less runs the risk of first dismissing and then missing the coming qualitative change and/or misconstruing it when it happens, three frequent errors associated with bourgeois ideology.

Metamorphosis is an organic movement of interaction within a system in which qualities (occasionally appearances but usually conditions or functions) of one part get transferred to other parts so that the latter can be referred to as forms of the former. What is essential is that this process of metamorphosis be large enough to include both what is changing and what it is changing into, so that the transformation becomes an internal movement. Thus when, through exchange, value metamorphoses into commodity or money, for example, and the latter assumes some of the alienated relationships embodied in value as its own, this is seen as a later stage in the development of value itself. Otherwise, operating with smaller abstractions, commodity or money could never actually become value, and speaking of them as "forms" of value could only be understood metaphorically.

The essentially synchronic character of metamorphosis, no matter the number of steps involved, is also dependent on the size of the abstraction used. To some it may appear that the various phases in the metamorphosis of value occur one after another, serially, but this is to assume a brief duration for each phase. When, however, all the phases of this metamorphosis are abstracted as ongoing, as Marx does in the case of value—usually as aspects of production abstracted as reproduction—then all phases of the cycle are seen as occurring simultaneously (1971, 279-80). Whereas stopping too soon, which means abstracting too short a period for each phase, leaves one with an incompleted piece of the interaction and inclines one to mistake what is an organic connection for a causal one.

Contradiction, perhaps the most important of the submovements treated by Marx, has its core in a union of two or more internally related processes that are simultaneously supporting and undermining one another—internally related, because, as Marx asserts, where there is "no inner connection," there can be no "hostile connection," no "contradiction" (1971, 503). In the contradiction between capital and labor, for example, capital, as the means of production used to produce value, helps bring into existence labor of a very special kind, that is, alienated labor, labor that will best serve its needs as capital, while labor, as the production of goods intended for the market, helps fashion capital in a form that enables it to continue its exploitation of labor. However, capital and labor also possess qualities that exert pressure in the opposite direction. With its unquenchable thirst for surplus-value, capital would drive labor to exhaustion, while labor, with its inherent tendencies toward working less hours, in better conditions, and so on, would render capital unprofitable. To avoid the temptation of misrepresenting contradiction as a simple opposition, tension, or dysfunction (common ideological misrepresentations of the origins, ramifications, and potential in any conflict), it is essential that the chief movements which reproduce the existing equilibrium as well as those which tend to undermine it be brought into the same overarching abstraction.

What determines the resolution of a contradiction, of course, is not its dialectical form, the fact that differences get abstracted as a contradiction, but its real content. However, such content is unlikely to reveal its secret to anyone who cannot read it as a contradiction. By including the undermining interaction of mutually supporting processes in the same unit, by expanding this unit to take in how these crisscrossing effects have developed and where they are tending, it is Marx's broad abstractions of extension that make it possible to grasp such varied movements as internal and necessary elements of real contradictions.

Level of Generality

The second main aspect of Marx's process of abstraction, or mode in which it occurs, is the abstraction of level of generality. In his unfinished Introduction to the *Critique of Political Economy,* Marx's only systematic attempt to present this method, great care is taken to distinguish "production" from "production in general" (1904, 268-74). The former takes place in a particular society, capitalism, and includes all the relations of this society that enable it to appear and function as it does. "Production in general," on the other hand, refers to whatever it is that work in all societies have in common—chiefly the purposive activity of human beings in transforming nature to satisfy human needs—leaving out everything that distinguishes different social forms of production from one another.

Marx makes a further distinction within capitalist production between "production as a whole," what applies to all kinds of production within capitalism, and "production as a specific branch of industry," what applies only to

Dialectics and Abstraction

production in that industry (1904, 270). It is clear that more than a change in extension is involved in making these distinctions, especially the first one. The relations of productive activity with those who engage in it as well as with its product are *internal* relations in both cases, but production in capitalism is united with producers and its products in their distinctive capitalist forms, while production in general is united with them in forms that share its own quality as a lowest common denominator.

The abstraction that Marx makes in moving from capitalist production to production in general, then, is not one of extension but one of level of generality. It is a move from a more specific understanding of production, which brings into focus the whole network of equally specific qualities in which it functions (and with it the period of capitalism in which all this takes place), to a more general understanding of production, which brings into focus the equally general state of those conditions in which it occurs (along with the whole of human history as the period in which these qualities are found).

Something very similar is involved in the distinction that Marx makes between "production as a whole" and "production in a particular branch of industry," though the movement here is away from what is more general in the direction of what is more specific. How a particular branch of industry— car manufacturing, for example—appears and functions involves a set of conditions that fall substantially short of applying to the entire capitalist epoch. What appears superficially like a whole/part distinction is, like the earlier distinction between "capitalist production" and "production in general," one of levels of generality. Both capitalist production (or production as a whole) and production in a particular industry are internally related to the rest of society, but each brings into focus a different period of history, the capitalist epoch in one case and what might be called "modern capitalism," or that period in which this branch of production has functioned in just this way, in the other.

In this Introduction, Marx comes out in favor of concentrating on production in its current historical forms, that is, on capitalist and modern capitalist production, and criticizes the political economists for contenting themselves with production in general when trying to analyze what is happening here and now. Then, falling for the all-too-common error of mistaking what is more general for what is more profound, the political economists treat the generalizations they have derived from examining various specific forms of production as the most important truths about each historical society in turn, and even as the cause of phenomena that are peculiar to each one. In this way, for example, the general truth that production in any society makes use of material nature, the most general form of property, is offered as an explanation and even a justification for how wealth gets distributed in capitalist society, where people who own property claim a right to part of what gets produced with its help (1904, 271-72).

While Marx's discussion of the political economists in this Introduction oscillates between modern capitalism, capitalism as such, and the human condition, much of what he says elsewhere shows that he can operate on still other levels of generality, and therefore that a more complex breakdown of what are in fact degrees of generality is required. Before offering such a breakdown, I would like to stress that the boundary lines which follow are all suggested by Marx's own practice in abstracting, a practice that is largely determined by his aim of capturing the double movement of the capitalist mode of production together with the special role he gives to production. In other words, there is nothing absolute about the particular divisions I have chosen. Other ways of distinguishing between levels of generality are possible, and for other kinds of problems may be very useful.

Keeping this in mind, there are seven major levels of generality into which Marx subdivides the world, seven planes of comprehension on which he places all the problems he investigates, seven different foci for organizing everything that is. Starting from the most specific, there is the level made up of whatever is unique about a person and situation. It is all that makes J. Smith different from everyone else, and so too all his/her activities and products. It is what gets summed up in a proper name and an actual address. With this level—call it level one—the here and now, or however long what is unique lasts, is brought into focus.

Level two distinguishes what is general to people, their activities and products, because they exist and function within modern capitalism, understood as the last twenty to fifty years. Here the unique qualities that justify using proper names, like J. Smith, are abstracted out of focus (we no longer see them), and the qualities that make us speak of an individual as an engineer or in terms of some other occupation that has emerged in modern capitalism are abstracted into focus. Bringing these slightly more general qualities into sight, we also end up considering more people, everyone to whom such qualities apply, and a longer period, the entire time during which these qualities have existed. We also bring into focus a larger area, usually one or a few countries, with whatever else has occurred there that has affected or been affected by the qualities in question during this period. Marx's abstraction of a "particular branch of production" belongs to this level.

Dialectics and Abstraction

Capitalism as such constitutes level three. Here, everything that is peculiar to people, their activity, and products due to their appearance and functioning in capitalist society is brought into focus. We encountered this level earlier in our discussion of "production as a whole." The qualities that J. Smith possesses which mark him/her as J. Smith (level one) and as an engineer (level two) are equally irrelevant. Front and center now are all that makes that person a typical worker in capitalism, including his/her relations to a boss, product, and so on. Productive activity is reduced to the denominator indicated by calling it "wage labor," and the product to the denominator indicated by calling it "commodity" and "value." Just as level two widens the area and lengthens the time span brought into focus as compared to level one, so too level three widens the focus so that it now includes everyone who partakes of capitalist relations anywhere that these relations obtain, and the entire five hundred or so years of the capitalist era.

After capitalism, still moving from the specific to the general, there is the level of class society, level four. This is the period of human history during which societies have been divided up into classes based on the division of labor. Brought into focus are the qualities which people, their activities, and products have in common across the five to ten thousand years of class history, or whatever capitalism, feudalism, and slavery share as versions of class society, and wherever these qualities have existed. Next, level five, is human society. It brings into focus—as we saw in the case of the political economists above—qualities which people, their activities, and products have in common as part of the human condition. Here, one is considering all human beings and the entire history of the species.

To make this scheme complete, two more levels will be added, but they are not nearly as important as the first five in Marx's writings. Level six is the level of generality of the animal world, for just as we possess qualities that set us apart as human beings (level five), we have qualities (including various life functions, instincts, and energies) that are shared with other animals. Finally, there is level seven, the most general level of all, which brings into focus our qualities as a material part of nature, including weight, extension, movement, and so on.

In acquiring an extension, all Marx's units of thought acquire in the same act of abstraction a level of generality. Thus, all the relations that are constituted as such by Marx's abstractions of extension, including the various classifications and movements they make possible, are located on one or another of these levels of generality. And though each of these levels brings into focus a different time period, they are not to be thought of as "slices of time," since the whole of history is implicated in each level, including the most specific. Rather, they are ways of organizing time, placing the period relevant to the qualities brought into focus in the front and treating everything that comes before as what led up to it, as origins.

It is important, too, to underline that all the human and other qualities discussed above are present simultaneously and are equally real, but that they can only be perceived and therefore studied when the level of generality on which they fall has been brought into focus. This is similar to what occurs in the natural sciences, where phenomena are abstracted on the basis of their biological or chemical or atomic properties. All such properties exist together, but one cannot see or study them at the same time. The significance of this observation is evident when we consider that all the problems from which we suffer, and everything that goes into solving them or keeping them from being solved, is made up of qualities that can only be brought into focus on one or another of these different levels of generality. Unfolding as they do over time, these qualities can also be viewed as movements and pressures of one sort or another—whether organized into tendencies, metamorphoses, contradictions, and so on—that, taken together, pretty well determine our existence. Consequently, it is essential, in order to understand any particular problem, to abstract a level of generality that brings the characteristics chiefly responsible for this problem into focus. We have already seen Marx declare that because the classical political economists abstract production at the level of generality of the human condition (level five) they cannot grasp the character of distribution in capitalist society (level three).

Given Marx's special interest in uncovering the double movement of the capitalist mode of production, most of what he writes on human beings and society falls on level three. Abstractions such as "capital," "value," "commodity," "labor," and "working class," whatever their extensions, bring out the qualities that these people, activities, and products possess as part of capitalism. Precapitalist and postcapitalist developments come into the analysis done on this level as the origins and likely futures of these capitalist qualities. What Marx refers to in the *Grundrisse* as "precapitalist economic formations" (the apt title of an English translation of some historical material taken from this longer work) are just that (1973, 471-513). The social formations that preceded capitalism are mainly viewed and studied here as early moments of capitalism abstracted as a process, as its origins extending back before enough of its distinctive structures had emerged to justify the use of the label "capitalism."

Marx also abstracts his subject matter on levels two (modern capitalism) and four (class society), though this is much less frequent. Where Marx operates on the level of generality of class society, capitalism, feudalism, and

Dialectics and Abstraction

slave society are examined with a view to what they have in common. Studies of feudalism on this level of generality emphasize the division of labor and the struggle between the classes to which it gives rise, as compared to the breakdown of the conditions underlying feudal production which gets most of the attention when examining feudalism as part of the origins of capitalism, that is, on level three (1958, part 8).

An example of Marx operating on level two, modern capitalism, can be found in his discussion of economic crisis. After examining the various ways that the capitalist system, given what it is and how it works, could break down, that is, after analyzing it on the level of capitalism as such (level three), he then shows how these possibilities had been actualized in the immediate past, in what was for him modern or developed capitalism (1968; 492-535). To explain why the last few crises occurred in just the ways they did, he has to bring into focus the qualities that apply to this particular time period and these particular places, that is, recent economic, social, and political history in specific countries. This is also an example of how Marx's analysis can play off two or more different levels of generalization, treating what he finds on the more specific level as the actualization of one among several possibilities present on the more general level(s).

It is instructive to compare Marx's studies of human beings and society conducted on levels two, three, and four (chiefly three, capitalism) with studies in the social sciences and also with common-sense thinking about these subjects, which typically operate on levels one (the unique) and five (the human condition). Where Marx usually abstracts human beings, for example, as classes (as *a* class on level four, as one of the main classes that emerge from capitalist relations of production—workers, capitalists, and sometimes landowners—on level three, and as one of the many classes and fragments of classes that exist in a particular country in the most recent period on level two), most non-Marxists abstract people as unique individuals, where everyone has a proper name (level one) or as a member of the human species (level five). In proceeding in their thinking directly from level one to level five, they may never even perceive, and hence have no difficulty in denying, the very existence of classes. But the question is not which of these different abstractions is true. They all are insofar as people possess qualities that fall on each of these levels of generality. The relevant question is, which is the appropriate abstraction for dealing with a particular set of problems? More specifically, if social and economic inequality, exploitation, unemployment, social alienation, and imperialist wars are due in large part to conditions associated with capitalist society, then they can only be understood and dealt with through the use of abstractions that bring out their capitalist qualities.

And that involves, among other things, abstracting people as capitalists and workers. Not to do so, to insist on sticking to levels one and five, leaves one blaming particular individuals (a bad boss, an evil president) or human nature as such for these problems.

To complete the picture, it must be admitted that Marx occasionally abstracts phenomena, including people, on levels one and five. There are discussions of specific individuals, such as Napoleon III and Palmerston, where he focuses on the qualities that make these people different, and some attention is given, especially in his earliest writings, to qualities that all human beings have in common, to human nature in general. But not only are such digressions an exception, but, more important for our purposes, Marx seldom allows the qualities that come from these two levels to enter into his explanation of social phenomena. Thus, when G. D. H. Cole (1966, 11) faults Marx for making classes more real than individuals, or Carol Gould (1980, 33) says individuals enjoy an ontological priority in Marxism, or, conversely, Althusser (1965, 225-58) denies the individual any theoretical space in Marxism whatsoever, they are all misconstruing the nature of a system that has places, levels of generality, for individuals, classes, and the human species. The very idea of attributing an ontological priority to either individuals, class, or the species assumes an absolute separation between them that is belied by Marx's conception of human beings in terms of social relations with qualities that fall on different levels of generality. None of these ways of thinking about human beings is more real or more fundamental than the others. If, despite this, class remains Marx's preferred abstraction for treating human beings, it is only because of its necessary ties to the kind, range, and, above all, level of generality of the phenomena he seeks to explain.

If all Marx's abstractions involve, as I have argued, a level of generality as well as an extension, if each level of generality organizes and even prescribes to some degree the analyses made with its help, that is, in its terms, if Marx abstracts this many levels of generality in order to get at different, though related problems (even though his abstraction of capitalism as such, level three, is the decisive one), then the conclusions of his studies, the theories of Marxism, are all located on one or another of these levels and must be viewed accordingly if they are to be correctly understood, evaluated, and where necessary revised.

Marx's labor theory of value, for example, is chiefly an attempt to explain why all the products of human productive activity in capitalist society have a price, not why a particular product costs such and such but why it costs anything at all. That everything humans produce has a price is an extraordinary

Dialectics and Abstraction

phenomenon peculiar to the capitalist era, whose social implications are even more profound because most people view it ahistorically, simply taking it for granted. Marx's entire account of this phenomena, which includes the history of how a society in which all products have a price has evolved, takes place on the level of generality of capitalism as such, which means that he only deals with the qualities of people, their activities, and products in the forms they assume in capitalism overall. The frequent criticism one hears of this theory, that it does not take account of competition in real market places and therefore cannot explain actual prices, is simply off the point, that is, the more general point that Marx is trying to make.

Marx's remarks on history are particularly vulnerable to being misunderstood unless they are placed on one or another of these levels of generality. The role Marx attributes to production and economics generally, for example, differs somewhat depending on whether the focus is on capitalism (including its origins), modern capitalism, class societies, or human societies. Starting with human societies, the special importance Marx accords to production is based on the fact that one has to do what is necessary in order to survive before attempting anything else, that production limits the range of material choices available just as, over time, it helps to transform them, and that production is the major activity which gives expression to and helps to develop our peculiarly human powers and needs (1958, 183-84; Marx and Engels 1964, 117; Ollman 1976, 98-101). In class society, production plays its decisive role primarily through the division of labor that comes into being in this period and the class divisions and antagonisms that it sets up (1959b, 772; Marx and Engels 1951, 9-10). In capitalism, the special role of production is shared by everything that goes into the process of capital accumulation (1958, part 8). In modern capitalism, it is usually what has happened in a particular phase or sector of capitalist production in a given country in the most recent period (like the development of railroads in India during Marx's time) that is treated as decisive (Marx and Engels n.d., 79).

Each of these interpretations of the predominant role of production applies only to the level of generality that it brings into focus. No single interpretation comes close to accounting for all that Marx believes needs to be explained, which is probably why, on one occasion, Marx denies that he has any theory of history whatsoever (Marx and Engels 1952, 278). It might be more accurate, however, to say that he has four complementary theories of history, one each for history as abstracted on these four different levels of generality. The effort by most of Marx's followers and virtually all of his critics to encapsulate the materialist conception of history into a single generalization regarding the role of production (or economics) has never succeeded, therefore, because it could not succeed.

Finally, the various movements that Marx investigates, some of which were discussed under abstraction of extension, are also located on particular levels of generality. That is, like everything else, the movements of quantity/quality, metamorphosis, and contradiction are composed of qualities that are unique or special to modern capitalism, or to capitalism, and so on, so that they only take shape as movements when the relevant level of generality is brought into focus. Until then, whatever force they exercise must remain mysterious and our ability to use or influence them virtually nil.

Two major questions relating to this mode of abstraction remain to be treated. One is, how do the qualities located on each level of generality affect those on the others? And second, what is the influence of the decision made regarding abstraction of extension on the level of generality that is abstracted, and vice versa? The effect of qualities from each level on those from others, moving from the most general (level seven) to the most specific (level one), is that of a context on the possibilities it contains. That is, each level, beginning with seven, establishes a range of possibilities for what can occur on the more specific levels that follow. The actualization of some of these possibilities on each level limits in turn what can come about on the levels next in line, all the way up to level one, that of the unique.

Each more general level, in virtue of what it is and contains, also makes one or a few of the many (though not infinite) alternative developments that it makes possible on less general levels more likely to be actualized. Capitalism, in other words, was not only a possible development out of class society, but made likely by the character of the latter, by the very dynamics inherent in the division of labor once it began. The same might be said of the relation between capitalism as such and the "modern" English capitalism in which Marx lived, and the relation between the latter and the unique events that Marx experienced.

It is within this framework, too, that the relation that Marx saw between freedom and determinism can best be understood. Whatever the level of abstraction—whether we are talking about a unique individual, a group in modern capitalism, workers throughout the capitalist era, any class, or human beings as such—there is always a choice to be made and some ability to make it. Hence, there is always some kind and some degree of freedom. On each level of generality, however, the alternatives among which people must choose are severely limited by the very nature of the overlapping contexts, which also make one or one set of alternatives more feasible and/or attractive, just as they condition the very personal, class, and human qualities

Dialectics and Abstraction

brought into play in making any choice. Hence, there is also a considerable degree of determinism. It is this relationship between freedom and determinism that Marx wishes to bring out when he says that it is people who make history but not in conditions of their own choosing (Marx and Engels 1951, 225). What seems like a relatively straightforward claim is complicated by the fact that both the people and the conditions referred to exist on various levels of generality, and depending on the level that is brought into focus, the sense of this claim—though true in each instance—will vary.

The view of determinism offered here is different from, but not in contradiction with, the view presented in our discussion of the philosophy of internal relations, where determinism was equated first with the reciprocal effect found in any organic system and then with the greater or special influence of any one process on the others. To this we can now add a third, complementary sense of determinism that comes from the limiting and prescribing effects of overlapping contexts on all the phenomena that fall within them. Marx's success in displaying how the latter two kinds of determinism operate in the capitalist mode of production accounts for most of the explanatory power that one finds (and feels) in his writings.

Affects of events on their larger contexts, that is, of qualities found on more particular levels on those that fall on more general ones, can also be discerned. Whenever Marx speaks of people reproducing the conditions of their existence, the reference is to how activities whose main qualities fall on one level of generality help to construct the various contexts, including those on other levels of generality, that make the continuation of these same activities both possible and highly likely. Such effects, however, can also be detrimental. In our time, for example, the unregulated growth of harmful features associated with modern capitalist production (level two) have begun to threaten the ecological balance necessary not only for the continuation of capitalism (level three), but also for the life of our species (level five).

As for the relation between the choice of extension and that of level of generality, there would seem to be a rough correspondence between narrow abstractions of extension and abstracting very low and very high levels of generality. Once the complex social relations in which a particular phenomenon is situated are put aside through an overly narrow abstraction of extension, there is little reason to bring these relations into better focus by abstracting the relevant level of generality. Thus, abstracting an extension that sets individuals apart from their social conditions is usually accompanied by an abstraction of level of generality that focuses on what is altogether different and unique about people (level one). With the social qualities that were abstracted from individuals in extension now attached to the groups to which they belong (viewed as externally related to their members), efforts at generalizing tend to bypass the levels on which these social qualities would be brought into focus (modern capitalism, capitalism, and class society) and move directly to the level of the human condition (level five). For bourgeois ideology people are either all different (level one) or all the same (level five), while for Marx, whose abstractions of extension usually include a significant number of social relations, privileging the levels of generality of capitalism, modern capitalism, and class society was both easy and obvious—just as giving special attention to these levels led to abstractions of extension that enabled him to take in at one sweep most of the connections that these levels bring into focus.

Vantage Point

The third mode in which Marx's abstractions occur is that of vantage point. Capitalists, as we saw, are referred to as "embodiments of capital"; but capital is also said to function as it does because it is in the hands of people who use it to make profit (1959b, 857-58, 794; 1959a, 79). The state is said to be an instrument of the ruling economic class; but Marx also treats it as a set of objective structures that respond to the requirements of the economy, as an aspect of the mode of production itself (Marx and Engels 1945, 15; Marx 1959a, 103). There are many similar, apparently contradictory positions taken in Marx's writings. They are the result of different abstractions, but not of extension or level of generality. They are due to different abstractions of vantage point. The same relation is being viewed from different sides, or the same process from different moments.

In the same mental act that Marx's units of thought obtain an extension and a level of generality, they acquire a vantage point or place from which to view the elements of any particular relation and, given its extension, from which to reconstruct the larger system to which this relation belongs. A vantage point sets up a perspective that colors everything which falls into it, establishing order, hierarchy, and priorities, distributing values, meanings, and degrees of relevance, and asserting a distinctive coherence between the parts. Within a given perspective, some processes and connections will appear large, some obvious, some important; others will appear small, insignificant and irrelevant; and some will even be invisible.

In discussing Marx's conception of relation, we saw that it was more than a simple connection. It was always a connection contained in its parts *as seen* from one or another side. So capital and labor, for example, were quoted as being "expressions of the same relation, only seen from the opposite pole"

Dialectics and Abstraction

(1971, 491). Or again, Marx says, capital has one "organizational differentiation or composition" (that of fixed and circulating capital) from the point of view of circulation, and another (that of constant and variable capital) from the point of view of production (1968, 579). Both circulation and production are part of the extended capital relation. A criticism of the political economists is that they try to understand capital only from the point of view of circulation, but to grasp the nature of wealth in capitalism, Marx believed, the decisive vantage point is that of production (1968, 578). Prioritizing one vantage point in this way does not mean that Marx cannot use others, and in his study of capital—as of labor, value, class, the state, and so on—Marx makes use of various vantage points.

It is clear that the decisions Marx makes regarding extension and levels of generality greatly affect the kind of vantage points which he abstracts, and vice versa. The amount of mutual dependence and process that is included in an abstraction of extension largely determines what can be seen and studied from this same abstraction taken as a vantage point. Giving production the extension of reproduction or capital the extension of capital accumulation, for example, enables Marx to bring into view and organize the system of which they are part in ways that would not be possible with narrower (or shorter) abstractions. Likewise, in abstracting a level of generality, Marx brings into focus an entire range of qualities that can now serve individually or collectively (depending on the abstraction of extension) as vantage points, just as other possible vantage points, organized around qualities from other levels of generality, are excluded. Conversely, any commitment as to vantage point predisposes Marx to abstract the extension and level of generality that correspond to it and enables him to make the most of it as a vantage point. In practice, these three decisions (really, three aspects of the same decision) as to extension, level of generality, and vantage point are usually made together and their effects are immediate, though on any given occasion one or another of them may appear to dominate.

In the social sciences, the notion of vantage point is most closely associated with the work of Karl Mannheim (1936, part 5). But for Mannheim a point of view is something that belongs to people, particularly as organized into classes. The conditions in which each class lives and works supplies its members with both a distinctive range of experiences and a distinctive point of view. Because of their different points of view, even the few experiences that are shared by people of opposing classes are not only understood but actually perceived in quite different ways. As far as it goes, this view—which Mannheim takes over from Marx—is correct. Marx's conception of point of view goes farther, however, by grounding each class's perceptions in the nature of its habitual abstractions, in order to show how starting out to make sense of society from just these mental units, within the perspectives that they establish, leads to different perceptual outcomes. In uncovering the cognitive link between class conditions and class perceptions, Marx helps us understand not only *why* Mannheim is right but *how* what he describes actually works. As part of this, point of view becomes an attribute of the abstraction as such (Marx speaks of the point of view or vantage point of accumulation, relations of production, money, etc.), and only secondarily of the person or class that adopts it (1963, 303; 1971, 156; 1973, 201).

We can now explain why Marx believed that workers have a far better chance to understand the workings of capitalism than do capitalists. Their advantage does not come from the quality of their lives and only in small part from their class interests (since the capitalists have an interest in misleading even themselves about how their system works). More importantly, given what constitutes the lives of workers, the abstractions with which they start out to make sense of their society are likely to include "labor," "factory," and "machine," and especially "labor," which puts the activity that is chiefly responsible for social change at the forefront of their thinking. Within the perspective set up by this abstraction, most of what occurs in capitalism is arranged as part of the necessary conditions and results of this activity. There is no more enlightening vantage point for making sense of what is, both as the outcome of what was and as the origins of what is coming into being. This is not to say, of course, that all workers will make these connections (there are plenty of reasons rooted in their alienated lives that militate against it), but the predisposition to do so coming from the initial abstraction of vantage point is there.

For capitalists, just the opposite is the case. Their lives and work incline them to start making sense of their situation with the aid of "price," "competition," "profit," and other abstractions drawn from the market place. Trying to put together how capitalism functions within perspectives that place labor near the end of the line rather than at the start simply turns capitalist dynamics around. According to Marx, in competition, "everything always appears in inverted form, always standing on its head" (1968, 217). What are predominantly the effects of productive activity appear here as its cause. It is demands coming from the market, itself the product of alienated labor, for example, that seem to determine what gets produced.

As with thinking in terms of processes and relations, common sense is not wholly devoid of perspectival thinking. People occasionally use expressions like "point of view," "vantage point," and "perspective" to refer to some part of what we have been discussing, but they are generally unaware of how

Dialectics and Abstraction

much their points of view affect everything they see and know, and of the role played by abstractions in arriving at this result. As with their abstractions of extension and levels of generality, most people simply accept as given the abstractions of vantage point that are handed down to them by their culture and particularly by their class. They examine their world again and again from the same one or few angles, while their ability to abstract new vantage points becomes atrophied. The one-sided views that result are treated as not only correct, but as natural, indeed as the only possible view.

Earlier we saw that one major variety of bourgeois ideology arises from using too narrow abstractions of extension (dismissing parts of both processes and relationships that are essential for accurately comprehending even what is included), and that a second comes from abstracting an inappropriate level of generality (inappropriate in that it leaves out of focus the main qualities in which the problem of concern is rooted). There is a third major form of bourgeois ideology that is associated with the abstraction of vantage point. Here, ideology results from abstracting a vantage point that either hides or seriously distorts the relations and movements that one has to perceive in order to comprehend adequately a particular phenomenon. Not everything we need or want to know emerges with equal clarity, or even emerges at all, from every possible vantage point.

A related form of ideology may also result from examining a phenomenon from only one perspective, no matter how crucial, when multiple perspectives are needed—all the while being unaware of the limits on what can be learned from this single perspective—and mistaking such a partial, lopsided view for a full understanding. This is what Hegel had in mind when he said, to think abstractly (in the ideological sense of the term) is "to cling to one predicate" (1966, 118). Murderers, servants, and soldiers, who serve as Hegel's examples, are all much more than what is conveyed by viewing them from the single vantage point associated with the label that we have given them. Marx is even more explicit when, for example, he berates the economist Ramsay, for bringing out all the factors but "one-sidedly" and "therefore incorrectly," or equates "wrong" with "one-sided" in a criticism of Ricardo (1971, 351; 1968, 470).

What needs to be stressed is that Marx never criticizes ideology as a simple lie or claims that what it asserts is completely false. Instead, ideology is generally described as overly narrow, partial, misfocused and/or one-sided, all of which are attributable to limitations in the abstractions of extension, level of generality, and vantage point that are used, where neither these abstractions nor their implications are grasped for what they are. While correctly pointing to the material roots of ideology in capitalist conditions and in the conscious manipulations of capitalists, and bringing out how it functions to serve capitalist interests, most discussions of ideology have completely ignored the misapplication of the process of abstraction that is responsible for its very forms.

Among the major vantage points associated with bourgeois ideology, where the error is not simply one of restricting analysis to a single perspective but where the one or few that are chosen either hide or distort the essential features of capitalism, are the following: the vantage point of the isolated individual, the subjective side of any situation (what is believed, wanted, intended, etc.), the results of almost any process, anything connected with the market, and all of what falls on level five of generality, particularly human nature. Marx, who on occasion made use of all these vantage points, favored vantage points connected with production, the objective side of any situation, historical processes generally, and social class, particularly at the level of generality of capitalist society. The reason that Marx privileges such vantage points varies, as does the extension he gives them, with the level of generality on which he is operating. But in almost every case, his choice of vantage point is determined by what is necessary to uncover some part of the organic or historical movement of the capitalist mode of production.

The easy facility that Marx shows in moving from one to the other is equally characteristic of his practice in abstracting vantage points. Aware of the limitations inherent in any single vantage point, even that of production, Marx frequently alters the angle from which he examines his chosen subject matter. While whole works and sections of works can be distinguished on the basis of the vantage point that predominates, changes of vantage point can also be found on virtually every page of Marx's writings. Within the same sentence, Marx can move from viewing wages from the vantage point of the worker to viewing them from the vantage point of society as a whole (1963, 108). Marx's analysis of the complex relations among production, distribution, exchange, and consumption, which has already come into this work on several occasions, also provides what is perhaps the best example of how often he changes his abstractions of both extension and vantage point, and how crucial this practice and his facility in it was for obtaining his results (1904, 274-92).

As with his abstractions of extension and level of generality, Marx's abstractions of vantage point play a decisive role in the development of all his theories. It is Marx's abstractions of vantage point that enable him to find identity in difference (and vice versa), to actually catch sight of the organic and historical movements made possible by his abstractions of extension, and

Dialectics and Abstraction 65

to classify and reclassify the world of his perceptions into the explanatory structures bound up in the theories of Marxism.

Earlier, in discussing Marx's theory of identity, we saw that abstracting an extension that is large enough to contain both identical and different qualities of two or more phenomena is what makes the coexistence of identity and difference possible, but one's ability to actually see and therefore to examine either set of qualities depends on the vantage point adopted for viewing them. Sticking with only one vantage point will restrict understanding any relation to its identical or different aspects when, in fact, it contains both. Marx, on the other hand, can approach the relation of profit, rent, and interest from the vantage point of surplus value, or what they have in common as the portion of value that is not returned to the workers who produced it, their identity, as well as from any of the vantage points located in differences arising from who holds these forms of surplus value and how each functions in the economic system.

Abstracting vantage points that bring out the differences between two or more aspects of an interactive system also highlights the asymmetry in their reciprocal effect. Granted such reciprocal effect, production was said to play the dominant role on all five levels of generality on which Marx operates. But it is only by abstracting production as a vantage point that its special influence on other economic processes and on society as a whole on each level can be seen for what it is. As Marx says, with the level of class societies in mind, the existence of the ruling class and their functions "can only be understood *from* the specific historical structure of their production relations" (1963, 285, emphasis added).

Along with his abstractions of extension, Marx's abstractions of vantage point play an equally important role in establishing the flexible boundaries that characterize all his theories. In Marx's division of reality into objective and subjective conditions, it is by abstracting a vantage point first in one, then in the other, that he uncovers the more objective aspects of what is ordinarily taken to be subjective (extending the territory of the objective accordingly), and vice versa. Together with the aforementioned theory of identity, it is the abstraction of the vantage point that enables Marx actually to see objective and subjective conditions as "two distinct forms of the same conditions" (1973, 832). Likewise, it is by abstracting a particular vantage point that Marx can see aspects of nature in society, or the forces of production in the relations of production, or economic in noneconomic structures, or the base in the superstructure, and vice versa, adjusting the abstraction of extension for each pairing accordingly. By looking at the relations of production from the vantage point of the forces of production, for example, even the cooperative power of workers can appear as a productive force (Marx and Engels 1964, 46).

Marx's various class divisions of society, based as we saw on different abstractions of extension for class, are also only discernible from the vantage point of the qualities (functions, opposition to other classes, consciousness, etc.) that serve as the criteria for constructing a given classification. That is, if class is a complex relation made up of a number of different aspects, and if the composition of any particular class depends on which ones Marx includes in his abstraction of extension and brings into focus through his abstraction of level of generality, then his ability to actually distinguish people as members of this class depends on his having abstracted just these aspects as his vantage points for viewing them. It also follows that as Marx's vantage point changes so does his operative division of society into classes. In this way, too, the same people, viewed from the vantage points of qualities associated with different classes, may actually fall in different classes. The landowner, for example, is said to be a capitalist insofar as s/he confronts labor as the owner of commodities, that is, functions as a capitalist vis-à-vis labor (rather than as a landowner vis-à-vis capitalists), and is viewed from this vantage point (1963, 51).

Viewed from the vantage point of any one of his/her qualities, the characterization of the individual is limited to what can be seen from this angle. The qualities that emerge from the use of other vantage points are ignored because, for all practical purposes, at *this* moment in the analysis, and for treating *this* particular problem, they simply do not exist. Hence, people abstracted as workers, that is, viewed from one or more of the qualities associated with membership in this class, where the object of study is capitalist political economy, are presented as not having any gender, nation, or race. People, of course, possess all these characteristics and more, and Marx, when dealing with other problems, can abstract vantage points (usually as part of noncapitalist levels of generality) that bring out these other identities.

Given Marx's flexibility in abstracting extension, he can also consider people from vantage points that play down their human qualities altogether in order to highlight some special relation. Such is the case when Marx refers to the buyer as a "representative of money confronting commodities," that is, views him/her from the vantage point of money inside an abstraction of extension that includes money, commodities, and people (1963, 404). The outstanding example of this practice is Marx's frequent reference to capitalists as "embodiments" or "personifications" of capital, where living human beings are considered from the vantage point of their economic function

Dialectics and Abstraction

(1958, 10, 85, and 592). The school of structuralist Marxism has performed an important service in recovering such claims from the memory hole in which an older, more class struggle-oriented Marxism had placed them. However useful decentering human nature in this manner is for grasping some of the role-determined behavior that Marx uncovered, there is as much that is volunteerist in his theories that requires the adoption of distinctively human vantage points, and only a dialectical Marxism that possesses sufficient flexibility in changing abstractions—of vantage point as of extension and level of generality—can make all the necessary adjustments.

If Marx's abstractions of extension are large enough to encompass how things happen as part of what they are, if such abstractions of extension also allow him to grasp the various organic and historical movements uncovered by his research as essential movements, then it is his abstractions of vantage point that make what is there—what his abstractions of extension have "placed" there—visible. The movement of the transformation of quantity into quality, for example, is made possible as an essential movement by an abstraction of extension that includes both quantitative changes and the qualitative change that eventually occurs. But this transformative process is not equally clear or even visible from each of its moments. In this case, the preferred vantage point is one that bridges the end of quantitative changes and the start of the qualitative change. Viewing the cooperation among workers, for example, from the vantage point of where its transformation into a qualitatively new productive power begins provides the clearest indication of whence this change comes as well as where the process that brought it about was heading.

The movement of metamorphosis, we will recall, is an organic movement in which qualities associated with one part of a system get transferred to its other parts. In the case of the metamorphosis of value, the main instance of this movement in Marx's writings, some of the central relationships that constitute value are taken up by commodity, capital, wage labor, and so on. Only an abstraction of extension large enough to include its different phases as internally related aspects of a single system allows us to conceive of metamorphosis as an internal movement and of its subsequent stages as forms of what it starts out as. But to observe this metamorphosis and, therefore, to study it in any detail, we must accompany this abstraction of extension with an abstraction of vantage point in the part whose qualities are being transferred. Thus, the metamorphosis of value into and through its various forms can only be observed as a metamorphosis from the vantage point of value.

As regards contradiction, Marx says, "in capitalism everything seems and in fact is contradictory" (1963, 218). It *is* so—in reality, and with the help of Marx's broad abstractions of extension which organize the parts as mutually dependent processes. But it *seems* so only from certain vantage points. From others, the incompatible development of the parts would be missed, misconstrued, or, at a minimum, seriously underestimated. The vantage point from which Marx observes contradictions is the intersection between the two or more processes said to be in contradiction. It is a composite vantage point made up of elements of all these processes. If one has not abstracted differences as processes and such processes as mutually dependent, there is no point of intersection on which to focus. People who operate with external relations and static units do not see contradictions because they cannot. They lack both the abstractions of extension and vantage point that are needed to do so.

What we have called the double movement of the capitalist mode of production can be approached, that is, viewed and studied, from any of the major contradictions that compose it, and in each case, given internal relations, the elements that are not directly involved enter into the contradiction as part of its extended conditions and results. In this way, the vantage point that is adopted organizes not only the immediate contradiction, but establishes a perspective in which other parts of the system acquire their order and importance. In the contradiction between exchange- and use-value, for example, the relations between capitalists and workers are part of the necessary conditions for this contradiction to take its present form and develop as it does, just as one result of this contradiction is the reproduction of the ties between capitalists and workers. Given the internal relations that Marx posits between all elements in the system, this makes capitalists and workers subordinate aspects of the contradiction between exchange- and use-value. The whole process can be turned around: adopting the vantage point of the contradiction between capitalists and workers transforms the relations between exchange- and use-value into its subordinate aspects. The actual links in each case, of course, need to be carefully worked out. Hence contradictions can be said to overlap; they cover much the same ground, but this ground is broken up in various ways, along a variety of axes, based on as many different foci.

Marx's laws offer still another illustration of the crucial role played by the abstraction of vantage point. All of Marx's laws are tendencies, arising from the very nature of whatever it is that is said to have them. In every case, it is Marx's abstraction of extension that brings the various organic and historical movements together under the same rubric, making the way that things happen a part of what they are, but it is his abstraction of vantage point

Dialectics and Abstraction 69

that enables him (and us) to actually view them as a single movement, as a tendency.

The law of the falling rate of profit, for example, is a tendency inherent in the relation of profit to the organic composition of capital, which is the ratio of constant to variable capital, or the amount of surplus labor that can be realized with a given amount of capital (1959b, part 3). Like all tendencies in Marx's work, it is subject to countertendencies (state subsidies, inflation, devaluation of existing capital, etc.), which are often strong enough to keep the falling rate of profit from finding expression in the balance sheet of businesspersons at the end of the year. To observe this tendency, therefore, and to be in a position to study the constant pressure which it exerts on the concentration of capital (another law) and through it on the entire capitalist system, one must follow Marx in abstracting an extension for profit that includes its relation over time to the organic composition of capital, and view this relation from the vantage point of this composition. Without such abstractions of extension *and* vantage point, one simply cannot see, let alone grasp, what Marx is saying. With them, one can see the law despite all the evidence presented in countertendencies. Hence, the irrelevance of various attempts by Marx's critics and followers alike to evaluate the law of the falling rate of profit based on analyses made from the vantage point of one of its possible results (the actual profits of real businesspersons), from capitalist competition or some other vantage point located in the market place. All the laws in Marxism can only be described, studied, and evaluated within the perspectives associated with the particular vantage points from which Marx both discovered and constructed them as laws.

The Role of Abstractions in the Debates over Marxism

It will have become evident by now that it is largely differences of vantage point that lay behind many of the great debates in the history of Marxist scholarship. In the *New Left Review* debate between Ralph Miliband and Nicos Poulantzas on the character of the capitalist state, for example, Miliband (1970) viewed the state chiefly from the vantage point of the ruling economic class, while Poulantzas (1969) viewed what are essentially the same set of relations from the vantage point of the socioeconomic structures that establish both the limits and the requirements for a community's political functions.[4] As a result, Miliband is better able to account for the traditional role of the state in serving ruling-class interests, while Poulantzas has an easier time explaining the relative autonomy of the state and why the capitalist state continues to serve the ruling class when the latter is not directly in control of state institutions.

The debate over whether capitalist economic crisis is caused by the tendency of the rate of profit to fall or by difficulties in the realization of value, where one side views the capitalist economy from the vantage point of the accumulation process and the other from the vantage point of market contradictions, is of the same sort (Mattick 1969; Baran and Sweezy 1966).[5] A somewhat related dispute over the centrality of the capitalist mode of production as compared to the international division of labor (the position of "world systems theory") for charting the history and future of capitalism is likewise rooted in a difference of preferred vantage points (Brenner 1977; Wallerstein 1974). So, too, is the debate over whether bourgeois ideology is mainly a reflection of alienated life and reified structures or the product of the capitalist consciousness industry, where one side views the construction of ideology from the vantage point of the material and social conditions out of which it arises, and the other from that of the role played by the capitalist class in promoting it (Mepham 1979; Marcuse 1965).

Earlier, in what is perhaps the most divisive dispute of all, we saw that those who argue for a strict determinism emanating from one or another version of the economic factor (whether simple or structured) and those who emphasize the role of human agency (whether individual or class) can also be distinguished on the basis of the vantage points which they have chosen for investigating the necessary interaction between the two (Althusser 1965; Sartre 1963). To be sure, each of these positions, here as in the other debates, is also marked by somewhat different abstractions of extension for shared phenomena based in part on what is known and considered worth knowing, but even these distinguishing features come into being mainly as a result of the vantage point that is treated as privileged.

The different levels of generality on which Marx operates are also responsible for their share of debates among interpreters of his ideas, the

---

4. Both thinkers seriously modified the views expressed in these articles in later works (Miliband 1977; Poulantzas 1978), and these revisions, too, can be explained in large part through changes in their abstractions of vantage point.

5. There are still other Marxist interpretations of capitalist crises (as, indeed, of the state) that are also largely dependent on the vantage point adopted. Here, as in the other debates mentioned, it was enough to refer to a single major cleavage to illustrate the general point regarding abstractions.

main one being over the subject of the materialist conception of history: is it all history or all of class history or the period of capitalism (in which earlier times are conceived as precapitalist) (Kautsky 1988; Korsch 1970)? Depending on the answer, the sense in which production is held to be primary will vary as will the abstractions of extension and vantage point used to bring this out.

Finally, the various abstractions of extension of such central notions as mode of production, class, state, and so on, have also led to serious disagreements among Marx's followers and critics alike, with most schools seeking to treat the boundaries they consider decisive as permanent. However, as evidenced by the quotations upon which practically every side in these disputes can draw, Marx is capable of pursuing his analysis not only on all social levels of generality and from various vantage points, but with units of differing extension, only giving greater weight to those which are most useful in revealing the particular dynamic he was investigating. The many apparently contradictory claims that emerge from his study are in fact complementary, and all are required to "reflect" the complex double movement (historical—including probable future—and organic) of the capitalist mode of production. Without an adequate grasp of the role of abstraction in dialectical method, and without sufficient skill and flexibility in making the needed abstractions of extension, level of generality, and vantage point, most interpreters of Marx have simply constructed versions of his theories that suffer in their very form from the same rigidity, inappropriate focus, and one-sidedness that Marx saw in bourgeois ideology.

In an often-quoted though little-analyzed remark in the Introduction to *Capital*, Marx says that value, as compared to larger, more complex notions, has proven so difficult to grasp because "the body, as an organic whole, is more easy to study than are the cells of that body." To make such a study, he adds, one must use the "force of abstraction" (1958, 8). Using the force of abstraction, as I have tried to show, is Marx's way of putting dialectics to work. It is the living dialectic, its process of becoming, the engine that sets other parts of his method into motion. In relation to this emphasis on abstraction, every other approach to studying dialectics stands on the outside looking in, treating the change and interaction that abstractions help to shape in one or another already completed form. The relations of contradiction, identity, law, and so on, which they study have all been constructed, ordered, brought into focus, and made visible through prior abstractions. Consequently, while other approaches may help us to understand what dialectics is and to recognize it, only an approach that puts the process of abstraction at the center enables us to think adequately about change and interaction, that is, to think dialectically, and to do research and engage in political struggle in a dialectical manner.

References

Acton H. B. 1962. *The Illusion of the Epoch*. London: Cohen and West.

Allen, J. 1983. "In Search of Method: Hegel, Marx and Realism," *Radical Philosophy*, no. 35 (Autumn): 26-33.

Althusser, L. 1965. *Pour Marx*. Paris: Maspero.

Baraka, A. (Jones, L.). 1966. *Home Social Essays*. New York: William Morrow and Co.

Baran, P., and Sweezy, P. 1966. *Monopoly Capital*. New York: Monthly Review Press.

Brenner, R. 1977. "The Origins of Capitalist Development: A Critique of Neo-Smithian Marxism," *New Left Review,* no. 104 (July-August): 25-92.

Cole, G. D. H. 1966. *The Meaning of Marxism*. Ann Arbor: University of Michigan Press.

Coleman, J. 1968. "The Mathematical Study of Change." In *Methodology in Social Research,* ed. H. and A. Blalock, 428-78. New York: McGraw Hill.

Dietzgen, J. 1928. *The Positive Outcome of Philosophy*. Trans. W. W. Craik. Chicago: Charles H. Kerr.

Dunayevskaya, R. 1982. *Philosophy and Revolution*. Atlantic Highlands, NJ: Humanities Press.

Gould, C. 1980. *Marx's Social Ontology*. Cambridge: MIT Press.

Hegel, G. W. F. 1966. *Hegel: Texts and Commentary,* Ed. and trans. W. Kaufman. Garden City, NY: Anchor.

Horvath, R. J., and Gibson, K. D. 1984. "Abstraction in Marx's Method." *Antipode* 16 (April): 12-25.

Hume, D. 1955. *Enquiry Concerning Human Understanding*. Indianapolis: Bobbs-Merrill.

Ilyenkov, E. V. 1982. *The Dialectics of the Abstract and the Concrete in Marx's 'Capital'*. Trans. S. Syrovatkin. Moscow: Progress Publishers.

James, W. 1978. *The Works of William James*. Cambridge: Harvard University Press.

Kautsky, K. 1988. *The Materialist Conception of History*. Trans. R. Meyer. New Haven: Yale University Press.

Korsch, K. 1970. *Marxism and Philosophy*. Trans. F. Halliday. New York: Monthly Review Press.

Lukács, G. 1971. *History and Class Consciousness*. Trans. R. Livingstone. Cambridge: MIT Press.

Mannheim, K. 1936. *Ideology and Utopia*. Trans. L. Wirth and E. Shils. New York: Harcourt, Brace, and Co.

Mao Tse Tung. 1968. *Four Essays on Philosophy*. Peking: Foreign Languages Press.

Marcuse, H. 1965. "Repressive Tolerance." In *A Critique of Pure Tolerance,* ed. R. W. Wolff, B. Moore, and H. Marcuse. Boston: Beacon Press.

Marx, K. 1904. *A Contribution to the Critique of Political Economy*. Trans. N. I. Stone. Chicago: Charles H. Kerr.

———. 1958. *Capital*, vol. 1. Trans. S. Moore and E. Aveling. Moscow: Foreign Languages Publishing House.

———. 1959a. *Economic and Philosophical Manuscripts of 1844*. Trans. M. Milligan. Moscow: Foreign Languages Publishing House.

———. 1959b. *Capital*, vol. 3. Moscow: Foreign Languages Publishing House.

———. 1963. *Theories of Surplus Value*, part 1. Trans. E. Burns. Moscow: Progress Publishers.

———. 1968. *Theories of Surplus Value*, part 1. Trans. S. Ryazanskaya. Moscow: Progress Publishers.

———. 1970. *Critique of Hegel's Philosophy of Right*. Ed. J. O'Malley. Trans. A. Jolin and J. O'Malley. Cambridge: Cambridge University Press.

———. 1971. *Theories of Surplus Value*, part 3. Trans. J. Cohen and S. W. Ryazanskaya. Moscow: Progress Publishers.

———. 1973. *Grundrisse*. Trans. M. Nicolaus. Harmondsworth: Penguin Books.

———. n.d. *The Poverty of Philosophy*. Moscow: Foreign Languages Publishing House.

Marx, K., and Engels, F. 1941. *Selected Correspondence*. Trans. D. Torr. London: Lawrence and Wishart.

———. 1945. *The Communist Manifesto*. Chicago: Charles H. Kerr.

———. 1950. *Briefwechsel*, vol. 3. Berlin: Dietz.

———. 1951. *Selected Works in Two Volumes*, vol. 1. Moscow: Foreign Languages Publishing House.

———. 1952. *The Russian Menace to Europe*. Ed. P. W. Blackstock and B. F. Hoselitz. Glencoe, IL: The Free Press.

———. 1961. *Werke*, vol. 4. Berlin: Dietz.

———. 1964. *The German Ideology*. Trans. S. Ryazanskaya. Moscow: Progress Publishers.

———. n.d. *On Colonialism*. Moscow: Foreign Languages Publishing House.

Mattick, P. 1969. *Marx and Keynes*. Boston: Porter Sargent Publishers.

Meikle, S. 1985. *Essentialism in the Thought of Karl Marx*. London: Open Court.

Mepham, J. 1979. "The Theory of Ideology in *Capital*," In *Issues in Marxist Philosophy*, vol. 3. Ed. J. Mepham and D. H. Ruben, 141-74. Atlantic Highlands, NJ: Humanities Press.

Miliband, R. 1970. "The Capitalist State: Reply to Nicos Poulantzas," *New Left Review*, no. 59 (January-February): 53-60.

———. 1977. *Marxism and Politics*. Oxford: Oxford University Press.

Moore, G. E. 1903. *Principia Ethica*. Cambridge: Cambridge University Press.

Novak, L. 1980. *The Structure of Idealization: Toward a Systemic Interpretation of the Marxian Idea of Science*. Dordrecht, Holland: Reidel Publishing Company.

Ollman, B. 1976. *Alienation: Marx's Conception of Man in Capitalist Society*. Cambridge: Cambridge University Press.

———. 1978. *Social and Sexual Revolution: Essays on Marx and Reich*. Boston: South End Press.

Poulantzas, N. 1969. "The Problem of the Capitalist State," *New Left Review,* no. 58 (November-December): 67-78.

———. 1978. *State, Power, Socialism.* Trans. P. Camiller. London: Verso.

Rader, M. 1979. *Marx's Interpretation of History.* Oxford: Oxford University Press.

Robinson, J. 1953. *On Re-reading Marx.* Cambridge: Students Bookshop.

Sartre, J.-P. 1963. *The Problem of Method.* Trans. H. E. Barnes. London: Methuen.

Sayers, A. 1981. "Abstraction: a Realist Interpretation." *Radical Philosophy,* no. 28 (Summer): 6-15.

Sayer, D. 1987. *The Violence of Abstraction.* London: Blackwell.

Sohn-Rethel, A. 1978. *Intellectual and Manual Labor.* London: Macmillan.

Sorel, G. 1950. *Reflexions sur la violence.* Paris: Marcel Riviere.

Wallerstein, I. 1974. *The Modern World System.* London: Academic Press.

[4]

The Unity of Science and Revolution: Marxism as Critique

Peter G. Stillman

Marx's predominant form of theoretical discourse is the critique (*Kritik*). His central and most famous work is labelled a critique: *Capital: A Critique of Political Economy* (1867).[1] He announced other works similarly: for instance, *The Holy Family, or Critique of Critical Criticism* (1844) and *A Contribution to the Critique of Political Economy* (1859). His major unpublished works also bear that title. His first important political work is *The Critique of Hegel's Philosophy of Right* (1843). His preferred title for the 1844 *Economic and Philosophical Manuscripts* was *A Critique of Politics and Political Economy*.[2] The full title of his next long, unprinted effort, *The German Ideology* (1845), included "critique."[3] While the frequent appearance of *Kritik* has often been noted, only rarely has anything more than a brief and superficial analysis been given.[4]

There is one sense of "critique" for which Marx is justly notorious: vitriolic destruction or devastation of the theoretical formulations of fellow socialists, would-be allies, and bourgeois opponents. No one can read Marx's works without being struck by his often vicious critical polemics and his continuing criticisms of others. Burdened with carbuncles, burning with indignation, and convinced of his own scientific accuracy, Marx took the theories of others, examined them, and then disagreed with, censured, and sometimes excoriated them, using as his basis

Marx's Enterprise of Critique   **253**

the conclusions that he had arrived at in the course of his own studies.[5]

As can be discerned in *Capital* and his other works titled *Kritik*, Marx also engages in "critique" in a different and technical sense of the term, with a complex, far-reaching, and unique meaning. For Marx, critique involves insightful assessment that can produce knowledge even in a society permeated by illusion and constrained by power, knowledge that can become part of the consciousness—and hence the bases for thought and action—of a part of that society, the proletariat. The presentation of Marx's sense of critique also indicates his indebtedness to his predecessors in philosophy and economics, like Hegel and Ricardo; shows how critique is integral to Marx's idea of science; reveals that critique forms the locus for his claim to unify theory and practice, science and revolution, knowledge of the world and action to change it; and suggests that attention to critique may help clarify some recurrent issues in the interpretation of Marx and Marxism.

1. THE MEANING OF CRITIQUE

As a technical term for Marx, critique encompasses three distinguishable steps of analysis and evaluation: immanent criticism, critical reconstruction, and critical supersession.[6] Each step occurs on two levels, consciousness and reality, as Marx indicates in the ambiguity of *Capital*'s full title: it is a "critique of political economy," where "political economy" refers both to those thinkers who analyze the economic order and to the actual workings of that economic order, i.e., to both economists and economics, both theory and the reality it describes.

As the first step (and using political economy as the example), critique involves an immanent criticism of contemporary economists and economy, pointing up errors, inconsistencies, and irrationalities. But such internal criticism is not merely negative and does not stop with the discovery of the errors of a Nassau Senior (CI, 224–29) or of the misleading appearances and practices of capitalism (CI, 583). Rather—and as the second step—critique includes the discovery and reconstruction of the way the economic world works, i.e., an interpretation of capital and its laws of motion (CI, 10). Since this theoretical reconstruction illuminates the historical and developmental aspect of capitalism, it includes some hints toward the reconstruction of reality, some suggestions of the new world of associated producers that will grow out of the old world of capital. In other words, critique reconstructs both theory and reality, as the reinterpretation of the laws of capital and completes the immanent criticism of the political economists, and the hints of the new society show the results of the immanent criticism of economic activity. Finally, critique takes on its concluding meaning: it is the criticism of political economy as such, as an autonomous enterprise of thought and action. Bound up with the bourgeois world, political economy is to be replaced by theories that account for the full range of human potentials and activities, and by practical human life and actions motivated by and aiming for more than money and capital.

The meaning of critique, with its three steps and two levels, needs to be described in more detail and with examples from the range of Marx's work.[7] At first, critique entails an analysis of theory, thought, or consciousness.[8] This immanent criticism does not look outside the theory but examines the theory's categories, statements, and conclusions with the intention of discovering internal limitations and defects: logical inconsistencies, insuperable internal contradictions or aporias, unasked questions or unexamined assumptions, gaps in reasoning, and failure to realize the goals posited for the theory. Thus, for instance, Marx criticizes Hegel's assertion that the bureaucracy is the universal class by showing how, in Hegel's own construction, the bureaucracy and bureacrats pursue their own particular interests (CHPR, 45–48, 50–51). Marx begins his essay "Alienated Labour" by accepting the "presuppositions" of British political economists; he notes, for instance, that "political economy begins with the fact of private property; it does not explain it"; and then he goes on to "explain" it, starting from their facts and ideas (EW, 120). His later analyses of Smith, Ricardo, and the others lead Marx to conclude that "it is the weak point of the classical school of Political Economy that it nowhere, expressly and with full consciousness, distinguishes between labour, as it appears in the value of a product and the same labour, as it appears in the use-value of that product" (CI,

Marx's Enterprise of Critique

80 n. 1). They fail even though both uses occur in their writings.

Critique also includes an analysis that builds on this immanent criticism of theories: having exposed the theory's problems, Marx does not rest content with an academic or polemic victory, but rather he asks *why* these inadequate theoretical categories and conclusions exist. To answer that question, Marx moves from the realm of pure theory to an examination of the society that can give rise to such internally insufficient or incoherent theoretical constructs. In other words, Marx does not allow his criticism to stay at the level of theory (GI, 148–49); he insists that consciousness is always consciousness *of* something (CI, 154–55; CIII, 313); and, even "if in all ideology men and their circumstances appear upside-down as in a *camera obscura*, this phenomenon arises just as much from their historical life-process as the inversion of objects on the retina does from their physical life-process" (GI, 154; CIII, 209). So Marx engages in an immanent criticism of the "historical life-process" of men.

For instance, Hegel's misunderstanding of the bureaucracy derives in part from the "uncritical idealism" that simply reproduces the institutions and conundrums of his world (CHPR, 3–10). Thus, "the criticism of the German philosophy of right and of the state . . . is at once the critical analysis of the modern state and of the reality connected with it, and the definitive negation of all the past forms of consciousness in German jurisprudence and politics" (ICHPR, 59). The inability of Adam Smith and James Mill to "explain" private property leads Marx to the concept of alienated labor (EW, 120, 129). To discover why Smith and Ricardo fail to understand the value form and hence the commodity, Marx examines the form of value in its different historical manifestations (CI, 80 n. 2) and is able to draw out the "two-fold nature" of labor and value in commodities (CI, 41). So the criticism of a theory gives insight into the "historical life-processes" of men and makes possible the criticism of these processes: the state's sovereignty is only "imagined" (EW, 14); labor in capitalism is alienated; and Ricardo's problems with value reflect the historical nature and complexity of the commodity itself.

Critique includes immediately a second step. Since a fully completed immanent criticism gives insights into the deficiences of theories of reality and of the reality they describe, it results in the clarification of reality: consequently, critique is reconstruction, as reality is redescribed by an alternate theory or interpretation. Since the immanent criticism of Hegel's political philosophy leads Marx to see that Hegel's "uncritical positivism and [equally] uncritical idealism" (EW, 201) simply reproduce the dilemmas of the bourgeois world he describes, Marx can then redescribe and reformulate that world, accounting for its (and Hegel's) contradictions, as a world in which civil society dominates the state. Throughout the 1844 *Economic and Philosophical Manuscripts,* Marx uses his immanent criticism to arrive at reformulations like alienated labor.

Similarly, in one important theme of *Capital,* Marx describes the liberal ideology of "liberty, equality, property, and Bentham" as the ideology and reality of the sphere of simple circulation (CI, 176) and then shows how that sphere (with that ideology) does not yield the answer to the question, posed by Smith and Ricardo via Marx, about where and how surplus value is created (CI, 166). Marx's analysis drives him to see that the sphere of circulation is the "phenomenon of a process taking place behind it" (G, 255), the sphere of production, in which, as Marx concludes four hundred pages after posing the question, the apparently equal and "ever repeated purchase and sale of labour-power is now the mere form; what really takes place is this—the capitalist again and again appropriates, without equivalent, a portion of the previously materialised labour of others, and exchanges it for a greater quantity of living labour" (CI, 583). Through the criticism of ideology and the world that produces it, Marx arrives at a theoretical recontruction of the process of the appropriation of labor.

Marx intends practical reconstruction also; he suggests the critical reconstruction of bourgeois society according to the possibilities implicit in his immanent criticism and theoretical reconstruction. Because reconstruction grows out of immanent criticism, Marx finds the image of the future in the present: as he wrote in a letter of 1843, "we do not attempt dogmatically to prefigure the future, but want to find the new world only through criticism of the old" (to Ruge, Sept. 1843); and in 1875, "what we have to deal with here is a communist society, not as it has *developed* on its own foundations, but, on the contrary,

Marx's Enterprise of Critique

257

just as it *emerges* from capitalist society . . . still stamped with the birth marks of the old society from whose womb it emerges" (Gotha, I).

For example, from his study of Hegel's political philosophy, Marx discovers the inadequacy of purely political emancipation (EW, 11–13) and the need for the proletariat as the revolutionary class (ICHPR, 64). The analysis in "Alienated Labor" leads Marx to see the inadequacy of "radical" measures like equality of wages (EW, 132) and the need to abolish the conditions of labor that result in alienation (EW, 132–33). *Capital* contains many allusions to a reconstructed society. Where capitalism imposes a limited form, Marx sees the possibility for breadth: "When the limited bourgeois form is stripped away, what is wealth other than the universality of individual needs, capacities, pleasures, productive forces, etc., created through universal exchange? The full development of human mastery over the forces of nature . . .? The absolute working-out of his creative potentialities . . ." (G, 488; CI, 645)? Where capitalism has introduced new possibilities but maintains them in destructive forms, Marx sees the potential: "Modern Industry . . . compels society, under penalty of death, to replace the detail-worker of to-day, crippled by life-long repetition of one and the same trivial operation, and thus reduced to the mere fragment of a man, by the fully developed individual, fit for a variety of labours, ready to face any change of production, and to whom the different social functions he performs, are but so many modes of giving free scope to his own natural and acquired powers" (CI, 488). Furthermore, Marx is clear about the means to be used to attain these goals: since the theoretical reconstruction of capitalism demonstrates the centrality of time (as in labor time), the "basic prerequisite" for the "true realm of freedom" is "the shortening of the working-day" (CIII, 820).

Finally, the last step of critique is critical supersession, in which the narrow area being criticized—whether it be philosophy, politics, or economics—is seen to be deficient as a theoretical and practical enterprise and therefore to be superseded or *aufgehoben*.[9] Thus, Marx wishes to "realize and abolish philosophy" (ICHPR, 59). He wishes, in 1844, to reverse the situation in which "everything which the economist takes from you in the way of life and humanity, he restores to you in the form of money and wealth" (EW, 171). In his later critiques, Marx continues his early theme. Following Hegel, Marx sees that political economy has arisen "out of the conditions of the modern world" (PR, 189R[10]; CI, 80 n. 2). For Marx, the theory of political economy is too narrow: it treats the worker as a worker, not as a man (EW, 76; CI, 407–409); it sees work only in a limited sense (G, 610–11; CI, 177–78); and it generally looks only to the economic (G, 650–52). Similarly, economic activity is too narrow: the capitalist lives by only one commandment—"Accumulate, accumulate! That is Moses and the prophets!" (CI, 595)—and the worker has only one existence—"it is self-evident that the labourer is nothing else, his whole life through, than labour-power to be devoted to the self-expansion of capital" (CI, 264). So Marx looks to a future society in which the narrow issues of political economy will be replaced by the central issues of human freedom and self-development (CM, II; Gotha, I), and political economy, like politics and philosophy, will no longer exist as a separate theoretical undertaking or distinct sphere of activity. While his contemporaries are writing the "principles of political economy," Marx writes about a specific historical form, capital, and engages in a critique of its theoretical and practical companion, political economy, in order to supersede them.

Marx's critique, then, involves three steps, each on the two levels of theory and reality. Writing more than half a century before Marx's "early writings," Kant presaged that "our age is the age of critique, to which everything must be subjected."[11] Kant's critiques, which discover the conditions for the proper employment of the faculties of knowledge, differ from Marx's critique, which examines what others know—their consciousness of the world and the world of which they are conscious. Marx's critique, nevertheless, aims at subjecting everything to the process of critique, so as to resolve the difficulties and realize the potentials of human knowing and acting.

2. THE NECESSITY FOR IMMANENT CRITICISM

Marx insists on and requires immanent criticism as the first step in critique because he sees that there can be no immediate

Marx's Enterprise of Critique

259

access to reality, no direct route to truth, "no royal road to science" (CI, 21). Both reality and the logic of access to it are in question. Marx faces exactly the same dilemma that Hegel sees confronting philosophy: "Philosophy misses an advantage enjoyed by the other sciences. It cannot like them rest the existence of its objects on the natural admissions of consciousness, nor can it assume that its method of cognition, either for starting or continuing, is one already accepted" (Enc. 1). German idealism since Kant recognized that human subjects participate in the constitution of the world, building up the world and knowledge of it at the same time that they create constraints and distortions—as each stage in Hegel's *Phenomenology* testifies. Marx follows Hegel in seeing that the world as it appears is the result of a prior social construction of reality (Enc. 41A). Appearances have been constituted or constructed by "everyday concepts" (CIII, 820) that "have already acquired the stability of natural, self-understood forms of social life" (CI, 75). As Marx is aware, in this world of appearances all facts gain their place and meaning for human discourse by the labels and categories that are attached to them: "brute" social facts, i.e., facts that exist independently of human categories, do not exist. The categories with which human beings order their observations and experiences are a "social product as much as language" (CI, 74). But, for Marx, this preconstituted world of appearances, categories, and mediated facts ultimately masks the essential relations of capital.

Moreover, the logic of analysis is not self-evident. German idealism since Kant had subjected previous modes of thought to critiques of reason, and Hegel did the same to Kant (Enc. 41–60). So all pre-Hegelian methods of cognition are problematical by Marx's youth, and Marx's critique of Hegel's *Philosophy of Right* and *Phenomenology* made clear to him that he could not just appropriate Hegel's logic outright (CHPR, 3–10; EW, 201; CI, 19–20).

As a result of the process of critique, Marx concludes that "the final pattern of economic relations as seen on the surface, in their real existence and consequently in the conceptions by which the bearers and agents of these relations seek to understand them, is very much different from, and indeed quite the reverse of, their inner but concealed essential pattern and the conception corresponding to it" (CIII, 209). Marx tries to discover and present logically the inner, concealed, and frequently inverted (CI, 537) "essential pattern" hidden behind "real existence" and "conceptions" of it.[12] He uses immanent criticism for the discovery.

But the voyage of discovery is difficult because, for Marx, capitalism produces "an enchanted, perverted, topsy-turvy world" (CIII, 830) in which appearances mask essence in a double way: the conceptions and ideas that actors hold about "capitalist relations" (CIII, 818) (or, synonymously, "real existence" [CIII, 209]) may be more or less accurate and unastigmatic representations of those relations; and those capitalist relations themselves frequently invert, hide, or otherwise mystify the "essential pattern" (or, synonymously, "essential relations" or "essence") of human interaction.

For Marx, "false appearance and illusion" (CIII, 830) characterize the conceptions "in the ordinary consciousness of the agents of production themselves" (CIII, 25) and in the texts of the vulgar political economists, whose theories are "no more than a didactic, more or less dogmatic, translation of everyday concepts of the actual agents of production" (CIII, 830; CI, 537). These illusions nonetheless are not simply "false"[13] but derive from observation and reasoning. Marx explains at some length how a superficial observer of a surface of capitalist relations could perceive these false appearances (CIII, 826–29); for instance, because capital increases productive forces, "all of labour's social productive forces appear . . . to issue from the womb of capital itself" (CIII, 827). If the superficial observer writes in justification of capitalism, as do the vulgar political economists, then illusions multiply: one example that releases Marx's indignation, learning, and sarcasm is Nassau Senior's replacement of "capital" with "abstinence" and J.S. Mill's further claim, that profits are "remuneration of abstinence" (CI, 596 n. 3 and 596–98).

The illusory conceptions of everyday life invade the consciousness of even the best economists, the school of "classical Political Economy . . . which, since the time of W. Petty, has investigated the real relations of production in bourgeois society" (CI, 80 n. 2). As Marx notes in connection with an important argument about wages and the value of labor power, clas-

Marx's Enterprise of Critique

sical economists "borrowed from every-day life the category of 'price of labour' without further criticism" (CI, 537) and "accepted uncritically the categories 'value of labour,' 'natural price of labour,' &c., as final and as adequate expressions for the value-relations under consideration, and [were] thus led . . . into inextricable confusion and contradiction" (CI, 538).

Even when conceptions conform to the "real existence" of "capitalist relations," the "real existence" may mask and mystify the essential pattern. In capitalist relations, exchange value exists, circulation of commodities exists, but "exchange-value . . . is only the mode of expression, the phenomenal form, of something contained in" the commodity (CI, 37); and circulation is the "phenomenon of a process taking place behind it" and is "pure semblance," not self-grounding, dependent on production (G, 255).

Commodities and other central aspects of capitalism are "enigmatic" (CI, 71) in other ways. For instance, "a commodity is . . . a mysterious thing . . . because the relation of the producers to the sum total of their own labour is presented to them as a social relation, existing not between themselves, but between the products of their labour" (CI, 72); human relations are reified relations. Similarly, the social becomes the natural: "The special difficulty in grasping money in its fully developed character as money . . . is that a social relation, a definite relation between individuals, here appears as a metal, a stone, a purely physical, external thing which can be found, as such, in nature, and which is indistinguishable in form from its natural existence" (G, 239). Human creations have power over humans in capitalism, "in which the process of production has the mastery over man, instead of being controlled by him" (CI, 81, 92–93). Finally, both reality and thought in capitalism are ahistorical. While money, commodities, and the like have evolved historically, "the intermediate steps of the process vanish in the result and leave no trace behind" (CI, 92; Phen. 68). So crucial economic forms have a social fixity because nothing remains of their "genesis" (CI, 47). Moreover, for Marx, even the best bourgeois political economist "seeks to decipher, not their historical character, for to him they are immutable, but their meaning" (CI, 75); the economist remains within the "bounds of the bourgeois horizon" (CI, 14), looks upon the "capitalist

PETER G. STILLMAN

regime . . . as the absolutely final form of social production, instead of as a passing historical phase of its evolution" (CI, 15), and thus evinces no interest in history and change except to treat them in the essentially ahistorical way that as "the Fathers of the Church treated pre-Christian religions" (CI, 81).

To accept appearances uncritically—to accede to common conceptions and to look only for "real existence"—is the mark of an inadequate science (CIII, 817; CI, 542), a vulgar political economy, or a radicalism manqué. Proudhon, for instance, failed as a radical thinker, according to Marx, because he accepted the categories of thought that appeared to him in bourgeois society and so he always spoke and thought in the concepts of a capitalist (G, 248; PofP, 161), with whom he shares the illusions of the epoch (GI, 165).

On the other hand, appearances must be taken seriously: they are not mere illusion or mere "real existence" unconnected or irrelevant to essence; rather, they are manifestations that both reveal and conceal essence. In Hegel's words, appearance is the "illusory being of essence itself" (Logic, 398): i.e., both illusory and being. As Marx wrote of some categories of British political economists, "these imaginary expressions arise from the relations of production themselves. They are categories for the phenomenal forms of essential relations" (CI, 537; CI, 586).

The discovery of essential relations behind appearances requires criticism of the categories or forms of thought in which appearance is cast. Marx agrees with Hegel that "forms of thought must be made an object for investigation" (Enc. 41; CI, 80 n. 2). So Marx analyzes the category of free laborer and discovers estranged labor (EW, 123), and he analyzes labor and value in order successfully to break labor conceptually into its relations with use value and exchange value (CI, 80 n. 1). Immanent criticism of theories—that discovers the inconsistencies and other inadequacies in their concepts—discloses deficient categories and exposes them as categories of appearance, in need of rejection or modification.

Marx needs previous philosophical and economic theories as a mine for his critical excursions. They also assist Marx because previous theories do contain partial insights or show where interpretive problems exist (CI, 542; CIII, 313). He also needs good prior philosophical and economic analyses that have asked important questions and have refined or resolved many major difficulties (CIII, 830). Both the number of reference footnotes in *Capital* and Marx's modesty about the number of his own theoretical insights [14] indicate his reliance on past theories; Marx is here like Hegel, for whom "the half-truth" should not be rejected as wrong but maintained as a "mere element . . . included in the truth" (Enc. 32A). Consequently, Marx is also like Hegel in wishing not to eliminate previous theories as though replacing falsehood with truth; rather, both Hegel and Marx see themselves as fulfilling the previous theoretical development and rendering the previous theories *aufgehoben*, both cancelled and preserved (HF, 38; Phen. 68). Marx is therefore a part of the traditions of German idealism and British political economy at the same time that he is trying to burst them open to discover their liberatory potentials.

Marx insists that criticism be immanent because, in the analysis of categories, he agrees with Hegel that criticism or "refutation must not come from the outside, that is, it must not proceed from assumptions lying outside the system in question and inconsistent with it. . . . The genuine refutation must penetrate the opponent's stronghold and meet him on his own ground; no advantage is gained by attacking him somewhere else and defeating him where he is not" (Logic, 580–81). The critic must, in a sense, know the theory better than its author, to discern its internal inadequacies and inconsistencies.

Thus, for Marx (as for Hegel), there is little value in criticizing one theory by holding it against another theory asserted dogmatically, as Marx knew from his youth (letter to Ruge, Sept. 1843; Enc. 32A). Equally, there is little point in criticizing a theory with moral imperatives or dogmas brought in from outside. Since the very need for critique stems from the problematic status of "reality" and the ubiquity of illusion, there is little point in opposing "reality" to the theory to be criticized. Nor is there need to discover new facts or ascertain if hypotheses can be falsified empirically with new data. Rather, immanent criticism analyzes and reconceives existing concepts and categories of theories and the real existence they reflect.[15]

In his concern with categories of analysis or forms of thought, Marx indicates how bourgeois ideology—with its categories that reflect the phenomenal appearances of capitalist society—permeates the very basis of the thinking of individuals in that society and thus how the illusions of the epoch are maintained and solidified; as Marx sees, cultures create and maintain illusion.[16] At the same time, concern with categories leads Marx to concern with logic. He demonstrates the intimate relation between form (or categories or concepts) and content: a content (like labor [CI, 177–85] or value [CI, 80 n. 2]) takes many different forms, each of which is characteristic of a specific historical period and involves different defining aspects. In his concern with forms, Marx rejects the Kantian approach that concepts are a priori categories of reasoning, fixed and immutable; he also rejects the alternative, empiricist formulation, that they are "mere" concepts, abstract generalizations arbitrarily abstracted from arbitrarily assembled empirical data or merely stipulated, as a convenient means to order data; and he rejects the approach of a formal logic that, seeing no inherent essence or necessary connections in the external world, develops in the human mind a set of principles that are then to be applied, from the outside, to the world. As I.I. Rubin has written:

> One cannot forget that on the question of the relation between content and form, Marx took the standpoint of Hegel, and not of Kant. Kant treated form as something external in relation to the content, and as something which adheres to the content from the outside. From the standpoint of Hegel's philosophy, the content is not in itself something to which forms adheres from the outside. Rather, through its development, the content itself gives birth to the form which is already latent in the content. Form necessarily grows out of the content itself.[17]

Whereas Hegel's *Logic* develops by a process of thought analyzing thought (Enc. 83), for Marx both content and form derive from human practical life. For instance, labor's content is universal: "it is the everlasting Nature-imposed condition of human existence, and thus is independent of every social phase of that existence, or rather, is common to every such phase" (CI, 184). As men relate to each other in different social phases, the form of labor differs: e.g., slavery, wage labor. So the form grows from the common content, differently in different social

3. THE VALIDATION OF CRITICAL RECONSTRUCTION

Immanent criticism needs to be followed by critical reconstruction. Marx is well aware of the limited value of "that kind of criticism which knows how to judge and condemn the present, but not how to comprehend it" (CI, 505 n.) Ever since Hegel's portrayal of master and slave (Phen. 228–40) showed how human beings create the relations that oppress them and demonstrated that the form of liberation is conditioned by the form of domination (G, 98), outrage at oppression must be matched by analysis of its exact form and legitimation. So, for instance, awareness that the capitalist "robs" the worker must be matched by the comprehension of how he "earns surplus value with full right."[19]

For Marx as for Hegel, however, immanent or philosophical criticism is not only negative but contributes to knowledge. As Hegel said, "For the negative, which emerges as the result of dialectic, is, because a result, at the same time the positive: it contains what it results from, absorbed into itself, and made part of its own nature" (Enc. 81A, 82; G, 90). Marx's youthful criticism of the political economist's "free laborer" led him to see "alienated labor." *Capital* as a whole stands as the central example of the positive contribution.

Capital is the critical reconstruction of the essential relations of capitalist interaction. Deriving from his immanent critique, it is justified in two ways. First, Marx claims that *Capital* is science—and by "science" Marx means systematic knowledge, the goal of German idealists and British political economists.[20] In other words, Marx's is an interpretive science.[21] Moreover, Marx asserts his science is superior to his predecessors'. By this, he makes multiple claims. His science is internally more consistent than theirs, for his immanent criticism has discovered the inconsistencies in classical political economy that his critical reconstruction can overcome. His science explains as wide or wider a scope than theirs, as is indicated by his continual references to their work, to show that he has mastered *their* scope. His science, finally, is a better reflection of reality, as Marx strikingly and unfortunately phrased it, using a metaphor that later positivists, "Marxist" or not, have misread: in an "adequate" description, "the life of the subject-matter is ideally reflected as in a mirror" (CI, 19). In discussing commodities, Marx gives an example of such a reflection: "When I state that coats or boots stand in a relation to linen, because it is the universal incarnation of abstract human labour, the absurdity of the statement is self-evident. Nevertheless, when the producers of coats and boots compare those articles with linen, or, what is the same thing, with gold or silver, as the universal equivalent, they express the relation between their own private labour and the collective labour of society in the same absurd form" (CI, 76; CIII, 25). Marx's mirror does not simply reflect nature, but restates the categories and the categorical relations in their essential pattern.

In his interpretive science, Marx does not reify laws or facts, i.e., he does not place them beyond human thought or activity. Even Marx's central laws are subject to recurring modifications and exceptions: of a law so important it is italicized, *"the absolute general law of capitalist accumulation"* (CI, 644), Marx writes: "Like all other laws it is modified in its workings by many circumstances, the analysis of which does not concern us here" (loc. cit.) Moreover, these "natural laws of capitalist production" can take forms that are "more brutal or more humane" and can be overthrown more rapidly by the effective formation of the proletariat into a class (CI, 8–10). Similarly, for Marx facts cannot be used immediately for evidence or falsification, because he distinguishes essence from appearance and because for him "brute" facts do not exist independent of the categories that subsume them and give them meaning.

But Marx does not scorn laws, for he does try to develop the essential pattern of capitalism. Nor does he dismiss facts; rather, he uses them to buttress and amplify the results of his interpretive science. As he wrote to a follower, Sigfried Meyer, about

Marx's Enterprise of Critique

Capital: "Besides the general scientific exposition, I describe in great detail, from hitherto unused *official* sources, the condition of the English agricultural and industrial proletariat *during the last 20 years*, ditto *Irish* conditions. You will, of course, understand that all this serves me only as an *argumentum ad hominem*'" (letter of 30 April 1867). So, for instance, Marx derives and presents "the absolute general law of capitalist accumulation," i.e., that "accumulation of wealth at one pole is . . . at the same time accumulation of misery, agony of toil, slavery, ignorance, brutality, mental degradation at the opposite pole" of laborers, paupers, and unemployed (CI, 644–45). Then he illustrates the law by presenting multiple types of evidence (CI, 648–712), such as statistics of all sorts, conclusions of economists, visible conditions like the terrible housing for the poor, quotations from government documents, reports in Tory newspapers, and the like.

While Marx's interpretive science does make distinctions between essence and appearance (CIII, 817) and does distinguish between capitalism's narrow view of human essence, wealth, and labor and communism's broad and exalted view (G, 611, 488), Marx would not consider these discriminations as "value judgments" or "normative statements" in the contemporary positivisitic, social science senses of the phrases. Rather, the "values" and "norms" are part and parcel of the interpretation itself: distinctions about relative importance are integral to any interpretive comprehension of any broad scope of human life; equally integral are reflections about human activities, human potentials, and the possible forms of social life. In other words, any interpretive science—Marx's, Ricardo's, Hegel's, anyone's—must include, explicitly or implicitly, a view of man. As sciences, they must be judged, not by the absence or prevalence of "value judgments" nor by the "realism" or "idealism" of those judgments, but by which interpretation can marshall the force of the better argument.

Marx does not, however, hinge the validity of his critique of political economy solely on its superiority as an interpretive science. He understands and explains the limited efficacy of persuasion and the limited validity of intersubjective agreement in a society marked by constrained communication and by individual self-understandings so firmly rooted in objective life sit-

268   PETER G. STILLMAN

uations as to be virtually unchangeable. Marx looks to the consciousness of the working class for his ultimate justification. Just as vulgar political economy represents the point of view of the businessman, so, Marx thinks, *Capital* represents the working class: "So far as . . . criticism [of 'the bourgeois economy'] represents a class, it can only represent the class whose vocation in history is the overthrow of the capitalist mode of production and the final abolition of all classes—the proletariat" (CI, 16; see PofP, 109). Marx here is restating his youthful stand: "Just as philosophy finds its *material* weapons in the proletariat, so the proletariat finds its *intellectual* weapons in philosophy" (ICHPR, 65).

In presenting the standpoint of the proletariat, Marx wishes to amplify and clarify the workers' feelings of unease, unfairness, or oppression and to recast them into systematic, scientific form. "Theory is only realized in a people so far as it fulfils the needs of the people" (ICHPR, 61). So *Capital* is the demonstration that the felt problems of the workers derive from the essential relations of capitalism, that oppression takes the form of the class exploitation inherent and necessary to capitalism (EW, 69–76; CI, 583), and that capitalism is a transitory economic system. Marx's systematic presentation, then, develops and expands the workers' thoughts, explains to them, "as in a mirror" (CI, 19), their situation, and gives them categories for thinking and acting that can illuminate the enigmatic face of capitalism. In other words, it is their critical self-consciousness.

But, for Marx, *Capital* requires self-clarification by the workers. The conclusions of *Capital* cannot simply be accepted and memorized by rote, or adopted immediately on authority "as if shot out of a pistol" (Phen. 89)—or, at least, they make little sense if they are (CI, 76).[22] While the laws of Newton's physics or Euclid's geometry can be memorized and applied, critique is a process in which existing categories and logic must be criticized and overthrown, new ones developed, and a system constructed. Consequently, Marx's science includes both the conclusions and the process by which they were reached, and the individual learning the science has to "go through the stages" (Phen. 89), i.e., has to engage in a formative education (*Bildung*) in which his whole perspective on the world may be changed.

Marx's Enterprise of Critique 269

Just as the character Socrates tries, in Plato's *Republic,* to speak directly to the particular characteristics and concerns of his interlocutors, Marx tries to speak directly to the interests of the workers, in order to persuade. This persuasion to new knowledge involves, for Socrates, a transformation of the souls of individuals to a new and just ordering and, for Marx, a *Bildung* that reorders the attitudes and activities of each of the workers who reads and comprehends *Capital.* Quietism, reconciliation, reformism—none of these is possible, Marx thinks, after *Capital* has been taken to heart (CI, 644, 583, 235); only possible is opposition to capital,[23] through action focusing on the shortening of the working day (CIII, 820).

Socrates sees the trip out of the cave as arduous and hazardous. Marx lacks the overpowering image but shares the concern: the power of bourgeois culture blocks comprehension and insight into cultural illusions. "The ideas of the ruling class are in every epoch the ruling ideas" (GI, 172). Whereas Socrates addresses himself to single individuals to convince them to undertake the struggle out of the cave, Marx makes clear to workers that opposition to capital can be effective only when they cooperate: "the isolated labourer, the labourer as 'free' vendor of his labour-power . . . succumbs without any power of resistance" (CI, 299). So the persuasion of workers aims at the formation of the proletariat into a class (CM, II), i.e., the creation of its consciousness of itself as a class.

As the action-orienting consciousness of the proletariat as a class, *Capital* is revolutionary; it entails the critical reconstruction of society in practice. As a systematic statement of interpretation, it is science, and involves the critical reconstruction of society in theoretical terms. Marx's critique of political economy is, as he wrote his friend Weydemeyer, "a scientific victory for our party" (letter of 1 Feb. 1859). While some might see a conflict between advocacy of revolution and science, Marx does not. He sees that all science has a bias or interest. Even at its most scientific and "unprejudiced," classical political economy supported the bourgeoisie against the "feudal aristocracy" (CI, 14). After about 1825, when the bourgeois-proletariat "class struggle, practically as well as theoretically, took on more and more outspoken and threatening forms" (CI, 15), major economists end up supporting either capital or labor in the struggle.

270 PETER G. STILLMAN

For Marx in 1867, this struggle has been "a civil war of half a century" (CI, 295) in which the capitalist has tried to expand and intensify the working day, the worker to reduce it. "There is here, therefore, an antinomy, right against right, both equally bearing the seal of the law of exchanges. Between equal rights [,] force decides" (CI, 235). Within the rules of capitalism, both capital and labor have equal right; like the characters in Aeschylus' *Oresteia* or the cultures in Hegel's world history, both sides have justifiable claims; without Athena or the world-spirit to constitute a tribunal or cast the deciding vote, parties claiming irreconcilable rights must resort to force. The political economist represents capital; Marx, the worker. Marx's science is inherently revolutionary.

4. THE PROMISE OF CRITICAL SUPERSESSION

For Marx, the proof of the effective unity of science and revolution is the transformation of society. "Man must prove the truth, that is, the reality and power, the this-sidedness of his thinking in practice" (Theses on Feuerbach, II). Marx expects that the victory of the proletariat will vindicate his interpretive science with its view of human life and activity. Then, his immanent criticism will be seen as accurate; his assessments will be shown to be not "value judgments" but valid comprehension; the horizons of bourgeois life will appear as constricting; and the separate spheres and divisions of bourgeois life, with their separate ideologies, will dissolve in a new society in which philosophy (and the critique of philosophy) and political economy (and its critique) will be superfluous because "the practical relation of every-day life offer to man none but perfectly intelligible and reasonable relations with regard to his fellowmen and to Nature" (CI, 79).

5. MARX'S CRITIQUE TODAY

Almost immediately after Marx's death, one important segment of his "disciples," the theoreticians of the Second International, dissolved Marxism into a dogmatic economics that

Marx's Enterprise of Critique

eliminated most dimensions of "critique" found in his thought, retaining only critique in the sense of polemics based on pre-established dogma. Leading the workers, these theoreticians—and their theoretical successors in the Soviet Union and elsewhere—drowned themselves like lemmings in a sea of positivistic social theory. The comment of a Dutch Marxist around the time of World War I has recurring accuracy: "Because the proletariat masses were still wholly ruled by a bourgeois mode of thought, after the collapse [of November 1918] they rebuilt with their own hands bourgeois domination."[24]

Among some Marxists ostracized by the "orthodox," a commitment to "critical theory" remained. But for the Frankfurt School, for instance, part of the justification of Marx's critique gradually became problematical, as the revolutionary character of the working class was questioned. Undermined on one side by uncritical ideologues and on the other by the apparent integration of the proletariat, what remains of Marx's critique today?

Since critique involves not only the bare conclusions but also the process by which they were discovered, the vital strands of Marx's critique today almost always include an emphasis on reflecting upon and thinking through again Marx's full theory. So theorists stressing critique usually do not ossify Marx's theoretical conclusions, much less his tactical remarks or the later accretions to his theory. Occasionally, theorists stressing critique may accept more or less uncritically Marx's own use of critique as the definition of "critical theory" or they may attempt to deduce from Marx's critique some method or methodology that is to be applied universally—in both instances, however, losing some essential aspects of Marx's process of critique.

But critique is alive today. Clearly, critique as immanent criticism of ideology and the reality that generates it does remain. This dimension of critique has been the self-appointed task of, among others, the Frankfurt School: for an American audience, Herbert Marcuse's *One-Dimensional Man* is probably the best-known exemplar.[25] The anguish of the book's last chapter, however, as well as Marcuse's later writings, suggest that critique as reconstruction and as supersession could not be or has not been maintained.

The critique of political economy also remains, whether as renewed critique of classical political economy, as critique of current economic thought, or as critique of current economic activity. At present, this last seems to be the most theoretically interesting and practically promising, in its Marxist and non-Marxist forms of workers' self-management. Concern with workers' participation and control grew in part from analysis of the relation of the worker to the process of production, the focus of Marx's critique in "Alienated Labour." André Gorz, for instance, has drawn on Marx's insights to make an immanent criticism of that relation and its ideological accompaniments and legitimations, and has attempted to construct some new modes of interaction on the basis of his criticisms.[26]

Marx's sense of critique is alive today in another way. Some contemporary theorists—of whom Jürgen Habermas is the most famous, but not the only nor necessarily the paradigmatic example—have tried to readdress the issue of critique by looking back to Marx and examining how he undertook the process of critique. So, for instance, Habermas has worked his way through the major philosophers since Kant, as well as other thinkers important to contemporary dilemmas, and subjected their theories to an immanent criticism that allows at least the reconstruction of a critical social theory with a practical intent. As Albrecht Wellmer has written, "Habermas's work is critical theory attempting, in a debate with analytical scientific theory and social science [and, since Wellmer wrote, with theories of linguistics and communication], to determine its critical position anew."[27] While Habermas's own work is marred by a number of problems from a Marxist—or Hegelian—point of view (including especially some Kantian turns), nonetheless he is following Marx's own development of critical theory.

In his attempt to respond theoretically to "a changed historical situation,"[28] Habermas is also following Marx's stance. For Hegel, "philosophy is its own time comprehended in thought" (PR, Preface); for Marx likewise, critique comprehends, analyzes, and evaluates its own time, to criticize, reconstruct, and —unlike Hegel—suspersede it. Both Hegel and Marx evince a radical concern with the present. Although interested in confronting questions that concerned their predecessors, they refuse to be bound by those questions. Hegel and Marx do not

Marx's Enterprise of Critique

ask, as their central explicit questions, Kant's question of the limits to reason or the Cartesian question about certain human knowledge. Rather, Hegel and Marx rephrase issues into their contemporary dilemmas and concerns. To follow through on Marx's critique in the late twentieth century poses the same challenge that Hegel put, in the Preface to the *Philosophy of Right*: "Hic Rhodus, hic salta!"

NOTES

1. Citations to Marx's works are usually in the text, in parentheses, and to page number (except as noted below). The most frequently cited texts are *Capital*, vol. I (abbreviated CI) and *Capital*, vol. III (abbreviated CIII) (New York: International Publishers, 1967). Other cited works, in the order Marx wrote them, are: J. O'Malley, ed., *Critique of Hegel's 'Philosophy of Right'* (Cambridge: Cambridge University Press, 1970), abbreviated as CHPR; "Introduction to the Critique of Hegel's 'Philosophy of Right'," abbreviated as ICHPR and cited according to Robert C. Tucker, ed., *The Marx-Engels Reader* (New York: Norton, 1978; second edition); "On the Jewish Question" and the 1844 *Economic and Philosophical Manuscripts*, in T.B. Bottomore, ed., *Karl Marx: Early Writings* (New York: McGraw-Hill, 1964), abbreviated as EW; *The Holy Family, or Critique of Critical Criticism* (Moscow: Progress, 1975), abbreviated as HF; *The German Ideology*, cited according to *The Marx-Engels Reader* and abbreviated as GI; *The Poverty of Philosophy* (Moscow: Progress, 1955), abbreviated as PofP; *The Communist Manifesto*, cited according to *The Marx-Engels Reader*, by section number, and abbreviated as CM; *Grundrisse*, Martin Nicolaus, trans. (New York: Vintage, 1973), abbreviated as G; and the *Critique of the Gotha Program*, cited according to *The Marx-Engels Reader*, by section number, and abbreviated as Gotha. Marx's letters can be found in Marx and Engels, *Selected Correspondence* (Moscow: Progress, 1975; third edition); they are cited by recipient and date. In cases of more than one citation in parentheses, the first is the origin of the quotation cited; other citations can be seen for elucidation.
2. Gary Teeple, "The Development of Marx's Critique of Politics, 1842–1847," doctoral dissertation, 1981, University of Sussex, p. 276, n. 12.*
3. *The German Ideology: A Critique of the New German Philosophy as represented by Feuerbach, B. Bauer, and Stirner, and of German Socialism and its various Prophets.* Other texts that are "critiques" in the tech-

274   PETER G. STILLMAN

nical sense are the *Poverty of Philosophy* (see HF, 38) and the "Theses on Feuerbach" (see the fourth thesis).

4. For the best treatments of critique, see Jürgen Habermas, "Between Philosophy and Science: Marxism as Critique" in his *Theory and Practice* (Boston: Beacon, 1973); Karl Korsch, *Three Essays on Marxism* (London: Pluto Press, 1971); Geoffrey Pilling, *Marx's Capital: Philosophy and Political Economy* (London: Routledge & Kegan Paul, 1980); and Teeple, "Marx's Critique of Politics."*On related topics, see Lucio Coletti, "Marxism: Science or Revolution?" and Norman Geras, "Marx and the Critique of Political Economy," both in Robin Blackburn, ed., *Ideology in Social Science* (New York: Vintage, 1973).

5. For one famous example, see the *Critique of the Gotha Program* (not Marx's title); also, CI, 224–29.

6. The German word *Kritik* can be translated as either "critique" or "criticism." In titles, it is usually translated as "critique," a practice I follow. I take advantage of the existence of two English words to use "critique" as the technical term and "criticism" (and its other grammatical forms) as a short synonym for "analysis, assessment, and evaluation."

7. While most of this chapter stresses the critique of political economy, because Marx saw that as central, in this section I use evidence from his *Critique of Hegel's 'Philosophy of Right'* and his 1844 *Economic and Philosophical Manuscripts* as well to indicate the basic stability of his use of critique. For a more detailed examination, see Teeple, "Marx's Critique of Politics."*

8. While "consciousness" is the umbrella term, I use these terms— and "ideology"—not synonymously but with overlapping ranges of meaning. I think that greater precision is not necessary for the arguments of this chapter, except for "science," for which see section 3 below.

9. Korsch, *Three Essays,* p. 41.

10. Citations to G.W.F. Hegel's works are also in the text, in parentheses. Hegel, [*Encyclopedia*] *Logic,* William Wallace, trans. (Oxford: Oxford University Press, 1892; second edition), abbreviated as Enc. and cited to section (not page) number; where an "R" follows the number, the citation is not to the main paragraph but to Hegel's written elucidatory "remarks"; where an "A," to students' notes of Hegel's lectures collated by them in posthumous editions; Hegel, *The Science of Logic,* A.V. Miller, trans. (London: George Allen & Unwin, 1969), abbreviated as Logic and cited to page number; Hegel, *The Phenomenology of Mind,* J.B. Baillie, trans. (London: Macmillan, 1931), abbreviated as Phen. and cited to page

Marx's Enterprise of Critique 275

number; and Hegel, *The Philosophy of Right*, T.M. Knox, trans. (Oxford: Oxford University Press, 1942), abbreviated as PR and cited as is the [*Encyclopedia*] *Logic*.

11. I. Kant, *Critique of Pure Reason*, Preface to the First Edition. See also Marx's letter to Ruge, Sept. 1843.

12. As is the case with many other issues, Hegel makes a similar distinction between "reality" and "actuality" (PR, Preface). Hegel is frequently cited and referred to because one subsidiary theme of this chapter is the close relation between Hegel's thought and *Capital*. Indeed, Hegel's idea of critique in much of the *Phenomenology* directly parallels Marx's technical sense of the term.

13. For Marx, I think, the opposite of "true" consciousness is not "false" consciousness (as though consciousness were wayward only by erring) but "mystified" consciousness (led astray by both illusion and error). Illusion can derive from a misperception of the world or from an accurate perception of mystified real existence.

14. See Marx's letters to Weydemeyer on 5 March 1852 and to Engels on 8 January 1868.

15. As is frequently apparent in the section on the fetishism of commodities (e.g., CI, 73, 75), existing concepts may well accurately reflect real existence, but that real existence itself is an inversion and mystification of essential human relations (G, 640), needing criticism.

16. Marx himself may have fallen victim to the objectivism of bourgeois society (CI, 57–85, 71–76), according to some critics like Albrecht Wellmer; see his "The Latent Positivism in Marx's Philosophy of History" in his *Critical Theory of Society* (New York: Seabury, 1974).

17. I.I. Rubin, *Essays on Marx's Theory of Value* (Detroit: Black and Red, 1972), p. 117; see Pilling, *Marx's Capital*, p. 74. For Hegel and Marx, the intimate connection between form and content means that logic can only be discovered in the process of undertaking science. To attempt a prior epistemology or critique of pure reason commits "the error of refusing to enter the water until you have learnt to swim" (Enc. 41R). To develop specific rules of sociological method before studying the subject matter results in the same problem.

18. A full statement of Marx's logic—especially in its relations to Kant's and Hegel's—would require writing the book that Marx promised but never started. Briefly, the distinction in this paragraph is between Hegel's logic of ideas and Marx's logic of practical (or material) life, i.e., between Hegel's idealism and Marx's materialism. One implication, central for *Capital*, is that, whereas Hegelian me-

276   **PETER G. STILLMAN**

diations between opposites produce a higher synthesis on the path to thought thinking thought, Marx's mediations can simply retain the conflict and opposition of what is (CHPR, 91–92; e.g., CI, 644).

19. Karl Marx, *Notes on Adolph Wagner*, pp. 185–186, in Terrell Carver, *Karl Marx: Texts on Method* (New York: Barnes & Noble, 1975).

20. Phen., 70–71; James Steuart, *Principles of Political Economy* (1767), Preface.

21. "Interpretive" in a sense like that of, for instance, Charles Taylor, "Interpretation and the Sciences of Man," *Review of Metaphysics*, XXV, no. 1 (Sept. 1971).

22. For Marx's concern about reaching the working class, see CI, 13 and 21.

23. As a part of persuading workers to see *Capital* as the scientific statement of their interests and consciousness, Marx uses rhetorical devices throughout: classical allusions, metaphors, tropes, irony, the whole range of expressive forms. As with Socrates in Plato's presentation of him, Marx's rhetoric should be seen as part of an appeal to the entire individual, not just to his rational or theoretical faculties—because both Socrates and Marx realize that individuals are not persuaded exclusively by logic, because both aim at the transformation of the whole individual (and not just his reason), and because both assert that their rhetoric is in the service of rationality. In other words, Marx's rhetoric is not primarily evaluative, subjective, or superfluous, but an essential element of a persuasive text.

24. Anton Pannekoek, "World Revoluti on and Communist Tactics" (1920), quoted in Russell Jacoby, "Toward a Critique of Automatic Marxism," *Telos*, no. 10 (Winter 1971), p. 125. See also Korsch's 1923 comment: "the neglect of the problem of philosophy [or critique] by the Marxists of the Second International [is] . . . related to the fact that problems of revolution hardly concerned them," in his *Marxism and Philosophy* (New York: Monthly Review Press, 1970), pp. 52–53.

25. Herbert Marcuse, *One-Dimensional Man* (Boston: Beacon, 1964).

26. André Gorz, *Strategy for Labor* (Boston: Beacon, 1967).

27. Wellmer, *Critical Theory of Society*, p. 53.

28. Ibid.

Editor's Note

*This dissertation has now been published as a book: Teeple, Gary. *Marx's Critique of Politics, 1842–1847*. Toronto: University of Toronto Press, 1984.

[5]

Karl Marx's "Enquête Ouvrière"

HILDE WEISS

It appears from Marx's letter of November 5, 1880, addressed to Sorge that the "Enquête Ouvrière" published in the *Revue Socialiste* on April 20, 1880, was the work of Marx himself. He writes: "I have prepared for him [Benoît Malon, the editor of the *Revue Socialiste*] the 'Questionneur' [*sic*] which was first published in the *Revue Socialiste* and afterwards distributed in a large number of copies throughout France." [1] Only the detailed questionnaire, containing a hundred questions, and the accompanying text seem to have survived. A note in a later issue of the *Revue Socialiste,* the style of which suggests that it may have been written by Marx, indicates that some replies had been received, and that when a sufficient number had come in they would be published. [2] The journal *Egalité*, which was published during this period, and which Marx described in the same letter to Sorge as the first "workers' paper" in France, repeatedly urged its readers to take part in the survey and included copies of the questionnaire. [3]

From Hilde Weiss, "Die 'Enquête Ouvrière' von Karl Marx," *Zeitschrift für Sozialforschung*, V (Paris: Félix Alcan, 1936), 76, 83–88, 91–97. Translated by Tom Bottomore. Published with the permission of Presses Universitaires de France.

[1] "Twenty-five thousand copies of this appeal were printed and were sent to all labor organizations, socialist and democratic groups, French newspapers and individuals who requested copies." (Note on the "Enquête Ouvrière" in *Revue Socialiste*, April 20, 1880).

[2] "Concerning the 'Enquête Ouvrière': A number of our friends have already responded to our questionnaire, and we are grateful to them. We urge those of our friends and readers who have not yet replied to do so quickly. In order to make the survey as complete as possible we shall defer our own work until a large number of questionnaires has been returned. We ask our proletarian friends to reflect that the completion of these 'cahiers du travail' is of the greatest importance, and that by participating in our difficult task they are working directly for their own liberation." *Revue Socialiste,* July 5, 1880.

[3] "In its last issue the *Revue Socialiste* has taken the initiative in an excellent project. . . . The significance of an investigation of working-class conditions as they have been created by bourgeois rule is to place the possessing caste on trial, to assemble the materials for a passionate protest against modern society, to display before the eyes of all the oppressed, all wage-slaves, the injustices of which they are the constant victims, and thereby to arouse in them the will to end such conditions." *L'Egalité*, April 28, 1880.

Karl Marx's "Enquête Ouvrière" 173

* * *

Marx's "Enquête Ouvrière" differs in three respects from previous investigations of social conditions. First, as is clear from the statement of its purpose, and from the questions themselves, it aimed to provide an exact description of actual social conditions. Secondly, it proposed to collect information only from the workers themselves. Thirdly, it had a didactic aim; it was meant to develop the consciousness of the workers in the sense expounded in Marx's social theory.

Marx also intended that his "Enquête Ouvrière" should diffuse among the general public a knowledge of the working and living conditions of the workers, and he had, therefore, some ulterior motives in undertaking his study. At the same time, however, his socialist views imposed upon him the obligation to depict as faithfully as possible the existing social misery. He assigns to social investigation the task of aiding the workers themselves to gain an understanding of their situation. For philanthropists the workers, as the most miserable stratum of society, were the object of welfare measures; but Marx saw in them an oppressed class which would become master of its own fate when once it had become aware of its situation. With the development of industrial capitalism, not only the misery of the proletariat, but also its will to emancipation increased. In his preface to the questionnaire Marx describes the "Enquête Ouvrière" as a basis for "preparing a reconstruction of society."

However, it is not only in its aims that Marx's "Enquête Ouvrière" differs from the private and official investigations that had preceded it, but also in the manner in which it was carried out. Earlier surveys, even if they had the intention, could not discover the real character of social evils, because they employed inadequate means to collect their information. They were addressed almost exclusively to factory owners and their representatives, to factory inspectors where there were such people, or to government officials (as in the case of Villeneuve-Bargement's inquiry).[4] Even where doctors or philanthropists who made such surveys went directly to working-class families, they were usually accompanied by factory owners or their representatives. Le Play, for example, recommends

---

[4] [Villeneuve-Bargement, *Economie politique chrétienne ou Recherches sur la nature et les causes du paupérisme en France et en Europe et sur les moyens de le soulager et de le prévenir*, 3 vols. (Paris: Paulin, 1834)—Ed.]

Hilde Weiss

visits to working class families ". . . with an introduction from some carefully selected authority"; and he advises extremely diplomatic behavior towards the family members, including the payment of small sums of money, or the distribution of presents, as a recompense. The investigator should ". . . praise with discrimination the cleverness of the men, the charm of the women, the good behavior of the children, and discreetly hand out small presents to all of them." [5] In the course of a thorough critical examination of survey methods that appears in Audiganne's account of the discussions in his circle of workers, it is said of Le Play: "Never was a more misleading course embarked upon, in spite of the very best intentions. It is simply a question of the approach. A false viewpoint and a false method of observation give rise to a completely arbitrary series of suppositions, which bear no relation whatsoever to social reality, and in which there is apparent an invincible partiality for despotism and constraint." [6] Audiganne indicates as one of the common mistakes in the conduct of surveys the pomp and ceremony which is adopted by investigators when they visit working-class families. "If there is not a single tangible result produced by any survey carried out under the Second Empire, the blame must be assigned, in large measure, to the pompous manner in which they were conducted." [7] Marx and Engels also described the methods by which workers were induced to give testimony through social research of this kind, even to the extent of presenting petitions against the reduction of their working hours.

Marx's questionnaire, which was addressed directly to the workers, was something unique. The article on social surveys in the *Dictionary of Political Economy* observes bluntly: "Those who are to be questioned should not be allowed to participate in the inquiry." [8] This justified Audiganne's criticism that ". . . people judge us without knowing us." [9]

Marx asks the workers alone for information about their social conditions, on the grounds that only they and not any "providential savior" know the causes of their misery, and they alone can discover effective means to eliminate them. In the preface to the question-

---

[5] *Les Ouvriers Européens,* Vol. I, p. 223.

[6] Audiganne, *Mémoires d'un ouvrier de Paris, 1871–1872* (Paris, 1873), p. 61.

[7] Audiganne, *op. cit.,* p. 93.

[8] *Dictionnaire de l'économie politique* (Paris, 1854), p. 706.

[9] Audiganne, *op. cit.,* p. 1.

Karl Marx's "Enquête Ouvrière"

naire he asks the socialists for their support, since they need, for their social reforms, exact knowledge of the conditions of life and work of the oppressed class, and this can only be brought to light by the workers themselves. He points out to them the historical role which the working class is called upon to play and for which no socialist utopia can provide a substitute.

This method of collecting information, by asking the workers themselves, represents a considerable progress over the earlier inquiries. It is, of course, understandable that Marx had to restrict himself to this method. Apart from the political and educational purposes which he wanted to combine with his investigation, his method of obtaining information directly from the workers was intended to open the eyes of the public and of the state. From the point of view of modern social research in this field, the restriction of such an inquiry into working conditions to the responses of workers themselves would be considered inadequate. This method of inquiry is still vitally important in modern social surveys; but the monographs that were to have resulted from the "Enquête Ouvrière" would need to be complemented, and their findings checked, by statistical materials, and by the data available from other surveys. . . .

The didactic purpose of the "Enquête Ouvrière" arises, as will be shown later, from the arrangement and formulation of the questions; but it is apparent also in the preface, and especially in the title that Marx gives to the monographs which it is proposed to write on the basis of the replies to the questionnaire; he calls them "cahiers du travail" ("labor-lists") in contrast to the "cahiers de doléances" ("grievance-lists") of 1789. The specific character of his survey is shown by his coining of this new term, which is connected with a living tradition of the French workers, the petitions of the Third Estate. But while the "cahiers de doléances" put forward trivial demands in a servile manner, the "cahiers du travail" were meant to contain a true and exact description of the condition of the working class and of the path to its liberation. Moreover, the accomplishment of this program is not to be left to the goodwill of a king; the workers are to struggle forthrightly and consciously for their human rights. It is not by chance that Marx also refers in this context to the "socialist democracy," whose first task is to prepare the "cahiers du travail." The workers, who have to wage a class struggle and to accomplish a renewal of society, must first of

176   *Hilde Weiss*

all become capable of recognizing their own situation and of seeing the readiness of individuals to work together in a common cause.

The "cahiers du travail," as I have noted, were not only to provide a better knowledge of working-class conditions, but were also to educate the workers in socialism. By merely reading the hundred questions, the worker would be led to see the obvious and commonplace facts that were mentioned there as elements in a general picture of his situation. By attempting seriously to answer the questions, he would become aware of the social determination of his conditions of life; he would gain an insight into the nature of the capitalist economy and the state, and would learn the means of abolishing wage labor and attaining his freedom. The questionnaire thus provides the outline of a socialist manual, which the worker can fill with a living content by absorbing its results.

Several of the questions are formulated in such a way—for instance, by the introduction of valuations—that the worker is led at once to the answer which the didactic purpose of the survey requires. Thus, Marx refers to the misuse of public power when it is a matter of defending the privileges of entrepreneurs; and a subsequent question asks whether the state protects the workers "against the exactions and the illegal combinations of the employers." The contrast is intended to make the worker aware of the class character of the state. Another example is provided by the case where workers share in the profits of the enterprise. The respondent is asked to consider whether business concerns with this apparently social orientation differ from other capitalist enterprises, and whether the legal position of the workers in them is superior. "Can they go on strike? Or are they only permitted to be the humble servants of their masters?" (Question 99). It should be said, however, that only a relatively small proportion of the questions seek to influence opinion so directly.

It is far more significant, in relation to the two aspects of the survey, that Marx was successful in setting out the questions in a clear and practical manner. They are easily intelligible and deal with matters of direct concern to the worker. The simplicity and exactness of the questions in the "Enquête Ouvrière" represent an advance over earlier surveys. Audiganne had observed quite rightly that these surveys asked questions that were far too comprehensive, abstract, and complicated, and compromised the answers on im-

Karl Marx's "Enquête Ouvrière" 177

portant issues by introducing irrelevant questions.[10] For the same reasons, the various private investigations could provide no better picture of the real social conditions and attitudes of the workers.

The content of the questions posed in the earlier surveys, as well as their aims and techniques of inquiry, corresponded very closely with the interests of employers. For example, the question whether workers were paid wholly in cash, or whether a part of their wages were given in the form of goods or rent allowances, was asked both in the government survey of 1872 and in the "Enquête Ouvrière"; but in the former case it was asked from the point of view of the employers, in the latter from the point of view of the workers. In the official survey, payments in the form of goods are treated as a "supplement" to wages, but Marx regards every form of wage payment other than in cash as a method of reducing wages.

Since Marx's survey does represent an advance over earlier attempts, it is all the more surprising that very few replies to the questionnaire were apparently received.[11] Two reasons may explain this failure: first, the scope of the questionnaire, and second, the circumstances of the time. Even today, it is not easy for the average worker, in his spare time, to answer a questionnaire containing a hundred questions; and it was all the more difficult in a period when workers were being asked to do this for the first time. Their ability to write and to express themselves was still limited; they read very little, and their newspapers were published in small editions, as well as being hampered by the censorship. Second, the French labor movement was still in the period of depression that followed the Paris Commune. Had there been at that time an independent labor movement, the survey could have been carried out much more effectively. It was, indeed, because of the backwardness of the labor movement and of the working class generally,[12] that Marx gave his survey the didactic purpose of awakening the workers

---

[10] For one example among many, see Ducarre, *Rapport sur les conditions du travail en France* (Versailles, 1875), p. 195: "What is the physical condition of the working population in your district, from the point of view of sanitary conditions, population increase, and expectation of life?" It is easy to imagine the prolixity of the replies.

[11] It has proved impossible to find even the few replies that did arrive, in spite of an active search for them.

[12] The reports compiled by workers on the occasion of the Vienna Exhibition (1873) show clearly how far the workers at that time were influenced by utopian ideas and by the views of employers.

178 *Hilde Weiss*

to a realization of their condition. Thus Marx's survey had at the same time to create the circumstances in which an inquiry could be carried out.

THE TEXT OF THE QUESTIONNAIRE [18]

No government—whether monarchical or bourgeois-republican—has dared to undertake a serious investigation of the condition of the French working class, although there have been many studies of agricultural, financial, commercial and political crises.

The odious acts of capitalist exploitation which the official surveys by the English government have revealed, and the legislative consequences of these revelations (limitation of the legal working day to ten hours, legislation concerning the labour of women and children, etc.), have inspired in the French bourgeoisie a still greater terror of the dangers which might result from an impartial and systematic inquiry.

While awaiting the time when the republican government can be induced to follow the example of the English monarchical government and inaugurate a comprehensive survey of the deeds and misdeeds of capitalist exploitation, we shall attempt a preliminary investigation with the modest resources at our disposal. We hope that our undertaking will be supported by all those workers in town and country who realize that only they can describe with full knowledge the evils which they endure, and that only they—not any providential saviours—can remedy the social ills from which they suffer. We count also upon the socialists of all schools, who, desiring social reform, must also desire *exact* and *positive* knowledge of the conditions in which the working class, the class to which the future belongs, lives and works.

These "labour-lists" ("cahiers du travail") represent the first task which socialist democracy must undertake in preparation for the regeneration of society.

The following hundred questions are the most important ones. The replies should follow the order of the questions. It is not necessary to answer all the questions, but respondents are asked to make their answers as comprehensive and detailed as possible. The name of the respondent will not be published unless specifically authorized, but it should be given together with the address, so that we can establish contact with him.

From T. B. Bottomore and Maximilien Rubel (editors), *Karl Marx: Selected Writings in Sociology and Social Philosophy* (London: C. A. Watts & Company Ltd., 1956), pp. 203–12. Copyright © 1956 C. A. Watts & Company Ltd. Reprinted with the permission of C. A. Watts & Company Ltd., and McGraw-Hill Book Company.

[18] [Hilde Weiss notes that this was, to her knowledge, the first German translation of the "Enquête Ouvrière." The first English translation of the questionnaire and of some passages from the prefatory statement was published in T. B. Bottomore and Maximilien Rubel, editors, *Karl Marx: Selected Writings in Sociology and Social Philosophy.*—Ed.]

Karl Marx's "Enquête Ouvrière"

The replies should be sent to the director of the *Revue Socialiste* (Monsieur Lécluse, 28 rue Royale, Saint-Cloud, near Paris).

The replies will be classified and will provide the material for monographs to be published in the *Revue Socialiste* and subsequently collected in a volume.

I

1. What is your occupation?
2. Does the workshop in which you are employed belong to a capitalist or to a joint-stock company? Give the names of the capitalist employers or of the directors of the company.
3. State the number of persons employed.
4. State their ages and sex.
5. What is the minimum age at which children (boys or girls) are employed?
6. State the number of supervisors and other employees who are not ordinary wage earners.
7. Are there any apprentices? How many?
8. Are there, in addition to the workers usually and regularly employed, others who are employed at certain periods?
9. Does your employer's industry work exclusively or primarily for the local market, for the national market, or for export?
10. Is the workshop in the country or in the town? Give the name of the place where it is situated.
11. If your workshop is in the country, does your industrial work enable you to live, or do you combine it with agricultural work?
12. Is your work done by hand or with the aid of machinery?
13. Give details of the division of labour in your industry.
14. Is steam used as motive power?
15. State the number of workshops in which the different branches of the industry are carried on. Describe the special branch in which you are employed, giving information not only about the technical aspects, but also about the muscular and nervous strain involved, and the general effects of the work on the health of the workers.
16. Describe the sanitary conditions in the workshop; size of the rooms, space assigned to each worker; ventilation, temperature, whitewashing of the walls, lavatories, general cleanliness; noise of machines, metallic dust, humidity, etc.
17. Is there any municipal or governmental supervision of the sanitary conditions in the workshops?
18. In your industry, are there any harmful fumes which cause specific illnesses among the workers?
19. Is the workshop overcrowded with machines?

Hilde Weiss

20. Are the machines, the transmission system, and the engines supplying power, protected so as to avoid any accidents?

21. Enumerate the accidents which have occurred in your personal experience.

22. If you work in a mine enumerate the preventive measures taken by your employer to ensure adequate ventilation and to prevent explosions and other dangerous accidents.

23. If you are employed in a chemical works, in a factory, in the metal-working industry, or in any other industry which is particularly dangerous, enumerate the safety measures introduced by your employer.

24. How is your factory lighted (by gas, paraffin, etc.)?

25. In case of fire, are there enough emergency exits?

26. In case of accidents, is the employer obliged *by law* to pay compensation to the worker or his family?

27. If not, has he ever paid compensation to those who have met with an accident while working to enrich him?

28. Is there a medical service in your workshop?

29. If you work at home, describe the condition of your work-room. Do you use only tools, or do you use small machines? Are you helped by your children or by any other people (adults or children, male or female)? Do you work for individual clients or for a contractor? Do you deal directly with the latter, or do you deal with a middleman?

II

30. State your daily hours of work, and working days in the week.

31. State the holidays during the year.

32. What are the breaks in the working day?

33. Are meals taken at regular intervals or irregularly? Are they taken in the workshop or elsewhere?

34. Do you work during the meal breaks?

35. If steam power is used, when is the power turned on, and when is it turned off?

36. Is there any night work?

37. State the hours of work of children and of young persons below the age of 16.

38. Are there shifts of children and young persons which replace each other during the hours of work?

39. Are the laws concerning the employment of children enforced by the government or the municipality? Are they respected by the employer?

40. Are there any schools for the children and young persons em-

Karl Marx's "Enquête Ouvrière"

ployed in your trade? If there are, what are the school hours? Who runs the schools? What is taught in them?

41. When work continues day and night how are the shifts organized?

42. What is the normal increase in hours of work during periods of great industrial activity?

43. Are the machines cleaned by workers specially employed for this work, or are they cleaned gratuitously by the workers who are employed on them during the working day?

44. What are the regulations and the penalties for lateness? At what time does the working day begin, and at what time does it begin again after meals?

45. How much time do you spend in getting to work and in returning home?

III

46. What kind of work contract do you have with your employer? Are you engaged by the day, by the week, by the month, etc.?

47. What are the conditions laid down for giving or receiving notice?

48. In the event of the contract being broken, what penalty is imposed on the employer if it is his fault?

49. What penalty is imposed on the worker if it is his fault?

50. If there are apprentices, what are the terms of their contract?

51. Is your work regular or irregular?

52. In your trade, is the work seasonal, or is it, in normal times, spread more or less evenly over the year? If your work is seasonal, how do you live in the periods between working?

53. Are you paid time rates or piece rates?

54. If you are paid time rates, are you paid by the hour or by the day?

55. Is there additional pay for overtime work? What is it?

56. If you are paid piece rates, how are the rates fixed? If you are employed in an industry in which the work performed is measured by quantity or weight, as is the case in the mines, does your employer or his representatives resort to trickery in order to defraud you of a part of your earnings?

57. If you are paid piece rates, is the quality of the article made a pretext for fraudulent deductions from your wages?

58. Whether you are paid piece rates or time rates, when are you paid, or in other words how long is the credit which you extend to your master before receiving the price of the work carried out? Are you paid at the end of a week, a month, etc.?

59. Have you noticed that the delay in paying your wages makes it necessary for you to resort frequently to the pawnbroker, paying a high rate of interest, and depriving yourself of things which

Hilde Weiss

you need; or to fall into debt to shopkeepers, becoming their victim because you are their debtor? Do you know any instances in which workers have lost their wages through the bankruptcy of their employers?

60. Are wages paid directly by the employer, or by middlemen (sub-contractors, etc.)?

61. If wages are paid by sub-contractors, or other middlemen, what are the terms of your contract?

62. What is your daily and weekly wage rate in money?

63. What are the wages of women and children working with you in the same workshop?

64. What was the highest daily wage in your workshop during the past month?

65. What was the highest piece-rate wage . . . ?

66. What was your wage during the same period, and if you have a family what were the wages of your wife and children?

67. Are wages paid entirely in money, or in some other way?

68. If you rent your dwelling from your employer, what are the conditions? Does he deduct the rent from your wages?

69. What are the prices of necessities such as:
    (a) rent of dwelling; conditions of letting; number of rooms, number of inhabitants, repairs and insurance: purchase and maintenance of furniture, heating, lighting, water;
    (b) food: bread, meat, vegetables, potatoes, etc., milk, eggs, fish, butter, oil, lard, sugar, salt, spices, coffee, chicory, beer, cider, wine, etc., tobacco;
    (c) clothing for parents and children, laundry, personal toilet, baths, soap, etc.;
    (d) various expenses: postage, loans and pawnbrokers' charges, children's school or apprenticeship fees, papers and books, contributions to friendly societies, or for strikes, co-operatives and defence societies;
    (e) expenses, if any, caused by your work;
    (f) taxes.

70. Try to draw up a budget of the weekly and annual income and expenditure of yourself and your family.

71. Have you noticed, in your personal experience, a greater rise in the price of the necessities of life, such as food and shelter, than in wages?

72. State the fluctuations in wage rates which are known to you.

73. State the wage reductions in periods of stagnation and industrial crisis.

74. State the wage increases in so-called periods of prosperity.

75. Note the interruptions of work resulting from changes of fashion and from particular and general crises. Give an account of your own experiences of involuntary unemployment.

Karl Marx's "Enquête Ouvrière"

76. Compare *the price of the article you produce,* or of the services you provide, with the price of your labour.

77. Quote any instance you know of workers being displaced by the introduction of machinery or by other improvements.

78. With the development of machinery and the productivity of labour, has the intensity and duration of work increased or diminished?

79. Do you know of any instance of an increase of wages in consequence of the progress of production?

80. Have you ever known any ordinary workers who were able to retire at the age of 50 and to live on the money acquired in their capacity as wage earners?

81. For how many years, in your trade, can a worker of average health continue to work?

IV

82. Are there any defence organizations in your trade, and how are they conducted? Send their statutes and rules.

83. How many strikes have occurred in your trade, in the course of your career?

84. How long did these strikes last?

85. Were they general or partial?

86. Was their aim an increase in wages, or were they organized to resist a wage reduction? Or were they concerned with the length of the working day, or caused by other factors?

87. What results did they achieve?

88. Say what you think of the actions of the *Prud'hommes* (arbitrators).[14]

89. Has your trade supported strikes by workers of other trades?

90. Give an account of the rules and penalties instituted by your employer for the government of his wage earners.

91. Have there been any combinations of employers for the purpose of imposing wage reductions, increasing working hours, or preventing strikes, or, in general, for getting their own way?

92. Do you know any instances in which the Government has misused the forces of the State, in order to place them at the disposal of employers against their employees?

93. Do you know any instances in which the Government has intervened to protect the workers against the exactions of the employers and their illegal combinations?

94. Does the Government apply against the employers the existing labour laws? Do its inspectors carry out their duties conscientiously?

[14] [The *conseil des prud'hommes* is a committee of arbitration in disputes between workers and employers—ED.]

Hilde Weiss

95. Are there, in your workshop or trade, any friendly societies for cases of accident, illness, death, temporary incapacity for work, old age, etc.? Send their statutes and rules.

96. Is membership of these societies voluntary or obligatory? Are their funds controlled exclusively by the workers?

97. If the contributions are obligatory and under the control of the employers, are they deducted from wages? Is interest paid on these contributions? Are they returned to the worker when he leaves or is dismissed? Do you know any instances in which workers have benefited from so-called retirement funds controlled by the employers, but whose capital is derived from the workers' wages?

98. Are there any co-operative societies in your trade? How are they managed? Do they employ workers from outside in the same way as the capitalists do? Send their statutes and rules.

99. Are there any workshops in your trade, in which the workers are remunerated partly by wages and partly by a so-called participation in the profits? Compare the sums received by these workers with those received by workers where there is no so-called participation in profits. State the obligations of workers living under this system. Can they go on strike? Or are they only permitted to be the humble servants of their masters?

100. What is the general physical, intellectual, and moral condition of men and women workers employed in your trade?

101. General comments.

Part II
Political Economy

[6]

From Financial Crisis to World Slump: Accumulation, Financialization, and the Global Slowdown
David McNally

This is an expanded version of a paper presented to the Plenary Session on "The Global Financial Crisis: Causes and Consequences" at the 2008 Historical Materialism Conference, "Many Marxisms," held at the University of London, November 8, 2008.[1]

1. From US Financial Crisis to World Slump

As the International Monetary Fund observed some months ago, we are living through "the largest financial crisis in the United States since the Great Depression." But that was to understate things in two ways. First, the financial crisis is no longer largely about the US. It has gone global, rocking the UK, the Eurozone, Japan, and the so-called "emerging market economies." A wave of devastating national and regional crises is just getting started, having already hit Iceland, Hungary, the Ukraine and Pakistan. Secondly, this is no longer simply a financial crisis; a global economic slump is now sweeping through the so-called "real economy," hammering the construction, auto and consumer goods sectors, and clobbering growth rates in China and India. Manufacturing output is sharply down in the US, Europe, Japan and China. The Detroit Three automakers, reeling from losses of $28.6 billion in the first half of this year, are teetering on the verge of collapse. World trade is in a stunning free fall.

Catastrophic forecasts of the sort that only handfuls of leftists indulged in, often all too glibly, have now become standard fare, with the chairman and CEO of Merrill Lynch and the former chairman of Goldman Sachs both talking of a global slowdown comparable to the Great Depression.[2] Extreme (and misleadingly ahistorical) as such predictions are, it is easy to see why world bankers are so shaken.

Over the past year, global stock markets have dropped by 50 per cent, wiping out perhaps $25 trillion in paper assets and plunging us into "the worst bear market since the 1930s."[3] All five of Wall Street's investment banks are gone – caput. More than 250,000 jobs have evaporated in the US financial services industry. And now, as noted above, the effects of

---

[1]   I would like to thank the editors of *Historical Materialism* for the opportunity to first present this paper at their conference. Thanks too to Sue Ferguson for comments on an earlier draft.

[2]   Greg Farrell, "Merrill chief see severe global slowdown," *Financial Times*, November 11, 2008; "Doom and Gloom rule on Wall Street," *Globe and Mail Report on Business*, November 13, 2008.

[3]   As of the end of October 2008, Standard and Poor's Index Service, estimated world stock market losses of $16.2 trillion. Since then, losses have climbed, and some analysts believe S&P's figures were already too low. The quote comes from John Authurs and Michael Mackenzie, "Worst bear market since 1930s dashes hopes, *Financial Times*, November 21, 2008.

global over-accumulation are turning financial crisis into world economic slump. Problems of over-accumulation – more factories, machines, buildings, fibre optic networks, and so on than can be operated profitably, and piles of goods that cannot profitably be sold – can only be resolved via bankruptcies, plant closings and mass layoffs. One analyst at Merrill Lynch, for instance, suggests that, to remain viable, GM will have to shut five of 12 North American car assembly plants and slash output of trucks, sports utility vehicles and cross-over utility vehicles by two-thirds. Altogether, these moves would eliminate the jobs of 59,000 out of 123,000 GM employees in the US, Mexico and Canada.[4] The ripple effects, in the auto parts industries and beyond, would be dramatic. Indeed, the Center for Automotive Research predicts that a 50 per cent contraction of Ford, Chrysler and GM would wipe out nearly two and a half million US jobs.[5] So, if the first phase of the global crisis centered on the financial sector, with a stunning series of bank collapses, the second phase will be dominated by failure, bailouts and/or massive downsizing of non-financial corporations. But those will then trigger big drops in global demand (as laid off workers cut back consumption and corporate demand retrenches), which in turn will hit firms in services (such as hotels and business assistance) and spark further problems for banks.

As world demand and sales dive, the effects of overcapacity (factories, machines, buildings that cannot be profitably utilized), which have been masked by credit creation over the past decade, will thus kick in with a vengeance. Experts are already predicting that US vehicle sales will plummet by at least three million in 2009, and quite possibly by twice that much, imperilling the very future of the US-based auto makers. World sales of personal computers, mobile phones, and semiconductors are collapsing by 10 per cent and more, inducing frantic price-cutting in order to generate corporate revenues.[6] In Japan industrial production dropped three percent in October, with government officials forecasting that November will see a sharp 6.4 per cent drop in factory output. Having tried to export its way back to economic health after its "lost decade," Japan now faces relapse into a downward economic spin as world markets contract. And contract they will, as October's one per cent drop in US consumer spending, just the seventh drop in half a century, indicates.

And just as China was the center of the wave of accumulation of the past 25 years, so it will be at the center of the over-accumulation storm. According to some predictions, Chinese industry is running at only 50 per cent of capacity, as huge numbers of factories and machines sit idle.[7] Sitting in Chinese warehouses are stockpiles of refrigerators equal to three years of world demand. Not surprisingly, steel output dropped 17 per cent in October, signalling a deepening slump in the appliance and machinery industries in particular.[8] Trying to manage an economy that needs economic growth rates of eight per cent a year just to absorb the massive flows of rural migrants into industrial centers, Chinese officials describe the employment

---

[4]   Greg Keenan, "Detroit Three rev up to plead case," *Globe and Mail*, December 2, 2008.

[5]   Nicholas Van Praet, "Auto industry collapse would crush U.S. economy: study," *Financial Post*, November 5, 2008.

[6]   Richard Waters, "Electronics bargains for US consumers spell trouble for the industry" *Financial Times*, November 20, 2008, and Chris Nuttall, "Semiconductor sales poised to slump next year," *Financial Times*, November 20, 2008.

[7]   See the estimates of Noboyuki Saji, chief economist for Mitsubishi UFI Securities.

[8]   Andrew Batson, "China's steel boom fizzles out," *Wall Street Journal*, November 26, 2008.

situation as "grim" and worry openly about social unrest.[9] India too is feeling the crunch, with exports plummeting 12 per cent in October and the Commerce Secretary predicting that half a million jobs will be lost in textiles by April of next year. With global overcapacity in play, the spectre that haunted Japan throughout the 1990s – deflation – has emerged; indeed, core prices in the US fell one per cent in October, the biggest drop since 1947, when records began. Over-accumulation, asset deflation and price-cutting now threaten a downward spiral in prices and profits that would spell a seriously prolonged global slump.

And we are very far from the endpoint. Despite a stunning series of bailouts of the banking system in the Global North approaching $10 trillion, or 15 per cent of world GDP, the international financial system continues to stagger.[10] Hundreds of billions more in losses will have to be written off by world banks. More banks will fail, more countries will be forced to turn to the IMF in order to stay afloat. Indeed, the global economy is now enmeshed in a classic downward feedback loop: financial meltdown having triggered a recession, a slump in the real economy will now spark a new round of banking crises, putting very big institutions at risk. In the wake of $65 billion in write-downs (with more to come), for instance, Citigroup, the second-largest bank in America has been kept afloat only thanks to a whopping $300 billion US government bailout.

The current crisis is unlike all the others of the past decade in terms of scope and depth. While previous financial shocks in the US were contained – the Savings and Loan meltdown of the early 1990s, the collapse of Long Term Capital Management (1998) or the bursting of the dotcom bubble (2000-1) – this one has moved from a financial meltdown to a generalized economic crisis. And unlike crises that were regionally confined – East Asia (1997), Russia (1998), Argentina (2000-1) – this is a globalizing crisis at the heart of the system. We confront, in other words, a *generalized global crisis* in specific forms for organizing the relations between capitals and the relations between capital and global labour that have characterized the neoliberal period. In short, the neoliberal reorganization of world capitalism is now systemically shaken.

And like any systemic crisis, it has produced an ideological one. Consider, for instance, the pronouncement from Alan Greenspan, who headed the Federal Reserve Bank of the US for 18 years, declaring that he is in "a state of shocked disbelief" as to how a system based on "the self-interest of lending institutions" could have found itself in this pickle. Or think about the report published by the Institute for Policy Analysis at the University of Toronto that bears

---

[9] Jonathan Manthorpe, "Chinese officials fear more unrest over job losses, *Vancouver Sun*, November 24, 2008. Late November also saw riots by laid off workers at a toy factory in southern China, in which the workers smashed factory windows and wrecked computers. See Marcus Gee, "China cuts rates by most in a decade," *Globe and Mail*, November 27, 2008.

[10] On the scale of the bailout, the Bank of England, *Financial Stability Report*, n. 24 (October 2008) estimated $7.2 trillion. But estimates by CreditSights that the US government had already committed $5 trillion by that point to keep the financial system afloat suggested a higher figure. See Elizabeth Moyer, "Washington's $5 Trillion Tab," *Forbes.com*, November 12, 2008. Then, in late November, the US government earmarked an additional $1.1 trillion to its bailouts, designating $300 billion to rescue Citigroup and another $800 billion to buy troubled" mortgage-backed securities and to extend credit for borrowers with student loans and credit card debt. Commentators are now suggesting that the price tag for the US bailouts has hit $7 trillion; see Barrie McKenna, "Millions, Billions, Trillions," *Globe and Mail*, November 26, 2008.

the title, "We don't have a clue and we're not going to pretend we do." Neoliberal claims for the magical properties of self-regulating markets are rapidly losing traction, even among their advocates.

In this context, the Left has an enormous opportunity to provide critical analysis, strategic vision, and mobilizational proposals. This paper largely restricts itself to the first of these: critical analysis of the crisis.

2. Capital Accumulation and the Question of Financialization

On the Left, most analyses of the crisis have tended to fall into one of two camps. On the one hand, we find a series of commentators who view the financial meltdown as just the latest manifestation of a crisis of profitability that began in the early 1970s, a crisis that has effectively persisted since that time. In another camp is a large number of commentators who see the crisis as essentially caused by an explosion of financial transactions and speculation that followed from de-regulation of financial markets over the past quarter-century.

Those interpretations that focus principally on the de-regulation of financial markets suffer from a failure to grasp the deep tendencies at the level of capital accumulation and profitability that underpin this crisis. They are unable to explain why this crisis has not been restricted to financial markets, or to probe its interconnection with problems of global over-accumulation. As a result, they are prone to describe the problem in terms of neoliberalism, rather than capitalism, and to advocate a return to some sort of Keynesian re-regulation of financial markets. Socialist politics remain effectively absent from these perspectives, displaced by arguments for "a renewed leashed capitalism" of the sort that is said to have prevailed after 1945.[11]

Those analyses that effectively read the current crisis in terms of a decline in the rate of profitability in the early 1970s at least focus on deeper problems at the level of capitalist accumulation.[12] But they tend for the most part to be amazingly static, ignoring the specific dynamics of capitalist restructuring and accumulation in the neoliberal period. After all, across the recessions of 1974-75 and 1981-82 and the ruling class offensive against unions and the Global South that ran through this period, severe capitalist restructuring did generate a new wave of capitalist growth. As analysts like Fred Moseley have shown, after 1982 a significant restoration of profitability took place,[13] and this underpinned major processes of expanded capitalist reproduction (particularly in China). It is true that profit rates did not

---

[11] Robert Pollin, "Resurrection of the Rentier," *New Left Review* 46 (July-August 2007), p. 153.

[12] The most celebrated and widely debated effort to analyze the global economy since 1945 in terms of a developing crisis of profitability is that offered by Robert Brenner, *The Economics of Global Turbulence* (London: Verso, 1998 and 2006) and *The Bubble and the Boom: The US in the World Economy* (London: Verso, 2002). I attempted to re-cast Brenner's analysis in terms of Marxian value theory in "Turbulence in the World Economy," *Monthly Review*, v. 51, n.2 (June 1999), pp. 38-52. A very important response to Brenner from a value theory standpoint, and one that raised the critical questions of credit and international finance, is that by Ben Fine, Costas Lapavitsas and Dimitris Milonakis, "Addressing the World Economy: Two Steps Back," *Capital and Class* 67 (1999), pp. 47-90.

[13] See the empirical evidence presented by Fred Moseley, "The United States Economy at the Turn of the Century: Entering a New Era of Prosperity?" *Capital and Class* 67 (1999) and his "Marxian Crisis Theory and the Postwar US Economy," in *Anti-Capitalism A Marxist Introduction*, ed. Alfredo Saad-

recover to their peak levels of the 1960s, and that overall growth rates were not as robust. But there was a dynamic period of growth, centered on industrial expansion in East Asia, which enabled capitalism to avoid a world crisis for twenty-five years. And this process of growth, and the unique financial forms that have underpinned it, have determined many of the specific features of the current crisis.

Inattention to the specific forms of industrial, monetary and financial reorganization that have characterized the neoliberal period, or the patterns of sustained capital accumulation that have taken place over the past quarter-century, prevents us from explaining how and why capitalism managed to avoid a generalized economic and financial slump for the quarter century after the two recessions (1974-75 and 1981-82) that followed upon the sharp decline in profitability at the end of the 1960s. It will not do to say that for 25 years crisis was "postponed" because credit was pumped into the system. If this was the whole answer, if everything had simply been credit-driven, a massive global financial crisis of the sort we are witnessing today ought to have occurred *much* earlier. There is simply no way that priming the pump of credit could have staved off crisis for 25 years after the recession of 1981-82. We need, therefore, to be able to explain the partial but real successes of capital in restoring profit rates throughout the 1980s; the generation of new centers of global accumulation, such as China[14] and the creation of huge new labour reserves (by means of ongoing "primitive accumulation"); and the associated metamorphoses in financial markets, all of which enabled neoliberal capitalism to avoid a generalized economic and financial slump for a quarter of a century – only to lay the grounds for new crises of over-accumulation and financial dislocation. In doing so, we will be able to better make sense of the unique forms and patterns of this crisis by relating them to specific changes in the neoliberal organization of capitalism – and the fault lines inherent in it.

As I shall suggest below, the partial recovery in profit rates in the early 1980s sustained a wave of capitalist expansion that began to falter in 1997, with the crisis in East Asia. After that regional crisis (and particularly after the bursting of the dotcom bubble in 2000-1) a massive expansion of credit *did* underpin rates of growth, concentrating profound sources of instability in the financial sector. So, while the entire period after 1982 cannot be explained in terms of credit creation, the postponement of a general crisis *after 1997* can. A decade long credit explosion delayed the day of reckoning. But as the credit bubble burst, beginning in the summer of 2007, it generated a major financial crisis. And because of underlying problems of over-accumulation that had first manifest themselves in 1997, this financial crisis necessarily triggered a profound global economic slowdown.

To summarize, then, as well to anticipate some details, my argument rests on the following claims: 1) the neoliberal offensive succeeded in raising the rate of exploitation and profits, thereby inducing a new wave of global accumulation (1982-2007); 2) this expansion took place in the framework of transformations in money and finance that enabled financial service industries to double their share of total corporate profits, creating increasingly "financialized"

Filho (London: Pluto Press, 2003), pp. 211-23. See also Charlie Post, "Crisis Theory – Root Causes of the Current Crisis," available at http://.marxsite.com/Charles%20Post%20crisis%20theory.html.

[14]   For helpful overviews of the often spectacular process of capitalist growth in China see David Harvey, *A Brief History of Neoliberalism* (Oxford: Oxford University Press, 2005), Ch. 5, and Andrew Glyn, *Capitalism Unleashed: Finance, Globalization and Welfare* (Oxford: Oxford University Press, 2006), pp. 88-95.

relations between capitals; 3) when the first signs of a new phase of over-accumulation set in, with the Asian Crisis of 1997, massive credit-expansion, fuelled after 2001 by record-low interest rates, postponed the day of reckoning, while greatly "financializing" relations between capital and labour; 4) but when financial markets started to seize up in the summer of 1997, the underlying weaknesses of accumulation and profitability meant that financial meltdown would trigger global slump; and 5) neoliberal transformations in money and finance have given this crisis a number of unique features, which the Left ought to be able to explain.

It is with this in mind that I want to clarify the idea of financialized capitalism. For there are deep and important reasons why this crisis began in the financial system, and why it has taken unique forms – and these must be explained if we wish to illuminate the concrete features of this slump. However, in many respects, the term *financialization* can be, and has been, highly misleading. To the degree to which it suggests that finance capitalists and their interests dominate contemporary capitalism, it is especially so. And where it has been taken to imply that late capitalism rests on the *circulation* rather than the production of goods – as if we could have one without the other – it has contributed to absurd depictions of the world economy today. Moreover, the lines between industrial and financial capital are in practice often quite blurred, with giant firms engaging in both forms of profit-making. General Electric, for instance, is as much a bank as it is a manufacturing corporation, while General Motors and Ford have increasingly relied on their finance divisions in order to make a profit. Prior to its collapse, Enron was essentially a derivative trading company, not an energy firm. All of these firms financialized themselves to important degrees in response to the rising profitability of the financial sector during the neoliberal period – a point to which I return.

What the term "financialization" ought to capture, in my view, is that set of transformations through which *relations between capitals and between capital and wage labour have been increasingly financialized* – i.e. increasingly embedded in interest-paying financial transactions. Understanding this enables us to grasp how it is that financial institutions have appropriated ever larger shares of surplus value. It is as a way of capturing these structural shifts that I intend to use the term financialization. In order to avoid misunderstanding – and to close off bad theorizing often associated with the concept – I will identify it specifically with the complex interconnections among three key phenomena of the neoliberal period that have underpinned the dizzying growth – and now the stunning collapse – of the financial sector. The three phenomena at issue are:

1. the mutation in the form of world money that occurred in the early 1970s;
2. the financial effects of neoliberal wage compression over the past 30 years; and
3. the enormous global imbalances (revolving around the US current account deficit) that have flooded the world economy with US dollars

Let me now briefly explore each of these in turn.

3. A Mutation in the Form of World Money

Commentators have rarely noted the curious conjunction that has defined capitalist globalization in the neoliberal era. On the one hand, globalizing capital has involved an intensification of capitalist value logics – removal of extra-market protections designed to subsidize prices of subsistence goods (e.g. food or fuel); weakening of labour market protections for workers; privatization of state-owned enterprises; deep cuts to non-market provision of healthcare and other social goods. On the other hand, this intensification of value logics has occurred through the medium of more unstable and volatile forms of money. As a result, *value forms have been extended at the same time as value measures (and predictions) have become more volatile.* This has given neoliberal globalization a number of distinct characteristics and a propensity to enormous credit bubbles and financial meltdowns of the sort we are witnessing at the moment. The following bullet points trace this second, and largely neglected side of the process.[15]

- The breakdown of Bretton Woods saw not only liberalization of capital flows, but also globalization alongside a weakening in the world money properties of the US dollar. Under Bretton Woods, the dollar was considered equivalent to $1/35^{th}$ of an ounce of gold, and major currencies were fixed in proportion to the dollar. Changes in these currency proportions (exchange rates) were infrequent and generally small. But with the end of dollar-gold convertibility in 1971 and the move to floating exchange rates (rates that literally fluctuate all day each and every day according to values determined on world markets), currency values, especially for the dollar, became much more volatile. As a result, the formation of values at the world level became much more uncertain and less predictable.

- With the end of convertibility, the dollar became a full-fledged international credit money – grounded in fictitious capital (the US national debt), and lacking any substantive grounding in past labour (in this case, gold). As we shall see, this produced fertile ground for financial speculation.

- As a result of the de-commodification of the dollar and the moving from fixed to floating exchange rates for currencies, the *measure of value* property of money – the capacity of money to express the socially necessary (abstract) labor times inherent in commodities – was rendered highly unstable.

- With increased uncertainty in value relations, the importance of risk assessment and hedging against risk became a crucial activity for all capitals, especially for those whose business activities required moving in and through multiple currencies (all of whose values were fluctuating more widely). It is in this context that markets for derivatives exploded. In the first instance, derivatives are instruments designed to hedge risk. They allow, for instance, a corporation to enter a contract that provides an option to buy a currency (dollars, yens, euros or whatever) at a set price. While this option contract costs a fee, it also provides greater financial predictability for the firm.

- But while this aspect of derivatives follows conventional business logic, there has been an amazing proliferation of such instruments to cover just about every imaginable risk. And, huge numbers of such derivative contracts represent nothing more than financial

---

[15] I recognize the telegraphic style of this argument, which will be developed systematically in a future study on world money.

gambling. This is because I can buy insurance against "risks" to assets I don't own. I can, for instance, purchase a derivative known as a Credit Default Swap (discussed further below) against the risk of GM defaulting – and I can do this even if I own none of GM's stocks or bonds. Rather than protecting my investment, then, in this case I am buying a CDS as a bet that GM *will* fail, hoping then to collect in the event of the company's failure. It is as if I could take out an insurance policy on someone I suspect to be dying, and then wait to collect. Thus, while their explosion follows on the new volatility of money since 1971, derivatives have also evolved as speculative bets on the movements of specific currencies, interest rates, stocks or bonds, even when I don't own any of these assets. I can thus buy a derivative contract simply as a bet on the weather pattern or the result of a sports event. Derivatives also create opportunities for speculators to exploit value gaps between markets (arbitrage), when currency movements make some asset relatively cheaper or pricier in one national market compared to another.

- This volatile regime of world money thus gave an enormous impetus to foreign exchange trading and to a whole plethora of options, hedges and swaps related to it. In fact, foreign exchange trading is now far and away the world's largest market, with an average daily turnover above \$4 trillion according to the Bank for International Settlements, which represents an 800 per cent increase since 1988. To that market must be added a currency derivatives market of more than half that much again.

- Meanwhile, derivatives markets have come to massively eclipse markets in stocks and bonds. In 2006, for instance, more than \$450 trillion in derivative contracts were sold. That compares with \$40 trillion for global stock markets, and about \$65 trillion of world bond markets in the same year. And the profits that can be made on selling derivatives are much higher than on selling stocks and bonds, thereby fuelling the growth of financial markets and the profits of the financial sector.[16]

- The heightened instability of world money, the explosion in foreign exchange trading, and the rise of instruments designed to hedge risk (derivatives) and, finally, the speculative activities associated with these have all encouraged a whole range of practices designed to financially capture *future values*, i.e. shares of surplus value that have not yet been produced. The result has been a proliferation of *fictitious capitals*, such as mortgage-backed securities and Collateralized Debt Obligations (which are discussed further below).

All of these developments, which are structurally related to the mutation in the form of world money that took place in the early 1970s, as any commodity basis to world money was abandoned and exchange rates were allowed to float, constitute an essential basis of financialization in the neoliberal period.[17]

---

[16] See Aaron Lucchetti, "'Innovation, imagination' drive derivatives-investment contracts," *Wall Street Journal*, March 20, 2007.

[17] My argument, to be clear, is not that the operation of the law of value requires a commodity money, but, rather, that the move to a full-fledged system of credit money at the world level comprises a major metamorphosis in the formation of values at the world level.

4. Neoliberal Wage Compression, Social Inequality and the Credit Explosion

It follows from this analysis that the financialization that defines capitalism in its neoliberal form consists in structural transformations that corresponds to a particular conjuncture, not a financial coup or the rebirth of the *rentier*.[18]

In the first instance, this is manifest in the doubling of the share of US corporate profits going to the financial sector compared to its share during the 1970s and 1980s. While the proportion of profits going to finance doubled to more than 28 percent by 2004, the share going to the broader financial (interest-bearing) services sector – Finance, Real Estate and Insurance (FIRE) – also doubled to nearly 50 per cent of all US corporate profits.[19]

The growth of financial markets and profitability is tied to processes of neoliberal wage compression that also underwrote the significant partial recovery of the rate of profit between 1982 and 2007. Wage compression – which is a key component of the increase in the rate of surplus value in the neoliberal period – was accomplished by way of social and spatial reorganization of labour markets and production processes. Five dynamics figure especially prominently here: 1) the geographic relocation of production, with significant expansion of manufacturing industries in dramatically lower wage areas of East Asia and, to a lesser degree, India, Mexico and so on; 2) the downward pressure on wages triggered by a huge expansion in the reserve army of global labour resulting from massive dispossession of peasants and agricultural labourers, particularly in China and India; 3) the increase in relative surplus value brought about by the boosts to labour productivity (output per worker per hour) resulting from the combined effects of lean production techniques and new technologies; 4) increases in absolute surplus value triggered by an increase in work hours, particularly in the United States; 5) sharp cuts to real wages brought about by union-busting, two-tiered wage systems, and cuts to the "social wage" in the form of a reduction in non-wage social benefits, such as health care, food and fuel subsidies, pensions and social assistance programs.

Where successful, all of these strategies have reduced the living standards of working class people while spectacularly concentrating wealth at the top of the economic ladder. Data from the United States are especially instructive in this regard. According to detailed studies, which may if anything underestimate the polarization, between 1973 and 2002, average real incomes for the bottom 90 per cent of Americans fell by nine percent. Incomes for the top one per cent rose by 101 per cent, while those for the top 0.1 per cent soared by 227 percent. These data have recently been updated to show additional increases in household inequality in the US all the way through 2006.[20] And a recent report from the Organization for Economic Cooperation and Development charts similar trends for most major capitalist societies.

---

[18]   The idea of a financial coup, dated to 1979 and ostensibly led by Paul Volcker, then head of the US Federal Reserve, has been advanced by Gérard Duménil and Dominque Lévy, *Capital Resurgent: Roots of the Neoliberal Revolution*, pp. 69 and 165.

[19] David Leonhardt, "Bubblenomics," *New York Times,* September 21, 2008. For the FIRE sector more broadly, see Greta R. Krippner, "The financialization of the American economy," *Socio-Economic Review* 3 (2005), pp. 173-208, and Duménil and Lévy, Ch. 13.

[20]   Thomas Picketty and Emmanuel Saez, November 2004 updated data for *Income Inequality in the United States, 1913-1998*, plus recent updates through 2006, available at http://elsa.berkeley.edu/saez/

Inevitably, even more unequal relations appear once we look beyond income to the ownership of corporate wealth. Whereas in 1991 the wealthiest one percent of Americans owned 38.7 percent of corporate wealth, by 2003 their share had soared to 57.5 per cent.[21] And similar effects are evident at the global level. According to the Boston Consulting Group, for example, since 2000, "the 16.5 percent of global households with at least $100,000 to invest have seen their assets soar 64 percent in value, to $84.5 trillion." The vast bulk of that wealth resides in the portfolios of millionaire households Although they comprise just 0.7 percent of the globe's total households, these millionaire households now hold over a third of the world's wealth.[22] And it is these households, particularly in the conditions of renewed over-accumulation of capital since the late 1990s, who have enormously boosted demand for interest-bearing financial assets.

Just as the wealthiest households demanded a plethora of financial instruments in which to invest, large numbers of working class people turned to credit markets – particularly in the context of dramatically lowered interest rates after 2001 – in order to sustain living standards. And the provision of greater amounts of credit to such working class people – in the forms of mortgage and credit card debt in particular – was underpinned by the provision of "cheap money" (low interest rates) designed to prevent the deepening of the slump that began in 1997 and was reactivated in 2001, and by growing demand from wealthy investors for "securitized" debt instruments (i.e. mortgage and credit card debt packaged like securities for purchase) that offered higher rates of return. The process of securitization of debt – repacking it as a purchasable income-generating "security" – enabled working class debt to comprise a significant source of new financial instruments for banks, pension funds, financialized corporations, wealthy investors and the like.

All of these trends led to a quadrupling of private and public debt in US, from slightly more than $10 trillion to $43 trillion, during the period of Alan Greenspan's tenure as President of the Federal Reserve (1987-2005).[23] And the great acceleration in this debt build-up came after 1997, as the recessionary dynamics of global over-accumulation became more evident. Moreover, as I discuss below, since 2000 the rate of credit creation in many economies has been much faster than that in the highly indebted US and UK, presaging a serious of local crises, of the sort we have already seen in Iceland, Hungary, the Ukraine and Pakistan.

5. Global Imbalances, Prolonged Slump

As I have suggested, a new wave of global capitalist expansion began in 1982, as two recessions (1974-75, 1981-82) coupled with mass unemployment, cuts to the social wage, an employers' offensive against unions, and the accelerated introduction of lean production methods all raised the rate of surplus value and general levels of profitability. Spatial restructuring of capital to take advantage of low wages, particularly in labour-intensive manufacturing and assembly, had the same effects. The center of the new wave of accumulation was East Asia.

---

[21] David Cay Johnston, "Corporate Wealth Share Rises for Top-Income Americans," *New York Times*, January 29, 2006.

[22] Boston Consulting Group, *Global Wealth 2007*.

[23] Kevin Phillips, "The Destructive Rise of Big Finance," *Huffington Post*, April 4, 2008.

And it was there, fifteen years into the new cycle of growth, that the first symptoms of a new crisis of over-capacity manifested themselves.

While many commentators treated the Asian crisis of 1997 as simply a matter of global flows of finance (which exited the region *en masse* at the time), the regional financial outflows reflected severe pressures of over-accumulation of capital, as I argued at the time.[24] The investment boom in East Asia created enormous excess capacity in computer chips, autos, semi-conductors, chemicals, steel, and fibre optics. One key indicator of this overcapacity is the *consumption deflator*, which measures prices in consumer goods. That index demonstrates that US prices for consumer durables –electronics, appliances, cars and more – began to decline in the autumn of 1995. This signal of rising productivity and over-production offers the best clues as to the structural underpinnings of the crisis that broke out in East Asia (the center of the manufacturing boom of the neoliberal era). Equally important, the consumption deflator shows that prices for consumer durables continued to fall from 1995 right into 2008, one of the reasons the rate of inflation was relatively low, though still positive, and a clear indication that problems of over-accumulation have not been resolved.[25]

It is at this point – after the Asian crisis of 1997 and the slide back toward recession following the bursting of the dotcom bubble in 2000-1 – that two interconnected phenomena become crucial to postponing a general slump: massive growth of debt loads; and the US current account deficit (its shortfall in trade in goods and services and interest payments with the rest of the world), which operated as the "Keynesian engine" of the global economy over the past decade. And here too, as we shall see, the new form of world money played a central role.

Although it may seem paradoxical, it was the recently-hammered East Asian economies (plus China) that drove the next decade of growth (1998-2007). Obeying the logic of capitalism, these economies were forced to cut exchange rates of local currencies, shed labor, reduce costs and dramatically restructure industry. Soon they were exporting their way back to growth, developing huge trade surpluses and soaring international reserves (mainly dollars). But this export-led growth was sustained overwhelmingly by the growing trade and current account deficits in the US. As commentators have noted, the American economy effectively became "the consumer of last resort." From 1980 to 2000, for instance, US imports rose 40 per cent, accounting for almost one-fifth of world exports, and four per cent of world gross domestic product. But by 2006, this level of consumption of foreign goods could only be sustained at the cost of an $857 billion US current account deficit (the shortfall in trade in goods and services and in interest payments with the rest of the world). The recovery after 1997, in other words, was built on the pillars of exceptionally low US interest rates, particularly from 2001; steady growth in consumer indebtedness; and a swelling US current account deficit. Absent those, there would have been no sustained recovery after 1997 – and across the related crises in Russia (1998), at Long Term Capital Management (1998), Brazil (1999) and Argentina (2000-1).

---

[24] David McNally, "Globalization on Trial: Crisis and Class Struggle in East Asia," *Monthly Review*, v. 50, n. 4 (September 1998).

[25] Bureau of Economic Analysis. Graham Turner, *The Credit Crunch: Housing Bubbles, Globalisation and the Worldwide Economic Crisis* (London: Pluto Press, 2008), pp. 21-22, is one of very commentators to underscore the significance of these developments. While I have differences with Turner's analytical framework, he does see the general problem of over-accumulation.

No other country but the US could have run sustained current account deficits of this magnitude for so long. And, had it not broken convertibility with gold, it would have been confronted by another run on US gold supplies. But operating now as inconvertible world money, dollars had to be accepted by those governments with whose economies the US was running a deficit. And because the euphoria of a "boom" built on asset bubbles, particularly in real estate,[26] created real investment opportunities – even if these were increasingly built on sand – foreign investors kept pouring funds into US markets. Foreign central banks, particularly in East Asia and the OPEC nations did the same, recycling the dollars used to cover American current account deficits into the US, therein subsidizing the credit-driven consumer boom. Because the US dollar is the main form of world money, it remained attractive, so long as the American economy looked vibrant, despite sustained – and unsustainable – current account deficits and a massive decline in US international net worth.

But – and this is a point that has eluded many analysts – as soon as the US bubble-driven boom showed signs of faltering, a flight from the dollar and the US economy was inevitable. And precisely this is what happened in 2007. First, US profits peaked in the third quarter of 2006, entering a period of decline. By the first half of 2007, private investors saw the writing on the wall. *Private capital flows into the US turned sharply negative in the third quarter of 2007, with an annualized outflow of $234 billion* – a stunning drop of $1.1 trillion from the previous quarter (when flows were positive to the tune of $823 billion).[27] A reversal of this sort was absolutely without precedent. And it indicated that, contrary to some pundits, capital could flee the US economy and its currency as readily as anywhere else. What saved the US economy from a dizzying collapse of the dollar and an even more brutal seizure of credit markets was continued investment (particularly in Treasury bills and bonds) by central banks in East Asia and oil-producing Middle Eastern states. Tellingly, if Chinese reports are to be believed, this was provided only after US president George Bush begged his Chinese counterpart, Hu Jintao, to keep up purchases of US bonds.[28]

But foreign capital had spoken. Belief in the US "boom" was evaporating. The real estate bubble began to deflate, mortgage-backed securities entered their free fall, hedge funds (first at Bear Stearns) collapsed, followed by investment banks. The rout was on – and it is far from over. In the process, the capacity of whopping US current account deficits, underpinned by debt-fuelled consumer spending, to buoy the world economy appears to be exhausted. Yet, to rebalance the global economy, to eliminate huge US deficits and enormous East Asian surpluses, means to destroy the source of demand that enabled growth in a period of over-accumulation (and it would also mean much larger falls in the US dollar). For this reason, short of a long slump that destroys massive amounts of capital, it will be extremely difficult for the world economy to find a new source of demand sufficient to restart sustained growth.

---

[26] For a hundred years after 1895, US house prices rose in tandem with the rate of inflation. Then, from 1995 to 2007 they rose 70% faster, creating an extra $8 trillion in paper wealth for US home owners, paper wealth that became the basis for the great borrowing binge of the period. See Dean Baker, "The Housing Bubble Pops," *The Nation*, October 1, 2007.

[27] Bureau of Economic Analysis. See the discussion in Turner, pp. 90-91.

[28] David Pilling, "How China can be more than 350 Albanias," *Financial Post*, November 20, 2008.

6. Fictitious Capital, Continuing Financial Crises

Meanwhile, we will continue to be treated to a great destruction of capitals, both real and fictitious. The concept of fictitious capital is developed by Marx with two key features in mind. First, fictitious capitals are paper claims to wealth that exist alongside the actual means of production, stocks of goods and reserves of labour-power that capitals mobilize. Yet, they can be bought and sold many times over as if they were that wealth itself (this is why the prices of stocks can come to bear an absurdly inflated relation to the actual value and profitability of a firm). Secondly, fictitious capitals lay claim to future wealth, i.e. to shares of profits or wages that have not yet come into existence. So, when a bank creates a financial asset that provides the right to the principal and interest payments from my credit card debt – a process, as we have seen, known as *securitization* – it is not selling an existing asset but a claim to income that *may* be created in the future. Should I lose my job, however, and default on my credit card debt, then the "asset" sold by the bank is revealed to be totally fictitious, a mere piece of paper – nothing more than an IOU that will never be repaid.

And during the neoliberal period, for the three reasons I have outlined, we have seen an extraordinary build-up of fictitious capitals (paper claims to future wealth) within the system. A key structural underpinning for this is the mutation in the form of world money that produced massive new industries devoted to currency trading, and the related derivative instruments – futures, options, swaps and the like – that have proliferated over the neoliberal era.[29] As much as there are sound structural reasons for a proliferation of risk-hedging derivatives in an era of floating exchange rates, derivatives have also provided a huge field for purely speculative activity – for financial gambling, as speculators make bets as to which currencies, commodities or national interest rates will rise or fall, and reap profits or losses according to the accuracy of their bets. Of course, the profits on the trading of such instruments have to come from somewhere – and that somewhere has been the non-financial corporate sector, whose share of total profits has systematically fallen across the neoliberal era, while the financial share has soared, as we have seen. Secondly, the massive polarization of incomes produced both a huge demand from the wealthy for interest-paying financial instruments, which was eventually met by the extension of massive amounts of credit (particularly for mortgages, housing-backed loans, and credit cards) to working class households desperate to sustain living standards. Since 2000, mortgage-backed "securities" have been the flavour of the month, often in the form of Collateralized Debt Obligations (CDOs), that is, debts backed up by collateral (in this case houses). But if the value of the underlying asset (houses) plummets, no longer equal to the paper debts themselves, then the "collateral" is largely fictitious. And that is exactly what has happened. As housing prices have fallen off a cliff in the US, Ireland, UK, Spain, and elsewhere, the actual values of CDOs have collapsed, forcing banks to write off billions of dollars in assets. At the moment, billions worth of CDOs are actually trading at prices between 20 and 40 cents on the dollar.

This is what it means when Marx says a crisis involves a destruction of capital. The "values" of fictitious capitals – stocks, bills and all kinds of paper assets – which were previously treated as if they were real assets (and against which financial institutions borrowed), enter a freefall.

---

[29]   I am well aware that futures and options contracts, mainly on raw commodities, have existed for a very long time. But the explosion in these instruments and the size of their markets is a phenomenon that follows on the move to floating exchange rates in 1971-73.

At the same time, real capital is destroyed, as factories are mothballed, corporations go bust and sell off their buildings, machines, land, customers lists and so on at bargain basement prices. And what is particularly troubling for the ruling class is that, even after something approaching $10 trillion in bailouts, the destruction of capital is still in the early innings.

It is quite clear that huge global companies, of the scale of GM and Chrysler, are going to collapse or be merged. The same will happen in the electronics industry. Factories will be permanently closed, millions of jobs will be eviscerated (the OECD estimates eight million additional job losses in the major economies next year, and so far every mainstream prediction as to the severity of this slump has under-estimated). And the earthquakes in the financial sector are far from over, meaning that more bank meltdowns are in store.

There are, after all, a lot more ticking time bombs in the financial system. Consider, for instance, the rising defaults on credit card debt. And then contemplate the mountain of commercial paper, much of which was sold to finance Leveraged Buy Outs (LBOs), i.e. corporate takeovers made possible by borrowing funds and issuing IOUs. As corporate profits plummet, it gets harder and harder for firms that floated such paper to meet their payments. Many will go under. For that reason, LBO commercial paper now trades at between 60 and 70 cents on the dollar.[30] Consider also the coming decline in commercial mortgages, as businesses, faced with falling sales and disappearing profits, can't keep up their mortgage payments on lands and buildings. Those losses will wobble more banks. But perhaps the biggest fault-line runs through the market in Credit Default Swaps. As we have seen, a CDS is essentially an insurance policy taken by a creditor as a protection against default by a debtor. When all is well in the economy, it is a nice source of revenues for the insuring party. But in a crisis, it can be deadly. It is as if a life insurance company all of a sudden had to pay out on a rapidly rising percentage of its policies. But, whereas death rates are relatively constant, in the midst of a financial crisis, default rates are not. To make matters worse, as noted above, any investor can buy a Credit Default Swap, even if they do not own a single share of the company in question. This encourages speculators to literally bet on the failure of a particular company. If you think GM will default on its debt, for instance, buying a CDS on GM debt is a great way to get a payout many times higher than what the CDS costs. As a result, as speculative bets build up, the insuring party (the seller of CDSs) is on the hook for a growing number of claims in the event of default. In crisis conditions, however, the insurer can quickly go under, unable to pay out to every claimant. But in that event, nobody is protected any longer against default of the toxic waste they might be holding. And that means complete and total financial market panic. That's the secret behind the US government bailout of AIG, the world's largest insurance company. AIG holds about $1 trillion in CDSs. In the early fall of 2008, it defaulted on just $14 billion in Credit Default Swaps. That was enough to wobble the market. The government had no real option, if it wanted to avoid a devastating panic cycle, but to bail out AIG. Yet, a mere five weeks after having injected $85 billion into the giant insurer, the US Treasury had to pump in $65 billion more, taking the total to $150 billion, the largest such bailout in history. Tellingly, of the government funds AIG has drawn, fully 95 per cent have

---

[30] Jenny Strasburg and Peter Lattman, "Bain shaken by steep credit fund losses," *Wall Street Journal*, October 23, 2008; "LBO debt," *Financial Times*, November 5, 2008.

been used to cover losses in a single sector of the Credit Default Swap market.[31] And there are likely to be bigger CDS losses to come, both at AIG and elsewhere, as there is another $54 trillion in CDSs out there, default on a small fraction of which could induce another major financial market collapse.[32]

And here, questions of market regulation and transparency become important. Because most derivatives, including CDSs, are sold outside regulated markets, nobody really knows who holds what, or how much. That is why banks have become so leery of lending to one another. Some institutions are sitting on time bombs, trying to conceal massive amounts of financial toxic waste. But no one knows exactly who it might be. As bankers at Lehman Brothers said to US government officials when the two groups reviewed Lehman's books, "We have no idea of the details of our derivatives exposure and neither do you."[33]

That's why, despite massive injections of liquidity into the banking system, credit markets are still stuck in low gear. There are very large financial crises yet to unfold. All parties involved know it. Until all of that junk is washed out of the system – which means the booking of massive losses of the sort Citigroup recently took – the financial crisis will not be over.

7. Capitalist Measurement, the Value Form and the Violence of Abstraction

This returns us to some of the specific features of the current crisis, which have too often been neglected on the Left. For, as money has become more volatile, its measure of value function has become more problematic, as I pointed out in section 3 above. While capitalist investment always involves wagers on future results, the conditions of such wagers have become riskier in a context in which the international values of national currencies have become less predictable and more unstable. After all, the profits made by foreign branches of a corporation – say in Korean *won* or Turkish *lira* – can be completely wiped out when repatriated to the home office, as a result of drops in the values of those currencies.

Derivatives, by allowing corporations to contract to buy a currency at a particular exchange rate some time in the future, or to purchase the right to borrow at a certain rate of interest in a given currency, have played a crucial role in helping capitalist enterprises manage these risks. Indeed, they have become the key financial instrument for doing so.[34] Moreover, as we have seen, with the proliferation of derivatives designed to hedge the risk of currency fluctuations has come an explosion of others meant to put a price on protection against any and every risk, from the effects of climate change on Florida's orange crop to the likelihood

---

[31]   Sinclair Stewart and Paul Waldie, "AIG's Journey: Bailout to Black Hole," *Globe and Mail*, November 11, 2008.

[32]   Christopher Cox, "Swapping Secrecy for Transparency, *New York Times*, October 19, 2008; see also Matthew Philips, "The Monster that Ate Wall Street," *Newsweek*, October 6, 2008

[33]   Francesco Guerrera and Nicole Bullock, "Struggle to unearth quake's epicentre," *Financial Times*, October 31, 2008.

[34]   It is the great merit of Dick Bryan's and Michael Rafferty's that they have attended to the significance of derivatives in late capitalism; see their, *Capitalism with Derivatives: A Political Economy of Financial Derivatives, Capital and Class* (New York: Palgrave Macmillan, 2006). I dissent from their view, however, that derivatives *are* money in late capitalism. Instead, I interpret them as financial instruments designed to bridge the spatio-temporal "gaps" in value measurement that characterize our era.

that Evo Morales's government in Bolivia will nationalize the hydrocarbons industry. And this requires that derivatives be capable of computing all concrete risks – climatological, political, monetary, and more – on a single metric. They must, in other words, be able to translate concrete risks into quantities of *abstract risk*.[35]

One recognizes here the logic of the value form as analyzed by Marx, in which all commodities, irrespective of their concrete characteristics, must be measurable on a single metric (value), and priced as mere quanta of money (the universal equivalent) – and in which all concrete labours must be treated as commensurable, i.e. as quantities of *abstract* human labour. But as the powers of money to do this pricing reliably – to provide relatively predictable measures of value – have declined (see Section 3), derivatives have increasingly filled in the gaps. *Now, however, a classic crisis of capitalist measurement is manifesting itself, in part in the form of a breakdown in derivatives pricing.*

During every crisis, value measurement is radically disrupted and destabilized. Pressures of over-accumulation and declining profitability induce a destruction of values that reorganize the foundations of capitalist production. In the process, existing capitals are de-valued, until a new and relatively stable valuation is found. In fact, for Marx, an essential feature of crises is that they destroy the old value relations that persisted through a period of boom, over-accumulation and declining profitability in order to lay the basis, through destruction and devaluation of capital and labour power, for a new set of value norms.[36] Today, as we have seen in Section 3, derivatives offer an indirect way of trying to measure value by way of measuring risk. But in the midst of this crisis, the risk measurement models that have guided derivatives markets have completely and utterly failed. This was admitted in an especially interesting way by Alan Greenspan:

> A Nobel Prize was awarded for the discovery of the pricing model that underpins much of the advance in derivatives markets. This modern risk management paradigm held sway for decades. The whole intellectual edifice, however, collapsed in the summer of last year . . .[37]

In trying to measure abstract risk, the models in question attempt to create indicators of current and future value relations by predicting the riskiness of investment or economic activity in a given situation (and the appropriate premium or "risk reward" that ought to be expected). Inherently, these models involve violent abstractions, to use Marx's term, insofar as they reduce concrete social, political, climatological and economic relations to a single scale of measurement, often with life-threatening implications, as we shall see. The process of abstraction these models undertake involves treating space and time as mathematical, as nothing more than different points on a grid. This homogenization of space and time assumes that what applied at any one spatio-temporal moment applies in principle at any other. Future events in multiple spaces are thus held to be predictable on the basis of past events. But crises destroy any basis for such assumptions – they bring about the "collapse" of

---

[35] See Edward Li Puma and Benjamin Lee, *Financial Derivatives and the Globalization of Risk* (Durham: Duke University Press, 2004), pp. 143-50.

[36] See for instance, Karl Marx, *Theories of Surplus Value*, v. 3 (Moscow: Progress Publishers, 1971), pp. 518-19.

[37] Alan Greenspan, Testimony to the House Committee on Oversight and Government Reform, October 23, 2008.

"the whole intellectual edifice" on which they rest, as Greenspan notes. As a result, nobody knows any longer the value of trillions of dollars worth of financial "assets" – Collateralized Debt Obligations, Asset Backed Commercial Paper, and much more. Consequently, lack of knowledge of "the details of . . . derivatives exposure" is not a problem unique to Lehman Brothers; it is a *systemic* problem that will not quickly or readily be resolved. As a result of financialization of neoliberal capitalism, therefore, the crisis of value measurement is expressed in the first instance in markets for financial instruments, like derivatives. But it is at root a classic case of a crisis of value measurement, caused by collapses in value brought on by over-accumulation, falling profits, and unsustainable build-ups in fictitious capitals.

8. Debt, Discipline, Dispossession: Value Struggles and the Crisis

Thus far, I have focussed on developments on the side of capital, abstracted from its (mutually constituting) relation with global labour.[38] But, of course, every crisis of capital also involves immense suffering and hardship for the world's workers. And this one is no different. At the same time, crises are also moments in which the subordination of labour to capital must be reorganized, and in which new spaces of resistance can be pried open. They are, in short, moments of great danger and opportunity for the world's workers. It is not within the bounds of this paper to attempt any sort of analysis of actual correlations of class forces and capacities. But it is worth drawing attention to a few salient features of the current moment.

Recall that this crisis is deeply related to debt markets, and that working class debt figures centrally here. Debt, of course, is one of the oldest class relations; repayment of loans has been a great mechanism for transferring wealth from direct producers to landlords and moneyed capitalists. In the neoliberal context, debt has become a powerful weapon for disciplining the working class in the Global North. After all, the pressure of debt repayment (based on the threat of losing houses, cars, etc. should one fail to make payments) forces extreme capitalist work discipline on people. Not only do pressures of financial payments push people to work long hours, but, in a context of growing use of casual, temporary, contract, and precarious employment, it also increases the sheer stress of juggling multiple jobs. While there is an element of exaggeration in the idea of "the real subsumption of labour to finance,"[39] the formulation does grasp the powerful disciplining effects of the increased financialization of relations between labour and capital, of the ever-greater incorporation of workers into financial and credit markets.

But the politics of massive government bailouts, in which the debt of major financial institutions is assumed by the state, raises important openings for campaigns to reduce and eliminate working class debt, particularly in the housing sector, just as it opens political space for mobilizations to use the massive funds designed to save banks in order instead to build

---

[38] For the record, by global labour I refer to all members of that social group, dispossessed of means of economic subsistence, which has no option but to *try* to sell their labour-power. This includes the unemployed, the casualized, and the majority of those eking out an existence in the so-called "informal sector."

[39] See Riccardo Bellofiore and Joseph Halevi, "The real subsumption of labour to finance and the changing nature of economic policies in contemporary capitalism," *Review of Radical Political Economics,* forthcoming.

social housing, nationalize failing industries, convert them to green production, and preserve jobs.

Debt is also, of course, a weapon of dispossession. Again, this is as old as class society itself. But in the neoliberal period, debt has been used at multiple scales to engage in processes of "accumulation by dispossession."[40] National debts have been occasions for the transfer of state assets in the South – electrical utilities, mines, national airlines and the like – to investors from the North, as Structural Adjustment Programs imposed by the IMF have mandated privatization of government holdings. And there can be little doubt that capital in the North will attempt to use impending financial and currency crises that in the Global South to similar ends. As prices plummet for food and raw materials – copper, oil, coffee, cocoa, timber, rubber and more – dozens of poorer countries will encounter big drops in their export earnings. This will inhibit their capacities to import food, medicine and other essentials, as well as to service existing debts. Trade and currency crises may ensue, driving poor nations into the dreaded hands of the IMF. Already, Iceland, Hungary, the Ukraine and Pakistan have had to turn to the IMF. And more will follow. Once again, the IMF will join with governments and banks in the North to set loan conditions that open countries in the South to plunder of their assets. The only alternative will be to repudiate debts, as Ecuador rightly plans to do, and to mobilize against the imperial order embodied in the domination of the IMF, the World Bank and financial institutions in the Global North.

Beyond the level of the global debts of states, debts on smaller scales continue to be used as levers to seize peasant lands and dispossess millions, thereby gaining capitalist access to oil, minerals, timber, lands for eco-tourism, and more, all the while swelling the global reserve army of labour.[41] Meanwhile, "natural disasters," from Katrina to the tsunami have provided ideal conditions for government sponsored displacement programs in the US, Thailand, Sri Lanka, and Indonesia that re-enact the economic violence of "primitive accumulation" as described by Marx.[42]

Such processes of accumulation have given rise to powerful movements of the rural poor – think of Via Campesina, the Landless Workers' Movement in Brazil, or the Save Narmada Movement in India, the latter of which has fought mass displacement by giant dam projects. Such movements are likely to resurge in many parts of the world as this crisis intensifies processes of dispossession. Indeed, recently, in the wake of the global financial crisis, major riots against displacement swept China's Gansu province.[43]

---

[40]   The term, of course, is David Harvey's resonant reformulation of Marx's concept of the "so-called primitive accumulation of capital." See Harvey, *The New Imperialism* (Oxford: Oxford University Press, 2003), Ch. 4. There are some unclarities in Harvey's deployment of this concept, however, as Ellen Meiksins Wood points out in "Logics of Power: A Conversation with David Harvey," *Historical Materialism* v. 14, n. 4 (2006), pp. 9-34.

[41]   See my *Another World is Possible: Globalization and Anti-Capitalism*, 2nd edn. (Winnipeg: Arbeiter Ring Publishing, and London: Merlin Press, 2006), pp. 96-108.

[42]   On Katrina see Michael Eric Dyson, *Come Hell or High Water: Hurricane Katrina and the Color of Disaster* (New York: Basic Civitas, 2006). On displacement after the tsunami see Naomi Klein, *The Shock Doctrine: The Rise of Disaster Capitalism* (Toronto: Alfred A. Knopf, 2007), pp. 476-87.

[43]   Jonathan Manthorpe, "Chinese officials fear more unrest over job losses, *Vancouver Sun*, November 24, 2008.

All such struggles, however much they can be derailed or diverted, implicitly challenge the domination of society by the capitalist value form. They assert the priority of life values – for land, water, food, housing, income – over the value abstraction and the violent economic and social crises it entails. And one of the tasks of the Left is to highlight this conflict – between life values and capitalist imperatives – that comes to the fore dramatically during times of crisis, in order to pose a socialist alternative that speaks directly and eloquently to the most vital needs of the oppressed.

It is, as we have seen, the logic of the value abstraction to express utter indifference to use values, notably to the needs of the concrete, sensuous beings who are bearers of labour power. What matters for capital is not the capacity of a given commodity to satisfy specific human needs; instead, what counts is its capacity to exchange for money, to turn a profit, to assist accumulation. Bread, steel, water, houses, clothing, computers and cars count only as potential sums of money; their specific use values are ultimately irrelevant to the drive to accumulate. Capital is thus indifferent to the concrete need-satisfying properties of particular goods. For capital, they are all interchangeable, merely potential sums of expandable wealth. The rich diversity of human needs is thus flattened out (abstracted) by the expansionary drive of capital. The question of food illustrates this particularly clearly.

In recent years, traders in raw commodities have come to treat four different use value groups as interchangeable. They claim to have effectively integrated commodities that serve as transportation energy; heat and power; materials for plastics and other goods; food and water. All four are said to have become part of a single equational system in which they are literally interchangeable, indeed in which they are effectively a single complex use-value that operates as if it were a *uni-commodity*. One commodity trader explains,

". . . we don't care what commodity you buy. We call it bushels-to-barrels-to BTUs convergence. Take corn: it can now create heating and transportation . . . And you can use petroleum to create plastics or to create fertilizer to grow food – suddenly we are indifferent to what commodity we are buying to meet our demands."[44]

But while capital is indifferent to the concrete commodity in question, working people are not. It matters enormously whether the corn being grown will be used for food, as opposed to fuel for trucks or for heating factories. Survival for millions can literally turn on market dictates in this regard. And this graphically underlines the value struggles at the heart of capitalism in general, which are posed with a dramatic urgency in the midst of a crisis such as this.

And it is not simply the "automatic" operations of capitalist markets that are at issue here. Similarly, the political decisions of the world's rulers obey the same market logics, as we have seen throughout the course of the global bailouts. Again, the case of food vividly illustrates this.

Last spring, as rising food prices pushed millions of people toward starvation, governments pledged $22 billion in emergency funding for the world's hungriest. While that was a paltry sum, even more paltry is the amount that was actually delivered – merely one tenth of what was pledged, or $2.2 billion, according to the UN Food and Agriculture Organization.[45] Yet,

---

[44] Doug Sanders, "What does oil have to do with the price of bread? A lot," *Globe and Mail*, October 25, 2008.

[45] Paul Waldie, "Food promises give way to financial reality," *Globe and Mail*, October 17, 2008.

somehow, governments in the Global North have in short order come up with about $10 trillion to bail out financial institutions – nearly 5000 times as much as they have anted up to feed the world's poor. Compressed in that simple fact is the most basic case for socialism.

And despite falling food prices, the current slump is going to deepen the global food crisis. Lack of credit with which to import food and production cutbacks by farmers in the face of falling prices are expected to exacerbate food shortages in much of the Global South. And, to make matters worse, governments in the South, squeezed by falling prices for the commodities they export, are trying to cut back on food imports, in order to avoid balance of payments crises. All of this foreshadows severe crises of hunger and starvation. Not surprisingly, the Food and Agriculture Organization now predicts that food riots "could again capture the headlines," the way they did in 2007 and early 2008.[46] Not only are such riots one of the most longstanding forms of plebeian revolt against the dictates of the market; they also pose the most fundamental questions about the nature of a society that condemns millions to starve while funnelling untold trillions into global banks.

9. Looking Forward

We are, in sum, entering the second stage of a profound systemic crisis of neoliberal capitalism. The first stage involved a staggering financial shock that toppled major banks and elicited a multi-trillion dollar bailout of the global financial system. The second stage will entail the collapse, merger, and/or effective nationalization of major corporations, especially in the auto and electronics industries. Unemployment will ratchet higher – much higher. And the ongoing collapse of sales and profits will topple more financial institutions.

It is impossible to predict exactly how this crisis will play out and how long the slump will last, though there is a strong possibility that it will be deep and protracted. Some things, however, are clear.

First, the crisis will induce massive centralization of capital. Already, banks have been merged on a huge scale. In Japan, the crisis of the 1990s saw three national banks emerge from a field that once boasted more than ten. In Britain, the merger of Lloyds bank with the Halifax Bank of Scotland will create a single institution with 40 per cent of all retail banking in the UK. Bank mergers in Brazil have produced one of the 20 largest banks in the world and the largest in Latin America. Meanwhile, pressure is growing for a merger of General Motors and Chrysler or for their merger with other firms, moves which would close large numbers of plants and axe tens of thousands of jobs. And in Japan, a merger of electronics giants Panasonic and Sanyo is also in the works. As they centralize, combining former rivals under one corporate owner, capitals try simultaneously to get a leg up on their competitors and to concentrate their power over labour, so as to drive down wages, benefits and total employment.

Second, this crisis will also pose again the question of the balance of global economic power and the role of the dollar. One of the key problems making for financial instability is the diminished capacity of the US dollar to act as a stable form of world money. In fact, despite its recent rise as a "safe haven" in the midst of financial panic, the dollar is likely to resume its downward movement in the near future, creating more instability for the world economy.

---

[46]   Javier Blas, "Another food crisis looms, says FAO," *Financial Times*, November 7, 2008.

This has prompted economists at the UN to advocate reforms to the international monetary system that would move towards a multi-currency regime of world money.[47] Notwithstanding the impressive rise of the euro in less than a decade – to the point that it exceeds the dollar in international bond markets and nearly equals it as a means of payment in cross-border transactions – there is no rival currency with the economic depth to displace the dollar. As a result, the world economy is likely to drift toward a more fractured regime of world money, with two or more currencies pushing for larger shares of global financial transactions. This could lead to pressures to develop an Asian currency bloc capable of rivalling the dollar and euro zones. It could also indicate new forms of competition between rival imperial projects – not the forms of territorial and military rivalry of the nineteenth and first half of the twentieth centuries, but competition between blocs for greater control of financial markets and global monetary privileges.[48] Interestingly, elements of this have been grasped by the US National Intelligence Council, whose *Global Trends 2025* predicts a world order characterized by "multipolarity," rather than simple US dominance.

Third, centralization of capital and competition between blocs will also be played out by way of attempts to spatially reorganize capital, so that economies in the Global North can displace the effects of crisis onto those in the South. There has been a major build up of credit in a whole number of "emerging market" economies in recent years, and these debt loads will produce a variety of crises. Especially vulnerable will be countries like Turkey and South Africa, where economic growth has been driven by huge inflows of foreign capital. At some point during this crisis, if investors become wary of the prospects of these economies in the midst of a world slump, capital outflows will trigger major financial and currency crises.[49] Those economies may then encounter their own version of the Asian crisis. And if the IMF is called in, western governments will press to buy up assets on the cheap, as was done to South Korea in particular in 1997, after IMF loan conditions facilitated perhaps "the biggest peacetime transfer of assets from domestic to foreign owners in the past fifty years anywhere in the world."[50] As sharp regional crises unfold, therefore, major conflicts between governments in the North and South may emerge (over loan repayment, IMF conditions requiring greater liberalization and privatization and so on), with the capacity to ignite powerful social struggles. In Latin America, where a number of governments – Bolivia, Venezuela, Ecuador and Argentina – already strike an oppositional stance towards the US-dominated economic order, such struggles may well assume an anti-imperial form. Campaigns for debt repudiation, bank nationalizations and the like could become part of significant social upheavals.

Fourth, just as nations at the top of the imperial order will try to inflict greater hardship on the South, so we can anticipate moves toward even more draconian restrictions on the movement of migrant labour. At the same time as they press for "free movement" of

---

[47] Harvey Morris, "UN team warns of hard landing for the dollar," *Financial Times*, December 1, 2008.

[48] See my "Global Crisis, World Finance and Challenges to the Dollar," *The Bullet*, n. 118, June 25, 2008, available at www.newsocialist.org or www.socialistproject.ca/bullet/

[49] For more extensive analysis in this area see Adam Hanieh, "Making the World's Poor Pay: The Economic Crisis and the Global South," *The Bullet*, n. 155, November 23, 2008. Available at www.socialistproject.ca/bullet/ or at www.newsocialist.org

[50] Robert Wade and Frank Veneroso, "The Asian Crisis: The High Debt Model versus the Wall Street-Treasury-IMF Complex," *New Left Review* 228 (1998), pp. 3-23.

capital, governments at the core of the system also demand tighter control and regulation of the movement of labour. With the deepening of the economic crisis, many have already started to play the anti-immigrant card. Britain, in particular, has signalled a tightening up of immigration policy, and others will surely follow. As businesses fail, factories close and unemployment mounts, immigrant-bashing is likely to become more widespread. Moreover, government officials and parties on the right are likely to fan xenophobic sentiments of the sort that were on display earlier this year in countries like South Africa, where migrants from Zimbabwe in particular suffered violent assaults, or in South Korea, where undocumented migrants from the Philippines have been subjected to mass deportation. This crisis will thus put a premium on a Left for which anti-racism and defence of migrant workers are absolutely central to a politics of resistance.

Finally, this crisis also puts a premium on Left responses that are clearly *socialist* in character. The notion of calling for a "leashed capitalism"[51] in the face of such a colossal failure of the capitalist market system represents an equally colossal failure of socialist imagination. If ever there was a moment to highlight the systemic failings of capitalism and the need for a radical alternative, it is now. True, the Left must be able to do this in a meaningful and accessible language, by way of formulating concrete socialist demands and strategies that speak eloquently and powerfully to real and compelling needs and interests of oppressed people. And this will certainly involve fighting for specific reforms – to save jobs, build social housing, cancel Third World debts, invest in ecologically sustainable industries, feed the poor. But, as Rosa Luxemburg pointed out more than a century ago, while Marxists have a duty to fight for social reforms, they ought to do so in a way that builds the revolutionary capacities of the world's workers to remake the world.[52] And one crucial part of this involves popular education and agitation for socialism. Not to advance the critique of capitalism as a system, and not to highlight the need for a systemic transformation that will break the hold of the capitalist value form over human life is to squander an opportunity that lurks within this moment of crisis. This is a moment that calls out for bold, thoughtful socialist responses, a moment when socialist theory, joined to practical struggles, can become "a material force" for changing the world. But this requires insisting, in the face of capitalist crisis, that another world really is possible.

---

[51]   Pollin, p. 153.

[52]   Where the goal is socialism, Luxemburg writes, "The struggle for reforms is its means; the social revolution its aim." See Rosa Luxemburg, "Reform or Revolution" in *Rosa Luxemburg Speaks* (New York: Pathfinder Press, 1970), p. 36.

[7]

Self-Sourcing
How Corporations Get Us to Work Without Pay!

MARTHA E. GIMENEZ

The expansion of the capitalist world economy, which accelerated after the fall of the socialist bloc, has produced everywhere drastic changes in the division of labor, occupational structure, and the quality and quantity of labor that is in demand. In the United States, public awareness about the causes of job losses (downsizing, capital flight, offshoring, and outsourcing) has vastly increased since it became widely known that these processes caused the loss not only of blue-collar but also of "middle-class" and "upper-middle-class" jobs; i.e., jobs requiring some degree of education and technical competence.

Politicians, academics, the media, and job seekers focus on downsizing, offshoring, and outsourcing as the main causes of unemployment and declining opportunities, even for college graduates. They neglect, however, the impact of *self-sourcing*, a term I apply to the complex and relatively unnoticed effects of the radical reorganization of our working and non-working time due to the widespread use of information technologies. In this essay, I will explore the significance of self-sourcing, which I define as the intensification of the process of transferring work from the sphere of production, where it is visible and paid, to the sphere of consumption, where it is invisible and unpaid. This process is not new and it is commonly understood as self-service. It is my contention that self-sourcing signals a qualitative change in the forces and the relations of production, consumption, and circulation, which merits theoretical and empirical investigation.

Self-sourcing is a relatively unnoticed basis for the growth of business profits even as average wages and salaries decline; it is an important contributor to unemployment and underemployment. Consumption increasingly requires the performance of tasks previously done by paid workers. Jobs are not disappearing just because of automation, downsizing, and outsourcing; they disappear because they are increasingly done without pay by millions of consumers while the people who previously held those low-paid service and clerical jobs find themselves unemployed and perhaps unemployable.

MARTHA E. GIMENEZ teaches sociology at the University of Colorado at Boulder.

I first became interested in these issues when, in the mid-1980s, the university where I worked subsidized the faculty's purchase of personal computers, a practice that still continues. As computers were quite expensive in those days, I wondered about the reasons for the university's decision. True, computer use enhanced faculty productivity, as word processing accelerated the writing process. Computers were fun to use and quickly become addictive, the source of a new "trained incapacity" which made previous forms of writing seem clumsy and cumbersome. More importantly, the use of computers changed the organization of intellectual production and the conditions for the reproduction of intellectual labor power. Computers created the need to use them and increased the ability of one person to do many things which, in "the old days," would have been time consuming and would have required the labor of staff workers. Faculty members were not given paid time off to retool themselves; instead, they spent a great deal of their theoretically "free" time learning new skills and reproducing their labor power at higher and higher levels of competence. Through speedup, they increased their future productivity on a scale that would have been difficult to attain without having access to research funds, research assistants, and secretaries. It also became easier for faculty to use the computer for all the paper work associated with teaching (e.g., bibliographies, memos for students and colleagues, syllabi, letters, book requests, handouts for students, exams, etc.) than to type or write by hand a draft to be typed by department secretaries.

In the last twenty-five years, computers have become smaller, ubiquitous, inexpensive, and far more efficient. Faculty have become their own typists, secretaries, research assistants, computer experts (to some extent), and webmasters; they hold virtual office hours, teach virtual courses, and increasingly incorporate information technologies in the classroom. The ease with which computers have become integrated in the processes of intellectual production and teaching masks the intermingling between professional and clerical work. The consumption of information technologies by faculty has long-term implications not only for their overall productivity but also for the employment of non-faculty personnel at the university. Faculty have taken on some of the work formerly done by research and teaching assistants, secretaries, typists, data analysts, work-study students, proofreaders, library employees, and others I may not have thought about. The transfer of unpaid clerical labor to the faculty is irreversible, and its quantity varies with the relative power of individuals and departments. These two kinds of la-

SELF-SOURCING

39

bor, unpaid clerical labor and paid professional labor, are inextricably combined and may not appear as separate domains in the consciousness of most faculty who simply enjoy their self-sufficiency and the ease with which work is done, without reflecting about the kind and quantity of work they do. These observations, which relate the use of computers to a process of speedup or intensification of professional labor via its combination with labor previously done by clerical workers and graduate students in various capacities, might be received with derision, as manifestations of elitism. What is at issue, however, is not what is proper or improper work for somebody with a PhD, but the implications of these changes for the skills, wages, and employment of staff workers. Speedup for the faculty means that, though their job description does not openly state it, they are now expected to perform a variable quantity of unrecognized and unpaid computer-related clerical labor which expands their working day without expanding their paychecks. Faculty speedup, as well as the speedup inherent in most clerical jobs, also means long-term changes in the employment prospects for people who, given their levels of education and training, can only aspire to middle- and low-level clerical employment.

An examination of self-sourcing in the context of educational institutions is a good starting point for theorizing the nature of this phenomenon. It is, in some ways, an extension of the now familiar practices of self-service and do-it-yourself, and the uncritical acceptance of the work entailed in many instances of consumption. While these practices are not new, in creating the concept of self-sourcing I want to call attention to the qualitative changes in the amount of work required by consumption. Feminists have called attention to the ways capital benefits from women's unpaid labor within and outside the household.[1] Others have written about the increase in household production, where mostly male unpaid labor enters in the process of delivery and assembly of unfinished goods and materials used in building, remodeling, repairing, and so forth.[2] But the development of online shopping for goods and services, and online self-management of finances, employment benefits, health insurance, etc. have taken self-service to a different plane. Cumbersome and maddening phone menus were an early stage in the process of replacing the paid labor of customer service employees with standardized information often irrelevant to the callers' problems. Phone menus are still there but increasingly direct people to Web sites where they can find or do what they need by themselves, without the paid labor of someone guiding them through the process.

I still refuse to get an ATM card, because there are people, mostly working women, who need jobs at the bank; and it is only recently that I learned how to pump gas into my car because I thought the teenager who did it needed the job. Now the service station, recently purchased by BP, charges $2.50 for full-service. But these, as well as the salad bars and self-service supermarkets, are the earliest forms of a process of transformation in the consumption process which increasingly demands more unpaid work from the consumer while jobs quietly disappear. Supermarkets are now diminishing the number of cashiers while replacing them with self-checking machines. Consumers now work not only as they select their groceries but as they bag and check them out, guided by a creepy mechanical voice that instructs them how to do it in alignment with the machine's requirements. Self-service check-in machines are not just in the airports (where passengers, after purchasing tickets online, pay for and receive boarding passes from a machine), but in hotel lobbies (where they dispense room keys and can be used by customers to check themselves out), theater lobbies, the post office, and, increasingly, in most settings where consumers do what was previously done by paid workers. The last time I traveled by air, the airline employee wanted me (and other passengers as well) to print the baggage claim and attach it to the suitcase! We, the passengers, had no idea how to do it and we had to complain loudly until someone finally took care of our luggage.

The growth of self-service online transactions covering every conceivable consumer need, the use of self-service kiosks in large, big box stores, and the technological upgrading of self-service everywhere can be experienced as fun and self-empowering. The concept of self-sourcing, however, calls attention to the actual significance of these applications of information technologies; they not only restructure occupations through the blurring of job descriptions but displace paid labor with unpaid labor. The fact that this unpaid labor is, depending on the context, blended in with paid labor (as in the case of teachers), or of such short duration as to be practically invisible, just one more aspect of a pleasurable consumption experience, obscures its significance as a source of profits—corporations and businesses of all sizes save money when they cut labor costs by having the consumers' unpaid labor replace the paid labor of retail clerks, cashiers, travel agents, hotel clerks, bank clerks, etc. While the unpaid labor time of each consumer is minimal, adding up the unpaid labor time of millions of consumers yields substantial cuts in labor costs for businesses, who see their profits grow through their appropriation of unpaid consumption labor.

SELF-SOURCING 41

It may be argued that the lost jobs, which are generally low-skill, low-paid jobs, should not be saved, and that automation opens up jobs with higher skills and better pay. Those better jobs, however, are usually beyond the skills of those who self-sourcing technology replaces and a large proportion is likely to be outsourced to countries where labor is cheaper. While the process of self-sourcing is irreversible, it should not be accepted uncritically. Self-sourcing is an important aspect of the "hollowing out" of the job market, which entails the creation of jobs at the top and the bottom of the occupational structure, while the jobs in the middle are increasingly outsourced, or self-sourced.

Consumers do not know that they are doing more than just consuming goods and services: they are working without pay, entering into relations of circulation and distribution independent of their will and outside their consciousness of themselves as free, self-empowered consumers. If the trend of the future is, as Scott Burns suggested, for consumers to do more of the producers' work, it is important to raise awareness of the productive moment of consumption or "productive consumption."[3] While it might provide "middle-class" consumers with great satisfactions, it turns them into a vast reservoir of unpaid workers who contribute to capital accumulation while consciously reproducing themselves as consumers and objectively reproducing themselves as unpaid workers. At the same time large numbers of working-class people fall between the cracks of the system, condemned to menial, poorly paid jobs, permanent underemployment, or unemployment.

Notes

1. See, for example, Nona Glazer, "Servants to Capital," *Review of Radical Political Economics* 16, no. 1 (1984): 61–87, and Martha E. Gimenez, "The Dialectics of Waged and Unwaged Work," in Jane L. Collins and Martha Gimenez, eds., *Work Without Wages* (New York: State University of New York Press, 1990).
2. See, for example, Scott Burns, *The Household Economy* (Boston, MA: Beacon Press, 1977).
3. For an illuminating discussion of the dialectical relationship between production and consumption see Karl Marx, *A Contribution to the Critique of Political Economy* (New York: International Publishers, 1970), 193–99.

[8]

THE REPRODUCTION OF DAILY LIFE

FREDY PERLMAN

The everyday practical activity of tribesmen reproduces, or perpetuates, a tribe. This reproduction is not merely physical, but social as well. Through their daily activities the tribesmen do not merely reproduce a group of human beings; they reproduce a tribe, namely a particular *social form* within which this group of human beings performs *specific* activities in a *specific* manner. The specific activities of the

2

tribesmen are not the outcome of "natural" characteristics of the men who perform them, the way the production of honey is an outcome of the "nature" of a bee. The daily life enacted and perpetuated by the tribesman is a specific *social* response to particular material and historical conditions.

The everyday activity of slaves reproduces slavery. Through their daily activities, slaves do not merely reproduce themselves and their masters physically; they also reproduce the instruments with which the master represses them, and their own habits of submission to the master's authority. To men who live in a slave society, the master-slave relation seems like a natural and eternal relation. However, men are not born masters or slaves. Slavery is a specific social form, and men submit to it only in very particular material and historical conditions.

The practical everyday activity of wage-workers reproduces wage labor and capital. Through their daily activities, "modern" men, like tribesmen and slaves, reproduce the inhabitants, the social relations and the ideas of their society; they reproduce the *social form* of daily life. Like the tribe and the slave system, the capitalist system is neither the natural nor the final form of human society; like the earlier social forms, capitalism is a specific response to material and historical conditions.

Unlike earlier forms of social activity, everyday life in capitalist society *systematically* transforms the material conditions to which capitalism originally responded. Some of the material limits to human activity come gradually under human control. At a high level of industrialization, practical activity creates its own material conditions as well as its social form. Thus the subject of analysis is not only how practical activity in capitalist society reproduces capitalist society, but also how this activity itself eliminates the material conditions to which capitalism is a response.

Daily Life in Capitalist Society

The social form of people's regular activities under capitalism is a response to a certain material and historical situation. The material and historical conditions explain the origin of the capitalist form, but do not explain why this form continues after the initial situation disappears. A concept of "cultural lag" is not an explanation of the con-

3

tinuity of a social form after the disappearance of the initial conditions to which it responded. This concept is merely a name for the continuity of the social form. When the concept of "cultural lag" parades as a name for a "social force" which determines human activity, it is an obfuscation which presents the outcome of people's activities as an external force beyond their control. This is not only true of a concept like "cultural lag." Many of the terms used by Marx to describe people's activities have been raised to the status of external and even "natural" forces which determine people's activity; thus concepts like "class struggle," "production relations" and particularly "The Dialectic," play the same role in the theories of some "Marxists" that "Original Sin," "Fate" and "The Hand of Destiny" played in the theories of medieval mystifiers.

In the performance of their daily activities, the members of capitalist society simultaneously carry out two processes: they reproduce the form of their activities, and they eliminate the material conditions to which this form of activity initially responded. But they do not know they carry out these processes; their own activities are not transparent to them. They are under the illusion that their activities are responses to natural conditions beyond their control, and do not see that they are themselves authors of those conditions. The task of capitalist ideology is to maintain the veil which keeps people from seeing that their own activities reproduce the form of their daily life; the task of critical theory is to unveil the activities of daily life, to render them transparent, to make the reproduction of the social form of capitalist activity visible within people's daily activities.

Under capitalism, daily life consists of related activities which reproduce and expand the capitalist form of social activity. The sale of labor-time for a price (a wage), the embodiment of labor-time in commodities (salable goods, both tangible and intangible), the consumption of tangible and intangible commodities (such as consumer goods and spectacles)—these activities which characterize daily life under capitalism are not manifestations of "human nature," nor are they imposed on men by forces beyond their control.

If it is held that man is "by nature" an uninventive tribesman and an inventive businessman, a submissive slave and a proud craftsman, an independent hunter and a dependent wage-worker, then either man's "nature" is an empty concept, or man's "nature" depends on material and historical conditions, and is in fact a response to those conditions.

4

Alienation of Living Activity

In capitalist society, creative activity takes the form of commodity production, namely production of marketable goods, and the results of human activity take the form of commodities. Marketability or salability is the universal characteristic of all practical activity and all products.

The products of human activity which are necessary for survival have the form of salable goods: they are only available in exchange for money. And money is only available in exchange for commodities. If a large number of men accept the legitimacy of these conventions, if they accept the convention that commodities are a prerequisite for money, and that money is a prerequisite for survival, then they find themselves locked into a vicious circle. Since they have no commodities, their only exit from this circle is to regard themselves, or parts of themselves, as commodities. And this is, in fact, the peculiar "solution" which men impose on themselves in the face of specific material and historical conditions. They do not exchange their bodies or parts of their bodies for money. They exchange the creative content of their lives, their practical daily activity, for money.

As soon as men accept money as an equivalent for life, the sale of living activity becomes a condition for their physical and social survival. Life is exchanged for survival. Creation and production come to mean sold activity. A man's activity is "productive," useful to society, only when it is sold activity. And the man himself is a productive member of society only if the activities of his daily life are sold activities. As soon as people accept the terms of this exchange, daily activity takes the form of universal prostitution.

The sold creative power, or sold daily activity, takes the form of *labor*. Labor is a historically specific form of human activity. Labor is abstract activity which has only one property: it is marketable, it can be sold for a given quantity of money. Labor is *indifferent* activity: indifferent to the particular task performed and indifferent to the particular subject to which the task is directed. Digging, printing and carving are different activities, but all three are *labor* in capitalist society. Labor is simply "earning money." Living activity which takes the form of labor is a means to earn money. Life becomes a *means of survival*.

This ironic reversal is not the dramatic climax of an imaginative

5

novel; it is a fact of daily life in capitalist society. Survival, namely self-preservation and reproduction, is not the means to creative practical activity, but precisely the other way around. Creative activity in the form of *labor,* namely *sold activity,* is a *painful necessity* for survival; labor is the means to self-preservation and reproduction.

The sale of living activity brings about another reversal. Through sale, the labor of an individual becomes the "property" of another, it is appropriated by another, it comes under the control of another. In other words, a person's activity becomes the activity of another, the activity of its owner; it becomes *alien* to the person who performs it. Thus one's *life,* the accomplishments of an individual in the world, the difference which his life makes in the life of humanity, are not only transformed into *labor,* a painful condition for survival; they are transformed into *alien* activity, activity performed by the buyer of that labor. In capitalist society, the architects, the engineers, the laborers, are not builders; the man who buys their labor is the builder; their projects, calculations and motions are alien to them; their living activity, their accomplishments, are his.

Academic sociologists, who take the sale of labor for granted, understand this alienation of labor as a feeling: the worker's activity "appears" alien to the worker, it "seems" to be controlled by another. However, any worker can explain to the academic sociologists that the alienation is neither a feeling nor an idea in the worker's head, but a real fact about the worker's daily life. The sold activity is *in fact* alien to the worker; his labor is *in fact* controlled by its buyer.

In exchange for his sold activity, the worker gets money, the conventionally accepted means of survival in capitalist society. With this money he can buy commodities, things, but he cannot buy back his activity. This reveals a peculiar "gap" in money as the "universal equivalent." A person can sell commodities for money, and he can buy the same commodities with money. He can sell his living activity for money, but he cannot buy his living activity for money.

The things the worker buys with his wages are first of all consumer goods which enable him to survive, to reproduce his labor-power so as to be able to continue selling it; and they are spectacles, objects for passive admiration. He consumes and admires the products of human activity passively. He does not exist in the world as an active agent who transforms it, but as a helpless, impotent spectator; he may call this state of powerless admiration "happiness," and since labor is

6

painful, he may desire to be "happy," namely inactive, all his life (a condition similar to being born dead). The commodities, the spectacles, *consume him;* he uses up living energy in passive admiration; he is consumed by things. In this sense, the more he has, the less he is. (An individual can surmount this death-in-life through marginal creative activity; but the population cannot, except by abolishing the capitalist form of practical activity, by abolishing wage-labor and thus de-alienating creative activity.)

The Fetishism of Commodities

By alienating their activity and embodying it in commodities, in material receptacles of human labor, people reproduce themselves and create Capital.

From the standpoint of capitalist ideology, and particularly of academic Economics, this statement is untrue: commodities are "not the product of labor alone"; they are produced by the primordial "factors of production," Land, Labor and Capital, the capitalist Holy Trinity, and the main "factor" is obviously the hero of the piece, Capital.

The purpose of this superficial Trinity is not analysis, since analysis is not what these Experts are paid for. They are paid to obfuscate, to mask the social form of practical activity under capitalism, to veil the fact that producers reproduce themselves, their exploiters, as well as the instruments with which they're exploited. The Trinity formula does not succeed in convincing. It is obvious that *land* is no more of a commodity producer than water, air, or the sun. Furthermore *Capital,* which is at once a name for a social relation between workers and capitalists, for the instruments of production owned by a capitalist, and for the money-equivalent of his instruments and "intangibles," does not produce anything more than the ejaculations shaped into publishable form by the academic Economists. Even the instruments of production which are the capital of one capitalist are primordial "factors of production" only if one's blinders limit his view to an isolated capitalist firm, since a view of the entire economy reveals that the capital of one capitalist is the material receptacle of the labor alienated to another capitalist. However, though the Trinity formula does not convince, it does accomplish the task of obfuscation by shifting the subject of the question: instead of asking why the activity of people under capitalism takes the form of wage-labor, potential analysts of capi-

7

talist daily life are transformed into academic house-Marxists who ask whether or not labor is the only "factor of production."

Thus Economics (and capitalist ideology in general) treats land, money, and the products of labor, as things which have the power to produce, to create value, to work for their owners, to transform the world. This is what Marx called the *fetishism* which characterizes people's everyday conceptions, and which is raised to the level of dogma by Economics. For the economist, living people are *things* ("factors of production"), and things *live* (money "works," Capital "produces").

The fetish worshipper attributes the product of his own activity to his fetish. As a result, he ceases to exert his own power (the power to transform nature, the power to determine the form and content of his daily life); he exerts only those "powers" which he attributes to his fetish (the "power" to buy commodities). In other words, the fetish worshipper emasculates himself and attributes virility to his fetish.

But the fetish is a dead thing, not a living being; it has no virility. The fetish is no more than a thing for which, and through which, capitalist relations are maintained. The mysterious power of Capital, its "power" to produce, its virility, does not reside in itself, but in the fact that people alienate their creative activity, that they sell their labor to capitalists, that they materialize or reify their alienated labor in commodities. In other words, people are bought with the products of their own activity, yet they see their own activity as the activity of Capital, and their own products as the products of Capital. By attributing creative power to Capital and not to their own activity, they renounce their living activity, their everyday life, to Capital, which means that people *give themselves,* daily, to the personification of Capital, the capitalist.

By selling their labor, by alienating their activity, people daily reproduce the personifications of the dominant forms of activity under capitalism, they reproduce the wage-laborer and the capitalist. They do not merely reproduce the individuals physically, but socially as well; they reproduce individuals who are sellers of labor-power, and individuals who are owners of means of production; they reproduce the individuals as well as the specific activities, the sale as well as the ownership.

Every time people perform an activity they have not themselves

8

defined and do not control, every time they pay for goods they produced with money they received in exchange for their alienated activity, every time they passively admire the products of their own activity as alien objects procured by their money, they give new life to Capital and annihilate their own lives.

The aim of the process is the reproduction of the relation between the worker and the capitalist. However, this is not the aim of the individual agents engaged in it. Their activities are not transparent to them; their eyes are fixed on the *fetish* that stands between the act and its result. The individual agents keep their eyes fixed on *things,* precisely those things for which capitalist relations are established. The worker as producer aims to exchange his daily labor for money-wages, he aims precisely for the thing through which his relation to the capitalist is re-established, the thing through which he reproduces himself as a wage-worker and the other as a capitalist. The worker as consumer exchanges his money for products of labor, precisely the things which the capitalist has to sell in order to realize his Capital.

The daily transformation of living activity into Capital is *mediated* by things, it is not *carried out by* the things. The fetish worshipper does not know this; for him labor and land, instruments and money, entrepreneurs and bankers, are all "factors" and "agents." When a hunter wearing an amulet downs a deer with a stone, he may consider the amulet an essential "factor" in downing the deer and even in providing the deer as an object to be downed. If he is a responsible and well-educated fetish worshipper, he will devote his attention to his amulet, nourishing it with care and admiration; in order to improve the material conditions of his life, he will improve the way he wears his fetish, not the way he throws the stone; in a bind, he may even send his amulet to "hunt" for him. His own daily activities are not transparent to him: when he eats well, he fails to see that it is his own action of throwing the stone, and not the action of the amulet, that provided his food; when he starves, he fails to see that it is his own action of worshipping the amulet instead of hunting, and not the wrath of his fetish, that causes his starvation.

The fetishism of commodities and money, the mystification of one's own daily activities, the religion of everyday life which attributes living activity to inanimate things, is not a mental caprice born in men's imaginations; it has its origin in the character of social relations under capitalism. Men do in fact relate to each other through things; the fetish is in fact the occasion for which they act collectively, and through which they reproduce their activity. But it is not the fetish that performs the activity. It is not Capital that transforms raw materials, nor Capital that produces goods. If living activity did not transform the materials, these would remain untransformed, inert, dead matter. If men were not disposed to continue selling their living activity, the impotence of Capital would be revealed; Capital would cease to exist; its last remaining potency would be the power to remind people of a bypassed form of everyday life characterized by daily universal prostitution.

The worker alienates his life in order to preserve his life. If he did not sell his living activity he would not get a wage and could not survive. However, it is not the wage that makes alienation the condition for survival. If men were collectively not disposed to sell their lives, if they were disposed to take control over their own activities, universal prostitution would not be a condition for survival. It is people's disposition to continue selling their labor, and not the *things* for which they sell it, that makes the alienation of living activity necessary for the preservation of life.

The living activity sold by the worker is bought by the capitalist. And it is only this living activity that breathes life into Capital and makes it "productive." The capitalist, an "owner" of raw materials and instruments of production, presents natural objects and products of other people's labor as his own "private property." But it is not the mysterious power of Capital that creates the capitalist's "private property"; living activity is what creates the "property," and the form of that activity is what keeps it "private."

Transformation of Living Activity into Capital

The transformation of living activity into Capital takes place *through* things, daily, but is not carried out *by* things. Things which are products of human activity *seem* to be active agents because activities and contacts are established for and through things, and because people's activities are not transparent to them; they confuse the mediating object with the cause.

In the capitalist process of production, the worker embodies or materializes his alienated living energy in an inert object by using

10

instruments which are embodiments of other people's activity. (Sophisticated industrial instruments embody the intellectual and manual activity of countless generations of inventors, improvers and producers from all corners of the globe and from varied forms of society.) The instruments in themselves are inert objects; they are material embodiments of living activity, but are not themselves alive. The only active agent in the production process is the living laborer. He uses the products of other people's labor and infuses them with life, so to speak, but the life is his own; he is not able to resurrect the individuals who stored their living activity in his instrument. The instrument may enable him to do more during a given time period, and in this sense it may raise his productivity. But only the living labor which is able to produce can be productive.

For example, when an industrial worker runs an electric lathe, he uses products of the labor of generations of physicists, inventors, electrical engineers, lathe makers. He is obviously more productive than a craftsman who carves the same object by hand. But it is in no sense the "Capital" at the disposal of the industrial worker which is more "productive" than the "Capital" of the craftsman. If generations of intellectual and manual activity had not been embodied in the electric lathe, if the industrial worker had to invent the lathe, electricity, and the electric lathe, then it would take him numerous lifetimes to turn a single object on an electric lathe, and no amount of Capital could raise his productivity above that of the craftsman who carves the object by hand.

The notion of the "productivity of capital," and particularly the detailed measurement of that "productivity," are inventions of the "science" of Economics, that religion of capitalist daily life which uses up people's energy in the worship, admiration and flattery of the central fetish of capitalist society. Medieval colleagues of these "scientists" performed detailed measurements of the height and width of angels in Heaven, without ever asking what angels or Heaven were, and taking for granted the existence of both.

The result of the worker's sold activity is a product which does not belong to him. This product is an embodiment of his labor, a materialization of a part of his life, a receptacle which contains his living activity, but it is not his; it is as alien to him as his labor. He did not decide to make it, and when it is made he does not dispose of it. If he wants it, he has to buy it. What he has made is not simply

11

a product with certain useful properties; for that he did not need to sell his labor to a capitalist in exchange for a wage; he need only have picked the necessary materials and the available tools, he need only have shaped the materials guided by his goals and limited by his knowledge and ability. (It is obvious that an individual can only do this marginally; men's appropriation and use of the materials and tools available to them can only take place after the overthrow of the capitalist form of activity.)

What the worker produces under capitalist conditions is a product with a very specific property, the property of salability. What his alienated activity produces is a *commodity*.

Because capitalist production is commodity production, the statement that the goal of the process is the satisfaction of human needs is false; it is a rationalization and an apology. The "satisfaction of human needs" is not the goal of the capitalist or of the worker engaged in production, nor is it a result of the process. The worker sells his labor in order to get a wage; the specific content of the labor is indifferent to him; he does not alienate his labor to a capitalist who does not give him a wage in exchange for it, no matter how many human needs this capitalist's products may satisfy. The capitalist buys labor and engages it in production in order to emerge with commodities which can be sold. He is indifferent to the specific properties of the product, just as he is indifferent to people's needs; all that interests him about the product is how much it will sell for, and all that interests him about people's needs is how much they "need" to buy and how they can be coerced, through propaganda and psychological conditioning, to "need" more. The capitalist's goal is to satisfy *his* need to reproduce and enlarge Capital, and the result of the process is the expanded reproduction of wage labor and Capital (which are not "human needs").

The commodity produced by the worker is exchanged by the capitalist for a specific quantity of money; the commodity is a *value* which is exchanged for an equivalent *value*. In other words, the living and past labor materialized in the product can exist in two distinct yet equivalent forms, in commodities and in money, or in what is common to both, *value*. This does not mean that value is labor. Value is the social *form* of reified (materialized) labor in capitalist society.

Under capitalism, social relations are not established directly;

14

they are established through value. Everyday activity is not exchanged directly; it is exchanged *in the form of value*. Consequently, what happens to living activity under capitalism cannot be traced by observing the activity itself, but only by following the metamorphoses of value.

When the living activity of people takes the form of *labor* (alienated activity), it acquires the property of exchangeability; it acquires the form of value. In other words, the labor can be exchanged for an "equivalent" quantity of money (wages). The deliberate alienation of living activity, which is perceived as necessary for survival by the members of capitalist society, itself reproduces the capitalist form within which alienation is necessary for survival. Because of the fact that living activity has the form of value, the products of that activity must also have the form of value: they must be exchangeable for money. This is obvious since, if the products of labor did not take the form of value, but for example the form of useful objects at the disposal of society, then they would either remain in the factory or they would be taken freely by the members of society whenever a need for them arose; in either case, the money-wages received by the workers would have no *value*, and living activity could not be *sold* for an "equivalent" quantity of money; living activity could not be alienated. Consequently, as soon as living activity takes the form of value, the products of that activity take the form of value, and the reproduction of everyday life takes place through changes or metamorphoses of value.

The capitalist sells the products of labor on a market; he exchanges them for an equivalent sum of money; he realizes a determined value. The specific magnitude of this value on a particular market is the *price* of the commodities. For the academic Economist, Price is St. Peter's key to the gates of Heaven. Like Capital itself, Price moves within a wonderful world which consists entirely of objects; the objects have human relations with each other, and are alive; they transform each other, communicate with each other; they marry and have children. And of course it is only through the grace of these intelligent, powerful and creative objects that people can be so happy in capitalist society.

In the Economist's pictorial representations of the workings of Heaven, the angels do everything and men do nothing at all; men simply enjoy what these superior beings do for them. Not only does

15

Capital produce and money work; other mysterious beings have similar virtues. Thus Supply, a quantity of things which are sold, and Demand, a quantity of things which are bought, together determine Price, a quantity of money; when Supply and Demand marry on a particular point of the diagram, they give birth to Equilibrium Price, which corresponds to a universal state of bliss. The activities of everyday life are played out by things, and people are reduced to things ("factors of production") during their "productive" hours, and to passive spectators of things during their "leisure time." The virtue of the Economic Scientist consists of his ability to attribute the outcome of people's everyday activities to things, and of his inability to see the living activity of people underneath the antics of the things. For the Economist, the things *through* which the activity of people is regulated under capitalism are themselves the mothers and sons, the causes and consequences of their own activity.

The magnitude of value, namely the price of a commodity, the quantity of money for which it exchanges, is not determined by things, but by the daily activities of people. Supply and demand, perfect and imperfect competition, are nothing more than social forms of products and activities in capitalist society; they have no life of their own. The fact that activity is alienated, namely that labor-time is sold for a specific sum of money, that it has a certain value, has several consequences for the magnitude of the value of the products of that labor. The value of the sold commodities must *at least* be equal to the value of the labor-time. This is obvious both from the standpoint of the individual capitalist firm, and from the standpoint of society as a whole. If the value of the commodities sold by the individual capitalist were smaller than the value of the labor he hired, then his labor expenditures alone would be larger than his earnings, and he would quickly go bankrupt. Socially, if the value of the laborers' production were smaller than the value of their consumption, then the labor force could not even reproduce itself, not to speak of a class of capitalists. However, if the value of the commodities were merely equal to the value of the labor-time expended on them, the commodity producers would merely reproduce themselves, and their society would not be a capitalist society; their activity might still consist of commodity production, but it would not be capitalist commodity production.

For labor to create Capital, the value of the products of labor

16

must be larger than the value of the labor. In other words, the labor force must produce a *surplus product,* a quantity of goods which it does not consume, and this surplus product must be transformed into *surplus value,* a form of value which is not appropriated by workers as wages, but by capitalists as profit. Furthermore, the value of the products of labor must be larger still, since living labor is not the only kind of labor materialized in them. In the production process, workers expend their own energy, but they also use up the stored labor of others as instruments, and they shape materials on which labor was previously expended.

This leads to the strange result that the value of the laborer's products and the value of his wage are different magnitudes, namely that the sum of money received by the capitalist when he sells the commodities produced by his hired laborers is different from the sum he pays the laborers. This difference is not explained by the fact that the used-up materials and tools must be paid for. If the value of the sold commodities were equal to the value of the living labor and the instruments, there would still be no room for capitalists. The fact is that the difference between the two magnitudes must be large enough to support a class of capitalists—not only the individuals, but also the specific activity that these individuals engage in, namely the purchase of labor. The difference between the total value of the products and the value of the labor spent on their production is surplus value, the seed of Capital.

In order to locate the origin of surplus value, it is necessary to examine why the value of the labor is smaller than the value of the commodities produced by it. The alienated activity of the worker transforms materials with the aid of instruments, and produces a certain quantity of commodities. However, when these commodities are sold and the used-up materials and instruments are paid for, the workers are not given the remaining value of their products as their wages; they are given less. In other words, during every working day, the workers perform a certain quantity of unpaid labor, *forced labor,* for which they receive no equivalent.

The performance of this unpaid labor, this forced labor, is another "condition for survival" in capitalist society. However, like alienation, this condition is not imposed by nature, but by the collective practice of people, by their everyday activities. Before the existence of unions,

17

an individual worker accepted whatever forced labor was available, since rejection of the labor would have meant that other workers would accept the available terms of exchange, and the individual worker would receive no wage. Workers competed with each other for the wages offered by capitalists; if a worker quit because the wage was unacceptably low, an unemployed worker was willing to replace him, since for the unemployed a small wage is higher than no wage at all. This competition among workers was called "free labor" by capitalists, who made great sacrifices to maintain the freedom of workers, since it was precisely this freedom that preserved the surplus value of the capitalist and made it possible for him to accumulate Capital. It was not any worker's aim to produce more goods than he was paid for. His aim was to get a wage which was as large as possible. However, the existence of workers who got no wage at all, and whose conception of a large wage was consequently more modest than that of an employed worker, made it possible for the capitalist to hire labor at a lower wage. In fact, the existence of unemployed workers made it possible for the capitalist to pay the lowest wage that workers were willing to work for. Thus the result of the collective daily activity of the workers, each striving individually for the largest possible wage, was to lower the wages of all; the effect of the competition of each against all was that all got the smallest possible wage, and the capitalist got the largest possible surplus.

The daily practice of all annuls the goals of each. But the workers did not know that their situation was a product of their own daily behavior; their own activities were not transparent to them. To the workers it seemed that low wages were simply a natural part of life, like illness and death, and that falling wages were a natural catastrophe, like a flood or a hard winter. The critiques of socialists and the analyses of Marx, as well as an increase in industrial development which afforded more time for reflection, stripped away some of the veils and made it possible for workers to see through their activities to some extent. However, in Western Europe and the United States, workers did not get rid of the capitalist form of daily life; they formed unions. And in the different material conditions of the Soviet Union and Eastern Europe, workers (and peasants) replaced the capitalist class with a state bureaucracy that purchases alienated labor and accumulates Capital in the name of Marx.

18

With unions, daily life is similar to what it was before unions. In fact, it is almost the same. Daily life continues to consist of labor, of alienated activity, and of unpaid labor, or forced labor. The unionized worker no longer settles the terms of his alienation; union functionaries do this for him. The terms on which the worker's activity is alienated are no longer guided by the individual worker's need to accept what is available; they are now guided by the union bureaucrat's need to maintain his position as pimp between the sellers of labor and the buyers.

With or without unions, surplus value is neither a product of nature nor of Capital; it is created by the daily activities of people. In the performance of their daily activities, people are not only disposed to alienate these activities, they are also disposed to reproduce the conditions which force them to alienate their activities, to reproduce Capital and thus the power of Capital to purchase labor. This is not because they do not know "what the alternative is." A person who is incapacitated by chronic indigestion because he eats too much grease does not continue eating grease because he does not know what the alternative is. Either he prefers being incapacitated to giving up grease, or else it is not clear to him that his daily consumption of grease causes his incapacity. And if his doctor, preacher, teacher and politician tell him, first, that the grease is what keeps him alive, and secondly that they already do for him everything he would do if he were well, then it is not surprising that his activity is not transparent to him and that he makes no great effort to render it transparent.

The production of surplus value is a condition of survival, not for the population, but for the capitalist system. Surplus value is the portion of the value of commodities produced by labor which is not returned to the laborers. It can be expressed either in commodities or in money (just as Capital can be expressed either as a quantity of things or of money), but this does not alter the fact that it is an expression for the materialized labor which is stored in a given quantity of products. Since the products can be exchanged for an "equivalent" quantity of money, the money "stands for," or represents, the same value as the products. The money can, in turn, be exchanged for another quantity of products of "equivalent" value. The ensemble of these exchanges, which take place simultaneously

19

during the performance of capitalist daily life, constitutes the capitalist process of circulation. It is through this process that the metamorphosis of surplus value into Capital takes place.

The portion of value which does not return to labor, namely surplus value, allows the capitalist to exist, and it also allows him to do much more than simply exist. The capitalist invests a portion of this surplus value; he hires new workers and buys new means of production; he expands his dominion. What this means is that the capitalist *accumulates new labor*, both in the form of the living labor he hires and of the past labor (paid and unpaid) which is stored in the materials and machines he buys.

The capitalist class as a whole accumulates the surplus labor of society, but this process takes place on a social scale and consequently cannot be seen if one observes only the activities of an individual capitalist. It must be remembered that the products bought by a given capitalist as instruments have the same characteristics as the products he sells. A first capitalist sells instruments to a second capitalist for a given sum of value, and only a part of this value is returned to workers as wages; the remaining part is surplus value, with which the first capitalist buys new instruments and labor. The second capitalist buys the instruments for the given value, which means that he pays for the total quantity of labor rendered to the first capitalist, the quantity of labor which was remunerated as well as the quantity performed free of charge. This means that the instruments accumulated by the second capitalist contain the unpaid labor performed for the first. The second capitalist, in turn, sells his products for a given value, and returns only a portion of this value to his laborers; he uses the remainder for new instruments and labor.

If the whole process were squeezed into a single time period, and if all the capitalists were aggregated into one, it would be seen that the value with which the capitalist acquires new instruments and labor is equal to the value of the products which he did not return to the producers. This accumulated surplus labor is *Capital*.

In terms of capitalist society as a whole, the total Capital is equal to the sum of unpaid labor performed by generations of human beings whose lives consisted of the daily alienation of their living activity. In other words Capital, in the face of which men sell their living days, is the product of the sold activity of men, and is re-

20

produced and expanded every day a man sells another working day, every moment he decides to continue living the capitalist form of daily life.

Storage and Accumulation of Human Activity

The transformation of surplus labor into Capital is a specific historical form of a more general process, the process of industrialization, the permanent transformation of man's material environment.

Certain essential characteristics of this consequence of human activity under capitalism can be grasped by means of a simplified illustration. In an imaginary society, people spend most of their active time producing food and other necessities; only part of their time is "surplus time" in the sense that it is exempted from the production of necessities. This surplus activity may be devoted to the production of food for priests and warriors who do not themselves produce; it may be used to produce goods which are burned for sacred occasions; it may be used up in the performance of ceremonies or gymnastic exercises. In any of these cases, the material conditions of these people are not likely to change, from one generation to another, as a result of their daily activities. However, one generation of people of this imaginary society may store their surplus time instead of using it up. For example, they may spend this surplus time winding up springs. The next generation may unwind the energy stored in the springs to perform necessary tasks, or may simply use the energy of the springs to wind new springs. In either case, the stored surplus labor of the earlier generation will provide the new generation with a larger quantity of surplus working time. The new generation may also store this surplus in springs and in other receptacles. In a relatively short period, the labor stored in the springs will exceed the labor time available to any living generation; with the expenditure of relatively little energy, the people of this imaginary society will be able to harness the springs to most of their necessary tasks, and also to the task of winding new springs for coming generations. Most of the living hours which they previously spent producing necessities will now be available for activities which are not dictated by necessity but projected by the imagination.

At first glance it seems unlikely that people would devote living hours to the bizarre task of winding springs. It seems just as unlikely, even if they wound the springs, that they would store them for future generations, since the unwinding of the springs might provide, for example, a marvelous spectacle on festive days.

However, if people did not dispose of their own lives, if their working activity were not their own, if their practical activity consisted of *forced labor,* then human activity might well be harnessed to the task of winding springs, the task of storing surplus working time in material receptacles. The historical role of Capitalism, a role which was performed by people who accepted the legitimacy of others to dispose of their lives, consisted precisely of storing human activity in material receptacles by means of forced labor.

As soon as people submit to the "power" of money to buy stored labor as well as living activity, as soon as they accept the fictional "right" of money-holders to control and dispose of the stored as well as the living activity of society, they transform money into Capital and the owners of money into Capitalists.

This double alienation, the alienation of living activity in the form of wage labor, and the alienation of the activity of past generations in the form of stored labor (means of production), is not a single act which took place sometime in history. The relation between workers and capitalists is not a thing which imposed itself on society at some point in the past, once and for all. At no time did men sign a contract, or even make a verbal agreement, in which they gave up the power over their living activity, and in which they gave up the power over the living activity of all future generations on all parts of the globe.

Capital wears the mask of a natural force; it seems as solid as the earth itself; its movements appear as irreversible as tides; its crises seem as unavoidable as earthquakes and floods. Even when it is admitted that the power of Capital is created by men, this admission may merely be the occasion for the invention of an even more imposing mask, the mask of a man-made force, a Frankenstein monster, whose power inspires more awe than that of any natural force.

However, Capital is neither a natural force nor a man-made monster which was created sometime in the past and which dominated human life ever since.

The power of Capital does not reside in money, since money is a social convention which has no more "power" than men are willing

22

to grant it; when men refuse to sell their labor, money cannot perform even the simplest tasks, because money does not "work."

Nor does the power of Capital reside in the material receptacles in which the labor of past generations is stored, since the potential energy stored in these receptacles can be liberated by the activity of living people whether or not the receptacles are Capital, namely alien "property." Without living activity, the collection of objects which constitute society's Capital would merely be a scattered heap of assorted artifacts with no life of their own, and the "owners" of Capital would merely be a scattered assortment of uncommonly uncreative people (by training) who surround themselves with bits of paper in a vain attempt to resuscitate memories of past grandeur. The only "power" of Capital resides in the daily activities of living people; this "power" consists of the disposition of people to sell their daily activities in exchange for money, and to give up control over the products of their own activity and of the activity of earlier generations.

As soon as a person sells his labor to a capitalist and accepts only a part of his product as payment for that labor, he creates conditions for the purchase and exploitation of other people. No man would willingly give his arm or his child in exchange for money; yet when a man deliberately and consciously sells his working life in order to acquire the necessities for life, he not only reproduces the conditions which continue to make the sale of his life a necessity for its preservation; he also creates conditions which make the sale of life a necessity for other people. Later generations may of course refuse to sell their working lives for the same reason that he refused to sell his arm; however each failure to refuse alienated and forced labor enlarges the stock of stored labor with which Capital can buy working lives.

In order to transform surplus labor into Capital, the capitalist has to find a way to store it in material receptacles, in new means of production, and he must hire new laborers to activate the new means of production. In other words, he must enlarge his enterprise, or start a new enterprise in a different branch of production. This presupposes or requires the existence of materials that can be shaped into new salable commodities, the existence of buyers of the new products, and the existence of people who are poor enough to be willing to sell their labor. These requirements are themselves created

23

by capitalist activity, and capitalists recognize no limits or obstacles to their activity; the democracy of Capital demands absolute freedom.

Imperialism is not merely the "last stage" of Capitalism; it is also the first.

Anything which can be transformed into a marketable good is grist for Capital's mill, whether it lies on the capitalist's land or on the neighbor's, whether it lies above ground or under, floats on the sea or crawls on its floor; whether it is confined to other continents or other planets. All of humanity's explorations of nature, from Alchemy to Physics, are mobilized to search for new materials in which to store labor, to find new objects that someone can be taught to buy.

Buyers for old and new products are created by any and all available means, and new means are constantly discovered. "Open markets" and "open doors" are established by force and fraud. If people lack the means to buy the capitalists' products, they are hired by capitalists and are paid for producing the goods they wish to buy; if local craftsmen already produce what the capitalists have to sell, the craftsmen are ruined or bought-out; if laws or traditions ban the use of certain products, the laws and the traditions are destroyed; if people lack the objects on which to use the capitalists' products, they are taught to buy these objects; if people run out of physical or biological wants, then capitalists "satisfy" their "spiritual wants" and hire psychologists to create them; if people are so satiated with the products of capitalists that they can no longer use new objects, they are taught to buy objects and spectacles which have no use but can simply be observed and admired.

Poor people are found in pre-agrarian and agrarian societies on every continent; if they are not poor enough to be willing to sell their labor when the capitalists arrive, they are impoverished by the activities of the capitalists themselves. The lands of hunters gradually become the "private property" of "owners" who use state violence to restrict the hunters to "reservations" which do not contain enough food to keep them alive. The tools of peasants gradually become available only from the same merchant who generously lends them the money with which to buy the tools, until the peasants' "debts" are so large that they are forced to sell land which neither they nor any of their ancestors had ever bought. The buyers of craftsmen's products gradually become reduced to the merchants who market the products, until the day comes when a merchant decides to house

24

"his craftsmen" under the same roof, and provides them with the instruments which will enable all of them to concentrate their activity on the production of the most profitable items. Independent as well as dependent hunters, peasants and craftsmen, free men as well as slaves, are transformed into hired laborers. Those who previously disposed of their own lives in the face of harsh material conditions cease to dispose of their own lives precisely when they take up the task of modifying their material conditions; those who were previously conscious creators of their own meager existence become unconscious victims of their own activity even while abolishing the meagerness of their existence. Men who were much but had little now have much but are little.

The production of new commodities, the "opening" of new markets, the creation of new workers, are not three separate activities; they are three aspects of the same activity. A new labor force is created precisely in order to produce the new commodities; the wages received by these laborers are themselves the new market; their unpaid labor is the source of new expansion. Neither natural nor cultural barriers halt the spread of Capital, the transformation of people's daily activity into alienated labor, the transformation of their surplus labor into the "private property" of capitalists. However, Capital is not a natural force; it is a set of activities performed by people every day; it is a form of daily life; its continued existence and expansion presuppose only one essential condition: the disposition of people to continue to alienate their working lives and thus reproduce the capitalist form of daily life.

[9]

The Rise and Future Demise of the World Capitalist System: Concepts for Comparative Analysis

IMMANUEL WALLERSTEIN

McGill University

The growth within the capitalist world-economy of the industrial sector of production, the so-called 'industrial revolution', was accompanied by a very strong current of thought which defined this change as both a process of organic development and of progress. There were those who considered these economic developments and the concomitant changes in social organization to be some penultimate stage of world development whose final working-out was but a matter of time. These included such diverse thinkers as Saint-Simon, Comte, Hegel, Weber, Durkheim. And then there were the critics, most notably Marx, who argued, if you will, that the nineteenth-century present was only an antepenultimate stage of development, that the capitalist world was to know a cataclysmic political revolution which would then lead in the fullness of time to a final societal form, in this case the classless society.

One of the great strengths of Marxism was that, being an oppositional and hence critical doctrine, it called attention not merely to the contradictions of the system but to those of its ideologists, by appealing to the empirical evidence of historical reality which unmasked the irrelevancy of the models proposed for the explanation of the social world. The Marxist critics saw in abstracted models concrete rationalization, and they argued their case fundamentally by pointing to the failure of their opponents to analyze the social whole. As Lukacs put it, 'it is not the primacy of economic motives in historical explanation that constitutes the decisive difference between Marxism and bourgeois thought, but the point of view of totality'.[1]

In the mid-twentieth century, the dominant theory of development in the core countries of the capitalist world-economy has added little to the theorizing of the nineteenth-century progenitors of this mode of analysis, except to quantify the models and to abstract them still further, by adding

---

[1] George Lukacs, 'The Marxism of Rosa Luxemburg', in *History and Class Consciousness* (London: Merlin Press, 1968), p. 27.

388   IMMANUEL WALLERSTEIN

on epicyclical codas to the models in order to account for ever further deviations from empirical expectations.

What is wrong with such models has been shown many times over, and from many standpoints. I cite only one critic, a non-Marxist, Robert Nisbet, whose very cogent reflections on what he calls the 'Western theory of development' concludes with this summary:

> [We] turn to history and only to history if what we are seeking are the actual causes, sources, and conditions of overt changes of patterns and structures in society. Conventional wisdom to the contrary in modern social theory, we shall not find the explanation of change in those studies which are abstracted from history; whether these be studies of small groups in the social laboratory, group dynamics generally, staged experiments in social interaction, or mathematical analyses of so-called social systems. Nor will we find the sources of change in contemporary revivals of the comparative method with its ascending staircase of cultural similarities and differences plucked from all space and time.[2]

Shall we then turn to the critical schools, in particular Marxism, to give us a better account of social reality? In principle yes; in practice there are many different, often contradictory, versions extant of 'Marxism'. But what is more fundamental is the fact that in many countries Marxism is now the official state doctrine. Marxism is no longer exclusively an oppositional doctrine as it was in the nineteenth century.

The social fate of official doctrines is that they suffer a constant social pressure towards dogmatism and apologia, difficult although by no means impossible to counteract, and that they thereby often fall into the same intellectual dead-end of ahistorical model-building. Here the critique of Fernand Braudel is most pertinent:

> Marxism is a whole collection of models. . . . I shall protest . . ., more or less, not against the model, but rather against the use to which people have thought themselves entitled to put it. The genius of Marx, the secret of his enduring power, lies in his having been the first to construct true social models, starting out from the long term (*la longue durée*). These models have been fixed permanently in their simplicity; they have been given the force of law and they have been treated as ready-made, automatic explanations, applicable in all places to all societies. . . . In this way has the creative power of the most powerful social analysis of the last century been shackled. It will be able to regain its strength and vitality only in the long term.[3]

Nothing illustrates the distortions of ahistorical models of social change better than the dilemmas to which the concept of stages gives rise. If we are to deal with social transformations over long historical time (Braudel's 'the long term'), and if we are to give an explanation of both continuity and transformation, then we must logically divide the long term into segments in order to observe the structural changes from time A to time B. These

---

[2] Robert A. Nisbet, *Social Change and History* (New York: Oxford University Press, 1969), pp. 302–3. I myself would exempt from this criticism the economic history literature.

[3] Fernand Braudel, 'History and the Social Sciences', in Peter Burke (ed.) *Economy and Society in Early Modern Europe* (London: Routledge and Kegan Paul, 1972), pp. 38–9.

THE WORLD CAPITALIST SYSTEM 389

segments are however not discrete but continuous in reality; *ergo* they are 'stages' in the 'development' of a social structure, a development which we determine however not *a priori* but *a posteriori*. That is, we cannot predict the future concretely, but we can predict the past.

The crucial issue when comparing 'stages' is to determine the units of which the 'stages' are synchronic portraits (or 'ideal types', if you will). And the fundamental error of ahistorical social science (including ahistorical versions of Marxism) is to reify parts of the totality into such units and then to compare these reified structures.

For example, we may take modes of disposition of agricultural production, and term them subsistence-cropping and cash-cropping. We may then see these as entities which are 'stages' of a development. We may talk about decisions of groups of peasants to shift from one to the other. We may describe other partial entities, such as states, as having within them two separate 'economies', each based on a different mode of disposition of agricultural production. If we take each of these successive steps, all of which are false steps, we will end up with the misleading concept of the 'dual economy' as have many liberal economists dealing with the so-called underdeveloped countries of the world. Still worse, we may reify a misreading of British history into a set of universal 'stages' as Rostow does.

Marxist scholars have often fallen into exactly the same trap. If we take modes of payment of agricultural labor and contrast a 'feudal' mode wherein the laborer is permitted to retain for subsistence a part of his agricultural production with a 'capitalist' mode wherein the same laborer turns over the totality of his production to the landowner, receiving part of it back in the form of wages, we may then see these two modes as 'stages' of a development. We may talk of the interests of 'feudal' landowners in preventing the conversion of their mode of payment to a system of wages. We may then explain the fact that in the twentieth century a partial entity, say a state in Latin America, has not yet industrialized as the consequence of its being dominated by such landlords. If we take each of these successive steps, all of which are false steps, we will end up with the misleading concept of a 'state dominated by feudal elements', as though such a thing could possibly exist in a capitalist world-economy. But, as André Gunder Frank has clearly spelled out, such a myth dominated for a long time 'traditional Marxist' thought in Latin America.[4]

Not only does the misidentification of the entities to be compared lead us into false concepts, but it creates a non-problem: can stages be skipped? This question is only logically meaningful if we have 'stages' that 'co-exist' within a single empirical framework. If within a capitalist world-economy, we define one state as feudal, a second as capitalist, and a third as socialist,

---

[4] See André Gunder Frank, Ch. IV (A), 'The Myth of Feudalism' in *Capitalism and Underdevelopment in Latin America* (New York: Monthly Review Press, 1967), 221–42.

390 IMMANUEL WALLERSTEIN

then and only then can we pose the question: can a country 'skip' from the feudal stage to the socialist stage of national development without 'passing through capitalism'?

But if there is no such thing as 'national development' (if by that we mean a natural history), and if the proper entity of comparison is the world-system, then the problem of stage-skipping is nonsense. If a stage can be skipped, it isn't a stage. And we know this *a posteriori*.

If we are to talk of stages, then—and we should talk of stages—it must be stages of social systems, that is, of totalities. And the only totalities that exist or have historically existed are mini-systems and world-systems, and in the nineteenth and twentieth centuries there has been only one world-system in existence, the capitalist world-economy.

We take the defining characteristic of a social system to be the existence within it of a division of labor, such that the various sectors or areas within are dependent upon economic exchange with others for the smooth and continuous provisioning of the needs of the area. Such economic exchange can clearly exist without a common political structure and even more obviously without sharing the same culture.

A mini-system is an entity that has within it a complete division of labor, and a single cultural framework. Such systems are found only in very simple agricultural or hunting and gathering societies. Such mini-systems no longer exist in the world. Furthermore, there were fewer in the past than is often asserted, since any such system that became tied to an empire by the payment of tribute as 'protection costs'[5] ceased by that fact to be a 'system', no longer having a self-contained division of labor. For such an area, the payment of tribute marked a shift, in Polanyi's language, from being a reciprocal economy to participating in a larger redistributive economy.[6]

Leaving aside the now defunct mini-systems, the only kind of social system is a world-system, which we define quite simply as a unit with a single division of labor and multiple cultural systems. It follows logically that there can, however, be two varieties of such world-systems, one with a common political system and one without. We shall designate these respectively as world-empires and world-economies.

It turns out empirically that world-economies have historically been unstable structures leading either towards disintegration or conquest by one group and hence transformation into a world-empire. Examples of such world-empires emerging from world-economies are all the so-called

[5] See Frederic Lane's discussion of 'protection costs' which is reprinted as Part Three of *Venice and History* (Baltimore: Johns Hopkins Press, 1966). For the specific discussion of tribute, see pp. 389–90, 416–20.

[6] See Karl Polanyi, 'The Economy as Instituted Process', in Karl Polanyi, Conrad M. Arsenberg and Harry W. Pearson (eds.), *Trade and Market in the Early Empire* (Glencoe: Free Press, 1957), pp. 243–70.

THE WORLD CAPITALIST SYSTEM 391

great civilizations of pre-modern times, such as China, Egypt, Rome (each at appropriate periods of its history). On the other hand, the so-called nineteenth-century empires, such as Great Britain or France, were not world-empires at all, but nation-states with colonial appendages operating within the framework of a world-economy.

World-empires were basically redistributive in economic form. No doubt they bred clusters of merchants who engaged in economic exchange (primarily long-distance trade), but such clusters, however large, were a minor part of the total economy and not fundamentally determinative of its fate. Such long-distance trade tended to be, as Polanyi argues, 'administered trade' and not market trade, utilizing 'ports of trade'.

It was only with the emergence of the modern world-economy in sixteenth-century Europe that we saw the full development and economic predominance of market trade. This was the system called capitalism. Capitalism and a world-economy (that is, a single division of labor but multiple polities and cultures) are obverse sides of the same coin. One does not cause the other. We are merely defining the same indivisible phenomenon by different characteristics.

How and why it came about that this particular European world-economy of the sixteenth century did not become transformed into a redistributive world-empire but developed definitively as a capitalist world-economy I have explained elsewhere.[7] The genesis of this world-historical turning-point is marginal to the issues under discussion in this paper, which is rather what conceptual apparatus one brings to bear on the analysis of developments within the framework of precisely such a capitalist world-economy.

Let us therefore turn to the capitalist world-economy. We shall seek to deal with two pseudo-problems, created by the trap of not analyzing totalities: the so-called persistence of feudal forms, and the so-called creation of socialist systems. In doing this, we shall offer an alternative model with which to engage in comparative analysis, one rooted in the historically specific totality which is the world capitalist economy. We hope to demonstrate thereby that to be historically specific is not to fail to be analytically universal. On the contrary, the only road to nomothetic propositions is through the historically concrete, just as in cosmology the only road to a theory of the laws governing the universe is through the concrete analysis of the historical evolution of this same universe.[8]

On the 'feudalism' debate, we take as a starting-point Frank's concept

---

[7] See my *The Modern World-System: Capitalist Agriculture and the Origins of the European World-Economy in the Sixteenth Century* (New York: Academic Press, 1974).

[8] Philip Abrams concludes a similar plea with this admonition: 'The academic and intellectual dissociation of history and sociology seems, then, to have had the effect of deterring both disciplines from attending seriously to the most important issues involved in the understanding of social transition'. 'The Sense of the Past and the Origins of Sociology', *Past and Present*, No. 55, May 1972, 32.

392 IMMANUEL WALLERSTEIN

of 'the development of underdevelopment', that is, the view that the economic structures of contemporary underdeveloped countries is not the form which a 'traditional' society takes upon contact with 'developed' societies, not an earlier stage in the 'transition' to industrialization. It is rather the result of being involved in the world-economy as a peripheral, raw material producing area, or as Frank puts it for Chile, 'underdevelopment . . . is the necessary product of four centuries of capitalism itself'.[9]

This formulation runs counter to a large body of writing concerning the underdeveloped countries that was produced in the period 1950–70, a literature which sought the factors that explained 'development' within non-systems such as 'states' or 'cultures' and, once having presumably discovered these factors, urged their reproduction in underdeveloped areas as the road to salvation.[10]

Frank's theory also runs counter, as we have already noted, to the received orthodox version of Marxism that had long dominated Marxist parties and intellectual circles, for example in Latin America. This older 'Marxist' view of Latin America as a set of feudal societies in a more or less pre-bourgeois stage of development has fallen before the critiques of Frank and many others as well as before the political reality symbolized by the Cuban revolution and all its many consequences. Recent analysis in Latin America has centered instead around the concept of 'dependence'.[11]

However, recently, Ernesto Laclau has made an attack on Frank which, while accepting the critique of dualist doctrines, refuses to accept the categorization of Latin American states as capitalist. Instead Laclau asserts that 'the world capitalist system . . . includes, *at the level of its definition*, various modes of production'. He accuses Frank of confusing the two concepts of the 'capitalist mode of production' and 'participation in a world capitalist economic system'.[12]

Of course, if it's a matter of definition, then there can be no argument. But then the polemic is scarcely useful since it is reduced to a question of semantics. Furthermore, Laclau insists that the definition is not his but that of Marx, which is more debatable. Rosa Luxemburg put her finger on a key element in Marx's ambiguity or inconsistency in this particular debate, the ambiguity which enables both Frank and Laclau to trace their thoughts to Marx:

Admittedly, Marx dealt in detail with the process of appropriating non-capitalist means of production [N.B., Luxemburg is referring to primary products produced in peripheral areas under conditions of coerced labor—I.W.] as well as with the transformation

[9] Frank, *op. cit.*, p. 3.

[10] Frank's critique, now classic, of these theories is entitled 'Sociology of Development and Underdevelopment of Sociology' and is reprinted in *Latin America: Underdevelopment or Revolution* (New York: Monthly Review Press, 1969), 21–94.

[11] See Theontonio Dos Santos, *La Nueva Dependencia*. (Buenos Aires: s/ediciones, 1968).

[12] Ernesto Laclau (h), 'Feudalism and Capitalism in Latin America', *New Left Review*, No. 67, May–June 1971, 37–8.

THE WORLD CAPITALIST SYSTEM 393

of the peasants into a capitalist proletariat. Chapter XXIV of *Capital*, Vol. 1, is devoted to describing the origin of the English proletariat, of the capitalistic agricultural tenant class and of industrial capital, with particular emphasis on the looting of colonial countries by European capital. Yet we must bear in mind that all this is treated solely with a view to so-called primitive accumulation. For Marx, these processes are incidental, illustrating merely the genesis of capital, its first appearance in the world; they are, as it were, travails by which the capitalist mode of production emerges from a feudal society. As soon as he comes to analyze the capitalist process of production and circulation, he reaffirms the universal and exclusive domination of capitalist production [N.B., that is, production based on wage labor—I.W.].[13]

There is, after all, a substantive issue in this debate. It is in fact the same substantive issue that underlay the debate between Maurice Dobb and Paul Sweezy in the early 1950s about the 'transition from feudalism to capitalism' that occurred in early modern Europe.[14] The substantive issue, in my view, concerns the appropriate unit of analysis for the purpose of comparison. Basically, although neither Sweezy nor Frank is quite explicit on this point, and though Dobb and Laclau can both point to texts of Marx that seem clearly to indicate that they more faithfully follow Marx's argument, I believe both Sweezy and Frank better follow the spirit of Marx if not his letter[15] and that, leaving Marx quite out of the picture, they bring us nearer to an understanding of what actually happened and is happening than their opponents.

What is the picture, both analytical and historical, that Laclau constructs? The heart of the problem revolves around the existence of free labor as the defining characteristic of a capitalist mode of production:

The fundamental economic relationship of capitalism is constituted by the *free* [italics mine] labourer's sale of his labour-power, whose necessary precondition is the loss by the direct producer of ownership of the means of production. . . .

[13] *The Accumulation of Capital* (New York: Modern Reader Paperbacks, 364–5). Luxemburg however, as is evident, lends herself further to the confusion by using the terminology of 'capitalistic' and 'non-capitalistic' modes of production. Leaving these terms aside, her vision is impeccable: 'From the aspect both of realising the surplus value and of producing the material elements of constant capital, international trade is a prime necessity for the historical existence of capitalism—an international trade which under actual conditions is essentially an exchange between capitalistic and non-capitalistic modes of production'. *Ibid.*, 359. She shows similar insight into the need of recruiting labor for core areas from the periphery, what she calls 'the increase in the variable capital'. See *ibid.*, p. 361.

[14] The debate begins with Maurice Dobb, *Studies in the Development of Capitalism* (London: Routledge and Kegan Paul, 1946). Paul Sweezy criticized Dobb in 'The Transition from Feudalism to Capitalism', *Science and Society*, XIV, 2, Spring 1950, 134–57, with a 'Reply' by Dobb in the same issue. From that point on many others got into the debate in various parts of the world. I have reviewed and discussed this debate *in extenso* in Chapter 1 of my work cited above.

[15] It would take us into a long discursus to defend the proposition that, like all great thinkers, there was the Marx who was the prisoner of his social location and the Marx, the genius, who could on occasion see from a wider vantage point. The former Marx generalized from British history. The latter Marx is the one who has inspired a critical conceptual framework of social reality. W. W. Rostow incidentally seeks to refute the former Marx by offering an alternative generalization from British history. He ignores the latter and more significant Marx. See *The Stages of Economic Growth: A Non-Communist Manifesto* (Cambridge: at the University Press, 1960).

394   IMMANUEL WALLERSTEIN

If we now confront Frank's affirmation that the socio-economic complexes of Latin America has been capitalist since the Conquest Period . . . with the currently available empirical evidence, we must conclude that the 'capitalist' thesis is indefensible. In regions with dense indigenous populations–Mexico, Peru, Bolivia, or Guatemala—the direct producers were not despoiled of their ownership of the means of production, while extra-economic coercion to maximize various systems of labour service . . . was progressively intensified. In the plantations of the West Indies, the economy was based on a mode of production constituted by slave labour, while in the mining areas there developed disguised forms of slavery and other types of forced labour which bore not the slightest resemblance to the formation of a capitalist proletariat.[16]

There in a nutshell it is. Western Europe, at least England from the late seventeenth century on, had primarily landless, wage-earning laborers. In Latin America, then and to some extent still now, laborers were not proletarians, but slaves or 'serfs'. If proletariat, then capitalism. Of course. To be sure. But is England, or Mexico, or the West Indies a unit of analysis? Does each have a separate 'mode of production'? Or is the unit (for the sixteenth–eighteenth centuries) the European world-economy, including England *and* Mexico, in which case what was the 'mode of production' of this world-economy?

Before we argue our response to this question, let us turn to quite another debate, one between Mao Tse-Tung and Liu Shao-Chi in the 1960s concerning whether or not the Chinese People's Republic was a 'socialist state'. This is a debate that has a long background in the evolving thought of Marxist parties.

Marx, as has been often noted, said virtually nothing about the post-revolutionary political process. Engels spoke quite late in his writings of the 'dictatorship of the proletariat'. It was left to Lenin to elaborate a theory about such a 'dictatorship', in his pamphlet *State and Revolution*, published in the last stages before the Bolshevik takeover of Russia, that is, in August 1917. The coming to power of the Bolsheviks led to a considerable debate as to the nature of the regime that had been established. Eventually a theoretical distinction emerged in Soviet thought between 'socialism' and 'communism' as two stages in historical development, one realizable in the present and one only in the future. In 1936 Stalin proclaimed that the U.S.S.R. had become a socialist (but not yet a communist) state. Thus we now had firmly established *three* stages after bourgeois rule: a post-revolutionary government, a socialist state, and eventually communism. When, after the Second World War, various regimes dominated by the Communist Party were established in various east European states, these regimes were proclaimed to be 'peoples' democracies', a new name then given to the post-revolutionary stage one. At later points, some of these countries, for example Czechoslovakia, asserted they had passed into stage two, that of becoming a socialist republic.

[16] Laclau, *op. cit.*, 25, 30.

THE WORLD CAPITALIST SYSTEM 395

In 1961, the 22nd Congress of the CPSU invented a fourth stage, in between the former second and third stages: that of a socialist state which had become a 'state of the whole people', a stage it was contended the U.S.S.R. had at that point reached. The Programme of the Congress asserted that 'the state as an organization of the entire people will survive until the complete victory of communism'.[17] One of its commentators defines the 'intrinsic substance (and) chief distinctive feature' of this stage: 'The state of the whole people is the first state in the world with no class struggle to contend with and, hence, with no class domination and no suppression'.[18]

One of the earliest signs of a major disagreement in the 1950s between the Communist Party of the Soviet Union and the Chinese Communist Party was a theoretical debate that revolved around the question of the 'gradual transition to Communism'. Basically, the CPSU argued that different socialist states would proceed separately in effectuating such a transition whereas the CCP argued that all socialist states would proceed simultaneously.

As we can see, this last form of the debate about 'stages' implicitly raised the issue of the unit of analysis, for in effect the CCP was arguing that 'communism' was a characteristic not of nation-states but of the world-economy as a whole. This debate was transposed onto the internal Chinese scene by the ideological debate, now known to have deep and long-standing roots, that gave rise eventually to the Cultural Revolution.

One of the corollaries of these debates about 'stages' was whether or not the class struggle continued in post-revolutionary states prior to the achievement of communism. The 22nd Congress of the CPSU in 1961 had argued that the U.S.S.R. had become a state without an internal class struggle, there were no longer existing antagonistic classes within it. Without speaking of the U.S.S.R., Mao Tse-Tung in 1957 had asserted of China:

The class struggle is by no means over. . . . It will continue to be long and tortuous, and at times will even become very acute. . . . Marxists are still a minority among the entire population as well as among the intellectuals. Therefore, Marxism must still develop through struggle. . . . Such struggles will never end. This is the law of development of truth and, naturally, of Marxism as well.[19]

If such struggles *never* end, then many of the facile generalizations about 'stages' which 'socialist' states are presumed to go through are thrown into question.

During the Cultural Revolution, it was asserted that Mao's report 'On the Correct Handling of Contradiction Among The People' cited above, as

---

[17] Cited in F. Burlatsky, *The State and Communism* (Moscow: Progress Publishers, n.d., *circa* 1961), p. 95.

[18] *Ibid.*, p. 97.

[19] Mao Tse-Tung, *On The Correct Handling of Contradictions Among The People*, 7th ed., revised translation (Peking: Foreign Languages Press, 1966), pp. 37–8.

396 IMMANUEL WALLERSTEIN

well as one other, 'entirely repudiated the "theory of the dying out of the class struggle" advocated by Liu Shao-Chi. . . .'[20] Specifically, Mao argued that 'the elimination of the system of ownership by the exploiting classes through socialist transformation is not equal to the disappearance of struggle in the political and ideological spheres'.[21]

Indeed, this is the logic of a *cultural* revolution. Mao is asserting that even if there is the achievement of *political* power (dictatorship of the proletariat) and *economic* transformation (abolition of private ownership of the means of production), the revolution is still far from complete. Revolution is not an event but a process. This process Mao calls 'socialist society' —in my view a somewhat confusing choice of words, but no matter—and 'socialist society covers a fairly long historical period'.[22] Furthermore, 'there are classes and class struggle throughout the period of socialist society'.[23] The Tenth Plenum of the 8th Central Committee of the CCP, meeting from September 24–7, 1962, in endorsing Mao's views, omitted the phrase 'socialist society' and talked instead of 'the historical period of proletarian revolution and proletarian dictatorship, . . . the historical period of transition from capitalism to communism', which it said 'will last scores of years or even longer' and during which 'there is class struggle between the proletariat and the bourgeoisie and struggle between the socialist road and the capitalist road'.[24]

We do not have directly Liu's counter-arguments. We might however take as an expression of the alternative position a recent analysis published in the U.S.S.R. on the relationship of the socialist system and world development. There it is asserted that at some unspecified point after the Second World War, 'socialism outgrew the bounds of one country and became a world system. . . .'[25] It is further argued that: 'Capitalism, emerging in the 16th century, became a world economic system only in the 19th century. It took the bourgeois revolutions 300 years to put an end to the power of the feudal elite. It took socialism 30 or 40 years to generate the forces for a new world system.'[26] Finally, this book speaks of 'capitalism's

[20] *Long Live The Invincible Thought of Mao Tse-Tung!*, undated pamphlet, issued between 1967 and 1969, translated in *Current Background*, No. 884, July 18, 1969, 14.

[21] This is the position taken by Mao Tse-Tung in his speech to the Work Conference of the Central Committee at Peitaiho in August 1962, as reported in the pamphlet, *Long Live . . .*, p. 20. Mao's position was subsequently endorsed at the 10th Plenum of the 8th CCP Central Committee in September 1962, a session this same pamphlet describes as 'a great turning point in the violent struggle between the proletarian headquarters and the bourgeois headquarters in China'. *Ibid.*, 21.

[22] Remarks made by Mao at 10th Plenum, cited in *ibid.*, 20.

[23] Mao Tse-Tung, 'Talk on the Question of Democratic Centralism', January 30, 1962, in *Current Background*, No. 891, Oct. 8, 1969, 39.

[24] 'Communiqué of the 10th Plenary Session of the 8th Central Committee of the Chinese Communist Party', *Current Background*, No. 691, Oct. 5, 1962, 3.

[25] Yuri Sdobnikov (ed.), *Socialism and Capitalism: Score and Prospects* (Moscow: Progress Publ., 1971), p. 20. The book was compiled by staff members of the Institute of World Economy and International Relations, and the senior contributor was Prof. V. Aboltin.

[26] *Ibid.*, p. 21.

THE WORLD CAPITALIST SYSTEM 397

international division of labor'[27] and 'international socialist co-operation of labor'[28] as two separate phenomena, drawing from this counterposition the policy conclusion: 'Socialist unity has suffered a serious setback from the divisive course being pursued by the incumbent leadership of the Chinese People's Republic', and attributes this to 'the great-power chauvinism of Mao Tse-Tung and his group'.[29]

Note well the contrast between these two positions. Mao Tse-Tung is arguing for viewing 'socialist society' as process rather than structure. Like Frank and Sweezy, and once again implicitly rather than explicitly, he is taking the world-system rather than the nation-state as the unit of analysis. The analysis by U.S.S.R. scholars by contrast specifically argues the existence of *two* world-systems with two divisions of labor existing side by side, although the socialist system is acknowledged to be 'divided'. If divided politically, is it united economically? Hardly, one would think; in which case what is the substructural base to argue the existence of the system? Is it merely a moral imperative? And are then the Soviet scholars defending their concepts on the basis of Kantian metaphysics?

Let us see now if we can reinterpret the issues developed in these two debates within the framework of a general set of concepts that could be used to analyze the functioning of world-systems, and particularly of the historically specific capitalist world-economy that has existed for about four or five centuries now.

We must start with how one demonstrates the existence of a single division of labor. We can regard a division of labor as a grid which is substantially interdependent. Economic actors operate on some assumption (obviously seldom clear to any individual actor) that the totality of their essential needs—of sustenance, protection, and pleasure—will be met over a reasonable time-span by a combination of their own productive activities and exchange in some form. The smallest grid that would substantially meet the expectations of the overwhelming majority of actors within those boundaries constitutes a single division of labor.

The reason why a small farming community whose only significant link to outsiders is the payment of annual tribute does not constitute such a single division of labor is that the assumptions of persons living in it concerning the provision of protection involve an 'exchange' with other parts of the world-empire.

This concept of a grid of exchange relationships assumes, however, a distinction between *essential* exchanges and what might be called 'luxury' exchanges. This is to be sure a distinction rooted in the social perceptions of the actors and hence in both their social organization and their culture. These perceptions can change. But this distinction is crucial if we are not to fall into the trap of identifying *every* exchange-activity as evidence of the

[27] *Ibid.*, p. 26.　　　[28] *Ibid.*, p. 24.　　　[29] *Ibid.*, p. 25.

398 IMMANUEL WALLERSTEIN

existence of a system. Members of a system (a mini-system or a world-system) can be linked in limited exchanges with elements located outside the system, in the 'external arena' of the system.

The form of such an exchange is very limited. Elements of the two systems can engage in an exchange of preciosities. That is, each can export to the other what is in *its* system socially defined as worth little in return for the import of what in its system is defined as worth much. This is not a mere pedantic definitional exercise, as the exchange of preciosities *between* world-systems can be extremely important in the historical evolution of a given world-system. The reason why this is so important is that in an exchange of preciosities, the importer is 'reaping a windfall' and not obtaining a profit. Both exchange-partners can reap windfalls simultaneously but only one can obtain maximum profit, since the exchange of surplus-value within a system is a zero-sum game.

We are, as you see, coming to the essential feature of a capitalist world-economy, which is production for sale in a market in which the object is to realize the maximum profit. In such a system production is constantly expanded as long as further production is profitable, and men constantly innovate new ways of producing things that will expand the profit margin. The classical economists tried to argue that such production for the market was somehow the 'natural' state of man. But the combined writings of the anthropologists and the Marxists left few in doubt that such a mode of production (these days called 'capitalism') was only one of several possible modes.

Since, however, the intellectual debate between the liberals and the Marxists took place in the era of the industrial revolution, there has tended to be a *de facto* confusion between industrialism and capitalism. This left the liberals after 1945 in the dilemma of explaining how a presumably non-capitalist society, the U.S.S.R., had industrialized. The most sophisticated response has been to conceive of 'liberal capitalism' and 'socialism' as two variants of an 'industrial society', two variants destined to 'converge'. This argument has been trenchantly expounded by Raymond Aron.[30] But the same confusion left the Marxists, including Marx, with the problem of explaining what was the mode of production that predominated in Europe from the sixteenth to the eighteenth centuries, that is before the industrial revolution. Essentially, most Marxists have talked of a 'transitional' stage, which is in fact a blurry non-concept with no operational indicators. This dilemma is heightened if the unit of analysis used is the state, in which case one has to explain why the transition has occurred at different rates and times in different countries.[31]

---

[30] See Raymond Aron, *Dix-huit leçons de la société industrielle* (Paris: Ed. Gallimard, 1962).

[31] This is the dilemma, I feel, of E. J. Hobsbawm in explaining his so-called 'crisis of the seventeenth century'. See his *Past and Present* article reprinted (with various critiques) in

THE WORLD CAPITALIST SYSTEM 399

Marx himself handled this by drawing a distinction between 'merchant capitalism' and 'industrial capitalism'. This I believe is unfortunate terminology, since it leads to such conclusions as that of Maurice Dobb who says of this 'transitional' period:

But why speak of this as a stage of capitalism at all? The workers were generally not proletarianized: that is, they were not separated from the instruments of production, nor even in many cases from occupation of a plot of land. Production was scattered and decentralized and not concentrated. *The capitalist was still predominantly a merchant* who did not control production directly and did not impose his own discipline upon the work of artisan-craftsmen, who both laboured as individual (or family) units and retained a considerable measure of independence (if a dwindling one).[32]

One might well say: why indeed? Especially if one remembers how much emphasis Dobb places a few pages earlier on capitalism as a mode of *production*—how then can the capitalist be primarily a merchant?—on the concentration of such ownership in the hands of a few, and on the fact that capitalism is not synonymous with private ownership, capitalism being different from a system in which the owners are 'small peasant producers or artisan-producers'. Dobb argues that a defining feature of private ownership under capitalism is that some are 'obliged to [work for those that own] since [they own] nothing and [have] no access to means of production [and hence] have no other means of livelihood'.[33] Given this contradiction, the answer Dobb gives to his own question is in my view very weak: 'While it is true that at this date the situation was transitional, and capital-to-wage-labour relations were still immaturely developed, the latter were already beginning to assume their characteristic features'.[34]

If capitalism is a mode of production, production for profit in a market, then we ought, I should have thought, to look to whether or not such production was or was not occurring. It turns out in fact that it was, and in a very substantial form. Most of this production, however, was not industrial production. What was happening in Europe from the sixteenth to the eighteenth centuries is that over a large geographical area going from Poland in the northeast westwards and southwards throughout Europe and including large parts of the Western Hemisphere as well, there grew up a world-economy with a single division of labor within which there was a world market, for which men produced largely agricultural products for sale and profit. I would think the simplest thing to do would be to call this agricultural capitalism.

This then resolves the problems incurred by using the pervasiveness of *wage*-labor as a defining characteristic of capitalism. An individual is

---

Trevor Aston (ed.), *The Crisis of the Seventeenth Century* (London: Routledge and Kegan Paul, 1965).

[32] Maurice Dobb, *Capitalism Yesterday and Today* (London: Lawrence and Wishart, 1958), p. 21. Italics mine.

[33] *Ibid.*, pp. 6–7.   [34] *Ibid.*, p. 21.

400 IMMANUEL WALLERSTEIN

no less a capitalist exploiting labor because the state assists him to pay his laborers low wages (including wages in kind) and denies these laborers the right to change employment. Slavery and so-called 'second serfdom' are not to be regarded as anomalies in a capitalist system. Rather the so-called serf in Poland or the Indian on a Spanish *encomienda* in New Spain in this sixteenth-century world-economy were working for landlords who 'paid' them (however euphemistic this term) for cash-crop production. This is a relationship in which labor-power is a commodity (how could it ever be more so than under slavery?), quite different from the relationship of a feudal serf to his lord in eleventh-century Burgundy, where the economy was not oriented to a world market, and where labor-power was (therefore?) in no sense bought or sold.

Capitalism thus means labor as a commodity to be sure. But in the era of agricultural capitalism, wage-labor is only one of the modes in which labor is recruited and recompensed in the labor market. Slavery, coerced cash-crop production (my name for the so-called 'second feudalism'), share-cropping, and tenancy are all alternative modes. It would be too long to develop here the conditions under which differing regions of the world-economy tend to specialize in different agricultural products. I have done this elsewhere.[35]

What we must notice now is that this specialization occurs in specific and differing geographic regions of the world-economy. This regional specialization comes about by the attempts of actors in the market to avoid the normal operation of the market whenever it does not maximize their profit. The attempts of these actors to use non-market devices to ensure short-run profits makes them turn to the political entities which have in fact power to affect the market—the nation-states. (Again, why at this stage they could not have turned to city-states would take us into a long discursus, but it has to do with the state of military and shipping technology, the need of the European land-mass to expand overseas in the fifteenth century if it was to maintain the level of income of the various aristocracies, combined with the state of political disintegration to which Europe had fallen in the Middle Ages.)

In any case, the local capitalist classes—cash-crop landowners (often, even usually, nobility) and merchants—turned to the state, not only to liberate them from non-market constraints (as traditionally emphasized by liberal historiography) but to create new constraints on the new market, the market of the European world-economy.

By a series of accidents—historical, ecological, geographic—northwest Europe was better situated in the sixteenth century to diversify its agricultural specialization and add to it certain industries (such as textiles, shipbuilding, and metal wares) than were other parts of Europe. Northwest

[35] See my *The Modern World-System, op. cit.*, Chap. 2.

THE WORLD CAPITALIST SYSTEM 401

Europe emerged as the core area of this world-economy, specializing in agricultural production of higher skill levels, which favored (again for reasons too complex to develop) tenancy and wage-labor as the modes of labor control. Eastern Europe and the Western Hemisphere became peripheral areas specializing in export of grains, bullion, wood, cotton, sugar— all of which favored the use of slavery and coerced cash-crop labor as the modes of labor control. Mediterranean Europe emerged as the semi-peripheral area of this world-economy specializing in high-cost industrial products (for example, silks) and credit and specie transactions, which had as a consequence in the agricultural arena share-cropping as the mode of labor control and little export to other areas.

The three structural positions in a world-economy—core, periphery, and semi-periphery—had become stabilized by about 1640. How certain areas became one and not the other is a long story.[36] The key fact is that given slightly different starting-points, the interests of various local groups converged in northwest Europe, leading to the development of strong state mechanisms, and diverged sharply in the peripheral areas, leading to very weak ones. Once we get a difference in the strength of the state-machineries, we get the operation of 'unequal exchange'[37] which is enforced by strong states on weak ones, by core states on peripheral areas. Thus capitalism involves not only appropriation of the surplus-value by an owner from a laborer, but an appropriation of surplus of the whole world-economy by core areas. And this was as true in the stage of agricultural capitalism as it is in the stage of industrial capitalism.

In the early Middle Ages, there was to be sure trade. But it was largely either 'local', in a region that we might call the 'extended' manor, or 'long-distance', primarily of luxury goods. There was no exchange of 'bulk' goods, of 'staples' across intermediate-size areas, and hence no production for such markets. Later on in the Middle Ages, world-economies may be said to have come into existence, one centering on Venice, a second on the cities of Flanders and the Hanse. For various reasons, these structures were hurt by the retractions (economic, demographic, and ecological) of the period 1300–1450. It is only with the creating of a *European* division of labor after 1450 that capitalism found firm roots.

Capitalism was from the beginning an affair of the world-economy and not of nation-states. It is a misreading of the situation to claim that it is only in the twentieth century that capitalism has become 'world-wide', although this claim is frequently made in various writings, particularly by Marxists. Typical of this line of argument is Charles Bettelheim's response to Arghiri Emmanuel's discussion of unequal exchange:

---

[36] I give a brief account of this in 'Three Paths of National Development in the Sixteenth Century', *Studies in Comparative International Development*, VII, 2, Summer 1972, 95–101.

[37] See Arghiri Emmanuel, *Unequal Exchange* (New York: Monthly Review Press, 1972).

402 IMMANUEL WALLERSTEIN

The tendency of the capitalist mode of production to become worldwide is manifested not only through the constitution of a group of national economies forming a complex and hierarchical structure, including an imperialist pole and a dominated one, and not only through the antagonistic relations that develop between the different 'national economies' and the different states, but also through the constant 'transcending' of 'national limits' by big capital (the formation of 'international big capital', 'world firms', etc. . . .).[38]

The whole tone of these remarks ignores the fact that capital has never allowed its aspirations to be determined by national boundaries in a capitalist world-economy, and that the creation of 'national' barriers—generically, mercantilism—has historically been a defensive mechanism of capitalists located in states which are one level below the high point of strength in the system. Such was the case of England *vis-à-vis* the Netherlands in 1660–1715, France *vis-à-vis* England in 1715–1815, Germany *vis-à-vis* Britain in the nineteenth century, the Soviet Union *vis-à-vis* the U.S. in the twentieth. In the process a large number of countries create national economic barriers whose consequences often last beyond their initial objectives. At this later point in the process the very same capitalists who pressed their national governments to impose the restrictions now find these restrictions constraining. This is not an 'internationalization' of 'national' capital. This is simply a new political demand by certain sectors of the capitalist classes who have at all points in time sought to maximize their profits within the real economic market, that of the world-economy.

If this is so, then what meaning does it have to talk of structural positions within this economy and identify states as being in one of these positions? And why talk of three positions, inserting that of 'semi-periphery' in between the widely-used concepts of core and periphery? The state-machineries of the core states were strengthened to meet the needs of capitalist landowners and their merchant allies. But that does not mean that these state-machineries were manipulable puppets. Obviously any organization, once created, has a certain autonomy from those who pressed it into existence for two reasons. It creates a stratum of officials whose own careers and interests are furthered by the continued strengthening of the organization itself, however the interests of its capitalist backers may vary. Kings and bureaucrats wanted to stay in power and increase their personal gain constantly. Secondly, in the process of creating the strong state in the first place, certain 'constitutional' compromises had to be made with other forces within the state-boundaries and these institutionalized compromises limit, as they are designed to do, the freedom of maneuver of the managers of the state-machinery. The formula of the state as 'executive committee of the ruling class' is only valid, therefore, if one bears in mind that executive committees are never mere reflections of

[38] Charles Bettelheim, 'Theoretical Comments' in Emmanuel, *op. cit.*, 295.

THE WORLD CAPITALIST SYSTEM 403

the wills of their constituents, as anyone who has ever participated in any organization knows well.

The strengthening of the state-machineries in core areas has as its direct counterpart the decline of the state-machineries in peripheral areas. The decline of the Polish monarchy in the sixteenth and seventeenth centuries is a striking example of this phenomenon.[39] There are two reasons for this. In peripheral countries, the interests of the capitalist landowners lie in an opposite direction from those of the local commercial bourgeoisie. Their interests lie in maintaining an open economy to maximize their profit from world-market trade (no restrictions in exports and access to lower-cost industrial products from core countries) and in elimination of the commercial bourgeoisie in favor of outside merchants (who pose no local political threat). Thus, in terms of the state, the coalition which strengthened it in core countries was precisely absent.

The second reason, which has become ever more operative over the history of the modern world-system, is that the strength of the state-machinery in core states is a function of the weakness of other state-machineries. Hence intervention of outsiders via war, subversion, and diplomacy is the lot of peripheral states.

All this seems very obvious. I repeat it only in order to make clear two points. One cannot reasonably explain the strength of various state-machineries at specific moments of the history of the modern world-system primarily in terms of a genetic-cultural line of argumentation, but rather in terms of the structural role a country plays in the world-economy at that moment in time. To be sure, the initial eligibility for a particular role is often decided by an accidental edge a particular country has, and the 'accident' of which one is talking is no doubt located in part in past history, in part in current geography. But once this relatively minor accident is given, it is the operations of the world-market forces which accentuate the differences, institutionalize them, and make them impossible to surmount over the short run.

The second point we wish to make about the structural differences of core and periphery is that they are not comprehensible unless we realize that there is a third structural position: that of the semi-periphery. This is not the result merely of establishing arbitrary cutting-points on a continuum of characteristics. Our logic is not merely inductive, sensing the presence of a third category from a comparison of indicator curves. It is also deductive. The semi-periphery is needed to make a capitalist world-economy run smoothly. Both kinds of world-system, the world-empire

---

[39] See J. Siemenski, 'Constitutional Conditions in the Fifteenth and Sixteenth Centuries', *Cambridge History of Poland, I*, W. F. Reddaway *et al.* (eds.), *From the Origins to Sobieski (to 1696)* (Cambridge: At the University Press, 1950), pp. 416–40; Janusz Tazbir, 'The Commonwealth of the Gentry', in Aleksander Gieysztor *et al.*, *History of Poland* (Warszawa: PWN—Polish Scientific Publ., 1968), pp. 169–271.

404 IMMANUEL WALLERSTEIN

with a redistributive economy and the world-economy with a capitalist market economy, involve markedly unequal distribution of rewards. Thus, logically, there is immediately posed the question of how it is possible politically for such a system to persist. Why do not the majority who are exploited simply overwhelm the minority who draw disproportionate benefits? The most rapid glance at the historic record shows that these world-systems have been faced rather rarely by fundamental system-wide insurrection. While internal discontent has been eternal, it has usually taken quite long before the accumulation of the erosion of power has led to the decline of a world-system, and as often as not, an external force has been a major factor in this decline.

There have been three major mechanisms that have enabled world-systems to retain relative political stability (not in terms of the particular groups who will play the leading roles in the system, but in terms of systemic survival itself). One obviously is the concentration of military strength in the hands of the dominant forces. The modalities of this obviously vary with the technology, and there are to be sure political prerequisites for such a concentration, but nonetheless sheer force is no doubt a central consideration.

A second mechanism is the pervasiveness of an ideological commitment to the system as a whole. I do not mean what has often been termed the 'legitimation' of a system, because that term has been used to imply that the lower strata of a system feel some affinity with or loyalty towards the rulers, and I doubt that this has ever been a significant factor in the survival of world-systems. I mean rather the degree to which the staff or cadres of the system (and I leave this term deliberately vague) feel that their own well-being is wrapped up in the survival of the system as such and the competence of its leaders. It is this staff which not only propagates the myths; it is they who believe them.

But neither force nor the ideological commitment of the staff would suffice were it not for the division of the majority into a larger lower stratum and a smaller middle stratum. Both the revolutionary call for polarization as a strategy of change and the liberal encomium to consensus as the basis of the liberal polity reflect this proposition. The import is far wider than its use in the analysis of contemporary political problems suggests. It is the normal condition of either kind of world-system to have a three-layered structure. When and if this ceases to be the case, the world-system disintegrates.

In a world-empire, the middle stratum is in fact accorded the role of maintaining the marginally-desirable long-distance luxury trade, while the upper stratum concentrates its resources on controlling the military machinery which can collect the tribute, the crucial mode of redistributing surplus. By providing, however, for an access to a limited portion of the

THE WORLD CAPITALIST SYSTEM 405

surplus to urbanized elements who alone, in pre-modern societies, could contribute political cohesiveness to isolated clusters of primary producers, the upper stratum effectively buys off the potential leadership of co-ordinated revolt. And by denying access to political rights for this commercial-urban middle stratum, it makes them constantly vulnerable to confiscatory measures whenever their economic profits become sufficiently swollen so that they might begin to create for themselves military strength.

In a world-economy, such 'cultural' stratification is not so simple, because the absence of a single political system means the concentration of economic roles vertically rather than horizontally throughout the system. The solution then is to have three *kinds* of states, with pressures for cultural homogenization within each of them—thus, besides the upper stratum of core-states and the lower stratum of peripheral states, there is a middle stratum of semi-peripheral ones.

This semi-periphery is then assigned as it were a specific economic role, but the reason is less economic than political. That is to say, one might make a good case that the world-economy as an economy would function every bit as well without a semi-periphery. But it would be far less *politically* stable, for it would mean a polarized world-system. The existence of the third category means precisely that the upper stratum is not faced with the *unified* opposition of all the others because the *middle* stratum is both exploited and exploiter. It follows that the specific economic role is not all that important, and has thus changed through the various historical stages of the modern world-system. We shall discuss these changes shortly.

Where then does class analysis fit in all of this? And what in such a formulation are nations, nationalities, peoples, ethnic groups? First of all, without arguing the point now,[40] I would contend that all these latter terms denote variants of a single phenomenon which I will term 'ethno-nations'.

Both classes and ethnic groups, or status-groups, or ethno-nations are phenomena of world-economies and much of the enormous confusion that has surrounded the concrete analysis of their functioning can be attributed quite simply to the fact that they have been analyzed as though they existed within the nation-states of this world-economy, instead of within the world-economy as a whole. This has been a Procrustean bed indeed.

The range of economic activities being far wider in the core than in the periphery, the range of syndical interest groups is far wider there.[41] Thus,

---

[40] See my fuller analysis in 'Social Conflict in Post-Independence Black Africa: The Concepts of Race and Status-Group Reconsidered' in Ernest W. Campbell (ed.), *Racial Tensions and National Identity* (Nashville: Vanderbilt Univ. Press, 1972), pp. 207–26.

[41] Range in this sentence means the number of different occupations in which a significant proportion of the population is engaged. Thus peripheral society typically is overwhelmingly agricultural. A core society typically has its occupations well-distributed over all of Colin Clark's three sectors. If one shifted the connotation of range to talk of style of life, consumption patterns, even income distribution, quite possibly one might reverse the correlation. In a typical peripheral society, the differences between a subsistence farmer and an urban professional are probably far greater than those which could be found in a typical core state.

406 IMMANUEL WALLERSTEIN

it has been widely observed that there does not exist in many parts of the world today a proletariat of the kind which exists in, say, Europe or North America. But this is a confusing way to state the observation. Industrial activity being disproportionately concentrated in certain parts of the world-economy, industrial wage-workers are to be found principally in certain geographic regions. Their interests as a syndical group are determined by their collective relationship to the world-economy. Their ability to influence the political functioning of this world-economy is shaped by the fact that they command larger percentages of the population in one sovereign entity than another. The form their organizations take have, in large part, been governed too by these political boundaries. The same might be said about industrial capitalists. Class analysis is perfectly capable of accounting for the political position of, let us say, French skilled workers if we look at their structural position and interests in the world-economy. Similarly with ethno-nations. The meaning of ethnic consciousness in a core area is considerably different from that of ethnic consciousness in a peripheral area precisely because of the different class position such ethnic groups have in the world-economy.[42]

Political struggles of ethno-nations or segments of classes within national boundaries of course are the daily bread and butter of local politics. But their significance or consequences can only be fruitfully analyzed if one spells out the implications of their organizational activity or political demands for the functioning of the world-economy. This also incidentally makes possible more rational assessments of these politics in terms of some set of evaluative criteria such as 'left' and 'right'.

The functioning then of a capitalist world-economy requires that groups pursue their economic interests within a single world market while seeking to distort this market for their benefit by organizing to exert influence on states, some of which are far more powerful than others but none of which controls the world-market in its entirety. Of course, we shall find on closer inspection that there are periods where one state is relatively quite powerful and other periods where power is more diffuse and contested, permitting weaker states broader ranges of action. We can talk then of the relative tightness or looseness of the world-system as an important variable and seek to analyze why this dimension tends to be cyclical in nature, as it seems to have been for several hundred years.

We are now in a position to look at the historical evolution of this capitalist world-economy itself and analyze the degree to which it is fruitful to talk of distinct stages in its evolution as a system. The emergence of the European world-economy in the 'long' sixteenth century (1450–

---

[42] See my 'The Two Modes of Ethnic Consciousness: Soviet Central Asia in Transition?' in Edward Allworth (ed.), *The Nationality Question in Soviet Central Asia* (New York: Praeger, 1973), pp. 168–75.

THE WORLD CAPITALIST SYSTEM 407

1640) was made possible by an historical conjuncture: on those long-term trends which were the culmination of what has been sometimes described as the 'crisis of feudalism' was superimposed a more immediate cyclical crisis plus climatic changes, all of which created a dilemma that could only be resolved by a geographic expansion of the division of labor. Furthermore, the balance of inter-system forces was such as to make this realizable. Thus a geographic expansion did take place in conjunction with a demographic expansion and an upward price rise.

The remarkable thing was not that a European world-economy was thereby created, but that it survived the Hapsburg attempt to transform it into a world-empire, an attempt seriously pursued by Charles V. The Spanish attempt to absorb the whole failed because the rapid economic-demographic-technological burst forward of the preceding century made the whole enterprise too expensive for the imperial base to sustain, especially given many structural insufficiencies in Castilian economic development. Spain could afford neither the bureaucracy nor the army that was necessary to the enterprise, and in the event went bankrupt, as did the French monarchs making a similar albeit even less plausible attempt.

Once the Hapsburg dream of world-empire was over—and in 1557 it was over forever—the capitalist world-economy was an established system that became almost impossible to unbalance. It quickly reached an equilibrium point in its relations with other world-systems: the Ottoman and Russian world-empires, the Indian Ocean proto-world-economy. Each of the states or potential states within the European world-economy was quickly in the race to bureaucratize, to raise a standing army, to homogenize its culture, to diversify its economic activities. By 1640, those in northwest Europe had succeeded in establishing themselves as the core-states; Spain and the northern Italian city-states declined into being semi-peripheral; northeastern Europe and Iberian America had become the periphery. At this point, those in semi-peripheral status had reached it by virtue of decline from a former more pre-eminent status.

It was the system-wide recession of 1650–1730 that consolidated the European world-economy and opened stage two of the modern world-economy. For the recession forced retrenchment, and the decline in relative surplus allowed room for only one core-state to survive. The mode of struggle was mercantilism, which was a device of partial insulation and withdrawal from the world market of *large* areas themselves hierarchically constructed—that is, empires within the world-economy (which is quite different from world-empires). In this struggle England first ousted the Netherlands from its commercial primacy and then resisted successfully France's attempt to catch up. As England began to speed up the process of industrialization after 1760, there was one last attempt of those capitalist

408 IMMANUEL WALLERSTEIN

forces located in France to break the imminent British hegemony. This attempt was expressed first in the French Revolution's replacement of the cadres of the regime and then in Napoleon's continental blockade. But it failed.

Stage three of the capitalist world-economy begins then, a stage of industrial rather than of agricultural capitalism. Henceforth, industrial production is no longer a minor aspect of the world market but comprises an ever larger percentage of world gross production—and even more important, of world gross surplus. This involves a whole series of consequences for the world-system.

First of all, it led to the further geographic expansion of the European world-economy to include now the whole of the globe. This was in part the result of its technological feasibility both in terms of improved military firepower and improved shipping facilities which made regular trade sufficiently inexpensive to be viable. But, in addition, industrial production *required* access to raw materials of a nature and in a quantity such that the needs could not be supplied within the former boundaries. At first, however, the search for new markets was not a primary consideration in the geographic expansion since the new markets were more readily available within the old boundaries, as we shall see.

The geographic expansion of the European world-economy meant the elimination of other world-systems as well as the absorption of the remaining mini-systems. The most important world-system up to then outside of the European world-economy, Russia, entered in semi-peripheral status, the consequence of the strength of its state-machinery (including its army) and the degree of industrialization already achieved in the eighteenth century. The independences in the Latin American countries did nothing to change their peripheral status. They merely eliminated the last vestiges of Spain's semi-peripheral role and ended pockets of non-involvement in the world-economy in the interior of Latin America. Asia and Africa were absorbed into the periphery in the nineteenth century, although Japan, because of the combination of the strength of its state-machinery, the poverty of its resource base (which led to a certain disinterest on the part of world capitalist forces), and its geographic remoteness from the core areas, was able quickly to graduate into semi-peripheral status.

The absorption of Africa as part of the periphery meant the end of slavery world-wide for two reasons. First of all, the manpower that was used as slaves was now needed for cash-crop production in Africa itself, whereas in the eighteenth century Europeans had sought to *discourage* just such cash-crop production.[43] In the second place, once Africa was part of

---

[43] A. Adu Boahen cites the instructions of the British Board of Trade in 1751 to the Governor of Cape Castle (a small British fort and trading-settlement in what is now Ghana) to seek to stop the local people, the Fante, from cultivating cotton. The reason given was the

THE WORLD CAPITALIST SYSTEM 409

the periphery and not the external arena, slavery was no longer economic. To understand this, we must appreciate the economics of slavery. Slaves receiving the lowest conceivable reward for their labor are the least productive form of labor and have the shortest life span, both because of undernourishment and maltreatment and because of lowered psychic resistance to death. Furthermore, if recruited from areas surrounding their workplace the escape rate is too high. Hence, there must be a high transport cost for a product of low productivity. This makes economic sense only if the purchase price is virtually nil. In capitalist market trade, purchase always has a real cost. It is only in long-distance trade, the exchange of preciosities, that the purchase price can be in the social system of the purchaser virtually nil. Such was the slave-trade. Slaves were bought at low immediate cost (the production cost of the items actually exchanged) and none of the usual invisible costs. That is to say, the fact that removing a man from West Africa lowered the productive potential of the region was of *zero* cost to the European world-economy since these areas were not part of the division of labor. Of course, had the slave trade totally denuded Africa of all possibilities of furnishing further slaves, then a real cost to Europe would have commenced. But that point was never historically reached. Once, however, Africa was part of the periphery, then the real cost of a slave in terms of the production of surplus in the world-economy went up to such a point that it became far more economical to use wage-labor, even on sugar or cotton plantations, which is precisely what transpired in the nineteenth-century Caribbean and other slave-labor regions.

The creation of vast new areas as the periphery of the expanded world-economy made possible a shift in the role of some other areas. Specifically, both the United States and Germany (as it came into being) combined formerly peripheral and semi-peripheral regions. The manufacturing sector in each was able to gain political ascendancy, as the peripheral subregions became less economically crucial to the world-economy. Mercantilism now became the major tool of semi-peripheral countries seeking to become core countries, thus still performing a function analogous to that of the mercantilist drives of the late seventeenth and eighteenth centuries in England and France. To be sure, the struggle of semi-peripheral countries to 'industrialize' varied in the degree to which it succeeded in the period before the First World War: all the way in the United States, only partially in Germany, not at all in Russia.

following: 'The introduction of culture and industry among the Negroes is contrary to the known established policy of this country, there is no saying where this might stop, and that it might extend to tobacco, sugar and every other commodity which we now take from our colonies; and thereby the Africans, who now support themselves by wars, would become planters and their slaves be employed in the culture of these articles in Africa, which they are employed in in America'. Cited in A. Adu Boahen, *Topics in West Africa History* (London: Longmans, Green and Co., 1966), p. 113.

410 IMMANUEL WALLERSTEIN

The internal structure of core-states also changed fundamentally under industrial capitalism. For a core area, industrialism involved divesting itself of substantially all agricultural activities (except that in the twentieth century further mechanization was to create a new form of working the land that was so highly mechanized as to warrant the appellation industrial). Thus whereas, in the period 1700–40, England not only was Europe's leading industrial exporter but was also Europe's leading agricultural exporter—this was at a high point in the economy-wide recession—by 1900, less than 10 percent of England's population were engaged in agricultural pursuits.

At first under industrial capitalism, the core exchanged manufactured products against the periphery's agricultural products—hence, Britain from 1815 to 1873 as the 'workshop of the world'. Even to those semi-peripheral countries that had some manufacture (France, Germany, Belgium, the U.S.), Britain in this period supplied about half their needs in manufactured goods. As, however, the mercantilist practices of this latter group both cut Britain off from outlets and even created competiton for Britain in sales to peripheral areas, a competition which led to the late nineteenth-century 'scramble for Africa', the world division of labor was reallocated to ensure a new special role for the core: less the provision of the manufactures, more the provision of the machines to make the manufactures as well as the provision of infra-structure (especially, in this period, railroads).

The rise of manufacturing created for the first time under capitalism a large-scale urban proletariat. And in consequence for the first time there arose what Michels has called the 'anti-capitalist mass spirit',[44] which was translated into concrete organizational forms (trade-unions, socialist parties). This development intruded a new factor as threatening to the stability of the states and of the capitalist forces now so securely in control of them as the earlier centrifugal thrusts of regional anti-capitalist landed elements had been in the seventeenth century.

At the same time that the bourgeoisies of the core countries were faced by this threat to the internal stability of their state structures, they were simultaneously faced with the economic crisis of the latter third of the nineteenth century resulting from the more rapid increase of agricultural production (and indeed of light manufactures) than the expansion of a potential market for these goods. Some of the surplus would have to be redistributed to someone to allow these goods to be bought and the economic machinery to return to smooth operation. By expanding the purchasing power of the industrial proletariat of the core countries, the world-economy was unburdened simultaneously of two problems: the

[44] Robert Michels, 'The Origins of the Anti-Capitalist Mass Spirit', in *Man in Contemporary Society* (New York: Columbia University Press, 1955), Vol. I, pp. 740–65.

THE WORLD CAPITALIST SYSTEM 411

bottleneck of demand, and the unsettling 'class conflict' of the core states—hence, the social liberalism or welfare-state ideology that arose just at that point in time

The First World War was, as men of the time observed, the end of an era; and the Russian Revolution of October 1917 the beginning of a new one—our stage four. This stage was to be sure a stage of revolutionary turmoil but it also was, in a seeming paradox, the stage of the *consolidation* of the industrial capitalist world-economy. The Russian Revolution was essentially that of a semi-peripheral country whose internal balance of forces had been such that as of the late nineteenth century it began on a decline towards a peripheral status. This was the result of the marked penetration of foreign capital into the industrial sector which was on its way to eliminating all indigenous capitalist forces, the resistance to the mechanization of the agricultural sector, the decline of relative military power (as evidenced by the defeat by the Japanese in 1905). The Revolution brought to power a group of state-managers who reversed each one of these trends by using the classic technique of mercantilist semi-withdrawal from the world-economy. In the process of doing this, the now U.S.S.R. mobilized considerable popular support, especially in the urban sector. At the end of the Second World War, Russia was reinstated as a very strong member of the semi-periphery and could begin to seek full core status.

Meanwhile, the decline of Britain which dates from 1873 was confirmed and its hegemonic role was assumed by the United States. While the U.S. thus rose, Germany fell further behind as a result of its military defeat. Various German attempts in the 1920s to find new industrial outlets in the Middle East and South America were unsuccessful in the face of the U.S. thrust combined with Britain's continuing relative strength. Germany's thrust of desperation to recoup lost ground took the noxious and unsuccessful form of Nazism.

It was the Second World War that enabled the United States for a brief period (1945–65) to attain the same level of primacy as Britain had in the first part of the nineteenth century. United States growth in this period was spectacular and created a great need for expanded market outlets. The Cold War closure denied not only the U.S.S.R. but Eastern Europe to U.S. exports. And the Chinese Revolution meant that this region, which had been destined for much exploitative activity, was also cut off. Three alternative areas were available and each was pursued with assiduity. First, Western Europe had to be rapidly 'reconstructed', and it was the Marshall Plan which thus allowed this area to play a primary role in the expansion of world productivity. Secondly, Latin America became the reserve of U.S. investment from which now Britain and Germany were completely cut off. Thirdly, Southern Asia, the Middle East and Africa had

412 IMMANUEL WALLERSTEIN

to be decolonized. On the one hand, this was necessary in order to reduce the share of the surplus taken by the Western European intermediaries, as Canning covertly supported the Latin American revolutionaries against Spain in the 1820s.[45] But also, these countries had to be decolonized in order to mobilize productive potential in a way that had never been achieved in the colonial era. Colonial rule after all had been an *inferior* mode of relationship of core and periphery, one occasioned by the strenuous late-nineteenth-century conflict among industrial states but one no longer desirable from the point of view of the new hegemonic power.[46]

But a world capitalist economy does not permit true imperium. Charles V could not succeed in his dream of world-empire. The Pax Britannica stimulated its own demise. So too did the Pax Americana. In each case, the cost of *political* imperium was too high economically, and in a capitalist system, over the middle run when profits decline, new *political* formulae are sought. In this case the costs mounted along several fronts. The efforts of the U.S.S.R. to further its own industrialization, protect a privileged market area (eastern Europe), and force entry into other market areas led to an immense spiralling of military expenditure, which on the Soviet side promised long-run returns whereas for the U.S. it was merely a question of running very fast to stand still. The economic resurgence of western Europe, made necessary both to provide markets for U.S. sales and investments and to counter the U.S.S.R. military thrust, meant over time that the west European state structures collectively became as strong as that of the U.S., which led in the late 1960s to the 'dollar and gold crisis' and the retreat of Nixon from the free-trade stance which is the definitive mark of the self-confident leader in a capitalist market system. When the cumulated Third World pressures, most notably Vietnam, were added on, a restructuring of the world division of labor was inevitable, involving probably in the 1970s a quadripartite division of the larger part of the world surplus by the U.S., the European Common Market, Japan, and the U.S.S.R.

Such a decline in U.S. state hegemony has actually *increased* the freedom of action of capitalist enterprises, the larger of which have now taken the form of multinational corporations which are able to maneuver against state bureaucracies whenever the national politicians become too responsive to internal worker pressures. Whether some effective links can be established between multinational corporations, presently limited to operating in certain areas, and the U.S.S.R. remains to be seen, but it is by no means impossible.

---

[45] See William W. Kaufman, *British Policy and the Independence of Latin America, 1804–28* (New Haven: Yale University Press, 1951).

[46] Cf. Cathérine Coquéry-Vidrovitch, 'De l'impérialisme britannique à l'impérialisme contemporaine—l'avatar colonial,' *L'Homme et la société*, No. 18, oct.–nov.–déc. 1970, 61–90.

THE WORLD CAPITALIST SYSTEM 413

This brings us back to one of the questions with which we opened this paper, the seemingly esoteric debate between Liu Shao-Chi and Mao Tse-Tung as to whether China was, as Liu argued, a socialist state, or whether, as Mao argued, socialism was a *process* involving continued and continual class struggle. No doubt to those to whom the terminology is foreign the discussion seems abstrusely theological. The issue, however, as we said, is real. If the Russian Revolution emerged as a reaction to the threatened further decline of Russia's structural position in the world-economy, and if fifty years later one can talk of the U.S.S.R. as entering the status of a core power in a *capitalist* world-economy, what then is the meaning of the various so-called socialist revolutions that have occurred in a third of the world's surface? First let us notice that it has been neither Thailand nor Liberia nor Paraguay that has had a 'socialist revolution' but Russia, China and Cuba. That is to say, these revolutions have occurred in countries that, in terms of their internal economic structures in the pre-revolutionary period, had a certain minimum strength in terms of skilled personnel, some manufacturing, and other factors which made it plausible that, within the framework of a capitalist world-economy, such a country could alter its role in the world division of labor within a reasonable period (say 30–50 years) by the use of the technique of mercantilist semi-withdrawal. (This may not be all that plausible for Cuba, but we shall see.) Of course, other countries in the geographic regions and military orbit of these revolutionary forces had changes of regime without in any way having these characteristics (for example, Mongolia or Albania). It is also to be noted that many of the countries where similar forces are strong or where considerable counterforce is required to keep them from emerging also share this status of minimum strength. I think of Chile or Brazil or Egypt—or indeed Italy.

Are we not seeing the emergence of a political structure for *semi-peripheral* nations adapted to stage four of the capitalist world-system? The fact that all enterprises are nationalized in these countries does not make the participation of these enterprises in the world-economy one that does not conform to the mode of operation of a capitalist market-system: seeking increased efficiency of production in order to realize a maximum price on sales, thus achieving a more favorable allocation of the surplus of the world-economy. If tomorrow U.S. Steel became a worker's collective in which all employees without exception received an identical share of the profits and all stockholders were expropriated without compensation, would U.S. Steel thereby cease to be a capitalist enterprise operating in a capitalist world-economy?

What then have been the consequences for the world-system of the emergence of many states in which there is no private ownership of the basic means of production? To some extent, this has meant an internal

414 IMMANUEL WALLERSTEIN

reallocation of consumption. It has certainly undermined the ideological justifications in world capitalism, both by showing the political vulnerability of capitalist entrepreneurs and by demonstrating that private ownership is irrelevant to the rapid expansion of industrial productivity. But to the extent that it has raised the ability of the new semi-peripheral areas to enjoy a larger share of the world surplus, it has once again depolarized the world, recreating the triad of strata that has been a fundamental element in the survival of the world-system.

Finally, in the peripheral areas of the world-economy, both the continued economic expansion of the core (even though the core is seeing some reallocation of surplus internal to it) and the new strength of the semi-periphery has led to a further weakening of the political and hence economic position of the peripheral areas. The pundits note that 'the gap is getting wider', but thus far no-one has succeeded in doing much about it, and it is not clear that there are very many in whose interests it would be to do so. Far from a strengthening of state authority, in many parts of the world we are witnessing the same kind of deterioration Poland knew in the sixteenth century, a deterioration of which the frequency of military coups is only one of many signposts. And all of this leads us to conclude that stage four has been the stage of the *consolidation* of the capitalist world-economy.

Consolidation, however, does not mean the absence of contradictions and does not mean the likelihood of long-term survival. We thus come to projections about the future, which has always been man's great game, his true *hybris*, the most convincing argument for the dogma of original sin. Having read Dante, I will therefore be brief.

There are two fundamental contradictions, it seems to me, involved in the workings of the capitalist world-system. In the first place, there is the contradiction to which the nineteenth-century Marxian corpus pointed, which I would phrase as follows: whereas in the short-run the maximization of profit requires maximizing the withdrawal of surplus from immediate consumption of the majority, in the long-run the continued production of surplus requires a mass demand which can only be created by redistributing the surplus withdrawn. Since these two considerations move in opposite directions (a 'contradiction'), the system has constant crises which in the long-run both weaken it and make the game for those with privilege less worth playing.

The second fundamental contradiction, to which Mao's concept of socialism as process points, is the following: whenever the tenants of privilege seek to co-opt an oppositional movement by including them in a minor share of the privilege, they may no doubt eliminate opponents in the short-run; but they also up the ante for the next oppositional movement created in the next crisis of the world-economy. Thus the cost of 'co-op-

THE WORLD CAPITALIST SYSTEM 415

tion' rises ever higher and the advantages of co-option seem ever less worthwhile.

There are today no socialist systems in the world-economy any more than there are feudal systems because there is only *one* world-system. It is a world-economy and it is by definition capitalist in form. Socialism involves the creation of a new kind of *world*-system, neither a redistributive world-empire nor a capitalist world-economy but a socialist world-government. I don't see this projection as being in the least utopian but I also don't feel its institution is imminent. It will be the outcome of a long struggle in forms that may be familiar and perhaps in very new forms, that will take place in *all* the areas of the world-economy (Mao's continual 'class struggle'). Governments may be in the hands of persons, groups or movements sympathetic to this transformation but *states* as such are neither progressive nor reactionary. It is movements and forces that deserve such evaluative judgments.

Having gone as far as I care to in projecting the future, let me return to the present and to the scholarly enterprise which is never neutral but does have its own logic and to some extent its own priorities. We have adumbrated as our basic unit of observation a concept of world-systems that have structural parts and evolving stages. It is within such a framework, I am arguing, that we can fruitfully make comparative analyses—of the wholes and of parts of the whole. Conceptions precede and govern measurements. I am all for minute and sophisticated quantitative indicators. I am all for minute and diligent archival work that will trace a concrete historical series of events in terms of all its immediate complexities. But the point of either is to enable us to see better what has happened and what is happening. For that we need glasses with which to discern the dimensions of difference, we need models with which to weigh significance, we need summarizing concepts with which to create the knowledge which we then seek to communicate to each other. And all this because we are men with hybris and original sin and therefore seek the good, the true, and the beautiful.

[10]

THE 'NEW' IMPERIALISM: ACCUMULATION BY DISPOSSESSION

DAVID HARVEY

The survival of capitalism for so long in the face of multiple crises and reorganizations accompanied by dire predictions, from both the left and the right, of its imminent demise, is a mystery that requires illumination. Lefebvre, for one, thought he had found the key in his celebrated comment that capitalism survives through the production of space, but he did not explain exactly how this might be so.[1] Both Lenin and Luxemburg, for quite different reasons and utilizing quite different forms of argument, considered that imperialism – a certain form of the production of space – was the answer to the riddle, though both argued that this solution was finite because of its own terminal contradictions.

The way I sought to look at this problem in the 1970s was to examine the role of 'spatio-temporal fixes' to the inner contradictions of capital accumulation.[2] This argument makes sense only in relation to a pervasive tendency of capitalism, understood theoretically by way of Marx's theory of the falling rate of profit, to produce crises of overaccumulation.[3] Such crises are registered as surpluses of capital and of labour power side by side without there apparently being any means to bring them profitably together to accomplish socially useful tasks. If system-wide devaluations (and even destruction) of capital and of labour power are not to follow, then ways must be found to absorb these surpluses. Geographical expansion and spatial reorganization provide one such option. But this cannot be divorced from temporal fixes either, since geographical expansion often entails investment in long-lived physical and social infrastructures (in transport and communications networks and education and research, for example) that take many years to return their value to circulation through the productive activity they support.

64   SOCIALIST REGISTER 2004

Global capitalism has experienced a chronic and enduring problem of over-accumulation since the 1970s. I find the empirical materials Brenner assembles to document this point generally convincing.[4] I interpret the volatility of international capitalism during these years, however, as a series of temporary spatio-temporal fixes that failed even in the medium run to deal with problems of overaccumulation. It was, as Gowan argues, through the orchestration of such volatility that the United States sought to preserve its hegemonic position within global capitalism.[5] The recent apparent shift towards an open imperialism backed by military force on the part of the US may then be seen as a sign of the weakening of that hegemony before the serious threat of recession and widespread devaluation at home, as opposed to the various bouts of devaluation formerly inflicted elsewhere (Latin America in the 1980s and early 1990s, and, even more seriously, the crisis that consumed East and South-East Asia in 1997 and then engulfed Russia and much of Latin America). But I also want to argue that the inability to accumulate through expanded reproduction on a sustained basis has been paralleled by a rise in attempts to accumulate by dispossession.[6] This, I then conclude, is the hallmark of what some like to call ' the new imperialism' is about.[7]

THE SPATIO-TEMPORAL FIX AND ITS CONTRADICTIONS

The basic idea of the spatio-temporal fix is simple enough. Overaccumulation within a given territorial system means a condition of surpluses of labour (rising unemployment) and surpluses of capital (registered as a glut of commodities on the market that cannot be disposed of without a loss, as idle productive capacity, and/or as surpluses of money capital lacking outlets for productive and profitable investment). Such surpluses may be absorbed by: (a) temporal displacement through investment in long-term capital projects or social expenditures (such as education and research) that defer the re-entry of current excess capital values into circulation well into the future, (b) spatial displacements through opening up new markets, new production capacities and new resource, social and labour possibilities elsewhere, or (c) some combination of (a) and (b).

The combination of (a) and (b) is particularly important when we focus on fixed capital of an independent kind embedded in the built environment. This provides the necessary physical infrastructures for production and consumption to proceed over space and time (everything from industrial parks, ports and airports, transport and communications systems, to sewage and water provision, housing, hospitals, schools). Plainly, this is not a minor sector of the economy and it is capable of absorbing massive amounts of capital and labour, particularly under conditions of rapid geographical expansion and intensification.

The reallocation of capital and labour surpluses to such investments requires the mediating help of financial and/or state institutions. These have the capacity to generate credit. A quantity of 'fictitious capital' is created that can be allocated away from current consumption to future-oriented projects in, say, highway

THE 'NEW' IMPERIALISM   65

construction or education, thereby re-invigorating the economy (including, perhaps, augmenting the demand for surplus commodities like shirts and shoes by teachers and construction workers).[8] If the expenditures on built environments or social improvements prove productive (i.e. facilitative of more efficient forms of capital accumulation later on) then the fictitious values are redeemed (either directly by retirement of debt or indirectly in the form of, say, higher tax returns to pay off state debt). If not, overaccumulations of values in built environments or education can become evident with attendant devaluations of these assets (housing, offices, industrial parks, airports, etc.) or difficulties in paying off state debts on physical and social infrastructures (a fiscal crisis of the state).

The role of such investments in stabilizing and destabilizing capitalism has been significant. I note, for example, that the starting point of the crisis of 1973 was a world-wide collapse of property markets (beginning with the Herstatt Bank in Germany which brought down the Franklin National in the United States), followed shortly thereafter by the virtual bankruptcy of New York City in 1975 (a classic case of social expenditures outrunning tax revenues); that the beginning of the decade-long stagnation in Japan in 1990 was a collapse of the speculative bubble in land, property and other asset prices, putting the whole banking system in jeopardy; that the beginning of the Asian collapse in 1997 was the bursting of the property bubbles in Thailand and Indonesia; and that the most important prop to the US and British economies after the onset of general recession in all other sectors from mid-2001 onwards has been the continued speculative vigour in property markets. Since 1998, the Chinese have kept their economy growing and sought to absorb their labour surpluses (and curb the threat of social unrest) by debt-financed investment in huge mega-projects that dwarf the already huge Three Gorges Dam (8,500 miles of new railroads, superhighways and urbanization projects, massive engineering works to divert water from the Yangtze to Yellow Rivers, new airports, etc.). It is, I think, passing strange that most accounts of capital accumulation (including Brenner's) either ignore these matters entirely or treat them as epiphenomal.

The term 'fix' has, however, a double meaning. A certain portion of the total capital becomes literally fixed in some physical form for a relatively long period of time (depending on its economic and physical lifetime). There is a sense in which social expenditures also become territorialized and rendered geographically immobile through state commitments. (In what follows, however, I will exclude social infrastructures from explicit consideration since the matter is complicated and would take too much text to elucidate). Some fixed capital is geographically mobile (such as machinery that can easily be unbolted from its moorings and taken elsewhere) but the rest is so fixed in the land that it cannot be moved without being destroyed. Aircraft are mobile but the airports to which they fly are not.

The spatio-temporal 'fix', on the other hand, is a metaphor for solutions to capitalist crises through temporal deferment and geographical expansion. The production of space, the organization of wholly new territorial divisions of

66 SOCIALIST REGISTER 2004

labour, the opening up of new and cheaper resource complexes, of new dynamic spaces of capital accumulation, and the penetration of pre-existing social formations by capitalist social relations and institutional arrangements (such as rules of contract and private property arrangements) provide multiple ways to absorb existing capital and labour surpluses. Such geographical expansions, reorganizations and reconstructions often threaten, however, the values fixed in place but not yet realized. Vast quantities of capital fixed in place act as a drag upon the search for a spatial fix elsewhere. The values of the fixed assets that constitute New York City were and are not trivial and the threat of their massive devaluation in 1975 (and now again in 2003) was (and is) viewed by many as a major threat to the future of capitalism. If capital does move out, it leaves behind a trail of devastation (the de-industrialization experienced in the 1970s and 1980s in the heartlands of capitalism, like Pittsburgh and Sheffield, as well as in many other parts of the world, such as Bombay illustrates the point). If overaccumulated capital does not or cannot move, on the other hand, then it stands to be devalued directly. The summary statement of this process I usually offer is this: capital necessarily creates a physical landscape in its own image at one point in time only to have to destroy it at some later point in time as it pursues geographical expansions and temporal displacements as solutions to the crises of overaccumulation to which it is regularly prone. Thus is the history of creative destruction (with all manner of deleterious social and environmental consequences) written into the evolution of the physical and social landscape of capitalism.

Another series of contradictions arises within the dynamics of spatio-temporal transformations more generally. If the surpluses of capital and labour power exist within a given territory (such as a nation state) and cannot be absorbed internally (either by geographical adjustments or social expenditures) then they must be sent elsewhere to find a fresh terrain for their profitable realization if they are not to be devalued. This can happen in a number of ways. Markets for commodity surpluses can be found elsewhere. But the spaces to which the surpluses are sent must possess means of payment such as gold or currency (e.g. dollar) reserves or tradable commodities. Surpluses of commodities are sent out and money or commodities flow back. The problem of overaccumulation is alleviated only in the short term; it merely switches the surplus from commodities to money or into different commodity forms, though if the latter turn out, as is often the case, to be cheaper raw materials or other inputs they can relieve the downward pressure on the profit rate at home temporarily. If the territory does not possess reserves or commodities to trade back, it must either find them (as Britain forced India to do by opening up the opium trade with China in the nineteenth century and thus extracting Chinese gold via Indian trade) or be given credit or aid. In the latter case a territory is lent or donated the money with which to buy back the surplus commodities generated at home. The British did this with Argentina in the nineteenth century and Japanese trade surpluses during the 1990s were largely absorbed by lending to the United States to support the consumerism that purchased Japanese goods. Plainly, market and credit transactions of this sort can

THE 'NEW' IMPERIALISM   67

alleviate problems of overaccumulation at least in the short term. They function very well under conditions of uneven geographical development in which surpluses available in one territory are matched by lack of supply elsewhere. But resort to the credit system simultaneously makes territories vulnerable to flows of speculative and fictitious capitals that can both stimulate and undermine capitalist development and even, as in recent years, be used to impose savage devaluations upon vulnerable territories.

The export of capital, particularly when accompanied by the export of labour power, works rather differently and typically has longer term effects. In this case, surpluses of (usually money) capital and labour are sent elsewhere to set capital accumulation in motion in the new space. Surpluses generated in Britain in the nineteenth century found their way to the United States and to the settler colonies like South Africa, Australia and Canada, creating new and dynamic centers of accumulation in these territories which generated a demand for goods from Britain. Since it may take many years for capitalism to mature in these new territories (if it ever does) to the point where they, too, begin to produce over-accumulations of capital, the originating country can hope to benefit from this process for a considerable period of time. This is particularly the case when the goods demanded elsewhere are fixed physical infrastructures (such as railroads and dams) required as a basis for future capital accumulation. But the rate of return on these long-term investments in the built environment eventually depends upon the evolution of a strong dynamic of accumulation in the receiving country. Britain lent to Argentina in this way during the last part of the nineteenth century. The United States, via the Marshall Plan for Europe (Germany in particular) and Japan, clearly saw that its own economic security (leaving aside the military aspect dependent on the Cold War) rested on the active revival of capitalist activity in these spaces.

Contradictions arise, because new dynamic spaces of capital accumulation ultimately generate surpluses and have to absorb them through geographical expansions. Japan and Germany became competitors with US capital from the late 1960s onwards, much as the US overwhelmed British capital (and helped pull down the British Empire) as the twentieth century dragged on. It is always interesting to note the point at which strong internal development spills over into a search for a spatio-temporal fix. Japan did so during the 1960s, first through trade, then through the export of capital as direct investment first to Europe and the United States and more recently through massive investments (both direct and portfolio) in East and South East Asia, and finally through lending abroad (particularly to the United States). South Korea suddenly switched outwards in the 1980s, shortly followed by Taiwan in the 1990s, in both cases exporting not only financial capital but some of the most vicious labour management practices imaginable as subcontractors to multinational capital throughout the world (in Central America, in Africa, as well as throughout the rest of South and East Asia). Even recently successful adherents to capitalist development have, therefore, quickly found themselves in need of

68 SOCIALIST REGISTER 2004

a spatio-temporal fix for their overaccumulated capital. The rapidity with which certain territories, like South Korea, Singapore, Taiwan and now even China moved from being net receiving to net exporting territories has been quite startling relative to the slower rhythms characteristic of former periods. But by the same token these successful territories have to adjust fast to the blowbacks from their own spatio-temporal fixes. China, absorbing surpluses in the form of foreign direct investments from Japan, Korea and Taiwan, is rapidly supplanting those countries in many lines of production and export (particularly of the lower value-added and labour intensive sort, but it is quickly moving up to the higher value-added commodities as well). The generalized overcapacity that Brenner identifies can in this way be disaggregated into a cascading and proliferating series of spatio-temporal fixes primarily throughout South and East Asia but with additional elements within Latin America – Brazil, Mexico and Chile in particular – supplemented now by Eastern Europe. And in an interesting reversal, explicable in large part by the role of the dollar as a secure global reserve currency which confers the power of seigniorage, the US has in recent years with its huge increase in indebtedness absorbed surplus capitals chiefly from East and South East Asia but also from elsewhere.[9]

The aggregate result, however, is increasingly fierce international competition as multiple dynamic centers of capital accumulation emerge to compete on the world stage in the face of strong currents of overaccumulation. Since they cannot all succeed in the long run, either the weakest succumb and fall into serious crises of devaluation, or geopolitical confrontations erupt in the form of trade wars, currency wars and even military confrontations (of the sort that gave us two world wars between capitalist powers in the twentieth century). In this case it is devaluation and destruction (of the sort that the US financial institutions visited on East and South East Asia in 1997-8) that is being exported, and the spatio-temporal fix takes on much more sinister forms. There are, however, some further points to make about this process in order to better understand how it actually occurs.

INNER CONTRADICTIONS

In *The Philosophy of Right*, Hegel notes how the inner dialectic of bourgeois society, producing an overaccumulation of wealth at one pole and a rabble of paupers at the other, drives it to seek solutions through external trade and colonial/imperial practices. He rejects the idea that there might be ways to solve the problem of social inequality and instability through internal mechanisms of redistribution.[10] Lenin quotes Cecil Rhodes as saying that colonialism and imperialism abroad were the only possible way to avoid civil war at home.[11] Class relations and struggles within a territorially bounded social formation drive impulses to seek a spatio-temporal fix elsewhere.

The evidence from the end of the nineteenth century is here of interest. Joseph Chamberlain ('Radical Joe' as he was known) was closely identified with the liberal manufacturing interests of Birmingham, and was initially opposed to

THE 'NEW' IMPERIALISM 69

imperialism (in the Afghan Wars of the 1850s, for example). He devoted himself to educational reform and improvements in the social and physical infrastructures for production and consumption in his home city of Birmingham. This provided, he thought, a productive outlet for surpluses that would be repaid in the long run. An important figure within the liberal conservative movement, he saw the rising tide of class struggle in Britain at first hand and in 1885 made a celebrated speech in which he called for the propertied classes to take cognizance of their responsibilities to society (i.e. to better the conditions of life of the least well off and invest in social and physical infrastructures in the national interest) rather than solely to promote their individual rights as property owners. The uproar that followed on the part of the propertied classes forced him to recant and from that moment on he turned to be the most ardent advocate for imperialism (ultimately, as Colonial Secretary, leading Britain into the disaster of the Boer War). This career trajectory was quite common for the period. Jules Ferry in France, an ardent supporter of internal reform, particularly education, in the 1860s, took to colonial advocacy after the Commune of 1871 (leading France into the mire of Southeast Asia that culminated in defeat at Dien Bien-Phu in 1954); Crispi sought to solve the land problem in the Italian south through colonization in Africa; and even Theodore Roosevelt in the United States turned, after Frederic Jackson Turner declared, erroneously, at least as far as investment opportunities were concerned, that the American Frontier was closed, to support imperial policies rather than internal reforms.[12]

In all of these cases, the turn to a liberal form of imperialism (and one that had attached to it an ideology of progress and of a civilizing mission) resulted not from absolute economic imperatives but from the political unwillingness of the bourgeoisie to give up any of its class privileges, thus blocking the possibility of absorbing overaccumulation through social reform at home. The fierce opposition by the owners of capital to any politics of redistribution or internal social amelioration in the United States today likewise leaves the country no option but to look outwards for solutions to its economic difficulties. Internal class politics of this sort forced many European powers to look outwards to solve their problems from 1884 to 1945, and this gave a specific coloration to the forms that European imperialism then took. Many liberal and even radical figures became proud imperialists during these years and much of the working-class movement was persuaded to support the imperial project as essential to their well-being. This required, however, that bourgeois interests should thoroughly command state policy, ideological apparatuses and military power. Arendt therefore interprets this Euro-centric imperialism, correctly in my view, as 'the first stage in political rule of the bourgeoisie rather than the last stage of capitalism' as Lenin depicted it.[13] I will consider this idea further in the conclusion.

70   SOCIALIST REGISTER 2004

MEDIATING INSTITUTIONAL ARRANGEMENTS FOR THE PROJECTION OF POWER OVER SPACE

In a recent article Henderson shows that the difference in 1997-8 between Taiwan and Singapore (which both escaped the crisis relatively unscathed except for currency devaluation) and Thailand and Indonesia (which suffered almost total economic and political collapse), turned on differences in state and financial policies.[14] The former territories were insulated from speculative flows into property markets by strong state controls and protected financial markets, whereas the latter were not. Differences of this sort plainly matter. The forms taken by the mediating institutions are productive of, as well as products of, the dynamics of capital accumulation.

Clearly, the whole pattern of turbulence in the relations between state, supra-state, and financial powers on the one hand, and the more general dynamics of capital accumulation (through production and selective devaluations) on the other, has been one of the most signal, and most complex, elements in the narrative of uneven geographical development and imperialist politics to be told of the period since 1973.[15] I think Gowan is correct to see the radical restructuring of international capitalism after 1973 as a series of gambles on the part of the United States to try to maintain its hegemonic position in world economic affairs against Europe, Japan and later East and South East Asia.[16] This began during the crisis of 1973 with Nixon's double strategy of high oil pricing and financial deregulation. The US banks were then given the exclusive right to recycle the vast quantities of petro-dollars being accumulated in the Gulf region. This re-centered global financial activity in the US and incidentally helped, along with the deregulation of the financial sector within the US, to rescue New York from its own local economic crisis. A powerful Wall Street/US Treasury financial regime[17] was created, with controlling powers over global financial institutions (such as the IMF) and able to make or break many weaker foreign economies through credit manipulations and debt management practices. This monetary and financial regime was used, Gowan argues, by successive US administrations 'as a formidable instrument of economic statecraft to drive forward both the globalization process and the associated neo-liberal domestic transformations.' The regime thrived on crises. 'The IMF covers the risks and ensures that the US banks don't lose (countries pay up through structural adjustments etc.) and flight of capital from localized crises elsewhere ends up boosting the strength of Wall Street ...'.[18] The effect was to project US economic power outwards (in alliance with others wherever possible), to force open markets, particularly for capital and financial flows (now a requirement for membership in the IMF), and impose other neoliberal practices (culminating in the WTO) upon much of the rest of the world.

There are two major points to be made about this system. First, free trade in commodities is often depicted as opening up the world to free and open competition. But this whole argument fails, as Lenin long ago pointed out, in the face of monopoly or oligopoly power (either in production or consumption). The US, for example, has repeatedly used the weapon of denial of access to the huge

THE 'NEW' IMPERIALISM   71

US market to force other nations to comply with its wishes. The most recent (and crass) example of this line of argument comes from the US Trade Representative Robert Zoellick to the effect that if Lula, the newly elected Workers Party President of Brazil, does not go along with US plans for free markets in the Americas, he would find himself having 'to export to Antarctica'.[19] Taiwan and Singapore were forced to sign on to the WTO, and thereby open their financial markets to speculative capital, in the face of US threats to deny them access to the US market. At US Treasury insistence, South Korea was forced to do the same as a condition for an IMF bail-out in 1998. The US now plans to attach a condition of financial institutional compatibility to the foreign aid it offers as 'challenge grants' to poor countries. On the production side, oligopolies largely based in the core capitalist regions, effectively control the production of seeds, fertilizers, electronics, computer software, pharmaceutical products, petroleum products and much more. Under these conditions, the creation of new market openings does not open up competition but merely creates opportunities to proliferate monopoly powers with all manner of social, ecological, economic and political consequences. The fact that nearly two-thirds of foreign trade is now accounted for by transactions within and between the main transnational corporations is indicative of the situation. Even something as seemingly benevolent as the Green Revolution has, most commentators agree, paralleled the increased agricultural outputs with considerable concentrations of wealth in the agrarian sector and higher levels of dependency upon monopolized inputs throughout South and East Asia. The penetration of the China market by US tobacco companies is set fair to compensate for their losses in the US market at the same time as it will surely generate a public health crisis in China for decades to come. In all of these respects, the claims generally made that neoliberalism is about open competition rather than monopoly control or limited competition within oligopolistic structures, turn out to be fraudulent, masked as usual by the fetishism of market freedoms. Free trade does not mean fair trade.

There is also, as even advocates of free trade readily acknowledge, a huge difference between freedom of trade in commodities and freedom of movement for finance capital.[20] This immediately poses the problem of what kind of market freedom is being talked about. Some, like Bhagwati, fiercely defend free trade in commodities but resist the idea that this necessarily holds good for financial flows. The difficulty here is this. On the one hand credit flows are vital to productive investments and reallocations of capital from one line of production or location to another. They also play an important role in bringing consumption needs – for housing, for example – into a potentially balanced relationship with productive activities in a spatially disaggregated world marked by surpluses in one space and deficits in another. In all of these respects the financial system, with or without state involvement, is critical to coordinate the dynamics of capital accumulation through uneven geographical development. But finance capital also embraces a lot of unproductive activity in which money is simply used to make more money through speculation on commodity futures, currency

72   SOCIALIST REGISTER 2004

values, debt, and the like. When huge quantities of capital become available for such purposes, then open capital markets become vehicles for speculative activity some of which, as we saw during the 1990s with both the 'dot.com' and the stock market 'bubbles', become self-fulfilling prophecies, just as the hedge funds, armed with trillions of dollars of leveraged money, could force Indonesia and even South Korea into bankruptcy no matter what the strength of their underlying economies. Much of what happens on Wall Street has nothing to do with facilitating investment in productive activities. It is purely speculative (hence the descriptions of it as 'casino', 'predatory' or even 'vulture' capitalism – with the debacle of Long Term Capital Management needing a $2.3 billion bail-out reminding us that speculations can easily go awry). This activity has, however, deep impacts upon the overall dynamics of capital accumulation. Above all, it facilitated the re-centering of political-economic power primarily in the United States but also within the financial markets of other core countries (Tokyo, London, Frankfurt).

How this occurs depends on the dominant form of the class alliances arrived at within the core countries, the balance of power between them in negotiating international arrangements (such as the new international financial architecture put in place after 1997-8 to replace the so-called Washington Consensus of the mid-1990s) and the political-economic strategies set in motion by dominant agents with respect to surplus capital. The emergence of a 'Wall Street-Treasury-IMF' complex within the United States, able to control global institutions and to project vast financial power across the world through a network of other financial and governmental institutions, has played a determinant and problematic role in the dynamics of global capitalism in recent years. But this power center can only operate the way it does because the rest of the world is networked and successfully hooked into (and effectively 'hooked on') a structured framework of interlocking financial and governmental (including supra-national) institutions. Hence the significance of collaborations between, for example, central bankers of the G7 nations and the various international accords (temporary in the case of currency strategies and more permanent with respect to the WTO) designed to deal with particular difficulties.[21] And if market power is not sufficient to accomplish particular objectives and to bring recalcitrant elements or 'rogue states' into line, then unchallengeable US military power (covert or overt) is available to force the issue.

This complex of institutional arrangements should in the best of all possible capitalist worlds be geared to sustain and support expanded reproduction (growth). But, like war in relation to diplomacy, finance capital intervention backed by state power can frequently become accumulation by other means. An unholy alliance between state powers and the predatory aspects of finance capital forms the cutting edge of a 'vulture capitalism' dedicated to the appropriation and devaluation of assets, rather than to building them up through productive investments. But how are we to interpret these 'other means' to accumulation or devaluation?

THE 'NEW' IMPERIALISM   73

ACCUMULATION BY DISPOSSESSION

In *The Accumulation of Capital,* Luxemburg focuses attention on the dual aspects of capitalist accumulation:

> One concerns the commodity market and the place where surplus value is produced – the factory, the mine, the agricultural estate. Regarded in this light accumulation is a purely economic process, with its most important phase a transaction between the capitalist and the wage labourer.... Here, in form at any rate, peace, property and equality prevail, and the keen dialectics of scientific analysis were required to reveal how the right of ownership changes in the course of accumulation into appropriation of other people's property, how commodity exchange turns into exploitation and equality becomes class rule. The other aspect of the accumulation of capital concerns the relations between capitalism and the non-capitalist modes of production which start making their appearance on the international stage. Its predominant methods are colonial policy, an international loan system – a policy of spheres of interest – and war. Force, fraud, oppression, looting are openly displayed without any attempt at concealment, and it requires an effort to discover within this tangle of political violence and contests of power the stern laws of the economic process.

These two aspects of accumulation, she argues, are 'organically linked' and 'the historical career of capitalism can only be appreciated by taking them together'.[22]

Marx's general theory of capital accumulation is constructed under certain crucial initial assumptions which broadly match those of classical political economy and which exclude primitive accumulation processes. These assumptions are: freely functioning competitive markets with institutional arrangements of private property, juridical individualism, freedom of contract and appropriate structures of law and governance guaranteed by a 'facilitative' state which also secures the integrity of money as a store of value and as a medium of circulation. The role of the capitalist as a commodity producer and exchanger is already well-established and labour power has become a commodity that trades generally at its value. 'Primitive' or 'original' accumulation has already occurred and accumulation now proceeds as expanded reproduction (albeit through the exploitation of living labour in production) within a closed economy working under conditions of 'peace, property and equality'. These assumptions allow us to see what will happen if the liberal project of the classical political economists or, in our times, the neo-liberal project of the neo-classical economists, is realized. The brilliance of Marx's dialectical method is to show that market liberalization – the credo of the liberals and the neo-liberals – will not produce a harmonious state in which everyone is better off. It will instead produce ever greater levels of social inequality, as indeed has been the global trend over the last thirty years of neoliberalism, particularly within those countries such as

74   SOCIALIST REGISTER 2004

Britain and the United States that have most closely hewed to such a political line. It will also, Marx predicts, produce serious and growing instabilities culminating in chronic crises of overaccumulation of the sort we are now witnessing.

The disadvantage of these assumptions is that they relegate accumulation based upon predation, fraud, and violence to an 'original stage' that is considered no longer relevant or, as with Luxemburg, as being somehow 'outside of' the capitalist system. A general re-evaluation of the continuous role and persistence of the predatory practices of 'primitive' or 'original' accumulation within the long historical geography of capital accumulation is, therefore, very much in order, as several commentators have recently observed.[23] Since it seems peculiar to call an ongoing process 'primitive' or 'original' I shall, in what follows, substitute these terms by the concept of 'accumulation by dispossession'.

A closer look at Marx's description of primitive accumulation reveals a wide range of processes. These include the commodification and privatization of land and the forceful expulsion of peasant populations; conversion of various forms of property rights – common, collective, state, etc. – into exclusive private property rights; suppression of rights to the commons; commodification of labour power and the suppression of alternative, indigenous, forms of production and consumption; colonial, neo-colonial and imperial processes of appropriation of assets, including natural resources; monetization of exchange and taxation, particularly of land; slave trade; and usury, the national debt and ultimately the credit system. The state, with its monopoly of violence and definitions of legality, plays a crucial role in both backing and promoting these processes and there is considerable evidence, which Marx suggests and Braudel confirms, that the transition to capitalist development was vitally contingent upon the stance of the state – broadly supportive in Britain, weakly so in France and highly negative, until very recently, in China.[24] The invocation of the recent shift towards primitive accumulation in the case of China indicates that this is an on-going issue and the evidence is strong, particularly throughout East and South East Asia, that state policies and politics (consider the case of Singapore) have played a critical role in defining both the intensity and the paths of new forms of capital accumulation. The role of the 'developmental state' in recent phases of capital accumulation has therefore been the subject of intense scrutiny.[25] One only has to look back at Bismarck's Germany or Meiji Japan to recognize that this has long been the case.

All the features that Marx mentions have remained powerfully present within capitalism's historical geography. Some of them have been fine-tuned to play an even stronger role now than in the past. The credit system and finance capital have, as Lenin, Hilferding and Luxemburg all remarked, been major levers of predation, fraud and thievery. Stock promotions, ponzi schemes, structured asset destruction through inflation, asset stripping through mergers and acquisitions, the promotion of levels of debt encumbrancy that reduce whole populations, even in the advanced capitalist countries, to debt peonage, to say nothing of corporate fraud, dispossession of assets (the raiding of pension funds and their

THE 'NEW' IMPERIALISM

decimation by stock and corporate collapses) by credit and stock manipulations – all of these are central features of what contemporary capitalism is about. The collapse of Enron dispossessed many people of their livelihoods and their pension rights. But above all we have to look at the speculative raiding carried out by hedge funds and other major institutions of finance capital as the cutting edge of accumulation by dispossession in recent times. By creating a liquidity crisis throughout South East Asia, the hedge funds forced profitable businesses into bankruptcy. These businesses could be purchased at fire-sale prices by surplus capitals in the core countries, thus engineering what Wade and Veneroso refer to as 'the biggest peacetime transfer of assets from domestic (i.e. South East Asian) to foreign (i.e. US, Japanese and European) owners in the past fifty years anywhere in the world.'[26]

Wholly new mechanisms of accumulation by dispossession have also opened up. The emphasis upon intellectual property rights in the WTO negotiations (the so-called TRIPS agreement) points to ways in which the patenting and licensing of genetic materials, seed plasmas, and all manner of other products, can now be used against whole populations whose environmental management practices have played a crucial role in the development of those materials. Biopiracy is rampant and the pillaging of the world's stockpile of genetic resources is well under way, to the benefit of a few large multinational companies. The escalating depletion of the global environmental commons (land, air, water) and proliferating habitat degradations that preclude anything but capital-intensive modes of agricultural production have likewise resulted from the wholesale commodification of nature in all its forms. The commodification of cultural forms, histories and intellectual creativity entails wholesale dispossessions – the music industry is notorious for the appropriation and exploitation of grassroots culture and creativity. The corporatization and privatization of hitherto public assets (like universities) to say nothing of the wave of privatization of water and other public utilities that has swept the world, constitute a new wave of 'enclosing the commons'. As in the past, the power of the state is frequently used to force such processes through even against the popular will. As also happened in the past, these processes of dispossession are provoking widespread resistance and this now forms the core of what the anti-globalization movement is about.[27] The reversion to the private domain of common property rights won through past class struggles (the right to a state pension, to welfare, or to national health care) has been one of the most egregious of all policies of dispossession pursued in the name of neo-liberal orthodoxy. The Bush administration's plan to privatize social security (and make pensions subject to the vagaries of the stock market) is a clear case in point. Small wonder that much of the emphasis within the anti-globalization movement in recent times has been focused on the theme of reclaiming the commons and attacking the joint role of the state and capital in their appropriation.

Capitalism internalizes cannibalistic as well as predatory and fraudulent practices. But it is, as Luxemburg cogently observed, 'often hard to determine, within the tangle of violence and contests of power, the stern laws of the economic process.' Accumulation by dispossession can occur in a variety of ways and there is much that is both contingent and haphazard about its modus operandi. Yet it is omnipresent in no matter what historical period and picks up strongly when crises of overaccumulation occur in expanded reproduction, when there seems to be no other exit except devaluation. Arendt suggests, for example, that for Britain of the nineteenth century, the depressions of the sixties and seventies initiated the push into a new form of imperialism in which the bourgeoisie realized 'for the first time that the original sin of simple robbery, which centuries ago had made possible "the original accumulation of capital" (Marx) and had started all further accumulation, had eventually to be repeated lest the motor of accumulation suddenly die down'.[28] This brings us back to relations between the drive for spatio-temporal fixes, state powers, accumulation by dispossession and the forms of contemporary imperialism.

THE 'NEW' IMPERIALISM

Capitalist social formations, often arranged in particular territorial or regional configurations and usually dominated by some hegemonic center, have long engaged in quasi-imperialist practices in search of spatio-temporal fixes to their overaccumulation problems. It is possible, however, to periodize the historical geography of these processes by taking Arendt seriously when she argues that the European-centered imperialism of the period 1884 to 1945 constituted the first stab at global political rule by the bourgeoisie. Individual nation-states engaged in their own imperialist projects to deal with problems of overaccumulation and class conflict within their orbit. Initially stabilized under British hegemony and constructed around open flows of capital and commodities on the world market, this first system broke down at the turn of the century into geopolitical conflicts between major powers pursuing autarky within increasingly closed systems. It erupted in two world wars in much the way that Lenin foresaw. Much of the rest of the world was pillaged for resources during this period (just look at the history of what Japan did to Taiwan or Britain did to the Witwatersrand in South Africa) in the hope that accumulation by dispossession would compensate for a chronic inability, which came to a head in the 1930s, to sustain capitalism through expanded reproduction.

This system was displaced in 1945 by a US led system that sought to establish a global compact among all the major capitalist powers to avoid internecine wars and find a rational way to deal collectively with the overaccumulation that had plagued the 1930s. For this to happen they had to share in the benefits of an intensification of an integrated capitalism in the core regions (hence US support for moves towards European Union) and engage in systematic geographical expansion of the system (hence the US insistence upon decolonization and 'developmentalism' as a generalized goal for the rest of the world). This second phase of global bourgeois rule was largely held together by the contingency of the Cold War. This entailed US military and economic leadership as the sole capitalist superpower. The effect was to construct a

THE 'NEW' IMPERIALISM   77

hegemonic US 'superimperialism' that was more political and military than it was a manifestation of economic necessity. The US was not itself highly dependent upon external outlets or even inputs. It could even afford to open its market to others and thereby absorb through internal spatio-temporal fixes, such as the interstate highway system, sprawling suburbanization, and the development of its South and West, part of the surplus capacity that began to emerge strongly in Germany and Japan during the 1960s. Strong growth through expanded reproduction occurred throughout the capitalist world. Accumulation by dispossession was relatively muted, though countries with capital surpluses, like Japan and West Germany, increasingly needed to look outwards for markets, including by competing for control of post-colonial developing markets.[29] Strong controls over capital export (as opposed to commodities) were, however, kept in place in much of Europe and capital imports into East Asia remained restricted. Class struggles within individual nation states over expanded reproduction (how it would occur and who would benefit) dominated. The main geopolitical struggles that arose were either those of the Cold War (with that other empire constructed by the Soviets) or residual struggles (more often than not cross-cut by Cold War politics that pushed the US to support many reactionary post-colonial regimes) which resulted from the reluctance of European powers to disengage from their colonial possessions (the invasion of Suez by the British and French in 1956, not supported at all by the US, was emblematic). Growing resentments of being locked into a spatio-temporal situation of perpetual subservience to the center did, however, spark anti-dependency and national liberation movements. Third world socialism sought modernization but on an entirely different class and political basis.

This system broke down around 1970. Capital controls became hard to enforce as surplus US dollars flooded the world market. Inflationary pressures resulting from the US trying to have both guns and butter in the midst of the Vietnam War became very strong while the level of class struggle in many of the core countries began to erode profits. The US then sought to construct a different kind of system, that rested upon a mix of new international and financial institutional arrangements to counter economic threats from Germany and Japan and to re-center economic power as finance capital operating out of Wall Street. The collusion between the Nixon administration and the Saudis to push oil prices sky-high in 1973 did far more damage to the European and Japanese economies than it did to the US, which at that time was little dependent upon Middle Eastern supplies.[30] US banks gained the privilege of re-cycling the petro-dollars into the world economy. Threatened in the realm of production, the US countered by asserting its hegemony through finance. But for this system to work effectively, markets in general and capital markets in particular had to be forced open to international trade – a slow process that required fierce US pressure backed by use of international levers such as the IMF and an equally fierce commitment to neo-liberalism as the new economic orthodoxy. It also entailed shifting the balance of power and interests within the bourgeoisie from

78 SOCIALIST REGISTER 2004

production activities to institutions of finance capital. This could be used to attack the power of working class movements within expanded reproduction either directly, by exerting disciplinary oversight on production, or indirectly by facilitating greater geographical mobility for all forms of capital. Finance capital was therefore central to this third phase of bourgeois global rule.

This system was much more volatile and predatory and visited various bouts of accumulation by dispossession – usually as structural adjustment programs administered by the IMF – as an antidote to difficulties in the realm of expanded reproduction. In some instances, such as Latin America in the 1980s, whole economies were raided and their assets recovered by US finance capital. The hedge funds' attack upon the Thai and Indonesian currencies in 1997, backed up by the savage deflationary policies demanded by the IMF, drove even viable concerns into bankruptcy and reversed the remarkable social and economic progress that had been made in much of East and South East Asia. Millions of people fell victim to unemployment and impoverishment as a result. The crisis also conveniently sparked a flight to the dollar, confirming Wall Street's dominance and generating an amazing boom in asset values for the affluent in the United States. Class struggles began to coalesce around issues such as IMF-imposed structural adjustment, the predatory activities of finance capital and the loss of rights through privatization.

Debt crises could be used to reorganize internal social relations of production in each country on a case-by-case basis in such a way as to favour the penetration of external capitals. Domestic financial regimes, domestic product markets and thriving domestic firms were, in this way, prized open for takeover by American, Japanese or European companies. Low profits in the core regions could thereby be supplemented by taking a cut out of the higher profits being earned abroad. Accumulation by dispossession became a much more central feature within global capitalism (with privatization as one its key mantras). Resistance to this became more central within the anti-capitalist and anti-imperialist movement.[31] But the system, while centered on the Wall Street-Treasury complex, had many multilateral aspects with the financial centers of Tokyo, London, Frankfurt and many other financial centers participating. It was associated with the emergence of transnational capitalist corporations which, though they may have a basis in one or other nation state, spread themselves across the map of the world in ways that were unthinkable in the earlier phases of imperialism (the trusts and cartels that Lenin described were all tied very closely to particular nation states). This was the world that the Clinton White House, with an all-powerful Treasury Secretary, Robert Rubin, drawn from the speculator side of Wall Street, sought to manage by a centralized multilateralism (epitomized by the so-called 'Washington Consensus' of the mid 1990s). It seemed, for a brief moment, that Lenin was wrong and that Kautsky might be right – an ultraimperialism based on a 'peaceful' collaboration between all the major capitalist powers – now symbolized by the grouping known as the G7 and the so-called 'new international financial architecture', albeit under the hegemony of US leadership – was possible.[32]

THE 'NEW' IMPERIALISM   79

But this system has now run into serious difficulties. The sheer volatility and chaotic fragmentation of power conflicts makes it hard, as Luxemburg earlier noted, to discern how the stern laws of economics are working behind all the smoke and mirrors (particularly those of the financial sector). But insofar as the crisis of 1997–8 revealed that the main center of surplus productive capacity lay in East and South East Asia (so that the US targeted that region specifically for devaluation), the rapid recovery of some parts of East and South East Asian capitalism has forced the general problem of overaccumulation back into the forefront of global affairs.[33] This poses the question of how a new form of the spatio-temporal fix (into China?) might be organized, or who will bear the brunt of a new round of devaluation. The gathering recession within the United States after a decade or more of spectacular (even if 'irrational') exuberance indicates that the US may not be immune. A major fault line of instability lies in the rapid deterioration in the balance of payments of the United States. 'The same exploding imports that drove the world economy' during the 1990s, writes Brenner, 'brought US trade and current account deficits to record levels, leading to the historically unprecedented growth of liabilities to overseas owners' and 'the historically unprecedented vulnerability of the US economy to the flight of capital and a collapse of the dollar'.[34] But this vulnerability exists on both sides. If the US market collapses then the economies that look to that market as a sink for their excess productive capacity will go down with it. The alacrity with which the central bankers of countries like Japan and Taiwan lend funds to cover US deficits, has a strong element of self-interest. They thereby fund the US consumerism that forms the market for their products. They may now even find themselves funding the US war effort.

But the hegemony and dominance of the US is, once more, under threat and this time the danger seems more acute. If, for example, Braudel (followed by Arrighi) is correct, and a powerful wave of financialization is a likely prelude to a transfer of dominant power from one hegemon to another then the US turn towards financialization in the 1970s would appear to exemplify a self-destructive historical pattern.[35] The deficits, both internal and external, cannot continue to spiral out of control indefinitely and the ability and willingness of others, primarily in Asia, to fund them, to the tune of $2.3 billion a day at current rates, is not inexhaustible. Any other country in the world that exhibited the macroeconomic condition of the US economy would by now have been subjected to ruthless austerity and structural adjustment procedures by the IMF. But, as Gowan remarks: 'Washington's capacity to manipulate the dollar price and to exploit Wall Street's international financial dominance enabled the US authorities to avoid doing what other states have had to do; watch the balance of payments; adjust the domestic economy to ensure high levels of domestic savings and investment; watch levels of public and private indebtedness; ensure an effective domestic system of financial intermediation to ensure the strong development of the domestic productive sector.' The US economy has had 'an escape route from all these tasks' and has become 'deeply distorted and unstable'

80   SOCIALIST REGISTER 2004

as a result.[36] Furthermore, the successive waves of accumulation by dispossession, the hallmark of the new US-centered imperialism, are sparking resistance and resentments wherever they happen to break, generating not only an active worldwide anti-globalization movement (quite different in form from class struggles embedded in processes of expanded reproduction) but also active resistance to US hegemony by formerly pliant subordinate powers, particularly in Asia (South Korea is a case in point), and now even in Europe.

The options for the United States are limited. The US could turn away from its current form of imperialism by engaging in a massive redistribution of wealth within its borders and seek paths to surplus absorption through temporal fixes internally (dramatic improvements in public education and repair of aging infrastructures would be good places to start). An industrial strategy to revitalize manufacturing would also help. But this would require even more deficit financing or higher taxation as well as heavy state direction and this is precisely what the bourgeoisie will refuse to contemplate, as was the case in Chamberlain's day; any politician who proposes such a package will almost certainly be howled down by the capitalist press and their ideologists and lose any election in the face of overwhelming money power. Yet, ironically, a massive counter-attack within the US as well as within other core countries of capitalism (particularly in Europe) against the politics of neo-liberalism and the cutting of state and social expenditures might be one of the only ways to protect Western capitalism internally from its self-destructive tendencies.

Even more suicidal politically, within the US, would be to try to enforce by self-discipline the kind of austerity program that the IMF typically visits on others. Any attempt by external powers to do so (by capital flight and collapse of the dollar, for example) would surely elicit a savage US political, economic and even military response. It is hard to imagine that the US would peacefully accept and adapt to the phenomenal growth of East Asia and recognize, as Arrighi suggests it should, that we are in the midst of a major transition towards Asia as the hegemonic center of global power.[37] It is unlikely that the US will go quietly and peacefully into that good night. It would, in any case, entail a reorientation – some signs of which already exist – of East Asian capitalism away from dependency on the US market to the cultivation of an internal market within Asia itself. This is where the huge modernization program within China – an internal version of a spatio-temporal fix that is equivalent to what the US did internally in the 1950s and 1960s – may have a critical role to play in gradually siphoning off the surplus capitals of Japan, Taiwan and South Korea and thereby diminishing the flows into the United States. Taiwan, for example, now exports more to China than to North America. The consequent diminution of the flow of funds for the US could have calamitous consequences.

And it is in this context that we see elements within the US political establishment looking to flex military muscle as the only clear absolute power they have left, talking openly of Empire as a political option (presumably to extract tribute from the rest of the world) and looking to control oil supplies as a means

THE 'NEW' IMPERIALISM   81

to counter the power shifts threatened within the global economy. The attempts by the US to gain better control of Iraqi and Venezuelan oil supplies – in the former case by purportedly seeking to establish democracy and in the latter by overthrowing it – make a lot of sense. They reek of a re-run of what happened in 1973, since Europe and Japan, as well as East and South East Asia, now crucially including China, are even more heavily dependent on Gulf oil than is the United States. If the US engineers the overthrow of Chavez as well as Saddam, if it can stabilize or reform an armed-to-the-teeth Saudi regime that is currently based on the shifting sands of authoritarian rule (and in imminent danger of falling into the hands of radicalized Islam – this was, after all, Osama bin Laden's primary objective), if it can move on, as seems likely, from Iraq to Iran and consolidate its position in Turkey and Uzbekistan as a strategic presence in relation to Caspian basin oil reserves, then the US, through firm control of the global oil spigot, might hope to keep effective control over the global economy and secure its own hegemonic position for the next fifty years.[38]

The dangers of such a strategy are immense. Resistance will be formidable, not least from Europe and Asia, with Russia not far behind. The reluctance to sanction US military invasion of Iraq in the United Nations, particularly by France and Russia who already have strong connections to Iraqi oil exploitation, was a case in point. And the Europeans in particular are far more attracted to a Kautskyian vision of ultra-imperialism in which all the major capitalist powers will supposedly collaborate on an equal basis. An unstable US hegemony that rests on permanent militarization and adventurism of a sort that could seriously threaten global peace is not an attractive prospect for the rest of the world. This is not to say that the European model is much more progressive. If Robert Cooper, a Blair consultant, is to be believed, it resurrects nineteenth century distinctions between civilized, barbarian and savage states in the guise of postmodern, modern and pre-modern states with the postmoderns, as guardians of decentred civilized behaviour, expected to induce by direct or indirect means obeisance to universal (read 'Western' and 'bourgeois') norms and humanistic (read 'capitalistic') practices across the globe.[39] This was exactly the way that nineteenth century liberals, like John Stuart Mill, justified keeping India in tutelage and exacting tribute from abroad while praising the principles of representative government at home. In the absence of any strong revival of sustained accumulation through expanded reproduction, this will entail a deepening politics of accumulation by dispossession throughout the world in order to keep the motor of accumulation from stalling entirely.

This alternative form of imperialism will hardly be acceptable to wide swathes of the world's population who have lived through (and in some instances begun to fight back against) accumulation by dispossession and the predatory forms of capitalism they have had to confront over the last few decades. The liberal ruse that someone like Cooper proposes is far too familiar to postcolonial writers to have much traction.[40] And the blatant militarism that the US is increasingly proposing on the grounds that this is the only possible response to global terrorism is not only fraught with danger (including dangerous precedents for 'pre-emptive strikes'); it is increasingly recognized as a mask for trying to sustain a threatened hegemony within the global system.

But perhaps the most interesting question concerns the internal response within the United States itself. On this point Hannah Arendt again makes a telling argument: imperialism abroad cannot for long be sustained without active repressions, even tyranny, at home.[41] The damage done to democratic institutions domestically can be substantial (as the French learned during the Algerian struggle for independence). The popular tradition within the United States is anti-colonial and anti-imperial and it has taken a very substantive conjuring trick, if not outright deception, to mask the imperial role of the US in world affairs or at least to clothe it in grand humanitarian intentions over the past few decades. It is not clear that the US population will generally support an overt turn to any long-term militarized Empire (any more than it ended up supporting the Vietnam War). Nor will it likely accept for long the price, already substantial given the repressive clauses inserted into the Patriot and the Homeland Security Acts, that has to be paid at home in terms of civil liberties, rights and general freedoms. If Empire entails tearing up the Bill of Rights then it is not clear that this trade off will easily be accepted. But the other side of the difficulty is that in the absence of any dramatic revival of sustained accumulation through expanded reproduction and with limited possibilities to accumulate by dispossession, the US economy will likely sink into a deflationary depression that will make the last decade or so in Japan fade into insignificance by comparison. And if there is a serious flight from the dollar, then the austerity will have to be intense – unless, that is, there emerges an entirely different politics of redistribution of wealth and assets (a prospect the bourgeoisie will contemplate with utter horror) which focuses on the complete reorganization of the social and physical infrastructures of the nation to absorb idle capital and labour into socially useful, as opposed to purely speculative, tasks.

The shape and form any new imperialism will take is therefore up for grabs. The only thing that is certain is that we are in the midst of a major transition in how the global system works and that there is a variety of forces in motion which could easily tip the balance in one or another direction. The balance between accumulation by dispossession and expanded reproduction has already shifted towards the former and it is hard to see this trend doing anything other than deepening, making this the hallmark of what the new imperialism is all about (and making overt claims about the new imperialism and the necessity of empire of great ideological significance). We also know that the economic trajectory taken by Asia is key, but that military dominance still lies with the United States. This, as Arrighi remarks, is a unique configuration and we may well be seeing in Iraq the first stage of how it might play out geopolitically on the world stage under conditions of generalized recession. The United States, whose hegemony was based on production, finance and military power in the immediate post-war period lost its superiority in production after 1970 and may well now

THE 'NEW' IMPERIALISM   83

be losing financial dominance leaving it with military might alone. What happens within the United States is therefore a vitally important determinant of how the new imperialism might be articulated. And there is, to boot, a gathering storm of opposition to the deepening of accumulation by dispossession. But the forms of class struggle which this provokes are of a radically different nature from the classic proletarian struggles within expanded reproduction (which continue though in somewhat more muted forms) upon which the future of socialism was traditionally supposed to rest. The unities beginning to emerge around these different vectors of struggle are vital to nurture, for within them we can discern the lineaments of an entirely different, non-imperialistic, form of globalization that emphasizes social well-being and humanitarian goals coupled with creative forms of uneven geographical development, rather than the glorification of money power, stock market values and the incessant accumulation of capital across the variegated spaces of the global economy by whatever means, but always ending up heavily concentrated in a few spaces of extraordinary wealth. The moment may be full of volatility and uncertainties; but that means it is also a moment of the unexpected and full of potential.

NOTES

1   H. Lefebvre, *The Survival of Capitalism: Reproduction of the Relations of Production*, St Martin's Press, New York: 1976.
2   Most of these essays from the 1970s and 1980s have been republished in David Harvey, *Spaces of Capital: Towards a Critical Geography*, New York: Routledge 2001. The main line of argument can also be found in Harvey, *The Limits to Capital*, Oxford: Basil Blackwell, 1982 (reprint version, London: Verso Press, 1999).
3   My own version of this theoretical argument is detailed in Harvey, *Limits*, chapters 6 and 7.
4   R. Brenner, *The Boom and the Bubble: The US in the World Economy*, London: Verso, 2002. The theory of overaccumulation in Brenner is very different from mine but I find his empirical evidence, so far as it goes, useful and for the most part convincing.
5   P. Gowan, *The Global Gamble: Washington's Bid for World Dominance*, London: Verso, 1999.
6   Since this is a lot to argue for in a short piece, I will proceed in a schematic and simplified way, leaving more detailed elaborations for a later publication. D. Harvey, *The New Imperialism*, Oxford: Oxford University Press, forthcoming.
7   The topic of the 'new imperialism' has been broached on the left by L. Panitch, 'The New Imperial State', *New Left Review*, 11(1), 2000; see also P. Gowan, L. Panitch and M. Shaw, 'The State, Globalization and the New Imperialism: A Round Table Discussion', *Historical Materialism*, 9, 2001.

84 SOCIALIST REGISTER 2004

    Other commentaries of interest are J. Petras and J. Veltmeyer, *Globalization Unmasked: Imperialism in the 21st Century*, London: Zed Books, 2001; R. Went, 'Globalization in the Perspective of Imperialism', *Science and Society*, 66(4), 2002-3; S. Amin, 'Imperialism and Globalization', *Monthly Review*, 53(2), 2001; conservative and liberal perspectives are laid out in M. Ignatieff, 'The Burden', *New York Times Magazine*, January 5th, 2003 and R. Cooper, 'The New Liberal Imperialism', *The Observer*, April 7, 2002.

8   Marx's concepts of 'fixed capital of an independent kind' and 'fictitious capital' are elaborated in Harvey, *Limits*, chapters 8 and 10 respectively and their geopolitical significance is taken up in Harvey, *Spaces*, chapter 15, 'The Geopolitics of Capitalism'.

9   The importance of siegnorage is examined in G. Carchedi, 'Imperialism, Dollarization and the Euro', *Socialist Register 2002*, London: Merlin Press, 2002.

10   G.W. Hegel, *The Philosophy of Right*, New York: Oxford University Press, 1967.

11   V.I. Lenin, 'Imperialism: The Highest Stage of Capitalism', in *Selected Works*, Volume 1, Moscow: Progress Publishers.

12   This whole common history of a radical shift from internal to external solutions to political-economic problems in response to the dynamics of class struggle across many capitalist states is told in a little known but quite fascinating collection by C.-A. Julien, J. Bruhat, C. Bourgin, M. Crouzet and P. Renouvin, *Les Politiques d'Expansion Imperialiste*, Paris: Presses Universitaires de France, 1949, in which the cases of Ferry, Chamberlain, Roosevelt, Crispi and others are all examined in comparative detail.

13   H. Arendt, *Imperialism*, New York: Harcourt Brace, 1968. There are many eerie resemblances between Arendt's analysis of the situation in the nineteenth century and our contemporary condition. Consider, for example, the following extract: 'Imperialist expansion had been touched off by a curious kind of economic crisis, the overproduction of capital and the emergence of 'superfluous' money, the result of oversaving, which could no longer find productive investment within the national borders. For the first time, investment of power did not pave the way for investment of money, but export of power followed meekly in the train of exported money, since uncontrolled investments in distant countries threatened to transform large strata of society into gamblers, to change the whole capitalist economy from a system of production into a system of financial speculation, and to replace the profits of production with profits in commissions. The decade immediately before the imperialist era, the seventies of the last century, witnessed an unparalleled increase in swindles, financial scandals and gambling in the stock market' (p. 15).

14   J. Henderson, 'Uneven Crises: Institutional Foundations of East Asian Economic Turmoil', *Economy and Society*, 28(3), 1999.

15   Brenner, *The Boom*, attempts the most general and synthetic account of this

THE 'NEW' IMPERIALISM   85

turbulence. Details of the East Asian meltdown can be found in R. Wade and F. Veneroso, 'The Asian Crisis: The High Debt Model versus the Wall Street-Treasury-IMF Complex', *New Left Review*, 228, 1998; Henderson, 'Uneven Crises'; C. Johnson, *Blowback: The Costs and Consequences of American Empire*, New York: Henry Holt, 2000, chapter 9; the special issue of *Historical Materialism*, 8, 2001, 'Focus on East Asia after the Crisis' (particularly P. Burkett and M. Hart-Landsberg, 'Crisis and Recovery in East Asia: The Limits of Capitalist Development').

16   Gowan, *Global Gamble*.

17   Various names have been proposed for this. Gowan prefers the Dollar Wall Street Regime but I prefer the Wall-Street-Treasury-IMF complex suggested by Wade and Veneroso, 'The Asian Crisis'.

18   Gowan, *Global Gamble*, pp. 23, 35.

19   Editorial, *The Buenos Aires Herald*, December 31st, 2002, p. 4.

20   J. Bhagwati, 'The Capital Myth: The Difference Between Trade in Widgets and Dollars', *Foreign Affairs*, 77(3), 1998, pp. 7-12.

21   Gowan, *Global Gamble* and Brenner, *The Boom* offer interesting parallel accounts without, however, ever referring to each other.

22   R. Luxemburg, *The Accumulation of Capital*, New York: Monthly Review Press, 1968, pp. 452-3. Luxemburg bases her account on a theory of underconsumption (lack of effective demand) which has rather different implications from theories of overaccumulation (lack of opportunities for profitable activity) with which I work. A full exploration of the concept of accumulation by dispossession and its relation to overaccumulation is given in Part Three of Harvey, *The New Imperialism*.

23   M. Perelman, *The Invention of Capitalism: Classical Political Economy and the Secret History of Primitive Accumulation*, Durham: Duke University Press, 2000. There is also an extensive debate in *The Commoner* (www.thecommoner.org) on the new enclosures and on whether primitive accumulation should be understood as a purely historical or a continuing process. DeAngelis (http://homepages.uel.ac.uk/M.DeAngelis/PRIMACCA.htm) provides a good summary.

24   K. Marx, *Capital*, Volume 1, New York: International Publishers, 1967, Part 8; F. Braudel, *Afterthoughts on Material Civilization and Capitalism*, Baltimore: Johns Hopkins University Press, 1977.

25   Wade and Veneroso, 'The Asian Crisis', p. 7 propose the following definition: 'high household savings, plus high corporate debt/equity ratios, plus bank-firm-state collaboration, plus national industrial strategy, plus investment incentives conditional on international competitiveness, equals the developmental state.' The classic study is C. Johnson, *MITI and the Japanese Miracle: The Growth of Industrial Policy, 1925-75*, Stanford: Stanford University Press, 1982; while the empirical impact of state policies upon relative rates of economic growth has been well-documented in M. Webber and D. Rigby, *The Golden Age Illusion: Rethinking Post-war*

86   SOCIALIST REGISTER 2004

Capitalism, New York: Guilford Press, 1996.

26   Wade and Veneroso, 'The Asian Crisis'.

27   The extent of resistance is indicated in B. Gills, ed., *Globalization and the Politics of Resistance*, New York: Palgrave, 2000; see also J. Brecher and T. Costello, *Global Village or Global Pillage? Economic Reconstruction from the Bottom Up*, Boston: South End Press, 1994. A crisp recent guide to the resistance is given in W. Bello, *Deglobalization: Ideas for a New World Economy*, London: Zed Books, 2002. The idea of globalization from below is presented most succinctly in R. Falk, *Predatory Globalization: A Critique*, Cambridge: Polity Press, 2000.

28   Arendt, *Imperialism*, p. 28.

29   By far the best account is given in P. Armstrong, A. Glyn and J. Harrison, *Capitalism Since World War II: The Making and Break Up of the Great Boom*, Oxford: Basil Blackwell, 1991.

30   Gowan, *Global Gamble*, pp. 21-2, cites the evidence for collusion between Nixon and the Saudis.

31   The left, embedded as it was (and still in many respect is) in the politics of expanded reproduction, was slow to recognize the significance of anti-IMF riots and other movements against dispossession. Walton's pioneering study on the pattern of anti-IMF riots stands out in retrospect. See J. Walton, *Reluctant Rebels: Comparative Studies on Revolution and Underdevelopment*, New York: Columbia University Press, 1984. But it also seems right that we do a far more sophisticated analysis to determine which of the myriad movements against dispossession are regressive and anti-modernizing in any socialist sense and which can be progressive or at least be pulled in a progressive direction by alliance formation. As ever, the way in which Gramsci analyzed the Southern question seems to be a pioneering study of this sort. Petras has recently emphasized this point in his critique of Hardt and Negri: see J. Petras, 'A Rose by Any Other Name? The Fragrance of Imperialism', *The Journal of Peasant Studies*, 29(2), 2002. Affluent peasants fighting against land reform are not the same as landless peasants fighting for the right to subsist.

32   P. Anderson, 'Internationalism: A Breviary', *New Left Review*, 14, 2002, p. 20, notes how 'something like Kautsky's vision' had come to pass and that liberal theorists, like Robert Keohane, also noticed the connection. On the new international financial architecture, see S. Soederberg, 'The New International Financial Architecture: Imposed Leadership and "Emerging Markets"', *Socialist Register 2002*, London: Merlin, 2002.

33   See Burkett and Hart-Landsberg, 'Crisis and Recovery'.

34   Brenner, *The Boom*, p. 3.

35   G. Arrighi and B. Silver, eds., *Chaos and Governance in the Modern World System*, Minneapolis: University of Minnesota Press, 1999, pp. 31-3.

36   Gowan, *Global Gamble*, p. 123.

37   Arrighi does not envisage any serious external challenge but he and his

THE 'NEW' IMPERIALISM   87

colleagues do conclude that the US 'has even greater capabilities than Britain did a century ago to convert its declining hegemony into exploitative domination. If the system eventually breaks down, it will be primarily because of US resistance to adjustment and accommodation. And conversely, US adjustment and accommodation to the rising economic power of the East Asian region is an essential condition for a non-catastrophic transition to a new world order.' See Arrighi and Silver, *Chaos and Governance*, pp. 288-9.

38 M. Klare, *Resource Wars: The New Landscape of Global Conflict*, New York: Henry Holt, 2002.

39 Cooper, 'New Liberal Imperialism'.

40 The critique mounted by U. Mehta, *Liberalism and Empire*, Chicago: Chicago University Press, 1999, is simply devastating when put up against Cooper's formulations.

41 Arendt, *Imperialism*, pp. 6-9; This has, interestingly, been a persistent internal source of concern against imperial ventures on the part of the United States, as William Appleman Williams points out in his *Empire as a Way of Life*, Oxford: New York, 1980.

Part III
State and Politics

[11]

The Constitution as an Elitist Document

Michael Parenti

Political scientist Michael Parenti is the author of *Power and the Powerless* (1978), *Inventing Reality: The Politics of the Mass Media* (1986), *Democracy for the Few* (5th ed. 1987), *The Sword and the Dollar: Imperialism, Revolution, and the Arms Race* (1989), and other works. He is currently completing *Make Believe Media*, a book on the politics of Hollywood film and television. Parenti resides in Washington, D.C., and lectures widely.

The following selection is reprinted, with emendations by the author for this edition, by permission of the American Enterprise Institute for Public Policy Research, from "The Constitution as an Elitist Document," in Robert A. Goldwin and William A. Schambra, eds., *How Democratic Is the Constitution?* (Washington, D.C.: American Enterprise Institute, 1980), 39–58.

How democratic is the Constitution? Not as democratic as we have been taught to believe. I will argue that the intent of the framers of the Constitution was to *contain* democracy, rather than give it free rein, and dilute the democratic will, rather than mobilize it. In addition, their goal was to construct a centralized power to serve the expanding interests of the manufacturing, commercial, landowning, and financial classes, rather than the needs of the populace. Evidence for this, it will be shown, can be found in the framers' opinions and actions and in the Constitution they fashioned. Finally, I will argue that the elitist design of the Constitution continues to function as intended, serving as a legitimating cloak and workable system for the propertied interests at the expense of the ordinary populace.

Class and Power in Early America

It is commonly taught that in the eighteenth and nineteenth centuries men of property preferred a laissez-faire government, one that kept its activities to

142 MICHAEL PARENTI

a minimum. In actuality, they were not against a strong state but against state restrictions on business enterprise. They never desired to remove civil authority from economic affairs but to ensure that it worked *for*, rather than against, the interests of property. This meant they often had to move toward new and stronger state formations.

Adam Smith, who is above suspicion in his dedication to classical capitalism, argued that, as wealth increased in scope, government would have to perform still greater services on behalf of the propertied class. "The necessity of civil government," he wrote, "grows up with the acquisition of valuable property."[1] More importantly, Smith argued seventy years before Marx, "Civil authority, so far as it is instituted for the security of property, is in reality instituted for the defense of the rich against the poor, or of those who have some property against those who have none at all."[2]

Smith's views of the purposes of government were shared by the rich and the wellborn who lived in America during the period between the Revolution and the framing of the Constitution. Rather than keeping their distance from government, they set the dominant political tone.

Their power was born of place, position, and fortune. They were located at or near the seats of government and they were in direct contact with legislatures and government officers. They influenced and often dominated the local newspapers which voiced the ideas and interests of commerce and identified them with the good of the whole people, the state, and the nation. The published writings of the leaders of the period are almost without exception those of merchants, of their lawyers, or of politicians sympathetic with them.[3]

The United States of 1787 has been described as an "egalitarian" society free from the extremes of want and wealth which characterized the Old World, but there were landed estates and colonial mansions that bespoke an impressive munificence. From the earliest English settlements, men of influence had received vast land grants from the crown. By 1700, three-fourths of the acreage in New York belonged to fewer than a dozen persons. In the interior of Virginia, seven persons owned a total of 1,732,000 acres.[4] By 1760, fewer than 500 men in five colonial cities controlled most of the commerce, banking, mining, and manufacturing on the eastern seaboard and owned much of the land.[5]

Here and there could be found farmers, shop owners, and tradesmen who, by the standards of the day, might be judged as comfortably situated. The bulk of the agrarian population were poor freeholders, tenants, squatters, and indentured and hired hands. The cities also had their poor—cobblers,

THE CONSTITUTION AS AN ELITIST DOCUMENT   143

weavers, bakers, blacksmiths, peddlers, laborers, clerks, and domestics, who worked long hours for meager sums.[6]

As of 1787, property qualifications left perhaps more than a third of the white male population disfranchised.[7] Property qualifications for holding office were so steep as to prevent most voters from qualifying as candidates. Thus, a member of the New Jersey legislature had to be worth at least 1,000 pounds, while state senators in South Carolina were required to possess estates worth at least 7,000 pounds, clear of debt.[8] In addition, the practice of oral voting, the lack of a secret ballot, and an "absence of a real choice among candidates and programs" led to "widespread apathy."[9] As a result, men of substance monopolized the important offices. "Who do they represent?" Josiah Quincy asked of the South Carolina legislature. "The laborer, the mechanic, the tradesman, the farmer, the husbandman or yeoman? No, the representatives are almost if not wholly rich planters."[10]

Dealing with Insurgency

The Constitution was framed by financially successful planters, merchants, lawyers, and creditors, many linked by kinship and marriage and by years of service in Congress, the military, or diplomatic service. They congregated in Philadelphia in 1787 for the professed purpose of revising the Articles of Confederation and strengthening the powers of the central government. They were impelled by a desire to do something about the increasingly insurgent spirit evidenced among poorer people. Fearful of losing control of their state governments, the framers looked to a national government as a means of protecting their interests. Even in a state like South Carolina, where the propertied class was distinguished by the intensity of its desire to avoid any strong federation, the rich and the well-born, once faced with the possibility of rule by the common people" and realizing that a political alliance with conservatives from other states would be a safeguard if the radicals should capture the state government . . . gave up 'state rights' for 'nationalism' without hesitation."[11] It swiftly became their view that a central government would be less accessible to the populace and would be better able to provide the protections and services that their class so needed.

The landed, manufacturing, and merchant interests needed a central government that would provide a stable currency; impose uniform standards for trade; tax directly; regulate commerce; improve roads, canals, and harbors; provide protection against foreign imports and against the discrimination

144   MICHAEL PARENTI

suffered by American shipping; and provide a national force to subjugate the Indians and secure the value of western lands. They needed a government that would honor at face value the huge sums of public securities they held and would protect them from paper-money schemes and from the large debtor class, the land-hungry agrarians, and the growing numbers of urban poor.

The nationalist conviction that arose so swiftly among men of property during the 1780s was not the product of a strange transcendent inspiration; it was not a "dream of nation-building" that suddenly possessed them as might a collective religious experience. (If so, they were remarkably successful in keeping it a secret in their public and private communications.) Rather, their newly acquired nationalism was a practical and urgent response to material conditions affecting them in a most immediate way. Gorham of Massachusetts, Hamilton of New York, Morris of Pennsylvania, Washington of Virginia, and Pinckney of South Carolina had a greater identity of interest with each other than with debt-burdened neighbors in their home counties. Their like-minded commitment to a central government was born of a common class interest stronger than state boundaries.

The rebellious populace of that day has been portrayed as irresponsible and parochial spendthrifts who never paid their debts and who believed in nothing more than timid state governments and inflated paper money. Little is said by most scholars of the period about the actual plight of the common people, the great bulk of whom lived at a subsistence level. Farm tenants were burdened by heavy rents and hard labor. Small farmers were hurt by the low prices merchants offered for their crops and by the high costs for merchandised goods. They often bought land at inflated prices, only to see its value collapse and to find themselves unable to meet their mortgage obligations. Their labor and their crops usually were theirs in name only. To survive, they frequently had to borrow money at high interest rates. To meet their debts, they mortgaged their future crops and went still deeper into debt. Large numbers were caught in that cycle of rural indebtedness which is the common fate of agrarian peoples in many countries to this day. The artisans, small tradesmen, and workers (or "mechanics," as they were called) in the towns were not much better off, being "dependent on the wealthy merchants who ruled them economically and socially." [12]

During the 1780s, the jails were crowded with debtors. Among the people, there grew the feeling that the revolution against England had been fought for naught. Angry, armed crowds in several states began blocking foreclosures

Containing the Spread of Democracy

and sales of seized property, and opening up jails. They gathered at county towns to prevent the courts from presiding over debtor cases. In the winter of 1787, farmers in western Massachusetts led by Daniel Shays took up arms. But their rebellion was forcibly put down by the state militia after some ragged skirmishes.[13]

Containing the Spread of Democracy

The specter of Shays' Rebellion hovered over the delegates who gathered in Philadelphia three months later, confirming their worst fears about the populace. They were determined that persons of birth and fortune should control the affairs of the nation and check the "leveling impulses" of that propertyless multitude which composed "the majority faction." "To secure the public good and private rights against the danger of such a faction," wrote James Madison in *Federalist* No. 10," and at the same time preserve the spirit and form of popular government is then the great object to which our inquiries are directed." Here Madison touched the heart of the matter: how to keep the *spirit* and *form* of popular government with only a minimum of the *substance,* how to provide the appearance of republicanism without suffering its leveling effects, how to construct a government that would win mass acquiescence but would not tamper with the existing class structure, a government strong enough both to service the growing needs of an entrepreneurial class while withstanding the egalitarian demands of the poor and propertyless.

The framers of the Constitution could agree with Madison when he wrote in the same *Federalist* No. 10 that "the most common and durable source of factions has been the various and unequal distribution of property. Those who hold and those who are without property have ever formed distinct interests in society." They were of the opinion that democracy was "the worst of all political evils," as Elbridge Gerry put it. Both he and Madison warned of "the danger of the leveling spirit." "The people," said Roger Sherman, "should have as little to do as may be about the Government." And according to Alexander Hamilton, "All communities divide themselves into the few and the many. The first are the rich and the well-born, the other the mass of the people. . . . The people are turbulent and changing; they seldom judge or determine right."[14]

The delegates spent many weeks debating their interests, but these were the differences of merchants, slave owners, and manufacturers, a debate of

146 MICHAEL PARENTI

haves versus haves in which each group sought safeguards within the new Constitution for its particular concerns. Added to this were the inevitable disagreements that arise over the best means of achieving agreed-upon ends. Questions of structure and authority occupied a good deal of the delegates' time: How much representation should the large and small states have? How might the legislature be organized? How should the executive be selected? What length of tenure should exist for the different officeholders? *Yet, questions of enormous significance, relating to the new government's ability to protect the interests of property, were agreed upon with surprisingly little debate.* For on these issues, there were no dirt farmers or poor artisans attending the convention to proffer an opposing viewpoint. The debate between haves and have-nots never occurred.

The portions of the Constitution giving the federal government the power to support commerce and protect property were decided upon after amiable deliberation and with remarkable dispatch considering their importance. Thus all of Article I, Section 8 was adopted within a few days.[15] This section gave to Congress the powers needed by the propertied class for the expansion of its commerce, trade, and industry, specifically the authority to (1) regulate commerce among the states and with foreign nations and Indian tribes, (2) lay and collect taxes and impose duties and tariffs on imports but not on commercial exports, (3) establish a national currency and regulate its value, (4) "borrow Money on the credit of the United States"—a measure of special interest to creditors,[16] (5) fix the standard of weights and measures necessary for trade, (6) protect the value of securities and currency against counterfeiting, (7) establish "uniform Laws on the subject of Bankruptcies throughout the United States," and (8) "pay the Debts and provide for the common Defense and general Welfare of the United States."

Some of the delegates were land speculators who expressed a concern about western holdings; accordingly, Congress was given the "Power to dispose of and make all needful Rules and Regulations respecting the Territory or other Property belong to the United States. . . ." Some delegates speculated in highly inflated and nearly worthless Confederation securities. Under Article VI, all debts incurred by the Confederation were valid against the new government, a provision that allowed speculators to make generous profits when their securities were honored at face value.[17]

In the interest of merchants and creditors, the states were prohibited from issuing paper money or imposing duties on imports and exports or interfering with the payment of debts by passing any "Law impairing the Obligation of

THE CONSTITUTION AS AN ELITIST DOCUMENT 147

Contracts." The Constitution guaranteed "Full Faith and Credit" in each state "to the Acts, Records, and judicial Proceedings" of other states, thus allowing creditors to pursue their debtors more effectively.

The property interests of slave owners were looked after. To give the slave-owning states a greater influence, three-fifths of the slave population were to be counted when calculating the representation deserved by each state in the lower house. The importation of slaves was allowed until 1808. Under Article IV, slaves who escaped from one state to another had to be delivered to the original owner upon claim, a provision unanimously adopted at the convention.

The framers believed the states acted with insufficient force against popular uprisings, so Congress was given the task of "organizing, arming, and disciplining the Militia" and calling it forth, among other reasons, to "suppress Insurrections." The federal government was empowered to protect the states "against domestic Violence." Provision was made for "the Erection of Forts, Magazines, Arsenals, dock-Yards and other needful Buildings" and for the maintenance of an army and navy for both national defense and to establish an armed federal presence within the potentially insurrectionary states—a provision that was to prove a godsend a century later when the army was used repeatedly to break strikes by miners, railroad employees, and factory workers.

In keeping with their desire to contain the majority, the founders inserted "auxiliary precautions" *designed to fragment power without democratizing it.* By separating the executive, legislative, and judiciary functions and then providing a system of checks and balances among the various branches, including staggered elections, executive veto, Senate confirmation of appointments and ratification of treaties, and a bicameral legislature, they hoped to dilute the impact of popular sentiments. They also contrived an elaborate and difficult process for amending the Constitution. *To the extent that it existed at all, the majoritarian principle was tightly locked into a system of minority vetoes, making sweeping popular actions nearly impossible.*

The propertyless majority, as Madison pointed out in *Federalist* No. 10, must not be allowed to concert in common cause against the established economic order.[18] First, it was necessary to prevent unity of public sentiment by enlarging the polity and then compartmentalizing it into geographically insulated political communities. The larger the nation, the greater the "variety of parties and interests" and the more difficult it would be for a majority to find itself and act in unison. As Madison argued, "A rage for paper money,

148 MICHAEL PARENTI

for an abolition of debts, for an equal division of property, or for any other wicked project will be less apt to pervade the whole body of the Union than a particular member of it. . . ." An uprising of impoverished farmers could threaten Massachusetts at one time and Rhode Island at another, but a national government would be large and varied enough to contain each of these and insulate the rest of the nation from the contamination of rebellion.

Political Diversity

Contemporary political scientists have said different things about the concept of political diversity. Some presume that a wide variety of interests produces moderation and compromise, it being argued that the "cross-pressured" lawmaker and voter and the multigroup polity are more likely to avoid the "extremist" solutions that are presumed to inflict those possessed of a single-minded, homogeneous political interest. In contrast, Madison welcomed diversity because it would produce not compromise but division. It would keep the mass of people divided against each other, unable to concert against the opulent class.

Political scientists have also feared that too great a multiplicity of interests makes compromise impossible, leading to the kind of factionalism and insta-bility that supposedly result when a vast array of irreconcilable demands are made on the polity. Here too, Madison was of a different mind. For him, the danger was centripetal, not centrifugal. The problem was not factional-ism, as such, but democracy. His concern was that the people might *not* be riddled with divisions, that they might unify in common cause as an oppres-sive majority "faction."

Here I would enter a qualification. A close reading of *Federalist* No. 10 actually uncovers two themes. The first is the one just mentioned, the one that occupied Madison's thoughts before and during the convention: the relation between the propertyless and the propertied, the division that was "the most common and durable source of factions," factions which "ever formed distinct interests in society." But in the same paragraph of that same great essay, Madison introduced another theme, shifting the focus from the divisions between the propertied and the propertyless to the divisions *among* the propertied. "A landed interest, a manufacturing interest, a mercantile interest, a moneyed interest grow up of necessity in civilized nations. . . ." For all his supposed concern for "factions," Madison was not too worried

THE CONSTITUTION AS AN ELITIST DOCUMENT   149

about *these* factions. Unlike the factionalism between the propertied and propertyless that necessitated the whole great effort in Philadelphia and the need for a central government, the minority factions of propertied interests caused him no alarm.

True, these minority factions might occasionally be a nuisance; they might "clog the administration" and even "convulse the society." But for some unstated reason, they would never be able "to sacrifice . . . the public good and the rights of other citizens," nor could any propertied faction "mask its violence under the forms of the Constitution." Only the majority faction was capable of such evils. Only the propertyless majority was capable of "improper and wicked projects" against property. The propertied interests, whatever their particular differences, would never advocate "an abolition of debts" or "an equal division of property"; they would never jeopardize the institution of property and wealth and the untrammeled uses thereof, which in their eyes—and Madison's—constituted the essence of "liberty."

There was, then, no need to impose constitutional checks upon the haves. If a larger polity would make it difficult for the populace to coalesce, it would do just the opposite for the propertied elites, allowing them to organize a centralized force to protect themselves from the turbulent plebeians within the various states. They would do well to settle their particular differences and work in unison to defend their common class interests. Indeed, in large part, that was what the Philadelphia convention was all about. Madison wanted what every elite has ever wanted, unity of purpose within his own class and divisions and conflicts within the other, larger one.

By focusing on Madison's second theme, the diversity of supposedly self-regulating propertied interests, modern-day political scientists discovered pluralism. By ignoring his first and major theme, the conflict between haves and have-nots, they have yet to discover class conflict.

It is interesting to note that Madison did not advocate minority rights as some abstract principle, although some of the language in the *Federalist Papers* seems to suggest so. He was concerned about protecting the *propertied* minority and not regional, racial, ethnic, or state minorities. In fact, on the question of representation he took a hardline majoritarian position. As a Virginian he repeatedly argued against giving the small states an equal voice in the Senate with the large ones. Representation should be proportional to population with no special provisions for the less populous states. On this question he evidenced not the slightest fear of majoritarian dominance, no

150   MICHAEL PARENTI

difficulty in brushing aside the anxieties of representational minorities in smaller states. To repeat, Madison's fear in Philadelphia was not of some abstract majority but of a particular *class* majority, a democracy.[19]

Besides preventing the people from finding *horizontal* cohesion, the Constitution was designed to dilute their *vertical* force, blunting its upward thrust upon government by interjecting indirect and staggered forms of representation. Thus, the senators from each state were to be elected by their respective state legislatures and were to have rotated terms of six years. The chief executive was to be selected by an electoral college voted by the people but, as anticipated by the framers, composed of men of substance and prominence who would gather in their various states and choose a president of their own liking. The Supreme Court was to be elected by no one, its justices being appointed to life tenure by the president and confirmed by the Senate.[20]

This system of checks would be the best safeguard against "agrarian attempts" and "symptoms of a leveling spirit," observed Madison at the convention. In those same remarks, he opposed a six-year term for the Senate, preferring a nine-year one because he believed the Senate should be composed of "a portion of enlightened citizens whose limited number and firmness might seasonably interpose against" popular impetuosity.[21] Exactly who were the "enlightened citizens"? Certainly not the tenants and squatters, nor even the average freeholder. Only the men of substance. If wealth were not a sufficient cause of enlightenment, it was almost always a necessary condition for Madison and his colleagues. Who else would have the breeding, education, and experience to govern? While often treated as an abstract virtue, "enlightened" rule had a real class meaning.

The only portion of government directly elected by the people was the House of Representatives. Many of the delegates would have preferred excluding the public entirely from direct representation. John Mercer observed that he found nothing in the proposed Constitution more objectionable than "the mode of election by the people. The people cannot know and judge of the characters of Candidates. The worst possible choice will be made." Others were concerned that demagogues would ride into office on a populist tide only to pillage the treasury and wreak havoc on all. "The time is not distant," warned Gouverneur Morris, "when this Country will abound with mechanics and manufacturers [industrial workers] who will receive their bread from their employers. Will such men be the secure and faithful Guardians of liberty? . . . Children do not vote. Why? Because they want prudence, because they have no will of their own. The ignorant and dependent can be as little trusted with the public interest."[22]

Several considerations softened the framers' determination to contain democracy. First and most important, the delegates recognized that there were limits to what the states would ratify. They also understood that if the federal government were to have any kind of stability, it must gain some measure of popular acceptance. Hence, for all their class biases, they were inclined to "leave something for the People," even if it were only "the *spirit* and *form* of popular government," to recall Madison's words. In addition, some delegates feared not only the tyranny of the many but the machinations of the few. It was Madison who reminded his colleagues that in protecting themselves from the multitude, they must not reintroduce a "cabal" or a monarchy, thus erring in the opposite direction.

Plotters or Patriots?

The question of whether the founders were motivated by financial or national interest has been debated since Charles Beard published *An Economic Interpretation of the Constitution* in 1913. It was Beard's view that the delegates were guided by their class interests. Arguing against Beard's thesis are those who believe that the framers were concerned with higher things than lining their purses and protecting their property. True, they were moneyed men who profited directly from policies initiated under the new Constitution, but they were motivated by a concern for nation building that went beyond their particular class interests, the argument goes.[23] To paraphrase Justice Holmes, these men invested their belief to make a nation; they did not make a nation because they had invested. "High-mindedness in not impossible to man," Holmes reminded us.

That is exactly the point: High-mindedness is one of man's most common attributes even when, or especially when, he is pursuing his personal and class interest. The fallacy is to presume that there is a dichotomy between the desire to build a strong nation and the desire to protect property and that the delegates could not have been motivated by both. In fact, like most other people, they believed that what was good for themselves was ultimately good for the entire society. Their universal values and their class interests went hand in hand; to discover the existence of the "higher" sentiment does not eliminate the self-interested one.

152   MICHAEL PARENTI

Most persons believe in their own virtue. The founders never doubted the nobility of their effort and its importance for the generations to come. Just as many of them could feel dedicated to the principle of "liberty for all" and at the same time own slaves, so could they serve both their nation and their estates. The point is not that they were devoid of the grander sentiments of nation building but that there was nothing in the concept of nation which worked against their class interest and a great deal that worked for it.

People tend to perceive things in accordance with the position they occupy in the social structure; that position is largely—although not exclusively—determined by their class status. Even if we deny that the framers were motivated by the desire for personal gain that moves others, we cannot dismiss the existence of their class interest. They may not have been solely concerned with getting their own hands in the till, although enough of them did, but they were admittedly preoccupied with defending the propertied few from the propertyless many—for the ultimate benefit of all, as they understood it. "The Constitution," as Staughton Lynd noted, "was the settlement of a revolution. What was at stake for Hamilton, Livingston, and their opponents, was more than speculative windfalls in securities; it was the question, what kind of society would emerge from the revolution when the dust had settled, and on which class the political center of gravity would come to rest."[24]

The small farmers, tradesmen, and debtors who opposed a central government have been described as motivated by self-serving parochial interests—as opposed to the supposedly higher-minded statesmen who journeyed to Philadelphia and others of their class who supported ratification. How or why the propertied rich became visionary nation builders is never explained. In truth, it was not their minds that were so much broader but their economic interests. Their motives were neither higher nor lower than those of any other social group struggling for place and power in the United States of 1787–1789. They pursued their material interests as single-mindedly as any small freeholder—if not more so. Possessing more time, money, information, and organization, they enjoyed superior results. How could they have acted otherwise? For them to have ignored the conditions of governance necessary for the maintenance of their enterprises would have amounted to committing class suicide—and they were not about to do that. They were a rising bourgeoisie rallying around a central power in order to advance their class interests. Some of us are quite willing to accept the existence of such

THE CONSTITUTION AS AN ELITIST DOCUMENT 153

a material-based nationalism in the history of other countries, but not in our own.

Among the mass of ordinary people there were some who supported the new Constitution. For instance some northern workers in cities like New York supported the provisions for stronger manufacturing and shipping protections.[25] This point has been made by latter-day apologists who wish to emphasize that the framers' work had popular support. Apparently suggestions that some *workers* supported the Constitution from direct economic interest is an acceptable datum, but to suggest that merchants, manufacturers, landowners, speculators, and creditors did so is a contention bred of the crudest economic determinism.

Finally, those who argue that the founders were motivated primarily by high-minded objectives consistently overlook the fact that the delegates repeatedly stated their intention to erect a government strong enough to protect the haves from the have-nots. They gave voice to the crassest class prejudices and never found it necessary to disguise the fact—as have latter-day apologists—that their uppermost concern was to diminish popular control and resist all tendencies toward class equalization (or "leveling," as it was called). Their opposition to democracy and their dedication to the propertied and moneyed interests were unabashedly and openly avowed. Their preoccupation was so pronounced that one delegate, James Wilson, did finally complain of hearing too much about how the purpose of government was to protect property. He wanted it noted that the ultimate objective of government was the ennoblement of mankind—a fine sentiment that evoked no opposition from his colleagues as they continued about their business.

An Elitist Document

More important than conjecturing about the framers' motives is to look at the Constitution they fashioned, for it tells a good deal about their objectives. It was, and still is, largely an elitist document, more concerned with securing property interests than personal liberties. Bills of attainder and ex post facto laws are expressly prohibited, and Article I, Section 9, assures us that "the Privilege of the Writ of Habeas Corpus shall not be suspended, unless when in Cases of Rebellion or Invasion the public Safety may require it," a restriction that leaves authorities with a wide measure of discretion. Other

154   MICHAEL PARENTI

than these few provisions, the Constitution that emerged from the Philadelphia Convention gave no attention to civil liberties.

When Colonel Mason suggested to the Convention that a committee be formed to draft "a Bill of Rights"—a task that could be accomplished "in a few hours"—the representatives of the various states offered little discussion on the motion and voted almost unanimously against it. The Bill of Rights, of course, was ratified only after the first Congress and president had been elected.

For the founders, liberty meant something different from democracy; it meant liberty to invest and trade and carry out the matters of business and enjoy the security of property without encroachment by king or populace. The civil liberties designed to give all individuals the right to engage actively in public affairs were of no central concern to the delegates and, as noted, were summarily voted down.

When asking how democratic the Constitution is, we need look not only at the Constitution but also at what we mean by "democracy," for different definitions have been ascribed to the term. Let us say that democracy is a system of governance that represents, both in form *and content*, the desires and interests of the ruled. This definition is more meaningful for the twentieth century—and at the same time somewhat closer to the eighteenth-century one—than the currently propagated view that reduces democracy to a set of procedures and "rules of the game." Democracy is a *social order* with a social class content—which is why the framers so disliked it. What they feared about democracy was not its forms but its content, the idea that the decisions of government might be of substantive benefit to the popular class at the expense of their own.

In a democracy, the people exercise a measure of control by electing their representatives and by subjecting them to the check of periodic elections, open criticism, and removal from office. In addition, a democratic people should be able to live without fear of want, enjoying freedom from economic, as well as political, oppression. In a real democracy, the material conditions of people's lives should be humane and roughly equal. It was this democratic vision that loomed as a nightmare for the framers and for so many of their spiritual descendants today.

Some people argue that democracy is simply a system of rules for playing the game, which allows some measure of mass participation and government accountability, and that the Constitution is a kind of rule book. One should not try to impose, as a precondition of democracy, particular class relations, economic philosophies, or other substantive arrangements on this open-ended game. This argument certainly does reduce democracy to a game. It presumes that formal rules can exist in a meaningful way independently of substantive realities. Whether procedural rights are violated or enjoyed, whether one is treated by law as pariah or prince, depends largely on material realities that extend beyond a written constitution or other formal guarantees of law. Whether a political system is democratic depends not only on its procedures but on its substantive outputs, that is, the actual material benefits and costs of policy and the kind of social justice, or injustice, that is propagated. By this view, a government that pursues policies that by design or neglect are so inequitable as to deny people the very conditions of life, is not fully democratic, no matter how many competitive elections it holds.

The twentieth-century concept of social justice, involving something more than procedural liberties, is afforded no place in the eighteenth-century Constitution. The Constitution says nothing about those conditions of like that have come to be treated by many people as essential human rights—for instance, freedom from hunger; the right to decent housing, medical care, and education regardless of ability to pay; the right to gainful employment, safe working conditions, and a clean, nontoxic environment. Under the Constitution, equality is treated as a *procedural* right without a *substantive* content. Thus, "equality of opportunity" means equality of opportunity to move ahead competitively and become unequal to others; it means a chance to get in the game and best others rather than to enjoy an equal distribution and use of the resources needed for the maintenance of community life.

If the founders sought to "check power with power," they seemed chiefly concerned with restraining mass power, while assuring the perpetuation of their own class power. They supposedly had a "realistic" opinion of the self-interested and rapacious nature of human beings—readily evidenced when they talked about the common people—yet they held a remarkably sanguine view of the self-interested impulses of their own class, which they saw as being inhabited by industrious, trustworthy, and virtuous men. Recall Hamilton's facile reassurance that the rich will "check the unsteadiness" of the poor and will themselves "ever maintain good government" by being given a "distinct permanent share" in it. Power corrupts others but somehow has the opposite effect on the rich and the wellborn.

If the Constitution is so blatantly elitist, how did it manage to win enough popular support for ratification? First, it should be noted that it did not have a wide measure of support, initially being opposed in most of the states. But

156 MICHAEL PARENTI

the same superiority of wealth, leadership, organization, control of the press, and control of political office that allowed the rich to monopolize the Philadelphia Convention worked with similar effect in the ratification campaign. Superior wealth also enabled the Federalists to bribe, intimidate, and, in other ways, pressure and discourage opponents of the Constitution. At the same time, there were some elements in the laboring class, especially those who hoped to profit from employment in shipping and export trades, who supported ratification.[26]

Above all, it should be pointed out that the Constitution never was submitted to popular ratification. There was no national referendum and none in the states. Ratification was by state convention composed of elected delegates, the majority of whom were drawn from the more affluent strata. The voters who took part in the selection of delegates were subjected to a variety of property restrictions. In addition, the poor, even if enfranchised, carried all the liabilities that have caused them to be underrepresented in elections before and since: a lack of information and organization, illiteracy, a sense of being unable to have any effect on events, and a feeling that none of the candidates represented their interests. There were also the problems of relatively inaccessible polls and the absence of a secret ballot. Even if two-thirds or more of the adult white males could vote for delegates, as might have been the case in most states, probably not more than 20 percent actually did.[27]

In sum, the framers laid the foundation for a national government, but it was one that fit the specifications of the propertied class. They wanted protection from popular uprisings, from fiscal uncertainty and irregularities in trade and currency, from trade barriers between states, from economic competition by more powerful foreign governments, and from attacks by the poor on property and on creditors. The Constitution was consciously designed as a conservative document, elaborately equipped with a system of minority checks and vetoes, making it hard to enact sweeping popular reforms or profound structural changes, and easy for entrenched interests to endure. It provided ample power to build the services and protections of state needed by a growing capitalist class but not the power for a transition of rule to a different class or to the public as a whole.

Democratic Concessions

For all its undemocratic aspects, the Constitution was not without its historically progressive features.[28] Consider the following:

THE CONSTITUTION AS AN ELITIST DOCUMENT 157

1. The very existence of a written constitution with specifically limited powers represented an advance over more autocratic forms of government.

2. No property qualifications were required for any federal officeholder, unlike in England and most of the states. And salaries were provided for all officials, thus rejecting the common practice of treating public office as a voluntary service, which only the rich could afford.

3. The President and all other officeholders were elected for limited terms. No one could claim a life tenure on any office.

4. Article VI reads: "No religious Test shall ever be required as a Qualification to any Office or public Trust under the United States," a feature that represented a distinct advance over a number of state constitutions which banned Catholics, Jews, and nonbelievers from holding office.

5. Bills of attainder, the practice of declaring by legislative fiat a specific person or group of people guilty of an offense, without benefit of a trial, were made unconstitutional. Also outlawed were ex post facto laws, the practice of declaring an act a crime and punishing those who had committed it *before* it had been unlawful.

6. As noted earlier, the framers showed no interest in a Bill of Rights, but supporters of the new Constitution soon recognized their tactical error and pledged the swift adoption of such a bill as a condition for ratification. So in the first session of Congress, the first ten amendments were swiftly passed and then adopted by the states; these rights included freedom of speech and religion; freedom to assemble peaceably and to petition for redress of grievances; the right to keep arms; freedom from unreasonable searches and seizures, self-incrimination, double jeopardy, cruel and unusual punishment, and excessive bail and fines; the right to a fair and impartial trial; and other forms of due process.

7. The Constitution guarantees a republican form of government and explicitly repudiates monarchy and aristocracy; hence, Article I, Section 9 states: "No title of Nobility shall be granted by the United States . . ." According to James McHenry, a delegate from Maryland, *at least 21 of the 55 delegates favored some form of monarchy.* Yet few dared venture in that direction out of fear of popular opposition. Furthermore, delegates like Madison believed that stability for their class order was best assured by a republican form of government. The time had come for the bourgeoisie to rule directly without the baneful intrusions of kings and nobles.

Time and again during the Philadelphia convention, this assemblage of men who feared and loathed democracy found it necessary to show some regard for popular sentiment (as with the direct election of the lower house). If the Constitution was going to be accepted by the states and if the new government was to have any stability, it had to gain some measure of popular acceptance; hence, the founders felt compelled to leave something for the people. While the delegates and their class dominated the events of 1787–89, they were far from omnipotent. The class system they sought to preserve was itself the cause of marked restiveness among the people.

158 MICHAEL PARENTI

Land seizures by the poor, food riots, and other violent disturbances occurred throughout the eighteenth century in just about every state and erstwhile colony.[29] This popular fomentation spurred the framers in their effort to erect a strong central government *but it also set a limit on what they could do.* The delegates "gave" nothing to popular interests; rather—as with the Bill of Rights—they reluctantly made concessions under the threat of democratic rebellion. They kept what they could and grudgingly relinquished what they felt they had to, driven not by a love of democracy but by a fear of it, not by a love of the people but by a prudent desire to avoid popular uprisings. The Constitution, then, was a product not only of class privilege but of class struggle—a struggle that continued and intensified as the corporate economy and the government grew.

With some democratizing changes, including the direct election of the Senate and the enfranchisement of women, the Constitution fashioned in 1787 has served its intended purpose. During the industrial strife of the late nineteenth century, when the state militias proved unreliable and state legislatures too responsive to the demands of workers, the military power of the federal government was used repeatedly to suppress labor insurgency. Where would the robber barons have been without a Constitution that provided them with the forceful services of the U.S. Army?[30]

Similarly, for over seventy years, the Supreme Court wielded a minority veto on social welfare, unionization, and taxation, preventing reform legislation that had been enacted in European countries decades earlier. The Court became—and with momentary exceptions remains—what the founders intended it to be, a nonelective branch staffed by persons of elitist political, legal, and business backgrounds, exercising a preponderantly conservative influence as guardian of existing class and property relations.

The Senate today qualifies as the "tinsel aristocracy" that Jefferson scorned, composed mostly of persons with large financial holdings, many of them millionaires, who vote their own interests with shameless regularity. The House is subdivided into a network of special-interest subcommittees, dominated by the concerns of banking, agribusiness, and big corporations, in what has become almost a parody of Madison's lesson on how to divide power in order to fragment mass pressures and protect the propertied few.[31]

The system of popular elections, an institution most of the founders never liked, has been safely captured by two political parties that are financed by moneyed interests and dedicated to the existing corporate social order. In modern times, especially at the national level, men of property have demon-

THE CONSTITUTION AS AN ELITIST DOCUMENT   159

strated their adeptness at financing elections, running for office, getting elected, and influencing those who are elected, in ways that would warm the heart of the most conservative Federalist. Electoral politics is largely a rich man's game and the property qualifications—as translated into campaign costs—are far steeper today than in 1787.

The endeavor the framers began in Philadelphia, for a stronger central government to serve the commercial and industrial class, has continued and accelerated. As industrial capitalism has expanded at home and abroad, the burden of subsidizing its endeavors and providing the military force needed to protect its markets, resources, and client states has fallen disproportionately on that level of government which is national and international in scope— the federal—and on that branch which is best suited to carry out the necessary technical, organizational, and military tasks—the executive. The important decisions increasingly are being made in federal departments and corporate boardrooms and in the advisory committees that are linked to the upper echelons of the executive branch, staffed by public policy makers and private representatives of the major industries. I described this in an earlier work:

One might better think of ours as a dual political system. First, there is the *symbolic* political system centering around electoral and representative activities including party conflicts, voter turnout, political personalities, public pronouncements, official role-playing and certain ambiguous presentations of some of the public issues which bestir Presidents, governors, mayors and their respective legislatures. Then there is the *substantive* political system, involving multibillion-dollar contracts, tax write-offs, protections, rebates, grants, loss compensations, subsidies, leases, giveaways and the whole vast process of budgeting, legislating, advising, regulating, protecting and servicing major producer interests, now bending or ignoring the law on behalf of the powerful, now applying it with full punitive vigor against heretics and "troublemakers." The symbolic system is highly visible, taught in the schools, dissected by academicians, gossiped about by newsmen. The substantive system is seldom heard of or accounted for.[32]

By offering well-protected havens for powerful special interests, by ignoring substantive rights and outcomes, by mobilizing the wealth and force of the state in a centralizing and property-serving way, by making democratic change difficult, the Constitution has served well an undemocratic military-industrial corporate structure. The rule of the "minority faction," the "persons of substance," the "propertied interest," the "rich and the well-born"—to mention a few of the ways the founders described their class—has prevailed. The

160   MICHAEL PARENTI

delegates would have every reason to be satisfied with the enduring nature of their work.

Notes

1. Adam Smith, *An Inquiry into the Nature and Causes of the Wealth of Nations* (Chicago: Encyclopaedia Britannica, Inc., 1952), p. 309.
2. Ibid., p. 311.
3. Merrill Jensen, *The New Nation* (New York: Random House, 1950), p. 178.
4. Sidney H. Aronson, *Status and Kinship in the Higher Civil Service* (Cambridge, Mass.: Harvard University Press, 1964), p. 35.
5. Ibid., p. 41.
6. Ibid., passim.
7. This is Beard's estimate regarding New York. Charles A. Beard, *An Economic Interpretation of the Constitution of the United States* (New York: Macmillan, 1935), pp. 67–68. In a few states like Pennsylvania and Georgia, suffrage was more widespread; in others it was even more restricted than New York; see Arthur Ekrich, Jr., *The American Democratic Tradition* (New York: Macmillan, 1963). For a pioneer work on this subject, see A. E. McKinley, *The Suffrage Franchise in the Thirteen English Colonies in America* (Philadelphia: B. Franklin, 1969, originally published 1905). Robert E. Brown makes the argument that Massachusetts was close to being both an economic and political democracy—which would have been alarming news to the Boston aristocracy of manufacturers, merchants, and large property holders. He conjectures that property requirements of a 40 shilling freehold could be easily met and that rural underrepresentation (during the same period that produced Shays' Rebellion) was due more to indifference than to disenfranchisement. See his *Middle-Class Democracy and the Revolution in Massachusetts* (Ithaca, N.Y.: Cornell University Press, 1955).
8. Beard, *An Economic Interpretation*, pp. 68, 70.
9. Aronson, *Status and Kinship*, p. 49.
10. Ibid., p. 49.
11. Merrill Jensen, *The Articles of Confederation* (Madison: University of Wisconsin Press, 1948), p. 30.
12. Ibid., pp. 9–10. "In addition to being frequently in debt for their lands," Beard noted, "the small farmers were dependent upon the towns for most of the capital to develop their resources. They were, in other words, a large debtor class, to which must be added, or course, the urban dwellers who were in a like unfortunate condition." Beard, *An Economic Interpretation*, p. 28.
13. For a study of this incident, see Monroe Stearns, *Shays' Rebellion, 1786–7: Americans Take Up Arms Against Unjust Laws* (New York: Franklin Watts, 1968).
14. The quotations by Gerry, Madison, Sherman, and Hamilton are taken from

THE CONSTITUTION AS AN ELITIST DOCUMENT 161

Max Farrand, ed., *Records of the Federal Convention* (New Haven: Yale University Press, 1927), vol. 1, passim. For further testimony by the Founding Fathers and other early leaders, see John C. Miller, *Origins of the American Revolution* (Boston: Little, Brown, 1943), pp. 491 ff. and Andrew C. McLaughlin, *A Constitutional History of the United States* (New York: Appleton-Century, 1935), pp. 141–144.

15. John Bach McMaster, "Framing the Constitution," in his *The Political Depravity of the Founding Fathers* (New York: Farrar, Straus, 1964, originally published in 1896), p. 137. Farrand refers to the consensus for a strong national government that emerged after the small states had been given equal representation in the Senate. Much of the work that followed "was purely formal" albeit sometimes time-consuming. See Max Farrand, *The Framing of the Constitution of the United States* (New Haven: Yale University Press, 1913), pp. 134–135.

16. The original working was "borrow money and emit bills." The latter phrase was deleted after Gouverneur Morris warned that "the Monied interest" would oppose the Constitution if paper notes were not prohibited. There was much strong feeling about this among creditors. In any case, it was assumed that the borrowing power would allow for "safe and proper" public notes should they be necessary. See Farrand, *The Framing of the Constitution*, p. 147.

17. See Beard, *An Economic Interpretation*, passim. The profits accrued to holders of public securities were in the millions. On the question of speculation in western lands, Hugh Williamson, a North Carolina delegate, wrote to Madison a year after the convention: "For myself, I conceive that my opinions are not biassed by private Interests, but having claims to a considerable Quantity of Land in the Western Country, I am fully persuaded that the Value of those Lands must be increased by an efficient federal Government." Ibid., p. 50. Critiques of Beard have been made by Robert E. Brown, *Charles Beard and the American Constitution* (Princeton, N.J.: Princeton University Press, 1956) and Forrest McDonald, *We the People—The Economic Origins of the Constitution* (Chicago: Chicago University Press, 1958).

18. *Federalist* No. 10 can be found in any of the good editions of *The Federalist Papers*. It is one of the most significant essays on American politics ever written. With clarity and economy of language, it explains, as do few other short works, how a government may utilize the republican principle to contain the populace and protect the propertied few from the propertyless many. It confronts, if not solves, the essential question of how government may reconcile the tensions between liberty, authority, and dominant class interest. In effect, the Tenth *Federalist* Paper maps out a method, relevant to this day, for preserving the existing undemocratic class structure under the legitimizing cloak of democratic forms.

19. See his lengthy comments of June 28 and July 14, 1787, in Madison's *The Debates in the Federal Convention of 1787 Which Framed the Constitution of the United States of America*, ed. Gaillard Hunt and James Brown Scott (New York: Oxford University Press, 1920), pp. 177–180, 256–258.

20. In time, of course, the electoral college proved to be something of a rubber

162   MICHAEL PARENTI

stamp, and the Seventeenth Amendment, adopted in 1913, provided for the popular election of the Senate.

21. Madison's speech of June 26, 1787, in *The Debates in the Federal Convention*, p. 167.

22. Farrand, *Records of the Federal Convention*, vol. 2, pp. 200 ff.

23. For some typical apologistic arguments on behalf of the "Founding Fathers" see Broadus Mitchell and Louise Pearson Mitchell, A *Biography of the Constitution of the United States* (New York: Oxford University Press, 1964), pp. 46–51, and David G. Smith, *The Convention and the Constitution* (New York: St. Martin's Press, 1965), chap. 3. Smith argues that the framers had not only economic motives but "larger" political objectives, as if the political had no relation to the economic or as if the economic interests were less selfish because they were national in financial scope.

24. Staughton Lynd, *Class Conflict, Slavery and the United States Constitution* (Indianapolis: Bobbs-Merrill, 1967), selection in Irwin Unger, ed., *Beyond Liberalism: The New Left Views American History* (Waltham, Mass.: Xerox College Publishing, 1971), p. 17. For discussions of the class interests behind the American Revolution, see Alfred F. Young, ed., *The American Revolution: Explorations in the History of American Radicalism* (DeKalb, Ill.: Northern Illinois University Press, 1976).

25. Beard, *An Economic Interpretation*, pp. 44–45.

26. See Jackson Turner Main, *The Antifederalists* (Chapel Hill: University of North Carolina Press, 1961).

27. See the studies cited by Beard, *An Economic Interpretation*, p. 242 ff.

28. This section on the progressive features of the Constitution is drawn from Herbert Aptheker, *Early Years of the Republic* (New York: International Publishers, 1976), pp. 71 ff. and passim.

29. Howard Zinn, A *People's History of the United States* (New York: Harper and Row, 1980), chapter 3.

30. See William Preston, Jr., *Aliens and Dissenters* (Cambridge, Mass.: Harvard University Press, 1963).

31. For a fuller exposition of these points see my *Democracy for the Few*, 5th ed. (New York: St. Martin's Press, 1987).

32. Ibid.

[12]

THE MONOPOLISTIC ECONOMY
Property and Contract

Franz Neumann

To understand the nature of the National Socialist economic system, a few considerations on the relation between property and contract will prove helpful. What is capitalism? How do we define it? Many identify capitalism with freedom of trade and contract, that is, with free competition. Capitalism is defined as an economy that is continuously maintained by the free initiative of a large number of entrepreneurs competing in a free market. It is thereby identified with one phase of its development, competitive capitalism. In that phase, free competition is held to be the distinguishing mark. This theory of capitalism is to a certain extent the classical one, though it has highly significant differences.

We propose to illustrate the nature of the economic system by an examination of the institution of property. By an institution, we mean an authoritarian or co-operative enduring association of men or of men and property, for the continuation of social life. This definition is purely descriptive. It has nothing to do with institutionalist philosophies, with pluralism, neo-Thomism, or syndicalism. Our definition covers all kinds of institutions: family, property, foundations, et cetera. Above all, it defines the major institution of modern society, private property in the means of production. Property, for a lawyer, is merely a subjective right that one man has against all others. It endows the proprietor with absolute defensive rights. The scope of man's power over the things he owns is, in principle, unlimited. The owner is a sovereign.

But the sociologist has to distinguish between various types of property. The man who owns a house in which he lives, furniture which he uses, clothes which he wears, food which he eats, an auto-

354   FASCISM AND COUNTERREVOLUTION

mobile which he drives, has no other power than the direct possession of the things he owns. He does not by virtue of his ownership control other men's lives. Houses, food, clothes, and automobiles are not institutions, are not intended to endure. They disappear or become valueless as they are consumed or used.

There is, however, a second type of property which is an institution, because it is an enduring and authoritarian organization for the perpetuation and reproduction of society: property of the means of production. In our language, domination over means of consumption and means of production is called by the same name: "property"; the term has thus become the legal mask behind which the owner of the means of production exercises power over other men. The term property (and ownership) never indicates what kind of object and what kind of power lies behind it, whether it is restricted to control over things or whether it also gives control over the fate of men. Property in the means of production gives power: power over workers, power over the consumers, power over the state. Property in the means of production is enduring, it aids in the continuous reproduction of society, it is the primary institution of modern society.

According to liberal ideas, if society is continuously to reproduce itself, there must be a free market. The prime requisites of the free market are free entrepreneurs, freedom of contract, and freedom of trade. The owner must be able to sell and to purchase, to lend and to borrow, to hire and to dismiss. Freedom of contract is, therefore, a supplementary or auxiliary guarantee of private property. It makes it possible for the owner of the means of production to produce and distribute. A competitive society must also be based on freedom of trade, the right to carry on one's business without interference and to establish a competing business. Freedom of trade is therefore another supplementary or auxiliary guarantee of property during the era of free competition. It, too, aids in the reproduction of society. In the process of competition, unfit competitors are thrown out, new establishments arise. Disturbances in equilibrium eliminate entrepreneurs who are not sufficiently rational in the conduct of their business; higher profits in one branch attract capital from other branches, thereby preserving the dynamic quality of a competitive society. Freedom of trade and freedom of contract are thus integral elements in a competitive society.

Hence property is surrounded by supplementary and auxiliary guarantees and by supplementary and auxiliary institutions, which make the operation of this major institution possible. They are at the service of the major institution, property, and are, in consequence, changed when the institution changes its function. Thus they are not merely juristic categories, as they are conceived to be today. The natural lawyers of the seventeenth century and the classical economists of the eighteenth century clearly realized that freedom of contract and freedom of trade are not simply legal categories but exercise specific social functions. Present-day apologists of economic liberalism maintain that freedom of contract implies the right to establish industrial combinations, to erect cartels, concerns, and trusts. They believe that freedom of trade exists even when a branch of industry is so completely monopolized that freedom of trade becomes a mere formal right. They maintain that competition implies the right to eliminate competing businesses and to establish the prerogative of a monopolistic group.

This was not the view held by the classical economists. "One individual must never prefer himself so much even to any other individual as to hurt or injure that other in order to benefit himself, though the benefit of the one should be much greater than the hurt or injury of the other." "In the race for wealth and honor and preferment, each may run as hard as he can and strain every nerve and every muscle in order to outstrip all his competitors, but if he should justle or throw down any of them, the indulgence of the spectators is entirely at an end." In these statements, Adam Smith introduces a distinction between two kinds of competition, one based on efficiency and the other based on the destruction of the competitor. He does not tolerate unfettered competition, since, in the theory of Adam Smith, competition is more than a right of the entrepreneur: it is the basic device for the continuous reproduction of society on an ever higher level. But this necessarily presupposes the absence of monopolies. Freedom of contract does not imply the right to establish industrial combinations; freedom of contract is the form of "free commodities." Where the commodities are not free, where they are monopolized, governmental interference must take place. "For a free commodity . . . there is no occasion for this [governmental interference], but it is necessary for bakers who may agree among themselves to make the quantity and prices what they please."

Yet the assumptions under which the classical economists are willing to guarantee freedom are still wider in character. They refer to the basic institution of society, to private property. Monopolies are repudiated as incompatible with the economic and social system, exceptions being allowed only for colonies, and even here only for a transitional period. As for the laws passed during the mercantilist period for protecting monopolies—"Like the laws of Draco, these laws may be said to be written in blood." Even the joint stock corporation is rejected in principle and allowed only for four economic activities: banking, insurance, the building and navigation of canals, and the water supply of great cities. It is characteristic of the profound sociological insight of Adam Smith that he considers joint stock corporations

356 FASCISM AND COUNTERREVOLUTION

legitimate only because in these activities the initiative of the entrepreneur has become unnecessary since the economic activity has been reduced to a mere routine.

The mechanism of the classical system is based, therefore, on the assumption of a large number of entrepreneurs of about equal strength, freely competing with each other on the basis of freedom of contract and freedom of trade, with the entrepreneur investing his capital and his labor for the purpose of his economic ends, and bearing the economic risks involved.

In this stage of society, freedom of contract was indeed the means by which society was held together. The contract was then the form through which the owner exercised his liberty and it was at the same time the means of ending the isolation in which each owner finds himself. "To bring about that I may own property, not only by means of a thing and my own subjective will but by means of another will and thereby a common will—this constitutes the sphere of contract." In Hegel's words, therefore, contract is the form in which society recognizes property and by which the property owners constitute society.

It is characteristic of the later development of capitalism that it completely divorced the juristic categories of freedom of contract and freedom of trade from the socio-economic background and thereby made the juristic categories absolute. Freedom of contract, the means by which free competition was secured, became the device by which it has been destroyed. Legal theory and practice, even more so in Europe than in the United States, separated the legal notion "freedom of trade" from the socio-economic requirements. Freedom of contract became the means of and the justification for the formation of industrial combinations, announcing the end of free competition. In the same way, freedom of trade degenerated into a mechanism for maintaining economic privileges and prerogatives. Its existence was asserted even in those branches of industry in which, because of the immense capital investment in one plant, no outsider could hope to establish a competing business, since he could not put up the necessary capital. Freedom of trade was perverted into a slogan for the defense of economic prerogatives and against state intervention.

This is one side of the development, but there is a second which is perhaps still more characteristic. Freedom of contract, although long disputed, implies the right to form trade unions and to oppose the power of the monopolist by the collective power of labor. Freedom of trade also implies the right of any entrepreneur to leave a combination and to re-establish his economic freedom, thereby endangering monopolistic possessions. Although it has lost much of its actual content, it still allows the establishment of competing business, once again endangering monopolistic privileges. These rights assume an especially dangerous form of monopolistic privileges in periods of recession and depression. The more perfect and rigid the structure of the economy becomes, the more sensitive it is to cyclical changes. A severe depression will inevitably shatter monopolistic positions. Cartels will be dissolved, outsiders will remain aloof, labor unions will fight off cuts in wages, protected by the sanctity of contracts. In such periods, the free contract, the freedom to keep aloof from the monopolists; turns into a major weapon against them.

Moreover, the new technology requires enormous investments, which involve risks and may give but uncertain returns. Only rich and powerful corporations will be able to make such investments, and their willingness to do so will depend upon what protection they receive—against cut-throat competition and the chiseler, even against competition as such. They may—and do—even demand specific guarantees from the state, in the form of guarantees of profit or turnover, of permission to write off investments in a short time, even in the form of outright subsidies. Outsiders, new competitors, labor unions—all these manifestations of freedom of trade and contract are then a nuisance. They must be destroyed.

For both sides, therefore—for the large masses and the small businessman on the one hand and the monopolistic powers on the other— state intervention in economic life becomes the major problem. The large masses and the small businessman will call in the state machinery for their protection. They will demand interference in the freedom of contract and freedom of trade in order to halt monopolization or even to dissolve existing industrial combines. By that demand they are merely drawing the consequences of the views of the classical economists. But in this situation monopolists will demand abrogation of freedom of contract and freedom of trade. They will insist that the right of industrial enterprises to leave cartels or to stay aloof from them means ruin for the economic system. They will point out that the freedom of labor to organize increases the costs of production and thereby the price of commodities. They will therefore demand complete abrogation of economic liberty.

In the period of monopolization, the new auxiliary guarantee of property is no longer the contract but the administrative act, the form in which the state interferes. But because that is so, it is the form and the content of the interventionist measure that now assumes supreme importance. Who is to interfere and on whose behalf becomes the most important question for modern society. The possession of the state machinery is thus the pivotal position around which everything else revolves. This is the only possible meaning of primacy of politics over economics. Shall the state crush monopolistic possessions, shall it restrict them for the sake of the masses, or shall interference be used

358 FASCISM AND COUNTERREVOLUTION

to strengthen the monopolistic position, to aid in the complete incorporation of all business activities into the network of industrial organizations? Shall the state become the weapon by which the masses will be made completely subservient to the policies of the industrial empires within it?

The aims of the monopolistic powers could not be carried out in a system of political democracy, at least not in Germany. The Social Democratic party and the trade unions, though they had lost their aggressive militancy, were still powerful enough to defend their gains. Their defensive strength made it impossible to place the whole machinery of the state at the service of one particular group in society. Similarly, the National Socialist party could not possibly carry out its economic policy on a democratic basis. Its propaganda and program were ostensibly aimed at protecting the small and medium-scale entrepreneur, handicraftsman, and trader—that is, those very groups that have suffered most under the National Socialist regime. The complete subjugation of the state by the industrial rulers could only be carried out in a political organization in which there was no control from below, which lacked autonomous mass organizations and freedom of criticism. It was one of the functions of National Socialism to suppress and eliminate political and economic liberty by means of the new auxiliary guarantees of property, by the command, by the administrative act, thus forcing the whole economic activity of Germany into the network of industrial combinations run by the industrial magnates.

The German economy of today has two broad and striking characteristics. It is a monopolistic economy—*and* a command economy. It is a private capitalistic economy, regimented by the totalitarian state. We suggest as a name best to describe it, "Totalitarian Monopoly Capitalism."

. . .

THE RULING CLASS

If one believes that Germany's economy is no longer capitalistic under National Socialism, it is easy to believe further that her society has become classless. This is the thesis of the late Emil Lederer. A brief analysis of his book will serve to introduce our discussion of the new German society.[1]

Lederer rejects attempts to define National Socialism as the last line of defense of capitalism, as the rule of the strong man, as the revolt of the middle classes, as domination by the army, or as the ascendency

---

[1] The book referred to by Emil Lederer is *State of the Masses: The Threat of the Classless Society* (New York, 1940).—*Ed.*

of the untalented. For him, it is a "modern political system which rests on amorphous masses." It is the masses "which sweep the dictator into power and keep him there" (page 18). The masses are therefore the actors, not the tools of a ruling class.

But who are the masses? They are the opposite of classes. They can be united solely by emotions (page 31); they tend to "burst into sudden action" (page 38), and being amorphous, they must be integrated by a leader who can articulate their emotions (page 39). As the very opposite of classes, the masses make up a classless society. The policy of National Socialism is to transfer a class-stratified society into masses by keeping the latter in a state of perpetual tension (page 105). Since the regime must also satisfy the material demands of the masses, it goes in for large-scale public spending and thus achieves full employment. National Socialism realizes that "people are filled with envy, with hatred for the rich and successful" (pages 110–11). The emotions can best be kept alive in the field of foreign affairs; for an aggressive foreign policy and preparation for foreign war prevent "the reawakening of thinking and of articulation into social groups" (page 123).

National Socialist society is thus composed of the ruling party and the amorphous masses (page 127). All other distinctions are removed. "It is on this psychological basis that the Fascist party has been built up. With their success they attract active mass-men who then are kept in a state of emotion and cannot return to their former ways of life. Even family cohesion is broken, the pulverization of society is complete. Masses make dictators, and dictators make masses the continuing basis of the state" (page 131). That is why the social stratification of society is of the utmost importance and why the Marxist theory of a classless society becomes so dangerous (page 138). National Socialism has completely destroyed the power of social groups and has established a classless society.

Were Lederer's analysis correct, our earlier discussion would be completely wrong. Social imperialism would then be not a device to ensnare the masses but an articulation of the spontaneous longing of the masses. Racism would not be the concern of small groups alone but would be deeply imbedded in the masses. Leadership adoration would be a genuine semi-religious phenomenon and not merely a device to prevent insight into the operation of the social-economic mechanism. Capitalism, finally, would be dead, since all particular groups have been destroyed and only leaders and masses remain.

Lederer is wrong, however, though a little of the truth sifts into some of his formulations. Occasionally one feels that even he realizes that the so-called spontaneity of the masses and their active participation in National Socialism are a sham and that the role of the people is merely to serve as an instrument of the ruling group. The problem

360 FASCISM AND COUNTERREVOLUTION

is perhaps the most difficult of all in an analysis of National Socialism. The difficulties lie not only in the paucity of information and the inadequacy of the sociological categories but also in the extraordinarily complicated character of the social relations themselves. Class structure and social differentiation are not identical—failure to recognize this point is the basic error underlying Lederer's analysis. A society may be divided into classes and yet not be socially differentiated in any other way. On the other hand, a classless society may have sharp differentiations.

The essence of National Socialist social policy consists in the acceptance and strengthening of the prevailing class character of German society, in the attempted consolidation of its ruling class, in the atomization of the subordinate strata through the destruction of every autonomous group mediating between them and the state, in the creation of a system of autocratic bureaucracies interfering in all human relations. The process of atomization extends even to the ruling class in part. It goes hand in hand with a process of differentiation within the mass party and within society that creates reliable élites in every sector. Through these élites, the regime plays off one group against the other and enables a minority to terrorize the majority.

National Socialism did not create the mass-men; it has completed the process, however, and destroyed every institution that might interfere. Basically, the transformation of men into mass-men is the outcome of modern industrial capitalism and of mass democracy. More than a century ago the French counter-revolutionaries, de Maistre and Bonald, and the Spaniard Donoso Cortes, asserted that liberalism, Protestantism, and democracy, which they hated, bore the seeds of the emotionally motivated mass-man and would eventually give birth to the dictatorship of the sword. Mass democracy and monopoly capitalism have brought the seeds to fruition. They have imprisoned man in a network of semi-authoritarian organizations controlling his life from birth to death, and they have begun to transform culture into propaganda and salable commodities.

National Socialism claims to have stopped this trend and to have created a society differentiated not by classes but according to occupation and training. That is absolutely untrue. In fact, National Socialism has carried to its highest perfection the very development it pretends to attack. It has annihilated every institution that under democratic conditions still preserves remnants of human spontaneity: the privacy of the individual and of the family, the trade union, the political party, the church, the free leisure organization. By atomizing the subject population (and to some extent the rulers as well), National Socialism has not eliminated class relations; on the contrary, it has deepened and solidified the antagonisms.

National Socialism must necessarily carry to an extreme the one process that characterizes the structure of modern society, bureaucratization. In modern anti-bureaucratic literature, this term means little more than the numerical growth of public servants, and especially of civil servants. Society is pictured as composed of free men and autonomous organizations on the one hand and of a bureaucratic caste, on the other hand, which takes over more and more political power. The picture is inaccurate, for society is not wholly free and unbureaucratic nor is the public bureaucracy the sole bearer of political and social power.

Bureaucratization, correctly understood, is a process operating in both public and private spheres, in the state as well as in society. It means that human relations lose their directness and become mediated relations in which third parties, public or private functionaries seated more or less securely in power, authoritatively prescribe the behavior of man. It is a highly ambivalent process, progressive as well as reactionary. The growth of bureaucracy in public life is not necessarily incompatible with democracy if the aims of the democracy are not limited to the preservation of individual rights, but also include the furtherance of certain social goals. Even in the social sphere the growth of private organizations is not entirely retrogressive. It brings some kind of order into an anarchic society and thereby rationalizes human relations that would otherwise be irrational and accidental.

If members of a trade union decide to change their labor conditions, they do so by accepting the recommendation of their officials, in whose hands the decision is left. When a political party formulates some policy, it is the party hierarchy that does so. In athletic organizations, the machinery of presidents, vice-presidents, secretaries, and treasurers goes into operation in arranging matches and carrying on the other activities of the group. This process of mediation and depersonalization extends to culture as well. Music becomes organized in the hands of professional secretaries who need not be musicians. The radio prescribes the exact amount of culture to be digested by the public, how much classical and how much light music, how much talk and how much news. The powers extend to the most intimate relations of man, to the family. There are organizations for large families and for bachelors, birth-control associations, advisory councils for the promotion of family happiness, consumers' co-operatives, giant food chain stores making a farce of the consumers' supposedly free choice.

There is, in short, a huge network of organizations covering almost every aspect of human life, each run by presidents and vice-presidents and secretaries and treasurers, each employing advertising agencies and publicity men, each out to interfere with, and to act as the mediator in, the relations between man and man. Civil liberties lose many of the

362 FASCISM AND COUNTERREVOLUTION

functions they had in a liberal society. Even the exercise of civil rights tends more and more to be mediated by private organizations. Whether it is a problem of defense in a political trial or protection of the rights of labor or the fight against unjust taxation, the average man, lacking sufficient means, has no other choice but to entrust his rights to some organization. Under democratic conditions, such mediation does not destroy his rights, as a rule, since the individual still has a choice between competing organizations. In a totalitarian society, however, even if his rights are still recognized on paper, they are completely at the mercy of private bureaucrats.

What National Socialism has done is to transform into authoritarian bodies the private organizations that in a democracy still give the individual an opportunity for spontaneous activity. Bureaucratization is the complete depersonalization of human relations. They become abstract and anonymous. On this structure of society, National Socialism imposes two ideologies that are completely antagonistic to it: the ideology of the community and the leadership principle.

[13]

The Worldwide Class Struggle

VINCENT NAVARRO

Neoliberalism as a Class Practice

A trademark of our times is the dominance of *neoliberalism* in the major economic, political, and social forums of the developed capitalist countries and in the international agencies they influence—including the IMF, the World Bank, the WTO, and the technical agencies of the United Nations such as the World Health Organization, Food and Agricultural Organization, and UNICEF. Starting in the United States during the Carter administration, neoliberalism expanded its influence through the Reagan administration and, in the United Kingdom, the Thatcher administration, to become an international ideology. Neoliberalism holds to a theory (though not necessarily a practice) that posits the following:

1. The state (or what is wrongly referred to in popular parlance as "the government") needs to reduce its interventionism in economic and social activities.
2. Labor and financial markets should be deregulated in order to liberate the enormous creative energy of the markets.
3. Commerce and investments should be stimulated by eliminating borders and barriers to allow for full mobility of labor, capital, goods, and services.

Following these three tenets, according to neoliberal authors, we have seen that the worldwide implementation of these practices has led to the development of a "new" process: a globalization of economic activity that has generated a period of enormous economic growth worldwide, associated with a new era of social progress. For the first time in history, we are told, we are witnessing a worldwide economy,

---

This essay is dedicated to the memory of my good friends Paul Sweezy and Harry Magdoff, who taught us an uncompromising critical evaluation of all that exists, uncompromising in the sense that our criticism fears neither its own results nor conflict with the powers that be.

Vincent Navarro is professor and director of the Public Policy Program of the Johns Hopkins University, USA–Pompeu Fabra University, Spain.

in which states are losing power and are being replaced by a worldwide market centered in multinational corporations, which are the main units of economic activity in the world today.

This celebration of the process of globalization is also evident among some sectors of the left. Michael Hardt and Antonio Negri, in their widely cited *Empire* (Harvard University Press, 2000), celebrate the great creativity of what they consider to be a new era of capitalism. This new period, they claim, breaks with obsolete state structures and establishes a new international order, which they define as an imperialist order. They further postulate that this new order is maintained without any state dominating or being hegemonic. Thus, they write:

> We want to emphasize that the establishment of empire is a positive step towards the elimination of nostalgic activities based on previous power structures; we reject all political strategies that want to take us back to past situations such as the resurrection of the nation-state in order to protect the population from global capital. We believe that the new imperialist order is better than the previous system in the same way that Marx believed that capitalism was a mode of production and a type of society superior to the mode that it replaced. This point of view held by Marx was based on a healthy despisement of the parochial localism and rigid hierarchies that preceded the capitalist society, as well as on the recognition of the enormous potential for liberation that capitalism had. (39)

Globalization (i.e., the internationalization of economic activity according to neoliberal tenets) becomes, in Hardt and Negri's position, an international system that is stimulating a worldwide activity that operates without any state or states leading or organizing it. Such an admiring and flattering view of globalization and neoliberalism explains the positive reviews that *Empire* has received from Emily Eakin, a book reviewer of the *New York Times*, and other mainstream critics, not known for sympathetic reviews of books that claim to derive their theoretical position from Marxism. Actually, Eakin describes *Empire* as the theoretical framework that the world needs to understand its reality.

Hardt and Negri applaud, along with neoliberal authors, the expansion of globalization. Other left-wing authors, however, mourn rather than celebrate this expansion, holding globalization as the cause of the world's growing inequalities and poverty. It is important to stress that even though the authors in this latter group—which includes, for example, Susan George and Eric Hobsbawm—lament globalization and criticize neoliberal thinking, they still share with neoliberal authors the basic assumption of neoliberalism: that states are losing power in an international order in which the power of multinational corporations has replaced that of states.

The Contradiction Between Theory and Practice in Neoliberalism

Let's be clear right away that neoliberal *theory* is one thing and neoliberal *practice* is another thing entirely. Most members of the Organisation for Economic Co-operation and Development (OECD) —including the U.S. federal government—have seen state intervention and state public expenditures *increase* during the last thirty years. My area of scholarship is public policy and I study the nature of state interventions in many parts of the world. I can testify to the expansion of state intervention in most countries in the developed capitalist world. Even in the United States, President Reagan's neoliberalism did not translate into a decline of the federal public sector. Instead, federal public expenditures increased under his mandate, from 21.6 to 23 percent of GNP, as a consequence of a spectacular growth in military expenditures from 4.9 to 6.1 percent of GNP (Congressional Budget Office National Accounts 2003). This growth in public expenditures was financed by an increase in the federal deficit (creating a burgeoning of the federal debt) and an increase in taxes. As the supposedly anti-tax president, Reagan in fact increased taxes for a greater number of people (in peace time) than any other president in U.S. history. And he increased taxes not once, but twice (in 1982 and 1983). In a demonstration of class power, he drastically reduced taxes for the 20 percent of the population with the highest incomes, while raising taxes for the majority of the population.

It is not accurate, therefore, to say that Reagan reduced the role of the state in the United States by reducing the size of the public sector and lowering taxes. What Reagan (and Carter before him) did was dramatically change the nature of state intervention, such that it benefited even more the upper classes and the economic groups (such as military-related corporations) that financed his electoral campaigns. Reagan's policies were indeed class policies that hurt the majority of the nation's working class. Reagan was profoundly anti-labor, making cuts in social expenditures at an unprecedented level. It bears repeating that Reagan's policies were not neoliberal: they were Keynesian, based on large public expenditures and large federal deficits. Also, the federal government intervened very actively in the nation's industrial development (mainly, but not exclusively, through the Defense Department). As Caspar Weinberger, secretary of defense in the Reagan administration, once indicated (in response to criticisms by the Democrats that the administration had abandoned the manufacturing sector), "Our Administration is the Administration that has a more advanced and extended industrial policy in the western world" (*Washington Post*, July 13, 1983). He was right. No other western government had such an extensive industrial policy. Indeed, the U.S. federal state is one of the most interventionist states in the western world.

There exists very robust scientific evidence that the United States is not a neoliberal society (as it is constantly defined) and that the U.S. state is not reducing its key role in developing the national economy, including in the production and distribution of goods and services by large U.S. corporations. This empirical evidence shows that federal government interventionism (in the economic, political, cultural, and security spheres) has *increased* over the last thirty years. In the economic sphere, for example, protectionism has not declined. It has grown, with higher subsidies to the agricultural, military, aerospace, and biomedical sectors. In the social arena, state interventions to weaken social rights (and most particularly labor rights) have increased enormously (not only under Reagan, but also under Bush Senior, Clinton, and Bush Junior), and surveillance of the citizenry has increased exponentially. Again, there has been no diminution of federal interventionism in the United States, but rather an even more skewed class character to this intervention during the last thirty years.

Neoliberal narratives about the declining role of the state in people's lives are easily falsified by the facts. Indeed, as John Williamson, one of the intellectual architects of neoliberalism, once indicated, "We have to recognize that what the U.S. government promotes abroad, the U.S. government does not follow at home," adding that "the U.S. government promotes policies that are not followed in the U.S." ("What Washington Means by the Policy Reform," in J. Williamson, ed., *Latin America Adjustment*, 1990, 213). It could not have been said better. In other words, if you want to understand U.S. public policies, look at what the U.S. government does, not what it says. This same situation occurs in the majority of developed capitalist countries. Their states have become more, not less, interventionist. The size of the state (measured by public expenditures per capita) has increased in most of these countries. Again, the empirical information on this point is strong. What has been happening is not a reduction of the state but rather a change in the nature of state intervention—further strengthening its class character.

Deterioration of the World Economic and Social Situation

Contrary to neoliberal dogma, neoliberal public policies have been remarkably unsuccessful at achieving their declared aims: economic efficiency and social well-being.

Table 1: Economic Growth, 1960–2000

	1960–1980	1980–2000
Rate of economic growth in developing countries (except China):		
Annual economic growth	5.5%	2.6%
Annual economic growth per capita	3.2%	0.7%
Rate of economic growth in China:		
Annual economic growth	4.5%	9.8%
Annual economic growth per capita	2.5%	8.4%

Sources: World Bank, *World Development Indicators,* 2001 CD-ROM; Robert Pollin, *Contours of Descent* (Verso, 2003) 131.

If we compare the period 1980–2000 (when neoliberalism reached its maximum expression*) with the immediately preceding period, 1960–1980, we can easily see that 1980–2000 was much less successful than 1960–1980 in most developed and developing capitalist countries. As table 1 shows, the rate of growth and rate of growth per capita in all developing (non-OECD) countries (excluding China) were much higher in 1960–1980 (5.5 percent and 3.2 percent) than in 1980–2000 (2.6 percent and 0.7 percent). Mark Weisbrot, Dean Baker, and David Rosnick have documented that the improvement in quality-of-life and well-being indicators (infant mortality, rate of school enrollment, life expectancy,

---

*The starting point of neoliberalism and of the growth of inequalities was July 1979, with Paul Volker's dramatic increase in interest rates that slowed down economic growth (plus the two oil shocks that particularly affected countries highly dependent on imported oil) (see David Harvey, *A Brief History of Neoliberalism,* Oxford University Press, 2005). Volker increased interest rates (thus creating a worldwide recession) as an anti-working-class move to weaken labor in the United States and abroad. The rate increase also initiated, as Giovanni Arrighi has noted (in "The African Crisis: World Systemic and Regional Aspects," *New Left Review* [May–June, 2002]), a flow of capital to the United States, making it very difficult for other countries, especially poor countries to compete for the limited capital. The fact that petrol Euro dollars (which increased enormously with the oil shocks) were deposited in the United States made the scarcity of capital particularly hard for poor countries to adapt to. This is the time when the stagnation of the poor countries started. The countries most affected by these neoliberal public policies were the Latin American countries, which followed these policies extensively, and the African countries (the poorest of the poor), which saw extremely negative economic growth. In 2000, twenty-four African countries had a smaller GNP per capita than twenty-five years earlier.

and others) increased faster during 1960–1980 than 1980–2000 (when comparing countries at the same level of development at the starting year of each period—*The Scorecard on Development,* Center for Economic and Policy Research, September 2005). And as table 2 shows, the annual rate of economic growth per capita in the developed capitalist countries was lower in 1981–99 than in 1961–80.

Table 2

A. Average Annual Rate of Per Capita Economic Growth in the OECD and Developing Countries		
	1961–80	1981–99
(A) OECD countries	3.5%	2.0%
(B) Developing countries (except China)	3.2%	0.7%
Growth differential (A/B)	0.3%	1.3%
B. Growth in World Income Inequalities, 1980–1998 (Excluding China)		
Income of richest 50% as share of poorest 50%	4% more unequal	
Income of richest 20% as share of poorest 20%	8% more unequal	
Income of richest 10% as share of poorest 10%	19% more unequal	
Income of richest 1% as share of poorest 1%	77% more unequal	

Sources: World Bank, *World Development Indicators,* 2001; Robert Sutcliffe, *A More or Less Unequal World?* (Political Economy Research Institute, 2003); Robert Pollin, *Contours of Descent* (Verso, 2003), 133.

But, what is also important to stress is that due to the larger annual economic growth per capita in the OECD countries than in the developing countries (except China), the difference in their rates of growth per capita has been increasing dramatically (table 2). This means, in practical terms, that income inequalities between these two types of countries have grown spectacularly, and particularly between the extremes (see table 2). But, most importantly, inequalities have increased dramatically not only among but *within* countries, developed and developing alike. Adding both types of inequalities (among and within countries), we find that, as Branco Milanovic has documented, the top 1 percent of the world population receives 57 percent of the world income, and the income difference between those at the top and those at the bottom has increased from 78 to 114 times (*Worlds Apart,* Princeton University Press, 2005).

It bears emphasizing that even though poverty has increased worldwide and within countries that are following neoliberal public policies, this does not mean the rich within each country (including developing countries) have been adversely affected. Instead, the rich saw their incomes and their distance from the non-rich increase substantially. Class inequalities have increased greatly in most capitalist countries.

Neoliberalism as a Class Practice: The Roots of Inequalities

In each of these countries, then, the income of those at the top has increased spectacularly as a result of state interventions. Consequently, we need to turn to some of the categories and concepts discarded by large sectors of the left: class structure, class power, class struggle, and their impact on the state. These scientific categories continue to be of key importance to understanding what is going on in each country. Let me clarify that a scientific concept can be very old but not antiquated. "Ancient" and "antiquated" are two different concepts. The law of gravity is very old but is not antiquated. Anyone who doubts this can test it by jumping from the tenth floor. There is a risk that some sectors of the left may pay an equally suicidal cost by ignoring scientific concepts such as class and class struggle simply because these are old concepts. We cannot understand the world (from Iraq to the rejection of the European Constitution) without acknowledging the existence of classes and class alliances, established worldwide between the dominant classes of the developed capitalist world and those of the developing capitalist world. *Neoliberalism is the ideology and practice of the dominant classes of the developed and developing worlds alike.*

But before we jump ahead, let's start with the situation in each country. Neoliberal ideology was the dominant classes' response to the considerable gains achieved by the working and peasant classes between the end of the Second World War and the mid-1970s. The huge increase in inequality that has occurred since then is the direct result of the growth in income of the dominant classes, which is a consequence of class-determined public policies such as: (a) deregulation of labor markets, an anti-working-class move; (b) deregulation of financial markets, which has greatly benefited financial capital, the hegemonic branch of capital in the period 1980–2005; (c) deregulation of commerce in goods and services, which has benefited the high-consumption population at the cost of laborers; (d) reduction of social public expenditures, which has hurt the working class; (e) privatization of services, which has benefited the richest 20 percent of the population at the expense of the well-being of the working classes that depend on public services; (f) promotion of individualism and consumerism, hurting the culture of solidarity; (g) development of a theoretical narrative and discourse that

The Primary Conflict in Today's World: Not Between North and South But Between an Alliance of Dominant Classes of North and South Against Dominated Classes of North and South

pays rhetorical homage to the markets, but masks a clear alliance between transnationals and the state in which they are based; and (h) promotion of an anti-interventionist discourse in clear conflict with the actual increased state interventionism to promote the interests of the dominant classes and the economic units—the transnationals—that foster their interests. Each of these class-determined public policies requires a state action or intervention that conflicts with the interests of the working and other popular classes.

The Primary Conflict in Today's World: Not Between North and South But Between an Alliance of Dominant Classes of North and South Against Dominated Classes of North and South

It has become part of the conventional wisdom that the primary conflict in the world is between the rich North and the poor South. The North and the South, however, have classes with opposing interests that have established alliances at the international level. This situation became clear to me when I was advising President Allende in Chile. The fascist coup led by General Pinochet was not, as was widely reported, a coup imposed by the rich North (the United States) on the poor South (Chile). Those who brutally imposed the Pinochet regime were the dominant classes of Chile (the bourgeoisie, petit bourgeoisie, and upper-middle professional classes), with the support not of the United States (U.S. society is not an aggregate of 240 million imperialists!) but of the Nixon administration, which was, at that time, very unpopular in the United States (having sent the army to put down the coalminers' strike in Appalachia).

A lack of awareness of the existence of classes often leads to condemnation of an entire country, frequently the United States. But, in fact, the U.S. working class is one of the first victims of U.S. imperialism. Some will say that the U.S. working class benefits from imperialism. Gasoline, for example, is relatively cheap in the United States (although increasingly less so). It costs me thirty-five dollars to fill my car in the United States and fifty-two euros to fill the same model in Europe. But, by contrast, public transportation is practically nonexistent in many regions of the United States. The working class of Baltimore, for example, would benefit much more from first-class public transportation (which it does not have) than having to depend on cars, whatever the price of gasoline. And let's not forget that the energy and automobile industry interests have been major agents in opposing and destroying public transportation in the United States. The U.S.

working class is a victim of its nation's capitalist and imperialist system. It is not by chance that no other country in the developed capitalist world has such an underdeveloped welfare state as the United States. More than 100,000 people die in the United States every year due to the lack of public health care.

The tendency to look at the distribution of power around the world while ignoring class power within each country is also evident in the frequent denunciations that the international organizations are controlled by the rich countries. It is frequently pointed out, for example, that 10 percent of the world population, living in the richest countries, has 43 percent of the votes in the IMF, but it is not true that the 10 percent of the population living in the so-called rich countries controls the IMF. It is the dominant classes of those rich countries that dominate the IMF, putting forward public policies that hurt the dominated classes of their own countries as well as of other countries. The director of the IMF, for example, is Rodrigo Rato, who while Spain's economy minister in the ultra-right government of José María Aznar (who partnered with Bush and Blair to support the Iraq war) carried out the brutal austerity policies that severely reduced the standard of living of the Spanish popular classes (Vincent Navarro, "Who is Mr. Rato?" *Counterpunch*, June 2004).

Let me also clarify another point. Much has been written about the conflict within the WTO between rich and poor countries. The governments of the rich countries, it is said, heavily subsidize their agriculture while raising protective barriers for industries such as textiles and foods that are vulnerable to products coming from the poor countries. While these obstacles to world trade do indeed adversely affect poor countries, it is wrong to assume that the solution is freer worldwide trade. Even without the barriers, the higher productivity of the rich countries would guarantee their success in world trade. What poor countries need to do is to change from export-oriented economies (the root of their problems) to domestic-oriented growth—a strategy that would require a major redistribution of income and is thus resisted by the dominant classes of those (and of the rich) countries. It is extremely important to realize that most countries already have the resources (including capital) to break with their underdevelopment. Let me quote from an unlikely source. The *New York Times*, on September 12, 1992 (when the population explosion was held to be the cause of world poverty), published a surprisingly candid assessment of the situation in Bangladesh, the poorest country in the world. In this extensive article,

Ann Crittenden touched directly on the root of the problem: the patterns of ownership of the production asset—the land:

> The root of the persistent malnutrition in the midst of relative plenty is the unequal distribution of land in Bangladesh. Few people are rich here by Western standards, but severe inequalities do exist and they are reflected in highly skewed land ownership. The wealthiest 16% of the rural population controls two thirds of the land and almost 60% of the population holds less than one acre of property.

Crittenden is not hopeful that the solution is technological. Quite to the contrary, technology can make things even worse:

> The new agricultural technologies being introduced have tended to favor large farmers, putting them in a better position to buy out their less fortunate neighbors.

Why does this situation persist? The answer is clear.

> Nevertheless, with the government dominated by landowners—about 75% of the members of the Parliament hold land—no one foresees any official support for fundamental changes in the system.

Let me add that in the U.S. State Department's classification of political regimes, Bangladesh is placed in the democratic column. Meanwhile, hunger and underweight are the primary cause of child mortality in Bangladesh. The hungry face of a child in Bangladesh has become the most common poster used by many charitable organizations to shame people in developed countries into sending money and food aid to Bangladesh. With what results?

> Food aid officials in Bangladesh privately concede that only a fraction of the millions of tons of food aid sent to Bangladesh has reached the poor and hungry in the villages. The food is given to the Government, which in turn sells it at subsidized prices to the military, the police, and the middle class inhabitants of the cities.

The class structure of Bangladesh and the property relations that determine it are the causes of the enormous poverty. As Ann Crittenden concludes:

> Bangladesh has enough land to provide an adequate diet for every man, woman and child in the country. The agricultural potential of this lush green land is such that even the inevitable population growth of the next 20 years could be fed easily by the resources of Bangladesh alone.

Most recently, Bangladesh has been much in the news as having undergone high economic growth due primarily to its exports in the world market. But that growth has been limited to a small, export-oriented sector of the economy and has left untouched the majority of the population. Malnutrition and hunger, meanwhile, have increased.

The States and Class Alliances

In the establishment of class alliances, states play a key role. U.S. foreign policy, for example, is oriented towards supporting the dominant classes of the South (where, incidentally, 20 percent of the world's richest persons live). These alliances include, on many occasions, personal ties among members of the dominant classes. Examples are many—among them, the traditional support of the Bush family for the Middle East feudal regimes; Clinton's support for the United Arab Emirates (UAE), one of the major supporters of the Clinton Library in Little Rock, Arkansas, and a major donor to Clinton in speaking fees (up to a million dollars) and to causes favoring Clinton (*Financial Times*, March 4, 2006). The UAE is one of the world's most oppressively brutal regimes. The dominant classes deny citizenship to 85 percent of the working population (called "guest workers"). Needless to say, international agencies (heavily influenced by the U.S. and European governments) promote such alliances based on the neoliberal rhetoric of free markets. Cutting social public expenditures, advocated by the IMF and the World Bank, is part of the neoliberal public policies pushed by the dominant classes of both the North and South at the expense of the well-being and quality of life of the dominated classes throughout the world. In all these examples, the states of the North and the South play a critical role.

Another example of alliances among dominant classes is the current promotion of for-profit health insurance by the Bush administration, both to the U.S. population and, increasingly, to the developing world. This is done with the advice and collaboration of conservative governments in Latin America on behalf of their dominant classes, which benefit from private insurance schemes that select clientele and exclude the popular classes. Those popular classes, in the United States and Latin America, profoundly dislike this push toward for-profit health care. (The movie *John Q* relates the hostility against health insurance companies among the U.S. working class.) The fact that the dominant classes in the developed and developing countries share class interests does not mean they see eye-to-eye on everything. Of course not. They have major disagreements and conflicts (just as there are disagreements and conflicts among the different components of the dominant classes in each country). But these disagreements cannot conceal the commonality of their interests as clearly exposed in the neoliberal forums (such as at Davos) and neoliberal instruments that have a hegemonic position (such as the *Economist* and the *Financial Times*).

Is There a Dominant State in the World Today?

More than globalization, what we are witnessing in the world today is the *regionalization* of economic activities around a dominant state: North America around the United States, Europe around Germany, and Asia around Japan—and soon China. Thus there is a hierarchy of states within each region. In Europe, for example, the Spanish government is becoming dependent on public policies of the European Union in which the German state predominates. This dependency creates an ambivalent situation. On the one hand, the states of the EU chose to delegate major policies (such as monetary policies) to a higher institution (the European Central Bank, which is dominated by the German Central Bank). But this does not necessarily mean that the Spanish state loses power. "Losing power" means you had more power before, which is not necessarily the case. Spain, for example, is more powerful with the euro as currency than it was with the peseta. Indeed, Spanish president Jose Luis Rodriguez Zapatero would have paid a very high price in his confrontation with Bush (in withdrawing Spanish troops from Iraq) if Spain still had the peseta as its national currency. Sharing sovereignty can increase power. On the other hand, the European government is frequently used by Europe's dominant classes as justification for unpopular policies that they want to implement (such as reducing public expenditures as a consequence of the European Stability Pact, which forces countries to maintain a central government deficit below 3 percent of GNP); these policies are presented as coming from European legislation rather than any of the member states, thus diluting the responsibility of each government. Class alliances at the European level are manifested through the operation of EU institutions committed to neoliberal ideology and policies. The "no" vote on the proposed European Constitution was the response of the working classes of some member states to the European institutions that operate as alliances for Europe's dominant classes.

Within the hierarchy of states, some are dominant. The U.S. state has a dominant place that is maintained through a set of alliances with the dominant classes of other states. Neoliberal ideology provides the linkage among these classes. Needless to say, there are conflicts and tensions among them. But these tensions cannot outweigh the commonality of their class interests. Among the practices that unite them are aggressive policies against the working class and left institutions. The 1980–2005 period was characterized by aggressive campaigns against left parties that had been successful in the 1960–1980 period. During the neoliberal period, the alliance of the dominant classes has promoted multi-class religious movements that have used religion as a motivating force to stop socialism or communism. It was the Carter administration that began to support the religious fundamentalists in Afghanistan against the communist-led government. From Afghanistan to Iraq, Iran, the Palestinian Territories, and many Arab countries, the dominant classes of the United States and Europe, through their governments, funded and supported the religious fundamentalists—often not only out of their own class interests, but out of their own religiosity. The "moral majority" in the United States was supposed to become the moral majority worldwide. These profoundly anti-left fundamentalist movements developed their own dynamics, making use of the enormous frustrations of the Arab masses with their oppressive, feudal regimes, to facilitate the capture of the state and the installation of regimes with equally oppressive religious theocracies, as has happened in many Arab countries.

But it is wrong to see the support by the dominant classes for the feudal regimes as simply a product of the Cold War. It was much more than that. It was a class response. The best evidence for this is that the support has continued even after the collapse of the Soviet Union. The Cold War was an excuse for carrying on the class struggle at the world level— as its continuation proves. Class war has indeed become an extremely active component of U.S. interventionism. It was the "shock therapy" pushed by Lawrence Summers and Jeffrey Sachs in Russia during the Clinton administration that led to the shortening of life expectancy in Russia, a consequence of the dramatic decline in the standard of living of the Russian popular classes. The increased privatization of major public assets was part of that class war in Russia—as it has been in Iraq.

The chief of the U.S. occupation in Iraq, Paul Bremer, fired half a million government workers, slashed business taxes, gave investors extraordinary new rights, and eliminated all import restrictions for all business except the oil industry. As Jeff Faux relates in *The Global Class War* (Wiley, 2006), the only laws from the brutal Iraqi dictatorship that the occupation retained were those that were anti-labor union, including a restrictive collective-bargaining agreement that took away all workers' bonuses and food and housing subsidies. As the *Economist* editorialized, the economic reforms in Iraq are a "capitalist's dream" (September 25, 2003).

Recently, another version of the North-South divide appears in the writings of one of the most influential thinkers in the United States, the philosopher John Rawls, who divides the countries of the world into "decent" and "non-decent" countries. The decent countries (mostly located in the developed capitalist world) are those that have democratic rights and institutions, while the non-decent countries (mostly located in the developing capitalist world) do not. After dividing the world into these two categories, he concludes that the non-decent countries had better be ignored, although he admits "a moral responsibility to help poor countries that are prevented by poverty from organizing themselves as liberal or decent societies." Such positions and statements testify to an overwhelming ignorance of past and present international relations, as well as of the class relations in each of those countries. Rawls further confuses governments with countries (a confusion that occurs frequently in the assumption that the primary conflict is between North and South). What he calls non-decent countries (characterized by brutal and corrupt dictatorships) have classes; their dominant classes have not been ignored in activities cultivated and supported by the dominant classes of the decent countries, which have also hurt the quality of life and well-being of their own dominated classes. Also, in Rawls's so-called non-decent countries, there are class-based movements that endure enormous sacrifices, carrying out a heroic struggle for change, struggling constantly while handicapped and opposed by the dominant classes of the so-called decent countries. It is remarkable (but predictable) that such an intellectual figure defines the moral compass of these indecent classes. The latest example of this indecency is the reported support by the U.S. and British governments for the King of Nepal, which grows out of their desire to stop a mass revolt led by leftist parties in a third world country.

Inequalities among Countries and Their Social Consequences

That inequalities contribute to a lack of social solidarity and increase social pathology is well documented. Many people, including myself, have documented this reality (*The Political Economy of Social Inequalities: Consequences for Health and Quality of Life*, Baywood, 2002). The scientific evidence supporting this position is overwhelming.

In any given society, the greatest number of deaths would be prevented by reducing social inequalities. Michael Marmot studied the gradient of heart disease mortality among professionals at different authority levels, and he found that the higher the level of authority, the lower the heart disease mortality (*The Status Syndrome*, 2005). And he further showed that this mortality gradient could not be explained by diet, physical exercise, or cholesterol alone; these risk factors explained only a small part of the gradient. The most important factor was the position that people held within the social structure (in which class, gender, and race play key roles) and the social distance between groups, and the differential control that people have over their own lives.

This enormously important scientific finding has many implications; one of them is that the major problem we face is not simply eliminating poverty but rather reducing inequality. The first is impossible to resolve without resolving the second. Another implication is that poverty is not just a matter of resources, as is wrongly assumed in World Bank reports that measure worldwide poverty by quantifying the number of people who live on a dollar a day. The real problem, again, is not absolute resources but the social distance and the different degrees of control over one's own resources. And this holds true in every society.

Let me elaborate. An unskilled, unemployed, young black person living in the ghetto area of Baltimore has more resources (he or she is likely to have a car, mobile phone, and TV, and more square feet per household and more kitchen equipment) than a middle-class professional in Ghana, Africa. If the whole world were just a single society, the Baltimore youth would be middle class and the Ghana professional would be poor. And yet, the first has a much shorter life expectancy (forty-five years) than the second (sixty-two years). How can that be, when the first has more resources than the second? The answer is clear. It is far more difficult to be poor in the United States (the sense of distance, frustration, powerlessness, and failure is much greater) than to be middle class in Ghana. The first is far below the median; the second is above the median.

Does the same mechanism operate in inequalities among countries? The answer is increasingly, yes. And the reason for adding "increasingly" is communication—with ever more globalized information systems and networks, more information is reaching the most remote areas of the world. And the social distance created by inequalities is becoming increasingly apparent, not only within but also among countries. Because this distance is more and more perceived as an outcome of exploitation, we are facing an enormous tension, comparable with that of the nineteenth and early twentieth centuries, when class exploitation became the driving force for social mobilization. The key element for defining the future is through what channels that mobilization takes place. What we have seen is an enormous mobilization, instigated and guided by an alliance of the dominant classes of the North and the South, aimed at—as mentioned earlier—stimulating multi-class religious or nationalistic mobilizations that leave key class relations unchanged. We saw this phenomenon at the end of the nineteenth and beginning of the twentieth centuries. Christian Democracy in Europe, for example, appears as the dominant classes' response to the threat of socialism and communism. The birth of Islamic fundamentalism was also stimulated for the same purposes.

The left-wing alternative must be centered in alliances among the dominated classes and other dominated groups, with a political movement that must be built upon the process of class struggle that takes place in each country. As Hugo Chávez of Venezuela said, "It cannot be a mere movement of protest and celebration like Woodstock." It is an enormous struggle, an endeavor in which organization and coordination are key, calling for a Fifth International. This is the challenge to the international left today.

[14]

The Economic and Social Functions of the Legal Institutions

KARL RENNER

Our enquiry, then, is not concerned with positive legal analysis, the systematic exposition of legal institutions, a field which has been amply covered by others. Nor are we investigating the problems of the creation of law. We shall refrain from analysing the questions as to how the norms originate which make up the legal institutions, how a legal norm grows from its economic background, and what are the economic causes of the creation of legal norms. This field, it is true, has not been cultivated, but we shall keep away from it. We propose to examine only the economic and social effect of the valid norm as it exists, so long as the norm does not change.

Those acquainted with socialist literature will at once perceive that we have taken as our subject the mutual relations between law and economics. The traditional Marxist school conceives the economic relations as the substructure and the legal institutions as the superstructure. "Substructure" and "superstructure" are metaphors, borrowed from architecture; it is obvious that they serve only to illustrate the connection, not to define it in exact terms. This superstructure, according to Marx's well-known formula,[1] comprises not only law but also ethics and culture, in fact every ideology. This terminology must therefore apply to many facts other than those relevant to the law, whose structures are completely

---

From Karl Renner, *The Institutions of Private Law and Their Social Functions* (London: Routledge & Kegan Paul Ltd., 1949), pp. 55–60. Reprinted with the permission of Routledge & Kegan Paul Ltd.

[1] Preface to Marx's *Critique of Political Economics*, transl. by N. I. Stone, N.Y. London, 1904. "The sum total of these relations of production constitutes the economic structure of society—the real foundations on which rise legal and political superstructures."

Friedrich Engels, Preface to Marx's *Der achtzehnte Brumaire,* 3rd edition, Hamburg, 1885: "The law according to which all struggle, whether in the political, religious, philosophical or any other ideological field, is in fact only the more or less clear expression of struggles among social classes whose existence and hence collisions are again conditioned by the degree of development of their economic position, their methods of production and their manner of exchange dependent thereon." And many other passages. . . .

124   *Karl Renner*

different and must be separately defined. The relation between the philosophy of an age and the economic substructure of that age is obviously determined by key concepts quite different from those of legal norm, exercise of a right, and the like. We must desist, therefore, from attempting to give a general exposition of the Marxist concept of superstructure. We must recognise that each of these social phenomena, which in their general aspects are quite aptly illustrated by Marx's metaphor, requires a specific investigation. We attempt this investigation in regard to law.

Our previous explanations have made it clear that the relation is not merely one of cause and effect. It would be no solution of our problem to say that the economic structure generates the norm. Such an assumption could apply only to one of the fields of learning, that concerned with the creation of laws. Yet the mechanism by which economy as the causal factor brings about the effect of law, is obscure and unexplored. It probably would not become intelligible by any ultimate abstraction, such as the application of the primitive categories of cause and effect, nor does Stammler's formula [Rudolf Stammler, *Wirtschaft und Recht nach der materialistischen Geschichtszauffassung* (Leipzig: 1896)] of the regulating form and the regulated substance make it any clearer. In the second province, that of positive legal analysis, the concepts of cause and effect generally mean little; the main concern here is obviously that of motive, means and ends, and the appropriate method of explanation is teleological, not causal. If we were to describe the superstructure of the law in the third field (that of the economic and social efficacy of the norms) as exclusively the effect of the social and economic substructure, our conclusions would be proved to be absurd by the very facts to which they refer.

It is mere platitude to say that laws can influence economy sufficiently to change it and can therefore be considered as causes of economic results. Marx, of course, was the last person to deny this. "The influence of laws upon the conservation of the relations of distribution and consequently their influence upon production must be specifically determined" (*Neue Zeit*, p. 744). [This quotation and the following one come from Marx's Introduction to the *Grundrisse*. The Introduction was first published by Karl Kautsky in the journal *Neue Zeit*, XXI (1), 1903, from which Renner quotes.—Ed.] Laws are made with the intention of producing economic results, and as a rule they achieve this effect. Social life is not so simple that we can

Economic and Social Functions of Law

grasp it, open it and reveal its kernel like a nut, by placing it between the two arms of a nutcracker called cause and effect. Although he was much occupied with legal problems, Marx never found time to "determine the influence of the laws" (as above); yet he saw the problem clearly as is proved in particular by the following methodological hint: "The really difficult point to be discussed here, however, is how the relations of production as relations of the law enter into a disparate development. An instance is Roman civil law in its relations to modern production" (ibid. p. 779). We make use of this hint in the formulation of our problem: (1) Law which continues unchanged in relation to changing economic conditions; (2) Changed economic conditions in relation to the new norms and the new law. Our study, however, will be concerned with the first part of the problem only.

We start with a definite legal system based upon a definite economic foundation as it appears at a given moment of history. All economic institutions are at the same time institutions of the law. All economic activities are either, like sale and purchase, acts-in-the-law, or, like farming one's own land, the mere exercise of a right; or if neither, like the work of a mill-hand at his loom, even though they are extra-legal activities, they are nevertheless performed within definite legal conditions. We see that the act-in-the-law and the economic action are not identical.

The process of eating has a physiological, an economic and a volitional aspect but it is not an act of will with the qualities of an act-in-the-law. Yet the conditions under which it takes place are determined to some extent by the law.

The circulation of goods in a capitalist society is mediated by sale and purchase and by ancillary contracts: these are transactions for which the law of obligations provides various forms. Production, however, is not in itself an act-in-the-law. It can be the mere exercise of the right of ownership, as in the case of the peasant. In the capitalist factory, however, the legal aspect of production is more complicated. For the capitalist, production is the exercise of his right of ownership, since factory and machines are his property. For the worker it is the fulfilment of a legal obligation which has been established by the contract of employment. In so far as it is the latter, it is an act-in-the-law; in so far as it is the former, it is the mere exercise of a right. Thus a simple economic category is equivalent to a combination of various legal categories, there is

126 *Karl Renner*

no point-to-point correspondence. A number of distinct legal institutions serves a single economic process. They play a part which I will call their economic function.

Yet every economic process which in theory is an isolated unit is only part of the whole process of social production and reproduction. If the economic function is related to this whole, it becomes the social function of the legal institution.

A comprehensive exposition of the functions fulfilled by the legal institutions at every stage of the economic process has been given in *Das Kapital,* Marx's principal work. No other investigator, either before or after him, was more aware of their importance for even the most minute details of this process. We shall see that no other economic theory gives so much insight into the connections between law and economics. Marx's predecessors and successors either refused to recognise the problem or could not do it full justice.

If we regard a social order as static and confine our attention to a certain moment of history, then the legal norms and the economic process merely appear as mutually conditioned and subservient to one another. Within the economic structure economic process and legal norm appear as the same thing: the former seen as an external, technico-natural event, the latter as an inherent relation of wills, seen from the point of view of individual will-formation. We call the external, technico-natural process the substratum of the norm. This sounds very plausible. But we can no more study the laws of gravity from a stone in a state of rest than we can learn the art of cooking from the cook who was pricked by the Sleeping Beauty's spindle. All that we can observe is that in a state of rest legal and economic institutions, though not identical, are but two aspects of the same thing, inextricably interwoven. We must define and describe this co-existence.

This observation, however, only stresses the fact that they are mutually determined. We must study the process in its historical sequence, the gradual transition of a social order from a given stage to the next. The inherent laws of development can only be revealed if the events are seen in motion, in the historic sequence of economic and legal systems. If we examine two consecutive periods, chosen at random, we may obtain results which, though they apply to these particular periods of transition, cannot claim to be generally valid. To decide the function of the law in general, we have to study inductively all social orders as they appear in the course of history, from the most primitive to the most highly devel-

Economic and Social Functions of Law 127

oped. By this method we obtain the general categories of the social order and at the same time the general functions of the law.

This procedure is legitimate in spite of the fact that every individual stage of development has its specific nature and is subject to its peculiar laws. Marx frequently refers to general principles of this kind, declaring them to be justified. "All periods of production have certain characteristics in common . . . production in general is an abstract concept, but a reasonable one in that it really establishes and emphasizes what is common, and thus saves us repetition." ". . . a unity brought about by the fact that the subject, mankind, and the object, nature, are always the same" (*Neue Zeit,* vol. 21, p. 712). Yet Marx disparages these general abstractions in economics often enough to fortify our objections against them. One of his reasons was the tendency of economists, which still exists, to regard the categories of the capitalist order as eternal and sacrosanct. Another reason lies in the limitations of his own task, viz. to explore and describe one individual period only. "Yet it is the very difference from what is general and common which is the essential element of a particular development." If Marx had concentrated upon the definition of peculiar characteristics of one epoch as he found them, he might have given a description in the manner of a research student, but the laws of social development would have remained hidden from him. Marx, however, seeks to explain the specific historical phenomenon alongside with previous individual forms as being merely an individual manifestation of the general principle. In this way he discovers inherent connections within the development.

The following may serve as an example: "Surplus labour is a general social phenomenon as soon as the productivity of human labour power exceeds the immediate needs of life, but its appearance in the feudal epoch differs from that in the capitalist epoch— in the former it is villeinage, in the latter surplus value."

We cannot dispense in our enquiry with a general survey of the functions performed by the legal institutions. Every individual function which is historically determined is correlated to the whole and can only be clearly understood within its context. A diagrammatic exposition of the functions at least clears the field. A concrete detail cannot be demonstrated otherwise than by relating it to the general whole. "A phenomenon is concrete because it integrates various determining factors, because it is a unity of multiplicity. If it is thought out, it appears as the product and result of an integrating process."

[15]

The Problem of the Capitalist State

Nicos Poulantzas

Ralph Miliband's recently published work, *The State in Capitalist Society*,[1] is in many respects of capital importance. The book is extremely substantial, and cannot decently be summarized in a few pages: I cannot recommend its reading too highly. I will limit myself here to a few critical comments, in the belief that only criticism can advance Marxist theory. For the specificity of this theory compared with other theoretical problematics lies in the extent to which Marxist theory provides itself, in the very act of its foundation, with the means of its own internal criticism. I should state at the outset that my critique will not be 'innocent': having myself written on the question of the State in my book *Pouvoir Politique et Classes Sociales*,[2] these comments will derive from epistemological positions presented there which differ from those of Miliband.

First of all, some words on the fundamental merits of Miliband's book. The theory of the State and of political power has, with rare exceptions such as Gramsci, been neglected by Marxist thought. This neglect has a number of different causes, related to different phases of the working-class movement. In Marx himself this neglect, more apparent than real, is above all due to the fact that his principal theoretical object was the capitalist mode of production, within which the economy not only holds the role of determinant in the last instance, but also the dominant role—while for example in the feudal mode of production, Marx indicates that if the economy still has the role of determinant in the last instance, it is ideology in its religious form that holds the dominant role. Marx thus concentrated on the economic level of the capitalist mode of production, and did not deal specifically with the other levels such as the State: he dealt only with these levels through their *effects* on the economy (for example, in the passages of *Capital* on factory legislation). In Lenin, the reasons are different: involved in direct political practice, he dealt with the question of the State only in essentially polemical works, such as *State and Revolution*, which do not have the theoretical status of certain of his tests such as *The Development of Capitalism in Russia*.

How, by contrast, is the neglect of theoretical study of the State in the Second International, and in the Third International after Lenin, to be explained? Here I would advance, with all necessary precautions, the following thesis: the absence of a study of the State derived from the fact that the dominant conception of these Internationals was a deviation, *economism*, which is generally accompanied by an absence of revolutionary strategy and objectives—even when it takes a 'leftist' or Luxemburgist form. In effect, economism considers that other levels of social reality, including the State, are simple epiphenomena reducible to the economic 'base'. Thereby a specific study of the State becomes superfluous. Parallel with this, economism considers that every change in the social system happens first of all in the economy and that political action should have the economy as its principal objective. Once again, a specific study of the State is redundant. Thus economism leads either to reformism and trade-unionism, or to forms of 'leftism' such as syndicalism. For, as Lenin showed, the principal objective of revolutionary action is *State power* and the necessary precondition of any socialist revolution is the destruction of the bourgeois State apparatus.

Economism and the absence of revolutionary strategy are manifest in the Second International. They are less obvious in the Third International, yet in my view what fundamentally determined the theory and practice of 'Stalinist' policy, dominant in the Comintern probably from 1928, was nevertheless the same economism and absence of a revolutionary strategy. This is true both of the 'leftist' period of the Comintern until 1935, and of the revisionist-reformist period after 1935. This economism determined the absence of a theory of the State in the Third International, and this *relation* (economism/absence of a theory of the State) is perhaps nowhere more evident than in its analyses of fascism—precisely where the Comintern had most need of such a theory of the State. Considerations of a concrete order both confirm and explain this.

---

[1] Weidenfeld and Nicholson, London 1969, 292 pp., 45/–.
[2] Maspero, Paris,

Since the *principal symptoms* of Stalinist politics were located in the relations between the State apparatus and the Communist Party in the USSR, symptoms visible in the famous Stalin Constitution of 1936, it is very comprehensible that study of the State remained a forbidden topic *par excellence*.

It is in this context that Miliband's work helps to overcome a major lacuna. As is always the case when a scientific theory is lacking, bourgeois conceptions of the State and of political power have pre-empted the terrain of political theory, almost unchallenged. Miliband's work is here truly *cathartic*: he methodically attacks these conceptions. Rigorously deploying a formidable mass of empirical material in his examination of the concrete social formations of the USA, England, France, Germany or Japan, he not only radically demolishes bourgeois ideologies of the State, but provides us with a positive knowledge that these ideologies have never been able to produce.

However, the procedure chosen by Miliband—a *direct* reply to bourgeois ideologies by the immediate examination of concrete fact—is also to my mind the source of the faults of his book. Not that I am against the study of the 'concrete': on the contrary, having myself relatively neglected this aspect of the question in my own work (with its some-what different aim and object), I am only the more conscious of the necessity for concrete analyses. I simply mean that a precondition of any scientific approach to the 'concrete' is to make explicit the epistemo-logical principles of its own treatment of it. Now it is important to note that Miliband nowhere deals with the Marxist theory of the State as such, although it is constantly implicit in his work. He takes it as a sort of 'given' in order to reply to bourgeois ideologies by examining the facts in its light. Here I strongly believe that Miliband is wrong, for the absence of explicit presentation of principles in the order of exposition of a scientific discourse is not innocuous: above all in a domain like the theory of the State, where a Marxist theory, as we have seen, has yet to be constituted. In effect, one has the impression that this absence often leads Miliband to attack bourgeois ideologies of the State whilst placing himself on their own terrain. Instead of *displacing* the epistemological terrain and submitting these ideologies to the critique of Marxist science by demonstrating their inadequacy to the real (as Marx does, notably in the *Theories of Surplus-Value*), Miliband appears to omit this first step. Yet the analyses of modern epistemology show that it is never possible simply to oppose 'concrete facts' to concepts, but that these must be attacked by other parallel concepts situated in a different problematic. For it is only by means of these new concepts that the old notions can be confronted with 'concrete reality'.

Let us take a simple example. Attacking the prevailing notion of 'plural elites', whose ideological function is to deny the existence of a ruling class, Miliband's reply, which he supports by 'facts', is that this plurality of *elites* does not exclude the existence of a ruling *class*, for it is precisely these elites that constitute this class:[3] this is close to Bottomore's response to the question. Now, I maintain that in replying to the

---

[3] Miliband, pp. 24 ff and 47.

adversary in this way, one places oneself on his ground and thereby risks floundering in the swamp of his ideological imagination, thus missing a scientific explanation of the 'facts'. What Miliband avoids is the necessary preliminary of a *critique of the ideological notion of elite* in the light of the scientific concepts of Marxist theory. Had this critique been made, it would have been evident that the 'concrete reality' concealed by the notion of 'plural elites'—the ruling class, the fractions of this class, the hegemonic class, the governing class, the State apparatus—can only be grasped if the very notion of elite is rejected. For concepts and notions are never innocent, and by employing the notions of the adversary to reply to him, one legitimizes them and permits their persistence. Every notion or concept only has meaning within a whole theoretical problematic that founds it: extracted from this problematic and imported 'uncritically' into Marxism, they have absolutely uncontrollable effects. They always surface when least expected, and constantly risk clouding scientific analysis. In the extreme case, one can be unconsciously and surreptitiously contaminated by the very epistemological principles of the adversary, that is to say the problematic that founds the concepts which have not been theoretically criticized, believing them simply refuted by the facts. This is more serious: for it is then no longer a question merely of external notions 'imported' into Marxism, but of principles that risk vitiating the use made of Marxist concepts themselves.

Is this the case with Miliband? I do not believe that the consequences of his procedure have gone so far. It nevertheless remains true that, as I see it, Miliband sometimes allows himself to be unduly influenced by the methodological principles of the adversary. How is this manifested? Very briefly, I would say that it is visible in the difficulties that Miliband has in comprehending social classes and the State as *objective structures*, and their relations as an *objective system of regular connections*, a structure and a system whose agents, 'men', are in the words of Marx, 'bearers' of it—*träger*. Miliband constantly gives the impression that for him social classes or 'groups' are in some way reducible to *inter-personal relations*, that the State is reducible to inter-personal relations of the members of the diverse 'groups' that constitute the State apparatus, and finally that the relation between social classes and the State is itself reducible to inter-personal relations of 'individuals' composing social groups and 'individuals' composing the State apparatus.

I have indicated, in an earlier article in NLR, that this conception seems to me to derive from a *problematic of the subject* which has had constant repercussions in the history of Marxist thought.[4] According to this problematic, the agents of a social formation, 'men', are not considered as the 'bearers' of objective instances (as they are for Marx), but as the genetic principle of the levels of the social whole. This is a problematic of *social actors*, of individuals as the origin of *social action*: sociological research thus leads finally, not to the study of the objective co-ordinates that determine the distribution of agents into social classes and the contradictions between these classes, but to the search for *finalist* explanations founded on the *motivations of conduct* of the individual actors.

---

[4] 'Marxist Political Theory in Great Britain', NLR 43.

This is notoriously one of the aspects of the problematic both of Weber and of contemporary functionalism. To transpose this problematic of the subject into Marxism is in the end to admit the epistemological principles of the adversary and to risk vitiating one's own analyses.

Let us now consider some of the concrete themes of Miliband's book in the light of this preamble.

1. The False Problem of Managerialism

The first problem which Miliband discusses, very correctly, is that of the *ruling class*, by way of reply to the current bourgeois ideologies of *managerialism*. According to these ideologies, the contemporary separation of private ownership and control has transferred economic power from entrepreneurs to managers. The latter have no interest as owners in the strict sense, and hence do not seek profit as their aim—in other words, profit is not a motivation of their conduct, but growth, or development. Since the ruling class is here defined by the quest for profit, and this quest no longer characterizes the directors of the economy, the ruling class itself no longer exists: we are now confronted with a 'plurality of elites', of which the managers are one. What is Miliband's response to this?[5] He takes these ideologies literally and turns their own arguments against them: in fact, managers do seek profit as the goal of their actions, for this is how the capitalist system works. Seeking private profit, they also make up part of the ruling class, for the contradiction of the capitalist system according to Marx, Miliband tells us, is 'the contradiction between its ever more social character and its enduringly private purpose'.[6] While not excluding the existence of some managerial goals relatively different from those of owners, Miliband considers managers as one among the distinct economic elites composing the ruling class.

I consider this a mistaken way of presenting the problem. To start with, the distinctive criterion for membership of the capitalist class for Marx *is in no way* a motivation of conduct, that is to say the search for profit as the 'aim of action'. For there may well exist capitalists who are not motivated by profit, just as there are non-capitalists (the petty-bourgeoisie in small-scale production, for instance) who by contrast have just such a motivation. Marx's criterion is the objective place in production and the ownership of the means of production. It should be remembered that even Max Weber had to admit that what defined the capitalist was not 'the lure of gain'. For Marx, profit is not a motivation of conduct—even one 'imposed' by the system—it is an objective category that designates a part of realized surplus value. In the same way, the fundamental contradiction of the capitalist system, according to Marx, is not at all a contradiction between its social character and its 'private purpose', but a contradiction between the socialization of productive forces and their *private appropriation*. Thus the characterization of the existing social system as capitalist in no way depends on the motivations of the conduct of managers. Furthermore: to characterize

---

[5] Miliband, ibid.
[6] Miliband, p. 34.

the class position of managers, one need not refer to the motivations of their conduct, but only to their place in production and their relation ship to the ownership of the means of production. Here both Bettleheim and myself have noted that it is necessary to distinguish, in the term 'property' used by Marx, formal legal property, which may not belong to the 'individual' capitalist, and *economic property or real appropriation*, which is the only genuine *economic power*.[7] This economic property, which is what matters as far as distribution into classes is concerned, still belongs well and truly to *capital*. The manager exercises only a functional delegation of it.

From this point of view, the managers as such do not constitute a distinct fraction of the capitalist class. Miliband, basing himself on the non-pertinent distinction of motivations of conduct, is led to consider the managers a distinct 'economic elite'. By doing so, he not only attributes to them an importance they do not possess, but he is prevented from seeing what is important. For in effect, what matters is not the differences and relations between 'economic elites' based on diverging aims, but something of which Miliband says virtually nothing, *the differences and relations between fractions of capital*. The problem is not that of a plurality of 'economic elites' but of fractions of the capitalist class. Can a Marxist pass over in silence the existent differences and relations, under imperialism, between comprador monopoly capital, national monopoly capital, non-monopoly capital, industrial capital, or financial capital?

2. The Question of Bureaucracy

The next problem that Miliband selects for discussion, again correctly, is that of the relation between the ruling class and the State. Here too Miliband's approach to the question is to provide a direct rebuttal of bourgeois ideologies. These ideologies affirm the *neutrality* of the State, representing the general interest, in relation to the divergent interests of 'civil society'. Some of them (Aron, for example) claim that the capitalist class has never truly *governed* in capitalist societies, in the sense that its members have rarely participated directly in the government; others claim that the members of the State apparatus, the 'civil servants', are neutral with respect to the interests of social groups. What is the general line of Miliband's response to these ideologies? Here too he is led to take up the reverse position to these ideologies, to turn their argument against them. He does so in two ways. First of all he establishes that the members of the capitalist class have in fact often directly participated in the State apparatus and in the government[8]. Then, having established the relation between members of the State apparatus and the ruling class, he shows (a) that the *social origin* of members of the 'summit' of the State apparatus is that of the ruling class, and (b) that *personal ties* of influence, status, and milieu are established between the members of the ruling class and those of the State apparatus.[9]

---

[7] Bettleheim, *La Transition vers l'Economie Socialiste*, and Poulantzas, *Pouvoir Politique et Classes Sociales*, pp. 23 ff.

[8] Miliband pp. 48–68.

[9] Ibid., pp. 69–145, especially 119–145.

I have no intention of contesting the value of Miliband's analyses, which on 'the contrary appear to me to have a capital *demystifying* importance. Yet however exact in itself, the way chosen by Miliband does not seem to me to be the most significant one. Firstly, because the *direct* participation of members of the capitalist class in the State apparatus and in the government, even where it exists, is not the important side of the matter. The relation between the bourgeois class and the State is an *objective relation*. This means that if the *function* of the State in a determinate social formation and the *interests* of the dominant class in this formation *coincide*, it is by reason of the system itself: the direct participation of members of the ruling class in the State apparatus is not the *cause* but the *effect*, and moreover a chance and contingent one, of this objective coincidence.

In order to establish this coincidence, it would have been necessary to make explicit the role of the State as a specific instance, a regional structure, of the social whole. Miliband, however, seems to reduce the role of the State to the conduct and 'behaviour' of the members of the State apparatus.[10] If Miliband had first established that the State is precisely *the factor of cohesion of a social formation and the factor of reproduction of the conditions of production of a system* that itself determines the domination of one class over the others, he would have seen clearly that the participation, whether direct or indirect, of this class in government *in no way changes things*. Indeed in the case of the capitalist State, one can go further: it can be said that the capitalist State best serves the interests of the capitalist class only when the members of this class do not participate directly in the State apparatus, that is to say when the *ruling class* is not the *politically governing class*. This is the exact meaning of Marx's analyses of 19th century England and Bismarckian Germany, to say nothing of Bonapartism is France. It is also what Miliband himself seems to suggest in his analyses of social-democratic governments.[11]

We come now to the problem of the *members of the State apparatus*, that is to say the army, the police, the judiciary and the administrative bureaucracy. Miliband's main line of argument is to try to establish the relation between the conduct of the members of the State apparatus and the interests of the ruling class, by demonstrating either that the social origin of the 'top servants of the State' is that of the ruling class, or that the members of the State apparatus end up united to this class by personal ties.[12] This approach, without being false, remains descriptive. More importantly, I believe that it prevents us from studying the specific problem that the State apparatus presents; *the problem of 'bureaucracy'*. According to Marx, Engels and Lenin, the members of the State apparatus, which it is convenient to call the 'bureaucracy' in the general sense, constitute a specific *social category*—not a class. This means that, although the members of the State apparatus belong, by their class origin, to different classes, they function according to a specific internal unity. Their class origin—*class situation*—recedes into the background in relation to that which unifies them—their *class*

---

[10] Ibid., pp. 68–118.
[11] Ibid., pp. 96 ff.
[12] Ibid., p. 119–45;.

position: that is to say, the fact that they belong precisely to the State apparatus and that they have as their *objective function* the actualization of the role of the State. This in its turn means that the bureaucracy, as a specific and relatively 'unified' social category, is the 'servant' of the ruling class, not by reason of its class origins, which are divergent, or by reason of its personal relations with the ruling class, but by reason of the fact that its internal unity derives from its actualization of the objective role of the State. The totality of this role itself coincides with the interests of the ruling class.

Important consequences follow for the celebrated problem of the *relative autonomy* of the State with respect to the ruling class, and thus for the equally celebrated question of the relative autonomy of the bureaucracy as a specific social category, with respect to that class. A long Marxist tradition has considered that the State is only a simple tool or instrument manipulated at will by the ruling class. I do not mean to say that Miliband falls into this trap, which makes it impossible to account for the complex mechanisms of the State in its relation to class struggle. However, if one locates the relationship between the State and the ruling class in the social origin of the members of the State apparatus and their inter-personal relations with the members of this class, so that the bourgeoisie almost physically 'corners' the State apparatus, one cannot account for the relative autonomy of the State with respect to this class. When Marx designated Bonapartism as the 'religion of the bourgeoisie', in other words as characteristic of *all* forms of the capitalist State, he showed that this State can only truly serve the ruling class in so far as it is relatively autonomous from the diverse fractions of this class, precisely in order to be able to organize the hegemony of the whole of this class. It is not by chance that Miliband finally admits this autonomy only in the extreme case of fascism.[13] The question posed is whether the situation today has changed in this respect: I do not think so, and will return to this.

3. The Branches of the State Apparatus

Miliband's approach thus to a certain extent prevents him from following through a rigorous analysis of the State apparatus itself and of the relations between different 'branches' or 'parts' of this apparatus. Miliband securely establishes that the State apparatus is not only constituted by the government, but also by special branches such as the army, the police, the judiciary, and the civil administration. Yet what is it that governs the *relations* between these branches, the respective importance and the relative predominance of these different branches among themselves, for example the relation between parliament and the executive, or the role of the army or of the administration in a particular form of State? Miliband's response seems to be the following:[14] the fact that one of these branches predominates over the others is in some way directly related to the 'exterior' factors noted above. That is to say, it is either the branch whose members are, by their class origin or connections, nearest to the ruling class, or the branch whose pre-

---

[13] Ibid., p. 93.
[14] Ibid., p. 119 ff.

dominance over the others is due to its immediate 'economic' role. An example of the latter case would be the present growth of the role of the army, related to the current importance of military expenditures.[15]

Here too, I cannot completely agree with Miliband's interpretation. As I see it, the State apparatus forms an *objective system* of special 'branches' whose relation presents a *specific internal unity* and obeys, to a large extent, *its own logic*. Each particular form of capitalist State is thus characterized by a particular form of relations among its branches, and by the predominance of one or of certain of its branches over the others: liberal State, interventionist State, Bonapartism, military dictatorship or fascism. But each particular form of capitalist State must be referred back, *in its unity*, to important modifications of the relations of production and to important stages of class struggle: competitive capitalism, imperialism, state capitalism. Only *after* having established the relation of a form of State as a unity, *that is as a specific form of the system of State apparatus as a whole*, with the 'exterior', can the respective role and the mutual internal relation of the 'branches' of the State apparatus be established. A *significant* shift in the predominant branch in the State apparatus, or of the relation between these branches, cannot be *directly* established by the immediate exterior role of this branch, but is determined *by the modification of the whole system of the State apparatus and of its form of internal unity as such*: a modification which is itself due to changes in the relations of production and to developments in the class struggle.

Let us take as an example the present case of the *army* in the advanced capitalist countries. I do not think that the 'immediate' facts of the growth of military expenditure and increasing inter-personal ties between industrialists and the military are sufficient to speak of a *significant* shift of the role of the army in the present State apparatus: besides, in spite of everything, Miliband himself is very reserved in this matter. In order for such a shift to occur, there would have to be an important modification of the form of State as a whole—without this necessarily having to take the form of 'military dictatorship'—a modification which would not be due *simply* to the growing importance of military expenditure, but to profound modifications of the relations of production and the class struggle, of which the growth of military expenditures is finally only the *effect*. One could thus establish the relation of the army not simply with the dominant class, but with the totality of social classes—a complex relation that would explain its role by means of a shift in the State as a whole. I believe that there is no more striking evidence of this thesis, in another context, than present developments in Latin America.

4. The Present Form of the Capitalist State

Can we then speak in the present stage of capitalism of a modification of the form of the State? I would answer here in the affirmative, although I do not believe that this modification is necessarily in the direction of a preponderant role of the army. Miliband also seems to

---

[15] Ibid., p. 130 ff.

give an affirmative reply to the question. How does he situate this present modification of the form of State?[16] If the relation between the State and the ruling class is principally constituted by the 'inter-personal' relations between the members of the State apparatus and those of the ruling class, the only approach that seems open is to argue that these relations are now becoming increasingly intense and rigid, that the two are practically interchangeable. In effect, this is just the approach which Miliband adopts. The argument seems to me, however, merely descriptive. Indeed, it converges with the orthodox communist thesis of *State monopoly capitalism*, according to which the present form of the State is specified by increasingly close inter-personal relations between the monopolies and the members of the State apparatus, by the 'fusion of State and monopolies into a single mechanism'.[17] I have shown elsewhere why and how this thesis, in appearance ultra-leftist, leads in fact to the most vapid revisionism and reformism.[18] In fact, the present modification of the form of State must mainly be sought and studied not in its simple effects, which are besides disputable, but in profound shifts of the articulation of economy and polity. This modification does not seem to me to alter the relative autonomy of the State which at present, as J. M. Vincent has recently noted in connection with Gaullism,[19] only assumes different forms. In brief, the designation of any existent State as the pure and simple agent of big capital seems to me, *taken literally*, to give rise to many misinterpretations—as much now as in the past.

5. The Ideological Apparatuses

Finally there is one last problem which seems to me very important, and which will provide me with the occasion to go further than I have done in my own work cited above. I wonder in effect if Miliband and myself have not stopped half-way on one critical question. This is the role of *ideology* in the functioning of the State apparatus, a question which has become especially topical since the events of May–June 1968 in France. The classic Marxist tradition of the theory of the State is principally concerned to show *the repressive role of the State,* in the strong sense of organized physical repression. There is only one notable exception, Gramsci, with his problematic of hegemony. Now Miliband very correctly insists in long and excellent analyses (*The process of legitimization*, I, II, pp. 179–264) on the role played by ideology in the functioning of the State and in the process of political domination: which I have tried to do from another point of view in my own work.

I think however that, for different reasons, we have both stopped half-way: which was not the case with Gramsci. That is to say, we have ended by considering that ideology only exists in ideas, customs or morals without seeing that ideology can be embodied, in the strong sense, in *institutions*: institutions which then, by the very process of institutionalization, belong to the system of the State whilst depending

---

[16] Ibid., expecially p. 123 ff.

[17] See the acts of the colloquy at Choisy-le-Roi on 'State Monopoly Capitalism' in *Economie et Politique*, Special Number.

[18] Poulantzas, op. cit. p. 297 ff.

[19] *Les Temps Modernes*, August-September 1968.

principally on the ideological level. Following the Marxist tradition, we gave the concept of the State a *restricted* meaning, considering the principally repressive institutions as forming part of the 'State', and rejecting institutions with a principally ideological role as 'outside of' the State, in a place that Miliband designates as the 'political system', distinguishing it from the State.[20]

Here is the thesis I would like to propose: the system of the State is composed of *several apparatuses or institutions* of which certain have a principally repressive role, in the strong sense, and others a principally ideological role. The former constitute the repressive apparatus of the State, that is to say the State apparatus in the classical Marxist sense of the term (government, army, police, tribunals and administration). The latter constitute the *ideological apparatuses of the State*, such as the Church, the political parties, the unions (with the exception of course, of the *revolutionary* party or trade union organizations), the schools, the mass media (newspapers, radio, television), and, from a certain point of view, the family. This is so whether they are *public* or *private*—the distinction having a purely juridicial, that is, largely ideological character, which changes nothing fundamental. This position is in a certain sense that of Gramsci himself, although one he did not sufficiently found and develop.

Why should one speak in the plural of the state ideological apparatuses, whilst speaking in the singular of the State repressive apparatus? Because the State repressive apparatus, the State in the classic Marxist sense of the term, possesses a very rigorous internal unity which directly governs the relation between the diverse branches of the apparatus. Whilst the State ideological apparatuses, by their principal function— ideological inculcation and transmission—possess a greater and more important autonomy: their inter-connections and relations with the State repressive apparatus appear, by relation to the mutual connections of the branches of the State repressive apparatus, vested with a greater independence.

Why should one speak of *State* ideological apparatuses; why should these apparatuses be considered as composing part of the State? I will mention four principal reasons:

1. If the State is defined as the instance that maintains the cohesion of a social formation and which reproduces the conditions of production of a social system by maintaining class domination, it is obvious that the institutions in question—the State ideological apparatuses—fill exactly the same function.

2. The condition of possibility of the existence and functioning of these institutions or ideological apparatuses, under a certain form, is the State repressive apparatus itself. If it is true that their role is principally ideological and that the State repressive apparatus does not in general intervene *directly* in their functioning, it remains no less true that this repressive apparatus is always present behind them, that it defends

---

[20] Miliband, p. 50 ff.

them and sanctions them, and finally, that their action is *determined* by the action of the State repressive apparatus itself. The student movement, in France and elsewhere, can testify to this for schools and universities today.

3. Although these ideological apparatuses possess a notable autonomy, among themselves and in relation to the State repressive apparatus, it remains no less true that they belong to the same system as this repressive apparatus. Every important modification of the form of the State has repercussions not only on the mutual relations of the State repressive apparatus, but also on the mutual relations of the State ideological apparatuses and of the relations between these apparatuses and the State repressive apparatus. There is no need to take the extreme case of fascism to prove this thesis: one need only mention the modifications of the role and relations of the Church, the parties, the unions, the schools, the media, the family, both among themselves and with the State repressive apparatus, in the diverse 'normal' forms through which the capitalist State had evolved.

4. Finally, for one last reason: according to Marxist-Leninist theory, a socialist revolution does not signify only a shift in *State power*, but it must equally *'break'*, that is to say radically change, the State apparatus. Now, if one includes ideological apparatuses in the concept of the State, it is evident why the classics of Marxism have—if often only in implicit fashion—considered it necessary to apply the thesis of the 'destruction' of the State not only to the State repressive apparatus, but *also to the State ideological apparatuses*: Church, parties, unions, school, media, family. Certainly, given the autonomy of the State ideological apparatuses, this does not mean that they must all be 'broken' in homologous fashion, that is, *in the same way* or at *the same time* as the State repressive apparatus, or that any one of them must be. It means that the 'destruction' of the ideological apparatuses has *its precondition* in the 'destruction' of the State repressive apparatus which maintains it. Hence the illusory error of a certain contemporary thesis, which considers it possible to pass here and now, to the 'destruction' of the university in capitalist societies, for instance. But it also means that the advent of socialist society cannot be achieved by 'breaking' only the State repressive apparatus whilst maintaining the State ideological apparatuses intact, taking them in hand as they are and merely changing their function.

This question evidently brings us closer to the problem of the *dictatorship of the proletariat* and of the *cultural revolution*: but I have the feeling that it takes us farther from Miliband. I do not however, want to enter here into the problem of the political conclusions of the Miliband's book, in which he shows himself very—too—discreet: the question remains open. I will end by recalling what I said at the beginning: if the tone of this article is critical, this is above all proof of the interest that the absorbing analyses of Miliband's work have aroused in me.

The Capitalist State:
Reply to Nicos Poulantzas

Ralph Miliband

I very much welcome Nicos Poulantzas's critique of *The State in Capitalist Society* in the last issue of NLR: this is exactly the kind of discussion which is most likely to contribute to the elucidation of concepts and issues that are generally agreed on the Left to be of crucial importance for the socialist project, yet which have for a very long time received altogether inadequate attention, or even no attention at all. While some of Poulantzas's criticisms are, as I shall try to show, unwarranted, my purpose in the following comments is only incidentally to 'defend' the book; my main purpose is rather to take up some general points which arise from his review and which seem to me of particular interest in the investigation of the nature and role of the state in capitalist society. I hope that others may be similarly provoked into entering the discussion.

1. The Problem of Method

The first such point concerns the question of method. Poulantzas suggests that, notwithstanding the book's merits (about which he is more than generous) the analysis which it attempts is vitiated by the absence of a 'problematic' which would adequately situate the concrete data it presents. In effect, Poulantzas taxes me with what C. Wright Mills called 'abstracted empiricism', and with which I myself, as it happens, tax pluralist writers.[1] Poulantzas quite rightly states that 'a precondition of any scientific approach to the "concrete" is to make explicit the epistemological principles of its own treatment of it'; and he then goes on to say that 'Miliband nowhere deals with the Marxist theory of the state as such, although it is constantly implicit in his work' (p. 69). In fact, I do quite explicitly give an outline of the Marxist theory of the state[2] but undoubtedly do so very briefly. One reason for this, quite apart from the fact that I have discussed Marx's theory of the state elsewhere,[3] is that, having outlined the Marxist theory of the state, I was concerned to set it against the dominant, democratic-pluralist view and to show the latter's deficiences in the only way in which this seems to me to be possible, namely in empirical terms. It is perfectly proper for Poulantzas to stress the importance of an appropriate 'problematic' in such an undertaking; and it is probably true that mine is insufficiently elucidated; but since he notes that such a 'problematic' is 'constantly implicit in my work', I doubt that my exposition is quite as vitiated by empiricist deformations as he suggests; i.e. that the required 'problematic' is not absent from the work, and that I am not therefore led 'to attack bourgeois ideologies of the State whilst placing [myself] on their own terrain' (p. 69).

Poulantzas gives as an example of this alleged failing the fact that, while I maintain against pluralist writers the view that a plurality of élites does not exclude the existence of a ruling class (and I do in fact entitle one chapter 'Economic Elites and Dominant Class') I fail to provide a critique of the ideological notion of élite and do therefore place myself inside the 'problematic' which I seek to oppose. Here too, however, I doubt whether the comment is justified. I am aware of the degree to which the usage of certain words and concepts is ideologically and politically loaded, and indeed I provide a number of examples of their far from 'innocent' usage;[4] and I did in fact, for this very reason, hesitate to speak of 'élites'. But I finally decided to do so, firstly because I thought, perhaps mistakenly, that it had by now acquired a sufficiently neutral connotation (incidentally, it may still have a much more ideological ring in its French usage than in its English one); and secondly because it seemed, in its neutral sense, the most convenient word at hand to suggest the basic point that, while there do exist such separate 'élites' inside the dominant class, which Poulantzas describes by the admittedly more neutral but rather weak word 'fractions', they are perfectly compatible with the existence of a dominant class, and are in fact parts of that class. He suggests that the 'concrete reality' concealed by the notion of 'plural élites' can only be grasped 'if the very notion of elite is rejected' (p. 70). I would say myself that the

---

[1] *The State in Capitalist Society*, p. 172.

[2] Ibid., pp. 5, 93.

[3] 'Marx and the State' in *The Socialist Register*, 1965.

[4] e.g. 'Governments may be solely concerned with the better running of "the economy". But the descriptions of systems as "the economy" is part of the idiom of ideology, and obscures the real process. For what is being improved is a *capitalist* economy; and this ensures that whoever may or may not gain, capitalist interests are least likely to lose' (op. cit. p. 79. Italics is original).

concrete reality can only be grasped if the concept of élite is turned against those who use it for apologetic purposes and shown to require integration into the concept of a dominant or ruling class: i.e. there *are* concepts of bourgeois social science which can be used for critical as well as for apologetic purposes. The enterprise may often be risky, but is sometimes legitimate and necessary.

However, the general point which Poulantzas raises goes far beyond the use of this or that concept. In fact, it concerns nothing less than the status of empirical enquiry and its relationship to theory. In this regard, I would readily grant that *The State in Capitalist Society* may be insufficiently 'theoretical' in the sense in which Poulantzas means it; but I also tend to think that his own approach, as suggested in his review and in his otherwise important book, *Pouvoir Politique et Classes Sociales*, a translation of which into English is urgently needed, errs in the opposite direction. To put the point plainly, I think it is possible, in this field at least, to be so profoundly concerned with the elaboration of an appropriate 'problematic' and with the avoidance of any contamination with opposed 'problematics', as to lose sight of the absolute necessity of empirical enquiry, and of the empirical demonstration of the falsity of these opposed and apologetic 'problematics'. Poulantzas declares himself not to be against the study of the 'concrete': I would go much farther and suggest that, of course on the basis of an appropriate 'problematic', such a study of the concrete, is a *sine qua non* of the kind of 'demystifying' enterpiise which, he kindly suggests, my book accomplishes. After all, it was none other than Marx who stressed the importance of empirical validation (or invalidation) and who spent many years of his life in precisely such an undertaking; and while I do not suggest for a moment that Poulantzas is unaware of this fact, I do think that he, and the point also goes for Louis Althusser and his collaborators, may tend to give it rather less attention than it deserves. This, I must stress, Is not a crude (and false) contraposition of empiricist versus non- or anti-empiricist approaches: it is a matter of emphasis— but the emphasis is important.

2. The Objective Nature of the State

Poulantzas's critique of my approach also underlies other points of difference between us. But before dealing with these, I should like to take up very briefly what he calls 'the false problem of managerialism'. Managerialism *is* a false problem in one sense, not in another. It is a false problem in the sense that the 'motivations' of managers (of which more in a moment) are not such as to distinguish the latter in any fundamental way from other members of the capitalist class: i.e. he and I are agreed that the thesis of the 'soulful corporation' is a mystification. But he also suggests that I attribute to the managers 'an importance they do not possess' (p. 72). This seems to me to underestimate the significance of the 'managerial' phenomenon in the internal organization of capitalist production (which, incidentally, Marx writing a hundred years ago, did not do).[5] Poulantzas for his own part chooses to

---

[5] In fact, *his* formulations may go rather further than is warranted: 'A large part of the social capital is employed by people who do not own it and who consequently

310 *Karl Marx*

stress 'the differences and relations between fractions of capital'. But while these *are* important and need to be comprehended in an economic and political analysis of contemporary capitalism I would argue myself that the emphasis which he gives to these differences and relations may well obscure the underlying cohesion of these various elements—and may well play into the hands of those who focus on these differences in order to deny the fundamental cohesion of the capitalist class in the conditions of advanced capitalism.

More important, however, Poulantzas also suggests that I attach undue importance, indeed that I am altogether mistaken in attaching *any* importance to the 'motivations' of the managers. Thus, 'the characterization of the existing social system as capitalist in no way depends on the motivations of the conduct of the managers . . . to characterize the class position of managers, one need not refer to the motivations of their conduct, but only to their place in production and their relation to the ownership of the means of production' (p. 71). I think myself that one must refer to both not because managerial 'motivations' are in themselves critical (and Poulantzas is mistaken in believing that I think they are)[6] but precisely in order to show why they are not. By ignoring them altogether, one leaves a dangerous gap in the argument which needs to be put forward against managerialist apologetics. This is why, I take it, Baran and Sweezy, for instance, devote a good deal of attention to 'business behaviour' in their *Monopoly Capital.*

This issue of 'motivations' also arises, in a much more significant and far-reaching way, in connection with what I have called the state élite and its relation to the ruling class. Poulantzas notes that, in order to rebut the ideologies which affirm the neutrality of the state, I bring forward evidence to show that members of that class are themselves involved in government, and also show the degree to which those who man the command posts of the various parts of the state system are, by social origin, status, milieu (and, he might have added, ideological dispositions) connected with the ruling class. But, he also adds, this procedure, while having a 'capital *demystifying* importance',[7] is 'not the most significant one' (p. 72). His reason for saying this is so basic that I must here quote him at some length: 'The relation between the bourgeois class and the State is an *objective relation.* This means that if the *function* of the State in a determinate social formation and the *interests* of the dominant class in this formation *coincide,* it is by reason of the system itself (p. 73).[8] Similarly, the members of the State apparatus 'function according to a specific internal unity. Their class origin—

---

tackle things quite differently than the owner' (*Capital,* Moscow 1962, III, p. 431) 'This is the abolition of the capitalist mode of production within the capitalist mode of production itself, and hence a self-dissolving contradiction, which *prima facie* represents a mere phase of transition to a new form of production' (ibid. p. 429).

[6] e.g. 'Like the vulgar owner-entrepreneur of the bad old days, the modern manager, however bright and shiny, must also submit to the imperative demands inherent in the system of which he is both master and servant; and the most important such demand is that he should make the 'highest possible" profits. Whatever his motives and aims may be, they can only be fulfilled on the basis of his success in this regard.' (*The State in Capitalist Society,* p. 34.)

[7] Italics in text.

[8] ditto.

class situation—recedes into the background in relation to that which unifies them—their *class position*: that is to say, the fact that they belong precisely to the State apparatus and that they have as their *objective function* the actualization of the role of the State. The totality of this role coincides with the interests of the ruling class' (pp. 73–4).[9]

I should like to make two comments about this. The first and less impoitant is that Poulantzas greatly under-estimates the extent to which I myself do take account of the 'objective relations' which affect and shape the role of the State. In fact, I repeatedly note how government and bureaucracy, irrespective of social origin, class situation and even ideological dispositions, are subject to the structural constraints of the system. Even so, I should perhaps have stressed this aspect of the matter more.

But however that may be, I believe—and this is my second point—that Poulantzas himself is here rather one-sided and that he goes much too far in dismissing the nature of the state élite as of altogether no account. For what his *exclusive* stress on 'objective relations' suggests is that what the state does is in every particular and at all times *wholly* determined by these 'objective relations': in other words, that the structural constraints of the system are so absolutely compelling as to turn those who run the state into the merest functionaries and executants of policies imposed upon them by 'the system'. At the same time, however, he also rejects the 'long Marxist tradition (which) has considered that the State is only a simple tool or instrument manipulated at will by the ruling class' (p. 74). Instead, he stresses the 'relative autonomy of the state'. But all that this seems to me to do is to substitute the notion of 'objective structures' and 'objective relations' for the notion of 'ruling' class. But since the ruling class is a dominant element of the system, we are in effect back at the point of total subordination of the state élite to that class; i.e. the state is not 'manipulated' by the ruling class into doing its bidding: it does so autonomously but totally because of the 'objective relations' imposed upon it by the system. Poulantzas condemns the 'economism' of the Second and Third Internationals and attributes to it their neglect of the State (p. 68). But his own analysis seems to me to lead straight towards a kind of structural determinism, or rather a structural super-determinism, which makes impossible a truly realistic consideration of the dialectical relationship between the State and 'the system'.

For my own part, I do believe that 'the state in these class societies is primarily and inevitably the guardian and protector of the economic interests which are dominant in them. Its "real" purpose and mission is to ensure their continued predominance, not to prevent it.'[10] But I also believe that within this 'problematic', the state élite is involved in a far more complex telationship with 'the system' and with society as a whole than Poulantzas's scheme allows; and that at least to a certain but definite and important extent that relationship is shaped by the kind of factors which I bring into the analysis and which Poulantzas dismisses as of no account.

---

[9] ditto.
[10] Op. cit. p. 265.

The political danger of structural super-determinism would seem to me to be obvious. For if the state élite is as totally imprisoned in objective structures as is suggested, it follows that there is *really* no difference between a state ruled, say, by bourgeois constitutionalists, whether conservative or social-democrat, and one ruled by, say, Fascists. It was the same approach which led the Comintern in its 'class against class' period fatally to under-estimate what the victory of the Nazis would mean for the German working-class movement. This is an ultra-left deviation which is also not uncommon today; and it is the obverse of a right deviation which assumes that changes in government, for instance the election of a social-democratic government, accompanied by some changes in the personnel of the state system, are sufficient to impart an entirely new character to the nature and role of the state. Both are deviations, and both are dangerous.

It is the same sort of obliteration of differences in the forms of government and state which appears in Poulantzas's references to the 'relative autonomy' of the state. He suggests that Marx designated Bonapartism as the 'religion of the bourgeoisie', and takes Marx to mean that Bonapartism was 'characteristic of *all* forms of the capitalist state' (p. 74).[11] I stand to be corrected but I know of no work of Marx which admits of such an interpretation; and if he had said anything which did admit of such an interpretation, he would have been utterly mistaken. For in any meaningful sense of the concept, Bonapartism has *not* been characteristic of all forms of the capitalist state —rather the reverse. What Marx did say was that Bonapartism in France 'was the only form of government possible at the time when the bourgeoisie had already lost, and the working class had not yet acquired, the faculty of ruling the nation'.[12] It is perfectly true that all states are in some degree 'autonomous', and Poulantzas misreads me when he suggests that I 'finally admit this autonomy only in the extreme case of Fascism' (p. 74).[13] What I do say is that Fascism is the extreme case of the state's autonomy in the context of capitalist society, which is not at all the same thing— and that between the kind of autonomy which is achieved by the state under Fascism, and that which is achieved by it under the conditions of bourgeois democracy, there is a large gulf, which it is dangerous to underestimate. This scarcely leads me to an apotheosis of bourgeois democracy. It leads me rather to say that 'the point of the socialist critique of "bourgeois freedoms" is not (or should not be) that they are of no consequence, but they are profoundly inadequate, and need to be extended by the radical transformation of the context, economic, social and political, which condemns them to inadequacy and erosion.'[14]

---

[11] Italics in text.

[12] *The Civil War in France*, in *Selected Works*, (Moscow, 1950) I, p. 469.

[13] It is, incidentally, this recognition on my part of the 'relative autonomy' of the state which leads me, *inter alia*, to suggest that Poulantzas also misreads me when he states that my analysis 'converges with the orthodox communist thesis of *State monopoly capitalism*, according to which the present form of the State is specified by increasingly close inter-personal relations between the monopolies and the members of the State apparatus, by the "fusion of State and monopolies into a single mechanism"'(p. 71). In fact, I think this scheme to be *simpliste* and explicitly question its usefulness (*The State in Capitalist Society*, p. 11, ft. 2).

[14] Ibid., p. 267.

3. The Ideological Institutions

Poulantzas's references to the sections of my book devoted to ideology also raises points of great substance. He suggests that both he and I 'have ended by considering that ideology only exists in ideas, customs and morals without seeing that ideology can be embodied, in the strong sense, in *institutions*' (p. 76).[15] I myself must plead not guilty to the charge. What he, again most generously, calls my 'long and excellent analyses' of the subject largely focus precisely on the institutions which are the purveyors of ideology, and on the degree to which they are part and parcel, as institutions, of the general system of domination —and I do this in relation to parties, churches, pressure groups, the mass media, education, and so on. What value my analyses may have lies, I think, in my attempted demonstration of the fact that 'political socialization' *is* a process performed by institutions, many of which never cease to insist on their 'un-ideological', 'un-political' and 'neutral' character.

The much more important point is that Poulantzas suggests that these institutions 'belong to the system of the State' and he proposes the thesis that this system of the State 'is composed of *several apparatuses or institutions* of which certain have a principally repressive role, and others a principally ideological role', and among these he lists the Church, political parties, unions, the schools, the mass media and, from a certain point of view, the family (p. 77).[16]

I am extremely dubious about this. I suggest in *The State in Capitalist Society* that the state is increasingly involved in the process of 'political socialization' and that it plays, in certain respects, an extremely important role in it.[17] But I also think that, just as it is necessary to show that the institutions mentioned earlier *are* part of a system of power, and that they are, as Poulantzas says, increasingly linked to and buttressed by the state, so is it important not to blur the fact that they are not, in bourgeois democracies, part of the state but of the political system. These institutions *are* increasingly subject to a process of 'statization'; and as I also note in the book, that process is likely to be enhanced by the fact that the state must, in the conditions of permanent crisis of advanced capitalism, assume ever greater responsibility for political indoctrination and mystification. But to suggest that the relevant institutions are actually part of the state system does not seem to me to accord with reality, and tends to obscure the difference in this respect between these political systems and systems where ideological institutions are indeed part of a state monopolistic system of power. In the former systems, ideological institutions do retain a very high degree of autonomy; and are therefore the better able to conceal the degree to which they do belong to the system of power of capitalist society. The way to show that they do, is not to claim that they are part of the state system, but to show how they do perform their ideological functions outside it; and this is what I have tried to do.

---

[15] Italics in Text.
[16] ditto.
[17] Op. cit. pp. 183 and ff.

Finally, Poulantzas notes that my book says very little by way of 'political conclusions'. If by 'political conclusions' is meant 'where do we go from here?' and 'how?', the point is well taken. I have no difficulties in suggesting that the aim of socialists is to create an' authentically democratic social order, a truly free society of self-governing men and women, in which, in Marx's phrase, the state will be converted "from an organ superimposed upon society into one completely subordinate to it"'.[18] But this obviously raises very large and complex questions which I did not believe it possible to tackle, let alone answer with any kind of rigour, at the tail-end of this particular book.

---

[18] Op. cit. p. 277.

[16]

The Marxist Case for Revolution Today

Ernest Mandel

I. WHAT IS A REVOLUTION?

Revolutions are historical facts of life. Almost all major states in today's world are born from revolutions. Whether one likes it or not, our century has seen something like three dozen revolutions—some victorious, others defeated—and there is no sign that we have come to the end of the revolutionary experience.

Revolutions have been, and will remain, facts of life because of the structural nature of prevailing relations of production and relations of political power. Precisely because such relations are *structural*, because they do not just "fade away"—as well as because ruling classes resist the gradual elimination of these relations to the very end—revolutions emerge as the means to overthrow these relations.

From the nature of a revolution as a sudden, radical overthrow of prevailing social and (or) political structures—leaps in the historical process—one should not draw the conclusion that an impenetrable Chinese wall separates evolution (or reforms) from revolution. Quantitative gradual social changes do occur in history, as do qualitative revolutionary ones. Very often the former prepare for the latter, especially in epochs of decay of a given mode of production. Prevailing economic and political power relations can be eroded, undermined, and increasingly challenged—or they can even slowly disintegrate—as a result of new relations of production and the political strength of revolutionary classes (or major class fractions) rising in their midst. This is what generally characterizes periods of prerevolutionary crises. But the erosion and decay of a given social or political order remains basically different from its overthrow. Evolution is not identical with

---

This article appeared in *The Socialist Register*, eds. Ralph Miliband, Leo Panitch, and John Saville (London: Merlin Press, 1989), p. 159.

180

revolution. It transforms dialectics into sophism when, from the fact that there is no rigid absolute distinction between evolution and revolution, the conclusion is drawn that there is no basic difference between them at all.

The sudden overthrow of ruling structures is, however, only one key characteristic of that social phenomenon. The other one is their overthrow through huge popular mobilization, through the sudden, massive, active intervention of ordinary people in political life and political struggle.[1]

One of the great mysteries of class society, based upon exploitation and oppression of the mass of direct producers by relatively small minorities, is why that mass in "normal" times by and large tolerates these conditions, be it with all kinds of periodic but limited reactions. Historical materialism tries, not without success, to explain that mystery. The explanation is many-dimensional, drawing upon a combination of economic compulsion, ideological manipulation, cultural socialization, political-juridical repression (including occasionally violence), and psychological processes (internalization, identification).

Generally, as one revolutionary newspaper wrote at the beginning of the French revolution of 1789, oppressed people feel weak before their oppressors, in spite of their numerical superiority, because they are on their knees.[2] A revolution can occur precisely when that feeling of weakness and helplessness is overcome, when the mass of the people suddenly thinks, "We won't take it any longer," and acts accordingly. In his interesting book, *The Social Bases of Obedience and Revolt*, Barrington Moore has tried to prove that suffering and consciousness of injustice are not sufficient to induce large-scale revolts (revolutions) in broader masses. In his opinion a decisive role is played by the conviction that suffered injustice is neither inevitable nor a "lesser evil," that is, that a better social set-up could be realized.[3] A concomitant brake upon direct challenges to a given social and/or political order, however, is the locally or regionally fragmented nature of revolts pure and simple. Revolts generally become revolutions when they are unified nationwide.

Such challenges can be explained, among other things, by that basic truth about class societies formulated by Abraham Lincoln, empirically confirmed throughout history, and which is at least one reason for historical optimism (belief in the possibility of human progress) when all is said and done: "You can fool all of the people some of the time and some of the people all the time. But you can't fool all of the people all of the time."

When the majority of the people refuse to be fooled and intimidated any longer; when they refuse to stay on their knees; when they recognize the fundamental weakness of their oppressors, they can become transformed overnight from seemingly meek, subdued, and helpless sheep into mighty lions. They strike, congregate, organize, and especially demonstrate in the

The Marxist Case for Revolution Today

streets in increasing numbers, even in the face of massive, gruesome, bloody repression by the rulers, who still have a powerful armed apparatus at their disposal. They often show unheard-of forms of heroism, self-sacrifice, and obstinate endurance.[4] This may end in their getting the better of the repressive apparatus, which starts to disintegrate. The first victory of every revolution is precisely such a disintegration. Its final victory calls for the substitution of the armed power of the revolutionary class (or of a major class fraction) for that of the former rulers.[5]

Such a descriptive definition of revolutions has to be integrated into an analytical/causal one. *Social revolutions* occur when prevailing relations of production can no longer contain the development of the productive forces, when they increasingly act as fetters upon them, when they cause a cancerous growth of destructiveness accompanying that development. *Political revolutions* occur when prevailing relations of political power (*forms* of state power) have likewise become fetters upon a further development of the productive forces within the framework of the prevailing relations of production, a development which is, however, still historically possible. That is why they generally consolidate a given social order instead of undermining it.

This materialist explanation of revolutions offered by Marxism seems indispensable for answering the question: "Why, and why just at the moment?" Revolutions have occurred in all types of class societies but not in a uniform way. It appears clearly illogical to attribute them either to permanently operating psychological factors (humanity's allegedly inborn aggression, "destructiveness," "envy," "greed," or "stupidity") or to accidental quirks of the political power structure: particularly inept, stupid, blind rulers meeting increasingly self-confident and active opponents. According to the particular school of history concerned, one can see that blind ineptitude in the excessive recourse to repression, in the excessive amplitude of suddenly introduced reforms, or in a peculiar explosive combination of both.[6]

There are, of course, kernels of truth in such psychological and political analyses. But they cannot explain in a satisfying way the regular and discontinuous occurrence of revolutions, their cyclical nature so to speak. *Why* do "inept" rulers at regular intervals succeed "adequate" ones, so many times in so many countries? This can surely not be caused by some mysterious genetic mutation cycle. The big advantage of the materialist interpretation of history is to explain that occurrence by deeper socioeconomic causes. It is not the ineptness of the rulers which produces the prerevolutionary crisis. It is the paralysis engendered by an underlying social-structural crisis which make rulers increasingly inept. In that sense Trotsky was absolutely right when he stressed that "revolutions are nothing but the final blow and *coup de grace* given to a paralytic."

182

Lenin summarized the underlying analysis in a classical way by stating that revolutions occur when those below no longer accept being ruled as before and those above cannot rule any longer as before. The inability of a ruling class or major fraction to continue to rule has basically objective causes. These reflect themselves in increasingly paralyzing internal divisions among the rulers, especially around the question about how to get out of the mess visible to the naked eye. It intertwines with growing self-doubt, a loss of faith in its own future, or an irrational search for peculiar culprits ("conspiracy theories") as a substitute for a realistic objective analysis of social contradictions. It is this combination which produces political ineptitude and counterproductive actions and reactions, if not sheer passivity. The basic cause always remains the rotting away of the system, not the peculiar psychology of a group of rulers.

One has obviously to distinguish the basic historical causes of revolutions from the factors (events) triggering them. The first ones are structural, the second ones conjunctural.[7]

But it is important to emphasize that, even as regards the structural causes, the Marxist understanding of revolutions is by no means monocausally "economistic." The conflict between the productive forces and the prevailing relations of production and/or political power relations isn't all purely economic. It is basically socioeconomic. It involves all main spheres of social relations. It even eventually finds its concentrated expression in the political and not in the economic sphere. The refusal of soldiers to shoot at demonstrators is a political-moral and not an economic act. It is only by digging deeper below the surface of that refusal that one discovers its material roots. These roots don't transform the political-moral decision into a pure "appearance" or a manifestation of mere shadowboxing. It has a clear reality of its own. But that substantial reality in its turn doesn't make the digging for the deeper material roots irrelevant, an exercise in "dogmatism," or an "abstract" analysis of only secondary interest.[8]

In any case the inability of the rulers to continue to rule is not only a socio-political fact, with its inevitable concomitant of an ideological moral crisis (a crisis of the prevailing "social values system"). It has also a precise technical-material aspect. To rule also means to control a material network of communications and a centralized repressive apparatus. When that network breaks down, the rule collapses in the immediate sense of the word.[9] We must never, therefore, underestimate the technical aspect of successful revolutions. But the Marxist theory of revolution also supersedes a peculiar variant of the conspiracy theory of history, which tends to substitute for an explanation of victorious revolutions an exclusive reference to the technical mechanism of successful insurrections or coups d'état.[10] Instead, it is the material interests of key social forces and their self-perception which provide the basic explanation of turning points of history.

The Marxist Case for Revolution Today   183

II. REVOLUTIONS AND COUNTER-REVOLUTIONS

While revolutions are historical facts of life, counter-revolutions are like-wise undeniable realities. Indeed, counter-revolutions seem regularly to follow revolutions as night follows day. Etymology confirms this paradox. The very concept of "revolution" originates from the science of astronomy. The planets move in an orbital manner, returning to the point of departure. Hence the suggested analogical conclusion: the role of revolutions as great accelerators, as locomotives of history, is just an optical illusion of short-sighted and superficial observers, not to say utopian daydreamers. Such an interpretation (denigration) of revolutions is compatible with the great Italian historian Vico's cyclical conception of world history.

Under the influence of the victorious counter-revolution in England in 1660, the great political philosophers of the 17th century, above all Hobbes and Spinoza, developed a basically pessimistic view of human destiny. Revolutions are doomed to fail: "Plus ça change, plus ça reste la même chose." ("The more things change, the more they remain the same.") Two thousand years earlier, Greek and Chinese political philosophers had arrived at similar conclusions. There is supposedly no way out for human destiny but the search for individual happiness under inevitably bad social condi-tions, be it happiness through self-discipline (Stoics, Confucians, Spinoza) or through hedonism (the Epicureans).[11]

In the 18th century the Enlightenment questioned both the empirical and the theoretical roots of dogmatic skeptical pessimism.[12] A belief re-emerged in the perfectibility of humankind (only sophists or dishonest critics identify perfectibility with attaining a final state of perfection, be it said in passing), in historical progress, and thus likewise in the progressive role of revolu-tions. Revolution, indeed, looked beautiful in times of reaction. But already, before the outbreak of the revolution of 1789, the camp of the Enlightenment had split between the basically skeptical and socially cau-tious, if not outright conservative, bourgeois like Voltaire ("cultivez votre jardin")[13] and the more radical petty-bourgeois ideologues like Rousseau, who would inspire the Jacobin revolutionists. This split deepened in the revolution itself. After the successive stages of counter-revolution (Thermi-dor, the Bonapartist Consulate, the Empire, the Bourbon restoration) the reversal to 17th-century skepticism became general, including erstwhile enthusiasts for revolution exemplified by the English poet Wordsworth (but not Shelley). Only a tiny minority continued to pin their hopes on future revolutions and to work for them.[14] The near consensus was: the overhead of revolutions is too large, especially given the fact that they achieve very little.[15]

The Russian revolution's Thermidor and its tragic aftermath, the horrors of Stalinism, reproduced the same revulsion toward revolutions, first in the

184

late 1930s and 1940s, then, after a temporary reprieve in the 1960s and the early 1970s, on a generalized scale from the middle '70s on. The Soviet military intervention in Czechoslovakia, and especially Cambodia and Afghanistan, but more generally the reflux of the revolutionary wave from 1968 to 1975 in Europe, from France through Czechoslovakia, Italy, and Portugal, strengthened this political retreat. The near consensus can again be summarized in the formula: revolutions are both useless and harmful from every point of view, including that of progress toward a more humane society. Indeed, this is one of the key platitudes of today's prevailing neo-conservative, neo-liberal, and neo-reformist ideologies.

It is, however, based upon obvious half-truths, if not outright mystifications. The idea that revolutions revert to their historical points of departure, if not to situations worse than the prerevolutionary ones, is generally based upon a confusion between social and political counter-revolution. While a few social counter-revolutions have indeed occurred, they are the exception, not the rule. Neither Napoleon nor Louis XVIII restored semi-feudal socioeconomic conditions in the French countryside, nor the political rule of a semi-feudal nobility. Stalin did not restore capitalism in Russia, nor did Deng Hsiao-ping in China.[16] The restoration in England was quickly followed by the Glorious Revolution. The compromise of the American Constitution did not lead eventually to the generalization of slave labor but to its suppression, after the Civil War. The list can be extended *ad libitum*.

To this objective balance-sheet the problems of subjective choice are closely related. They confront the skeptics and the pessimists with a real dilemma. Counter-revolutions are not simply "natural" reactions to revolutions, the products of an inevitable mechanical yo-yo movement, so to speak. They originate from the same exacerbation of a system's inner contradictions which give rise to the revolution, but with a specific shift in socio-political relations of forces. They reflect the relative decline of political mass activity and efficiency. There is indeed a "natural law" operating here. As genuine popular revolutions generally imply a qualitatively increased level of political mass activity, this cannot be sustained indefinitely, for obvious material and psychological reasons. You have to produce in order to eat, and when you demonstrate and participate in mass meetings, you don't produce. Also, great masses of people cannot live permanently at a high level of excitement and expenditure of nervous energy.[17]

To this relative decline of mass activity there corresponds a relative rise of activity and efficiency of the old ruling classes or strata and their various supporters and hangers-on. The initiative shifts from the "left" to the "right," at least momentarily (and not necessarily with total success: there have been defeated counter-revolutions as there have been defeated revolutions).[18] There are likewise preventive counter-revolutions: Indone-

The Marxist Case for Revolution Today   185

sia 1965 and Chile 1973 may be taken as examples. But these preventive counter-revolutions clearly reveal the skeptic's dilemma. They are generally very costly in human lives and human happiness—much more costly than revolutions. It stands to reason that much more repression, much more bloodletting, much more cruelty, including torture, is needed to suppress a highly active, broad mass of ordinary people than to neutralize a small group of rulers. So, by abstaining from intervention against a rising counter-revolution—on the pretext that revolution itself is useless and bad—one actually becomes a passive if not active accomplice of bloody counter-revolution and large-scale mass suffering.

This is morally revolting, as it means tolerating, aiding, and abetting the violence and exploitation of the oppressors, while finding all kinds of rationalizations for refusing to assist the oppressed in their self-defense and attempted emancipation. And it is politically counter-productive as well as obnoxious. In the end it often proves to be suicidal from the point of view of the skeptics' alleged devotion to the defense of democratic institutions and reforms.

The most tragic example in that respect was of German social democracy at the end of World War One. Under the alleged motive of "saving democracy," Ebert and Noske kept the Imperial Army's hierarchy and the Prussian officer corps intact. They conspired with it against the workers—first in Berlin itself, then in the whole country. They made the generals of the *Reichswehr* into the political arbiters of the Weimer Republic. They permitted them to create and consolidate the *Freikorps* from which a good part of the later S.A. and S.S. cadres were recruited. They thereby paved the way for the rise and eventual conquest of power by the Nazis, which in turn led to the social democracts' destruction. They thought they could contain regression and reaction in the framework of a democratic counter-revolution.[19] History taught the bitter lesson that democratic counter-revolutions in the end often lead to much more authoritarian and violent ones, when the sharpening of the socioeconomic contradictions makes a total instead of a partial suppression of the mass movement into an immediate goal of the ruling class.

This again is not accidental but corresponds to a deeper historical logic. The essence of revolution is often identified with a widespread explosion of violence and mass killings. This is, of course, a false picture. The essence of revolution is not the use of violence in politics but a radical, qualitative challenge—and eventually the overthrow—of prevailing economic or political power structures. The larger the number of people involved in mass actions targeting these structures, the more favorable the relationship of forces between revolution and reaction, the greater the self-confidence of the first and the moral-ideological paralysis of the second, and the less the

186

masses are inclined to use violence. Indeed, widespread use of violence is counter-productive for the revolution at that precise phase of the historical process.

But what does occur most often, if not always, at some point of the revolutionary process is the desperate recourse to violence by the most radical and the most resolute sectors of the rulers' camp, intent on risking everything before it is too late, while they still have human and material resources left to act in that way. At some culminating point, the confrontation between revolution and counter-revolution thus generally *does* assume a violent character, although the degree of violence depends largely upon the overall relationship of forces. In answer to reaction's violence, the masses will tend toward armed self-defense. Disintegration, paralysis, and the disarming of the counter-revolution paves the way toward revolutionary victory. The victory of the counter-revolution depends upon a disarming of the mass.[20]

When the chips are down, when power relations are stripped of all mediations and are nakedly reduced to bare essentials, Friedrich Engels's formula is then borne out by empirical evidence: in the final analysis, the state *is*, indeed, a gang of armed people. The class or layer which has the monopoly of armed force possesses (either keeps or conquers) state power. And that again is what revolution and counter-revolution are all about. Sitting on the sidelines cannot prevent this confrontation. Nor can it help delay forever the day of reckoning. In the last analysis the skeptics' and reformists' revulsion against revolution covers an implicit choice: the conservation of the status quo is a lesser evil compared to the costs and consequences of its revolutionary overthrow. This choice reflects social conservatism. It is not a rational judgment of the empirically verifiable balance-sheets of the "costs" of historical, that is, real, revolutions and counter-revolutions.

No normal human being prefers to achieve social goals through the use of violence. To reduce violence to the utmost in political life should be a common endeavor for all progressive and socialist currents. Only profoundly sick persons—totally unable to contribute to the building of a real classless society—can actually enjoy advocating and practicing violence on a significant scale. Indeed, the increasing rejection of violence in a growing number of countries is a clear indicator that at least some moral-ideological progress has occurred in the last 70 to 75 years. One only has to compare the wild and brazen justification of war by nearly all the leading Western intellectuals and politicians in the 1914–18 period to the near universal revulsion toward war today in the same milieu to note that progress.

Double moral standards still reign supreme in inter-class and interstate relations, but the legitimacy of the widespread use of violence by rulers is at

The Marxist Case for Revolution Today 187

least increasingly questioned in a systematic and consistent way by a much greater number of people than in 1914–18 or 1939–45. The future, indeed the very physical survival of humankind, depends upon the outcome of this race between increasing consciousness about the necessary rejection of armed confrontation on the one hand and the increasing de facto destructiveness of existing and future weapons on the other. If the first does not eliminate the second through successful political action, the second will eventually destroy not only the first but all human life.

But such a political action can only be revolutionary and thus implies the use of at least limited armed force. To believe otherwise is to believe that the rulers will let themselves be disarmed peacefully, without using the arms they still control. This is to deny the threat of any violent counter-revolution, which is utterly utopian in the light of historical experience. It is to assume that ruling classes and strata are exclusively and always represented by mild, well-meaning liberals. Go tell that to the prisoners of the Warsaw ghetto and of Auschwitz, to the million victims of Djakarta, to the oppressed non-white population of South Africa, to the Indochinese peoples, to the Chilean and Salvadoran workers and peasants, to the murdered participants of the *Intifada*, to the millions and millions of victims of reaction and counter-revolution throughout the world since the colonial wars of the 19th century and the Paris Commune.

The elementary human-moral duty in the face of that terrifying record is to refuse any retreat into (re)privatization and to assist the oppressed, the exploited, the humiliated, and downtrodden to struggle for their emancipation by any means necessary. In the long run this also makes the individual participant a more human, happier person, provided he does not make any pseudo-*Realpolitik* concessions and observes unrestrictedly the rule: fight everywhere and always against any and every social and political conditions which exploits and oppresses human beings.

III. THE POSSIBILITY OF REVOLUTION IN THE WEST

Revolutions and counter-revolutions, being real historical processes, always occur in actual social-economic conditions, which are always specific. No two countries in the world are exactly alike, if only because their basic social classes and the major fractions of these classes are products of the specific history of each of these countries. Hence the character of each revolution reflects a unique combination of the general and the specific. The first derives from the logic of revolutions as sketched above. The second derives from the specificity of each particular set of prevailing relations of production and relations of political power in a given country, at a given moment, with its own inner contradictions and a specific dynamic of their exacerbation.

188

A revolutionary strategy[21] represents the conscious attempt by revolutionists to influence, through their political actions, the outcome of objectively revolutionary processes in favor of a victory of the exploited and the oppressed—in today's world essentially the wage-earning proletariat, its allies, and the poor peasantry. In turn, it must therefore be specific to have a minimum chance of success. It has to be attuned to the differentiated social reality which prevails in today's world. We can use the formula of the "three sectors of world revolution" to designate significantly different strategic tasks, that is, roughly: the proletarian revolution in the imperialist countries; the combined national-democratic, anti-imperialist, and socialist revolution in the "third world" countries; and the political revolution in the post-capitalist social formations.[22] We shall consider each of these in turn.

Regarding the industrialized metropolises of capitalism, a formidable objection is raised with regard to the possible effectiveness of revolutionary strategy. Many skeptics and reformists do not limit themselves to alleging that revolutions are useless and harmful. They add that revolutions are impossible in these countries, that they won't occur anyway, that to hope for them or expect them is utterly utopian; that to try to prepare for them or to further them is a total waste of time and energy.

This line of reasoning is based on two different—and basically contradictory—assumptions. The first one (which is still true) states that no *victorious* revolution has ever occurred in a purely imperialist country. The case of Russia in 1917 is seen as exceptional, a unique combination of underdevelopment and imperialism. But it is irrational, even childish, to recognize as revolutions only those that have been successful. Once one accepts that revolutionary processes did occur in 20th-century imperialist countries, surely the logical conclusion for a revolutionist is to study them carefully so as to be able to map out a course which will make defeat unlikely when they occur again.

The second assumption is that whatever triggered past revolutions (revolutionary crises and processes)[23] will never happen again. Bourgeois society—the capitalist economy and parliamentary democracy—are supposed to have achieved such a degree of stability, and "integrated" the mass of wage earners to such an extent, that they won't be seriously challenged in the foreseeable future.[24] This assumption, which already prevailed during the postwar boom (as an obvious result of the undeniable increase in living standards and social security which was its by-product for the Western proletariat), was seriously challenged in May 1968 and its immediate aftermath, at least in Southern Europe (and partially in Britain in the early 1970s). It regained a powerful credibility in the wake of the retreat of the proletariat in the metropolitan countries toward essentially defensive struggles after 1974–75.

The Marxist Case for Revolution Today 189

We should understand the nub of the question. The seemingly a-prioristic assumption is in reality a prediction which will be historically either verified or falsified. It is in no way a final truth. It is nothing but a working hypothesis. It assumes a given variant of the basic trends of development of capitalism in the latter part of the 20th century: the variant of *declining contradictions*, of the ability of the system to avoid explosive crises, not to say catastrophes.

In that sense it is strikingly similar to the working hypothesis of the classical version of reformism in its rejection of a revolutionary perspective and revolutionary strategy: that of Eduard Bernstein. In his book which launched the famous "revisionism debate," he clearly posited a growing objective decline in acuity of inner contradictions of the system as the premise for his reformist conclusions: fewer and fewer capitalist crises; fewer and fewer tendencies toward war; fewer and fewer authoritarian governments; fewer and fewer violent conflicts in the world.[25] Rosa Luxemburg answered him succinctly that precisely the opposite would be the case. Under the influence of the Russian revolution of 1905, Kautsky came the nearest to revolutionary Marxism and was the undisputed mentor of Lenin, Rosa Luxemburg, and Trotsky.[26] He also explicitly identified the perspective of *inevitable catastrophes* to which capitalism was leading as one of the main pillars of Marxism's revolutionary perspectives.[27] When he moved away from revolutionary Marxism, he started to consider these catastrophes as becoming more and more unlikely, that is, he started to share Bernstein's euphoric working hypothesis.[28]

What does the historical record reveal? Two world wars, the economic crisis of 1929 and onwards, fascism, Hiroshima, innumerable colonial wars, hunger and disease in the third world, the ongoing ecological catastrophe, and the new long economic depression. It is Rosa Luxemburg who has been proven more right than Bernstein; and it is the Kautsky of 1907 who has been proven right by history and not the Kautsky of the 1914 "ultra-imperialism" theory. Today it seems truer than ever, to paraphrase a famous formula of Jean Jaures, that late capitalism carries within itself a succession of grave crises and catastrophes, as clouds carry storms.[29]

One transforms that obvious truth—obvious in the sense that is borne out by solid historical evidence for three-quarters of a century—into a meaningless caricature when one insinuates that revolutionary Marxists expect or predict *permanent* catastrophes every year in every imperialist country, so to speak. Leaving aside the lunatic fringe, serious Marxists have never taken that stand, which doesn't mean that they have never been guilty of false analysis and erroneous evaluations regarding particular countries. If one soberly analyzes the ups and downs of economic, social, and political crisis in the West and Japan since 1914, what emerges is a pattern of *periodic*

190

upsurges of mass struggles in *some* metropolitan countries, which have at times put revolutionary processes on the agenda. In our view the mechanisms leading in that direction remain operative today as they were since the period of the historical decline of the capitalist mode of production was first posited by Marxists. The burden of proving that this is no longer the case rests upon those who argue that today's bourgeois society is somehow *basically* different from that of 1936, not to say that of 1968. We haven't yet seen any persuasive argumentation of that nature.

The concept of *periodically and not permanently* possible revolutionary explosions in imperialist countries logically leads to a *topology of possible revolutions in the West*, which sees these revolutions essentially as a qualitative "transcroissance" of the mass struggles and mass experiences of nonrevolutionary times. We have often sketched this process of "overgrowing," based not upon speculation or wishful thinking but on the experience of prerevolutionary and revolutionary explosions which have really occurred in the West.[30] We can therefore limit ourselves to summarizing the process in the following chain of events: mass strikes; political mass strikes; a general strike; a general sit-down strike; coordination and centralization of democratically elected strike committees; and transformation of the "passive" into an "active" general strike, in which strike committees assume a beginning of state functions, beginning with the public and the financial sectors. (Public-transport regulation, access to telecommunications, access to savings and bank accounts limited to strikers, free hospital services under that same authority, and "parallel" teaching in schools by teachers under strikers' authority are examples of such inroads into the realm of the exercise of quasi-state functions growing out of an "active" general strike.) This leads to the emergence of a de facto generalized dual power situation with emerging self-defense bodies of the masses.

Such a chain of events generalizes trends already visible at high points of mass struggles in the West: 1920 in northern Italy; July 1927 in Austria; June 1936 in France; July 1948 in Italy; May 1968 in France; the "hot autumn" of 1969 in Italy; and the high points of the Portuguese revolution 1974–75. Other general strike experiences[31] involving a similar chain of events were those of Germany 1920 and Spain (especially Catalonia) in 1936–37. (Albeit in a very different social context, the tendency of the industrial proletariat to operate in the same general sense in revolutionary situations can also be seen in Hungary in 1956, Czechoslovakia in 1968–69, and Poland in 1980–81).

Such a view of proletarian revolutionary behavior in the imperialist countries makes it easier to solve a problem which has haunted revolutionary Marxists since the beginning of the 20th century: the relation between the struggle for reforms (economic as well as political-democratic) and the preparation for revolution. The answer given to that problem by Rosa

The Marxist Case for Revolution Today   191

Luxemburg in the beginning of the debate remains as valid today as it was then.[32] The difference between reformists and revolutionists does not lie in the rejection of reforms by the latter and the struggle for reforms by the former. On the contrary: serious revolutionists will be the most resolute and efficient fighters for all reforms which correspond to the needs and the recognizable preoccupations of the masses. The real difference between reformists and revolutionary Marxists can be thus summarized:

1. Without rejecting or marginalizing legislative initiatives, revolutionary socialists prioritize the struggle for reforms through broad, direct, extra-parliamentary mass actions.
2. Without negating the need to take into consideration real social-political relations of forces, revolutionary socialists refuse to limit the struggle for reforms to those which are acceptable to the bourgeoisie or, worse, which don't upset the basic social and political relations of power. For that reason reformists tend to fight less and less for serious reforms whenever the system is in crisis, because, like the capitalists, they understand the "destabilizing" tendency of these struggles. For the revolutionists the priority is the struggle for the masses' needs and interests and not the defense of the system's needs or logic nor the conservation of any consensus with capitalists.
3. Reformists see the limitation or elimination of capitalism's ills as a process of gradual progress. Revolutionists, on the contrary, educate the masses in the inevitability of crises that will interrupt the gradual accumulation of reforms and will periodically threaten the suppression of past conquests.
4. Reformists will tend to brake, oppose, or even repress all forms of direct mass actions which transcend or threaten bourgeois state institutions. Revolutionists, on the contrary, will systematically favor and try to develop self-activity and self-organization of the masses, even in daily struggles for immediate reforms, regardless of "destabilizing" consequences, thereby creating a tradition, an experience of broader and broader mass struggle, which facilitates the emergence of a dual power situation when generalized mass struggles—a general strike—occur. Thereby, proletarian revolutions of the type sketched above can be seen as an organic product—or climax—of broader and broader mass struggles for reforms in prerevolutionary or even nonrevolutionary times.
5. Reformists will generally limit themselves to propagating reform. Revolutionary Marxists will combine a struggle for reforms with constant and systematic anti-capitalist propaganda. They will educate the masses in the system's ills and advocate its revolutionary overthrow. The formulation and struggle for transitional demands (which, while corresponding to the masses' needs, cannot be realized within the framework of the system) plays a key role here.

192

Doesn't such a view of "really feasible revolution" in the West seriously underestimate the obstacle posed by the Western proletariat's obvious attachment to parliamentary democracy? Doesn't this block the overthrow of bourgeois institutions, without which no victorious revolution is possible? We don't think so.

In the first place, many aspects of the legitimate attachment of the masses to democratic rights and freedom are not attachments to bourgeois state institutions. To use a clarifying formula of Trotsky, they express the presence of nuclei of proletarian democracy inside the bourgeois state.[33] The larger the masses' self-activity, self-mobilization, and self-organization, the more the butterfly of democratic workers' power tends to appear out of its "bourgeois" chrysalis. The fundamental issue will be growing confrontation between the "naked core" of bourgeois state power (the central government, the repressive apparatus, etc.) and the masses' attachment to democratic institutions *which they themselves control*.

In the second place, there is no reason to counterpose, in an absolute and dogmatic way, organs of direct workers' and popular power and organs resulting from undifferentiated universal franchise. Workers and popular councils and their centralized coordination (local, regional, national, international council congresses) can be more efficient and democratic forms, making possible the direct exercise of political, economic, and social power by millions of toilers. But if it is necessary to reject parliamentary cretinism, it is likewise necessary to reject anti-parliamentary cretinism. Whenever and wherever the masses clearly express their wish to have parliamentary-type power organs elected by universal franchise—the cases of Hungary, Poland, and Nicaragua are clear—revolutionists should accept that verdict. These organs need not supersede the power of soviets, insofar as the masses have learned through their own experiences that their councils can give them more democratic rights and more real power than the broadest parliamentary democracy alone; and insofar as the precise functional division of labor between soviet-type and parliamentary-type organs is elaborated into a constitution under conditions of workers' power.

Of course, soviet institutions can and should also be elected on the basis of universal franchise. The fundamental difference between parliamentary and soviet democracy is not the mode of election but the mode of functioning. Parliamentary democracy is essentially representative, that is, indirect, democracy and to a large extent limited to the legislative field. Soviet democracy contains much higher doses of direct democracy, including the instrument of "binding mandates" of the electors for their representative and the right to instant recall of these representatives by their electors. In addition, it implies a large-scale unification of legislative and executive

The Marxist Case for Revolution Today   193

functions, which, combined with the principle of rotation, actually enables the majority of the citizens to exercise state functions.

The multiplication of functional assemblies with a division of competence serves the same purpose. A key specificity of soviet democracy is also that it is a producers' democracy, that is, that it ties economic decision-taking to work places and federated work places (at local, regional, and branch levels etc.), giving those who work the right to decide on their workload and the allocation of their products and services. Why should workers make sacrifices in spending time, nerves, and physical strength for increasing output, when they generally feel that the results of these additional efforts don't benefit them and they have no way of deciding about the distribution of its fruits? Producers' democracy appears more and more as the only way to overcome the declining motivation (sense of responsibility) for production, not to say the economy in its totality, which characterizes both the capitalist market economy and the bureaucratic command economy.

IV. THE LESSONS OF THIRD-WORLD REVOLUTIONS

The revolutionary processes in the third world since World War II have confirmed the validity of the strategy of permanent revolution. Wherever these processes have climaxed in a full break with the old ruling classes and with international capital, the historical tasks of the national-democratic revolution (national unification, independence from imperialism) have been realized. This was the case of Yugoslavia, Indochina, China, Cuba, and Nicaragua. Wherever the revolutionary process did not culminate in such a full break, key tasks of the national-democratic revolution remain unfulfilled. This was the case of Indonesia, Bolivia, Egypt, Algeria, Chile, and Iran.

The theory (strategy) of permanent revolution is counterposed to the traditional Comintern/C.P. strategy since the middle 1920s, to wit the "revolution by stages," in which a first phase of "bloc of four classes" (the "national" bourgeoisie, the peasantry, the urban petty-bourgeoisie, and the proletariat) is supposed to eliminate by a common political struggle the semi-feudal and oligarchic power structures, including foreign imperialist ones. Only in a second phase is the proletarian struggle for power supposed to come to the forefront. This strategy first led to disaster in China in 1927. It has led to grave defeats ever since. It is increasingly challenged inside many C.P.s.

It is of no avail to avoid making this fundamental choice by the use of abstract formulas. The formulas, "workers' and farmers' government" or, worse, "people's power" or "broad popular alliance under the hegemony of the working class," just evade the issue. What revolutions are all about is

194

state power. The class nature of state power—and the question of which major fraction of a given class exercises state power—is decisive. Either the formulas are synonymous with the overthrow of the bourgeois-oligarchic state, its army, and its repressive apparatus, and with the establishment of a workers' state, or the formulas imply that the state apparatus is not to be "immediately" destroyed—in which case the class nature of the state remains bourgeois-oligarchic and the revolution will be defeated.

When it is said that without the conquest of power by the working class, without the overthrow of the state of the former ruling classes, the historical tasks of the national-democratic revolution will not be fully realized, this does not mean that *none* of these tasks can be initiated under bourgeois or petty-bourgeois governments. After World War II, most of the previously colonial countries did, after all, achieve political national independence without overthrowing the capitalist order. In some cases, at least, India being the most striking one, this was not purely formal but also implied a degree of economic autonomy from imperialism, which made at least initial industrialization under national bourgeois ownership possible. Starting with the late 1960s, a series of semi-colonial countries succeeded in launching a process of semi-industrialization that went much farther (South Korea, Taiwan, Brazil, Mexico, Singapore, and Hong Kong are the most important cases), often supported by substantial land reforms as indispensable launching pads. The famous controversy of the 1950s and 1960s on the "dependencia" theory—the impossibility of any serious degree of industrialization without a total break with imperialism—has thus been settled by history.

It is likewise incorrect to interpret the theory of the permanent revolution as implying that the overthrow of the old state order and the radical agrarian revolution must perforce *coincide with* the complete destruction of capitalist private property in industry. It is true that the working class can hardly be supposed to tolerate its own exploitation at the factory level while it is busy, or has already succeeded in, disarming the capitalists and eliminating their political power. But from this it flows only that the victorious socialist revolution in underdeveloped countries will start making "despotic inroads" into the realm of capitalist private property, to quote a famous sentence of the *Communist Manifesto*. The rhythm and the extent of these inroads will depend on the political and social correlation of forces and on the pressure of economic priorities. No general formula is applicable here for all countries at all moments.

The question of the rhythm and the extent of the expropriation of the bourgeoisie is in turn tied to the question of the worker-peasant alliance, a key question of political strategy in most of the third-world countries. Keeping capitalist property intact to the extent of not fulfilling the poor

The Marxist Case for Revolution Today   195

peasants' thirst for land is obviously counter-productive. Hitting private property to the extent of arousing fear among the middle peasants that they too will lose their property is counter-productive from an economic point of view (it could become also counter-productive politically).

On balance, however, experience confirms what the theory suggests. It is impossible to achieve genuine independence from imperialism and genuinely motivate the working class for the socialist reconstruction of the nation without the expropriation of big capital in industry, banking, agriculture, trade, and transportation—be it international or national capital. The real difficulties only arise when the borderline between that expropriation and the tolerance of small and medium-sized capital (with all its implications for economic growth, social equality, and direct producers' motivation) has to be determined.

The historical record shows that a peculiar form of dual power, of confrontation between the old and the new state order, has appeared during all victorious socialist revolutions in underdeveloped countries: dual power reflecting a territorial division of the country into liberated zones, in which the new state is emerging, and the rest of the country, where the old state still reigns. This peculiar form of dual power expresses in turn the peculiar form of the revolutionary (and counter-revolutionary) processes themselves, in which armed struggle (guerrilla warfare, people's war) occupied a central place. In the cases of China, Yugoslavia, and Vietnam, this resulted from the fact that the revolution started as a movement of national liberation against a foreign imperialist aggressor/invader, while becoming increasingly intertwined with civil war between the poor and the well-to-do, that is, with social revolution. In the cases of Cuba and Nicaragua, the revolution started likewise as armed struggle against a viciously repressive and universally hated and despised dictatorship, again growing over into a social revolution.

One should, of course, not simplify the pattern emerging from these experiences. At least in Cuba and in Nicaragua (to some extent also in the beginning of the Indochinese revolution and in several stages of the Yugoslav revolution) urban insurrections played an important role. A successful general strike and a successful urban insurrection decided the outcome of the Cuban and the Nicaraguan revolutions. The proponents of the strategy of armed struggle today generally adopt a more sophisticated and complex strategy than in the 1960s, combining guerrilla warfare, the creation of liberated zones, and the mobilization of mass organizations in urban zones (including forms of armed self-defense) in order to lead the revolution to victory. This combination seems reasonable in many semi-colonial countries, where state repression under prerevolutionary conditions leaves no alternative to revolutionary strategy. We believe, however, that this pattern

196

should not be considered unavoidable in all third-world countries, regardless of specific circumstances and particular social-political relationships of forces at given moments.

V. POLITICAL REVOLUTION IN SO-CALLED SOCIALIST SOCIETIES

The concept of political (antibureaucratic) revolution in the bureaucratized societies in transition between capitalism and socialism (bureaucratized workers' states) was first formulated by Trotsky in 1933. It resulted from the diagnosis of the growing contradictions of Soviet society, and the prediction that these contradictions could no longer be removed through reforms; and it was related, therefore, to the prediction that a self-reform of the bureaucracy was impossible.[34] Most left tendencies considered this concept, and the premises on which it was based, as either a fantasy or objectively a call for counter-revolution. The overthrow of the bureaucratic dictatorship could only lead to a restoration of capitalism: that was the assumption.

These objections were unfounded. Trotsky's prognosis of political revolution, like his analysis of the contradictions of Soviet society, appear as one of his most brilliant contributions to Marxism. Since 1953 we have witnessed a chain of revolutionary crises in Eastern Europe: the G.D.R. in June 1953; Hungary in 1956; Czechoslovakia in 1968; Poland in 1980–81. One can discuss whether similar crises didn't also occur in China, in the 1960s and 1970s. (Mikhail Gorbachev himself calls his *perestroika* a revolution and compares it with the political revolutions which occurred in France in 1830, 1848, and 1870.)[35] In all these concrete revolutionary processes there was no prevalent tendency to restore capitalism. This did not result only from the objective fact that the overwhelming majority of the combatants were workers, who have no interest in restoring capitalism. It was subjectively determined by the very demands of these combatants, who in Hungary set up workers' councils, with the Central Workers Council of Budapest leading the struggle. Similar developments occurred in Czechoslovakia and in Poland. The line of march of the political revolution in the U.S.S.R. will be quite similar.

On the other hand it cannot be denied that attempts at self-reform of the bureaucracy have been many—the most spectacular of them being the introduction of workers' self-management at the factory level in Yugoslavia in 1950. While often instrumental in triggering a "thaw" of the bureaucracy's stranglehold on society and enabling a revival of mass activity and mass politization at various degrees, these attempts have always failed to solve the basic ills of these societies. This was especially true for the historically most important attempt, the one initiated by Khrushcheve in

The Marxist Case for Revolution Today 197

the U.S.S.R. Indeed, most "liberal" and "left" Soviet historians and intellectuals today agree that the reason for the failure of Khrushchev was insufficent activity from below. This, incidentally, is also Gorbachev's official version of the Khrushchev experience.

So the historical balance-sheet is again clear: attempts at self-reform can start a movement of change in the bureaucratized workers' states. They can even facilitate the beginning of a genuine mass movement. But they cannot bring about a successful culmination of such change and movement. For this, a genuine popular revolution is indispensable. Self-reform of the enlightened wing of the bureaucracy cannot be a substitute for such a revolution.

The bureaucracy is a hardened *social* layer, enjoying huge material privileges which depend fundamentally on its monopoly of the exercise of political power. But that same bureaucracy does not play any indispensable or useful role in society. Its role is essentially parasitic. Hence its rule is more and more wasteful. It tends to become the source of a succession of specific economic, social, political, and ideological-moral crises. The need to remove it from its ruling position is an objective necessity for unblocking the march toward socialism. For this, a revival of mass activity, in the first place political activity of the working class, is needed. While a revolution will have many implications in the field of the economy, it will basically consolidate and strengthen the system of collective ownership of the means of production and of socialized planning—far from overthrowing it. That is why we speak of a "political revolution" instead of "social revolution."[36]

To a large extent the bureaucracy rules as a result of the political passivity of the working class; Trotsky even said through passive "tolerance" by the working class. The historical-social origins of that passivity are well-known: the defeats of the international revolution; the pressure of the scarcity of consumer goods and of a lack of culture born from the relative backwardness of Russia; the consequences of the Stalinist terror; and a disappointment of historical dimensions, leading to a lack of historical alternatives to the bureaucracy's rule. But the very progress of Soviet society during the last half-century, achieved on the basis of the remaining conquests of the October revolution and in spite of the bureaucracy's misrule, slowly undermines the basis of that passivity. The stronger, more skilled, and more cultivated the working class becomes, the greater its resentments and expectations clash with the slow-down of economic growth and the manifold social crises which the bureaucracy's misrule and waste provoke. Conditions emerge which tend to revive the activity of the working class.

Timothy Garton Ash quotes a remarkable memorandum by the new Polish Prime Minister, Mieczyslaw F. Rakowski, which concludes with the prediction that if the "socialist formation" does not find the strength to

198

reform itself, "the further history of our formation will be marked by shocks and revolutionary explosions, initiated by an increasingly enlightened people." Indeed. But as Ash himself clearly indicates, in spite of Rakowski's favoring reforms moving toward a restoration of capitalism tempered by a "liberal" democracy, the difficulty lies precisely in the social correlation of forces: the working class is not ready to pay the price for a return to capitalism, that is, massive unemployment and inequality. So you can't have a generalized market economy plus political democracy. You can only have a partial market economy plus partial repression. So you can't have radical reforms. So the likelihood that you'll have a political revolution is growing. Ash himself rather cynically concludes: "It seems reasonable to suggest that the reform has a rather higher chance of minimal success—that is, of averting revolution—if only because of the further diversification of social interests which it will promote. The freeing of the private sector, in particular, means that Hungary might yet have an entrepreneurial bourgeoisie that will go to the barricades—against the revolting workers. Capitalists and Communists, shoulder to shoulder against the proletariat: a suitably Central European outcome for socialism. To estimate the percentage chance of peaceful transformation, by contrast, requires only the fingers of one hand."[37]

Yet, precisely because the bureaucracy is not a new ruling class but a parasitic cancer on the working class and society as a whole, its removal through a political revolution by the workers does not require the type of armed conflict which until now has accompanied revolutions in class societies, including modern capitalist ones. It is more in the nature of a surgical operation. This was confirmed in the case of Hungary in 1956, which went the farthest toward a victorious political revolution. A significant part of the C.P. apparatus and practically the whole Army went over to the camp of the workers (of the people). Only a tiny handful of secret police agents opposed the victorious masses in open armed provocations, thereby provoking an overt conflict (and their own sad fate), which otherwise could have been avoided. In Czechoslovakia in 1968 a similar trend was set in motion. In fact, in all cases of such political revolutions witnessed up till now, only foreign military intervention could prevent it from becoming victorious nearly without bloodshed. One does not see what force could replace such a foreign military intervention in the case of the U.S.S.R., probably not the Soviet Army. And the capacity of the K.G.B. to repress 265 million people seems dubious, to say the least.

History has also confirmed the utopian character of the idea that the construction of socialism could be fully achieved in a single country or a small number of countries. It has confirmed that the U.S.S.R. (and the "socialist camp") cannot escape the pressure of the world market (of inter-

The Marxist Case for Revolution Today 199

national capitalism), the pressure of wars and the permanent arms race, the pressure of constant technological innovations, and the pressure of changing consumption patterns for the mass of the producers. But, far from being an unavoidable result of that pressure, the bureaucratic dictatorship undermines the revolution's objective and subjective capacity of resistance. A victorious political revolution in the U.S.S.R. and Eastern Europe would considerably strengthen that resistance. It would make new advances toward socialism possible. But we should not fall into the illusion that it could actually achieve a classless society on its own, independently of revolutionary developments elsewhere.

VI. WORLD REVOLUTION TODAY

The concept of the three sectors of world revolution refers to the different strategic-historical tasks that confront the revolutionary process today. But this only represents the first step toward a full appreciation of the concept of world revolution. The question of these sectors and their interaction, and hence their growing unity, also has to be raised.

For decades the apologists of the Stalinist dictatorship used to say that revealing the dark side of the Soviet (the Eastern European, the Chinese) reality discourages the workers in the West from fighting to overthrow capitalism. But history has fully confirmed that it is impossible to conduct a fight for a good cause on the basis of lies, half-truths, or the hiding of truth. As it was impossible, in the long run, to hide the revolting aspects of Soviet reality, the mass of the workers in the West and Japan (including those adhering to or voting for the Communist parties) ended by assimilating them. What really discouraged and demoralized them was not the revelation of these facts but the facts themselves—including their decades-long suppression by the Communist parties and their fellow travellers. One of the biggest subjective obstacles to a new development of revolutionary consciousness among the Western working class is the repulsive mask which Stalinism has put on socialism (communism). By contributing to tearing off that mask, a victorious political revolution in the East greatly advances the cause of socialism the world over. It strengthens the struggle against capitalism and imperialism instead of weakening it.

The idea that, somehow, such a revolution would at least weaken the U.S.S.R. (or the "socialist camp") at the state level and thereby change the military relationship of forces worldwide in favor of imperialism is likewise unfounded. It is an undeniable fact that the existence of the U.S.S.R., in spite of the bureaucratic dictatorship with its policies of "peaceful coexistence," objectively contributed to the victory and especially the consolidation of the Chinese revolution and to the downfall of the colonial empires.

200

But parallel to that objective function is the fact that the Soviet bureaucracy tried to obstruct the victory of the Chinese revolution through the strategy it advocated, and that it played a key role in the post-World War II consolidation of capitalism in Western Europe.

Furthermore, it is impossible to disconnect military strength from its economic and social basis and from the political nature of governments. A Soviet Union, not to say a "socialist camp," governed through pluralistic socialist democracy and a broad consensus of the majority of the toilers would be much more efficient economically, far more influential in the world, and thereby much stronger militarily than the U.S.S.R. of today.[38]

The concept of unity between the three sectors of world revolution is supported by the fact that while victorious revolutions in third-world countries can weaken imperialism, they cannot overthrow it. In the epoch of nuclear weapons it is obvious that imperialism can only be overthrown inside the metropolis itself. But the main obstacle to that overthrow is not the objective strength of capitalism or the bourgeois state, nor the absence of periodically explosive contradictions inside the metropolis. The main obstacle is subjective: the level of Western (and Japanese) working-class consciousness and the political quality of its leadership. Precisely for that reason, new qualitative advances toward socialism in the U.S.S.R. and Eastern Europe, and the removal of the bureaucratic dictatorships, would greatly assist in the solution of the problem.

On the other hand, any leap toward a victorious proletarian revolution in the West or in the most advanced semi-industrialized third-world countries (like Brazil), which will occur under immeasurably more favorable objective and cultural conditions than the Russian October revolution, will usher in material and social changes which will operate as a powerful stimulant for the toilers of all countries, beginning with the Soviet toilers if they have not yet overthrown the bureaucracy's yoke. To mention just one key aspect of any future victorious proletarian revolution in an economically advanced country: the realization of the half workday would play the same role that the slogan "Land, Bread, Peace" played in the Russian revolution. If that were realized, what sector of the working class the world over could stay impervious to the conquest?

The potential interaction—we say potential because it is obviously not yet a fact—between the three sectors of world revolution is premised on the historical/social unity of the world working class and the strength of the forces operating toward the development of the conscious awareness of that unity. We know perfectly well how strong the obstacles are on the road toward that political consciousness. They have been enumerated and analyzed a thousand times. What we want to stress is that they can be overcome by the operation of still stronger objective trends.

The Marxist Case for Revolution Today 201

The unity of the process of world revolution is related to the growing internationalization of the productive forces and of capital—exemplified in the emergence of the transnational corporation as the late-capitalist firm predominant in the world market—which leads unavoidably to a growing internationalization of the class struggle. Hard material reality will teach the international working class that retreating toward purely national defensive strategies (exemplified by protectionism) leaves all the advantages to capital and increasingly paralyzes even the defense of a given standard of living and of political rights. The only efficient answer to an internationalization of capital's strength and maneuvers is international coordination, solidarity, and the organization of the working class.

During recent decades the objective need for world revolution as a unity of the three world sectors of revolution has received a new and frightening dimension through the growth of the destructive potential of contemporary technological and economic trends, resulting from the survival of capitalism beyond the period of its historical legitimacy. The accumulation of huge arsenals of nuclear and chemical weapons; the extension of nuclear power; the destruction of tropical forests; the pollution of air and water the world over; the destruction of the ozone layer; the desertification of large tracts of Africa; the growing famine in the third world: all these trends threaten disasters which put a question mark on the physical survival of humankind. None of these disasters can be stopped or prevented at the national or even continental level. They all call for solutions on a worldwide scale. Consciousness about the global nature of humanity's crisis and the need for global solutions, largely overlapping nation-states, has been rapidly growing.

Mikhail Gorbachev and his main advisers and intellectual supporters, from a correct perception of the globalization of problems and of the absolute necessity to prevent a nuclear war, tend to draw the conclusion that, progressively, these global problems will be solved through an increased collaboration between imperialist and "socialist" states. They base themselves on two assumptions in that regard. First, they believe that a course toward world revolution would exacerbate interstate relations to the point where the outbreak of a world war would become more likely, if not unavoidable. Second, they tacitly presume that the inner contradictions of capitalism will tend to decrease, that the real class struggle will become less explosive, that trends toward increased class collaboration will prevail in the 21st century. Both these assumptions are utterly unrealistic. They are of the same type as the hope to achieve the building of a really socialist society in a single country, of which they represent in a certain sense the logical continuation.

The fact is that while victorious or even unfolding revolutions have undoubtedly led to counter-revolutionary interventions by imperialist

202

powers, they have on several occasions prevented larger wars from occurring. Without the German revolution of 1918–19, the revolutionary general strike in that country in 1920, and the preparations for a general strike in Britain that same year, a major war of all imperialist powers against Soviet Russia would probably have occurred. Without the victory of the October revolution, World War I would probably have been prolonged. The revolutionary upsurge in Spain, France, and Czechoslovakia in 1936 significantly slowed the march toward World War II. If it had been victorious only in Spain, not to say in France and Czechoslovakia as well, World War II could have been prevented. So, to identify revolutions with unavoidable war is just a misreading of the historical record. In fact, a victorious revolution in France and Britain today, not to say in the U.S.A., would be the surest way to make world war impossible.

The real reasoning of the neo-reformist Gorbachev version of "globalization" is based on the classical reformist illusion of a decline in the explosiveness and intensity of the inner contradictions of capitalism and of bourgeois society. We have already dealt with the unrealistic character of that assumption. It errs especially by not taking into account the structural link between the destructive uses of technology and economic resources on the one hand and competitive attitudes, competitive strife, private property, and the market economy on the other hand. Bourgeois society can never lead and will never lead toward a world without weapons and without technological innovations applied, regardless of their costs, to the natural and human ecology. You need socialism to achieve these goals. And you have to achieve these goals if humanity is to survive. The strongest justification for world revolution today is that humankind is literally faced with the long-term dilemma: either a world socialist federation or death.

Notes

1. Precisely because the Marxist concept of revolution encompasses the necessary dimension of mass action, the concept of "revolution from above" is not strictly accurate, although it was used by Engels and has, of course, a well circumscribed significance. Joseph II's reforms in Austria, Tsar Alexander II's abolition of serfdom, Bismarck's unification of Germany, and the Meiji "revolution" in Japan were historical attempts to pre-empt revolutions from below through radical reforms from above. To what extent they were successful in that purpose must be analyzed in each specific case. The same applies *mutatis mutandis* to Gorbachev's reform course in the Soviet Union today.
2. This was the epigram of the weekly *Revolutions de Paris*, which started to appear from the end of August 1789 in Paris.
3. See Barrington Moore Jr., *The Social Bases of Obedience and Revolt* (White Plains, N.Y.: M.E. Sharpe, 1978).
4. This was the case during the days in 1979 preceding the downfall of the Shah of

The Marxist Case for Revolution Today   203

Iran in the streets of Teheran, a spectacle largely forgotten because of the subsequent developments in that country.

5. This does not automatically flow from the disintegration and disarmament of the former army. The ruling class can attempt to substitute a new bourgeois army for the old one, as it did in Cuba after the downfall of Batista and in Nicaragua after the fall of Somoza, but without success.

6. This is the currently prevailing explanation of the reasons for the Shah's downfall: the combination of the "white revolution" destabilizing traditional Iranian society and the savagery of SAVAK.

7. In Russia the cause of the February–March 1917 revolution was the rottenness of tsarism and the tremendous parasitical weight of the peasants' exploitation upon the overall economic development of the country. The triggering factors of that revolution were hunger riots by the Petrograd women workers, which the Cossacks refused to repress. This expressed the emergence of de facto alliance between the working class and the peasantry, contrary to what had occurred in the repression of the 1905 revolution. There is, however, also a deeper dialectical mediation between structure and conjuncture. The specific social-political order in tsarist Russia determined both its participation in the First World War and its increasing incapacity to cope with the material and political prerequisites of successful warfare. This incapacity in turn deepened the social crisis in a dramatic way—leading to chronic food shortages, to hunger riots, and hence to the outbreak of the February–March 1917 revolution. A similarly multi-layered analysis is needed to understand contemporary revolutionary moments— including unsuccessful ones, such as May 1968 in France. What went on in France during the climax of the mass upsurge and the general strike deserves to be seen as a revolution, although it was defeated. The triggering factor of the student revolt in Paris must itself be seen in the context of a deeper structural crisis of social and political relations. Useful here is the remarkable study by the Soviet sociologist Alex D. Khlopin, *New Social Movements in the West: Their Causes and Prospects of Developments* which complements Western Marxist analyses.

8. In Russia the material interests of the Cossacks as sons of peasants, the connections of these interests to political awareness on the one hand and to the explosive crisis of the relations of production in the countryside on the other hand, all converge to explain the Cossacks' peculiar shift in behavior at a given moment in a given place.

9. It is, of course, possible that this breakdown is only temporary and only lasts some weeks or months. But this doesn't make the collapse less real. In Germany—not only but of course especially in Berlin—this is what occurred in November–December 1918. In France this is what occurred at the climax of May 1968. Indeed, it was recently confirmed that, at that moment, General de Gaulle couldn't phone General Massu, the commander of the French Army in Germany: he had lost control of the whole telecommunications system in Paris as a result of an effective general strike. An anonymous woman telephone operator, whom he finally succeeded in speaking to personally, refused to obey his order. The decision of the strike committee prevailed. These are the unknown heroines and heroes of revolution. This is the stuff proletarian revolutions are made of.

10. See Edward Luttwack, *Coup D'Etat: A Practical Handbook* (Cambridge: Harvard University Press, 1979); cf. interview with *Stampa-Sera*, August 8, 1988.

204

11. Nevertheless, Spinoza, who was himself skeptical about the outcome of revolutions, explicitly proclaimed the people's right to revolution, more than a century before that same right was ensconced in the Preamble of the American Declaration of Independence, and afterwards in the French Declaration of the Rights of Men and Citizens. To our knowledge the Yugoslav Constitution is today the only one which not only contains that right explicitly but even adds to it *the duty* to make a revolution under specific conditions.

12. The dogma of the basic "evil" of humankind is based in the West on the superstition of Original Sin. Of late it has received a pseudo-scientific veneer with the Konrad Lorenz school of the alleged universal aggressiveness of human beings, which some psychologists tend to generalize into a human trend toward self-destruction. Better psychologists, in the first place Sigmund Freud, pointed out that the human psyche combines both a trend toward cooperation and a trend toward self-destruction, Eros and Thanatos, to love and to kill. If only the second one had prevailed, humankind would have disappeared a long time ago instead of showing an impressive demographic-biological expansion.

13. Two thousand years ago the Jewish philosopher Hillel expressed the contradictions of individual skepticism in a succinct way: "If I am not for myself, who is for me? And if I am for myself alone, what then am I? And if not now, then when?" Kant tried to escape that dilemma through his categorical imperative, but failed to apply it convincingly to social conflicts (see his attitude toward the French Revolution). Marx found the solution in his categorical imperative to struggle against all social conditions in which human beings are debased, oppressed, and alienated.

14. Revolutionary continuity was maintained by a handful of followers of Babeuf, who, through the person of Buonarotti, helped to inspire Auguste Blanqui's *Societe des Pouvres*, which gave rise to a new revolutionary organization in the 1830s. But for nearly 40 years there were very few organized revolutionaries in the country, which witnessed five revolutions in a century.

15. The debate goes on, of course. Rene Sedillot (*Le coût de la revolution française* (Paris: Perrin, 1987) is the most brazen of the latter-day dragon-killers, who continue the good fight against the French Revolution after two centuries. The bases of his argumentation are revealed by the fact that he adds the victims of counter-revolution, in the first place of Napoleon's wars, to the cost of the revolution. But he does not compare these "costs" to those of the Ancien Regime's dynastic wars: the devastation of a quarter of Germany, the big famine in France at the beginning of the 18th century, etc.

16. The inclusion of Deng Hsiao-ping in this list is, of course, open to serious challenge. Mao was not Lenin; he was rather a unique combination of the traits of both Lenin and Stalin. Deng Hsiao-ping, in spite of many right-wing tendencies in his policies, cannot be considered the Chinese revolution's Thermidorian equivalent of Stalin.

17. Incidentally, this is one of the objective bases for the second "law of permanent revolution" formulated by Trotsky. For the revolutionary process to continue after it starts to recede in a given country, its center of gravity must shift to another one.

18. Classical examples of defeated counter-revolutionary coups are the Kornilov one in Russia, August 1917, the Kapp-von Luttwitz *putsch* in Germany in 1920, and the Spanish military-fascist uprising in July 1936 in Catalonia, Madrid, Valencia, Malaga, the Basque country, etc.

The Marxist Case for Revolution Today 205

19. A democratic counter-revolution seeks to maintain the essential features of bourgeois democracy, including a legal mass labor movement, universal franchise, and a broadly free press, after having beaten back the workers' attempts to conquer power and to arm themselves. Of course, while engaged in suppressing the German revolution, Ebert, Noske, and Co. systematically curtailed democratic freedoms, forbade political parties, suspended newspapers, requisitioned strikers, and even outlawed strikes to preserve the bourgeois state. Moreover, Ebert cynically lied before the All-German Congress of Workers' and Soldiers' Councils (December 1918) when he denied having brought soldiers to Berlin for repressive purposes. He had actually done so, in direct connection with the Imperial Army's High Command, behind the back of his fellow "people's commissars" (ministers) of the Independent Socialist Party. The repression started a few days later.

20. This occurred in Germany throughout the country, starting with January 1919 in Berlin. It occurred in Barcelona after the May days in 1937, in Greece starting with December 1944, and in Indonesia in 1965, to quote some examples. Courageous left socialists like the prewar Austrian social democrats and Salvador Allende in Chile did not refuse to fight counter-revolution, arms in hand, but they refused to organize and prepare the masses systematically for this unavoidable showdown and deliberately left the initiative to the enemy, which meant courting disaster.

21. Revolutionists cannot "cause revolutions," nor can they "provoke" them artificially (this is the basic difference between a revolution and a *putsch*). Engels went even further: "Die Leute die sich ruhmen, eine Revolution *gemacht* zu haben, haben immer noch am Tage darauf gesehen, dass sie nicht wussten was sie taten, das die 'gemachte' Revolution, jener die sie hatten machen wollen, durchaus nicht ahnlich sah" (letter to Verra Sassulitch of April 23, 1885 [MEW], Berlin: Dietz-Verlag, Vol. 36, p. 307).

22. The concept of "combined revolution" also applies to some imperialist countries, but with a different weight of the combined elements from that of third-world countries: the combination of proletarian revolution and self-determination of oppressed national minorities in Spain; the combination of proletarian revolution and Black and Hispanic liberation in the United States.

23. For example, in Finland in 1917–18; in Austria in 1918–19, 1927, and 1934; in Germany in 1918–23; in Italy in 1919–20, 1944–45, and 1969; in Spain in 1931–37; in France in 1936 and 1968; and in Portugal in 1974–75.

24. Some argue that the impossibility of escaping "technology compulsion" (*technologischer Sachzwang*) constitutes an unsurpassable obstacle on the road to proletarian revolution and "Marxian socialism." This is an unproven assumption, based upon the *petitio principii* that technology somehow develops and is applied independently from the social interests of those who have the means (under large-scale commodity production: the capital) to apply it.

25. See Eduard Bernstein: *Die Voraussetzungen des Sozialismus und die Aufgaben der Sozialdemokratie* (Stuttgart, 1899).

26. On Kautsky's evolutions away from revolutionary Marxism in 1909–10, its turning point (his capitulation to the *Parteivorstand* on the censorship that body applied to his booklet *The Road to Power*), and its political outcome in his opposition to Rosa Luxemburg's campaign in favor of political mass strikes, see Massimo Salvadori, *Karl Kautsky and the Socialist Revolution* (London: NBL, 1979), pp. 123ff.

206

27. Karl Kautsky, *Les Trois Sources du Marxisme* (1907) (Paris: Spartacus, 1969), pp. 12–13.

28. Kautsky's articles on ultra-imperialism, in which he considered inter-imperialist wars more and more unlikely, started to appear in 1912. The final one had the unfortunate fate of appearing in *Die Neue Zeit* after the outbreak of World War I.

29. We have developed this idea further in our article "The Reasons for Founding the Fourth International and Why They Remain Valid Today," *International Marxist Review* (Summer-Autumn, 1988). (See pp. 143–78 of this volume.)

30. Ernest Mandel, *Revolutionary Marxism Today* (London: New Left Books, 1979).

31. The case of the German workers' answer to the Kapp-von Luttwitz coup of 1920 and of the Spanish workers' answer to the fascist-military uprising of July 1936—in a more limited way also the Italian workers' uprising of 1948—helps to integrate into this topology the question of the proletariat's capacity to answer massively counter-revolutionary initiatives by the bourgeoisie. This will remain on the agenda in the West in the future as it was in the past. But this does not justify any refusal to recognize that the process of proletarian revolutions likely to occur in the West and in Japan will most probably be quite different from these examples, as well as from the revolutionary processes which we witnessed in Yugoslavia, China, Indochina, Cuba, and Nicaragua during and after World War II.

32. See Norman Geras, *The Legacy of Rosa Luxemburg* (London: New Left Books, 1976), on this and on Luxemburg being one of the founders, together with Trotsky, of a theory of dual power emerging from workers' mass strikes.

33. Trotsky, "What Next? Vital Questions for the German Proletariat" (January 1932) *The Struggle Against Fascism in Germany* (New York: Pathfinder Press, 1972), p. 142.

34. Leon Trotsky first formulated that conclusion in 1933 in his article "The Class Nature of the Soviet State" (October 1, 1933) *Writings of Leon Trotsky 1933–1934* (New York: Pathfinder Press, 1975), p. 101f.

35. On the question of how far that characterization is legitimate, see Ernest Mandel, *Beyond Perestroika* (London: Verso, 1988).

36. On the theoretical foundations of the definition of "political revolution" and the analysis which leads to it, see Ernest Mandel, "Bureaucratie et production marchande," *Quatrieme Internationale*, 24 (April 1987).

37. *The New York Review of Books*, October 27, 1988.

38. The Mexican sociologist Pablo Gonzales Casanova has tried to refute the legitimacy of political revolution in the bureaucratized workers states on the basis of a hierarchy of revolutionary tasks on a world scale. As long as imperialism survives, revolutionists (socialists, anti-imperialists) everywhere in the world should give priority to the fight against that monster over and above all other struggles. (See his "La Penetraction metafisica en el Marxismo europeo," in *Sabado*, magazine supplement to the Mexican daily *Unomasuno*, 8/1/1983). Underlying that reasoning is the hypothesis that an ongoing, not to say a victorious, political revolution in a bureaucratized workers' state somehow weakens the fight against imperialism. But that supposition is completely unfounded, for the reason we have advanced.

Part IV
The Individual and Society

[17]

Psychoanalysis and Sociology

Erich Fromm

The problem of the relations between psychoanalysis and sociology, about which I will speak in the Institute's courses, has two sides. The first is the application of psychoanalysis to sociology, the second that of sociology to psychoanalysis. Of course, it is not possible even to list in a few minutes all the problems and themes that result from both sides. Therefore, I shall merely attempt to make a few fundamental remarks about the principles which seem to apply to the scientific treatment of psychoanalytic-sociological problems.

The application of psychoanalysis to sociology must definitely guard against the mistake of wanting to give psychoanalytic answers where economic, technical, or political facts provide the real and sufficient explanation of sociological questions. On the other hand, the psychoanalyst must emphasize that the subject of sociology, society, in reality consists of individuals, and that it is these human beings, rather than an abstract society as such, whose actions, thoughts, and feelings are the object of sociological research. Human beings do not have one "individual psyche," which functions when a person performs as an individual and so becomes the object of psychoanalysis, contrasted to a completely separate "mass psyche" with all sorts of mass instincts, as well as vague feelings of community and solidarity, which springs into action whenever a person performs as part of mass, and for which the sociologist creates some makeshift concepts for psychoanalytical facts unknown to him. There aren't two minds within a person's head, but only one, in which the same mechanisms and laws apply whether a person performs as an individual or people appear as a society, class, community, or what have you. What

---

Translated by Mark Ritter

38 / Erich Fromm

psychoanalysis can bring to sociology is the knowledge—though still imperfect—of the human psychic apparatus, which is a determinant of social development alongside technical, economic, and financial factors, and deserves no less consideration than the other factors mentioned. The common task of both sciences is to investigate in what way and to what extent the psychic apparatus of the human being causally affects or determines the development or organization of society.

Let me mention here only one essential concrete problem. It is necessary to investigate what role the instinctual and the unconscious play in the organization and development of society and in individual social facts, and to what extent the changes in mankind's psychological structure, in the sense of a growing ego-organization and thus a rational ability to cope with the instinctual and natural, is a sociologically relevant factor.

Now the other side of the problem: the application of sociological approaches to psychoanalysis. However important it may be to point out to sociologists the banal fact that society consists of living people and that psychology is one of the factors affecting social development, it is equally important that psychology not underestimate the fact that the individual person in reality exists only as a socialized person. Psychoanalysis, in contrast to some other schools of psychology, can claim that it has understood this fact from the beginning. Indeed, the recognition that there is no *homo psychologicus,* no psychological Robinson Crusoe, is one of the foundations of its theory. Psychoanalysis is predominantly oriented to questions of genesis; it devotes its special interest to human childhood, and it teaches us to interpret a very essential part of the development of the human psychological apparatus on the basis of people's attachment to mother, father, siblings, in short to the family, and thus to society. Psychoanalysis interprets the development of individuals precisely in terms of their relationship to their closest and most intimate surroundings; it considers the psychological apparatus as formed most decisively by these relationships.

Certainly, this is only a beginning, and from it a series of further important problems result, which have so far scarcely been attacked; for instance, the question of to what extent the family is itself the product of a particular social system, and how a socially conditioned change in the family as such might influence the development of the psychic apparatus of the individual. Or there is the question of what influence the growth of technology—i.e., an ever increasing gratification, or a decreasing deprivation, of the instincts—has on the psyche of the individual.

The classification from which we proceed, into problems that result from the application of psychoanalysis to sociology and of sociology to psychoanalysis, is of course only a crude one, which corresponds to practical needs. In keeping with the reciprocal interaction of person and

Psychoanalysis and Sociology / 39

society, there are a whole series of further problems. Some of the most important ones are precisely those where it is impossible to apply one method to the other, but where a set of facts, which are equally psychological and social in character, can be investigated by both methods and can be understood only by employing both perspectives. It is just such a problem of how much certain concerns of psychology, which are simultaneously sociological, such as religion, depend on the material development of mankind in their appearance and decline, that constitutes the subject of the latest book by Freud.

There Freud advances the idea that religion is the psychic correlative to mankind's helplessness in the face of nature. From there he opens a perspective onto a problem which may be considered one of the most important psychologic-sociological questions: What connections exist between the social, especially the economic-technical, development of humanity, and the development of the psychic apparatus, especially the ego-organization, of the human being? In short, he raises the question of the developmental history of the psyche. Psychoanalysis has so far asked and answered this question only for the individual. Freud in his latest book has extended this genetic inquiry to the psychic development of society, and has thus given important guidance to future psychoanalytic-sociological work.

In summary, I would like to say: Psychoanalysis, which interprets the human being as a socialized being, and the psychic apparatus as essentially developed and determined through the relationship of the individual to society, must consider it a duty to participate in the investigation of sociological problems to the extent the human being or his/her psyche plays any part at all. In this effort, one may quote the words, not of a psychologist, but of (Karl Marx) the greatest sociologist of all: "History does nothing, it possesses no immense wealth, it fights no battles. It is instead the human being, the real living person, who does everything, who owns everything, and who fights all battles."

[18]

THE USES AND ABUSES OF 'CIVIL SOCIETY'

ELLEN **MEIKSINS** WOOD

We live in curious times. Just when intellectuals of the Left in the West have a rare opportunity to do something useful, if not actually world-historic, they – or large sections of them– are in full retreat. Just when reformers in the Soviet Union and Eastern Europe are looking to Western capitalism for paradigms of economic and political success, many of us appear to be abdicating the traditional role of the Western left as critic of capitalism. Just when more than ever we need a Karl **Marx** to reveal the inner workings of the capitalist system, or a Friedrich **Engels** to expose its ugly realities 'on the ground', what we are getting is an army of 'post-Marxists' one of whose principal functions is apparently to conceptualize away the problem of capitalism.

The 'post-modem' world, we are told, is a pastiche of fragments and 'difference'. The systemic unity of capitalism, its 'objective structures' and totalizing imperatives, have given way (if they ever existed) to a bricolage of multiple social realities, a pluralistic structure so diverse and flexible that it can be rearranged by discursive construction. The traditional capitalist economy has been replaced by a 'post-Fordist' fragmentation, where every fragment opens up a space for emancipatory struggles. The constitutive class relations of capitalism represent only one personal 'identity' among many others, no longer 'privileged' by its historic centrality. And so on.

Despite the diversity of current theoretical trends on the left and their various means of conceptually dissolving capitalism, they often share one especially serviceable concept: 'civil society'. After a long and somewhat tortuous history, after a series of milestones in the works of **Hegel,** Marx and **Gramsci,** this versatile idea has become an all-purpose catchword for the left, embracing a wide range of emancipatory aspirations, as well – it must be said – as a whole set of excuses for political retreat. However constructive its uses in defending human liberties against state oppression, or in marking out a terrain of social practices, institutions and relations neglected by the 'old' Marxist left, 'civil society' is now in danger of becoming an alibi for capitalism.

The Idea of Civil Society: A Brief Historical Sketch
The current usage of 'civil society' or the conceptual opposition of 'state' and 'civil society', has been inextricably associated with the development of

ELLEN MEIKSINS WOOD

capitalism. There has certainly been a long intellectual tradition in the West, even reaching back to classical antiquity, which has in various ways delineated a terrain of human association, some notion of 'society', distinct from the body politic and with moral claims independent of, and sometimes opposed to, the state's authority. Whatever other factors have been at work in producing such concepts, their evolution has been from the beginning bound up with the development of private property as a distinct and autonomous locus of social power. For example, although the ancient Romans, like the Greeks, still tended to identify the state with the community of citizens, the 'Roman people', they did produce some major advances in the conceptual separation of state and 'society', especially in the Roman Law which distinguished between public and private spheres and gave private property a legal status and clarity it had never enjoyed **before.**[1] In that sense, the modem concept of 'civil society', its association with the specific property relations of capitalism, is a variation on an old theme. At the same time, any attempt to dilute the specificity of this 'civil society', to obscure its differentiation from earlier conceptions of 'society', risks disguising the particularity of capitalism itself as a distinct social form with its own characteristic social relations, its own modes of appropriation and exploitation, its own rules of reproduction, its own systemic imperatives.*

The very particular modem conception of 'civil society' – a conception which appeared systematically for the first time in the eighteenth century – is something quite distinct from earlier notions of 'society': civil society represents a separate sphere of human relations and activity, differentiated from the state but neither public nor private or perhaps both at once, embodying not only a whole range of social interactions apart from the private sphere of the household and the public sphere of the state, but more specifically a network of distinctively **economic** relations, the sphere of the market-place, the arena of production, distribution and exchange. A necessary but not sufficient precondition for this conception of civil society was the modem idea of the state as an abstract entity with its own corporate identity, which evolved with the rise of European absolutism; but the full conceptual differentiation of 'civil society' required the emergence of an autonomous 'economy', separated out from the unity of the 'political' and 'economic' which still characterized the absolutist state.

Paradoxically – or perhaps not so paradoxically – the early usages of the term 'civil society' in the birthplace of capitalism, in early modem England, far from establishing an opposition between civil society and the state, conflated the two. In 16th and 17th century English political thought, 'civil society' was typically synonymous with the 'commonwealth' or 'political society'. This conflation of state and 'society' represented the subordination of the state to the community of private-property holders (as against both monarch and 'multitude') which constituted the political nation. It reflected a unique political dispensation, in which the dominant class depended for its wealth and power increasingly on purely 'economic' modes of appropriation, instead of on directly coercive 'extra-economic' modes of accumulation by political and military means, like feudal rent-taking or absolutist taxation and office-holding as primary instruments of private appropriation.

But if English usage tended to blur the distinction between state and civil society, it was English conditions – the very same system of property relations and capitalist appropriation, but now more advanced and with a more highly developed market mechanism – which made possible the modem conceptual opposition between the two. When **Hegel** constructed his conceptual dichotomy, Napoleon was his inspiration for the 'modem' state; but it was primarily the capitalist economy of England – through the medium of classical political economists like Smith and Steuart – that provided the model of 'civil society' (with certain distinctively Hegelian corrections and improvements). **Hegel's** identification of 'civil' with 'bourgeois' society was more than just a fluke of the German language. The phenomenon which he designated by the term *burgerliche Gesellschaft* was a historically specific social **form.** Although this 'civil society' did not refer exclusively to purely 'economic' institutions(it was, for example, supplemented by **Hegel's** modem adaptation of medieval corporate principles), the modem 'economy' was its essential condition. For **Hegel,** the possibility of preserving both individual freedom and the 'universality' of the state, instead of subordinating one to the other as earlier societies had done, rested on the emergence of a new class and a whole new sphere of social existence: a distinct and autonomous 'economy'. It was in this new sphere that private and public, particular and universal, could meet through the interaction of private interests, on a terrain which was neither household nor state but a mediation between the two.

Marx, of course, transformed **Hegel's** distinction between the state and civil society by denying the universality of the state and insisting that the state expressed the particularities of 'civil society' and its class relations, a discovery which compelled him to devote his life's work to exploring the anatomy of 'civil society' in the form of a critique of political economy. The conceptual differentiation of state and civil society was thus a precondition to Mam's analysis of capitalism, but the effect of that analysis was to deprive the Hegelian distinction of its rationale. The state-civil society dualism more or less disappeared from the mainstream of political discourse.

It required Gramsci's reformulation to revive the concept of civil society as a central organizing principle of socialist theory. The object of this new formulation was to acknowledge both the complexity of political power in the parliamentary or constitutional states of the West, in contrast to more openly coercive autocracies, and the difficulty of supplanting a system of class domination in which class power has no clearly visible point of concentration in the state but is diffised throughout society and its cultural practices. Gramsci thus appropriated the concept of civil society to mark out the terrain of a new kind of struggle which would take the battle against capitalism not

ELLEN MEIKSINS WOOD

only to its economic foundations but to its cultural and ideological roots in everyday life.

The New Cult of Civil Society

Gramsci's conception of 'civil society' was unambiguously intended as a weapon against capitalism, not an accommodation to it. Despite the appeal to his authority which has become a staple of the 'new revisionism', the concept in its current usage no longer has this unequivocally anti-capitalist intent. It has now acquired a whole new set of meanings and consequences, some very positive for the emancipatory projects of the left, others far less so. The two contrary impulses *can* be summed up in this way: the new concept of 'civil society' signals that the left has **learned** the lessons of liberalism about the dangers of state oppression, but we seem to be forgetting the lessons we once learned from the socialist tradition about the oppressions of civil society. On the one hand, the advocates of civil society are strengthening our defence of non-state institutions and relations against the power of the state; on the other hand, they are tending to weaken our resistance to the coercions of capitalism.

The concept of 'civil society' is being mobilized to serve so many varied purposes that it is impossible to isolate a single school of thought associated with it; but some common dominant themes have emerged. 'Civil **society'** is generally intended to identify an arena of (at least potential) freedom outside the state, a space for autonomy, voluntary association and plurality or even conflict, guaranteed by the kind of 'formal democracy' which has evolved in the West. The concept is also meant to reduce the capitalist system (or the 'economy') to one of many spheres in the plural and heterogeneous complexity of modem society. The concept of 'civil society' *can* achieve this effect in one of two principal ways. It *can* be made to designate that multiplicity itself as against the coercions of both state and capitalist economy; or, more commonly, it *can* encompass the 'economy' within a larger sphere of a multiple non-state institutions and relations.3 In either case, the emphasis is on the plurality of social relations and practices among which the capitalist economy takes its place as one of many.

The principal current usages – which will be the main focus of this discussion – proceed from the distinction between civil society and state. 'Civil society' is defined by the advocates of this distinction in terms of a few simple oppositions: for example, 'the state (and its military, policing, legal, administrative, productive, and cultural organs) and the non-state (market-regulated, privately controlled or voluntarily organized) realm of civil **society';[4]** or 'political' vs. 'social' power, 'public' vs. 'private' law, 'state-sanctioned **(dis)information** and propaganda' vs. 'freely circulated public **opinion.'[5]** In this definition, 'civil society' encompasses a very wide range of institutions and relations, from households, trade unions, voluntary associations, hospitals, churches, to the market, capitalist enterprises, indeed the whole capitalist economy. The significant antitheses are simply state and non-state, or perhaps political and social.

This dichotomy apparently corresponds to the opposition between coercion, as embodied in the state, and freedom or voluntary action, which belongs – in principle if not necessarily in practice – to civil society. Civil society may be in various ways and degrees submerged or eclipsed by the state, and different political systems or **whole** 'historical regions' may vary according to the degree of 'autonomy' which they accord to the non-state sphere. It is a special characteristic of the West, for example, that it has given rise to a uniquely well-developed separation of state and civil society, and hence a particularly advanced form of political freedom.

The advocates of this state-civil society distinction generally ascribe to it two principal benefits. First, it focuses our attention on the dangers of state oppression and on the need to set proper limits on the actions of the state, by organizing and reinforcing the pressures against it within society. In other words, it revives the liberal concern with the limitation and legitimation of political power, and especially the control of such power by freedom of association and autonomous organization within society, too often neglected by the Left in theory and practice. Second, the concept of civil society recognizes and celebrates difference and diversity. Its advocates make *pluralism* a primary good, in contrast, it is claimed, to Marxism, which is, they say, essentially monistic, reductionist, economistic.6 This new pluralism invites us to appreciate a whole range of institutions and relations neglected by traditional socialism in its preoccupation with the economy and class.

The impetus to the revival of this conceptual dichotomy has come from several directions. The strongest impulse is now undoubtedly coming from Eastern Europe, where 'civil society' has become a major weapon in the ideological arsenal of opposition forces against state oppression. Here, the issues are fairly clear: the state – including both its political and economic apparatuses of domination – can be more or less unambiguously set against a (potentially) free space outside the state. The civil **society/state** antithesis can, for example, be said to correspond neatly to the opposition of Solidarity to Party and **State.**7

The crisis of the Communist states has, needless to say, also left a deep impression on the Western left, **converging** with other influences: the limitations of social democracy, with its unbounded faith in the state as the agent of social improvement, as well as the emergence of emancipatory struggles by social movements, not based on class, with a sensitivity to dimensions of human experience all too often neglected by the traditional socialist left. These heightened sensitivities to the dangers posed by the state and to the complexities of human experience have been associated with a wide range of activisms, taking in everything from feminism, ecology and peace, to constitutional reform. Each of these projects has often drawn upon the concept of civil society.

ELLEN MEIKSINS WOOD 65

No socialist can doubt the value of these new sensitivities, but there must be serious misgivings about this particular method of focusing our attention on them. We are being asked to pay a heavy price for the all-embracing concept of 'civil society'. This conceptual portmanteau, which indiscriminately lumps together everything from households and voluntary associations to the economic system of capitalism, confuses and disguises as much as it reveals. In Eastern Europe, it can be made to apprehend everything from the defence of political rights and cultural freedoms to the marketization of **post-capitalist** economies or even the restoration of capitalism. 'Civil society' **can** serve as a code-word or **cover** for capitalism, and the market can be lumped together with other less ambiguous goods like political and intellectual liberties as an unequivocally desirable goal.

But if the dangers of this conceptual strategy and of assigning the market to the free space of 'civil society' appear to pale before the enormity of Stalinist oppression in the East, problems of an altogether different order arise in the West, where capitalism does actually exist and where state-oppression is not an immediate and massive evil which overwhelms all other social ills. Since in this case 'civil society' is made to **encompass** a whole layer of social reality which does not exist in post-capitalist societies, the implications of its usage are in some important respects even more problematic.

Here, the danger lies in the fact that the totalizing logic and the coercive power of capitalism become invisible, when the whole social system of capitalism is reduced to one set of institutions and relations among many others, on a wnceptual par with households or voluntary associations. Such a reduction is, indeed, the principal distinctive feature of 'civil society' in its new incarnation. Its effects is to conceptualize away the problem of capitalism, by disaggregating society into fragments, with no over-arching power structure, no totalizing unity, no systemic coercions – in other words, no capitalist system, with its expansionary drive and its capacity to penetrate every aspect of social life.

It is a typical strategy of the 'civil society' argument – indeed, its *raison d'être* – to attack Marxist 'reductionism' or 'ewnomism'. Marxism, it is said, reduces civil society to the 'mode of production', the capitalist economy. 'The importance of *other* institutions of civil society – such as households, churches, scientific and literary associations, prisons and hospital – is **devalued.'8**

Whether or not Marxists have habitually paid too little attention to these 'other' institutions, the weakness of this juxtaposition (the capitalist economy and 'other institutions' like hospitals?) should be immediately apparent. It must surely be possible even for non-Marxists to acknowledge, for example, the very simple truth that in the West hospitals are situated within a capitalist economy which has profoundly affected the organization of health care and **the** nature of medical institutions. But is it possible to conceive of an analogous proposition about the effects of hospitals on capitalism? Does **Keane's** statement mean that **Marx** did not value households and hospitals, or

THE SOCIALIST REGISTER 1990

is it rather that he did not attribute to them the same historically determinative force? Is there no basis for distinguishing among these various 'institutions' on all sorts of quantitative and qualitative grounds, from size and scope to social power and historical efficacy? In the usage adopted here by John Keane – which is far from atypical – the concept of civil society evades questions like this. It also has the effect of confusing the moral claims of 'other' institutions with their determinative power, or-rather of dismissing altogether the essentially empirical question of historical and social determinations.

There is another **version** of the argument which, instead of simply evading the systemic totality of capitalism, explicitly denies it. The very existence of other modes of domination than class relations, other principles of stratification than class inequality, other social struggles than class struggle, is taken to demonstrate that capitalism, whose wnstitutive relation is class, is not a totalizing system. The Marxist preoccupation with 'economic' relations and class at the expense of other social relations and identities is understood to demonstrate that the attempt to **'totalize[d]** all society from the standpoint of one sphere, the economy or the mode of production,' is misconceived for the simple reason that other 'spheres' self-evidently **exist.**[9]

This argument is circular and question-begging. To deny the totalizing logic of capitalism, it is not enough merely to indicate the plurality of social identities and relations. The class relation which constitutes capitalism is not, after all, just a personal identity, nor even just a principle of 'stratification' or inequality. It is not only a specific system of power relations but also the wnstitutive relation of a distinctive social process, the dynamic of accumulation and the self-expansion of capital. Of course it can be easily – self-evidently – shown that class is not the only principle of 'stratification', the only form of inequality and domination. But this tells us virtually nothing about the totalizing logic of capitalism. To substantiate the denial of that logic, it would have to be convincingly demonstrated that these other 'spheres' do not come – or not in any significant way – within the determinative force of capitalism, its system of social property relations, its expansionary imperatives, its drive for accumulation, its commodification of all social life, its creation of the market as a necessity, a compulsive mechanism of self-sustaining 'growth', and so on. But 'civil society' arguments (or, indeed, 'post-Marxist' arguments in general) do not typically take the form of historically and empirically refuting the determinative effects of capitalist relations. Instead, (when they do not take the simple circular form: capitalism is not a totalizing system because other spheres exist) they tend to proceed as abstract philosophical arguments, as internal critiques of Marxist theory, or, most commonly, as moral prescriptions about the dangers of devaluing 'other' spheres of human experience.

In one form or another, capitalism is cut down to the size and weight of 'other' singular and specific institutions and disappears into a conceptual night where all cats are grey. The strategy of dissolving capitalism into an

ELLEN MEIKSINS WOOD

unstructured and undifferentiated plurality of social institutions and relations cannot help but weaken both the analytic and the normative force of 'civil society', its capacity to deal with the limitation and legitimation of power, as well as its usefulness in guiding the 'new social movements'. The current theories occlude 'civil society' in its distinctive sense as a social form specific to capitalism, a systemic totality within which all 'other' institutions are situated and all social forces must find their way, a specific and unprecedented sphere of social power, which poses wholly new problems of legitimation and control, problems not addressed by traditional theories of the state nor by contemporary liberalism.

Capitalism, 'Formal Democracy', and the Specificity of the West
One of the principal charges levelled against Marxism by the advocates of 'civil society' is that it endangers democratic freedoms by identifying Western 'formal democracy' — the legal and political forms which guarantee a free space for 'civil society' — with capitalism: 'civil' = 'bourgeois' society. The danger, they claim, is that we might be tempted to throw out the baby with the bath water, to reject liberal democracy together with **capitalism**.[10] We should instead, they argue, acknowledge the benefits of formal democracy, while expanding its principles of individual freedom and equality by *dissociating* them from capitalism in order to deny that capitalism is the sole or best means of advancing these principles.

It must be said that criticism of contemporary Western Marxism on these grounds must disregard the bulk of Marxist political theory since the sixties, and especially since the theory of the state was revived by the **'Miliband-Poulantzas'** debate. Certainly civil liberties were a major preoccupation of both the principals in that controversy, and of many others who have followed in their train. Even the contention that 'classical' Marxism — in the person of **Marx** or **Engels** — was too indifferent to civil liberties is open to question. But without reducing this discussion to a merely textual debate about the Marxist ('classical' or contemporary) attitude to 'bourgeois' liberties, let us accept that all socialists, Marxist or otherwise, must uphold civil liberties (now commonly, if somewhat vaguely, called 'human rights'), principles of legality, freedom of speech and association, and the protection of a 'non-state' sphere against incursions by the state. We must acknowledge that some institutional protections of this kind are necessary *conditions* of any democracy, even though we may not accept the *identification* of democracy with, or its confinement to, the formal safeguards of 'liberalism', and even if we may believe that 'liberal' protections will have to take a different institutional form in socialist democracy than under **capitalism**.[11]

Difficulties nevertheless remain in the 'civil society' argument. There are other ways (indeed the principal ways in Marxist theory) of associating 'formal democracy' with capitalism than by rejecting the one with the other. We can recognize the historical and structural connections without denying the value

THE SOCIALIST REGISTER 1990

of civil liberties. An understanding of these connections neither compels us to devalue civil liberties, nor does it oblige us to accept capitalism as the sole or best means of maintaining individual autonomy; and it leaves us perfectly free also to acknowledge that capitalism, while in certain historical conditions conducive to 'formal democracy', can easily do without it – as it has done more than once in recent history.

There are, on the contrary, real dangers in failing to see the connections or mistaking their character. There are real dangers in giving an account of Western democracy as an autonomous development, independent of the historical processes which produced capitalism. And the dangers affect both sides of the equation, limiting our understanding of both democracy and capitalism.

The historical and structural connection between formal democracy and capitalism can be formulated in terms of the separation of the state from civil **society.**[12] Much depends, however, on how we interpret that separation and the historical process which brought it about. There is a view of history, and a concomitant interpretation of the state-civil society separation, which cannot see the evolution of capitalism as anything but progressive. It is a view of history commonly associated with liberalism or 'bourgeois' ideology, but one which seems increasingly to underlie conceptions of democracy on the Left.

Let us sketch the traditional liberal version first. A few essential characteristics stand out: 1) a tendency to view history as a process of progressive individuation, generally associated with the evolution of private property, as communal or 'gentile' institutions and property-forms increasingly give way to more individualized modes of appropriation and consciousness; 2) a conception of the state as a response to this evolution from communal principles to individuality and private property, which calls for new, political institutions to replace old communal forms inadequate to deal with this degree of individuation; 3) a view of history, progress and the evolution of freedom which locates the principle of historical motion in the contradiction between individual and state, or perhaps between state and civil society – as an aggregate of (often mutually antagonistic) individuals – in contrast, for example, to a focus on class contradictions or relations of exploitation; 4) a tendency to identify milestones in the ascent of the propertied classes as the principal landmarks of history: **Magna** Carta, 1688, the establishment of constitutional principles whose object was to strengthen the hand of the propertied classes against both monarchical power and the **multitude.**[13] At some critical point, these developments begin to be called 'democratic' – so that, for example, American and European school-children are taught to think of such advances in the power of the landed aristocracy as the pivotal moments in the evolution of democracy. Such a definition of democracy would never have occurred to the major participants in the relevant historical events, for whom consolidating the power of the landed classes was, by definition, for good or for evil, anti-democratic.

ELLEN MEIKSINS WOOD

Marx himself did not subject the liberal view of history to the same thorough critique that he applied to classical political **economy.**[14] But from the **beginning,** there was a different view of history at the core of his own distinctive life's work: history as the development of exploitative relations and the progressive separation of producers from the conditions of labour, property as alienation, the specificity of capitalism and its laws of motion – in short, everything implied by the critique of political economy. What we seem to be witnessing now is a new left version of the old liberal history without this other side.

The historical presuppositions underlying the advocacy of 'civil society' are seldom explicitly spelled out. There is, however, a particularly useful and sophisticated account by a Hungarian scholar, recently published in English in a volume devoted to reviving 'civil society' (East and West), which may serve as a model of the relevant historical interpretation.

In an attempt to characterize three different 'historical regions of Europe' – Western and Eastern Europe and something in between – Jeno **Szücs** (following Istvan Bibo) offers the following account of the 'Western' model, in 'a search for the deepest roots of a "democratic way of organizing society"'.[15] The most distinctive 'characteristic of the West is the structural – and theoretical – separation of "society" from the **"state"**[16], a unique development which lies at the heart of Western democracy, while its corresponding absence in the East accounts for an evolution from autocracy to totalitarianism. The roots of this development, according to **Szücs,** lie in Western feudalism.

The uniqueness of Western history lay, according to this argument, in 'an entirely unusual "take-off" in the rise of civilizations. This take-off took place amidst disintegration instead of integration, and amidst declining civilization, re-agrarianization and mounting political anarchy.'[17] This fragmentation and disintegration were the preconditions of the separation of 'society' and 'state'. In the high civilizations of the East, where no such separation took place, the political function continued to be exercised 'downwards from above'.

In the process of feudal 'fragmentation' in the West, the old political relations of states and subjects were replaced by new social ties, of a contractual nature, between lords and vassals. This substitution of **social-**contractual relations for political relations had among its major consequences a new principle of human dignity, freedom and the 'honour' of the individual. And the territorial disintegration into small units each with its own customary law produced a decentralization of law which could resist '"descending" mechanisms of exercising **power'.**[18] When sovereignty was later reconstructed by the Western monarchies, the new state was essentially constituted 'vertically from **below'.**[19] It was a 'unity in plurality' that made 'freedoms' the 'internal organizing principles' of Western social structure 'and led to something which drew the line so sharply between the medieval West and many other civilizations: the birth of "society" as an autonomous **entity.'**[20]

THE SOCIALIST REGISTER 1990

There is much in this argument that is truly illuminating, but equally instructive is the bias in its angle of vision. Here, in fact, are all the staples of liberal history: the progress of civilization (at least in the West) as an unambiguous ascent of individual 'freedom' and 'dignity' (if there is a critical difference between Sziics's account and the traditional liberal view, it is that the latter is more frank about the identification of individuality with private property); the prime focus on the tension between individual or 'society' and the state as the moving force of history; even – and perhaps especially – the tendency to associate the advance of civilization, and democracy itself, with milestones in the ascent of the propertied classes. Although there was nothing democratic about the medieval West, Sziics concedes, this is where the 'deepest roots' of democracy are to be found. It is as if the 'constitutive idea' of modern democracy were *lordship*.

The same **'fragmentation'**, the same replacement of political relations by social and contractual bonds, the same **'parcellization'** of sovereignty, the same 'autonomy of society', even while their uniqueness and importance in the trajectory of Western development are acknowledged, can be seen in a different light, with rather different consequences for our appreciation of 'civil society' and the development of Western democracy.

Suppose we look at the same sequence of events from a different angle. The divergence of the 'West' from the 'Eastern' pattern of state-formation began, of course, much earlier than medieval feudalism. It could be traced as far back as early Greek antiquity, but for our purposes a critical benchmark can be identified in ancient **Rome**[21]. This divergence, it needs to be stressed, had to do not only with political forms but above all with modes of appropriation – and here developments in the Roman system of private property were decisive. (It is a curious but 'symptomatic' feature of Sziics's argument that modes of appropriation and exploitation do not figure centrally, if at all, in his differentiation of the three historical regions of Europe – which may also explain his insistence on a radical break between antiquity and feudalism. At the very least, the survival of Roman law, the quintessential symbol of the Roman property regime, should have signalled to Sziics some fundamental continuity between the Western 'autonomy' of civil society and the Roman system of appropriation.)

Rome represents a striking contrast to other 'high' civilizations – both in the ancient world and centuries later – where access to great wealth, to the surplus labour of others on a large scale, was typically achieved through the medium of the state (for example, late-imperial China, which had a highly developed system of private property but where great wealth and power resided not in land so much as in the state, in the bureaucratic hierarchy whose pinnacle was the court and imperial officialdom). Rome was distinctive in its emphasis on private property, on the acquisition of massive land-holdings, as a means of appropriation. The Roman aristocracy had an insatiable appetite for land which created unprecedented concentrations of wealth and a predatory

ELLEN MEIKSINS WOOD

imperial power unrivalled by any other ancient empire in its hunger not simply for tribute but for *territory*. And it was Rome which extended its regime of private property throughout a vast and diverse empire, governed without a massive bureaucracy but instead through a 'municipal' system which effectively constituted a federation of **local** aristocracies. The result was a very specific combination of a strong imperial state and a dominant propertied class autonomous from it, a strong state which at the same time encouraged, instead of impeding, the autonomous development of private property. It was Rome, in short, which firmly and self-consciously established private property as an autonomous locus of social power, detached from, while supported by, the state.

The 'fragmentation' of feudalism must be seen in this light, as rooted in the privatization of power already inherent in the Roman property system and in the Empire's fragmented 'municipal' administration. When the tensions between the Roman imperial state and the autonomous power of private property were finally resolved by the disintegration of the central state, the autonomous power of property remained. The old political relations of rulers and subjects were gradually dissolved into the 'social' relations between lords and vassals, and more particularly, lords and peasants. In the institution of lordship, political and economic powers were united as they had been where the state was a major source of private wealth; but this time, that unity existed in a fragmented and privatized **form.**

Seen from this perspective, the development of the West can hardly be viewed as simply the rise of individuality, the rule of law, the progress of freedom or power from 'below'; and the autonomy of 'civil society' acquires a different meaning. The very developments described by **Szücs** in these terms are also, and at the same time, the evolution of new forms of exploitation and domination (the constitutive 'power from below' is, after all, the power of lordship), new relations of personal dependence and bondage, the privatization of surplus extraction and the transfer of ancient oppressions from the state to 'society' – that is, a transfer of power relations and domination from the state to private property. This new division of labour between state and 'society' also laid a foundation for the increasing separation of private appropriation from public responsibilities which came to fruition in capitalism.

Capitalism then represents the culmination of a long development, but it also constitutes a qualitative break (which occurred 'spontaneously' only in the particular historical conditions of England). Not only is it characterized by a transformation of social power, a new division of labour between state and private property or class, but it also marks the creation of a completely new form of coercion, the market – the market not simply as a sphere of opportunity, freedom, and choice, but as a compulsion, a necessity, a social discipline, capable of subjecting all human activities and relationships to its requirements.

'Civil Society' and the Devaluation of Democracy

It is not, then, enough to say that democracy can be expanded by detaching the principles of 'formal democracy' from any association with capitalism. Nor is it enough to say that capitalist democracy is incomplete, one stage in an unambiguously progressive development which must be perfected by socialism and advanced beyond the limitations of 'formal democracy'. The point is rather that the association of capitalism with 'formal democracy' representsa contradictory unity of advance and retreat, both an enhancement and a devaluation of democracy.* To put it briefly, capitalism has been able to tolerate an unprecedented distribution of political goods, the rights and liberties of citizenship, because it has also for the first time made possible a form of citizenship, civil liberties and rights which can be abstracted from the distribution of social power. In this respect, it contrasts sharply with the profound transformation of class power expressed by the original Greek conception of democracy as rule by the demos, which represented a specific distribution of class power summed up in Aristotle's definition of democracy as rule by the poor. Access to political rights in societies where surplus extraction occurs by 'extra-economic' means and the power of economic exploitation is inseparable from juridical and political status and privilege has a very different meaning from what it does in capitalism, with its expropriated direct producers and a form of appropriation not directly dependent on juridical or political standing. In other words, in Athens, where citizenship remained a critical determinant in relations of exploitation, there could be no such thing as purely 'formal' political rights or purely 'formal' equality. It was capitalism which for the first time made possible a purely 'formal' political sphere, with purely 'political' rights and liberties.

That historical transformation laid the foundation for a redefinition of the word 'democracy'. If capitalism made this reconceptualization possible, political developments in a sense made it necessary. As it became more difficult for dominant classes simply to denounce democracy, with the intrusion of the 'masses' into the political sphere, the concept of democracy began to lose its social connotations, in favour of essentially procedural or 'formal' criteria. The concept was, in other words, domesticated, made acceptable to dominant classes who could now claim commitment to 'democratic' principles without fundamentally endangering their own dominance. Now, the purely 'formal' principles of liberalism have come to be *identified* with democracy. In other words, these formal principlesare treated not simply as good in themselves, nor even as necessary conditions for democracy in the literal sense of popular rule, but as synonymous with it or as its outer limit. More than that, it has now become possible even to describe undemocratic practices – like the restriction of trade union rights by Thatcher or Reagan – as democratic, while denouncing 'extra-parliamentary' popular politics as 'undemocratic'. 'Formal democracy', in shoat, certainly represents an

ELLEN MEIKSINS WOOD

improvement on political forms lacking civil liberties, the rule of law and the principle of representation. But it is also, equally and at the same time, a subtraction from the substance of the democratic idea, and one which is historically and structurally associated with **capitalism.**[23]

The 'civil society' argument insists that we should not allow our conception of human emancipation to be constrained by the identification of 'formal democracy' with capitalism. Yet the irony is that this very argument, by obscuring the connections, may have the effect of allowing capitalism to limit our conception of democracy. And if we think of human emancipation as little more than an extension of liberal democracy, then we may in the end be persuaded to believe that capitalism is after all its surest guarantee.

The separation of the state and civil society in the West has certainly given rise to new forms of freedom and equality, but it has also created new modes of domination and coercion. One way of characterizing the specificity of 'civil society' as a particular social form unique to the modem world – the particular historical conditions which made possible the modem distinction between state and civil society – is to say that it constituted a new form of social power, in which many coercive functions that once belonged to the state were relocated in the 'private' sphere, in private property, class exploitation, and market imperatives. It is,, in a sense, this 'privatization' of public power which has created the historically novel realm of 'civil society'. 'Civil society' constitutes not only a wholly new relation between 'public' and 'private' but more precisely a wholly new 'private' realm, with a distinctive 'public' presence and oppressions of its own, a unique structure of power and domination, and a ruthless systemic logic. It represents a particular network of social relations which does not simply stand in opposition to the coercive, 'policing' and 'administrative' functions of the state but represents the relocation of these functions, a new division of labour between the 'public' sphere of the state and the 'private' sphere of capitalist property and the imperatives of the market, in which appropriation, exploitation and domination are detached from public authority and social responsibility.

'Civil society' has given private property and its possessors a command over people and their daily lives, a power accountable to no one, which many an old tyrannical state would have envied.** Those activities and experiences which fall outside the immediate command structure of the capitalist enterprise, or outside the political power of capital, are regulated by the dictates of the market, the necessities of competition and profitability. Even when the market is not, as it commonly is in advanced capitalist societies, merely an instrument of power for giant conglomerates and multinational corporations, it is still a coercive force, capable of subjecting all human values, activities and relationships to its imperatives. No ancient despot could have hoped to penetrate the personal lives of his subjects – their choices, preferences, and relationships – in the same comprehensive and minute detail, not only in the workplace but in every comer of their lives. Coercion, in other words,

THE SOCIALIST REGISTER 1990

has been not just a *disorder* of 'civil society' but one of its constitutive principles.

This historical reality tends to undermine the neat distinctions required by current theories which ask us to treat civil society as, at least in principle, the sphere of freedom and voluntary action, the antithesis of the irreducibly coercive principle which intrinsically belongs to the state. These theories do, of course, acknowledge that civil society is not a realm of perfect freedom or democracy. It is, for example, marred by oppression in the family, in gender relations, in the workplace, by racist attitudes, homophobia, and so on. But these oppressions are treated as *dysfunctions* in civil society. In principle, coercion belongs to the state while civil society is where freedom is rooted, and human emancipation, according to these arguments, consists in the autonomy of civil society, its expansion and enrichment, its liberation from the state, and its protection by formal democracy. What tends to disappear from view, again, is the relations of exploitation and domination which irreducibly *constitute* civil society, not just as some alien and correctible disorder but as its very essence, the particular structure of domination and coercion that is specific to capitalism as a systemic totality.

The New Pluralism and the Politics of 'Identity'

The rediscovery of liberalism in the revival of civil society thus has two sides. It is admirable in its intention of making socialists more sensitive to civil liberties and the dangers of state oppression. But the cult of civil society also tends to reproduce the mystifications of liberalism, disguising the coercions of civil society and obscuring the ways in which state oppression itself is rooted in the exploitative and coercive relations of civil society. What, then, of its dedication to *pluralism?* How does the concept of civil society fare in dealing with the diversity of social relations and 'identities'?

It is here that the cult of civil society, its representation of civil society as the sphere of difference and diversity, speaks most directly to the dominant preoccupations of the new new left. If **anything** unites the various 'new revisionisms' – from the most abstruse 'post-Marxist' and 'post-modemist' theories to the activisms of the 'new social movements' – it is an emphasis on diversity, 'difference', pluralism. The new pluralism goes beyond the traditional liberal recognition of diverse interests and the toleration (in principle) of diverse opinions in three major ways: 1) its conception of diversity probes beneath the externalities of 'interest' to the psychic depths of 'subjectivity' or 'identity' and extends beyond political 'behaviour' or 'opinion' to the totality of 'life-styles'; 2) it no longer assumes that some universal and undifferentiated principles of right can accommodate all diverse identities and life-styles (women, for example, require different rights from men in order to be free and equal); 3) the new pluralism rests on a view that the essential characteristic, the historical *differentia specifica,* of the contemporary world – or, more specifically, the contemporary capitalist

ELLEN MEIKSINS WOOD

75

world – is not the totalizing, homogenizing drive of capitalism but the unique heterogeneityof 'post-modem' society, its unprecedenteddegree of diversity, even fragmentation, **requiring** new, more complex pluralistic principles.

The arguments run something like this: contemporary society is characterized by an increasing fragmentation, a diversificationof social relationsand experiences, a plurality of life-styles, a multiplication of personal identities. In other words, we are living in a 'post-modem' world, a world in which diversity and difference have dissolved all the old certainties and all the old universalities. (Here, some post-Marxist theories offer an alternative to the concept of civil society by insisting that it is no longer possible to speak of society at all, because that concept suggests a closed and unified **totality.**[25]) Old solidarities – and this, of course, means especially class solidarities – have broken down, and social movements based on other identities and against other oppressions have proliferated – having to do with gender, race, **ethnicity,** sexuality, and so on. At the same time, these developments have vastly extended the scope of individual choice, in consumption patterns and life-styles. This is what some people have called a tremendous expansion of 'civil **society'.** [26] The Left, the argument goes, needs to acknowledge these developments and build on them. It needs to construct a politics based on this diversity and difference. It needs both to celebrate difference and to recognize the plurality of oppressions or forms of domination, the multiplicity of emancipatory struggles. The Left needs to respond to this multiplicity of social relations with complex concepts of equality, which acknowledge people's different needs and **experiences.**[27]

There are variations on these themes, but in broad outline, this is a fair summary of what has become a substantial current on the left. And the general direction in which it is pushing us is to give up the idea of socialism and replace it with – or at least subsume it under – what is supposed to be a more inclusive category, democracy, a concept which does not 'privilege' class, as traditional socialism does, but treats all oppressions equally.

Now as a very general statement of principle, there are some admirable things here. No socialist can doubt the importance of diversity, or the multiplicity of oppressions that need to be abolished. And democracy is – or ought to be – what socialism is about. But an emancipatory theory is more than just a statement of general principles and good intentions. It also involves a critical view of the world as it is, a map of the existing terrain which informs our understanding of the obstacles to be overcome, an insight into the conditions of struggle. And an emancipatory theory takes us beyond the limiting and **mystifying** ideological categories which support existing dominations and oppressions.

What, then, does the cult of civil society tell us about the world as it is? How far does it take us beyond the ideological limits of current oppressions? We can test the limits of the new pluralism by exploring the implications of its **constitutive** principle. What we are looking for is a general concept which

THE SOCIALIST REGISTER 1990

can encompass – equally and without prejudice or privilege – everything from gender to class, from ethnicity or race to sexual preference. For lack of a better word, let us call it by its currently most fashionable name, 'identity'.

For the sake of brevity, we *can* assess the value of this all-embracing concept (or any analogous one) by conducting a thought experiment. Imagine a democratic community which acknowledges all kinds of difference, of gender, culture, sexuality, which encourages and celebrates these differences, but without allowing them to become relations of domination and oppression. Imagine these diverse human beings united in a democratic community, all free and equal, without suppressing their differences or denying their special needs. Now try to think in the same terms about *class* differences. Is it possible to imagine class differences without exploitation and domination? Does our imaginary democratic society celebrate class differences as it does diversities of life styles, culture, or sexual preference? Can we construct a conception of freedom or equality which accommodates class as it does gender differences? Would a conception of freedom or equality which *can* accommodate class differences satisfy our conditions for a democratic society?

There are serious problems in the concept of identity as applied to any of these social relations, but there is a particular problem in the case of class. When I perform this thought experiment, the results I get for class are very different from those I get for other 'identities'. I can conceive of a democratic society with gender or ethnic diversity, but a democracy with class difference seems to me a contradiction in terms. This already suggests that some important differences are being concealed in a catch-all category like 'identity' which is meant to cover very diverse social relations like class, gender or ethnicity.

But let us go on to the connection between the concept of identity and the idea of equality, and consider the notion of a 'complex' or pluralist equality which purports to accommodate diversity and difference. What happens when we try to apply the concept of equality to various different forms of domination? Clearly, class equality means something different and requires different conditions from gender or racial equality. In particular, the abolition of class inequality would by definition mean the end of capitalism. But is the same necessarily true about the abolition of gender or racial inequality? Gender and racial equality are not in principle incompatible with capitalism. The disappearance of class inequalities, on the other hand, by definition *is* incompatible with capitalism. At the same time, although class exploitation is *constitutive* of capitalism as gender or racial inequality are not, capitalism subjects *all* social relations to its requirements. It can co-opt and reinforce inequalities and oppressions which i t did not create and use them in the interests of class **exploitation.**[28]

How should we deal theoretically with these complex realities? One possibility is to retain a concept of equality that does not raise the problem of capitalism – perhaps the old liberal concept of *formal* legal and political

ELLEN **MEIKSINS** WOOD

equality, or some notion of so-called 'equality of opportunity', which presents no fundamental challenge to capitalism and its system of class relations. **This** concept of equality gives no privileged status to class. It may even have radical implications for gender or race, because in respect to these differences, no capitalist society has yet reached the limits even of the restricted **kind** of equality which capitalism allows. But formal equality cannot have the same radical implications for class differences in a capitalist society. In fact, it is a specific feature of capitalism that it has created a particular **kind** of universal equality *without* such radical implications – that is, precisely, a formal equality, having to do with political and legal principles and procedures rather than with the disposition of social or class power. Formal equality in this sense would have been impossible in pre-capitalist societies where appropriation and exploitation were inextricably bound up with juridical, political and military power.

If the liberaldemocratic conception of formal equality seems unsatisfactory, what about 'complex' or 'pluralist' conceptions as a way of dealing with diverse inequalities in a capitalist society without 'privileging' class? These differ from the liberal-democratic idea in that they are directed at a whole range of social inequalities (including class) but also in that they acknowledge the complexities of social reality by applying different criteria of equality to different circumstances and relations. In this respect, pluralist notions of this **kind** may have certain advantages over more universalistic principles, even if they may lose some of the benefits of such universal **standards.**[29] The trouble is that these 'complex' or 'pluralistic' conceptions beg the question of capitalism because they fail to deal with its overarching totality as a social system, which is *constituted* by class exploitation but which shapes all our social relations.

There is another possibility: to differentiate not **less** but much more radically among various **kinds** of inequality and oppression than even the new pluralism allows. We can acknowledge that, while all oppressions may have equal moral claims, class exploitation has a different *historical* status, a more strategic location at the heart of capitalism; and class struggle may have a more universal reach, a greater potential for advancing not only class emancipation but other emancipatory struggles too. But this is just the kind of differentiation the new pluralism will not permit, because it suggests that class is somehow privileged. If we want, then, to avoid giving class any **kind** of privileged historical status, if we want to avoid differentiating in this way among different inequalities, we shall have to accommodate ourselves to capitalism; and we shall also be obliged very drastically to limit our emancipatory project. Is that really what we want?

It is possible that the new pluralism, like other 'new revisionisms', is leaning toward the acceptance of capitalism, at least as the best social order we are likely to get. The crisis of the post-capitalist states has undoubtedly done

THE SOCIALIST REGISTER 1990

more than anything else to encourage the spread of this view. At least, it has become increasingly common to argue that, however pervasive capitalism may be, its old rigid structures have more or less disintegrated, or become so permeable, opened up so many large spaces, that people are free to construct their own social realities in uprecedented ways. That is precisely what some people mean when they talk about the vast expansion of civil society in modem ('post-Fordist'?) **capitalism**.[30]

But even if we stop short of openly embracing capitalism, we can simply evade the issue. That is the effect of all-purpose concepts like 'identity' or 'civil society' as they are currently used. The capitalist system, its totalizing unity, can be conceptualized away by adopting loose conceptions of civil society or by submerging class, in catch-all categories like 'identity' and by disaggregating the social world into particular and separate realities. The social relations of capitalism can be dissolved into an unstructured and fragmented plurality of identities and differences. Questions about historical causality or political efficacy can be side-stepped, and there is no need to ask how various identities are situated in the prevailing social structure because the existence of the social structure can be denied altogether.

In a sense, the concept of 'identity' has simply replaced the 'interest groups' of pluralist theories in conventional political science, whose object was to deny the importance of class in capitalist democracies. **According** to both the old and the new pluralisms 'interest groups' or 'identities' are separate but equal, or at least equivalent, *plural* rather than *different*. And our democracy is a kind of market-place where these interests or identities meet and compete, though they may come together in loose alliances or political parties. Both pluralisms, of course, have the effect of denying the systemic unity of capitalism, or its very existence as a social system; and both insist on the heterogeneity of capitalist society, while losing sight of its increasingly global power of homogenization.

The irony is that the new pluralism, with its demand for complex ideas of freedom and equality which acknowledge the multiplicity of oppressions, ends up by *homogenizing* these differences. What we get is *plurality* instead of difference. And here is an even more curious paradox. One of the distinctive features of the new social movements is supposed to be their focus on *power,* an antagonism to all power relations in all their diverse forms. Yet here, in these theories one of whose principal claims is their capacity to speak for the new social movements, we find a conceptual framework which, just like the old pluralism, has the effect of making invisible the power relations which constitute capitalism, the dominant structure of coercion which reaches into every comer of our lives, public and private.

The final irony is that this latest denial of capitalism's systemic and totalizing logic is in some respects a reflection of the very thing which it seeks to deny. The current preoccupation with 'post-modem' diversity and fragmentation undoubtedly expresses a reality in contemporary capitalism, but it is a reality

ELLEN MEIKSINS WOOD

seen through the distorting lens of ideology. It represents the ultimate 'commodity fetishism', the triumph of 'consumer society', in which the diversity of 'life-styles', measured in the sheer quantity of commodities and varied patterns of consumption, disguises the underlying systemic unity, the imperatives which create that diversity itself while at the same time imposing a deeper and more global homogeneity.

What is alarming about these theoretical developments is not that they violate some doctrinaire Marxist prejudice concerning the privileged status of class. Of course, the whole object of the exercise is to side-line class, to dissolve it in all-embracing categories which deny it any privileged status, or even any political relevance at all. But that is not the real problem. The problem is that theories which do not differentiate – and, yes, 'privilege', if that means ascribing causal or explanatory priorities – among various social institutions and 'identities' cannot deal critically with capitalism at all. The consequence of these procedures is to sweep the whole question under the rug. And whither capitalism, so goes the socialist idea. Socialism is the specific alternative to capitalism. Without capitalism, we have no need of socialism; we can make do with very diffuse and indeterminate concepts of democracy which are not specifically opposed to any identifiable system of social relations, in fact do not even recognize any such system. What we are left with then is a fragmented plurality of oppressions and a fragmented plurality of **emancipatory** struggles. Here is another irony: what claims to be a more universalistic project than traditional socialism is actually less so. Instead of the universalist project of socialism and the integrative politics of the struggle against class exploitation, we have a plurality of essentially disconnected particular struggles.

This is a serious business. Capitalism is constituted by class exploitation, but capitalism is more than just a system of class oppression. It is a ruthless totalizing process which shapes our lives in every conceivable aspect, and everywhere, not just in the relative opulence of the capitalist North. Among other things, and even leaving aside the sheer power of capital, it subjects all social life to the abstract requirements of the market, through the commodification of life in all its aspects. This makes a mockery of all our aspirations to autonomy, freedom of choice, and democratic self-government. For socialists, it is morally and politically unacceptable to advance a conceptual framework which makes this system invisible, or reduces it to one of many fragmented realities, just at a time when the system is more pervasive, more global than ever.

The replacement of socialism by an indeterminate concept of democracy, or the dilution of diverse and different social relations into catch-all categories **like** 'identity' or 'difference', or loose conceptions of 'civil society', represent a *surrender* to capitalism and its ideological mystifications. By all means let us have diversity, difference, and pluralism; but not this kind of *undifferentiated* and unstructured pluralism. What we need is a pluralism which does indeed

THE SOCIALIST REGISTER 1990

acknowledge diversity and difference – and that means not just *plurality* or *multiplicity*. It means a pluralism which also **recognizes** historical realities, which does not deny the systemic unity of capitalism, which can tell the difference between the constitutive relations of capitalism and *other* inequalities and oppressions with *different* relations to capitalism, a *different* place in the systemic logic of capitalism, and therefore a different role in our struggles against it. The socialist project should be *enriched* by the resources and insights of the new social movements, not **impoverished** by resorting to them as an excuse for disintegrating the struggle against capitalism. We should not confuse respect for the plurality of human experience and social struggles with a complete dissolution of historical causality, where there is nothing but diversity, difference, and contingency, no unifying structures, no logic of process, no capitalism and therefore no negation of it, no universal project of human emancipation.

Postscript

In the face of the current crisis in the post-capitalist world, it is easy for the Western left to lose its nerve. We certainly have a lot of rethinking to do. But while we are about it, the apologists of capitalism are having a field day. There could hardly have been a more welcome and timely diversion from various troubles at home. There is nothing like the trumpet of triumphalism to drown out the womsome noises from our own backyard. The very wildness of these triumphalist pronouncements should make us suspicious. Not just the triumph of capitalism or liberal democracy over socialism, long before the game is over, but even the end of **history??**[31]

Of course Stalinism was a disaster for the Soviet Union, Eastern Europe, and the whole socialist movement. But let us put things into perspective. In the 'richest country in the world', the capital city is riddled with poverty and crime, as sleek civil servants cohabit with beggars. In the first half of 1989, the infant mortality rate in Washington D.C. apparently rose by 40% over the previous year, in large part because of the spread of crack-cocaine addiction. At 32.3 deaths per **1000** births, this mortality rate exceeds, among others, those of China, Chile, Jamaica, Mauritius, Panama, and Uruguay, according to World Bank statistics. One end of the country is dominated by a city, New York, the heartland of the nation's wealth, where unparalleled **luxury** coexists with the most abject squalor, poverty, crime, drug addiction and homelessness. At the other end, in **Los** Angeles, the city's core is being eaten away by drugs and gang-warfare, while privileged whites increasingly retreat into fortified enclaves where every manicured lawn sports a notice that its owner is protected by one of many and multiplying security services, with the menacing announcement: 'Armed Response'. In many places, the school system is a shambles, producing illiterate graduates; and millions of Americans cannot afford health care. It is estimated that 20 million workers in the US take illegal drugs (not to mention many

ELLEN MEIKSINS WOOD 81

more with alcohol problems), and that drug and alcohol abuse is costing US companies more than **$100** billion a year *(Guardian,* November 17, 1989). In Britain, the birthplace of capitalism, under a government more implacably committed than any other to the values of 'free enterprise', the infrastructure crumbles, mass unemployment persists, public services decline, education even at the primary level becomes less accessible, and squalor deepens, while the poor and homeless multiply. The much vaunted 'economic miracle' in Italy has spawned a large and growing population of near-slaves in the form of Third World immigrants, many of them illegal, who have become the objects of yet another lucrative trade for the Mafia. In Japan, the well-spring of consumerism, ordinary citizens typically work longer hours than in any other developed country, live in postage-stamp-size flats, and take no holidays. As I write, here in prosperousToronto, the richest city in Canada, one of the city's two major newspapers is conducting a food drive to feed the hungry – not in Ethiopia, but in Metropolitan Toronto, where property developers are making a killing while people go hungry because 70% of their income goes to pay **impossibly** high rents. **The** Daily Bread Food Bank, representing 175 emergency food programmes, today helpfully **supplied** paper bags with every newspaper, inscribed with the following information: '**217,000** people a year **[84,000** a month, according to the Toronto Star] in Metro need food help [out of a population of about 3.4 million]. Half of them have gone without food for a day or more. One Metro [MetropolitanToronto] child in seven belongs to a family who needed food help last year. Daily Bread now distributes as much food in a week as it did in all 1984.'

And that is just in the prosperous comers of capitalism. If these are the successes of capitalism, what standards should we use in comparing its failures to those of the communist world? Would it be an exaggeration to say that more people live in abject poverty and degradation within the ambit of capitalism than in the Soviet Union or **Eastern** Europe? How should we weigh the well-fed and highly educated East Germans streaming into the West against, say, the shanty-town dwellers of **São** Paolo or the rubber-tappers of the Amazon – or, for that matter, against the millions in advanced capitalist countries who 'escape' from intolerable conditions by means of drug addiction and violent crime? (In fact, maybe we need to consider how to balance such apolitical reactions to the oppressions of 'civil society' against political resistance to a repressive state.) And if anyone objects that East Germany vs. Brazil is not comparing like with like, perhaps they should consider the 'third-world' areas of the Soviet **Union** itself. How about Tashkent as against Calcutta? Or what about this: if destruction of the environment in the post-capitalist world has resulted from gross neglect, massive inefficiency, and a reckless urge to catch up with Western industrial development in the shortest possible time, how are we to judge this against the capitalist West, where a far more wide-ranging

THE SOCIALIST REGISTER 1990

ecological vandalism is not an index of failure but a token of success, the inevitable by-product of a system whose constitutive principle is the subordination of all human values to the drive for accumulation and the requirements of profitability?

Solidarity's new minister of finance, seeking a model for the regeneration of Poland, looks to South Korea, a repressive regime whose 'human rights' record hardly represents an improvement over that of the regime which Solidarity was so keen to replace, and whose economic 'miracle' was achieved by means of a low-wage economy, with a working class even more overexploited and overworked than the Japanese (never mind that Poland, if the project of 'restoring capitalism' works at all, may turn out to be not a 'successful' South Korea but a squalid peripheral capitalism on a Latin American model). It is perhaps time for us in the West to tell a few home truths about capitalism, instead of hiding them discreetly behind the screen of 'civil society'.

NOTES

For an argument that the Romans, specifically in the person of **Cicero,** had a concept of 'society', see Neal **Wood,** *Cicero's Social and Political Thought,* Berkeley and **Los Angeles 1988,** esp. pp. **136–42.**

Much of John Keane's argument in *Democracy and Civil Society,* London **1988,** is, **for** example, predicated on a criticism of Marxism for its identification of 'civil society' with capitalism, which he opposes by invoking the long tradition of conceptions of 'society' in the West.

Something like the first conception can, for example, be extracted from Jean L. Cohen, *Class and Civil Society: The Limits of Marxian Critical Theory,* **Amherst 1982.** The second view is elaborated by John Keane in *Democracy and Civil Society.* (For his criticism of Cohen's **conception,** see p. 86n.)

4.   John Keane ed., *Civil Society and the State,* London **1988,** p. **1.**
5.   Keane, *Civil Society and the State,* p. **2.**
6.   Norman **Geras** debunks such myths about Marxism in this volume.
7.   For the application of 'civil society' to events in Poland, see Andrew Arato, 'Civil Society Against the State: Poland **1980–81',** *Telos* **47, 1981,** and 'Empire versus Civil Society: Poland **1981–82',** *Telos* **50,1982.**
8.   Keane, *Democracy and Civil Society,* p. *32.*
9.   Cohen, p. **192.**
10.   See, for example, Cohen, p. **49;** Keane, *Democracy and Civil Society,* p. **59;** Agnes **Heller,** 'On Formal Democracy', in Keane, *Civil Society and the State,* p. **132.**
11.   *I* have discussed these points at greater length in my *The Retreat from Class: A New 'True' Socialism,* London **1986,** chap. **10.**
12.   The rest of this section is drawn largely from a paper delivered at the Roundtable 'Socialism in **the** World', Cavtat, Yugoslavia, October **1988.**
13.   The tendency to conflate aristocratic 'constitutionalist' principles with democracy is very widespread and not confined to the English language. Another notable example is the canonization of the Huguenot resistance tracts, in particular the *Vindiciae Contra Tyrannos,* as classics of democratic political thought, when they more precisely represent the reassertion of feudal rights especially by lesser provincial nobles – those who benefitted least from the favours of the

ELLEN **MEIKSINS** WOOD

Court and from access to **high** state office – against an encroaching monarchy. 'Constitutionalism' has, in **fact,** historically **often been** aristocratic, **even** feudal, **in** its motivations; and while this does not disqualify it as an **important** contribution to the **development** of 'limited' and **'responsible' government,** a certain caution should attend any effort to identify it with 'democracy'.

14. For a powerful discussion of this point, see Gwrge **Comninel,** *Rethinking the French Revolution: Marxism and the Revisionist Challenge,* London, **1987,** chapters 3, 5 and 6.

15. Jeno **Sziics,** 'Three Historical Regions of Europe', in Keane, *Civil Society and the State,* p. 294.

16. **Sziics,** p. 295.

17. **Sziics,** p. 2%.

18. **Sziics,** p. 302.

19. **Sziics,** p. **304.**

20. **Sziics,** p. **306.**

21. I have discussed the specificity of Greece in *Peasant-Citizen and Slave,* London 1988, where the relation between this unique formation and the growth of chattel slavery is also explored.

22. I develop this point at greater length in 'Capitalism and Human Emancipation', *New Left Review* 167, **January/February 1988,** especially pp. 8–14.

23. The defence of formal democracy is sometimes explicitly **accompanied** by an attack on **'substantive'** democracy. Agnes Heller, in 'On Formal Democracy', writes: 'The statement of Aristotle, a **highly** realistic analyst, that all democracies are immediately transformed into **anarchy,** the latter **into** tyranny, was a statement of fact. not an aristocratic slanderine by an anti-democrat. The Roman reoublic was not for a moment democratic. **And I** should like to add to **all** that that kven if the degradation of modem democracies into tyrannies is far from being excluded (we were witness to it in the cases of German and Italian Fascism), the endurance of modem democracies is due precisely to their formal character.' (p. 130) Let us take each sentence in **turn.** The denunciation of ancient democracy as the inevitable forerunner of anarchy and tyranny (which is, incidentally, more typical of **Plato** or **Polybius** than Aristotle) is, precisely, an anti-democratic slander. For one thing, it bears no relation to real historical sequences, causal or even chronological. Athenian democracy brought an end to the institution of tyranny, and went on to survive nearly two centuries, only to be defeated not by anarchy but by a superior military power. During those centuries, of course, Athens produced an astonishingly fruitful and influential culture which survived its defeat and also laid the foundation for **Western** conceptions of citizenship and the rule of law. The Roman republic was indeed 'not for a moment democratic', and the most notable result of its aristocratic regime was the demise of the republic and its replacement by autocratic imperial **rule.** (That undemocratic **Republic** was, incidentally, a major **inspiration** for what Heller calls a 'constitutive' document of **modern democracy, the U S** Constitution.) To say that the 'degradation of modem democracies into tyrannies is far **from** being excluded' seems a bit coy in conjunction with a (parenthetical) reference to Fascism – not to mention the history of war and imperialism which has been inextricably associated with the regime of 'formal democracy'. As for endurance, it is surely worth mentioning that there does not yet exist a 'formal democracy' whose life-span equals, let alone exceeds, the duration of the Athenian democracy. No European 'democracy', by **Heller's** criteria, is even a century old (in Britain, for example, plural voting **survived** until 1948); and the American republic, which she credits with the 'constitutive idea' of formal democracy, took a long time to improve on the Athenian exclusion of women and slaves, while free working men – full citizens

THE SOCIALIST REGISTER 1990

in the Athenian democracy — cannot be said to have gained full admission even to 'formal' citizenship until the last state property qualifications were removed in the nineteenth century (not to mention the variety of stratagems to discourage voting by the poor in general and blacks in particular, which have not been exhausted to this day). Thus, at best (and for white men only), an endurance record of perhaps one century and a half for modem 'formal democracies'.

24. This paragraph is drawn largely from my article on civil society in *New Statesman and Society*, **6** October, **1989**.
25. This is, for example, the view of **Ernesto** Laclau and Chantal Mouffe in *Hegemony and Socialist Strategy*, London **1985**.
26. See, for example, Stuart Hall in *Marxism Today*, October **1988**.
27. The notion of complex equality is primarily the work of Michael **Walzer,** *Spheres of Justice: A Defence of Pluralism and Equality*, London **1983**. See also Keane, *Democracy and Civil Society*, p. **12**.
28. These points are developed in my 'Capitalism and Human Emancipation', *New Left Review* **167, January/February 1988**.
29. For a discussion of both the advantages and disadvantages in **Walzer's** conception of complex equality, see Michael **Rustin,** *For a Pluralist Socialism*, London **1985**, pp. **76–95**.
30. Such an analysis of capitalism, for example, constitutes the core of *Marxism Today's* conception of 'New Times', which purports to provide a platform for a modem Communist Party in Britain. See the special issue, *New Times*, October **1988**, and A *Manifesto for New Times*, June **1989**.
31. The argument that we have reached a kind of **Hegelian** end of history, with the triumph of liberal democracy over all other ideologies, is the latest conceit of the American right, as elaborated by Francis Fukuyama in *National Interest*, Summer **1989**.

[19]

LABOR MARKET AND PENAL SANCTION: THOUGHTS ON THE SOCIOLOGY OF CRIMINAL JUSTICE

Georg Rusche *
Translated by Gerda Dinwiddie **

Editors' Introduction

The following English translation of Georg Rusche's "Arbeitsmarkt und Strafvollzug" (1933) appears in print for the first time. Originally submitted as a research proposal to the Frankfurt Institute of Social Research in 1931, Rusche's article laid the foundation for the book, Punishment and Social Structure, *which he later co-authored with Otto Kirchheimer. First published in 1939 by Columbia University Press, the book was re-issued in 1968 by Russell and Russell Company.*

Punishment and Social Structure *continues to be neglected by American criminologists. Barnes and Teeters (*New Horizons in Criminology, *Prentice-Hall, 1943) and Edwin Sutherland (*Principles of Criminology, *4th Edition, 1947) are the only two "older" textbooks that acknowledge its existence. While Sutherland merely listed the work as suggested reading, Barnes and Teeters at least recognized the importance of the book: "In a stimulating and provocative work on the subject, Rusche and Kirchheimer have given us a clear idea of how changing social and economic systems fundamentally altered the ways of thinking and acting in relation to crime and punishment."*

The only American criminologist to employ the thesis developed in Punishment and Social Structure *was Thorsten Sellin in* Pioneering in Penology *(1944) and in his most recent work,*

---

* George Rusche (1900–?) studied law, philosophy, economics and the social sciences in Paris, London and at several German universities, graduating from Cologne University in 1924. He pursued his studies at that same university and completed his thesis on economic theory in 1929, followed by the writing of "Arbeitsmarkt und Strafvollzug" in 1931 (published in 1933). After Hitler came to power, Rusche left Germany and experienced years of difficult exile from Paris to London, then to Palestine, and back to London. Interned in a camp in Great Britain, Rusche was later released and was on his way to Canada when his ship was torpedoed. He was returned to London where he remained, at least until March 1941. There is no further information on Georg Rusche.

** Gerda Dinwiddie is a graduate student in German literature at the University of California, Berkeley.

Slavery and the Penal System *(1976). (See the review essay of Sellin's writings by Greg Shank in this issue of the journal.) Sellin was also familiar with Rusche's "Arbeitsmarkt und Strafvollzug" (see Sellin's* Research Memorandum on Crime in the Depression, *Social Science Research Council, Bulletin 27, 1937).*

In a review essay of Punishment and Social Structure *in* Crime and Social Justice 9 *(Spring–Summer 1978), Dario Melossi points out how Rusche's writings in Chapters II through VIII, which carefully follow the hypothesis laid down in "Arbeitsmarkt und Strafvollzug," were re-worked by Otto Kirchheimer. Rusche was less than enthusiastic about what had been done to his portion of the book. For this reason,* Crime and Social Justice *made the decision to print an English translation of how Rusche originally viewed his plan of research.*

This English translation is almost a faithful reproduction from the original German. We have, however, modernized the language and idioms without fundamentally altering the original meaning. It is apparent that Rusche was embarking on a radically new kind of analysis and, therefore, his vocabulary and categories of analysis are sometimes unclear and tentative.

I.

The study of crime and crime control is a fruitful field for sociological research. We are dealing with phenomena here which are determined to a large extent by social forces. Consequently, on the one hand, they practically compel an explanation derived from social relationships; on the other hand, they lend themselves especially well to an illumination of these relationships. The reason for this is that mystification and cover-up, which make the investigation of other social interconnections so very difficult, are to a great extent forced aside by the brutality of these phenomena and by conflicts which must necessarily be fought in the open.

Surprisingly, research has made only minimal use of the possibilities offered here. Sociological considerations have been included extensively in the examination of criminological problems. However, they have not been done justice in any way. For, even if the relationship between socioeconomic phenomena and the problems of crime and crime control are obvious to sociologists, there is still a long way to go from the naïve recognition of this fact to making use of it in a systematic and scientific fashion.

This failure is explained by the fact that, in general, the researchers who devote themselves to criminological problems are not familiar with the fundamental principles of the social sciences, but approach them more from the outside. They are usually jurists or doctors. When they employ sociological categories in their work, they are derived from naïve experience or, at best, if these categories are scientifically founded, they rely exclusively on social psychology.

Certainly the more recent criminology, partially stimulated by psychoanalysis, has produced valuable insights about the individual and social causes of crime and about the sociopsychological functions of punishment. But these studies lack a foundation in the basic principles of sociological knowledge. They are neither connected to economic theory, nor are they historically oriented. Rather, they imply a fixed social structure which does not exist in reality, and they unconsciously characterize the social system as eternal and unchanging rather than as a historical process.

The social function of crime and criminal justice can be clarified far beyond previous research, if simple axioms of economic theory are used and one does not presuppose a more or less static and ahistorical system of class relations. In this paper, some basic ideas for research along these lines will be proposed and discussed.

Although highly complex and somewhat independent circumstances influence the field of criminology, especially biological and psychological aspects, nevertheless economic theory and historical observation can clarify many questions. The dependency of crime and crime control on economic and historical conditions does not, however, provide a total explanation. These forces do not alone determine the object of our investigation and by themselves are limited and incomplete in several ways. For example, the penal system and the ritual of criminal procedure are shaped by various forces, including religious and sexual phenomena. Similarly, our method of investigation is not sufficient to explain the specific fate of a single individual who becomes a criminal and his particular punishment. But, within these limits, certain mechanisms can be discovered by economic-historical analysis with sufficient accuracy.

II.

It can be said without contradiction that crimes are acts which are forbidden in society. Debates about the meaning of punishment will not be addressed here. I shall not discuss whether the goal of punishment is retribution, deterrence or reform of the criminal. One thing, though, is certain: no society wants its penal system to incite the commission of crimes. In other words, punishment has to be constituted in such a way that those people who appear to be criminally inclined or inclined to commit acts that are undesirable to the society, are at least not encouraged to do so by the prospect of being discovered and punished. On the contrary, it is even hoped that the prospect of punishment will deter if not all members of this class, then at least a substantial part.

Indeed, the anticipation of future suffering and painful reprisal, which by far exceed the possible pleasurable gain, should be an effective counterbalance for any rational person. Now experience teaches us that most crimes are committed by members of those strata who are burdened by strong social pressures and who are relatively disadvantaged in satisfying their needs when compared to other classes. Therefore, a penal sanction, if it is not to be counter-productive, must be constituted in such a way that the classes which are most criminally inclined prefer to abstain from the forbidden acts than become victims of criminal punishment.

Perhaps, one could argue that such a proposition does not sufficiently consider the impact of the sense of honor and fear of disgrace associated with punishment. Indeed, the solidity of the social structure does in no way depend only on the strength of external measures of coercion which are supposed to guarantee the continuation of society. The great majority of people has to be psychically willing to accommodate to the existing society, to regard the state as their state, the law as their law. But, according to experience, there are classes for whom this adjustment and identification break down.

Criminality certainly occurs throughout all social classes. But disregarding persons for whom social inhibitions are without effect, or a few crimes which are not affected by social position, such as slander or political and related offenses or isolated cases of sensational trials, then it becomes clear that the criminal law and the daily work of the criminal courts are directed almost exclusively against those people whose class background, poverty, neglected education, or demoralization drove them to crime. It is rarely maintained anymore today that the individual alone is responsible for his crime. On the other hand, not everybody necessarily becomes a criminal even under the heaviest social pressure. Thus, the range of possibilities extends from law-abiding people in a wretched environment to confirmed criminals in a bourgeois milieu. Indeed, the power of resistance can be abnormally low or the inducement overly high in an individual case. At any rate, an extremely high capacity for resistance is expected of the lower strata, of whom large masses are regularly deprived of their livelihood by long, severe winters, inflation and crises, and the spiritually and physically weakest are thrown into the path of crime. If penal sanctions are supposed to deter these strata from crime in an effective manner, they must appear even worse than the strata's present living conditions. One can also formulate this proposition as follows: all efforts to reform the punishment of criminals are inevitably limited by the situation of the lowest socially significant proletarian class which society wants to deter from criminal acts. All reform efforts, however humanitarian and well-meaning, which attempt to go beyond this restriction, are condemned to utopianism. If penal reforms should be demanded by public opinion and carried out, the reforms would have to be undermined by a more subtle deterioration of prison conditions. For, a genuine improvement in the conditions of imprisonment beyond this limit would no longer deter such large groups of people, and, as a consequence, the purpose of punishment would be destroyed. George Bernard Shaw once said:

> When we get down to the poorest and most oppressed of our population we find the conditions of their life so wretched that it would be impossible to conduct a prison humanely without making the lot of the criminal more eligible than that of many free citizens. If the prison does not underbid the slum in human misery, the slum will empty and the prison will fill.[1]

III.

The preceding analysis, though abstract and formal, has been stated often enough.[2] Naturally, it should not be assumed that this proposition will be exactly reproduced in society in the manner in which it has been expressed here. It is only a principle of investigation, a guide to approach the subject matter. We will then find that there are very peculiar and unpredictable events, often strangely intertwined and quite different in conception and execution, which determine the course of real life.

If we want to make concrete the proposition that effective penal sanctions must deter the lower social classes which are the most criminally inclined, we must clarify what economic categories determine the fate of these classes. It is not at first easy to realize that these classes have no other goods at their disposal but their ability to sell their labor power and that, therefore, the labor market is the determining category. The situation of the working class is different in an economy in which a large reserve army of starving proletariat follows the employers and drives the wage for each job opportunity offered down to a minimum, than

---

[1]   See the Forward to Sidney and Beatrice Webb, *English Prisons Under Local Government,* London, 1922, p. *xi.*

[2]   The most concise example is found in Kriegsmann, *Einführung in die Gefängniskunde (Introduction to Penology),* Heidelberg, 1912, p. 175: "The care must not go so far, that the prisoner is being spoiled, that the prison becomes el dorado of the poorest classes of the population."

in an economy in which workers are scarce, as for example where free land is available and therefore nobody is forced to earn a living through dependent labor, and the employers compete for the few available workers and drive wages up.

Naturally, the scarcity of surplus of workers does not *unequivocally* determine the nature of the labor market. Political interventions can correct the fluctuation of supply and demand. When there is a lack of workers, for instance, the employers can try to compensate for the lack of economic incentives by introducing slavery or other forms of forced labor, or by setting maximum wages or taking similar measures pertaining to labor law. When there is a surplus of workers, the unions can protect wages from falling by withholding the supply of labor, or the state can do so through sociopolitical measures, particularly payment of aid to the unemployed. Depending on which of these situations prevails, the criminal justice apparatus will have to meet different tasks.

Unemployed masses, who tend to commit crimes of desperation because of hunger and deprivation, will only be stopped from doing so through cruel penalties. The most effective penal policy seems to be severe corporal punishment, if not ruthless extermination. In China, where there is a huge reserve army of wretched and starving proletariat which pours into the cities and is forced to sell its labor for any price (if it can find work at all), large gangs of mercenaries are always fighting one another. Under these conditions, the mere fact of being given food would make prison an enticement, not a deterrent. Prison sentences, therefore, only exist where European influence has asserted itself, and they are an indescribable cruelty. "Every socially thinking person who comes to China," writes Agnes Smedley in a report, "*Prisons in China*,"[3] "receives an extremely sad, depressing impression when he must see how lowly an ordinary human life weighs. This disregard becomes particularly clear when one realizes that criminals of any kind, who are caught here, are being shot, hanged or beheaded, and that these executions arouse hardly more than fleeting notice."

In a society in which workers are scarce, penal sanctions have a completely different function. They do not have to stop hungry masses from satisfying elementary needs. If everybody who wants to work can find work, if the lowest social class consists of unskilled workers and not of wretched unemployed workers, then punishment is required to make the unwilling work, and to teach other criminals that they have to content themselves with the income of an honest worker. Even more: when workers are scarce, the wages will be high. But then it will be profitable to lock up criminals and let them work for food only, since the costs of guarding and enforcement will still be less than the normal wage. Therefore, there is in all societies in which workers are scarce a tendency away from corporal punishment and the extermination of the criminal. Where the criminal's labor is valuable, exploitation is preferred to capital punishment, and forced labor is the corresponding mode of punishment.

IV.

This economic theory of punishment which has been developed here in a broad outline seems to me to be the key to understanding the criminal law. It would be quite wrong, however, to apply it to the present in exactly the same way as it has been presented here.

---

[3]   *Frankfurter Zeitung,* September 15, 1930.

Important peculiarities in the contemporary criminal law cannot be explained without a historical framework.... That our criminal law exists in its present-day form is to a great extent comprehensible only through an appreciation of its origins and development. Its present form is, so to speak, a projection of the past. In spite of fluctuations in the political economy, the criminal law has not become insignificant and, though adjusted to a great extent to present-day tasks, it exerts far-reaching effects. This cannot be comprehended if one tries to understand the penal system only from the viewpoint of today. Without a historical overview, it is impossible to rationally explain an incomprehensible state of affairs. That means, however, that our economic theory has to be supplemented by a historical analysis without which the present system of crime control is incomprehensible. This work has not been done so far by legal historians. The history of law, as it is practiced at the moment, is far too much a brand of positivist jurisprudence to be capable of analyzing it socio-historically.

The history of the penal system is more than a history of the alleged independent development of legal "institutions." It is the history of the relations of the "two nations," as Disraeli called them, that constitute a people – the rich and the poor. The unproductive and conventional notions which legal historians usually hang onto hinder more often than help a truly scientific explanation. And when jurists rise above the juristic horizon, they often treat their object of interest in the manner of a meticulous collector of curiosities, without any criteria for the selection of the significant, because they do not question the legitimacy of traditional archives. But historians record things which appear important and remarkable to them, while we, however, are interested in day-to-day events. It is the same with reports about sensational legal cases which fill all the newspapers but tell us little about the actual criminality of the masses.

Often, legal historians are guided not by an unprejudiced analysis of social laws, but by an evolutionary conception of the development of legal institutions: from barbaric cruelty to the humanitarianism of the relatively perfect legal system which we supposedly enjoy today. They overlook that we are dealing with a very long, now halting, now regressive movement. Accordingly, they are often rather generous with praise for the eras which confirm their theory and at the same time scathing about those centuries which do not fit into it – a procedure which does not always promote the understanding of facts.

Therefore, the task has been to study the historical relationship between criminal law and economics, the history of class struggle, and to utilize these interrelationships to analyze the present prison system. At this point, only a short overview of the results of this research can be given, as much as is necessary to explain the logic of this essay....

V.

In the history of punishment, three epochs succeed one another. They are characterized by the prevalence of quite different methods of punishment: penance and monetary fines are practically the only form of punishment in the early Middle Ages; they are replaced in the late Middle Ages by a system of cruel corporal punishment and death sentences, which in turn make way for prison sentences in the 17th century. If one compares these phases in the history of penology with changes in social history, one finds surprising interconnections.

The early medieval system of fines and penance corresponded to the needs of a thinly populated, peasant economy. The possibility of settling on free land hindered any strong social pressure on the lower classes and led to a relatively even distribution of society's wealth. Thus, there were few crimes against property, for a farmer would hardly take things from his neighbor which he could produce himself at a much lesser cost in psychic expenditure. What led to crimes were rather the primitive stirrings of sexuality and hatred. A real deterrent at this time was the fear of private revenge by the injured party. In order to prevent this situation from degenerating into blood feuds and anarchy, society strove for accommodation. Crime was regarded as a form of war and the goal of legislators was the reconciliation of the enemies by recognized principles rather than crime control as we know it today.

In the later Middle Ages, the situation changed completely. If, until then, as Schmoller says, "people were more in demand than property,"[4] now there is a growth in population, the land is settled and a crowding of the available living space occurs. A separation of classes into rich and poor begins; propertyless workers drive down wages; and, for the first time, a quasi-capitalistic mode of production emerges; armies of beggars, social unrest and revolts, culminating in the peasant wars are the result. The nature of criminality is completely changed: a rapid increase in property crimes occurs and hordes of beggars, thieves and robbers flourish. As a result, the sphere of action of criminal justice had to be completely altered. If in the Middle Ages fines were preferred over corporal punishment, now the traditional system of monetary fines had outlived its usefulness because these criminals had no possessions with which they could pay. Gradually, traditional punitive methods were replaced by whippings, mutilation and killing, at first still redeemable through money, later the universal means of punishment of and protection against the criminality of the gathering crowds of have-nots. The most gruesome imagination is hardly sufficient to visualize the justice of that time, which soon plunged vagabonds into destruction side by side with bandits and murderers and ended with the extermination of the jobless proletariat.

Around 1600, the conditions of the labor market again changed fundamentally. The supply of labor became scarcer as a result of the expansion of trade and new markets, the influx of precious metals from the New World, and wars and plagues, especially the Thirty Years' War and its decimation of the population. A period of noticeable shortage of workers occurred; workers' wages rose and the standard of living of the lowest class improved considerably. People became valuable and workers thought twice before putting their labor power at anybody's disposal. As the gains of the contractors receded and the "economy" declined, force replaced economic incentive. The whole social structure is determined by this effort and, as a consequence of it, the system of mercantilism emerges. From this perspective, it is easy to interpret the well-known fact that until then it had been easy to collect soldiers in sufficient numbers simply through the "propaganda drum," for jobless proletarians streamed together in crowds wherever they saw a possibility for continuing their existence. But now they had to be enlisted with force and trickery because they could find more favorable conditions outside the military. In this situation of constant scarcity of workers, where everybody's labor is valuable, it would be an economically "senseless" cruelty to keep destroying criminals. Confinement to prison takes over the role of corporal punishment and death sentences, "humanitarianism" replaces cruelty; wherever there used to be gallows, now prisons stand. This humanitarianism was absolutely profitable: "What good is a thief, who has been hanged because of 50 Gulden,

---

[4] *Grundriss der Allgemeinen Volkswirtschaftslehre (Principles of General Economy),* Volume II, Leipzig, 1901, p. 513.

either for himself or for the one he stole it from, when he can earn four times that amount in one year in a workhouse?" asks a distinguished labor economist of that time, J.J. Becher.[5]

This "humanitarian" system of punishment lost its utility when the Industrial Revolution, the replacement of the worker by the machine at the turn of the 18th century, removed the scarcity of workers, and the industrial reserve army came into existence. The lower classes sank into misery, underbid each other on the labor market, and compulsory measures lost their meaning. Prisons were no longer profitable. When wages were high, they had brought high gains; but when workers voluntarily offered their labor for a minimum existence, it was no longer worth it to come up with the cost for confinement and supervision. The proceeds of prisoners' labor were not even sufficient for the upkeep of the building and the maintenance of the guards and prisoners. The prison failed in two ways: again, as in the Middle Ages, the criminality of the pauperized masses rose and the penitentiary no longer terrorized them. Some advocated the return to medieval methods of punishment. Though it was demanded loud enough, it did not materialize because hard-earned humanitarian ideals hindered it and political wisdom kept the ruling class from overstraining an already revolutionary situation with such open provocation. Penal punishment remained a leftover from a previous and quite different epoch, but adjusted by necessity to changing needs. Institutions of forced labor, penitentiaries became places of pure torture, suitable to deter even the most wretched. Prisoners were insufficiently clothed and were cramped together. Work, having become unprofitable, served as torture: loads of stone had to be lugged without purpose from one place to another by the prisoners: they had to work waterpumps which let the water flow back again, or treadmills which were not used for any purpose. The discipline of this routine was reenforced by the deterrent effect of beatings.

The introduction of solitary confinement was only an apparent reform. It too was a punitive device which could arouse fear even in the hungry and act as a deterrent for people who did not know how to stay alive. For there is hardly a greater torment than the feeling of total dependency and helplessness, being cut off from all stimulations and distractions, which is induced by solitary confinement. Only in form did the idea of deterrence differ from the corporal punishments of the Middle Ages, but the conscience of the reformers could be at peace. In solitary confinement they could see, not torture, but the reform of the penitentiaries.

In America, punishment developed differently than in Europe because there was a greater demand for workers than during mercantilism. The free land and industrial development created a vacuum in the labor market which immigration could not fill. Everybody who was the least bit useful could find work, wages were high, possibilities of upward mobility were not closed to any capable person. The lowest socially important class were the unskilled, recent immigrants or the native colored workers. Public assistance for the unemployed was not needed. For the sick and weak, and those unable to work, private philanthropy was enough. The number of crimes was low and the form of punishment could take this into account. As under mercantilism, prisons became very profitable places of production whose main task was to transform criminals through education into useful members of society, i.e. industrious workers. Consequently, reformers were able to make surprising gains – education, learning of skills, hygiene, indeterminate sentencing, conditional pardon, probation, parole, separate

---

[5]   Johann Joachim Becher, *Politischer Discurs: Von den eigentlichen Ursachen dess Auff und Abnehmens der Städt, Länder und Republicken (Political Discourse: Of the Actual Causes of the Rise and Fall of Cities, Countries and Republics),* Frankfurt, 1688, p. 245.

treatment of juvenile delinquents and first offenders all had their starting point here. Also, scientific organizations investigated the individual and social causes of crime and methods of crime control through welfare and prevention.

Only when the situation improved somewhat in Europe, when the pressure of the unemployed which had weighed on the labor market since the Industrial Revolution slowly subsided, when unemployment as a permanent phenomenon disappeared, when social welfare lessened the misery of the helpless and, therefore, the rate of criminality went down considerably, was the American example slowly and hesitatingly followed, more perhaps in theory than in praxis. The development, for example, of effective aid for released prisoners in the period before the war was motivated by the scarcity of agricultural labor and employers' willingness to accept any labor force, provided that they contented themselves with sufficiently low wages. Thus, there was an urgent demand for vagabonds and criminals, as well as foreigners.

VI.

After the war, when there was chronic unemployment, a breakdown of the labor market in the countries which were most affected was avoided by unemployment assistance. Wages and the standard of living did not sink as low as they would have in an unregulated economy. Even those who dropped out of the production process were assured of satisfying their most immediate needs and, generally, they did not need to become criminals. Consequently, the penal system was saved from the task, which it had to perform several times in its history, of containing criminals for whom prison would not be intimidating, given the regular supply of food. Disregarding the short period of inflation, criminality did not rise above its prewar level; it even showed until recently a declining tendency. As a result, penal reforms which began even before the war did not at first have to be given up, but were partially continued, given the favourable political climate....

This effort, which was carried out in the last few years with considerable public participation, shall not be discussed at this point. As far as the results can be estimated, it is not necessary to abandon the simple heuristic maxim to which we evidently owe so many correct results.

In Germany, the class which is the most criminally endangered is the unemployed on relief, particularly young singles who keep house on their relief alone and at the moment receive about seven to eight Mark per week for all their living needs. Besides this class, there exists a group of people who do not receive assistance, for to a great extent the effectiveness of our very humane welfare laws is undermined by the apparatus created for their realization. A large part of the welfare law in Germany demands a high degree of a personal sense of responsibility from the officials. Given that the administration is cutting back personnel, establishing written records, and asking for the centralization of authority, the justification of aid in each case means a new burden for the functionaries, a burden which can be avoided by a simple denial of aid to the petitioner. Anyway, considering the extremely limited budget of public welfare, the officials are encouraged to make a negative decision and to refuse aid in case of doubt. Therefore, strong motives exist for an unfavourable decision in any case.

The class of the unaided supplies the beggars, vagabonds, peddlers, prostitutes, pimps and those who lower the wages for occasional work of any kind – guests of the hostels and asylums, when they have "sleeping money," otherwise without shelter, desperately awaiting the morning in waiting rooms and hallways.[6]

According to our heuristic maxim, we should assume that in the interest of deterring these classes, punishment must mean a hell which they would not voluntarily exchange for their living conditions. But until now, the satisfaction of the elementary needs of food and warmth does not seem to have been denied the prisoners too much. On the contrary, they receive "appropriate nourishment," which perhaps would even compare favourably with the nutrition of the unemployed (the price of food in the prisons is about .70 Reichsmark per day). The degradation, the meaninglessness of penal labor, the prison discipline with its enforced order, the exclusion of all normal sexual activity, as well as the hostility of the overworked guards – in short, the deprivation of freedom – appears to be effective enough so far. According to the scandalous trials of the last few years, a similar state of affairs must be assumed for education in juvenile reformatories. Naturally, the forces which bring about this state of affairs are anything else than conscious intent.

There is, however, an extraordinary confirmation of the proposition expressed here: the dramatic breakdown of "humane" punishment in America. In the United States today, the high level of unemployment is not absorbed by the welfare system. Consequently, there is an unimaginable rise in crime, an unimaginable brutality of repression, the breakdown of all humanitarian reforms, the overcrowding of the prisons, hunger, filth, joblessness, hopelessness and despair, leading to these penitentiary revolts, these outbreaks of madness, which for a time shocked world opinion.[7]

So far, the treatment of prisoners in Germany, though not as humane as some people assume, is nevertheless not as harsh as in America. But our humanitarianism is hardly effective enough to lift punishment out of the sphere of that fatal dependency on which we based our theoretical premise.

---

[6]   The released prisoners should not be driven into joining these classes, but are to receive welfare; but even then enough of them wind up among these groups: those who do not know their rights or do not know how to defend them in a suitable manner, those who cannot register with the police because of previously committed crimes, namely runaways from juvenile reformatories.

[7]   Compare my essay, "Zuchthausrevolten oder Sozialpolitik" ("Penitentiary Revolts or Social Politics"), *Frankfurter Zeitung,* June 1, 1930. No. 403.

[20]

The Injuries of Class

MICHAEL D. YATES

The Class-Divided Society

We live in a complex, divided society. We are divided by wealth, income, education, housing, race, gender, ethnicity, religion, and sexual orientation. These divisions are much discussed; in the last two years, there have been entire series in our major newspapers devoted to the growing income divide. The wealth-flaunting of today's rich was even the subject of a recent Sunday *New York Times Magazine* article ("City Life in the New Gilded Age," October 14, 2007).

What is seldom talked or written about is to me our most fundamental division, one at the center of our economic system, namely the division of our society into a very large class of working men, women, and children, the working class; and a much smaller class of owners that employs the former, the capitalist class. These two great classes make the world go round, so to speak.

Workers and owners are fundamentally connected and antagonistic along a number of dimensions:

♦It is through the labor of the working class that the goods and services necessary for our survival are produced.

♦It is through the ownership of society's productive wealth (land, machines, factories, etc.) that the owning class is able to compel that this labor be done. Workers must sell their capacity to work in order to gain access to this productive wealth, since no one can live without such access.

♦In terms of society's "reproduction" the relationship between labor and capital is essential. So much of what we do presupposes the suc-

---

MICHAEL D. YATES is associate editor of *Monthly Review*. He was for many years professor of economics at the University of Pittsburgh at Johnstown. He is most recently the editor of *More Unequal: Aspects of Class in the United States* (2007) and the author of *Cheap Motels and a Hotplate* (2006), both published by Monthly Review Press.

This is adapted from a talk delivered at the Labor Center of the University of Massachusetts Amherst on November 1, 2007.

cessful sale of labor power. Without the money from such a sale, nothing appears to exist.

♦The essence of production in capitalism is the ceaseless accumulation of capital, the making of profits and the use of such profits to increase the capital at the owners' disposal. Competition among capitals both drives accumulation and is driven by it, in a relentless dance.

♦But to accumulate capital, employers must make sure that workers cannot claim possession of all they produce. This means that employers must strive for maximum control of the entire apparatus of production and any and all social forces and institutions that might interfere with this control (for example, the state, schools, and media). At all costs, workers must be prevented from getting the idea that they have rights to the output they produce.

This organization of capital and labor in our society has negative effects on working people. I want to talk about some of these negative effects. However, before I do, I would like to point out that the whole process of accumulation, beginning with the extraction of a surplus from the labor of the workers, is, especially in the United States, hidden from view, so that workers do not know or are confused about what is happening to them. This is the result in part of the public school system and the tireless promotion of individualism and nationalism at its core.

As Peter McLaren and Ramin Farahmandpur explain:

> Today urban schools are adroitly organized around the same principles as factory production lines. According to [Jonathan] Kozol "rising test scores," "social promotion," "outcome-based objectives," "time management," "success for all," "authentic writing," "accountable talk," "active listening," and "zero noise" constitute part of the dominant discourse in public schools. Most urban public schools have adopted business and market "work related themes" and managerial concepts that have become part of the vocabulary used in classroom lessons and instruction. In the "market-driven classrooms," students "negotiate," "sign contracts," and take "ownership" of their own learning. In many classrooms, students can volunteer as the "pencil manager," "soap manager," "door manager," "line manager," "time manager," and "coat room manager." In some fourth-grade classrooms, teachers record student assignments and homework using "earning charts"....[Jonathan] Kozol writes that in the market-driven model of public education, teachers are viewed as "floor managers" in public schools, "whose job it is to pump some 'added-value' into undervalued children." ("The Pedagogy of Oppression," *Monthly Review*, July–August, 2006)

REVIEW OF THE MONTH

Racism/sexism, imperialism, media propaganda, and repression further distort the social matrix and hide its class basis:

♦Endless war magnifies and deepens nationalism and promotes both racism and male chauvinism. Wars send workers back to society badly damaged in mind and body.

♦Imperialism does the same thing as war and is, of course, the root cause of it.

♦Constant Orwellian propaganda by the media, think tanks, politicians, and business leaders denies the class polarization of capitalist society. An important element of this misinformation campaign is the mythology surrounding the "free market" economy.

♦As in the earliest stages of capitalism, naked violence ultimately serves to suppress class consciousness and sow seeds of doubt among workers who might otherwise be inclined to mutiny against the system.

Unveiling the Injuries of Class

Against this background, let me now talk about the "injuries of class." Consider first unemployment. The separation of workers from productive wealth creates the possibility that workers will be unemployed, that is, unable to find a buyer for their labor power. In addition, we know from studying the history of capitalist economies that it is not uncommon for them periodically to sink into recession or depression. Such crises are part of the nature of the system. In such circumstances, unemployment rises dramatically. Furthermore, capital is always searching the heavens for sunny skies (higher profits), and if it finds them somewhere other than where it is currently situated, it shuts down one operation and opens another. Plant contractions and closings will therefore be regular occurrences.

What these things mean for working people is a pervasive sense of insecurity and fear that even what seems to be the most stable employment will "melt into air." Fear and insecurity not uncommonly produce two responses: a kind of joyless penury or a present-orientation that often takes the self-destructive forms of debt, drinking, and the like. In a recent essay, referring to the workers in the mining town in which I was born, I wrote:

> Mining towns in the United States were typically owned by the mining companies, and the companies exerted a near totalitarian control over the residents. They owned the houses, the only store (the infamous "company store"), all utilities, the schools, the library, everything. They

had their own private police (the Coal and Iron Police in Pennsylvania) sanctioned by state law. The climate in such a town is one of perpetual insecurity and fear, emotions compounded by the danger of the work in the mines....It is difficult to overstate the power of fear and poverty in shaping how working men and women think and act. Fear of losing a job. Fear of not finding a job. Fear of being late with bill payments. Fear of the boss's wrath. Fear your house might burn down. Fear your kids will get hurt. I inherited these emotions. ("Class: A Personal Story," *Monthly Review,* July-August 2006)

Should a person face an extended bout of unemployment or a plant closing, the potential injuries of class are many, as has been amply demonstrated: suicide, homicide, heart attack, hypertension, cirrhosis of the liver, arrest, imprisonment, mental illness.

The members of the owning class are almost always better situated to withstand the storms of economic crisis or even unemployment, so these are injuries that the system does not inflict on them. Recently Michael Gates Gill, a wealthy former advertising executive who lost his job, was featured in the *New York Times* in connection with his book, *How Starbucks Saved My Life: A Son of Privilege Learns to Live Like Everyone Else.* Gill gets a job in a Starbucks, and in it he learns about ordinary people. By most accounts the book is not very good. But the author had connections, and not only managed to get it published by a trade press (Gotham/Penguin) but reviewed in our premier newspaper. The chances of this happening to "everyone else" is as close to zero as you can get. The stories of job losses are written in the litany of woes that are an everyday reality for most people; such stories are anything but exotic and receive almost no public attention.

Unemployment in our society is a constant threat to the employed and a torment to those who lose their jobs as many do periodically. To be unemployed is almost to drop out of society; since to have no relation to the market is not to exist.

I add here that those who do unpaid labor, especially homemakers, must certainly experience something akin to that of the unemployed. Their work is so devalued that an estimate of its value is not included in the Gross Domestic Product. The unpaid labor of poor single women with children is considered so worthless that they have been forced to give it up and seek wage labor, often taking care of the children of others while their own kids are attended haphazardly or not at all.

Workers comprise the subordinate class. They are normally in the position of having to react to decisions made by others. They are de-

REVIEW OF THE MONTH

pendent upon employers, and they are at the same time apprehensive of them, since employers hold the power to deny to workers the life-sustaining connection to the means of production. Exploitation, dependence, and insecurity—in a system where workers are bombarded with the message that they and they alone make the decisions that determine their circumstances—make for a toxic brew, which when drunk often enough, creates a personality lacking in self-confidence, afraid to take chances, easily manipulated and shamed (of course, on the bright side, these injuries have given rise to a massive "self-help" industry).

The very subordination of workers, combined with the market mechanism that ratifies and reinforces it, means that capitalist societies will display ineradicable inequalities in variables of great importance: wealth, income, schooling, health care, housing, child care, and so forth. What is more, the market will, absent powerful countervailing forces, not only reproduce inequalities but deepen them, as we have seen so clearly in the United States over the past thirty years. This inequality itself generates its own class injuries. In my book, *Naming the System*, I cite research comparing the impact of inequality across the United States. It was discovered that, all else being equal, the greater the inequality of income within a state (as measured by the share of income going to the poorest 50 percent of households in each state), the higher the mortality rate. It appears that the psychological damage done to poor people as they contemplate the gap between themselves and those at the top of the income distribution has an independent effect on a wide variety of individual and social health outcomes. Everything we know about the correlation between health and other social indicators and income (a decent though not perfect proxy for class) tells us that working people will suffer in every way.

You may have heard it said that the only thing worse than having a job is not having one. This is true, but what does it say about work? Work in capitalism is a traumatic affair. We all have the capacity to conceptualize what we do before we do it. This capability, when applied to work, has allowed human beings to transform the world around them in profound ways: to invent tools and machines and to socially divide our labor so that the riches of the earth can be unlocked and a cornucopia of output produced. As we have done these things, we have also transformed ourselves, becoming ever more conscious of causes and effects and better able to understand the world. Put another way, our capacity to think and to do makes us human. It is integral to our being.

In capitalism, however, this human mastery of the physical world is reserved for only a few. The capacity to think and to do implies control, and control by workers cannot be contemplated by capitalists. In fact, the essence of management in capitalism is the monopolization of control by the owners, control especially of the labor process—the work—and its denial to the workers.

We don't have time today to discuss all the various control tactics used by employers: the herding of workers into factories, the detailed division of labor, mechanization, Taylorism, personnel management, lean production—all of which deny workers their humanity, their capacity to conceptualize and carry out their plans, to actually "own" what they make. However, let us look at a sampling of jobs in modern America:

Auto workers: There are about 1.1 million auto workers. Not only are they facing rapidly rising insecurity, they are also confronted every day with a work regimen so Taylorized that they must work fifty-seven of every sixty seconds. What must this be like? What does it do to mind and body? In this connection, it is instructive to read Ben Hamper's *Rivethead* (1992), a startling account of working in auto plants. Hamper worked in an old plant, where the norm was about forty-five seconds of work each minute. He eventually got a job in a new, "lean production" facility. He called it a "gulag." In her book, *On the Line at Subaru-Isuzu* (1995), sociologist Laurie Graham tells us about her work routine in one of these gulags. Below, I have skipped a lot of the steps, because I just want to give readers a sense of the work. Remember as you read it that the line is relentlessly moving while she is working:

1. Go to the car and take the token card off a wire on the front of the car.
2. Pick up the 2 VIN (vehicle identification number) plates from the embosser and check the plates to see that they have the same number.
3. Insert the token card into the token card reader.
4. While waiting for the computer output, break down the key kit for the car by pulling the 3 lock cylinders and the lock code from the bag.
5. Copy the vehicle control number and color number onto the appearance check sheet....

8. Lift the hood and put the hood jig in place so it will hold the hood open while installing the hood stay....

22. Rivet the large VIN plate to the left-hand center pillar.
23. Begin with step one on the next car.

This work is so intense that it is not possible to steal a break much less learn your workmate's job so that you can double-up, then rest while she does both jobs. Within six months of the plant's start-up, a majority of the workers had to wear wrist splints for incipient carpal tunnel. Necks and backs ache from bodies being twisted into unnatural positions for eight hours a day. Supervisors recommend exercises and suggest that workers who cannot deal with the pain are sissies.

What is true for auto workers is true for all who do this type of labor—whether it be in beef processing plants or on chicken disassembly lines where workers labor with slippery blood and gore on the floor and on their bodies. And where cuts lead to infections and disease.

Clerks: There are about 15 million clerks in the United States. Many years ago I was on a television show with former secretary of labor Robert Reich. In response to my claim that a lot of the jobs being created were not all that desirable, he said that there were a lot of good jobs available, ones in which workers had a real say about their jobs (no doubt referring to the "quality circles" so popular then). One such job was that of "clerk." I blurted out in a loud and incredulous voice, CLERKS! I suggested that perhaps Mr. Reich had never noticed the splints on the writs of many clerks, signs of epidemic carpal tunnel syndrome. Since that time, I have actually worked as a clerk, at the Lake Hotel in Yellowstone National Park. I describe the experience and what I learned in my book *Cheap Motels and Hot Plate: An Economist's Travelogue*. Clerks work long hours; they are on their feet all day; they take regular abuse from customers; they are exposed in full view of supervisors with no place to hide; they are accorded no respect (think about customers on cell phones in grocery lines); their pay is low; their benefits negligible. After a hard day at the front desk, I only wanted a few drinks and a warm bed. The stress level was extraordinary.

Restaurant Workers: There are 11 million of these, growing in number every year. Next to personal care and service workers, those who prepare and serve our food are most likely to experience a "major depressive episode." Restaurant workers in Manhattan's Chinatown log as many as one hundred hours a week, for less than minimum wage. The pace of the work, the pressure of it are unbelievable. Check out the arms and legs of a kitchen worker. They are full of cuts and burns. Substance abuse is widespread.

Secretaries, Administrative Assistants, and Office Support: These workers are 23 million strong. They are poorly paid, many in sick buildings, stuck in badly designed chairs, staring at computer screens for hours, taking orders all day long (usually women from men), and often heavily Taylorized. These workers, whose working conditions are satirized so skillfully on the television series *The Office,* have to contend with daily degradations, including all too prevalent sexual harassment. Here is what my sister said about her work:

> I, too, share some of your fears and anxieties. As one of the administrative assistants you talk about, I can relate to the long days of sitting at the typewriter (in years past) and now at the computer. I am sure that is the cause of my neck and shoulder pain and the many headaches from which I suffer. Although I basically like my job and the people with whom I work, after thirty years I am anxious to move on to something else. I look forward to retirement in about three to four years, moving to the city, maybe working part-time, and finding meaningful things in which to participate.

Security workers: Three million men and women watch over others in prisons, malls, gated communities, in occupied Iraq, and on our city streets. This is a type of work guaranteed to be stressful and to generate not only an extremely jaundiced and pejorative view of the rest of society but also an extreme, macho personality, prone to violence.

Custodial workers: There are 4 million building and grounds workers, many of them immigrants, keeping our buildings clean and the grounds swept and manicured. Often they are hired by contractors who are themselves employed by the buildings' owners. It has taken monumental efforts by the SEIU to organize some of these exploited workers, who must often labor in close proximity to dangerous cleaning fluids, solvents, and chemical fertilizers.

Medical workers: There are more than 13 million people laboring in our hospitals, urgicare centers, and nursing homes, as well as in individual residences. With the exception of those at the top, including health care administrators and most of the physicians, health care is a minefield of poor working conditions. Even nursing has been degraded and deskilled so much that the nursing shortage could be nearly filled simply by the return of disaffected nurses to their profession. At the request of the California Nurses Association, I spoke this summer to nurses in four Texas cities. I heard many tales of woe: sixteen hour days, two weeks straight of twelve-hour days, insane patient loads, constant cost-cutting that damages patient health, demeaning treatment by administrators, etc. Conditions only worsen as one goes down the health care occupation ladder.

Working Stiffs

Work in today's exploitative society takes its toll on mind and body. It saps our creativity, bores us to death, makes us anxious, encourages us to be manipulative, alienates us in multiple ways (from coworkers, from products, from ourselves), makes us party to the production of debased and dangerous products, subjects us to arbitrary authority, makes us sick, and injures us. I remember my dad saying, when emphysema (the result of too many cigarettes, too much asbestos, and too much silica dust) had sapped his health, that he hadn't expected retirement to be like this. He and how many hundreds of millions of others? It is not the CEO who suffers depression, hypertension, and heart attacks from being too long on the job; it is instead the assembly line worker, the secretary, the kitchen laborer. Those who cannot control their work hurt the most. And with all of these injuries of class, I haven't even touched upon the compound misery endured by black workers, Hispanic workers, women workers, gay workers, and workers without the proper national documents. And I have not described some of the worst types of labor: farm labor, domestic work, labor in recycling plants, and many others, which get truly demonic as we move outside the rich nations and into the poor ones. It is no wonder that people do not need much convincing to believe that happiness lies not in the workplace but in the shopping mall.

The daily debasement heaped upon working men and women breeds anger and rage. Often rage is turned inward and shows itself as depression, addiction, or suicide. Frequently it is directed against children, spouses, lovers, or against some great mass of "others," like immigrants, women, radical minorities, or gay people. But sometimes it is correctly aimed at the class enemy and takes the form of riots, sabotage, strikes, demonstrations, even revolution. And then the creativity bound and gagged for so long bursts forth as people try to take control of their labor and their lives. This is what I think of as the "miracle of class struggle."

I am not going to end by talking at length about how important it is to keep the struggles of the past fresh in the present, how it is necessary to educate the working class, of how it is essential to build a working-class movement and not just to organize workers into unions, about how there are any number of hopeful signs that such a movement can be built, of why we must always fan the flames of dissent and revolution. You have heard all this before.

Instead I am going to say something different. The injuries of class are deep and long lasting. The poor education that is the lot of most working-class children leaves lasting scars that will not be healed by a picket line. The love lost when the factory-working father spent too much time in bars does not come back after a demonstration. I have been a radical, highly educated and articulate, but the fears and anxieties of my working-class parents are like indelible tattoos on my psyche. The dullness of mind and weariness of body produced by assembly line, store, and office do not go away after the union comes to town. The prisoner might be freed but the horror of the prison cell lives on.

Wilhelm Reich, the German psychoanalyst, was kicked out of the psychoanalytic society because he was a communist. Ironically he was also expelled from the Communist Party because he was a therapist who believed that the minds of working people, ravaged by the injuries of class, would have to be healed. It would take real effort to help workers regain their humanity. I think Reich was right. We ignore the injuries of class at our peril.

My friend Sam Gindin, former chief economist for the Canadian Auto Workers, has argued for years that all labor organizing and all union and labor movement activities, in fact, all efforts to transform societies, must aim at developing the capacities of working men and women, their ability to take control of their lives and the larger society. This means, for example, that inside a union, there has to be as much rank-and-file democracy and control as possible, and inside workplaces there has to be an active network of shop stewards. The union must have a vibrant and empowering education program. Politically unions and all working-class organizations must aim to promote a working-class way of thinking about the world and must fight for any and all public programs that empower workers, from national health care to paid vacations and leaves for all to free adult education programs. Reducing hours of work must become central to labor's agenda as must the nature of work itself. The idea that our labor power is just another commodity must be rejected. Finally, all movements for radical social change must address aggressively the prison-industrial and military-industrial complexes. Imperialism, war, and a domestic police state are an unholy triad that magnify enormously the injuries of class.

[21]

Sports and Cultural Politics:
The Attraction of Modern Spectator Sports

Sut Jhally and Bill Livant

The socialist tradition is based upon a vision of a society of "freely associated producers," a society founded upon cooperative productive relations and the extension of cooperation to the whole of social life. Consequently, the socialist tradition has tended to view competitive productive relations and competition in social life negatively. Progress in social relations (the progress towards socialism) is seen as a movement away from competition and toward cooperation. Socialists evaluate social progress as the elimination, "the withering away," of competition from social life. The struggle for socialism is the struggle to remove the competitive fetters to cooperation: first and foremost the competition of classes.

It is because socialists wish to eliminate competition in practice (i.e., wish that it were not there) that they also tend to erase it in theory and examine presently existing competition through a "biased" haze. This makes it difficult to consider competition *dialectically*, to examine the mutual relations, the interdependence of competition and cooperation in any particular sphere of social life. Nowhere is this undialectical consideration of competition clearer than in the critical analysis of *sports*, one of the areas of social life in which competition is most prominent and visible and to which it seems intrinsic under present conditions. Sports are an area in which the repugnance of critical socialists to competition is most manifest. Indeed, for a long time even the very importance of sports was ignored. However, as spectator sports have become one of the most prevalent features of modern societies, radical thinkers have turned their critical attention to it (albeit largely to deplore it). Competition in sports is seen as a mirror reflection of capitalist productive and gender relations. Examined *culturally* mass-spectator televised professional sports are part of the system of legitimation of contemporary capitalism. As British

122 *Jhally and Livant*

cultural critic Garry Whannel writes in his book *Blowing the Whistle:* "Sport offers a way of seeing the world. It is part of the system of ideas that supports, sustains and reproduces capitalism. It offers a way of seeing the world that makes our very specific form of social organization seem natural, correct and inevitable" (1983, 27). Spectator sports thus are *part of the problem* of contemporary social life and, aside from a few derogatory comments, their analysis is not high on the agenda of a progressive cultural politics.

Within the domain of progressive publications, ZETA magazine, a Boston-based monthly, is therefore quite unique in that it has a semiregular column that deals with sports in a serious way, and in the June 1989 issue Matthew Goodman poses a fundamental question to those of us on the Left who like/watch/follow/enjoy sports: are U.S. sports worth supporting? Positing two views of sport, one based on cooperation and camaraderie, the other on greed, individualism, and competition, Goodman notes with dismay that American sports are being pushed more and more in the latter direction, and consequently (and sorrowfully) he is having serious doubts about his fanship. In raising these important questions, Goodman is raising the paradox that Ike Balbus identified as long ago as 1973 (in his review of Paul Hoch's *Rip-off the Big Game*) when he pointed to the phenomenon of the "radical as sports fan"—the person who criticizes all institutions of capitalist society but who still loves sports.

While Goodman has raised an important point, he may have posed the wrong question. It is not a matter of whether one should or should not support sports but what form the struggle over their definition should take. Unless one simply wishes to abandon sport as an area of contestation, the question is really one of *cultural politics:* are sports worth struggling over? We believe they are, because sports may not simply be part of the problem, but also *part of the solution* to the transition to a more just society. Above all sports are a realm of *popular pleasure* in contemporary life. It is tapping into the nature of the attraction that may give us an answer to the question concerning the role that sports can play in a progressive cultural politics. Indeed, we believe that at the heart of the attraction of modern sports lies a vision of *socialism* and *socialist competition*. The struggle is over how to recover presently existing competitive sports for a positive socialist vision and to show how this vision is itself central to the attraction to sports, to the love of sports in the population. This requires that we examine closely the way in which competition presents itself in sports and daily life as both different and identical.

The Difference Between Sports and Life: The Heaven of Sports

There is an intrinsic relation between sports and competition. Sports are fundamentally about competition. Any attempt to clarify the nature of sports and their immense appeal must clarify the nature of competition. To do this we must first put away our petit-bourgeois panic about competition and ask the important question, "how does competition appear to the population in sports compared with daily life such that people identify and seek refuge in sports competition?" There are three aspects to the comparison:

First, in daily life, competition is very rarely direct but is experienced in a *mediated* form. We compete for jobs, raises, promotions, for security, for status, against a foggy field of competitors whom we do not even know. Most of our behavior in markets is in just this situation. In sports, on the other hand, competition is most often *direct and unmediated*. We can see the competitors, we can see the interdependedness of their performances. The competitors and their interdependence seem to us direct, in contrast to the pea soup of mediations that mask our competition in daily life.

Second, in daily life, the *basis* of competition is obscure. We are mostly in the dark about what it takes to succeed at it, to win or even to survive. The process of capitalism itself constantly mystifies the basis of success, and constantly generates new mysteries. People have little secure basis that whatever they are doing will give them a better chance to succeed. The basis of competition is mystified. In sports the basis of competition seems to be present, to be open to observation. The rules are clear and there seems to an objective basis for the judgment of competition. This is rare in competition in daily life.

Third, in daily life, because the competition is mediated and because the basis of competition is obscure, our emotional involvement is highly *unpleasant*. We have to compete against competitors largely unknown, on an unknown basis, with little idea of what we have to do to win. And we *have* to compete. If we fail to compete, or if we do compete and then fail, very unpleasant things happen to us. We lose "face," money, position, power . . . even sexual attractiveness (for men). The field of competition is obscure, the penalties severe. Because we cannot see clearly, and because it matters so much, the state of our emotions is both intense and confused. The state of our emotions is unpleasant. But in sports this is not so. Our emotional involvement is highly *pleasant*. The competition seems clear to us and we think we know what it is about. When we as spectators enter it, identify with it, our emotions are focused and not muddled. Best of all, we can "play" and not lose, just because we are spectators.

The secret then of the immense attractiveness of sports is that they present a *spectacle of unmystified competition*. It is around this image that people unite. In sport, it seems to us, that unlike life, we can see how society works, we can see who are the competitors, we can see what "it takes" to win. To see these things has enormous effects on us. It makes us feel smart, it makes us feel sane. In short it makes us happy. Sports cannot show us how our society *really works*. But they can show us how we *desire* it to work. We desire a society of unmystified competition. The attraction of sports is founded upon its seeming clarification of the alienated relations of competition of modern society.

At the same time, these sports also socialize us into tolerating and enduring competition as we experience it in daily life, by encouraging us to conceive our chaotic, obscure conditions of daily competition along the model of sports competition. But what is this model and whence does it come? We have argued above that competition in sports seems to be unmystified and that we can "really know" how it works. Indeed, where in our everyday grapplings with competition are we granted the luxury, the clarity of an *instant replay,* a replay that gives us a basis to sit in judgment—*informed judgment*—not only on the players but on the very authorities constituted to judge the game? This constitutes power, the *power of reason.* (The controversy over whether or not to allow instant replays into the sport itself is itself very interesting, i.e., how to handle the contradiction between reason and con-stituted authority?) And we participate in this power of reason; it empowers *us.* Where in everyday capitalist life can we sit in judgment on the invisible powers who sit in judgment on us? The seeming reason of competition in sports empowers us in another way. Because the competition seems clear, *justice can be done.* The outcome is "fair," the win was "earned," the winner "deserved" to win. In sports competition, it seems to us that Reason prevails, Justice is done, and we can understand it all. And we hunger for this. Sports competition is the *Heaven* of competitive reason and justice, as life is its *Hell.* Hence sports are immensely attractive. They provide both an *escape* from Hell and a *socialization* into living with it. Hidden in our hunger for this Heaven is the hope that the present Hell could be remade in the image of Heaven. In fact, hidden in our love of sports is the hope of *socialism.*

We can see the great difference between competition in Sport and Life if we turn the tables. Try to imagine sports competition with the mystified characteristics we find in real life. We find it impossible to do. Sports would not work in such darkness. But capitalism does, day after day. This is the reason why our rulers propagate the image of competition in sports as indeed the image of competition in life. In every sphere of life (including war) Nixon, Reagan, and Bush reach for the language of sports to describe the most atrocious deeds. (To explain his in-transigence concerning negotiations during the Persian Gulf War, George Bush reverted to the explanation of "having a game plan and sticking by it" and the jock-culture machoism of "kicking ass." Indeed, especially during the early weeks of the war, the language of sports was very visible in media reports.) The Terrible Simplifiers "make life clearer" by describing them as sport. There is a good basis for this: sports competition *is* clearer. Hence our rulers try to get us to imagine real competition, our real darkness, with the clarified characteristics we find in sports competition. We are attracted to sports because their competition is different from our present social life. Sports are clear, our social life is dark. But we are forced to live that life whose ruling ideology only makes it darker. We are constantly told that the dark competition of our lives is as clear as sport.

The Identity of Sports and Life:
The Private Appropriation of Collective Activity

So far we have stressed the difference between competition in sports and daily life. But of course sport is ultimately a part of life. Where this life is dark there will be a limit to the light that sport can shed on the nature of competition. It is important to discover this limit, this "boundary of light from darkness," because it is in fact a boundary between *resistance* and *submission* to the system of social life in the sphere of sport. To discover this boundary we need to separate the *division of labor* in sport from its *appropriation*. We noted above that in sports one can see the competition in an unmediated fashion. In fact, examined closely, we can see that competition (any competition) is a *collective* activity, a collective labor in which the contributions of the winner and the loser are interdependent. The collective nature of competition is central to the experience of sports. One-sided contests in which the collective activity is subordinated are uninteresting. We need only ask the television networks about the drop in viewers during an event as one side overwhelms the other. As all professional sports leagues know, it is competitive balance that is vital to the health and profitability of a league. (In the United States the draft system is the most obvious tool towards this competitive balance.) The great sports events of our culture are those that have balanced competition at their heart.

For example, one of the most historic and memorable tennis matches in recent history was the 1980 Wimbledon final in which Bjorn Borg defeated John McEnroe. What that match indicated was not that Borg was a great player but just how great in fact he was. Borg needed McEnroe to push him to new heights of achievement. If Borg had routinely won in four sets as at one time looked likely, that match would not stand out in our collective sports memory. But because McEnroe won the fourth set tiebreaker 18–16, he forced Borg to be even better. Whatever *beauty* we perceive in the realm of sports is dependent on both competitors. In his superb autobiography *The Game,* Ken Dryden, ex-goaltender for the Montréal Canadiens hockey team, writes of how his greatest moments occurred against Boston teams, that without the tremendous opposition they provided he could not have performed as he did. He needed their competition for the fulfillment of his own dreams.

What people are attracted to in sports then is the beauty of collective activity. They are drawn to the *process* of competition rather than to its results. We see beauty as a property of the personality, of the competitor, *in competition*. Not apart from the competition but within it. Beauty therefore is a property *of the competition* which is manifest through the competitors. When we perceive beauty in sports, the beauty of the competitors is the *figure,* the beauty of the competition is the *ground*.

In a capitalist society, however, it is the private appropriation of social labor that is the determining feature, and hence in capitalized sports it is the winners who appropriate the results of the process of competition. The winners go on to something better. They will appear again next week. They can convert their winning notoriety into sponsorship of commodities and so reap greater benefits and even more visibility for their appropriation of the results of collective activity. The losers disappear from view, their fate too desperate to be contemplated. As George Allen remarked in reflecting the ethos of U.S. culture: "Losing is worse than death. You have to live with losing." The more this private appropriation occurs, the more the

126   *Jhally and Livant*

very existence of this ground, not to speak of its collective character, is suppressed and the more the beauty is presented to us *only* as the property *of the competitors*. It is the private nature of appropriation that suppresses the collective character of beauty. It suppresses the beautiful character of the competitive *process* and reproduces beauty as an "attribute" of the competing *subjects*.

The rejection of competitive sports by critical socialists is based upon a failure to distinguish the process from the appropriation of its results. When we cannot distinguish between the process and the competitors, it will appear to us that properties that belong to the labor process as such belong only to the competitors. The labor process, the cooperative-competitive process, then appears only as a scene in which these *pre-existing* properties of the competitors simply display themselves. Hence, what is really *social* labor appears decomposed into merely *individual* labor. Because the winner takes all it appears that he or she does all, a process that we can label as the "personalization of competition."

Personalization might almost be called a U.S. trademark, a concept at the core of all its major cultural conceptions. It is inevitable in a society that virtually denies that classes exist. This is the point of identity between our sports and our social life. Sports may be clear and open to everyone in specifying their competitors, in framing their rules, in recording and measuring their process and their outcomes. In all this they make competition "light." But they share the mystification, they reproduce the "darkness" of competition in the personalization of competition.

The North American sports-media complex embodies a highly *capitalized* system of sport. The more capitalized is sport, the greater the contradiction between the cooperative labor of the competitive process in sport and the private appropriation of its result. The greater this contradiction, the more the image of competition is personalized. This process of personalization is important; it forms the major basis on which the audience identifies with the sport. A particularly horrendous example is the behavior of many parents, contrasted with their children, in Little League. The kids, as often as not, focus on the competition. They want to play the game. But the parents do not. Wedded to the personification of competition is parental attachment to the child; perhaps through the child to the parent's own ego. The kids wish to be left alone to play and enjoy the game. The innocent want the process while their parents want the result.

To summarize: the image of competition in sport, unlike its image almost everywhere else, is an image of *fair* competition. This is not merely an image; to an important degree sport *embodies* this. But this is a limited fairness. Sports reproduce the social mystification of competition by personalizing a process of social cooperation. In fact, we may argue, that in this fundamental respect, sports are "darker" than competition in everyday life. Precisely because sports competition is "fair," it personalizes competition *more* than does everyday competition, in all its darkness. Thus sports are an area of capitalist social life with contradictory possibilities for changing that life. And we can only begin to grasp the outlines of the nature of socialist sport and socialist competition. Socialist competition in sport

Remarx   127

is *uncapitalized* competition. As such, it makes manifest, makes visible what now must be extracted from the present structure of competition by analytical labor—the actual basis of competition as cooperative social labor. Such *unalienated, unmystified competition* is in fact compatible with the fact that competition continues under socialism: from each according to their ability, to each according to their work.

The Battle for Definitions of Sports

In this paper we have stressed the progressive possibilities that exist in sports. The visions that we see in sports, the visions that attract us to it (and there are others we have not listed, such as the cooperation involved in team sports), are visions of what a progressive socialist society would look like. Socialists should take advantage of these possibilities, for at the very heart of the mass spectacles that are designed to narcotize the population from open rebellion are images of what a transformed capitalism could look like. Sports provide images of what competition and cooperation would look like in another social setting. Role models with these potentialities should not be ignored. The definitions of what sports are about are definitions that should be fought and struggled over. As Gramsci noted, the "superstructures" are the *site* of class struggle and we should not ignore an institution that shows in spectacular fashion the nature of a progressive society that might follow the present one. We should especially not ignore this possibility when people identify themselves so strongly with that world. If only the nature of the attraction could be made clear and a course outlined where life would imitate in a true fashion the utopian dream of sports. That is the political struggle over sports. It is one of the crucial sites of a progressive cultural politics.

References

Balbus, I. 1973. "The American Game of Life." *The Nation* (7 May).
Dryden, K. 1983. *The Game*. Toronto: Totem.
Whannel, G. 1983. *Blowing the Whistle*. London: Pluto Press.

Part V
Culture and Religion

[22]

The Culture Industry:
Enlightenment as Mass Deception

Max Horkheimer and Theodor W. Adorno
Translated by Edmund Jephcott

The sociological view that the loss of support from objective religion and the disintegration of the last precapitalist residues, in conjunction with technical and social differentiation and specialization, have given rise to cultural chaos is refuted by daily experience. Culture today is infecting everything with sameness. Film, radio, and magazines form a system. Each branch of culture is unanimous within itself and all are unanimous together. Even the aesthetic manifestations of political opposites proclaim the same inflexible rhythm. The* decorative administrative and exhibition buildings of industry differ little between authoritarian and other countries. The bright monumental structures shooting up on all sides show off the systematic ingenuity of the state-spanning combines, toward which the unfettered entrepreneurial system, whose monuments are the dismal residential and commercial blocks in the surrounding areas of desolate cities, was already swiftly advancing. The older buildings around the concrete centers already look like slums, and the new bungalows on the outskirts, like the flimsy structures at international trade fairs, sing the praises of technical progress while inviting their users to throw them away after short use like tin cans. But the town-planning projects, which are supposed to perpetuate individuals as autonomous units in hygienic small apartments, subjugate them only more completely to their adversary, the total power of capital.* Just as the occupants of city centers are uniformly summoned there for purposes of work and leisure, as producers and consumers, so the living cells crystallize into homogenous, well-organized complexes. The conspicuous unity of macrocosm and microcosm confronts human beings with a model of their culture: the false identity of universal and particular. All mass culture under monopoly is identical, and the contours of its skeleton, the conceptual armature fabricated by monopoly, are beginning to stand out. Those in charge no longer take much trouble to conceal the structure, the power of which increases the more bluntly its existence is admitted. Films and radio no longer need to present themselves as art. The truth that they are nothing but business is used as an ideology to legitimize the trash they intentionally produce. They call themselves industries, and the published figures for their directors' incomes quell any doubts about the social necessity of their finished products.

Interested parties like to explain the culture industry in technological terms. Its millions of participants, they argue, demand reproduction processes which inevitably lead to the use of standard products to meet the same needs at countless locations. The technical antithesis between few production centers and widely dispersed reception necessitates organization and planning by those in control. The standardized forms, it is claimed, were originally derived from the needs of the consumers: that is why they are accepted with so little resistance. In reality, a cycle of manipulation and retroactive need is unifying the system ever more tightly. What is not mentioned is that the basis on which technology is gaining power over society is the power of those whose economic position in society is strongest.* Technical rationality today is the rationality of domination. It is the compulsive character of a society alienated from itself. Automobiles, bombs, and films hold the totality together until their leveling element demonstrates its power against the very system of injustice it served. For the present the technology of the culture industry confines itself to standardization and mass production and sacrifices what once distinguished the logic of the work from that of society. These adverse effects, however, should not be attributed to the internal laws of technology itself but to its function within the economy today.* Any need which might escape the central control is repressed by that of individual consciousness. The step from telephone to radio has clearly distinguished the roles. The former liberally permitted the participant to play the role of subject. The latter democratically makes everyone equally into listeners, in order to expose them in authoritarian fashion to the same programs put out by different

96   The Culture Industry

stations. No mechanism of reply has been developed, and private transmissions are condemned to unfreedom. They confine themselves to the apocryphal sphere of "amateurs," who, in any case, are organized from above. Any trace of spontaneity in the audience of the official radio is steered and absorbed into a selection of specializations by talent-spotters, performance competitions, and sponsored events of every kind. The talents belong to the operation long before they are put on show; otherwise they would not conform so eagerly. The mentality of the public, which allegedly and actually favors the system of the culture industry, is a part of the system, not an excuse for it. If a branch of art follows the same recipe as one far removed from it in terms of its medium and subject matter; if the dramatic denouement in radio "soap operas"* is used as an instructive example of how to solve technical difficulties—which are mastered no less in "jam sessions" than at the highest levels of jazz—or if a movement from Beethoven is loosely "adapted" in the same way as a Tolstoy novel is adapted for film, the pretext of meeting the public's spontaneous wishes is mere hot air. An explanation in terms of the specific interests of the technical apparatus and its personnel would be closer to the truth, provided that apparatus were understood in all its details as a part of the economic mechanism of selection.* Added to this is the agreement, or at least the common determination, of the executive powers to produce or let pass nothing which does not conform to their tables, to their concept of the consumer, or, above all, to themselves.

If the objective social tendency of this age is incarnated in the obscure subjective intentions of board chairmen, this is primarily the case in the most powerful sectors of industry: steel, petroleum, electricity, chemicals. Compared to them the culture monopolies are weak and dependent. They have to keep in with the true wielders of power, to ensure that their sphere of mass society, the specific product of which still has too much of cozy liberalism and Jewish intellectualism about it, is not subjected to a series of purges.* The dependence of the most powerful broadcasting company on the electrical industry, or of film on the banks, characterizes the whole sphere, the individual sectors of which are themselves economically intertwined. Everything is so tightly clustered that the concentration of intellect reaches a level where it overflows the demarcations between company names and technical sectors. The relentless unity of the culture industry bears witness to the emergent unity of politics. Sharp distinctions like those between A and B films, or between short stories published in magazines in different price segments, do not so much reflect real differences as assist in the classification, organization, and identification of consumers. Something is provided for everyone so that no one can escape; differences are hammered home and propagated. The hierarchy of serial qualities purveyed to the public serves only to quantify it more completely. Everyone is supposed to behave spontaneously according to a "level" determined by indices and to select the category of mass product manufactured for their type. On the charts of research organizations, indistinguishable from those of political propaganda, consumers are divided up as statistical material into red, green, and blue areas according to income group.

The schematic nature of this procedure is evident from the fact that the mechanically differentiated products are ultimately all the same. That the difference between the models of Chrysler and General Motors is fundamentally illusory is known by any child, who is fascinated by that very difference. The advantages and disadvantages debated by enthusiasts serve only to perpetuate the appearance of competition and choice. It is no different with the offerings of Warner Brothers and Metro Goldwyn Mayer. But the differences, even between the more expensive and cheaper products from the same firm, are shrinking—in cars to the different number of cylinders, engine capacity, and details of the gadgets, and in films to the different number of stars, the expense lavished on technology, labor and costumes, or the use of the latest psychological formulae. The unified standard of value consists in the level of conspicuous production, the amount of investment put on show. The budgeted differences of value in the culture industry have nothing to do with actual differences, with the meaning of the product itself. The technical media, too, are being engulfed by an insatiable uniformity. Television aims at a synthesis of radio and film, delayed only for as long as the interested parties cannot agree. Such a synthesis, with its unlimited possibilities, promises to intensify the impoverishment of the aesthetic material so radically that the identity of all industrial cultural products, still scantily disguised today, will triumph openly tomorrow in a mocking fulfillment of Wagner's dream of the total art work. The accord between word, image, and music is achieved so much more perfectly than in *Tristan* because the sensuous elements, which compliantly document only the surface of social reality, are produced in prin-

98   The Culture Industry

ciple within the same technical work process, the unity of which they express as their true content. This work process integrates all the elements of production, from the original concept of the novel, shaped by its sidelong glance at film,* to the last sound effect. It is the triumph of invested capital. To impress the omnipotence of capital on the hearts of expropriated job candidates as the power of their true master is the purpose of all films, regardless of the plot selected by the production directors.

Even during their leisure time, consumers must orient themselves according to the unity of production. The active contribution which Kantian schematism still expected of subjects—that they should, from the first, relate sensuous multiplicity to fundamental concepts—is denied to the subject by industry. It purveys schematism as its first service to the customer. According to Kantian schematism, a secret mechanism within the psyche preformed immediate data to fit them into the system of pure reason. That secret has now been unraveled. Although the operations of the mechanism appear to be planned by those who supply the data, the culture industry, the planning is in fact imposed on the industry by the inertia of a society irrational despite all its rationalization, and this calamitous tendency, in passing through the agencies of business,* takes on the shrewd intentionality peculiar to them. For the consumer there is nothing left to classify, since the classification has already been preempted by the schematism of production. This dreamless· art for the people fulfils the dreamy idealism which went too far for idealism in its critical form. Everything comes from consciousness—from that of God for Malebranche and Berkeley, and from earthly production management for mass art. Not only do hit songs, stars, and soap operas conform to types recurring cyclically as rigid invariants, but the specific content of productions, the seemingly variable element, is itself derived from those types. The details become interchangeable. The brief interval sequence which has proved catchy in a hit song, the hero's temporary disgrace which he accepts as a "good sport," the wholesome slaps the heroine receives from the strong hand of the male star, his plain-speaking abruptness toward the pampered heiress, are, like all the details, ready-made clichés, to be used here and there as desired and always completely defined by the purpose they serve within the schema. To confirm the schema by acting as its constituents is their sole *raison d'être*. In a film, the outcome can invariably be predicted at the start—who will be rewarded, punished, forgotten—and in light music the prepared ear can always guess the continuation after the first bars of a hit song and is gratified when it actually occurs. The average choice of words in a short story must not be tampered with. The gags and effects are no less calculated than their framework. They are managed by special experts, and their slim variety is specifically tailored to the office pigeonhole. The culture industry has developed in conjunction with the predominance of the effect, the tangible performance, the technical detail, over the work, which once carried the idea and was liquidated with it. By emancipating itself, the detail had become refractory; from Romanticism to Expressionism it had rebelled as unbridled expression, as the agent of opposition, against organization. In music, the individual harmonic effect had obliterated awareness of the form as a whole; in painting the particular detail had obscured the overall composition; in the novel psychological penetration had blurred the architecture. Through totality, the culture industry is putting an end to all that. Although operating only with effects, it subdues their unruliness and subordinates them to the formula which supplants the work. It crushes equally the whole and the parts. The whole confronts the details in implacable detachment, somewhat like the career of a successful man, in which everything serves to illustrate and demonstrate a success which, in fact, it is no more than the sum of those idiotic events. The so-called leading idea is a filing compartment which creates order, not connections. Lacking both contrast and relatedness, the whole and the detail look alike. Their harmony, guaranteed in advance, mocks the painfully achieved harmony of the great bourgeois works of art. In Germany even the most carefree films of democracy were overhung already by the graveyard stillness of dictatorship.

The whole world is passed through the filter of the culture industry. The familiar experience of the moviegoer, who perceives the street outside as a continuation of the film he has just left, because the film seeks strictly to reproduce the world of everyday perception, has become the guideline of production. The more densely and completely its techniques duplicate empirical objects, the more easily it creates the illusion that the world outside is a seamless extension of the one which has been revealed in the cinema. Since the abrupt introduction of the sound film, mechanical duplication has become entirely subservient to this objective. According to this tendency, life is to be made indistinguishable from the sound film. Far

100 *The Culture Industry*

more strongly than the theatre of illusion, film denies its audience any dimension in which they might roam freely in imagination—contained by the film's framework but unsupervised by its precise actualities—without losing the thread; thus it trains those exposed to it to identify film directly with reality. The withering of imagination and spontaneity in the consumer of culture today need not be traced back to psychological mechanisms. The products themselves, especially the most characteristic, the sound film, cripple those faculties through their objective makeup. They are so constructed that their adequate comprehension requires a quick, observant, knowledgeable cast of mind but positively debars the spectator from thinking, if he is not to miss the fleeting facts. This kind of alertness is so ingrained that it does not even need to be activated in particular cases, while still repressing the powers of imagination. Anyone who is so absorbed by the world of the film, by gesture, image, and word, that he or she is unable to supply that which would have made it a world in the first place, does not need to be entirely transfixed by the special operations of the machinery at the moment of the performance. The required qualities of attention have become so familiar from other films and other culture products already known to him or her that they appear automatically. The power of industrial society* is imprinted on people once and for all. The products of the culture industry are such that they can be alertly consumed even in a state of distraction. But each one is a model of the gigantic economic machinery,* which, from the first, keeps everyone on their toes, both at work and in the leisure time which resembles it. In any sound film or any radio broadcast something is discernible which cannot be attributed as a social effect to any one of them, but to all together. Each single manifestation of the culture industry inescapably reproduces human beings as what the whole has made them. And all its agents, from the producer to the women's organizations, are on the alert to ensure that the simple reproduction of mind does not lead on to the expansion of mind.

The complaints of art historians and cultural attorneys over the exhaustion of the energy which created artistic style in the West are frighteningly unfounded. The routine translation of everything, even of what has not yet been thought, into the schema of mechanical reproducibility goes beyond the rigor and scope of any true style—the concept with which culture lovers idealize the precapitalist past as an organic era. No

Palestrina could have eliminated the unprepared or unresolved dissonance more puristically than the jazz arranger excludes any phrase which does not exactly fit the jargon. If he jazzes up Mozart, he changes the music not only where it is too difficult or serious but also where the melody is merely harmonized differently, indeed, more simply, than is usual today. No medieval patron of architecture can have scrutinized the subjects of church windows and sculptures more suspiciously than the studio hierarchies examine a plot by Balzac or Victor Hugo before it receives the imprimatur of feasibility. No cathedral chapter could have assigned the grimaces and torments of the damned to their proper places in the order of divine love more scrupulously than production managers decide the position of the torture of the hero or the raised hem of the leading lady's dress within the litany of the big film. The explicit and implicit, exoteric and esoteric catalog of what is forbidden and what is tolerated* is so extensive that it not only defines the area left free but wholly controls it. Even the most minor details are modeled according to this lexicon. Like its adversary, avantgarde art, the culture industry defines its own language positively, by means of prohibitions applied to its syntax and vocabulary. The permanent compulsion to produce new effects which yet remain bound to the old schema, becoming additional rules, merely increases the power of the tradition which the individual effect seeks to escape. Every phenomenon is by now so thoroughly imprinted by the schema that nothing can occur that does not bear in advance the trace of the jargon, that is not seen at first glance to be approved. But the true masters, as both producers and reproducers, are those who speak the jargon with the same free-and-easy relish as if it were the language it has long since silenced. Such is the industry's ideal of naturalness. It asserts itself more imperiously the more the perfected technology reduces the tension between the culture product and everyday existence. The paradox of routine travestied as nature is detectable in every utterance of the culture industry, and in many is quite blatant. A jazz musician who has to play a piece of serious music, Beethoven's simplest minuet, involuntarily syncopates, and condescends to start on the beat only with a superior smile. Such "naturalness," complicated by the ever more pervasive and exorbitant claims of the specific medium, constitutes the new style, "a system of nonculture to which one might even concede a certain 'unity of style' if it made any sense to speak of a stylized barbarism."[1]

102   The Culture Industry

The general influence of this stylization may already be more binding than the official rules and prohibitions; a hit song is treated more leniently today if it does not respect the thirty-two bars or the compass of the ninth than if it includes even the most elusive melodic or harmonic detail which falls outside the idiom. Orson Welles is forgiven all his offences against the usages of the craft because, as calculated rudeness, they confirm the validity of the system all the more zealously. The compulsion of the technically conditioned idiom which the stars and directors must produce as second nature, so that the nation may make it theirs, relates to nuances so fine as to be almost as subtle as the devices used in a work of the avant-garde, where, unlike those of the hit song, they serve truth. The rare ability to conform punctiliously to the obligations of the idiom of naturalness in all branches of the culture industry becomes the measure of expertise. As in logical positivism, what is said and how it is said must be verifiable against everyday speech. The producers are experts. The idiom demands the most prodigious productive powers, which it absorbs and squanders. Satanically, it has rendered cultural conservatism's distinction between genuine and artificial style obsolete. A style might possibly be called artificial if it had been imposed from outside against the resistance of the intrinsic tendencies of form. But in the culture industry the subject matter itself, down to its smallest elements, springs from the same apparatus as the jargon into which it is absorbed. The deals struck between the art specialists and the sponsor and censor over some all-too-unbelievable lie tell us less about internal, aesthetic tensions than about a divergence of interests. The reputation of the specialist, in which a last residue of actual autonomy still occasionally finds refuge, collides with the business policy of the church or the industrial combine producing the culture commodity. By its own nature, however, the matter has already been reified as negotiable even before the various agencies come into conflict. Even before Zanuck* acquired her, Saint Bernadette gleamed in the eye of her writer as an advert aimed at all the relevant consortia. To this the impulses of form have been reduced. As a result, the style of the culture industry, which has no resistant material to overcome, is at the same time the negation of style. The reconciliation of general and particular, of rules and the specific demands of the subject, through which alone style takes on substance, is nullified by the absence of tension between the poles: "the extremes which touch" have become a murky identity in which the general can replace the particular and vice versa.

Nevertheless, this caricature of style reveals something about the genuine style of the past. The concept of a genuine style becomes transparent in the culture industry as the aesthetic equivalent of power. The notion of style as a merely aesthetic regularity is a retrospective fantasy of Romanticism. The unity of style not only of the Christian Middle Ages but of the Renaissance expresses the different structures of social coercion in those periods, not the obscure experience of the subjects, in which the universal was locked away. The great artists were never those whose works embodied style in its least fractured, most perfect form but those who adopted style as a rigor to set against the chaotic expression of suffering, as a negative truth. In the style of these works expression took on the strength without which existence is dissipated unheard. Even works which are called classical, like the music of Mozart, contain objective tendencies which resist the style they incarnate. Up to Schönberg and Picasso, great artists have been mistrustful of style, which at decisive points has guided them less than the logic of the subject matter. What the Expressionists and Dadaists attacked in their polemics, the untruth of style as such, triumphs today in the vocal jargon of the crooner, in the adept grace of the film star, and even in the mastery of the photographic shot of a farm laborer's hovel. In every work of art, style is a promise. In being absorbed through style into the dominant form of universality, into the current musical, pictorial, or verbal idiom, what is expressed seeks to be reconciled with the idea of the true universal. This promise of the work of art to create truth by impressing its unique contours on the socially transmitted forms is as necessary as it is hypocritical. By claiming to anticipate fulfillment through their aesthetic derivatives, it posits the real forms of the existing order as absolute. To this extent the claims of art are always also ideology. Yet it is only in its struggle with tradition, a struggle precipitated in style, that art can find expression for suffering. The moment in the work of art by which it transcends reality cannot, indeed, be severed from style; that moment, however, does not consist in achieved harmony, in the questionable unity of form and content, inner and outer, individual and society, but in those traits in which the discrepancy emerges, in the necessary failure of the passionate striving for identity. Instead of exposing itself to this failure, in which the style of the great work of art has always negated itself, the inferior work has relied on its similarity to others, the surrogate of identity. The culture industry has finally posited this imitation as absolute. Being nothing other than style, it divulges style's secret: obedience to the social

104 *The Culture Industry*

hierarchy. Aesthetic barbarism today is accomplishing what has threatened intellectual formations since they were brought together as culture and neutralized. To speak about culture always went against the grain of culture. The general designation "culture" already contains, virtually, the process of identifying, cataloging, and classifying which imports culture into the realm of administration. Only what has been industrialized, rigorously subsumed, is fully adequate to this concept of culture. Only by subordinating all branches of intellectual production equally to the single purpose of imposing on the senses of human beings, from the time they leave the factory in the evening to the time they clock on in the morning, the imprint of the work routine which they must sustain throughout the day, does this culture mockingly fulfill the notion of a unified culture which the philosophers of the individual personality held out against mass culture.

The culture industry, the most inflexible style of all, thus proves to be the goal of the very liberalism which is criticized for its lack of style. Not only did its categories and contents originate in the liberal sphere, in domesticated naturalism no less than in the operetta and the revue, but the modern culture combines are the economic area in which a piece of the circulation sphere otherwise in the process of disintegration, together with the corresponding entrepreneurial types, still tenuously survives. In that area people can still make their way, provided they do not look too closely at their true purpose and are willing to be compliant. Anyone who resists can survive only by being incorporated. Once registered as diverging from the culture industry, they belong to it as the land reformer does to capitalism. Realistic indignation is the trademark of those with a new idea to sell. Public authority in the present society* allows only those complaints to be heard in which the attentive ear can discern the prominent figure under whose protection the rebel is suing for peace. The more immeasurable the gulf between chorus and leaders, the more certainly is there a place among the latter for anyone who demonstrates superiority by well-organized dissidence. In this way liberalism's tendency to give free rein to its ablest members survives in the culture industry. To open that industry to clever people is the function of the otherwise largely regulated market, in which, even in its heyday, freedom was the freedom of the stupid to starve, in art as elsewhere. Not for nothing did the system of the culture industry originate in the liberal industrial countries, just as all its characteristic media, especially cinema, radio, jazz, and magazines, also triumph there. Its progress, however, stems from the general laws of capital. Gaumont and Pathé,* Ullstein and Hugenberg* did not follow the international trend to their own disadvantage; Europe's economic dependence on the USA after the war and the inflation also made its contribution. The belief that the barbarism of the culture industry is a result of "cultural lag," of the backwardness of American consciousness in relation to the state of technology, is quite illusory. Prefascist Europe was backward in relation to the monopoly of culture. But it was precisely to such backwardness that intellectual activity owed a remnant of autonomy, its last exponents their livelihood, however meager. In Germany the incomplete permeation of life by democratic control had a paradoxical effect. Many areas were still exempt from the market mechanism which had been unleashed in Western countries. The German educational system, including the universities, the artistically influential theatres, the great orchestras, and the museums were under patronage. The political powers, the state and the local authorities who inherited such institutions from absolutism, had left them a degree of independence from the power of the market as the princes and feudal lords had done up to the nineteenth century. This stiffened the backbone of art in its late phase against the verdict of supply and demand, heightening its resistance far beyond its actual degree of protection. In the market itself the homage paid to not yet marketable artistic quality was converted into purchasing power, so that reputable literary and musical publishers could support authors who brought in little more than the respect of connoisseurs. Only the dire and incessant threat of incorporation into commercial life as aesthetic experts finally brought the artists to heel. In former times they signed their letters, like Kant and Hume, "Your most obedient servant," while undermining the foundations of throne and altar. Today they call heads of government by their first names and are subject, in every artistic impulse, to the judgment of their illiterate principals. The analysis offered by de Tocqueville a hundred years ago has been fully borne out in the meantime. Under the private monopoly of culture tyranny does indeed "leave the body free and sets to work directly on the soul. The ruler no longer says: 'Either you think as I do or you die.' He says: 'You are free not to think as I do; your life, your property—all that you shall keep. But from this day on you will

106   *The Culture Industry*

be a stranger among us.'"[2] Anyone who does not conform is condemned to an economic impotence which is prolonged in the intellectual powerlessness of the eccentric loner. Disconnected from the mainstream, he is easily convicted of inadequacy. Whereas the mechanism of supply and demand is today disintegrating in material production, in the superstructure it acts as a control on behalf of the rulers. The consumers are the workers and salaried employees, the farmers and petty bourgeois. Capitalist production hems them in so tightly, in body and soul, that they unresistingly succumb to whatever is proffered to them. However, just as the ruled have always taken the morality dispensed to them by the rulers more seriously than the rulers themselves, the defrauded masses today cling to the myth of success still more ardently than the successful. They, too, have their aspirations. They insist unwaveringly on the ideology by which they are enslaved. The pernicious love of the common people for the harm done to them outstrips even the cunning of the authorities. It surpasses the rigor of the Hays Office,* just as, in great epochs, it has inspired renewed zeal in greater agencies directed against it, the terror of the tribunals. It calls for Mickey Rooney* rather than the tragic Garbo, Donald Duck rather than Betty Boop. The industry bows to the vote it has itself rigged. The incidental costs to the firm which cannot turn a profit from its contract with a declining star are legitimate costs for the system as a whole. By artfully sanctioning the demand for trash, the system inaugurates total harmony. Connoisseurship and expertise are proscribed as the arrogance of those who think themselves superior, whereas culture distributes its privileges democratically to all. Under the ideological truce between them, the conformism of the consumers, like the shamelessness of the producers they sustain, can have a good conscience. Both content themselves with the reproduction of sameness.

Unending sameness also governs the relationship to the past. What is new in the phase of mass culture compared to that of late liberalism is the exclusion of the new. The machine is rotating on the spot. While it already determines consumption, it rejects anything untried as a risk. In film, any manuscript which is not reassuringly based on a best-seller is viewed with mistrust. That is why there is incessant talk of ideas, novelty and surprises, of what is both totally familiar and has never existed before. Tempo and dynamism are paramount. Nothing is allowed to stay as it was, everything must be endlessly in motion. For only the universal victory of

Enlightenment as Mass Deception 107

the rhythm of mechanical production and reproduction promises that nothing will change, that nothing unsuitable will emerge. To add anything to the proven cultural inventory would be too speculative. The frozen genres—sketch, short story, problem film, hit song—represent the average of late liberal taste threateningly imposed as a norm. The most powerful of the culture agencies, who work harmoniously with others of their kind as only managers do, whether they come from the ready-to-wear trade or* college, have long since reorganized and rationalized the objective mind. It is as if some omnipresent agency* had reviewed the material and issued an authoritative catalog tersely listing the products available. The ideal forms are inscribed in the cultural heavens where they were already numbered by Plato—indeed, were only numbers, incapable of increase or change.

Amusement and all the other elements of the culture industry existed long before the industry itself. Now they have been taken over from above and brought fully up to date. The culture industry can boast of having energetically accomplished and elevated to a principle the often inept transposition of art to the consumption sphere, of having stripped amusement of its obtrusive naiveties and improved the quality of its commodities. The more all-embracing the culture industry has become, the more pitilessly it has forced the outsider into either bankruptcy or a syndicate; at the same time it has become more refined and elevated, becoming finally a synthesis of Beethoven and the Casino de Paris.* Its victory is twofold: what is destroyed as truth outside its sphere can be reproduced indefinitely within it as lies. "Light" art as such, entertainment, is not a form of decadence. Those who deplore it as a betrayal of the ideal of pure expression harbor illusions about society.* The purity of bourgeois art, hypostatized as a realm of freedom contrasting to material praxis, was bought from the outset with the exclusion of the lower class; and art keeps faith with the cause of that class, the true universal, precisely by freeing itself from the purposes of the false. Serious art has denied itself to those for whom the hardship and oppression of life make a mockery of seriousness and who must be glad to use the time not spent at the production line in being simply carried along. Light art has accompanied autonomous art as its shadow. It is the social bad conscience of serious art. The truth which the latter could not apprehend because of its social premises gives the former an appearance of objective justification. The split between them is

108   *The Culture Industry*

itself the truth: it expresses at least the negativity of the culture which is the sum of both spheres. The antithesis can be reconciled least of all by absorbing light art into serious or vice versa. That, however, is what the culture industry attempts. The eccentricity of the circus, the peep show, or the brothel in relation to society is as embarrassing to it as that of Schönberg and Karl Kraus. The leading jazz musician Benny Goodman therefore has to appear with the Budapest String Quartet, more pedantic rhythmically than any amateur clarinetist, while the quartet play with the saccharine monotony of Guy Lombardo.* What is significant is not crude ignorance, stupidity or lack of polish. The culture industry has abolished the rubbish of former times by imposing its own perfection, by prohibiting and domesticating dilettantism, while itself incessantly committing the blunders without which the elevated style cannot be conceived. What is new, however, is that the irreconcilable elements of culture, art, and amusement have been subjected equally to the concept of purpose and thus brought under a single false denominator: the totality of the culture industry. Its element is repetition. The fact that its characteristic innovations are in all cases mere improvements to mass production is not extraneous to the system. With good reason the interest of countless consumers is focused on the technology, not on the rigidly repeated, threadbare and half-abandoned content. The social power revered by the spectators manifests itself more effectively in the technically enforced ubiquity of stereotypes than in the stale ideologies which the ephemeral contents have to endorse.

Nevertheless, the culture industry remains the entertainment business. Its control of consumers is mediated by entertainment, and its hold will not be broken by outright dictate but by the hostility inherent in the principle of entertainment to anything which is more than itself. Since the tendencies of the culture industry are turned into the flesh and blood of the public by the social process as a whole, those tendencies are reinforced by the survival of the market in the industry. Demand has not yet been replaced by simple obedience. The major reorganization of the film industry shortly before the First World War, the material precondition for its expansion, was a deliberate adaptation to needs of the public registered at the ticket office, which were hardly thought worthy of consideration in the pioneering days of the screen. That view is still held by the captains of the film industry, who accept only more or less phenomenal box-office success as evidence and prudently ignore the counterevidence, truth. Their ideology is business. In this they are right to the extent that the power of the culture industry lies in its unity with fabricated need and not in simple antithesis to it—or even in the antithesis between omnipotence and powerlessness. Entertainment is the prolongation of work under late capitalism. It is sought by those who want to escape the mechanized labor process so that they can cope with it again. At the same time, however, mechanization has such power over leisure and its happiness, determines so thoroughly the fabrication of entertainment commodities, that the off-duty worker can experience nothing but after-images of the work process itself. The ostensible content is merely a faded foreground; what is imprinted is the automated sequence of standardized tasks. The only escape from the work process in factory and office is through adaptation to it in leisure time. This is the incurable sickness of all entertainment. Amusement congeals into boredom, since, to be amusement, it must cost no effort and therefore moves strictly along the well-worn grooves of association. The spectator must need no thoughts of his own: the product prescribes each reaction, not through any actual coherence—which collapses once exposed to thought—but through signals. Any logical connection presupposing mental capacity is scrupulously avoided. Developments are to emerge from the directly preceding situation, not from the idea of the whole. There is no plot which could withstand the screenwriters' eagerness to extract the maximum effect from the individual scene. Finally, even the schematic formula seems dangerous, since it provides some coherence of meaning, however meager, when only meaninglessness is acceptable. Often the plot is willfully denied the development called for by characters and theme under the old schema. Instead, the next step is determined by what the writers take to be their most effective idea. Obtusely ingenious surprises disrupt the plot. The product's tendency to fall back perniciously on the pure nonsense which, as buffoonery and clowning, was a legitimate part of popular art up to Chaplin and the Marx brothers, emerges most strikingly in the less sophisticated genres. Whereas the films of Greer Garson and Bette Davis can still derive some claim to a coherent plot from the unity of the socio-psychological case represented, the tendency to subvert meaning has taken over completely in the text of novelty songs,* suspense films, and cartoons. The idea itself, like objects in comic and horror films, is massacred and mutilated. Novelty songs have always lived on con-

110 *The Culture Industry*

tempt for meaning, which, as both ancestors and descendants of psychoanalysis, they reduce to the monotony of sexual symbolism. In crime and adventure films the spectators are begrudged even the opportunity to witness the resolution. Even in nonironic examples of the genre they must make do with the mere horror of situations connected in only the most perfunctory way.

Cartoon and stunt films were once exponents of fantasy against rationalism. They allowed justice to be done to the animals and things electrified by their technology, by granting the mutilated beings a second life. Today they merely confirm the victory of technological reason over truth. A few years ago they had solid plots which were resolved only in the whirl of pursuit of the final minutes. In this their procedure resembled that of slapstick comedy. But now the temporal relations have shifted. The opening sequences state a plot motif so that destruction can work on it throughout the action: with the audience in gleeful pursuit the protagonist is tossed about like a scrap of litter. The quantity of organized amusement is converted into the quality of organized cruelty.* The self-elected censors of the film industry, its accomplices, monitor the duration of the* atrocity prolonged into a hunt. The jollity dispels the joy supposedly conferred by the sight of an embrace and postpones satisfaction until the day of the pogrom. To the extent that cartoons do more than accustom the senses to the new tempo, they hammer into every brain the old lesson that continuous attrition, the breaking of all individual resistance, is the condition of life in this society. Donald Duck in the cartoons and the unfortunate victim in real life receive their beatings so that the spectators can accustom themselves to theirs.

The enjoyment of the violence done to the film character turns into violence against the spectator; distraction becomes exertion. No stimulant concocted by the experts may escape the weary eye; in face of the slick presentation no one may appear stupid even for a moment; everyone has to keep up, emulating the smartness displayed and propagated by the production. This makes it doubtful whether the culture industry even still fulfils its self-proclaimed function of distraction. If the majority of radio stations and cinemas were shut down, consumers probably would not feel too much deprived. In stepping from the street into the cinema, they no longer enter the world of dream in any case, and once the use of these institutions was no longer made obligatory by their mere existence, the urge to use them might not be so overwhelming.* Shutting them down in this way would not be reactionary machine-wrecking. Those who suffered would not be the film enthusiasts but those who always pay the penalty in any case, the ones who had lagged behind. For the housewife, despite the films which are supposed to integrate her still further, the dark of the cinema grants a refuge in which she can spend a few unsupervised hours, just as once, when there were still dwellings and evening repose, she could sit gazing out of the window. The unemployed of the great centers find freshness in summer and warmth in winter in these places of regulated temperature. Apart from that, and even by the measure of the existing order, the bloated entertainment apparatus does not make life more worthy of human beings. The idea of "exploiting" the given technical possibilities,* of fully utilizing the capacities for aesthetic mass consumption, is part of an economic system which refuses to utilize capacities when it is a question of abolishing hunger.

Notes

[94] "The" / 1944: "The German and Russian pavilions at the Paris World Exposition (of 1937, Ed.) seemed of the same essence, and the."

[94] "the total power of capital" / 1944: "monopoly."

[95] "those whose . . . strongest" / 1944: "capital."

[95] "economy today" / 1944: "profit economy."

[96] "Soap operas": alludes to the fact that such programs were originally broadcast at times when housewives were at home doing their washing (It. tr.).

[96] "selection" / 1944: "selection. The operations of the large studios, including the quality of the highly paid human material populating them, is a product of the monopoly system into which it is integrated."

[96] "subjected . . . purges" / 1944: "expropriated even before fascism."

[98] "at film" / 1944: "at the film monopoly."

[98] "agencies . . . business" / 1944: "monopolistic agencies."

[100] "industrial society" / 1944: "the machinery."

[100] "gigantic economic machinery" / 1944: "gigantic machinery of monopoly."

[101] "tolerated" / 1944: "tolerated, used by monopoly."

1. Nietzsche, *Unzeitgemässe Betrachtungen. Werke*, Leipzig 1917, Vol. I, p. 187.

[102] "Zanuck": Film producer, cofounder of 20th Century Pictures.

[104] "present society" / 1944: "monopoly society."

Notes 269

[105] "Pathé": French film magnates.

[105] "Hugenberg": Founders of German publishing combines.

2. A. de Tocqueville, *De la Démocratie en Amérique*, Paris 1864, Vol. II, p. 151.

[106] "Hays Office": Voluntary censorship agency (It. tr.), set up in 1934 in Hollywood.

[106] "Mickey Rooney": See note [126], p. 271.

[107] "ready-to-wear trade or" / 1944: "Jewish clothing trade or the Episcopal."

[107] "some omnipresent agency" / 1944: "a Rockefeller Institute, only slightly more omnipresent than the one in Radio City,"—"Radio City": the name given since the early 1930s to a part of the Rockefeller Center in New York containing several theatres, radio studios, and the Radio City Music Hall.

[107] "Casino de Paris": Music hall in Paris, famous for its luxurious furnishings.

[107] "society" / 1944: "class society."

[108] "Lombardo": Orchestra leader especially known for his annual musical broadcasts on New Year's Eve.

[109] "novelty songs": Hit songs with comic elements.

[110] "cruelty" / 1944: "lust for murder."

[110] "of the" / 1944: "of the kiss, but not of the."

[111] ". . . overwhelming": The idea expressed here dates from a time when television was not in widespread use (It. tr.).

[111] "possibilities" / 1944: "productive forces."

© 2005 Filip Noterdaeme

[23]

MUSEUM, INC: INSIDE THE GLOBAL ART WORLD
(OVER-THE-CLIFF NOTES).
by Paul Werner.

All quotes in italics are from Museum Inc: Inside the Global Art World (*Prickly Paradigm Press, 2005*) a*nd are used with permission of the publisher. An expanded, annotated bibliography can be found at* http://museuminc.net.

I) Looking for class in all the wrong places.

Nothing makes the Long March through the Institutions a little less long than the awareness that you might be out of an institution tomorrow. I knew this from the day I was hired as a lecturer at the Guggenheim Museum in Manhattan, a job like any other in the culture industry: the money's not bad and you're doing what you like and you wake up one morning and realize you've chosen between the institution and your self-respect, and if it's the self-respect you're sleeping late. I knew this from the first, and from the first my challenge was to see how long I'd stick it out while sticking it to the man and sticking to my own agenda. *My new assignment (from me to me, with love), was to demystify the art and the experience, and if that meant a critique of the museum itself, of its shady doings, its myths, its manipulations, and if I could do that and make you smile and think, and bring us all a step closer to World Revolution, then* a sus órdenes, Señor.

Walter Pater, the aesthete, wrote, "What makes revolutionists is either self-pity, or indignation for the sake of others, or a sympathetic perception of the dominant undercurrent of progress in things. The nature before us is revolutionist from the direct sense of personal worth, that pride of life, which to the Greeks was a heavenly grace." Self-pity? Bad idea. As for "sympathetic perception," that sounded at the time like the red-star-eyed opportunism that went out of style when Gramsci got busted: there wasn't much to be opportunistic about in the 'nineties, least of all at the Guggenheim under its director Tom Krens, the man *Time* called *"The CEO of Culture, Inc.": the man who was doing for the Art World what the new monster corporations were doing to the Global Economy.* The most opportunistic (or prophetic), aspect of my book was my claim that Krens and his free-market model were spinning on air like Wile E. Coyote. Which left the third and only valid excuse for working in the belly of the beast: belief in the class struggle – you know, the thing that the history of all hitherto existing society has been the history *of*? Everybody knew there was no class struggle back then because there was no class to be found, least of all at a fashionable avant-garde museum. How can you stand up for something you're not even sure exists? *The Guggenheim was the equivalent of Clintonian Neo-Liberalism and Krens its Bubba. Krens had borrowed Clinton's rosycheeked trappings all right: the utopianism, the surface populism, and most of all the innocent faith that all of the barriers of class had come down like so many Berlin Walls of Culture.*

Museums are like universities, it's okay to talk about class conflict as long as it's always happening somewhere else to someone else; that's why the young and the wealthy like to confuse class struggles with Class Warfare, as if you're only truly struggling when you're rushing the Winter Palace. But I'd read the early Marx closely enough to understand that

426 *Karl Marx*

objectivity, whether artistic or political, does not consist in wearing someone else's theory or your shoulder but in working out the contradictions of your own, subjective, lived experience from within the experience itself. *Feuerbach Thesis II*: Look it up. You play the hand you're dealt, you paint your canvas with the paints at hand; and you take on the struggles in the clothes they wear when these ghosts rise up before you. Class struggle is lived not as class but as struggle, and that might be the subjective experience, but it's the only one you'll live so you keep your eye on the struggle, not the class, because it's subjective class relations that create classes, not the other way around. So you retool the concept of *habitus*, as taken over by Pierre Bourdieu from the art historian Erwin Panofsky — the concept goes back to Aristotle Habitus: the set of practices and definitions that are accepted and enforced within a group, and whose acceptance and exclusiveness define the group against outsiders. Habitus is the talk the walk these groups take on to hide from themselves the meaning of their own struggles often by presenting themselves as the exact opposite of what they're about, which pretty much describes the artworld avant-garde.[1] *Most thought of themselves as the next Lenin, sniffing the winds at the Finland Station of Culture. Most actually were dull CEOs floating on a cloud illusion that economics are the scientific mapping of an inevitable upward spiral and they need only know the science in order to drift upwards with it.* The art-world rebels are always happy to claim there is a tide in the affairs of men, so long as it's the latest fashion trend. *Krens made a big production of revolutionizing the staid museum world; The press picked up and began to block out verbal gunfights in which Philippe de Montebello, tradition-bound Director of the Metropolitan Museum of Art... met Krens at high noon.*

If jobs are so much work it's usually because they're a protracted game of Class Conflict Gaslight: "Class conflict? What class conflict? You ahre imagining theengs!" But it doesn't take much to hear the muffled footsteps in the attic: a Marxist in the workplace is like a shrink who listens with his inner ear or an art historian seeing with her inner eyeball. *And when I began to notice how intimidated people were by museums I started working with that. And if people were intimidated by admission prices, well — we had our ways.* Culture wars are class wars. So I helped a few visitors get over, and it was good. And like so many others I could have kept engaging in these small guerrilla acts forever — and I still do, as do others in many museums in many countries, so *nu?* I was marching along with everyone who thinks Marxism begins and ends with the concept of surplus value, which makes of Marxism a form of Capitalism with a human face. Marxism, then, means little more than tinkering with the system so that every participant gets a fairer shake. I was giving a few museum visitors an easier access to culture than before, like a state-owned enterprise that hands over to the workers a greater share of what they produce – not even that: I wasn't treating them as producers, I was merely giving them a greater opportunity to consume Culture without changing their relationship to Culture. They remained consumers in a consumer society. I was working from assumptions about the reason people visit museums, or have visited museums, or should visit museums, and from deductive theories about what people see, or should see there. To rethink my praxis I needed to rethink myself in practice, as a producer of museum visitors and art lovers, a producer of producers: *servus servorum*.

---

1 Pierre Bourdieu. "The field of cultural production, or: the economic world reversed." *Poetics* vol. 12, nos. 4-5 (1983), pp. 311-56...

There are a number of theories about museum audiences and their purpose, some of them Marxist, some of them left-wing, almost all derived from a *redemptive theory out of Friedrich Schiller. A few years into the French Revolution a shocked Schiller argued, 'It is through Beauty that we arrive at Freedom', as opposed to the less subtle procedures in vogue at that time.* According to this theory the purpose of art is *"to cement the bonds of union between the richer and the poorer orders of the state"* — cue the last scene from *Metropolis* (1927), in which the workers, instead of tearing the place apart, are tamed by the Power of LOVE. For "Love," substitute "ART." In case of Communism, substitute "Party" for "richer" and "Masses" for poorer. Or, you can cobble from the renegade Jürgen Habermas or the errant, Hannah Arendt the claim that looking at art among like-minded others is the equivalent of the Public Sphere: Democracy at Work, the People United, the Museum as town meeting, a place to contemplate the fair form of Freedom or the Five-Year Plan. The avowed mission of museums is to bring us all together, as Schiller dreamt, in submission to a "Higher Ideal," which, being a higher ideal and all that, dispenses us all from the nasty world of economics and social strife. *That conflict might come spontaneously from the lower classes seems empirically ludicrous to those who choose the empirical data; and the opposite is so obvious it isn't worth discussing: that conflict comes from the top down; that it's as unremitting as the resistance it provokes from below; and that cultural institutions and practices (especially museums) have been for centuries sites for the joining or soothing of conflict between the rich and the poor.* Which is another way of saying that in the Museum as elsewhere, class relations are the visible aspect of the tensions borne of the evolving relationship between 1) productive forces (folks who do the producing), and 2) instruments of productions, viz., the apparently neutral techniques and technologies that the folks who do the producing do the producing with — or without, depending. For Schiller as for Marx and Pater, the whole point of Art was to appear to be outside of History; for Marx at least, the difficulty consists in seeing through this:[2] it's amazing, really, the number of serious thinkers who, confronted with a work of art, freeze their brain functions like boys to boobs.

Of course you can worm out of your own ignorance by claiming that art and culture exist outside the realm of production and consumption: *even Adam Smith couldn't figure how art fit into his tight little scheme.* Or, you can claim that culture's merely part of the "superstructure," which means little except, and including, the same thing. Or you can fantasize that culture is not part of the production process because it doesn't involve factories and tractors. By an amazing coincidence, the apologists of capital and the Ananiases of Marxism end up agreeing that 1) Culture's not about the money; b) Resistance is futile; and c) The real production's always happening elsewhere, back at the old University Department where the real work happens. All of which amounts to the fantasy that class relations do not originate in relationships among producers of culture but in the instruments of cultural production themselves, and that those instruments (Culture, *Kultur*, *La Culture*, Technè, Technique, Technology) are all "bourgeois" in their essential essence. Asking how museums are "bourgeois" is like trying to determine the gender of angels or the class-consciousness of tractors.

---

2   Karl Marx. *Grundrisse. Foundations [Outlines] of the critique of political economy* [1857]. http://marxists.org/archive/marx/works/1857/grundrisse

Nor was the museum visitor as powerless as all that to resist being "determined" by Art: *visitors usually bring their desires and agendas to the museum, and when it comes to writing their own script they can play Walter Mitty with the best of them, damn the curator full speed ahead. I never metanarrative I didn't like.* When museumgoers produce interpretations it's in a shared struggle to interpret: time and again one finds interpretation itself treated as a form of production. In the late nineteenth century, for instance, at the Cleveland Museum of Art or at New York's Metropolitan Museum of Art, there was strong pressure from founders and trustees to turn museums into training grounds for a skilled immigrant work force – training at once intellectual, practical and, of course, ethical. In France a similar approach was proposed very briefly, in the late nineteenth century and again during the Popular Front. This view of the function of culture might be called "productivist" in the sense that it sees museums and art as active instruments for technological and social development, not simply as sites of abstract utopian contemplation, left, liberal or fascist.[3]

II) Well there ain't no use to sit and value how, babe.

Charlie was *so* naïve. In a letter concerning an early reviewer of *Capital* he wrote to Engels:

> ...It is strange that the fellow does not sense [among the] fundamentally new elements of the book:
> [...] That the economists, without exception, have missed the simple point that if the commodity has a double character — use-value and exchange-value — then the labour represented by the commodity must also have a twofold character... This is, in fact, the whole secret of the critical conception.[*January 8, 1868*]

Why Marx would find this strange is beyond me: missing this simple point is the business of the culture industry, and the business of the culture industry is the culture of the business industry. Truth is, *Art is a lousy investment: there's no consistent or predictable demand, the value's all on paper, actual prices fluctuate wildly, and you get no interest or dividends. Plus the cost of maintaining your assets is huge: at least gold ingots and stock certificates don require acres of storage or proper cleaning and restoration and insurance, or commissions on sales and acquisitions, or the cost of hiking up the price of your investment by bidding against your best buddies at auction, or any of the many ways of building your pool of potential buyer. by hype and by buzz. [...] Like the pants with three legs in the Orchard Street joke, art isn something you use, it's something you buy, you sell, you buy, you sell.* It's all exchange-value and zero use-value. But then you go to the museum, and presto, art is all use-value and zero exchange-value, it's no longer something for you to buy and sell, it's something you use to make yourself feel good, and you enter that "realm of freedom" from economics that Schiller promised – that must be the reason these institutions call themselves "non-profits," because can't think of any other. The secret mission of Art is to not be a commodity (no mean trick!), and the joint mission of the Museum, the critic and the artist is to declare Mission Accomplished The art-critical powers accused, and still accuse, Tom Krens of being too "commercial" in his directorship, as though being uncommercial was the goal and glorious achievement of

---

3   Margaret A. Rose. *Marx's lost aesthetic. Karl Marx and the visual arts*. Cambridge: Cambridge University Press, 1984.

the art world, when in fact "not being commercial" is a code-word for accumulation through use-value (sometimes called "symbolic accumulation") in the service of the usual forms of accumulation through exchange-value. *The American art museum turns art into buzz the way its owners turn pork bellies into pork-belly futures*: Michael Kimmelman, chief art critic for the *New York Times*, was uncommonly candid when he demanded of Tom Krens *"less democracy, less blurring of the line between commerce and content, and a reassertion of authority on the part of museums."* Translation: the secret of relations of power in museums (suppression of democracy, assertion of authority), lies in the movement between the use-value and the exchange-value of art. Marx couldn't have said it better — oh, right...

Or again: if artworks are, among other things, commodities, then the purpose of museums is to repress the two-fold character inherent to all commodities. *When someone says a work of art is priceless they mean it, not in the sense that is has no value but that its value is not immediately apprehensible except dialectically, which puts it beyond the ideological competency of most art historians, and of most liberal economists as well, come to think of it. The system of valuation and exchange involved in a work of art (or any item of cultural production) hinges on simultaneously denying the liquidity of the object, inventing a new, other, exclusionary explanation for its existence and, finally, revaluing the object in terms of other criteria, unfathomable to anyone but yourself and a few trusted accomplices. It's a system so much more complex than anything an economist could dream up that you have to forgive the Montebellos of this world for falling back on smug prattle. The beauty of capitalism is that it has such a limited range of explanations for what goes on during a financial transaction. The beauty of art lies in the unending depth and range of interpretations thrown up whenever a work of art passes before your eyes or mine. Well, mine, anyhow.*

Art folks love to talk about Commodity Fetishism since by comparing artworks to commodities they can pretend they've explained everything about artworks while explaining nothing about commodities – call it the Fetish of Commodity Fetishism. What the wannabe wevolutionawies don't seem to wealize is that the "Commodity Fetish" is not the essence of "the commodity" but its subjective appearance as mediated by social relationships (*Fetischcharakter der Ware*). In Marx's Heraclitan world it's not the commodity that's a fetish but the activity of fetishizing: not reification but the reifying of human labor; not the artworks themselves but their use-value in denying or affirming "democracy" and "authority." Inside or outside the Museum, among critics and gallery lecturers and others, ninety percent of art-talk is there to jack up the exchange-value of art by talking about its use-value. This is the logic behind current justifications of cultural looting: the reason we're morally obligated to acquire a looted Iraqi statue is that we understand its use-value ("Exquisite!" "Inspiring!" "A cultural treasure!") better than its present or original owners, who only thought of it as bringing rain or inspiring to battle. Use-value: Priceless.

There's a lovely term in economics, "externalities," meaning anything economics is either not designed to cover, or designed to not cover. Museums are instruments of the second activity, tools for the encryption of one value (cash) as another (symbolic capital). .... And this manipulation, this movement back and forth between symbolic capital and capital tout court, *is the endless occupation of the museum.* But from the mid-nineteenth century on the concept of "Greed" (or, more politely, "self-interest"), acquired a metaphysical status; it's by that metaphysical status that the vulgar economists in the high-falutin' stink-tanks shore up their empire on the ruins of other disciplines. They meet no resistance in the Art Department, which harbors its own form of liberal aesthetics, a mishmash of screaming Schillerics and spurious Kant. The critical quislings have no trouble accepting or bemoaning that art is a commodity after all — or conversely that it's not a commodity in a metaphysical essence, it just happens to be treated like one. *By the 'nineties it was open museum warfare between the partisans of "Greed is Good" and "Greed, it's Not." The American Museum Establishment had been establishmented to repress the painful awareness that museums, like other parts of the system, serve the selfish interests of a narrow segment of the population. Kimmelman and kin thought this was all under threat from Krens, but the Guggenheim followed the same operating principles they did: authority to define what was to be consumed or circulated; encouragement of consumption for consumption's sake; and a deep, abiding interest in dissimulating class distinctions behind a system of consumption. Montebello, Krens and Kimmelman serviced the same john, it's just that Krens wasn't as much of a hypocrite.*

III) Control freaks.

The best points in my book are:
1) The twofold character of labor; according to whether it is expressed in use-value or exchange-value. (All understanding of the facts depends upon this.) [*Marx to Engels, August 24, 1867*].

Pierre Bourdieu has brilliantly shown how the Kantian concept of "disinterested interest" pervades the museum experience; less brilliant in not pursuing the various forms this "interest" would take if it were as interested as it really is. *The Museum as we know it was explicitly set up to demonstrate that the "real" value of artworks transcends at once their past use-value and their exchange value*, which is to say that the real work of the museum, at the admissions desk, in the trustees' dining-room or in the museum's relationship with the community and the government, is to manipulate these concepts: to obfuscate the "twofold character of labor," the use-value and exchange-value inherent in the real relationship of the visitor to the artwork, of the artist to the artwork, of the museum trustees to the artwork and of the museum as a whole to the State. "Authority" is the device by which *trustees and sponsors can at once protect their assets, jack up the value by holding the museum's assets off the market, further hype the value of their own holdings by promoting the museum's holdings, and earn brownie points ("symbolic capital") for proclaiming from the rooftops that their assets are Above Mere Financial Worth.* Disinterested interest is an interest-bearing investment.

With the introduction - however limited, however ambiguous - of aesthetic sentiment into the worker's universe, the very foundation of the whole political order is placed in question. [*Jacques Rancière*].[4]

---

4   quoted in Kristin Ross, *May 1968 and its afterlives* (Chicago: University of Chicago Press, 2002), p. 129.

Hit Reload, Jacques. I don't have much of a quarrel with the argument implied in Pater's statement that the "pride of life" has some sort of liberatory potential — hey, I'm a dialectical girl in a material world. I do contest the very distinct proposition (also Schiller's), that this sentiment needs to be "introduced," and that the museum's authority must derive from its monopolistic expertise in that area, much as the power of the Party must derive from its own expertise. As Bourdieu saw and as Rancière refuses to see, a visitor or curator who approaches the artwork from the common Kantian perspective of the transcendental ego is repressing the fact that in a class-based society some egos will be transcendentaler than others. As Rousseau knew, relationships of authority are inherent in the very fact of standing before a painting: *"Democracy" is okay to the extent that it divides people into spectators and participants.* Or, as Karl Korsch put it in a passage that had a lasting, possibly fatal, influence on Walter Benjamin,

> The advantage gained by the capitalist in this business derives not from economics but from his privileged social position as the monopolist owner of the material means of production, which permits him to exploit, for the production of commodities in his workshop, the specific use value of a labor-power which he has purchased at its economic 'value' (exchange value).[5]

Or, in the case of art, the particular exchange-value he has purchased at its non-economic, or use, value. What Korsch is saying, and Marx, is that capitalism isn't merely the exploitation of a supposedly neutral value, it's the process dependent on the power to modify and control value through the control of the relations among producers. Value is part and parcel of the process of cultural production, it's not something you put on display in the museum, it's the displaying in the museum; it's the museum itself — which is why that favorite game of postmodern artists, the representation of fetishization, was and ever will remain a malicious exercise in calculated pointlessness as long as the representation of fetishization collapses at the museum or elsewhere into the fetishizing it pretends to condemn. Symbolic capital? Guess what, all capital is symbolic in the first instance, and the difference between Krens and Montebello wasn't over who had his hands clean of economic imperatives, it was over different and competing models for extracting symbolic capital from museum operations — capital that translated into the same hard, cold cash for each museum's respective group of patrons or trustees. In the traditional view (Montebello's, for instance), *the role of the American art museum is to launder the money of its trustees and sponsors, not, as you may think, by turning one asset ("cocaine," for instance) into another asset (say, "Rembrandts"), but by turning artworks into objects of authority and trust — objects that mediate and are mediated by the worth of money.* At Montebello's Met, for instance, the percentage of revenues and expenses devoted to building up the symbolic value of the artworks far exceeds the percentage involved in getting visitors to come and squeezing admissions fees out of them. *Because, just as it's good banking policy to uphold the meaning of money (especially among those who don't have any), so, too, the museum's policy is to uphold the meaning of art by reinforcing in its audience those values that make the work of art desirable to begin with, and first among these values is being an audience. Karl Marx was speaking of art when he wrote of providing "a subject for the object,*

---

5   quoted Walter Benjamin, *The Arcades Project*, ed. Rolf Tiedemann (Cambridge, MA: Bellknap Press, 1991), p. 666.

and an object for the subject," before he turned his attention to money. Just as a circus attracts an audience by hiring the funniest clowns and can afford to hire the funniest clowns because it attracts the biggest audience, so too, the Met claims to attract audiences by having the artiest art while arguing that its art is the artiest of all because it awes the audiencest audience and the crickiest art critics from the newsiest newspapers—Arthur Ochs Sulzberger, former chair and publisher of the *New York Times*, is Chairman Emeritus of its Board of Trustees. What upset Montebello about Krens was that he claimed he could pull this off without benefit of art, or of major newspapers in his pocket. *The return on his investment—the justification for the gamble—was made out to be the spontaneous appearance of hordes of visitors through the galleries. As surely as laissez-faire economics dreams up goods moving unfettered through a system, so, too, the laissez-faire museum imagines artworks spontaneously moving through the perceptual equipment of the public.*

It was Benjamin again, in one of the most thoroughly misunderstood essays of the twentieth century, who argued that the "aura," the sense of authority attached to art objects, would survive even in the Age of Mechanical Reproduction but that it would require new strategies for its enforcement or transformation, not simply new labels; but the art-world fetish freaks still fantasize the "aura" as an ineffable essence of art, attracting audiences *like flies to poop.* Krens, too, believed in the Magic of the Marketplace: since art was a commodity like any other its use-value was a gimme, that mysterious "scarcity" which, in vulgar freakonomics, provides the constant that economics seeks to "regulate." *Krens imagined that circulating new objects (bikes or blouses) through auratic channels (museums) would automatically confer an aura on them and authority on the museum.* He thought he could accumulate symbolic capital by sticking a ham sandwich in a gallery, and he had plenty of curators and critics to back him up: Ham Sandwich Art, along with Ham Sandwich Literature and Ham Sandwich Music," may turn out to be the dominant art form of the first decades of the twenty-first century. *His critics were wrong to claim Krens was trying to commodify culture: he was trying to culturificate commodities, and he failed.*

Both Krens and Montebello considered the museum audience a commodity to be traded in the bond market of culture: *The point of attendance figures is to brag about spontaneous demand for the product, not about the money raised through admissions. It's about delivering numbers, not about the numbers themselves.* Only Krens seemed to think you didn't need collateral — the artworks themselves — to bring in the crowds. *Traditional museums (which usually look like old-style banks to begin with) are about preserving cultural capital by maintaining assets through good conservation, supporting the scholarship that maintains the value of the assets, sponsoring the shows that support the scholarship that maintains or raises the value of assets, leveraging their assets through loans and exhibitions that drive up attendance and consolidate the symbolic value of these assets and this type of asset in general. In contrast, Krens seemed to be gambling on a collateral he blew out of his ears like a junk-bond gambler.* But then, Krens wasn't looking for funds from the traditional well-heeled art-lovers and collectors and rich artists who make up the backbone of the Met's Board of Trustees: his great, first and only success had been the planning, construction and operation of a branch museum in Northern Spain. *The Guggenheim Bilbao opened in 1997, the visual centerpiece of a master plan for the economic redevelopment of the Basque Region... The Guggenheim Bilbao was wildly successful*

— *at least for the Basque Regional Government that originally commissioned it. Then again, the Basque region was in the midst of a political crisis and its government had bigger fish in mind than pulsating rhythms and passionate impastos: to replace a collapsing industrial base; to encourage tourism; to weaken cultural and economic isolationism and relieve political pressures for autonomy. [...] The Basque Government claimed to have recouped its initial investment within a year, apart from the political payoff, but the Basque Government had gone in with this double balance sheet in mind, trading off political against financial gains. The Guggenheim had no such fallback position: trading financial loss for ideological gain was simply not a part of its mission, it was actually a contradiction of its mission*, which was to trade the imaginary use-value of attendance for the financial support of its patrons.

It was a case of Ham Sandwich Art meets Potlatch Architecture: Krens was a model for every local booster, every speculator, corporation or sovereign state eager to contract out their own Bilbao project in the sands of Arabia or the beaches of Rio. *Bilbao was supposed to demonstrate that the Guggenheim had amassed a certain experience in attracting audiences, and the Guggenheim was saying it could sell that intangible experience — that was its equities. The name "Guggenheim" (with attendant services and architectural ecstasies) was to be used primarily, not to attract more visitors, ...but to attract major patrons and financing institutions with some kind of a stake in the museum's ability to attract visitors. ... The Guggenheim's stated mission was no longer making art available to an audience, it was delivering "its" audience to a new sponsor...* Which is to say that the Museum's function veered further and further away from content (the artworks), as its dependency grew on those social relations supposed to be inherent in the use-value of architectural constructions.

IV) Another art world is possible.

Kimmelman had obscurely seen the "twofold character of labor" in the struggle between "democracy" and "authority." Unlike Kimmelman I was free to follow the conflicting relationships among producers of culture from the Admissions desk to the gallery floor to the boardroom and beyond; to trace the meaning of art objects as they gyrated between use-value and exchange-value though the transfer of values from one producer to the other. I began to work with visitors, colleagues, artists, curators and critics to uncover our own roles in the production of symbolic capital, the manner in which each of us was called upon to mediate between artworks and their value.

A museum educator is expected to apply the paradigms of academic Art History to the objects on view; traditionally these paradigms divide approaches and academics between the stylistic approach and the sociological, or, to borrow the old phraseology, between *formalism* (as a rule explicitly reactionary) and *contextual history* — outwardly progressive and implicitly an empty promise. To break down these paradigms for the visitor, the colleague, or the boss meant to break down the relations among producers that these paradigms enforced: *The cliché that museums are not "about having fun" hides another meaning: that your visit will not be structured to help you enjoy better what you already know, or to know better what you already enjoy; or to tell you what you don't know. In the final instance it will be about being told that there are things you don't know and that are knowable, only not to you. You doubt me?*

Rent one of those audio-guides that have no solid information whatsoever except to go back and forth about the Hand of the Master on his Quivering Piece. Or read any number of art critics who have mastered the art of saying nothing while conveying an unbreachable sense of authority. Listen to a docent waving her hands while you regress to the state of a ten-year-old, wondering as you did back then if the purpose of education is to answer your questions or to make sure you never ask again.

Daniel Boorstin, the late, politically conservative Librarian of Congress, noted with alarm that the mission of cultural, not-for-profit institutions was gradually shifting away from research and intellectual productivity towards providing an "educational" experience. What he did not notice (being a conservative and all that), was that the shift was a movement todwards the monopolization of the distribution of Culture. More and more, the new globalizing museums describe their functions as "educational," and the educational experience they propose is not skills but an Educational Experience, the Ivy-League ideal of forming consumer-graduates who don't accumulate technique in their four years of College, only symbolic capital: Odd, that those who so oppose the Nanny State have no quarrel with Nanny Learning. The museum-going experience, like the Ivy-League degree, has become, *to use Paulo Freire's term, primarily bankable*: its purpose is to help its audience acquire social capital through the consumption of the "museum experience." *At the Guggenheim and elsewhere the museum-going experience was all fashion (also known as art appreciation), and fashion consisted in watching yourself looking at art.* (It's okay, Mr. Bush, you've earned your Gentleman's "See.")

In opposition I developed a model of art-learning as symbolic labor: labor on the part of the producer of art, of course, on the part of the art-student as well, but also on the part of the museum visitor and user, as if the accumulation of art-knowledge and art-skills were a form of production, not merely the consumption of museum services; not merely the reproduction of class distinctions through consumption. To explain art meant to clarify the role of the visitor, the role of the art and the role of the museum as an institution. That wasn't too hard since most museum visitors prefer the acquisition of practical knowledge to the accumulation of class brownie points — something that's occasionally true of college students as well. Besides, in a period of rapid technological change like ours the valuation of social capital is unreliable, and many visitors sense this. I was teaching museum visitors and art students how to confront and survive the ideologies of art and museums, to identify the cognitive and technical tools of various cultures and various histories, because the only type of activism that's worthwhile is the one that changes relationships among producers. My epiphany came during the infamous Motorcycle show at the Guggenheim: *It's a humbling experience to explain v-twin cylinders to a couple thousand pounds of studs and leather and body hair that happens to know more about the topic and in different ways than you could ever dream of, and isn't exactly afraid to say so. In other terms (those of Paulo Freire again), our interaction was dialogical: cooperative, born of a mutual exchange, reaching the participants where they lived and thought.* But to change those relationships I had to begin by treating visitors as producers of meanings, not as accumulators of symbolic capital. *And the visitors loved it and came back for more because they got something worth their money, even if it wasn't ideologically fruitful for the institution... Especially if it wasn't ideologically fruitful for the institution.* Periodically, a few visitors raged that I wasn't teaching anything, meaning I actually was, and where was the advantage in that? Here in America we earn our social capital the old-fashioned way: we buy it.

Pater again: "All art constantly aspires toward the condition of music." Actually, all art aspires to all kinds of things, depending; and in the last few years (and not for the first time, either), museums have aspired to be buildings: abstracted symbolic power, *authority regardless of content*. The figure of the "creative" personality popularized by a thousand CEOs in the pages of the *New York Times* and *Wall Street Journal* differs little from the figure of the Architect in that dumbass novel by the hysteric-Schilleric Ayn Rand. But when all art tends to the condition of real estate, all art ends up collapsing along with the real-estate bubble. 'Justice' was done, and the CEO of the Immortals, in Capitalist phrase, had ended his sport with Tom by the time my book came out. Today, with the ongoing deflation of Reaganomics and free-market ideology, there are new opportunities to channel the museum's function. Sticker shock and awe may be the intention of the museum in the global economy, but they're not a sure thing: if wishes were motorcycles, museum directors would ride on a hog donated by their corporate sponsors. And, as in the Big Bad Socialist Takeover of Wall Street, so, too, in the museum world: what we begin to see seems to be merely more of the change that changes nothing, All-That-Is-Solid-Melts-Into-Air, All-The-Time, as long as relations among producers are unaffected. The Global Museum Bubble *wasn't about art or the money, it was about creating an insatiable field for speculation in real estate, in services, in ideological control and manipulation.... Now the monster's out of the box: as the actual use-value of the art declines (meaning its ability to draw visitors), its investment value increases because it takes more and more cash to continue to valorize the art and that calls for more speculation, which in turn brings in more speculators: the dog notices it has a tail, and wags it.* Except the wagging has started to look and feel at times like the threatening swing of a dinosaur's tail.

> At a certain stage of development, the material productive forces of society come into conflict with the existing relations of production. From forms of development of the productive forces these relations turn into their fetters. Then begins an era of social revolution.[6]

What I see daily now, among artists and art students, among museum visitors – sometimes even among politicians — is an awareness that the productive forces are aligned, once again, the makers against the speculators, and that the museum, once again, is one among many sites of struggle, one of many fetters. In the next few years I foresee the usual gangs of "revolutionary" artists storming the museum's barricades to demand more of the same, once again, except for themselves, now: a change of labels, a change of bosses, relationships unchanged. Then again, we could get lucky. Another world is possible, even if it is Art.

© 2012 Paul Werner

---

6   Karl Marx, *A Contribution to the Critique of Political Economy* [1859].

[24]

The Cultural Logic of

Late Capitalism

Fredric Jameson

The last few years have been marked by an inverted millenarianism in which premonitions of the future, cat-astrophic or redemptive, have been replaced by senses of the end of this or that (the end of ideology, art, or social class; the "crisis" of Leninism, social democracy, or the welfare state, etc., etc.); taken together, all of these perhaps constitute what is increasingly called postmodernism. The case for its existence depends on the hypothesis of some radical break or *coupure*, generally traced back to the end of the 1950s or the early 1960s.

As the word itself suggests, this break is most often related to notions of the waning or extinction of the hundred-year-old modern movement (or to its ideological or aesthetic repudiation). Thus abstract expres-sionism in painting, existentialism in philosophy, the final forms of rep-resentation in the novel, the films of the great *auteurs*, or the modernist school of poetry (as institutionalized and canonized in the works of Wallace Stevens) all are now seen as the final, extraordinary flowering of a high-modernist impulse which is spent and exhausted with them. The enumeration of what follows, then, at once becomes empirical, chaotic, and heterogeneous: Andy Warhol and pop art, but also photorealism, and beyond it, the "new expressionism"; the moment, in music, of John Cage, but also the synthesis of classical and "popular" styles found in composers like Phil Glass and Terry Riley, and also punk and new wave rock (the Beatles and the Stones now standing as the high-modernist moment of that more recent and rapidly evolving tradition); in film, Godard, post-Godard, and experimental cinema and video, but also a whole new type of commercial film (about which more below); Bur-roughs, Pynchon, or Ishmael Reed, on the one hand, and the French *nouveau roman* and its succession, on the other, along with alarming

2 POSTMODERNISM

new kinds of literary criticism based on some new aesthetic of textuality or *écriture* . . . The list might be extended indefinitely; but does it imply any more fundamental change or break than the periodic style and fashion changes determined by an older high-modernist imperative of stylistic innovation?

It is in the realm of architecture, however, that modifications in aesthetic production are most dramatically visible, and that their theoretical problems have been most centrally raised and articulated; it was indeed from architectural debates that my own conception of postmodernism—as it will be outlined in the following pages—initially began to emerge. More decisively than in the other arts or media, postmodernist positions in architecture have been inseparable from an implacable critique of architectural high modernism and of Frank Lloyd Wright or the so-called international style (Le Corbusier, Mies, etc), where formal criticism and analysis (of the high-modernist transformation of the building into a virtual sculpture, or monumental "duck," as Robert Venturi puts it)[1] are at one with reconsiderations on the level of urbanism and of the aesthetic institution. High modernism is thus credited with the destruction of the fabric of the traditional city and its older neighborhood culture (by way of the radical disjunction of the new Utopian high-modernist building from its surrounding context), while the prophetic elitism and authoritarianism of the modern movement are remorselessly identified in the imperious gesture of the charismatic Master.

Postmodernism in architecture will then logically enough stage itself as a kind of aesthetic populism, as the very title of Venturi's influential manifesto, *Learning from Las Vegas*, suggests. However we may ultimately wish to evaluate this populist rhetoric,[2] it has at least the merit of drawing our attention to one fundamental feature of all the postmodernisms enumerated above: namely, the effacement in them of the older (essentially high-modernist) frontier between high culture and so-called mass or commercial culture, and the emergence of new kinds of texts infused with the forms, categories, and contents of that very culture industry so passionately denounced by all the ideologues of the modern, from Leavis and the American New Criticism all the way to Adorno and the Frankfurt School. The postmodernisms have, in fact, been fascinated precisely by this whole "degraded" landscape of schlock and kitsch, of TV series and *Reader's Digest* culture, of advertising and motels, of the late show and the grade-B Hollywood film, of so-called paraliterature, with its airport paperback categories of the gothic and the romance,

Culture   3

the popular biography, the murder mystery, and the science fiction or fantasy novel: materials they no longer simply "quote," as a Joyce or a Mahler might have done, but incorporate into their very substance.

Nor should the break in question be thought of as a purely cultural affair: indeed, theories of the postmodern—whether celebratory or couched in the language of moral revulsion and denunciation—bear a strong family resemblance to all those more ambitious sociological generalizations which, at much the same time, bring us the news of the arrival and inauguration of a whole new type of society, most famously baptized "postindustrial society" (Daniel Bell) but often also designated consumer society, media society, information society, electronic society or high tech, and the like. Such theories have the obvious ideological mission of demonstrating, to their own relief, that the new social formation in question no longer obeys the laws of classical capitalism, namely, the primacy of industrial production and the omnipresence of class struggle. The Marxist tradition has therefore resisted them with vehemence, with the signal exception of the economist Ernest Mandel, whose book *Late Capitalism* sets out not merely to anatomize the historic originality of this new society (which he sees as a third stage or moment in the evolution of capital) but also to demonstrate that it is, if anything, a purer stage of capitalism than any of the moments that preceded it. I will return to this argument later; suffice it for the moment to anticipate a point that will be argued in chapter 2, namely, that every position on postmodernism in culture—whether apologia or stigmatization—is also at one and the same time, and *necessarily*, an implicitly or explicitly political stance on the nature of multinational capitalism today.

A last preliminary word on method: what follows is not to be read as stylistic description, as the account of one cultural style or movement among others. I have rather meant to offer a periodizing hypothesis, and that at a moment in which the very conception of historical periodization has come to seem most problematical indeed. I have argued elsewhere that all isolated or discrete cultural analysis always involves a buried or repressed theory of historical periodization; in any case, the conception of the "genealogy" largely lays to rest traditional theoretical worries about so-called linear history, theories of "stages," and teleological historiography. In the present context, however, lengthier theoretical discussion of such (very real) issues can perhaps be replaced by a few substantive remarks.

One of the concerns frequently aroused by periodizing hypotheses is that these tend to obliterate difference and to project an idea of the his-

4 POSTMODERNISM

torical period as massive homogeneity (bounded on either side by inexplicable chronological metamorphoses and punctuation marks). This is, however, precisely why it seems to me essential to grasp postmodernism not as a style but rather as a cultural dominant: a conception which allows for the presence and coexistence of a range of very different, yet subordinate, features.

Consider, for example, the powerful alternative position that postmodernism is itself little more than one more stage of modernism proper (if not, indeed, of the even older romanticism); it may indeed be conceded that all the features of postmodernism I am about to enumerate can be detected, full-blown, in this or that preceding modernism (including such astonishing genealogical precursors as Gertrude Stein, Raymond Roussel, or Marcel Duchamp, who may be considered outright postmodernists, avant la lettre). What has not been taken into account by this view, however, is the social position of the older modernism, or better still, its passionate repudiation by an older Victorian and post-Victorian bourgeoisie for whom its forms and ethos are received as being variously ugly, dissonant, obscure, scandalous, immoral, subversive, and generally "antisocial." It will be argued here, however, that a mutation in the sphere of culture has rendered such attitudes archaic. Not only are Picasso and Joyce no longer ugly; they now strike us, on the whole, as rather "realistic," and this is the result of a canonization and academic institutionalization of the modern movement generally that can be traced to the late 1950s. This is surely one of the most plausible explanations for the emergence of postmodernism itself, since the younger generation of the 1960s will now confront the formerly oppositional modern movement as a set of dead classics, which "weigh like a nightmare on the brains of the living," as Marx once said in a different context.

As for the postmodern revolt against all that, however, it must equally be stressed that its own offensive features—from obscurity and sexually explicit material to psychological squalor and overt expressions of social and political defiance, which transcend anything that might have been imagined at the most extreme moments of high modernism—no longer scandalize anyone and are not only received with the greatest complacency but have themselves become institutionalized and are at one with the official or public culture of Western society.

What has happened is that aesthetic production today has become integrated into commodity production generally: the frantic economic urgency of producing fresh waves of ever more novel-seeming goods (from clothing to airplanes), at ever greater rates of turnover, now assigns

Culture 5

an increasingly essential structural function and position to aesthetic innovation and experimentation. Such economic necessities then find recognition in the varied kinds of institutional support available for the newer art, from foundations and grants to museums and other forms of patronage. Of all the arts, architecture is the closest constitutively to the economic, with which, in the form of commissions and land values, it has a virtually unmediated relationship. It will therefore not be surprising to find the extraordinary flowering of the new postmodern architecture grounded in the patronage of multinational business, whose expansion and development is strictly contemporaneous with it. Later I will suggest that these two new phenomena have an even deeper dialectical interrelationship than the simple one-to-one financing of this or that individual project. Yet this is the point at which I must remind the reader of the obvious; namely, that this whole global, yet American, postmodern culture is the internal and superstructural expression of a whole new wave of American military and economic domination throughout the world: in this sense, as throughout class history, the underside of culture is blood, torture, death, and terror.

The first point to be made about the conception of periodization in dominance, therefore, is that even if all the constitutive features of postmodernism were identical with and continuous to those of an older modernism—a position I feel to be demonstrably erroneous but which only an even lengthier analysis of modernism proper could dispel—the two phenomena would still remain utterly distinct in their meaning and social function, owing to the very different positioning of postmodernism in the economic system of late capital and, beyond that, to the transformation of the very sphere of culture in contemporary society.

This point will be further discussed at the conclusion of this book. I must now briefly address a different kind of objection to periodization, a concern about its possible obliteration of heterogeneity, one most often expressed by the Left. And it is certain that there is a strange quasi-Sartrean irony—a "winner loses" logic—which tends to surround any effort to describe a "system," a totalizing dynamic, as these are detected in the movement of contemporary society. What happens is that the more powerful the vision of some increasingly total system or logic —the Foucault of the prisons book is the obvious example—the more powerless the reader comes to feel. Insofar as the theorist wins, therefore, by constructing an increasingly closed and terrifying machine, to that very degree he loses, since the critical capacity of his work is thereby paralyzed, and the impulses of negation and revolt, not to speak of those

6 POSTMODERNISM

of social transformation, are increasingly perceived as vain and trivial in the face of the model itself.

I have felt, however, that it was only in the light of some conception of a dominant cultural logic or hegemonic norm that genuine difference could be measured and assessed. I am very far from feeling that all cultural production today is "postmodern" in the broad sense I will be conferring on this term. The postmodern is, however, the force field in which very different kinds of cultural impulses—what Raymond Williams has usefully termed "residual" and "emergent" forms of cultural production—must make their way. If we do not achieve some general sense of a cultural dominant, then we fall back into a view of present history as sheer heterogeneity, random difference, a coexistence of a host of distinct forces whose effectivity is undecidable. At any rate, this has been the political spirit in which the following analysis was devised: to project some conception of a new systematic cultural norm and its reproduction in order to reflect more adequately on the most effective forms of any radical cultural politics today.

The exposition will take up in turn the following constitutive features of the postmodern: a new depthlessness, which finds its prolongation both in contemporary "theory" and in a whole new culture of the image or the simulacrum; a consequent weakening of historicity, both in our relationship to public History and in the new forms of our private temporality, whose "schizophrenic" structure (following Lacan) will determine new types of syntax or syntagmatic relationships in the more temporal arts; a whole new type of emotional ground tone—what I will call "intensities"—which can best be grasped by a return to older theories of the sublime; the deep constitutive relationships of all this to a whole new technology, which is itself a figure for a whole new economic world system; and, after a brief account of postmodernist mutations in the lived experience of built space itself, some reflections on the mission of political art in the bewildering new world space of late or multinational capital.

I

We will begin with one of the canonical works of high modernism in visual art, Van Gogh's well-known painting of the peasant shoes, an example which, as you can imagine, has not been innocently or randomly chosen. I want to propose two ways of reading this painting, both of which in some fashion reconstruct the reception of the work in a two-stage or double-level process.

Culture 7

I first want to suggest that if this copiously reproduced image is not to sink to the level of sheer decoration, it requires us to reconstruct some initial situation out of which the finished work emerges. Unless that situation—which has vanished into the past—is somehow mentally restored, the painting will remain an inert object, a reified end product impossible to grasp as a symbolic act in its own right, as praxis and as production.

This last term suggests that one way of reconstructing the initial situation to which the work is somehow a response is by stressing the raw materials, the initial content, which it confronts and reworks, transforms, and appropriates. In Van Gogh that content, those initial raw materials, are, I will suggest, to be grasped simply as the whole object world of agricultural misery, of stark rural poverty, and the whole rudimentary human world of backbreaking peasant toil, a world reduced to its most brutal and menaced, primitive and marginalized state.

Fruit trees in this world are ancient and exhausted sticks coming out of poor soil; the people of the village are worn down to their skulls, caricatures of some ultimate grotesque typology of basic human feature types. How is it, then, that in Van Gogh such things as apple trees explode into a hallucinatory surface of color, while his village stereotypes are suddenly and garishly overlaid with hues of red and green? I will briefly suggest, in this first interpretative option, that the willed and violent transformation of a drab peasant object world into the most glorious materialization of pure color in oil paint is to be seen as a Utopian gesture, an act of compensation which ends up producing a whole new Utopian realm of the senses, or at least of that supreme sense—sight, the visual, the eye—which it now reconstitutes for us as a semiautonomous space in its own right, a part of some new division of labor in the body of capital, some new fragmentation of the emergent sensorium which replicates the specializations and divisions of capitalist life at the same time that it seeks in precisely such fragmentation a desperate Utopian compensation for them.

There is, to be sure, a second reading of Van Gogh which can hardly be ignored when we gaze at this particular painting, and that is Heidegger's central analysis in *Der Ursprung des Kunstwerkes*, which is organized around the idea that the work of art emerges within the gap between Earth and World, or what I would prefer to translate as the meaningless materiality of the body and nature and the meaning endowment of history and of the social. We will return to that particular gap or rift later on; suffice it here to recall some of the famous phrases that model the

8 POSTMODERNISM

process whereby these henceforth illustrious peasant shoes slowly re-create about themselves the whole missing object world which was once their lived context. "In them," says Heidegger, "there vibrates the silent call of the earth, its quiet gift of ripening corn and its enigmatic self-refusal in the fallow desolation of the wintry field." "This equipment," he goes on, "belongs to the *earth*, and it is protected in the *world* of the peasant woman. . . . Van Gogh's painting is the disclosure of what the equipment, the pair of peasant shoes, *is* in truth. . . . This entity emerges into the unconcealment of its being,"[3] by way of the mediation of the work of art, which draws the whole absent world and earth into revelation around itself, along with the heavy tread of the peasant woman, the loneliness of the field path, the hut in the clearing, the worn and broken instruments of labor in the furrows and at the hearth. Heidegger's account needs to be completed by insistence on the renewed materiality of the work, on the transformation of one form of materiality —the earth itself and its paths and physical objects—into that other materiality of oil paint affirmed and foregrounded in its own right and for its own visual pleasures, but nonetheless it has a satisfying plausibility.

At any rate, both readings may be described as *hermeneutical*, in the sense in which the work in its inert, objectal form is taken as a clue or a symptom for some vaster reality which replaces it as its ultimate truth. Now we need to look at some shoes of a different kind, and it is pleasant to be able to draw for such an image on the recent work of the central figure in contemporary visual art. Andy Warhol's *Diamond Dust Shoes* evidently no longer speaks to us with any of the immediacy of Van Gogh's footgear; indeed, I am tempted to say that it does not really speak to us at all. Nothing in this painting organizes even a minimal place for the viewer, who confronts it at the turning of a museum corridor or gallery with all the contingency of some inexplicable natural object. On the level of the content, we have to do with what are now far more clearly fetishes, in both the Freudian and the Marxian senses (Derrida remarks, somewhere, about the Heideggerian *Paar Bauernschuhe*, that the Van Gogh footgear are a heterosexual pair, which allows neither for perversion nor for fetishization). Here, however, we have a random collection of dead objects hanging together on the canvas like so many turnips, as shorn of their earlier life world as the pile of shoes left over from Auschwitz or the remainders and tokens of some incomprehensible and tragic fire in a packed dance hall. There is therefore in Warhol no way to complete the hermeneutic gesture and restore to these oddments that whole larger lived context of the dance hall or the ball, the

Culture 9

world of jetset fashion or glamour magazines. Yet this is even more paradoxical in the light of biographical information: Warhol began his artistic career as a commercial illustrator for shoe fashions and a designer of display windows in which various pumps and slippers figured prominently. Indeed, one is tempted to raise here—far too prematurely—one of the central issues about postmodernism itself and its possible political dimensions: Andy Warhol's work in fact turns centrally around commodification, and the great billboard images of the Coca-Cola bottle or the Campbell's soup can, which explicitly foreground the commodity fetishism of a transition to late capital, *ought* to be powerful and critical political statements. If they are not that, then one would surely want to know why, and one would want to begin to wonder a little more seriously about the possibilities of political or critical art in the postmodern period of late capital.

But there are some other significant differences between the high-modernist and the postmodernist moment, between the shoes of Van Gogh and the shoes of Andy Warhol, on which we must now very briefly dwell. The first and most evident is the emergence of a new kind of flatness or depthlessness, a new kind of superficiality in the most literal sense, perhaps the supreme formal feature of all the postmodernisms to which we will have occasion to return in a number of other contexts.

Then we must surely come to terms with the role of photography and the photographic negative in contemporary art of this kind; and it is this, indeed, which confers its deathly quality to the Warhol image, whose glacéd X-ray elegance mortifies the reified eye of the viewer in a way that would seem to have nothing to do with death or the death obsession or the death anxiety on the level of content. It is indeed as though we had here to do with the inversion of Van Gogh's Utopian gesture: in the earlier work a stricken world is by some Nietzschean fiat and act of the will transformed into the stridency of Utopian color. Here, on the contrary, it is as though the external and colored surface of things —debased and contaminated in advance by their assimilation to glossy advertising images—has been stripped away to reveal the deathly black-and-white substratum of the photographic negative with subtends them. Although this kind of death of the world of appearance becomes thematized in certain of Warhol's pieces, most notably the traffic accidents or the electric chair series, this is not, I think, a matter of content any longer but of some more fundamental mutation both in the object world itself—now become a set of texts or simulacra—and in the disposition of the subject.

10 POSTMODERNISM

All of which brings me to a third feature to be developed here, what I will call the waning of affect in postmodern culture. Of course, it would be inaccurate to suggest that all affect, all feeling or emotion, all subjectivity, has vanished from the newer image. Indeed, there is a kind of return of the repressed in *Diamond Dust Shoes*, a strange, compensatory, decorative exhilaration, explicitly designated by the title itself, which is, of course, the glitter of gold dust, the spangling of gilt sand that seals the surface of the painting and yet continues to glint at us. Think, however, of Rimbaud's magical flowers "that look back at you," or of the august premonitory eye flashes of Rilke's archaic Greek torso which warn the bourgeois subject to change his life; nothing of that sort here in the gratuitous frivolity of this final decorative overlay. In an interesting review of the Italian version of this essay,[4] Remo Ceserani expands this foot fetishism into a fourfold image which adds to the gaping "modernist" expressivity of the Van Gogh-Heidegger shoes the "realist" pathos of Walker Evans and James Agee (strange that pathos should thus require a team!); while what looked like a random assortment of yesteryear's fashions in Warhol takes on, in Magritte, the carnal reality of the human member itself, now more phantasmic than the leather it is printed on. Magritte, unique among the surrealists, survived the sea change from the modern to its sequel, becoming in the process something of a postmodern emblem: the uncanny, Lacanian foreclusion, without expression. The ideal schizophrenic, indeed, is easy enough to please provided only an eternal present is thrust before the eyes, which gaze with equal fascination on an old shoe or the tenaciously growing organic mystery of the human toenail. Ceserani thereby deserves a semiotic cube of his own:

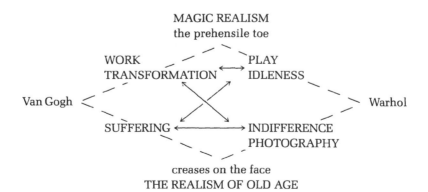

Culture 11

Walker Evans, "Floyd Burroughs' Work Shoes"
(Photograph removed)

The waning of affect is, however, perhaps best initially approached by way of the human figure, and it is obvious that what we have said about the commodification of objects holds as strongly for Warhol's human subjects: stars—like Marilyn Monroe—who are themselves commodified and transformed into their own images. And here too a certain brutal return to the older period of high modernism offers a dramatic shorthand parable of the transformation in question. Edward Munch's painting *The Scream* is, of course, a canonical expression of the great modernist thematics of alienation, anomie, solitude, social fragmentation, and isolation, a virtually programmatic emblem of what used to be called the age of anxiety. It will here be read as an embodiment not merely of the expression of that kind of affect but, even more, as a virtual deconstruction of the very aesthetic of expression itself, which seems to have dominated much of what we call high modernism but to have vanished away—for both practical and theoretical reasons—in the world of the postmodern. The very concept of expression presupposes indeed some separation within the subject, and along with that a whole metaphysics of the inside and outside, of the wordless pain within the monad and the moment in which, often cathartically, that "emotion" is then projected out and externalized, as gesture

12 POSTMODERNISM

or cry, as desperate communication and the outward dramatization of inward feeling.

This is perhaps the moment to say something about contemporary theory, which has, among other things, been committed to the mission of criticizing and discrediting this very hermeneutic model of the inside and the outside and of stigmatizing such models as ideological and metaphysical. But what is today called contemporary theory—or better still, theoretical discourse—is also, I want to argue, itself very precisely a postmodernist phenomenon. It would therefore be inconsistent to defend the truth of its theoretical insights in a situation in which the very concept of "truth" itself is part of the metaphysical baggage which poststructuralism seeks to abandon. What we can at least suggest is that the poststructuralist critique of the hermeneutic, of what I will shortly call the depth model, is useful for us as a very significant symptom of the very postmodernist culture which is our subject here.

Overhastily, we can say that besides the hermeneutic model of inside and outside which Munch's painting develops, at least four other fundamental depth models have generally been repudiated in contemporary theory: (1) the dialectical one of essence and appearance (along with a whole range of concepts of ideology or false consciousness which tend to accompany it); (2) the Freudian model of latent and manifest, or of repression (which is, of course, the target of Michel Foucault's programmatic and symptomatic pamphlet *La Volonté de savoir* [*The history of Sexuality*]); (3) the existential model of authenticity and inauthenticity whose heroic or tragic thematics are closely related to that other great opposition between alienation and disalienation, itself equally a casualty of the poststructural or postmodern period; and (4) most recently, the great semiotic opposition between signifier and signified, which was itself rapidly unraveled and deconstructed during its brief heyday in the 1960s and 1970s. What replaces these various depth models is for the most part a conception of practices, discourses, and textual play, whose new syntagmatic structures we will examine later on; let it suffice now to observe that here too depth is replaced by surface, or by multiple surfaces (what if often called intertextuality is in that sense no longer a matter of depth).

Nor is this depthlessness merely metaphorical: it can be experienced physically and "literally" by anyone who, mounting what used to be Raymond Chandler's Bunker Hill from the great Chicano markets on Broadway and Fourth Street in downtown Los Angeles, suddenly confronts the great free-standing wall of Wells Fargo Court (Skidmore,

Karl Marx 449

Culture 13

Wells Fargo Court (Skidmore, Owings and Merrill)
(Photograph removed)

Owings and Merrill)—a surface which seems to be unsupported by any volume, or whose putative volume (rectangular? trapezoidal?) is ocularly quite undecidable. This great sheet of windows, with its gravity-defying two-dimensionality, momentarily transforms the solid ground on which we stand into the contents of a stereopticon, pasteboard shapes profiling themselves here and there around us. The visual effect is the same from all sides: as fateful as the great monolith in Stanley Kubrick's *2001* which confronts its viewers like an enigmatic destiny, a call to evolutionary

14 POSTMODERNISM

mutation. If this new multinational downtown effectively abolished the older ruined city fabric which is violently replaced, cannot something similar be said about the way in which this strange new surface in its own peremptory way renders our older systems of perception of the city somehow archaic and aimless, without offering another in their place?

Returning now for one last moment to Munch's painting, it seems evident that *The Scream* subtly but elaborately disconnects its own aesthetic of expression, all the while remaining imprisoned within it. Its gestural content already underscores its own failure, since the realm of the sonorous, the cry, the raw vibrations of the human throat, are incompatible with its medium (something underscored within the work by the homunculus's lack of ears). Yet the absent scream returns, as it were, in a dialectic of loops and spirals, circling ever more closely toward that even more absent experience of atrocious solitude and anxiety which the scream was itself to "express." Such loops inscribe themselves on the painted surface in the form of those great concentric circles in which sonorous vibration becomes ultimately visible, as on the surface of a sheet of water, in an infinite regress which fans out from the sufferer to become the very geography of a universe in which pain itself now speaks and vibrates through the material sunset and landscape. The visible world now becomes the wall of the monad on which this "scream running through nature" (Munch's words)[5] is recorded and transcribed: one thinks of that character of Lautréamont who, growing up inside a sealed and silent membrane, ruptures it with his own scream on catching sight of the monstrousness of the deity and thereby rejoins the world of sound and suffering.

All of which suggests some more general historical hypothesis: namely, that concepts such as anxiety and alienation (and the experiences to which they correspond, as in *The Scream*) are no longer appropriate in the world of the postmodern. The great Warhol figures—Marilyn herself or Edie Sedgewick—the notorious cases of burnout and self-destruction of the ending 1960s, and the great dominant experiences of drugs and schizophrenia, would seem to have little enough in common any more either with the hysterics and neurotics of Freud's own day or with those canonical experiences of radical isolation and solitude, anomie, private revolt, Van Gogh-type madness, which dominated the period of high modernism. This shift in the dynamics of cultural pathology can be characterized as one in which the alienation of the subject is displaced by the latter's fragmentation.

Such terms inevitably recall one of the more fashionable themes in

Culture 15

contemporary theory, that of the "death" of the subject itself—the end of the autonomous bourgeois monad or ego or individual—and the accompanying stress, whether as some new moral ideal or as empirical description, on the *decentering* of that formerly centered subject or psyche. (Of the two possible formulations of this notion—the historicist one, that a once-existing centered subject, in the period of classical capitalism and the nuclear family, has today in the world of organizational bureaucracy dissolved; and the more radical poststructuralist position, for which such a subject never existed in the first place but constituted something like an ideological mirage—I obviously incline toward the former; the latter must in any case take into account something like a "reality of the appearance.")

We must however add that the problem of expression is itself closely linked to some conception of the subject as a monadlike container, within which things felt are then expressed by projection outward. What we must now stress, however, is the degree to which the high-modernist conception of a unique *style*, along with the accompanying collective ideals of an artistic or political vanguard or avant-garde, themselves stand or fall along with that older notion (or experience) of the so-called centered subject.

Here too Munch's painting stands as a complex reflection on this complicated situation: it shows us that expression requires the category of the individual monad, but it also shows us the heavy price to be paid for that precondition, dramatizing the unhappy paradox that when you constitute your individual subjectivity as a self-sufficient field and a closed realm, you thereby shut yourself off from everything else and condemn yourself to the mindless solitude of the monad, buried alive and condemned to a prison cell without egress.

Postmodernism presumably signals the end of this dilemma, which it replaces with a new one. The end of the bourgeois ego, or monad, no doubt brings with it the end of the psychopathologies of that ego—what I have been calling the waning of affect. But it means the end of much more—the end, for example, of style, in the sense of the unique and the personal, the end of the distinctive individual brush stroke (as symbolized by the emergent primacy of mechanical reproduction). As for expression and feelings or emotions, the liberation, in contemporary society, from the older *anomie* of the centered subject may also mean not merely a liberation from anxiety but a liberation from every other kind of feeling as well, since there is no longer a self present to do the feeling. This is not to say that the cultural products of the postmodern

16 POSTMODERNISM

era are utterly devoid of feeling, but rather that such feelings—which it may be better and more accurate, following J.-F. Lyotard, to call "intensities"—are now free-floating and impersonal and tend to be dominated by a peculiar kind of euphoria, a matter to which we will want to return later on.

The waning of affect, however, might also have been characterized, in the narrower context of literary criticism, as the waning of the great high modernist thematics of time and temporality, the elegiac mysteries of *durée* and memory (something to be understood fully as much as a category of the literary criticism associated with high modernism as with the works themselves). We have often been told, however, that we now inhabit the synchronic rather than the diachronic, and I think it is at least empirically arguable that our daily life, our psychic experience, our cultural languages, are today dominated by categories of space rather than by categories of time, as in the preceding period of high modernism.[6]

Notes

1 Robert Venturi and Denise Scott-Brown, *Learning from Las Vegas*, (Cambridge, Mass. 1972).

2 The originality of Charles Jencks's pathbreaking *Language of Post-Modern Architecture* (1977) lay in its well-nigh dialectical combination of postmodern architecture and a certain kind of semiotics, each being appealed to to justify the existence of the other. Semiotics becomes appropriate as a mode of analysis of the newer architecture by virtue of the latter's populism, which does emit signs and messages to a spatial "reading public," unlike the monumentality of the high modern. Meanwhile, the newer architecture is itself thereby validated, insofar as it is accessible to semiotic analysis and thus proves to be an essentially aesthetic object (rather than the transaesthetic constructions of the high modern). Here, then, aesthetics reinforces an ideology of communication (about which more will be observed in the concluding chapter), and vice versa. Besides Jencks's many valuable contributions, see also Heinrich Klotz, *History of Postmodern Architecture* (Cambridge, Mass., 1988); Pier Paolo Portoghesi, *After Modern Architecture* (New York, 1982).

3 Heidegger, "The Origin of the Work of Art," in Albert Hofstadter and Richard Kuhns, eds. *Philosophies of Art and Beauty* (New York, 1964), p. 663.

4 Remo Ceserani, "Quelle scarpe di Andy Warhol," *Il Manifesto* (June 1989).

5 Ragna Stang, *Edvard Munch* (New York, 1979), p. 90.

6   This is the moment to confront a significant translation problem and to say why, in my opinion, the notion of a postmodern spatialization is not incompatible with Joseph Frank's influential attribution of an essentially "spatial form" to the high modern. In hindsight, what he describes is the vocation of the modern work to invent a kind of spatial mnemonics—reminiscent of Frances Yates's *Art of Memory*, a "totalizing" construction in the stricter sense of the stigmatized, autonomous work, whereby the particular somehow includes a battery of re- and pre-tensions linking the sentence or the detail to the Idea of the total form itself. Adorno quotes a remark about Wagner by the conductor Alfred Lorenz in precisely this sense: "If you have completely mastered a major work in all its details, you sometimes experience moments in which your consciousness of time suddenly disappears and the entire work seems to be what one might call 'spatial,' that is, with everything present simultaneously in the mind with precision" (W. 36/33). But such mnemonic spatiality could never characterize postmodern texts, in which "totality" is eschewed virtually by definition. Frank's modernist spatial form is thus synedochic, whereas it is scarcely even a beginning to summon up the word *metonymic* for postmodernism's universal urbanization, let alone its nominalism of the here-and-now.

[25]

Aroma and Shadow:
Marx vs. Nietzsche on Religion

Ishay Landa

The struggle against religion is . . . indirectly a fight against
the world of which religion is the spiritual *aroma.*
—Karl Marx
God is dead; but given the way of men, there may still be caves
for thousands of years in which his shadow will be shown.—
And we—we still have to vanquish his shadow, too.
—Friedrich Nietzsche

The names of Karl Marx and Friedrich Nietzsche, despite all
that separates them in other respects, are often mentioned together
in relation to a joint atheism, antimetaphysical materialism, and
caustic denunciation of religion. Here, it is argued, the ideas of
the two mighty nineteenth-century thinkers had much in common.
Both, as Foucault classically put it, are the great "masters of suspicion," along with Freud (1998, 269–78)[1]; both fearlessly decon-
struct religion and naturalize the world, purging it of the despotic
phantoms of traditional idealist morality, which is replaced by an
unflinching materialism, a sober, almost cynical, view of things,
weaned of bourgeois sentimentalism. Having a common enemy
in religion, Marx and Nietzsche thus fight shoulder to shoulder
to bring about secular modernity.[2] This juxtaposition, however,
obscures more than it clarifies. It legitimately highlights certain

462 *NATURE, SOCIETY, AND THOUGHT*

epistemological similarities, but at the cost of obscuring a crucial ideological discrepancy. My point is not simply that Marx and Nietzsche cannot be said to have embraced a similar political cause; this would be a fairly trivial claim, in spite of the numerous attempts, over the last decades, to bring them ideologically together.[3] Nor do I argue merely that, given that Marx and Nietzsche criticized different facets of religion, their respective critiques are different, or even incompatible. Rather, I claim that Nietzschean atheism is radically *antithetical* to the Marxist one. Far from accompanying or completing Marx in any way, Nietzsche's atheism needs to be understood as a thorough alternative to Marxism, devised specifically to destroy it and take its place.

Nietzsche and Marx were at war (not a personal one, needless to say; there is no indication that Nietzsche ever read Marx, and Marx and Engels, for their part, wrote the *Communist Manifesto* when Nietzsche was four years old). I hope to show how the religious "shadow" that Nietzsche sought to chase away was, at bottom, the *Marxist variant of atheism*; conversely, the Nietzschean brand of atheism should be seen as just one of many odors associated with that religious "aroma" that Marx and Engels found offensive. Indeed, one might go as far as to argue that for both atheistic camps, the fundamental adversary was not so much religion *per se* but the profane *worldly* way in which it was being put to use.

To understand this ideological conflict it is necessary to bring the abstraction of "atheism" into its concrete historical context. I suggest, to start with, distinguishing between two distinctive forms of atheism. Nietzsche became immensely (in)famous following the resonant announcement of the death of God he put in the mouth of the madman in aphorism 125 of *The Gay Science* (1882). This proclamation has gone down in the history of philosophy as the slogan of Nietzsche's ruthless crusade against religion. When "God is dead" is placed back in historical perspective, however, at least some of the iconoclastic significance usually attached to it must be retracted. Western culture at the time *The Gay Science* was published, twenty-three years after Darwin's *On the Origin of Species*, was already imbued with atheism, and

Marx vs. Nietzsche on Religion   463

a growing secularization was a trend dominating all aspects of contemporary life and thought. Nietzsche's atheism as such could therefore hardly have produced such a shock. And if the public then and generations of subsequent readers since were indeed shocked, one must look for reasons other than the mere refutation of God's existence. Not the fact of God's "death" caused such scandal, but what the madman made of the "historical event" of God's murder, the Nietzschean interpretation of its significance. Such interpretation—the whole complex of conceptions, insights, judgments, and imagery that makes up Nietzsche's particular brand of atheism—was ultimately conceived of in response to, not to say retaliation against, an atheistic tradition that preceded it. To understand Nietzsche's atheism, therefore, we must first of all have at least a general notion of the ideological pith of the atheism it rose up against, namely socialist atheism.

Humanization vs. dehumanization of the universe

To simplify matters, I would posit Marx and Engels's atheism as representative of the basic tenets of socialist and revolutionary understanding of religion in general (just as Nietzsche's version of atheism could be seen as representative of other "theological" positions of a comparable nature). The ideas are fairly well known, but it would be helpful to summarize them briefly. The founders of Marxism wholeheartedly and unreservedly embraced secularization; it was for them a vital step in deposing religion as a prime means of class domination, the most important Ideological State Apparatus (Althusser's terminology) of the nineteenth century: "The criticism of religion is the premise of all criticism" (Marx 1975a, 175). Within bourgeois hierarchy, God's role was that of the ultimate overseer, keeping a watchful eye on the workers to guarantee their obedience. This was true metaphorically and sometimes even literally, as illustrated by the following catechism of an English Sunday school for working-class children (early nineteenth century):

> *Questions.* Is it honest for workmen to waste and destroy the materials and implements which they make use of? (Ans. No.) Who do these things belong to? (Ans. Their

464   NATURE, SOCIETY, AND THOUGHT

master.) Whose eyes see you when your master is not by? (Ans. God's.) . . . Who sees people when they are pilfering tea and sugar and such things? (Ans. God.) Does God approve of such actions? (Ans. No.) What would God do to thieves of all kind? (Ans. Punish them.)[4]

Thus, Marx and Engels understandably rejoiced over Darwin's theories, as they welcomed any blow aimed at the religious exegesis of the universe and of society. Taking on Feuerbach, they believed that to be rid of God would mean to enthrone humanity. This atheism was put in a nutshell by Engels: "The question has previously always been: what is God? and German philosophy has answered the question in this sense: God is man" (1975, 464). If, as Nietzsche would proclaim, God is indeed dead, then the Marxist corresponding claim was from the start, "Long live man!" A fiction told by humans, God has come to dominate its creator; alienated from humanity and raised above it, God became humanity's oppressor, backed up by a corrupt clerical hierarchy. Now at long last, humanity has attained the conceptual and emotional maturity needed to break free of its self-imposed chains and overcome estrangement. It no longer needs the mediation of a divinity to address itself. At last realizing that it was God who was created in the human image and not the other way around, humanity can finally become the measure of its own world, its sole meaning and purpose: "*All* emancipation is a *reduction* of the human world and relationships to *man himself*" (Marx 1975c, 168). Secularization hence means an ideological and epistemological (as opposed to ontological) humanization of the world. The political implications of this process of humanization are also clear: "the criticism of heaven turns into the criticism of the earth, the *criticism of religion* into the *criticism of law* and the *criticism of theology* into the *criticism of politics*" (Marx 1975a, 176). The masses, once awakened from the opiate dream of a blissful afterlife, would rise to claim a paradise on earth, brushing aside those who use religion to shield the status quo. Atheism was on that account deemed a vital vehicle of political transformation, the *sine qua non* of revolution. These two tenets at the heart of the Marxist critique of religion—the revolutionary appeal to

Marx vs. Nietzsche on Religion   465

the masses and the humanizing emphasis—are condensed in the following famous passage:

> The weapon of criticism cannot, of course, replace criticism by weapons, material force must be overthrown by material force; but theory also becomes a material force as soon it has gripped the masses. Theory is capable of gripping the masses as soon as it demonstrates *ad hominem*, and it demonstrates *ad hominem* as soon as it becomes radical. To be radical is to grasp things by the root of the matter. But for man the root is man himself. The evident proof of the radicalism of German theory, and hence of its practical energy, is that it proceeds from a resolute *positive* abolition of religion. The criticism of religion ends with the teaching that *man is the highest being for man*, hence with the *categorical imperative to overthrow all relations* in which man is a debased, enslaved, forsaken, despicable being. (Marx 1975a, 182)

This is the gist of the Marxist endeavor to equip the masses with a radical, secular theory, with the aid of which a new, *revolutionary* and *humanistic* society can be created.

On the opposite pole of the political spectrum stood those who were bound by conviction and interest to the present state of things and did not wish to see it altered, let alone radically turned upside down. For them, to keep the masses piously slumbering was a high priority. Historical developments, however, proved by and large unfavorable to their cause. The Enlightenment's emphasis on rational enquiry and scientific progress, requisite for bolstering the bourgeois social revolution as well as for expediting industrial technological progress, severely limited the sway of religion as a social myth. As Engels could affirm with gratification as early as 1844 (the year of Nietzsche's birth):

> [Thomas Carlyle] knows very well that rituals, dogmas, litanies and Sinai thunder cannot help, that all the thunder of Sinai does not make the truth any truer, nor does it frighten any sensible person, that we are far beyond the religion of fear. (1975, 457)

466   NATURE, SOCIETY, AND THOUGHT

The influential Victorian conservative, John Henry Cardinal Newman, son of a banker, likewise recognized the social effects of liberal atheism, but from a clerical, anxious point of view. Listing a series of logical inferences, he usefully registered the inexorable progress of rational atheism, from the initial refutation of the Church's authority up to the pernicious outcome of mass democracy, as the following selection illustrates:

> 4. It is dishonest in a man to make an act of faith in what he has not had brought home to him by actual proof.
>
> Therefore, e.g., the mass of men ought not absolutely to believe in the divine authority of the Bible.
>
> 5. It is immoral in a man to believe more than he can spontaneously receive as being congenial to his moral and mental nature.
>
> Therefore, e.g., a given individual is not bound to believe in eternal punishment.
>
> 6. No revealed doctrines or precepts may reasonably stand in the way of scientific conclusions.
>
> Therefore, e.g., Political Economy may reverse our Lord's declarations about poverty and riches. . . .
>
> 16. It is lawful to rise in arms against legitimate princes.
>
> Therefore, e.g., the Puritans in the seventeenth century, and the French in the eighteenth, were justified in their Rebellion and Revolution respectively.
>
> 17. The people are the legitimate source of power.
>
> Therefore, e.g., Universal Suffrage is among the natural rights of man. (1986, 1030–32)

As against this objective development, two basic theological responses took shape. The first was conservative, clinging tenaciously to the sacrosanct tenets of religious belief and reaffirming them in the face of danger. The second was more realistic and more ingenious; it took in the unfortunate balance of things and realized the need for developing an adequate, innovative response to the atheistic tide. To the former group belonged those, like the Victorian Bishop Samuel Wilberforce and his followers, who became infuriated over Darwin's publications and struggled to minimize

Marx vs. Nietzsche on Religion   467

the damages of the earthquake that ensued; Nietzsche, on the other hand, became one of the principal spokesmen of the latter camp.

Nietzsche's atheism, it is important to understand, was a belated one, atheism after the fact. It was also very much a reluctant atheism, very different from the unconditional endorsement and celebration of secularity of the socialists (or of those proponents of scientific and technological progress who were continuing the rationalistic impetus of the Enlightenment, although less and less in their social views). Nietzsche's reaction to the death of God was by no means one of sheer jubilation. Rather, it included an acute awareness that much that was valuable went under along with the deceased deity, not least of which was religion's priceless capacity to sustain hierarchy. Nietzsche therefore sought—in the aftermath of God's elimination—to harness and divert the advance of atheism, so as to impede its progress towards an egalitarian revolution. If the supernatural can no longer validate the existing social order, the natural may just as well fulfill this role, under the mediation of a social Darwinism combined with Schopenhauerian pessimism. Nietzsche expressed his consternation over this general secularizing process on numerous occasions, making it clear that the secularization of the masses was especially regrettable on account of its political, revolutionary consequences:

> The philosopher as we understand him, we free spirits . . . will make use of the religions for his work of education and breeding, just as he will make use of existing political and economic conditions. . . . To ordinary men . . . the great majority, who exist for service and general utility and who *may* exist only for that purpose, religion gives an invaluable contentment with their nature and station, manifold peace of heart, an ennobling of obedience. . . . Perhaps nothing in Christianity and Buddhism is so venerable as their art of teaching even the lowliest to set themselves through piety in an apparently higher order of things and thus to preserve their contentment with the real order, within which they live hard enough lives—and necessarily have to! (1990a, 86–87)

468   NATURE, SOCIETY, AND THOUGHT

In view of such ideas, we can already begin to appreciate how Nietzsche's assessment of religion constitutes the very ethical mirror image of that expounded by Marx and Engels. We say "ethical," because in terms of a realistic evaluation of the sociopolitical function of religion, their views are remarkably similar. For Nietzsche, just as for the Marxists, religion is one more department of the superstructure, alongside other "existing political and economic conditions," the specific function and "art" of which is to instill servility in the masses and reconcile them to their wretched conditions of life. Whereas the Marxist assault on religion was aimed at its role in upholding the class system, Nietzsche was nostalgic for the good old times when it was still able to "venerably" benumb the masses. Conversely, when Nietzsche turned to criticize Christianity, his reproaches were directed precisely at its other, and far less creditable side—its alleged *undermining* of hierarchy and its ignition of revolution. As in the following quotation, the likes of which could be multiplied many times over:

> With that I have done and pronounce my judgement. I *condemn* Christianity, I bring against the Christian Church the most terrible charge any prosecutor has ever uttered. To me it is the extremest thinkable form of corruption. . . . — "Equality of souls before God," this falsehood, this *pretext* for the *rancune* of all the base-minded, this explosive concept which finally became revolution, modern idea and the principle of the decline of the entire social order—is *Christian* dynamite. (1990b, 198)

Nietzsche wanted to exploit the demise of Christianity as a historic opportunity to transvalue egalitarian values. Once God is removed, it becomes vital to ensure that it is the ideal of social equality, and not that of hierarchy, that passes away with him. As Zarathustra declares, it is not the leveling mob that shall profit from atheism but the *Übermensch* (overman or Superman):

> "You higher men"—thus the mob blink—"there are no higher men, we are all equal, man is man; before God we are all equal!"

Marx vs. Nietzsche on Religion 469

Before God! But now this god has died. And before the mob we do not want to be equal. . . .

Before God! . . . You higher men, this god was your greatest danger. It is only since he lies in his tomb that you have been resurrected. Only now the great noon comes; only now the higher man becomes—lord.

. . . God died: now *we* desire the overman to live. (1995, 286–87)

Nietzsche's atheism was above all a repudiation of what he perceived as the egalitarian legacy of Christianity, and it was only consistent that he had a far better opinion of other, allegedly less egalitarian, religions, such as early Judaism or Hinduism.[5] Nietzsche was thus at bottom not really antireligious, and not altogether anti-Christian either. His critique of Christianity addressed exclusively its perceived function as a slave religion while applauding its historical role of keeping slaves under control.

The main task Nietzsche had to accomplish in his attempt to transform the nature of revolutionary atheism was to do away with its deep-seated humanistic optimism, and install in its place a pessimistic, tragic, and conservative mode of secularization. The event of God's death was hence described, at least in part, as inaugurating a dismal epoch of existential human solitude. This pessimistic, tragic approach to God's death is most eloquently expressed in the renowned passage in which the madman runs into the marketplace and seeks God with his lantern. Here we find poetically encapsulated the clash between the two forms of atheism, the optimistic and humanizing vs. the pessimistic and dehumanizing. On the one side stands in heroic isolation the pessimistic madman who is a despairing, anxious atheist. At the beginning of the scene, as a matter of fact, the madman is not an atheist at all, but still an apprehensive believer, seeking to recover God. He confronts the optimistic, shallow multitude in the marketplace: they, already atheists, belittle the significance of God's absence and jest at the madman's seemingly ridiculous quest.

At this point the madman suddenly acknowledges the death of God: "'Whither is God?' he cried; 'I will tell you. *We have killed him*—you and I. All of us are his murderers'" (1974, 181). But of

470   *NATURE, SOCIETY, AND THOUGHT*

all deicides, the madman alone experiences pangs of conscience. He alone is intensely aware of the tragic implications of this momentous deed. He discloses a distressing truth that has to do precisely with the place of humans in the world in the postreligious era. After the twilight of God, a new dawn breaks, but one utterly different from the cheerful sunrise foreseen by Feuerbach and the Marxists, who believed that humankind is poised to become at long last master of its destiny. The human hopes of freedom and mastery are categorically refuted. The universe will not gain in humanness after God's dismissal, as the optimists guarantee, but rather be utterly *deprived of it*. Since God was a human invention, his presence had humanized the universe; his love and protection, however figments of the imagination, have endowed the world with a comforting semblance of humanness. Now that the spell was recklessly broken by optimistic and shallow atheists, human beings must face the horrifying emptiness of the bare universe. The madman proclaims the absurdity of existence:

> Whither are we moving? Away from all suns? Are we not plunging continually? Backward, sideward, forward, in all directions? Is there still any up and down? Are we not straying through an infinite nothing? Do we not feel the breath of empty space? Has it not become colder? Is not night continually closing in on us? (1974, 181)

Instead of the joyful, proud independence promised by the optimistic atheists, the pessimistic madman decrees humanity's existential orphanhood. The universe is an infinite and empty space, its emptiness asphyxiating, cold, and thoroughly nonhuman. Atheism is profoundly transformed; it is not the human being that succeeds divinity. If God is dead, then long live *nature*! Humankind cannot impose itself on the universe, but must rather yield to the chaotic, amoral, indifferent nature of the cosmos in which humankind is a trifle. The ultimate consequence of such submission would be effectively to *dehumanize* the universe: "When will we complete our de-deification of nature? When may we begin to '*naturalize*' humanity in terms of a pure, newly discovered, newly redeemed nature?" (1974, 169) But what does such "naturalization" of humanity mean? It is very easy to mistake this suggestion,

Marx vs. Nietzsche on Religion   *471*

especially when presented in isolation, for a typical secular exhortation for humanity to "become natural," as it were, to get rid of religious inhibitions and prudish self-denial, and to glory in that which is "naturally" human, happy, and healthy. But the truth of the matter is quite different. It was only right that Nietzsche should place the word *naturalization* in quotation marks, for what he proposed thereby was the very opposite of what is conventionally meant by the term. For him, to naturalize humanity meant to *deny* human nature, since nature and humanity have nothing in common. Nature and humans stand as complete opposites; nature is a silent rock upon which all human concepts, ideas, and hopes crash and dissipate like so many feeble waves:

> The total character of the world, however, is in all eternity chaos—in the sense not of a lack of necessity but of a lack of order, arrangement, form, beauty, wisdom, and whatever other names there are for our aesthetic anthropomorphisms. . . . [H]ow could we reproach or praise the universe? Let us beware of attributing to it heartlessness and unreason or their opposites: it is neither perfect nor beautiful, nor noble, nor does it wish to become any of those things; it does not by any means strive to imitate man. (1974, 168)

What is important from an ideological point of view in these conceptions of nature is not the denial of the (very romantic) idea that nature possesses human attributes or the assertion that humans tend to project their own needs and emotions onto their natural surroundings, i.e., to anthropomorphize them. It is rather the contention that we must somehow start to "naturalize humanity." For one thing, what could such naturalization actually mean given the concomitant assertion that humanity and nature are inexorably cut apart? The very idea of such naturalization would seem senseless, unless by another act of anthropomorphism. Indeed it could be argued that the entire passage quoted above, in which nature is described as an eternal chaos, is itself but another, though very subtle, "aesthetic anthropomorphism," another romantic elegy for nature. The only other apparent option is for humankind to forfeit entirely its unnatural humanity and immerse itself definitely in nature by the act of dying (and, as we shall shortly see, this is not

472 NATURE, SOCIETY, AND THOUGHT

entirely alien to Nietzsche's argument). But even assuming that such naturalization is somehow possible while humans are still alive, why is it at all a recommendable, indeed urgent, mission that we should set out to complete without delay? What could be the enticement, for a human being, of uniting himself or herself with an entity that is said to be devoid of "order, arrangement, form, beauty, wisdom, and whatever other names there are for our aesthetic anthropomorphisms"? Thus, when Nietzsche speaks about a "newly discovered, newly redeemed nature" and the need for humanity to conduct itself according to its rules, he actually demands that human nature should be subordinated to nature as such, which is profoundly nonhuman. In a remarkable theoretical move, Nietzsche contends that to become natural we must deny and transcend our humanity. We can see that Nietzsche's interpretation of the place of human beings in the world following God's demise is never just a description; it is equally a prescription. It is not enough for Nietzsche to claim that the universe and nature are indifferent and meaningless, that the universe "does not by any means strive to imitate man"; he rather insists, in effect, that *humans* should *imitate the universe*, bow before the indifference and absurdity of existence and rearrange their lives accordingly. And this second proposition by no means follows logically or necessarily from the first. There is, furthermore, an element of duplicity behind the ostensible despair at God's murder. For Nietzsche, in fact, also celebrates the nothingness of the universe. The "infinite empty space" gaping at humanity may be cold and depressing, but it is also the supreme object of admiration:

> *In the horizon of the infinite.*—We have left the land and have embarked. We have burned our bridges behind us—indeed, we have gone further and destroyed the land behind us. Now, little ship, look out! Beside you is the ocean. . . . [H]ours will come before you realize that it is infinite and that there is nothing more awesome than infinity. (1974, 180)

Thus, it does not suffice to affirm that the world is nonhuman; somehow we must also exult in this nonhumanity, come to applaud the magnificence of the void; we may even wish to consider a glorious plunge into its "chaotic" depths. And here the political

Marx vs. Nietzsche on Religion   473

coordinator operating underneath Nietzsche's narrative can be glimpsed. The objective ideological purpose and function become clear. Whereas for the Marxists, secular humanization of the universe meant preparing the ground for revolution, Nietzsche's secular dehumanization is meant to impede it. Socialist atheism was bound with the conviction of human sovereignty and dignity, whereas Nietzsche's theory of nature is directed purposely against such illusions. This is demonstrated in a passage where Nietzsche enumerates several typical human misconceptions that must be redressed. One of these errors is the failure to admit the proper—that is, negligible—place of humans in the natural scheme:

> Third, [man] placed himself in a false order of rank in relation to animals and nature. . . . If we removed the effects of these four errors, we should also remove humanity, humanness and "human dignity." (1974, 174)

It is as if Nietzsche's theory was written in specific rebuttal of Marx's contention that "the criticism of religion ends with the teaching that *man is the highest being for man*" (1975a, 182). For Nietzsche, the criticism of religion rather ends by the realization, "One has no right to existence or to work, to say nothing of a right to 'happiness': the individual human being is in precisely the same case as the lowest worm" (1968, 398–99). While Marx has animated his readers *"to overthrow all relations* in which man is a debased, enslaved, forsaken, despicable being" (1975a, 182), Nietzsche strives to create precisely such a new condition, for which the existential insignificance of humanity will serve as a presupposition. Nietzsche's solution to the political problem of humanizing atheism is to an attempt to develop a dehumanizing atheism. By introducing a form of atheism-cum-pantheism that places nature above humanity, one can deny the political demands of humanistic socialism. François Bédarida, in an informative essay, has characterized National Socialism as an *Ersatzreligion* that was meant to take the place of Christianity. It was, moreover, a "naturalistic religion," substituting immanency and this-worldliness for transcendentalism and the afterlife. At the heart of this "secular religion" lay a project—we may add, a *Nietzschean* project, one that is compatible with Nietzsche's teaching—of a "naturalized humanity":

474   *NATURE, SOCIETY, AND THOUGHT*

> Such a world stands completely under the sign of naturalism. Man is only a part of nature. "The earth will continue to spin," claims Hitler, "whether man kills the tiger or the other way around; the world does not change. Its laws are eternal." The only thing that counts is to adapt to these laws. (Bédarida 1997, 161)

Philippe Burrin likewise stresses the naturalistic character of Nazi ideology as a means of "re-enchanting" a world that has dangerously gone secular, combined with an effort to dehumanize the world:

> The human species is a part of nature and subject to its "eternal laws." The important thing is the struggle for survival and the selection of the strongest. The role of this desacralized and nature-fixated mode of thought cannot be overestimated when considering the crimes of the regime. . . . Auschwitz is the culminating point of a specific anti-humanistic re-enchantment attempt, as the mythical-symbolic inspiration of Nazism clearly shows. (1997, 181–82)[6]

National Socialism as *Ersatzreligion* was but one historical instance of this naturalistic fetishism, though surely the most far-reaching and extravagant one. But the general principle of applying the reputed inhumanity of nature to legitimize the inhumanity of society was an ideological stratagem ubiquitous throughout the West in the form of social Darwinism and its diverse sociological, anthropological, and cultural manifestations. The "divine scheme" of the past was everywhere replaced, or at any rate complemented, by the "natural plan," according to which the strong "naturally" prevail and the weak "naturally" perish, and any intervention in that process amounts to heresy against the pagan yet monotheistic deity of Nature. A degree of "naturalism" was (and remains) an integral part of most hegemonic ideologies under capitalism, and Nietzsche's bid to naturalize humanity, though compatible with the Nazi version of naturalism, is similarly harmonious with other, less extreme, historical realizations. Hence we can establish the part played by Nietzsche's philosophy in the creation of a new, pantheistic, quasi-religion.

Marx vs. Nietzsche on Religion   475

Such a view of nature as the silent, omnipotent opposite of the human being has indeed established itself as the predominant modern conception, enjoying almost uncontested supremacy, at least in secular circles. It has become so much the accepted outlook that one would hardly think of linking it, even potentially, with an ideological position of any kind. It is postulated as a mere fact, a transhistorical given, bared before us with the advances of science. Even a Marxist and Hegelian like Frederic Jameson embraced this view, in reference to the stance of Marxism vis-à-vis existentialism: "that life is meaningless is not a proposition that need be inconsistent with Marxism, whose affirmation is the quite different one that History is meaningful, however absurd organic life may happen to be. The real issue is not the propositions of existentialism, but rather their charge of affect" (1981, 261). For Jameson, what separates a Marxist from an existentialist (Nietzsche, for our purposes) on this point is not an ontological disagreement but an epistemological, more specifically an ideological, one. The question is: once the objective place of human beings in the universe has been asserted, what should be their response, how should they live their lives and configure their society in the aftermath of metaphysics?

Original Marxism, however, was more ambitious. It should be remembered that for the young Marx it was quite pertinent to attempt to transcend the rigid dichotomy of humans and nature and bring about a Hegelian reconciliation between them. Far from being an eternal fact of life exposed by modernity, the separation of human beings and nature was for Marx *a symptom of modernity*, a social problem of the first degree that his vision of communism was to overcome.[7] It is illuminating to recall Marx's remarks on the matter from the *Economic and Philosophic Manuscripts of 1844,* which throw into vivid relief the ways in that his version of naturalism differs from the modern take on nature:

> This communism, as fully developed naturalism, equals humanism, and as fully developed humanism equals naturalism; it is the *genuine* resolution of the conflict between man and nature and between man and man—the true resolution of the strife between existence and essence, between

476   NATURE, SOCIETY, AND THOUGHT

objectification and self-confirmation, between freedom and necessity, between the individual and the species. Communism is the riddle of history solved, and it knows itself to be this solution. (1975b, 296–97)

For the youthful Marx, therefore, more was at stake than a simple "charge of affect." Communism, for him, offered the concrete possibility of a grand utopian resolution of human estrangement from nature. To modern ears this may sound like a beautiful epiphany that ugly history has grimly discarded. But we ought, perhaps, to remind ourselves that Marx's idea of communism in these passages was a political order that would eventually supersede "crude communism," whether "despotic or democratic," attaining a true abolition of private property and going beyond capital materially, spiritually, and psychologically. It remains difficult, however, to grasp how eliminating private property might possibly impinge on, let alone heal, the rift between humans and nature, which we now understand as two strictly separate sets of problems, the one political and social, the other existential or spiritual. But for Marx, the issue of the human being's position versus nature is not at all a "natural matter," so to speak, decided a priori by some given natural laws, but rather a thoroughly sociopolitical question that humanity itself must resolve by way of conscious revolutionary action. For Marx, the notion that nature was something "out there," an alien, nonhuman, or even antihuman essence, was but another aspect of the modern situation in which, for the isolated individual monad, society is felt as inhuman, alien, and oppressive:

Activity and enjoyment, both in their content and in their *mode of existence*, are *social*: *social* activity and social enjoyment. The *human* aspect of nature exists only for *social* man; for only then does nature exist for him as a *bond* with *man*—as his existence for the other and the other's existence for him—and as the life-element of human reality. Only then does nature exist as the *foundation* of his own *human* existence. Only here has what is to him his *natural* existence become his *human* existence, and nature become man for him. Thus *society* is the complete unity

Marx vs. Nietzsche on Religion   477

of man with nature—the true resurrection of nature—the accomplished naturalism of man and the accomplished humanism of nature. (1975b, 298)

Just like Nietzsche, Marx calls for a "naturalism of man," but for him it is the same as calling for a "humanism of nature." The antithesis (the conceptual resemblances notwithstanding) could not be more complete. Since humans are not properly social under present conditions, but enclosed within the egotistic shells created by private-property institutions, *therefore* the "human aspect of nature" does not exist for them. For Marx, to humanize nature makes perfect sense for the simple reason that human beings themselves *are nature*, and, while transforming and humanizing themselves, they are consequently, and by necessity, transforming and humanizing nature as well. To claim, like Nietzsche, that humans must adapt themselves to nature, which is inhuman—chaotic, senseless, indifferent, etc.—would be from Marx's viewpoint not only an impossible or undesirable proposition, but first and foremost an *unnatural* one. Humans would become thereby unnatural, not natural, for they will be banished from their natural habitat of history and society and thrown into some reified vacuum where no development is possible. The whole drift of Marx's argument is to supersede dialectically the distinction between nature and humanity and perceive their actual unity. It is in this sense that we should understand his famous claim that even the senses, allegedly bequeathed to humans by alienated nature as they are once and for all, to remain unchanged, are in fact subjected to historical transformation and undergo inexorable humanization; this is not some offense against nature but the most natural thing, for humans:

> The abolition of private property is therefore the complete *emancipation* of all human senses and qualities; but it is this emancipation precisely because these senses and attributes have become, subjectively and objectively, *human*. The eye has become a *human* eye, just as its *object* has become a social, *human* object—an object made by man for man. The *senses* have therefore become directly in their practice *theoreticians*. They relate themselves to the

478   *NATURE, SOCIETY, AND THOUGHT*

> *thing* for the sake of the thing, but the thing itself is an *objective human* relation to itself and to man. . . . Need or enjoyment has consequently lost its *egotistical* nature, and nature has lost its mere *utility* by use becoming *human* use. (1975b, 300)

And, similarly:

> Only through the objectively unfolded richness of man's essential being is the richness of subjective *human* sensibility. . . either cultivated or brought into being. For not only the five senses but also the so-called mental senses, the practical senses (will, love, etc.), in a word, *human* sense, the human nature of the senses, comes to be by virtue of *its* object, by virtue of *humanised* nature. (301–2)

Finally, and most expressively: "All history is the history of preparing and developing '*man*' to become the object of *sensuous* consciousness, and turning the requirements of 'man as man' into his needs. History itself is a *real* part of *natural history*—of nature's developing into man" (304). We need not, at this point at least, necessarily decide between Marx's naturalism and Nietzsche's. All we have to do is distinguish between them as fully as possible and register their radical difference at all points, epistemological as well as political. For Marx, naturalism meant the dialectical unity of humans and nature, resulting in the call for the humanization of nature and the naturalization of humans; for Nietzsche, nature and humans are divorced and the latter must submit to the former. The sociopolitical significance is likewise diametrically opposed. For Marx: recognition of the social nature of humans and the building of a human society by the abolition of private property relations. For Nietzsche: a denial of the social nature of humans (denounced as herd-mentality/morality), defense of the status quo, and vindication of property relations:

> But there will always be too many who have possessions for socialism to signify more than an attack of sickness—and those who have possessions are of one mind on one article of faith: "one must possess something inrder to *be* something." But this is the oldest and healthiest of all instincts:

Marx vs. Nietzsche on Religion   479

I should add, "one must want to have more than one has in order to *become* more." For this is the doctrine preached by life itself to all that has life: the morality of development. To have and to want to have more—*growth*, in one word—that is life itself. (1968, 77)

The tarantulas of equality

There can be no doubt that Nietzsche was deeply aware of the significance and role of his atheism as a *counter*-atheism. Perhaps nowhere in his writings is the difference between the uprightness of his unique brand of materialistic atheism and the perversity of the socialist one as energetically and militantly broadcast as in the passage dealing with what Zarathustra bitterly refers to as "the tarantulas." Nietzsche's prophet takes great care to distinguish his position from theirs: "My friends, I do not want to be confused with others or taken for what I am not" (1969, 124). He makes a distinction between two doctrines of life, a genuine and a counterfeit one: "There are those who preach my doctrine of life: yet are at the same time preachers of equality, and tarantulas." Like most founders of new religions, Zarathustra makes a claim for originality and primacy; he declares that the tarantulas, as false prophets are wont to do, preach and pervert *his* doctrine of life. For the sake of historical justice, however, it should be stated that it was rather Zarathustra (Nietzsche) who has reacted to the life-doctrine, spurious or not, of the tarantulas (the socialists). But who are the tarantulas and what does Nietzsche find so reprehensible about them? For one thing, as we have heard, they promulgate the creed of equality, the very anathema of Zarathustra's doctrine.

I do not wish to be mixed up and confused with these preachers of equality. For, to *me*, justice speaks thus: 'Men are not equal.' Nor shall they become equal! What would my love of the overman be if I spoke otherwise? (1995, 101)

The upholders of equality, namely the revolutionaries and socialists, can pretend to speak on behalf of life only because they rise up against the current establishment, founded on Christian morality:

480   NATURE, SOCIETY, AND THOUGHT

> Although they are sitting in their holes, these poisonous spiders, with their backs turned on life, they speak in favor of life, but only because they wish to hurt. They wish to hurt those who now have power, for among these the preaching of death is still most at home. (1995, 101)

Zarathustra acknowledges that the tarantulas possess some power of persuasion. Their life-rhetoric is effective because it is directed against Christianity, which is a life-denying religion. It is only in comparison to the lifeless Christians that the socialists can gain the appearance of liveliness although, in truth, they themselves "sit in their caves with their backs turned on life." With the demise of religion, socialism, with its promise of earthly happiness, becomes an enticing option. And it is here that Zarathustra intervenes to offer an alternative to the alternative. Against socialism he musters two main arguments, which happen to be contradictory, but their joint effect, in spite of the inconsistency, is quite powerful. The first argument is negative, dismissing what the socialists have to offer. Zarathustra claims that the socialists are frauds and hypocrites; they speak of justice and are ready to punish the strong and overturn the social order while they themselves are motivated by revengefulness and lust for power: "when they call themselves the good and the just, do not forget that they would be pharisees, if only they had—power" (100). Thus the revolutionaries can be condemned from the point of view of conventional pre-Zarathustrian morality, from *within* the bounds of *good and evil*: they are *evil*, firstly, and their evil, furthermore, expresses itself in their *obsession with power*; they promise justice and happiness but will fail to deliver, proving themselves to be tyrannical. This argument remains quite consistent with the habitual, conservative critique of revolutionaries since the French Revolution, directed at their cruelty and inhumanity, as they exact and mete out punishment against their betters:

> I counsel you my friends: Mistrust all in whom the impulse to punish is powerful. They are people of a low sort and stock; the hangman and the bloodhound look out of their faces. (100)

Marx vs. Nietzsche on Religion 481

But Zarathustra is not merely an advocator of old times; such timid admonitions, purely negative, cannot serve as a good defense against the optimistic tide of the socialists. It is difficult to defend present iniquity simply by the prediction of a future one. If Zarathustra is to justify his claims for a radical New Testament, and exceed the worn-out cautions of a Burke, a Bonald, or a de Maistre, he has to offer the masses a merchandise at least as exciting as what the socialists publicize, something bold and affirmative as opposed to passive and preventive. And at this point Zarathustra becomes the prophet of life. It is principally for this reason, no doubt, that the metaphor of the tarantulas was applied in the first place: the revolutionaries must be denuded of their glamorous, if ruthless, halo. They must be exposed as true enemies of life; venomous, weak, and disgusting creatures; necessarily hiding their true, pathetic selves. A lantern in hand, Zarathustra escorts the reader to the dark hiding-place of the socialist enemy of life and invites him to establish the latter's true nature: "Behold, this is the hole of the tarantula. Do you want to see the tarantula itself? Here hangs its web: touch it, that it tremble" (99).

The socialist is thereby deprived of power and stature; he is not only wicked but also weak and despicable. The tarantulas are the hateful forgers of materialism, who have done away with God but not to enable the development of natural, ascending life; instead, they launch a neomoralistic, neo-Christian crusade against life, in the name of the feeble and the sick. Zarathustra is the one who truly celebrates life. This is Zarathustra's assertive proposal, which happens to contradict his former, negative caveat. Earlier, he has claimed that the socialists will only replace power as it now exists with a new tyranny; their pledge for the abolition of injustice and suffering was therefore dismissed as unrealistic and illusory. But presently, Zarathustra tacitly acknowledges that such elimination of strife might actually materialize. Socialism is now deemed feasible but—*undesirable*. This is a point to reckon with, particularly in the context of Nietzsche's enthusiastic reception by numerous interpreters, who have praised his prophetic utterances against the horrors of twentieth-century communism, the totalitarian abuses of state

482   NATURE, SOCIETY, AND THOUGHT

power.[8] Leaving aside the relative value of such forewarnings on the part of a philosopher who encouraged the elite to subjugate the majority scrupulously and who made it perfectly clear that such subjugation will entail not only the exploitation but also "the annihilation of millions of failures" (Nietzsche 1968, 506), it is important to take heed of the fact that this critique of totalitarianism was only Nietzsche's *first line of defense*; that beyond the possibility of socialist *failure*, Nietzsche apprehended the prospect of a socialist *success*; and that he found the likelihood of a socialist *abuse* of power no more intimidating than the scenario of a socialist *elimination* of power. Put in Marx's terms, Nietzsche was targeting not only the dystopia of "despotic communism" that we have come to know during the twentieth century, but also "true communism," *the socialist utopia* as such.[9] For if, according to Zarathustra, the revolutionaries succeed and truly and abidingly eliminate conflict, exploitation, and war, this will prove humanity's catastrophe, since peace and equality, once attained, will cripple life, not enhance it:

> They shall throng to the future, and ever more war and inequality shall divide them: thus does my great love make me speak. In their hostilities they shall become inventors of images and ghosts, and with their images and ghosts they shall yet fight the highest fight against one another. Good and evil, and rich and poor, and high and low, and all the names of values—arms shall they be and clattering signs that life must overcome itself again and again.
>
> Life wants to build itself up into the heights with pillars and steps; it wants to look into vast distances and out toward stirring beauties: therefore it requires height. And because it requires height, it requires steps and contradiction among the steps and the climbers. Life wants to climb and to overcome itself climbing. (101)

The tarantulas turn their backs on life, for they refuse to admit the necessity of strife and suffering; they become ascetic enemies of life who, by suspending conflict and imposing equality, check the rise of ascending life:

Marx vs. Nietzsche on Religion   483

> And behold, my friends: here where the tarantula has its hole, the ruins of an ancient temple rise; behold it with enlightened eyes! Verily, the man who once piled his thoughts to the sky in these stones—he, like the wisest, knew the secret of all life. That struggle and inequality are present even in beauty. . . . [L]et us be enemies too, my friends! Let us strive against one another like gods! (101–2)

This is Zarathustra's innovation and the crux of Nietzsche's *Lebensphilosophie*. To minimize conflict and danger is to downgrade life; war produces the sublime *Übermensch,* whereas peace leads to the pathetic last man. But the paradoxes underpinning such *Lebensphilosophie* also come into view. To start with, it becomes clear that, in social terms, Nietzsche's *Jasagen zum Leben* means accepting, rather than combating, life's cruelty, injustice and, ultimately, life's termination—death. Thus, a *yes-saying to death*, indeed a cult of death, is never too far away from the philosophy-of-life. Consider, for example, section 109 of *The Gay Science*, where Nietzsche warns us against "thinking that the world is a living thing" (1974, 167). He then argues that the world has no "instinct for self-preservation," and proceeds to question the traditional dichotomy between life and death: "Let us beware of saying that death is opposed to life. The living is merely a type of what is dead, and a very rare type." These are not merely philosophical ruminations; rather, they are also a prescription as to the way humanity must take in accordance with nature. The section ends with the above discussed call to finally "'naturalize' humanity in terms of a pure, newly discovered, newly redeemed nature." And if humans are to be naturalized, it follows logically that they must renounce self-preservation as a supreme value. Once "demonstrated" to be lacking in nature as a guiding principle, self-preservation must be correspondingly abolished as a *social* principle. As Zarathustra will exclaim, against the mob rule of democracy and socialism:

> What is womanish, what derives from the servile and especially the mob hodgepodge: *that* now would now become master of all human destiny. O nausea! Nausea! Nausea! *That* asks and asks and never grows weary: "How is man

484   *NATURE, SOCIETY, AND THOUGHT*

to be preserved best, longest, most agreeably?" With that—they are the masters of today.

Overcome these masters of today, O my brothers—these small people: *they* are the overman's greatest danger!

You higher men, overcome the small virtues, the small prudences . . . the "happiness of the greatest number"! (1995, 287–88)

Here we find an indispensable clue to decipher the otherwise totally obscure death cult of fascism, quintessentially expressed by the Francoist battle-cry of *¡Viva la muerte!* To counter socialist and liberal humanist doctrines, the sanctity of human life had to be devalued. Self-preservation at all costs was consequently denigrated as a kind of superstition, a human, all-too-human weakness. Real, authentic life does not shun death as its opposite; only decadent, cowardly life does. Humans have to live grandiosely, courageously, healthily, and "naturally"—that is, in imitation of the universe: above pain, above "petty" emotions, and, finally, above life. It is in the context of such programmatic dehumanization that even death, the ultimate negation of human existence, is vindicated as at least as "natural" as life. In some senses, it is even more natural; life is an exception, a passing illusion, a mere *phenomenon*; death is the rule, the abiding reality, the *thing in itself.*

A further paradoxical feature of *Lebensphilosophie* is its fetishizing of life. With Nietzsche, life turns into something independent of the many concrete cases of living organisms, into a metaphysical, disembodied essence. Though formerly warning us against anthropomorphisms, Nietzsche now avows that life "wants," "needs," and "raises itself." It is as if each individual organism contains a piece of life and for that reason falls into the illusion of identifying itself, the means, with the goal, with *life* as a general, abstract force. Consequently the organism strives to preserve the life in its possession at all costs. But the cause of *life* is greater than the cause of all the little lives. From the lofty perspective of *life,* individuals having a share of it are merely tenants, expedient instruments, "steps and pillars" that it uses in order to ascend and overcome itself. In order to serve *life* in the abstract, therefore, it is sensible to sacrifice innumerable lives *in the concrete*, to have them perish in conflicts and wars. This

Marx vs. Nietzsche on Religion   485

is also the logic behind the idea of the *Übermensch*: since he is the utmost expression of *life*, its finest masterpiece, it makes sense for lesser people to sacrifice themselves for his sake: "I love those," says Zarathustra,

> ... who sacrifice themselves for the earth, that the earth may some day become the overman's.
> I love him who lives to know, and who wants to know so that the overman may live some day. And thus he wants to go under. (1995, 15)

And it is from the same vantage point that the weak and sickly are amiably entreated to forsake their pitiful, insignificant lives, so that *life* be advanced.

> To create a new responsibility, that of the physician, in all cases in which the highest interest of life, of *ascending* life, demands the most ruthless suppression and sequestration of degenerating life—for example in determining the right to reproduce, the right to be born, the right to live. . . . When one *does away* with oneself one does the most estimable thing possible: one thereby almost deserves to live. . . . Society—what am I saying! *life* itself derives more advantage from that than from any sort of "life" spent in renunciation, green-sickness and other virtues—one has freed others from having to endure one's sight, one has removed an objection from life. (1990b, 99–100)

Nietzsche thus discards self-preservation, the instinct of clinging on to life, as an *anti*life instinct. Ironically, the party of antilife socialists and egalitarians is the one that seeks to preserve life, whereas the philosopher of life, promoting a *Partei des Lebens* [party of the life], sanctions the sacrifice of countless lives: "The degree of 'progress' can actually be *measured* according to the mass of that which had to be sacrificed to it. Mankind in the mass sacrificed to the prosperity of a single *stronger* species of man—that *would be* a progress" (1988, 315). *Life* becomes a new absolute monarch, in fact a new God, to whose eternal glory every individual must dedicate his or her (little) life, which he or she must be ready to sacrifice if need arises. This is another subtle way by which the atheistic humanization of the world can be circumvented by use of dehumanizing atheism. The scheme can even boast of an odd egalitarianism: everyone, "good and evil, rich and poor, noble and mean," remains equally the humble servant of a greater cause, the perfection of *life*. Hence Zarathustra's kindly, amiable gestures, his talk of his "great love," and the frequent appeal to his readers/listeners with the cordial "my friends." We learn that, deceptive appearances aside, there is nothing self-serving in the social hierarchy, with its corresponding unequal division of pleasures and privileges, as well as toils and hardships. One is paid, rather, in accordance with the service rendered to *life*:

> The natural value of egoism depends on the physiological value of him who possesses it: it can be very valuable, it can be worthless and contemptible. Every individual may be regarded as representing the *ascending or descending line of life*. . . . If he represents the ascending line his value is in fact extraordinary—and for the *sake of the life-collective*, which with him takes a step *forward*, the care expended on his preservation, on the creation of optimum conditions for him, may even be extreme. . . . If he represents the descending development, decay, chronic degeneration, sickening . . . , then he can be accorded little value, and elementary fairness demands that he *takes away* as little as possible from the well-constituted. He is not better than a parasite on them. (1990b, 97)

The vast usefulness of such a *Weltanschauung* for justifying capitalism is obvious. Exploitation is metaphysically vindicated. What to the unaided eye seems simple "egoism" reveals itself, under the scrutiny of *life*'s superior lens, as "elementary fairness."

Marx and Engels's refutation of the Übermensch

So far, I have argued that Nietzsche's critique of religion was an attempt to corner the market of Western atheism with a new, dehumanizing product, devised specifically to bankrupt the socialist

Marx vs. Nietzsche on Religion 487

competitors. However ingenious such a move was, I contend that it did not catch its adversaries completely by surprise. As a matter of fact, both Marx and Engels, the latter perhaps more patently, foresaw the outlines of such a development and even provided essential arguments with which to counteract it.

In their first collaborative book, written in 1844, *The Holy Family, or Critique of Critical Criticism* (1975), Marx and Engels dedicated a chapter to a detailed analysis of one of the most popular novels of the time—Eugène Sue's *The Mysteries of Paris* (1844). This chapter, written by Marx, contains material that is highly valuable for our purposes, as it can help substantiate our understanding of the similarities as well as the crucial discrepancies between the Marxist and the Nietzschean critiques of religion.

Marx confronts religion as the main ideological accessory of the ruling classes in the nineteenth century. Although a power in decline, it is still able to exercise a strong influence on the popular imagination. Christian moralizing is a predominant ingredient in Sue's novel, which Marx regards as deeply conservative. The novel recounts the adventures of the worthy Prince Rudolph in the Parisian underworld, and his dealings with a host of low-lifes. Some of these criminals—like Fleur de Marie, the prostitute, or Chourineur, the bully—he is able to reform and recruit to the ranks of righteousness. Others, like the demonic and irredeemable *"Maître d'école,"* he brutally punishes. And both reward and chastisement are doled out in the name of Christian morality and in accord with bourgeois ideology, educating the lower classes about the benefits of virtue. The bulk of Marx's atheistic critique is directed at the sanctimony of the novel's "pious" message. In doing so, he speaks in a language that occasionally bears striking resemblance to the future Nietzschean demolition of Christianity, for instance when pitying the wretched Marie, who is *"enslaved by the consciousness of sin"* (Marx and Engels 1975, 174), or when denouncing the priestly debasement of nature and its smothering of life's exuberance:

> The priest has already succeeded in changing Marie's immediate naive pleasure in the beauties of nature into a *religious* admiration. For her, *nature* has already become

488   *NATURE, SOCIETY, AND THOUGHT*

> devout, *Christianised* nature, debased to *creation*. The transparent sea of space is desecrated and turned into the dark symbol of stagnant *eternity*. She has already learnt that all human manifestations of her being were *"profane,"* devoid of religion, of real consecration, that they were impious and godless. The priest must soil her in her own eyes, he must trample underfoot her natural, spiritual resources and means of grace, in order to make her receptive to the supernatural means of grace he promises her, *baptism*. (172)

This rings akin to Nietzsche's condemnation of Christianity as an antilife religion, subjecting existence to the yoke of metaphysical morality and banishing all natural drives. But, in crucial distinction to Nietzsche, Marx at all times sees religion as a *dehumanizing* force in the service of hierarchy. Nietzsche, as we saw, highly praised the aptitude of religion to sedate the masses and teach them "to preserve their contentment with the real order." This "holy lie" was needed to keep the multitude dutifully serving the elite, so that the latter would be free to elevate *life*. But Marx sees nothing life-enhancing about the Church's administration of tranquilizers to the poor. He disdainfully cites the priest's sermon to the former prostitute as the expression of the hollow Christian promise of the hereafter:

> The grey-headed slave of religion answers: "You must renounce hope of effacing this desolate page from your life, but you must trust in the *infinite mercy of God*. Here *below*, my poor child, you will have tears, remorse and penance, but one day *up above*, forgiveness and *eternal bliss*!" (174)

Far from finding such a ploy honorable, as Nietzsche did, Marx dismisses it as "hypocritical sophistry." Importantly, in *The Holy Family* we can also find Marx proposing to go beyond the conventional Christian dichotomy of good and evil, again in apparent consonance with Nietzsche. But for Marx, the moralizing discourse of good and evil is not a stratagem devised by the weak slaves to resist the power of the strong. On the contrary, it is one more means of domination wielded by the ruling classes, who

Marx vs. Nietzsche on Religion   489

loftily preach to the poor the commandment to do good, while simultaneously imposing upon them the material necessity to commit crime:

> [The priest] proves, as the commonest of bourgeois would, that she could have remained good: "There are many virtuous people in Paris today." The hypocritical priest knows quite well that at any hour of the day, in the busiest streets, those virtuous people of Paris pass indifferently by little girls of seven or eight years who sell *allumettes* and the like until about midnight as Marie herself used to do and who, almost without exception, will have the same fate as Marie. (172)

In opposition to this notion of good and evil, Marx advances what may be counted as their own version of *beyond good and evil*:

> *Good* and *evil*, as Marie conceives them, are not the *moral abstractions* of good and evil. She is *good* because she has never caused *suffering* to anyone, she has always been *human* towards her inhuman surroundings. She is *good* because the sun and the flowers reveal to her her own sunny and blossoming nature. She is *good* because she is still *young,* full of hope and vitality. Her situation is *not good,* because it puts an unnatural constraint on her, because it is not the expression of her human impulses, not the fulfillment of her human desires; because it is full of torment and without joy. She measures her situation in life by her *own individuality,* her *essential nature,* not by the *ideal of what is good.* . . . [Marie] is neither good nor bad, but *human.* (169–70)

To move in a Marxist way *beyond good and evil* is to access the *human, all too human.* Superseding dehumanizing Christian morality equals quitting the realm of metaphysical and supernatural injunctions, and asserting the natural and the human. Nature is not posited as the cold, senseless antithesis of humanity, as in Nietzsche, but rather as a mirror in which humanity can legitimately recognize its own reflection. Anthropomorphism is

490   NATURE, SOCIETY, AND THOUGHT

therefore sanctioned, not in an ontological sense but as a legitimate human need. Marie is fully entitled to measure "her situation in life by her *own individuality*, her *essential nature*." The human perspective is consciously given priority. It never occurs to Marx to suggest that men, or women, should *naturalize* themselves, in Nietzsche's sense of *denying* their own human nature, of becoming the *Übermensch*. On the contrary, Marx at all times espouses the effort to *humanize* nature, a process for which he used the term "objectification" (*Vergegenständlichung*): "man's natural means of projecting himself through his productive activity into nature. . . . [It] affords a free man the possibility of contemplating himself in a world of his own making."[10]

This is an example of how Nietzscheanism was not a clean break with nineteenth-century mores and norms, but also a continuation, in many regards a tactical adjustment more than a strategic transformation. If, in the nineteenth century, the priest was above humanity, urging it to go beyond its nature, in the twentieth century, this role was entrusted to the *Übermensch*. Nietzsche substituted atheistic dehumanization for a religious one. In this way he sought to repel the danger that atheism would proceed to revolutionize society, and to divert its potentially radical thrust into favorable channels.

Although Marx's proposals in *The Holy Family* are seen to contradict Nietzscheanism, they are nonetheless still posited vis-à-vis the old morality, the traditional defense of hierarchy. Only indirectly and in retrospect can we read into them an alternative to Nietzsche's new morality, preempting the beyond-good-and-evil gospel. Remarkably, however, Engels has provided us with what can be counted a well-nigh explicit rejection of Nietzscheanism and the ideal of the *Übermensch*. One of Engels's early pamphlets is a discussion of an embryonic form of Nietzscheanism, the ideas of Thomas Carlyle. In his social sympathies, Carlyle, like Nietzsche, was essentially an aristocratic antagonist to capitalism, coming from the ranks of the Tories. As Engels establishes, it is only his position as an outsider to the bourgeois world that enables him to criticize it. The Tory, "whose power and unchallenged dominance have been broken by industry . . . hates

Marx vs. Nietzsche on Religion   *491*

it and sees in it at best a necessary evil" (1975, 447). The Whigs, in comparison, being as they are wholly committed to English industry, the firm bedrock of their socioeconomic prevalence, cannot rise above their vested interests and critically confront the social order. This is the class standpoint that permits Carlyle to unfold his ruthless critique of English society, the profane cult of Mammon, the material as well as moral degeneration brought about by the Industrial Revolution. Engels accepts, even applauds, the diagnosis as such:

> This is the condition of England according to Carlyle . . . a total disappearance of all general human interests, a universal despair of truth and humanity and in consequence a universal isolation of men in their own "brute individuality," . . . a war of all against all, . . . a disproportionately strong working class, in intolerable oppression and wretchedness, in furious discontent and rebellion against the old social order, and hence, a threatening, irresistibly advancing democracy—everywhere chaos, disorder, anarchy, dissolution of the old ties of society. . . . Thus far, if we discount a few expressions that have derived from Carlyle's particular standpoint, we must allow the truth of all he says. He, alone of the "respectable" class, has kept his eyes open at least towards the facts, he has at least correctly apprehended the immediate present, and that is indeed a very great deal for an "educated" Englishman. (1975, 456)

Engels is even willing to assume that the shortcomings in Carlyle's diagnosis are not a result of an inherent reactionary standpoint, but merely of a romantic failure to come to terms with Hegelianism as a genuine, rational, and historical overcoming of religion. It is against the background of such a favorable overall evaluation that Engels's *firm rejection* of Carlyle's *positive* project stands out with particular clarity. Carlyle, like Nietzsche after him, confronts the bourgeois reality with deep aversion. And, like his German counterpart, he finds repulsive above all else the moral and cultural conditions dominating under bourgeois rule. These for him form the basic problem, rather than any material suffering, however acute, endured by the proletariat.[11] Carlyle

492   *NATURE, SOCIETY, AND THOUGHT*

conceives of modern "atheism" as a symptom of a general process that is very similar to what Nietzsche would later refer to as "nihilism"— namely, an erosion of values and loss of meaning, a gradual sinking into an axiological and epistemological morass.[12] In the words of Engels:

> But we have seen what Carlyle calls atheism: it is not so much disbelief in a personal God, as disbelief in the inner essence, in the infinity of the universe, disbelief in reason, despair of the intellect and the truth; his struggle is not against the disbelief in the revelation of the Bible, but against the most frightful disbelief, the disbelief in the "Bible of Universal History." (457)

The solution Carlyle envisions is not material but some moral regeneration, to be worked out within the existing framework of capitalism. For all his contempt at the rule of money, he does not contemplate the overthrow of bourgeois rule and the abolition of its material premise, private property, but rather emotionally clamors for the arrival of the noble capitalists, the heroic "captains of industry." He intends to remedy the moral affliction of the age by founding a new religion, a new popular cult, the cult of heroes, under which "work"—made a fetish by Carlyle, having recourse to Goethe's "religion of work"—will recover its meaning and dignity. Capitalism as a cultural phenomenon is somehow to be eliminated without ousting capitalism as a mode of production:

> In order to effect this organisation [of work], in order to put true guidance and true government in the place of false guidance, Carlyle longs for a "true aristocracy," a "hero-worship," and puts forward the second great problem to discover the άριςτοι, the best, whose task it is to combine "with inevitable Democracy indispensable Sovereignty." (460)

For this sort of project, Engels can feel no sympathy and he must part ways with Carlyle. The effort to exceed humanity by way of the hero he regards a neoreligious, pantheistic move, still positing a suprahuman entity above humans instead of accepting once

Marx vs. Nietzsche on Religion   493

and for all the human as such: "a new religion, a pantheistic hero-worship, a cult of work, ought to be set up or is to be expected; but this is impossible; all the possibilities of religion are exhausted" (462). As the antidote to Carlyle's mysticism, Engels advocates the principled acknowledgment of humanity's intrinsic value, in noteworthy sentences that might have been written with Nietzsche's *Übermensch* in mind:

> We want to put an end to atheism, as Carlyle portrays it, by giving back to man the substance he has lost through religion; not as a divine but as a human substance. . . . We want to sweep away everything that claims to be supernatural and superhuman [*übermenschlich*] and thereby to get rid of untruthfulness, for the root of all untruth and lying is the pretension of the human and the natural to be superhuman and supernatural. (463)

It may be argued that Engels's notion of what is *übermenschlich* and Nietzsche's use of the term bear only a superficial resemblance, since Nietzsche meant his *Übermensch* to be non-religious, indeed antireligious, as well as perfectly natural. Yet Engels's discussion of the residues of the supernatural in Carlyle unmistakably includes the "secular" notion of the *man above man*, the hero. For Engels, this allegedly "natural" hero is just as metaphysical as any entity claiming supernatural origins:

> Carlyle has still enough religion to remain in a state of unfreedom; pantheism still recognises something higher than man himself. Hence his longing for a "true aristocracy," for "heroes"; as if these heroes could at best be more than *men*. (466)

Significantly, Engels does not conceive of "man himself" in terms of a necessary compromise, a down-to-earth acquiescence with austere reality at the expense of the grandeur of heroic fantasy. Rather, the human being is celebrated as being *unsurpassable in magnificence*: "Man's own substance is far more splendid and sublime than the imaginary substance of any conceivable 'God,' who is after all only the more or less indistinct and distorted image of man himself" (465). It seems quite safe to assume that Nietzsche's

494 NATURE, SOCIETY, AND THOUGHT

Übermensch would have been regarded by Engels as one more exhibit in this stock of possible gods. What is more, as Engels proceeds to ponder the political and social implications of Carlyle's hero, he emphatically impugns the concrete, proto-Nietzschean justification of hierarchy attendant on such a hero:

> If he [Carlyle] had understood man as man in all his infinite complexity, he would not have conceived the idea of once more dividing mankind into two lots, sheep and goats, rulers and ruled, aristocrats and the rabble, lords and dolts, he would have seen the proper social function of talent not in ruling by force, but acting as a stimulant and taking the lead. (466)

Though a firm critic of bourgeois parliamentarism, Engels defends the objectives of democracy against Carlyle's attacks:

> Mankind is surely not passing through democracy to arrive back eventually at the point of departure. . . . Democracy, true enough, is only a transitional stage, though not towards a new, improved aristocracy, but towards real human freedom; just as the irreligiousness of the age will eventually lead to complete emancipation from everything that is religious, superhuman and supernatural, and not to its restoration. (466)

Finally, Engels puts his finger on the decisive difference between his own critique of capitalism and Carlyle's, a difference that is not confined to the realm of philosophical theory, but comes down to their respective approaches to the social question of property relations. Carlyle's ultimate failure to go beyond the superhuman and affirm the human is ascribed to his inability to envisage a move beyond capital. "Carlyle recognises the inadequacy of 'competition, demand' and 'supply, Mammonism,' etc. . . . So why has he not drawn the straightforward conclusion from all these assumptions and rejected the whole concept of property? How does he think he will destroy 'competition,' 'supply and demand,' Mammonism, etc., as long as the root of all these things, private property, exists?" (466). This decisive allegiance to capital, then, is what conditions, according to Engels, the hero-worship that Carlyle—and, at a second remove, Nietzsche—advocates.

Marx vs. Nietzsche on Religion   495

And so, if Nietzsche regarded the socialist tarantulas as still lurking in the shadow of God, the socialists themselves could just as surely sniff God's aroma emanating from the concept of Nietzsche's *Übermensch*. Strangely, this is a theological debate that is not really about religion, but about its profane uses here on earth. But this, perhaps, is the true nature of all theology. The general perseverance of the superhuman that Marx argued against was also that of the *Nietzschean* superhuman and the elitism-cum-capitalism attendant on it, while the God that Nietzsche sought to expel was very much the persistence of Christianity through socialism. This is not to say that we are permitted to reduce Nietzsche's (proto)existential composite of yearnings and anxieties, like those of his generation and of subsequent ones, to a clever ruse to parry the offensive of socialism. The anxieties were real enough, grounded in the reality of a disenchanted, desacralized world, just as the yearnings for wholeness and meaning were natural and genuine responses to this very same modern "void."[13]

Not so much were the questions as such ideological, but the answers; not the realization that modernity is indeed an ambivalent "progress" is here analyzed as an ideological means of class struggle, but the proposed "solutions" of principled irrationalism, pantheism, vitalism, etc. Having said that, it should be clear that not even the questions raised by incipient existentialism were simply, as often construed, the universal expression of the concerns of "modern man." The death of God, even to the extent that it can be seen as a universal catastrophe, as opposed to an event of a limited, local scale, must be evaluated in its social, rather than metaphysical, context. Not all classes of society responded equally, as abstract "human beings," to the sight of God's corpse. For it must be borne in mind that with God, the ruling classes had lost not only a spiritual helmsman and guarantor of meaning but also a material provider and social patron. To be sure, for the subordinate classes too, the weakening of religion as a mass doctrine was not bereft of painful consequences. But for them the political implications, at least to start with, seemed very different: a great oppressive force was removed from their path, revealing before them the promising

496   NATURE, SOCIETY, AND THOUGHT

horizon of a better future. God was too much part of the *ancien régime* to be truly grieved for.

At a later historical stage, as God was being replaced ever more effectively in hegemonic doctrines with a social Darwinist Nature, relentlessly weeding the "misfits" and rewarding "the entrepreneurial spirit," the ruling classes were conspicuously relieved of some of the early existential desolation to reembrace liberal secularism, whereas the masses, "stubbornly" and "ignorantly," often retained belief in a merciful God, pledged to the underdog. Hence the perplexing phenomenon, throughout the twentieth century and into the twenty-first, of God freely shifting alliances and crossing over to the side of the working class and of colonized "Third World" nations, against Western, secular, market-pantheism, as shown by his support for such diverse movements as those inspired by liberation theology in Africa and Latin America, or by the (indeed quite disparate) theologies of what is generally known as "Islamic fundamentalism." God nowadays—as borne out perhaps most tellingly by the events of September 11, 2001—fights on both sides of the "clash-of-civilizations" divide. It is a schizophrenic God, rising to "save America" from the terrorist attacks he himself had launched, surviving some 150 years of atheistic onslaught. This is, indeed, a God—*both* aroma *and* shadow.

Ben Gurion University
Beer Sheva, Israel

NOTES

1. A comparable position was expressed by Gilles Deleuze (1985, 142–49).

2. For a book-length exposition of such an approach from a Christian perspective, see Merold Westphal's accessible, well-written and often compellingly argued study (1998). Here Marx and Nietzsche are frequently linked together as advancing different but nonetheless complementary critiques of Christianity (22–24, 228, 232, 236, 243, 245). For a somewhat similar, if shorter, argument, see Hull (1997).

3. For a persuasive general argument against the ubiquitous attempt on the part of "left Nietzscheans" to reconcile Marxism and Nietzscheanism, stressing their essential incongruity, see Gedő (1998).

Marx vs. Nietzsche on Religion   497

4. Quoted in Bendix (1974, 67). It is necessary to clarify that this account of the function of religion in the eighteenth and nineteenth centuries in Europe addresses the hegemonic, institutional role of religion, and does not dispute either the existence or importance of counterhegemonic religious undercurrents, embodied—in the case of England—in such dissenting sects as the Quakers, the Camisards, or the Moravians. For a nuanced discussion of the uses and abuses of religion, as a major instrument for instilling quietism and work discipline in the working class, on the one hand, and as preserving a popular ethos of dissent, on the other, see chaps. 2 and 11 of E. P. Thompson's classic study, *The Making of the English Working Class* (1991).

5. On Nietzsche's appreciation of Hinduism, see Smith (2004) and Etter (1987).

6. Consider also the following commentary:

> For the Nazis, especially, the concept of "humanity" is biological nonsense, for man, "species-man," is part of nature. . . .[I]n place of God and any ideas of divine humanity, Nazism puts life itself. This in effect downgrades man: "Man is nothing special, nothing more than a piece of earth," Himmler tells us. (Neocleous 1997, 76)

Elsewhere in this excellent introduction to fascist ideology, the author briefly refers to Nietzsche's important contribution to the making of the fascist world-view (3–13).

7. Two fairly recent studies arguing the case for Marx as a pioneer of ecological thought are Burkett (1999) and Foster (2000).

8. See, for example, Roderick Stackelberg's commendation of Nietzsche as "a clairvoyant critic of impending totalitarianism" (2002, 311).

9. This is also the main weakness in Merold Westphal's account of Nietzsche's critique of religion as targeting the self-righteous vengefulness of the weak. This leads him to conclude that Marx and Nietzsche are complementary: "Taken together, Marx and Nietzsche remind us of this truth. Masters may be wicked sinners, but that does not make their slaves into saints" (1998, 230). In an idealist manner, the author believes that the gist of Nietzsche's opposition to religious *ressentiment* was just such an aversion to the self-deception of the slaves, and he credits Nietzsche with all sorts of stringent moral and intellectual virtues. "Nietzsche," we are at one place assured, "treats honesty and intellectual integrity like some kind of Kantian categorical imperative" (1998, 237). He completely overlooks Nietzsche's *social* commitment to the cause of the "masters" and his interest in guaranteeing their rule; Nietzsche's partial *affirmation* of Christianity as a means for ruling is nowhere noted. Westphal fails to grasp that Nietzsche did not level his critique at some excess of Christian-cum-revolutionary zeal, but rather at the revolutionary project as such. His ultimate aim, in other words, was not to civilize revolution, but to discredit altogether the very movement toward an egalitarian society. It is important to add that, extracted from the counter-revolutionary ideology in which they are firmly embedded, Nietzsche's insights into the potential mendaciousness of radical leaders or preachers, religious or otherwise, and his questioning of the purity of their motives are by no means to be dismissed.

10. Lucio Colletti's exposition of the term (1974, 431).

498   *NATURE, SOCIETY, AND THOUGHT*

11. To be sure, Carlyle's critique of capitalism far surpassed anything that Nietzsche ever put forward, if not in regard to substance, then at least as far as apparent sincerity of emotion and intention are concerned. Although a number of Nietzsche's utterances sympathizing with the working class are virtually plagiarized from Carlyle, they never quite generate the same sort of moral indignation, but give the impression of being merely tongue-in-cheek attempts at winning over the workers' trust. For Carlyle's influence on Nietzsche in that respect, compare, for instance, the closing section of Carlyle's *Chartism* (1839), titled "Impossible," in which he analyzes the working-class problem in Europe and proposes the solution of mass emigration, with Nietzsche's section from *Daybreak* (1881), titled "The Impossible Class," in which he analyzes the working-class problem in Europe and proposes the solution of mass emigration. And this "parallel" is by no means a single case.

12. See Nietzsche's distinction between the passive nihilism of the weak, characteristic of mass society, and the active nihilism of the strong, which he saw far more positively (1968, 17, 316–18). For a discussion of the concept of nihilism in Nietzsche see, for example, White (1987).

13. Cf. Fredric Jameson's thoughtful remarks on Nietzschean existentialism as a response to capitalist instrumentalization and the perceived erosion of values during the nineteenth century (1981, 251–52).

REFERENCE LIST

Bédarida, François. 1997. *Nationalsozialistische Verkündigung und säkulare Religion*. In *Der National-Sozialismus als politische Religion*, edited by Michael Ley and Julius H. Schoeps, 153–67. Frankfurt am Main: Philo.

Bendix, Reinhard. 1974. *Work and Authority in Industry. Ideologies of Management in the Course of Industrialization*. Berkeley, CA: Univ. of California Press.

Burkett, Paul. 1999. *Marx and Nature: A Red and Green Perspective*. New York: Palgrave Macmillan.

Burrin, Philippe. 1997. *Die politischen Religionen: Das Mythologisch-Symbolische in einer säkularisierten Welt*. In *Der National-Sozialismus als politische Religion*, edited by Michael Ley and Julius H. Schoeps, 168–85. Frankfurt am Main: Philo.

Colletti, Lucio. 1974. Glossary of Key Terms. In *Early Writings*, by Karl Marx, 429–32. Harmondsworth, UK: Penguin.

Deleuze, Gilles. 1985. *Nomad Thought*. In *The New Nietzsche*, edited by David B. Allison, 142–49. Cambridge, MA: MIT Press.

Engels, Frederick. 1975. The Condition of England: *Past and Present* by Thomas Carlyle, London 1843. In vol. 3 of Marx and Engels 1975–2005, 444–68.

Etter, Annemarie. 1987. Nietzsche und das Gesetzbuch des Manu. *Nietzsche Studien* 16:340–52.

Foster, John Bellamy. 2000. *Marx's Ecology: Materialism and Nature*. New York: Monthly Review Press.

Marx vs. Nietzsche on Religion   499

Foucault, Michel. 1998. Nietzsche, Freud, Marx. In *Essential Works of Foucault 1954–1984*. Vol. 2, *Aesthetics, Method, and Epistemology*, edited by J. D. Faubion, 269–78. New York: New Press.

Gedő, András. 1998. Why Marx or Nietzsche? *Nature, Society, and Thought* 11, 3:331–46.

Hull, John M. 1997. Atheism and the Future of Religions Education. In *Crossing the Boundaries: Essays in Biblical Interpretation in Honour of Michael D. Goulder*, edited by Stanley E. Porter, Paul Joyce, and David E. Orton, 357–75. Leiden: Brill Academic Publishers.

Jameson, Fredric. 1981. *The Political Unconscious*: *Narrative as a Socially Symbolic Act*. Ithaca, NY: Cornell Univ. Press.

Marx, Karl. 1975a. *Contribution to the Critique of Hegel's Philosophy of Law. Introduction*. In vol. 3 of Marx and Engels 1975–2005. 175–87.

———. 1975b. *Economic and Philosophic Manuscripts of 1844*. In vol. 3 of Marx and Engels 1975–2005, 229–347.

———. 1975c. On the Jewish Question. In vol. 3 of Marx and Engels 1975–2005, 146–74.

Marx, Karl, and Frederick Engels. 1975. *The Holy Family, or Critique of Critical Criticism: Against Bruno Bauer and Company*. In vol. 4 of Marx and Engels 1975–2005, 3–211.

———. 1975–2005. *Collected Works*. New York: International Publishers.

Neocleous, Mark. 1997. *Fascism*. Minneapolis: Univ. of Minnesota Press.

Newman, John Henry. 1986. *Apologia Pro Vita Sua,* from *Liberalism*. In *The Norton Anthology of English Literature*, 1030–32. 5th ed. New York: Norton.

Nietzsche, Friedrich. 1968. *The Will to Power*. New York: Vintage.

———. 1974. *The Gay Science*. New York: Vintage.

———. 1988. *Sämtliche Werke. 5. Kritische Studienausgabe in 15 Einzelbänden*. Edited by Giorgio Colli und Mazzino Montinari. Berlin: Walter de Gruyter.

———. 1990a. *Beyond Good and Evil*. Harmondsworth, UK: Penguin.

———. 1990b. *Twilight of the Idols and the Anti-Christ*. Harmondsworth, UK: Penguin.

———. 1995. *Thus Spoke Zarathustra*. New York: Modern Library.

Smith, David. 2004. Nietzsche's Hinduism, Nietzsche's India: Another Look. *Journal of Nietzsche Studies*, no. 28:37–56.

Stackelberg, Roderick. 2002. Critique as Apologetics: Nolte's Interpretation of Nietzsche. In *Nietzsche, Godfather of Fascism? On the Uses and Abuses of a Philosophy,* edited by Jacob Golomb and Robert S. Wistrich, 301–20. Princeton, NJ: Princeton Univ. Press.

Sue, Eugène. 1844. *The Mysteries of Paris*. New York: J. Winchester, 1844.

Thompson, Edward P. 1991. *The Making of the English Working Class*. Harmondsworth, UK: Penguin.

Westphal, Merold. 1998. *Suspicion and Faith: The Religious Uses of Modern Atheism*. New York: Fordham Univ. Press.

White, Alan. 1987. Nietzschean Nihilism: A Typology. *International Studies in Philosophy* 14, no. 2:29–44.

Part VI
History

[26]

EXPLOITATION

E.P. Thompson

JOHN THELWALL WAS not alone in seeing in every "manu-factory" a potential centre of political rebellion. An aristo-cratic traveller who visited the Yorkshire Dales in 1792 was alarmed to find a new cotton-mill in the "pastoral vale" of Aysgarth—"why, here now is a great flaring mill, whose back stream has drawn off half the water of the falls above the bridge":

With the bell ringing, and the clamour of the mill, all the vale is disturb'd; treason and levelling systems are the discourse; and rebellion may be near at hand.

The mill appeared as symbol of social energies which were destroying the very "course of Nature". It embodied a double threat to the settled order. First, from the owners of industrial wealth, those upstarts who enjoyed an unfair advantage over the landowners whose income was tied to their rent-roll:

If men thus start into riches; or if riches from trade are too easily procured, woe to us men of middling income, and settled revenue; and woe it has been to all the Nappa Halls, and the Yeomanry of the land.

Second, from the industrial working population, which our traveller regarded with an alliterative hostility which betrays a response not far removed from that of the white racialist towards the coloured population today:

The people, indeed, are employ'd; but they are all abandon'd to vice from the throng. . . . At the times when people work not in the mill, they issue out to poaching, profligacy and plunder. . . .[1]

The equation between the cotton-mill and the new industrial society, and the correspondence between new forms of produc-tive and of social relationship, was a commonplace among observers in the years between 1790 and 1850. Karl Marx was

[1] *The Torrington Diaries,* ed. C. B. Andrews (1936), III, pp. 81-2.

190 THE MAKING OF THE WORKING CLASS

only expressing this with unusual vigour when he declared: "The hand-mill gives you society with the feudal lord: the steam-mill, society with the industrial capitalist." And it was not only the mill-owner but also the working population brought into being within and around the mills which seemed to contemporaries to be "new". "The instant we get near the borders of the manufacturing parts of Lancashire," a rural magistrate wrote in 1808, "we meet a fresh race of beings, both in point of manners, employments and subordination . . ."; while Robert Owen, in 1815, declared that "the general diffusion of manufactures throughout a country generates a new character in its inhabitants . . . an essential change in the general character of the mass of the people."

Observers in the 1830s and 1840s were still exclaiming at the novelty of the "factory system". Peter Gaskell, in 1833, spoke of the manufacturing population as "but a Hercules in the cradle"; it was "only since the introduction of steam as a power that they have acquired their paramount importance". The steam-engine had "drawn together the population into dense masses" and already Gaskell saw in working-class organisations an " 'imperium in imperio' of the most obnoxious description".[1] Ten years later Cooke Taylor was writing in similar terms:

The steam-engine had no precedent, the spinning-jenny is without ancestry, the mule and the power-loom entered on no prepared heritage: they sprang into sudden existence like Minerva from the brain of Jupiter.

But it was the human consequence of these "novelties" which caused this observer most disquiet:

As a stranger passes through the masses of human beings which have accumulated round the mills and print works . . . he cannot contemplate these "crowded hives" without feelings of anxiety and apprehension almost amounting to dismay. The population, like the system to which it belongs, is NEW; but it is hourly increasing in breadth and strength. It is an aggregate of masses, our conceptions of which clothe themselves in terms that express something portentous and fearful . . . as of the slow rising and gradual swelling of an ocean which must, at some future and no distant time, bear all the elements of society aloft upon its bosom, and float them Heaven

---

[1] P. Gaskell, *The Manufacturing Population of England* (1833), p. 6; Asa Briggs, "The Language of 'Class' in Early Nineteenth-century England", in *Essays in Labour History*, ed. Briggs and Saville (1960), p. 63.

EXPLOITATION 191

knows whither. There are mighty energies slumbering in these masses. . . . The manufacturing population is not new in its formation alone: it is new in its habits of thought and action, which have been formed by the circumstances of its condition, with little instruction, and less guidance, from external sources. . . .[1]

For Engels, describing the *Condition of the Working Class in England in 1844* it seemed that "the first proletarians were connected with manufacture, were engendered by it . . . the factory hands, eldest children of the industrial revolution, have from the beginning to the present day formed the nucleus of the Labour Movement."

However different their judgements of value, conservative, radical, and socialist observers suggested the same equation: steam power and the cotton-mill = new working class. The physical instruments of production were seen as giving rise in a direct and more-or-less compulsive way to new social relationships, institutions, and cultural modes. At the same time the history of popular agitation during the period 1811-50 appears to confirm this picture. It is as if the English nation entered a crucible in the 1790s and emerged after the Wars in a different form. Between 1811 and 1813, the Luddite crisis; in 1817 the Pentridge Rising; in 1819, Peterloo; throughout the next decade the proliferation of trade union activity, Owenite propaganda, Radical journalism, the Ten Hours Movement, the revolutionary crisis of 1831-2; and, beyond that, the multitude of movements which made up Chartism. It is, perhaps, the scale and intensity of this multiform popular agitation which has, more than anything else, given rise (among contemporary observers and historians alike) to the sense of some *catastrophic* change.

Almost every radical phenomenon of the 1790s can be found reproduced tenfold after 1815. The handful of Jacobin sheets gave rise to a score of ultra-Radical and Owenite periodicals. Where Daniel Eaton served imprisonment for publishing Paine, Richard Carlile and his shopmen served a total of more than 200 years imprisonment for similar crimes. Where Corresponding Societies maintained a precarious existence in a score of towns, the post-war Hampden Clubs or political unions struck root in small industrial villages. And when this popular agitation is recalled alongside the dramatic pace of change in the

[1] W. Cooke Taylor, *Notes of a Tour in the Manufacturing Districts of Lancashire* (1842), pp. 4-6.

192 THE MAKING OF THE WORKING CLASS

cotton industry, it is natural to assume a direct causal relationship. The cotton-mill is seen as the agent not only of industrial but also of social revolution, producing not only more goods but also the "Labour Movement" itself. The Industrial Revolution, which commenced as a description, is now invoked as an explanation.

From the time of Arkwright through to the Plug Riots and beyond, it is the image of the "dark, Satanic mill" which dominates our visual reconstruction of the Industrial Revolution. In part, perhaps, because it is a dramatic visual image —the barrack-like buildings, the great mill chimneys, the factory children, the clogs and shawls, the dwellings clustering around the mills as if spawned by them. (It is an image which forces one to think first of the industry, and only secondly of the people connected to it or serving it.) In part, because the cotton-mill and the new mill-town—from the swiftness of its growth, ingenuity of its techniques, and the novelty or harshness of its discipline—seemed to contemporaries to be dramatic and portentous: a more satisfactory symbol for debate on the "condition-of-England" question than those anonymous or sprawling manufacturing *districts* which figure even more often in the Home Office "disturbance books". And from this both a literary and an historical tradition is derived. Nearly all the classic accounts by contemporaries of conditions in the Industrial Revolution are based on the cotton industry—and, in the main, on Lancashire: Owen, Gaskell, Ure, Fielden, Cooke Taylor, Engels, to mention a few. Novels such as *Michael Armstrong* or *Mary Barton* or *Hard Times* perpetuate the tradition. And the emphasis is markedly found in the subsequent writing of economic and social history.

But many difficulties remain. Cotton was certainly the pace-making industry of the Industrial Revolution,[1] and the cotton-mill was the pre-eminent model for the factory-system. Yet we should not assume any automatic, or over-direct, correspondence between the dyamic of economic growth and the dynamic of social or cultural life. For half a century after the "breakthrough" of the cotton-mill (around 1780) the mill workers remained as a minority of the adult labour force in the cotton industry itself. In the early 1830s the cotton hand-loom weavers alone still outnumbered all the men and women in spinning

[1] For an admirable restatement of the reasons for the primacy of the cotton industry in the Industrial Revolution, see E. J. Hobsbawm, *The Age of Revolution* (1962), Ch. 2.

EXPLOITATION 193

and weaving mills of cotton, wool, and silk combined.[1] Still, in 1830, the adult male cotton-spinner was no more typical of that elusive figure, the "average working man", than is the Coventry motor-worker of the 1960s.

The point is of importance, because too much emphasis upon the newness of the cotton-mills can lead to an underestimation of the continuity of political and cultural traditions in the making of working-class communities. The factory hands, so far from being the "eldest children of the industrial revolution", were late arrivals. Many of their ideas and forms of organisation were anticipated by domestic workers, such as the woollen workers of Norwich and the West Country, or the small-ware weavers of Manchester. And it is questionable whether factory hands—except in the cotton districts—"formed the nucleus of the Labour Movement" at any time before the late 1840s (and, in some northern and Midland towns, the years 1832-4, leading up to the great lock-outs). Jacobinism, as we have seen, struck root most deeply among artisans. Luddism was the work of skilled men in small workshops. From 1817 onwards to Chartism, the outworkers in the north and the Midlands were as prominent in every radical agitation as the factory hands. And in many towns the actual nucleus from which the labour movement derived ideas, organisation, and leadership, was made up of such men as shoemakers, weavers, saddlers and harnessmakers, booksellers, printers, building workers, small tradesmen, and the like. The vast area of Radical London between 1815 and 1850 drew its strength from no major heavy industries (shipbuilding was tending to decline, and the engineers only made their impact later in the century) but from the host of smaller trades and occupations.[2]

Such diversity of experiences has led some writers to question both the notions of an "industrial revolution" and of a "working class". The first discussion need not detain us here.[3] The term is serviceable enough in its usual connotations. For the second, many writers prefer the term working *classes*, which emphasises the great disparity in status, acquisitions, skills, conditions, within the portmanteau phrase. And in this they echo the complaints of Francis Place:

[1] Estimates for U.K., 1833. Total adult labour force in all textile mills, 191,671. Number of cotton hand-loom weavers, 213,000. See below, p. 311.

[2] Cf. Hobsbawm, op. cit., Ch. 11.

[3] There is a summary of this controversy in E. E. Lampard, *Industrial Revolution*, (American Historical Association, 1957). See also Hobsbawm, op. cit., Ch. 2.

194 THE MAKING OF THE WORKING CLASS

If the character and conduct of the working-people are to be taken from reviews, magazines, pamphlets, newspapers, reports of the two Houses of Parliament and the Factory Commissioners, we shall find them all jumbled together as the 'lower orders', the most skilled and the most prudent workman, with the most ignorant and imprudent labourers and paupers, though the difference is great indeed, and indeed in many cases will scarce admit of comparison.[1]

Place is, of course, right: the Sunderland sailor, the Irish navvy, the Jewish costermonger, the inmate of an East Anglian village workhouse, the compositor on *The Times*—all might be seen by their "betters" as belonging to the "lower classes" while they themselves might scarcely understand each others' dialect.

Nevertheless, when every caution has been made, the outstanding fact of the period between 1790 and 1830 is the formation of "the working class". This is revealed, first, in the growth of class-consciousness: the consciousness of an identity of interests as between all these diverse groups of working people and as against the interests of other classes. And, second, in the growth of corresponding forms of political and industrial organisation. By 1832 there were strongly-based and self-conscious working-class institutions—trade unions, friendly societies, educational and religious movements, political organisations, periodicals—working-class intellectual traditions, working-class community-patterns, and a working-class structure of feeling.

The making of the working class is a fact of political and cultural, as much as of economic, history. It was not the spontaneous generation of the factory-system. Nor should we think of an external force—the "industrial revolution"—working upon some nondescript undifferentiated raw material of humanity, and turning it out at the other end as a "fresh race of beings". The changing productive relations and working conditions of the Industrial Revolution were imposed, not upon raw material, but upon the free-born Englishman—and the free-born Englishman as Paine had left him or as the Methodists had moulded him. The factory hand or stockinger was also the inheritor of Bunyan, of remembered village rights, of notions of equality before the law, of craft traditions. He was the object of massive religious indoctrination and the creator of new political traditions. The working class made itself as much as it was made.

[1] Cit. M. D. George, *London Life in the 18th Century* (1930). p. 210.

EXPLOITATION

To see the working class in this way is to defend a "classical" view of the period against the prevalent mood of contemporary schools of economic history and sociology. For the territory of the Industrial Revolution, which was first staked out and surveyed by Marx, Arnold Toynbee, the Webbs and the Hammonds, now resembles an academic battlefield. At point after point, the familiar "catastrophic" view of the period has been disputed. Where it was customary to see the period as one of economic disequilibrium, intense misery and exploitation, political repression and heroic popular agitation, attention is now directed to the rate of economic growth (and the difficulties of "take-off" into self-sustaining technological reproduction). The enclosure movement is now noted, less for its harshness in displacing the village poor, than for its success in feeding a rapidly growing population. The hardships of the period are seen as being due to the dislocations consequent upon the Wars, faulty communications, immature banking and exchange, uncertain markets, and the trade-cycle, rather than to exploitation or cut-throat competition. Popular unrest is seen as consequent upon the unavoidable coincidence of high wheat prices and trade depressions, and explicable in terms of an elementary "social tension" chart derived from these data.[1] In general, it is suggested that the position of the industrial worker in 1840 was better in most ways than that of the domestic worker of 1790. The Industrial Revolution was an age, not of catastrophe or acute class-conflict and class oppression, but of improvement.[2]

The classical catastrophic orthodoxy has been replaced by a new anti-catastrophic orthodoxy, which is most clearly distinguished by its empirical caution and, among its most notable exponents (Sir John Clapham, Dr. Dorothy George, Professor Ashton) by an astringent criticism of the looseness of certain writers of the older school. The studies of the new orthodoxy have enriched historical scholarship, and have qualified and revised in important respects the work of the classical school. But as the new orthodoxy is now, in its turn, growing old and entrenched in most of the academic centres,

---

[1] See W. W. Rostow, *British Economy in the Nineteenth Century* (1948), esp. pp.122-5.

[2] Some of the views outlined here are to be found, implicitly or explicitly, in T. S. Ashton, *Industrial Revolution* (1948) and A. Radford, *The Economic History of England* (2nd edn. 1960). A sociological variant is developed by N. J. Smelser, *Social Change in the Industrial Revolution* (1959), and a knockabout popularisation is in John Vaizey, *Success Story* (W.E.A., n.d.).

196　THE MAKING OF THE WORKING CLASS

so it becomes open to challenge in its turn. And the successors of the great empiricists too often exhibit a moral complacency, a narrowness of reference, and an insufficient familiarity with the actual movements of the working people of the time. They are more aware of the orthodox empiricist postures than of the changes in social relationship and in cultural modes which the Industrial Revolution entailed. What has been lost is a sense of the whole process—the whole political and social context of the period. What arose as valuable qualifications have passed by imperceptible stages to new generalisations (which the evidence can rarely sustain) and from generalisations to a ruling attitude.

The empiricist orthodoxy is often defined in terms of a running critique of the work of J. L. and Barbara Hammond. It is true that the Hammonds showed themselves too willing to moralise history, and to arrange their materials too much in terms of "outraged emotion".[1] There are many points at which their work has been faulted or qualified in the light of subsequent research, and we intend to propose others. But a defence of the Hammonds need not only be rested upon the fact that their volumes on the labourers, with their copious quotation and wide reference, will long remain among the most important source-books for this period. We can also say that they displayed throughout their narrative an understanding of the political context within which the Industrial Revolution took place. To the student examining the ledgers of one cotton-mill, the Napoleonic Wars appear only as an abnormal influence affecting foreign markets and fluctuating demand. The Hammonds could never have forgotten for one moment that it was also a war against Jacobinism. "The history of England at the time discussed in these pages reads like a history of civil war." This is the opening of the introductory chapter of *The Skilled Labourer*. And in the conclusion to *The Town Labourer*, among other comments of indifferent value, there is an insight which throws the whole period into sudden relief:

At the time when half Europe was intoxicated and the other half terrified by the new magic of the word citizen, the English nation was in the hands of men who regarded the idea of citizenship as a challenge to their religion and their civilisation; who deliberately sought to make the inequalities of life the basis of the state, and to emphasise and perpetuate the position of the workpeople as a subject class. Hence it happened that the French Revolution has divided the

---

[1] See E. E. Lampard, op. cit., p. 7.

EXPLOITATION

people of France less than the Industrial Revolution has divided the people of England. . . .

"Hence it happened . . .". The judgement may be questioned. And yet it is in this insight—that the revolution which did *not* happen in England was fully as devastating, and in some features more divisive, than that which did happen in France —that we find a clue to the truly catastrophic nature of the period. Throughout this time there are three, and not two, great influences simultaneously at work. There is the tremendous increase in population (in Great Britain, from 10·5 millions in 1801 to 18·1 millions in 1841, with the greatest rate of increase between 1811-21). There is the Industrial Revolution, in its technological aspects. And there is the political *counter-revolution*, from 1792-1832.

In the end, it is the political context as much as the steam-engine, which had most influence upon the shaping consciousness and institutions of the working class. The forces making for political reform in the late 18th century—Wilkes, the city merchants, the Middlesex small gentry, the "mob"—or Wyvill, and the small gentry and yeomen, clothiers, cutlers, and tradesmen—were on the eve of gaining at least some piecemeal victories in the 1790s: Pitt had been cast for the rôle of reforming Prime Minister. Had events taken their "natural" course we might expect there to have been some show-down long before 1832, between the oligarchy of land and commerce and the manufacturers and petty gentry, with working people in the tail of the middle-class agitation. And even in 1792, when manufacturers and professional men were prominent in the reform movement, this was still the balance of forces. But, after the success of *Rights of Man*, the radicalisation and terror of the French Revolution, and the onset of Pitt's repression, it was the plebeian Corresponding Society which alone stood up against the counter-revolutionary wars. And these plebeian groups, small as they were in 1796, did nevertheless make up an "underground" tradition which ran through to the end of the Wars. Alarmed at the French example, and in the patriotic fervour of war, the aristocracy and the manufacturers made common cause. The English *ancien régime* received a new lease of life, not only in national affairs, but also in the perpetuation of the antique corporations which misgoverned the swelling industrial towns. In return, the manufacturers received important concessions: and notably the abrogation or repeal

198 THE MAKING OF THE WORKING CLASS

of "paternalist" legislation covering apprenticeship, wage-regulation, or conditions in industry. The aristocracy were interested in repressing the Jacobin "conspiracies" of the people, the manufacturers were interested in defeating their "conspiracies" to increase wages: the Combination Acts served both purposes.

Thus working people were forced into political and social *apartheid* during the Wars (which, incidentally, they also had to fight). It is true that this was not altogether new. What was new was that it was coincident with a French Revolution: with growing self-consciousness and wider aspirations (for the "liberty tree" had been planted from the Thames to the Tyne): with a rise in population, in which the sheer sense of numbers, in London and in the industrial districts, became more impressive from year to year (and as numbers grew, so deference to master, magistrate, or parson was likely to lessen): and with more intensive or more transparent forms of economic exploitation. More intensive in agriculture and in the old domestic industries: more transparent in the new factories and perhaps in mining. In agriculture the years between 1760 and 1820 are the years of wholesale enclosure, in which, in village after village, common rights are lost, and the landless and—in the south—pauperised labourer is left to support the tenant-farmer, the landowner, and the tithes of the Church. In the domestic industries, from 1800 onwards, the tendency is widespread for small masters to give way to larger employers (whether manufacturers or middlemen) and for the majority of weavers, stockingers, or nail-makers to become wage-earning outworkers with more or less precarious employment. In the mills and in many mining areas these are the years of the employment of children (and of women underground); and the large-scale enterprise, the factory-system with its new discipline, the mill communities—where the manufacturer not only made riches out of the labour of the "hands" but could be *seen* to make riches in one generation—all contributed to the transparency of the process of exploitation and to the social and cultural cohesion of the exploited.

We can now see something of the truly catastrophic nature of the Industrial Revolution; as well as some of the reasons why the English working class took form in these years. The people were subjected simultaneously to an intensification of two intolerable forms of relationship: those of economic exploitation

EXPLOITATION

and of political oppression. Relations between employer and labourer were becoming both harsher and less personal; and while it is true that this increased the potential freedom of the worker, since the hired farm servant or the journeyman in domestic industry was (in Toynbee's words) "halted half-way between the position of the serf and the position of the citizen", this "freedom" meant that he felt his *unfreedom* more. But at each point where he sought to resist exploitation, he was met by the forces of employer or State, and commonly of both.

For most working people the crucial experience of the Industrial Revolution was felt in terms of changes in the nature and intensity of exploitation. Nor is this some anachronistic notion, imposed upon the evidence. We may describe some parts of the exploitive process as they appeared to one remarkable cotton operative in 1818—the year in which Marx was born. The account—an Address to the public of strike-bound Manchester by "A Journeyman Cotton Spinner"—commences by describing the employers and the workers as "two distinct classes of persons":

"First, then, as to the employers: with very few exceptions, they are a set of men who have sprung from the cotton-shop without education or address, except so much as they have acquired by their intercourse with the little world of merchants on the exchange at Manchester; but to counterbalance that deficiency, they give you enough of appearances by an ostentatious display of elegant mansions, equipages, liveries, parks, hunters, hounds, &c. which they take care to shew off to the merchant stranger in the most pompous manner. Indeed their houses are gorgeous palaces, far surpassing in bulk and extent the neat charming retreats you see round London . . . but the chaste observer of the beauties of nature and art combined will observe a woeful deficiency of taste. They bring up their families at the most costly schools, determined to give their offspring a double portion of what they were so deficient in themselves. Thus with scarcely a second idea in their heads, they are literally petty monarchs, absolute and despotic, in their own particular districts; and to support all this, their whole time is occupied in contriving how to get the greatest quantity of work turned off with the least expence. . . . In short, I will venture to say, without fear of contradiction, that there is a greater distance observed between the master there and the spinner, than there is between the first merchant in London

200   THE MAKING OF THE WORKING CLASS

and his lowest servant or the lowest artisan. Indeed there is no comparison. I know it to be a fact, that the greater part of the master spinners are anxious to keep wages low for the purpose of keeping the spinners indigent and spiritless . . . as for the purpose of taking the surplus to their own pockets.

"The master spinners are a class of men unlike all other master tradesmen in the kingdom. They are ignorant, proud, and tyrannical. What then must be the men or rather beings who are the instruments of such masters? Why, they have been for a series of years, with their wives and their families, patience itself—bondmen and bondwomen to their cruel taskmasters. It is in vain to insult our common understandings with the observation that such men are free; that the law protects the rich and poor alike, and that a spinner can leave his master if he does not like the wages. True; so he can: but where must he go? why to another, to be sure. Well: he goes; he is asked where did you work last: 'did he discharge you?' No; we could not agree about wages. Well I shall not employ you nor anyone who leaves his master in that manner. Why is this? Because there is an abominable *combination existing amongst the masters*, first established at Stockport in 1802, and it has since become so general, as to embrace all the great masters for a circuit of many miles round Manchester, though not the little masters: they are excluded. They are the most obnoxious beings to the great ones that can be imagined. . . . When the combination first took place, one of their first articles was, that no master should take on a man until he had first ascertained whether his last master had discharged him. What then is the man to do? If he goes to the parish, that grave of all independence, he is there told—We shall not relieve you; if you dispute with your master, and don't support your family, we will send you to prison; so that the man is bound, by a combination of circumstances, to submit to his master. He cannot travel and get work in any town like a shoe-maker, joiner, or taylor; he is confined to the district.

"The workmen in general are an inoffensive, unassuming, set of well-informed men, though how they acquire their information is almost a mystery to me. They are docile and tractable, if not goaded too much; but this is not to be wondered at, when we consider that they are trained to work from six years old, from five in a morning to eight and nine at night. Let one of the advocates for obedience to his master take his stand in

EXPLOITATION

an avenue leading to a factory a little before five o'clock in the morning, and observe the squalid appearance of the little infants and their parents taken from their beds at so early an hour in all kinds of weather; let him examine the miserable pittance of food, chiefly composed of water gruel and oatcake broken into it, a little salt, and sometimes coloured with a little milk, together with a few potatoes, and a bit of bacon or fat for dinner; would a London mechanic eat this? There they are, (and if late a few minutes, a quarter of a day is stopped in wages) locked up until night in rooms heated above the hottest days we have had this summer, and allowed no time, except three-quarters of an hour at dinner in the whole day: whatever they eat at any other time must be as they are at work. The negro slave in the West Indies, if he works under a scorching sun, has probably a little breeze of air sometimes to fan him: he has a space of ground, and time allowed to cultivate it. The English spinner slave has no enjoyment of the open atmosphere and breezes of heaven. Locked up in factories eight stories high, he has no relaxation till the ponderous engine stops, and then he goes home to get refreshed for the next day; no time for sweet association with his family; they are all alike fatigued and exhausted. This is no over-drawn picture: it is literally true. I ask again, would the mechanics in the South of England submit to this?

"When the spinning of cotton was in its infancy, and before those terrible machines for superseding the necessity of human labour, called steam engines, came into use, there were a great number of what were then called *little masters*; men who with a small capital, could procure a few machines, and employ a few hands, men and boys (say to twenty or thirty), the produce of whose labour was all taken to Manchester central mart, and put into the hands of brokers. . . . The brokers sold it to the merchants, by which means the master spinner was enabled to stay at home and work and attend to his workmen. The cotton was then always given out in its raw state from the bale to the wives of the spinners at home, when they heat and cleansed it ready for the spinners in the factory. By this they could earn eight, ten, or twelve shillings a week, and cook and attend to their families. But none are thus employed now; for all the cotton is broke up by a machine, turned by the steam engine, called a devil: so that the spinners wives have no employment, except they go to work in the factory all day at

THE MAKING OF THE WORKING CLASS

what can be done by children for a few shillings, four or five per week. If a man then could not agree with his master, he left him, and could get employed elsewhere. A few years, however, changed the face of things. Steam engines came into use, to purchase which, and to erect buildings sufficient to contain them and six or seven hundred hands, required a great capital. The engine power produced a more marketable (though not a better) article than the little master could at the same price. The consequence was their ruin in a short time; and the overgrown capitalists triumphed in their fall; for they were the only obstacle that stood between them and the complete controul of the workmen.

"Various disputes then originated between the workmen and masters as to the fineness of the work, the workmen being paid according to the number of hanks or yards of thread he produced from a given quantity of cotton, which was always to be proved by the overlooker, whose interest made it imperative on him to lean to his master, and call the material coarser than it was. If the workman would not submit *he must summon his employer before a magistrate*; the whole of the acting magistrates in that district, with the exception of two worthy clergymen, being gentlemen who have sprung from the *same* source with the master cotton spinners. The employer generally contented himself with sending his overlooker to answer any such summons, thinking it beneath him to meet his servant. The magistrate's decision was generally in favour of the master, though on the statement of the overlooker only. The workman dared not appeal to the sessions on account of the expense. . . .

"These evils to the men have arisen from that dreadful monopoly which exists in those districts where wealth and power are got into the hands of the few, who, in the pride of their hearts, think themselves the lords of the universe."[1]

This reading of the facts, in its remarkable cogency, is as much an *ex parte* statement as is the "political economy" of Lord Brougham. But the "Journeyman Cotton Spinner" was describing facts of a different order. We need not concern ourselves with the soundness of all his judgements. What his address does is to itemise one after another the grievances felt by working people as to changes in the character of capitalist exploitation: the rise of a master-class without traditional authority or obligations: the growing distance between master

[1] *Black Dwarf*, 30 September 1818.

EXPLOITATION

and man: the transparency of the exploitation at the source of their new wealth and power: the loss of status and above all of independence for the worker, his reduction to total dependence on the master's instruments of production: the partiality of the law: the disruption of the traditional family economy: the discipline, monotony, hours and conditions of work: loss of leisure and amenities: the reduction of the man to the status of an "instrument".

That working people felt these grievances at all—and felt them passionately—is itself a sufficient fact to merit our attention. And it reminds us forcibly that some of the most bitter conflicts of these years turned on issues which are not encompassed by cost-of-living series. The issues which provoked the most intensity of feeling were very often ones in which such values as traditional customs, "justice", "independence", security, or family-economy were at stake, rather than straight-forward "bread-and-butter" issues. The early years of the 1830s are aflame with agitations which turned on issues in which wages were of secondary importance; by the potters, against the Truck System; by the textile workers, for the 10-Hour Bill; by the building workers, for co-operative direct action; by all groups of workers, for the right to join trade unions. The great strike in the north-east coalfield in 1831 turned on security of employment, "tommy shops", child labour.

The exploitive relationship is more than the sum of grievances and mutual antagonisms. It is a relationship which can be seen to take distinct forms in different historical contexts, forms which are related to corresponding forms of ownership and State power. The classic exploitive relationship of the Industrial Revolution is depersonalised, in the sense that no lingering obligations of mutuality—of paternalism or deference, or of the interests of "the Trade"—are admitted. There is no whisper of the "just" price, or of a wage justified in relation to social or moral sanctions, as opposed to the operation of free market forces. Antagonism is accepted as intrinsic to the relations of production. Managerial or supervisory functions demand the repression of all attributes except those which further the ex-propriation of the maximum surplus value from labour. This is the political economy which Marx anatomised in *Das Kapital*. The worker has become an "instrument", or an entry among other items of cost.

In fact, no complex industrial enterprise could be conducted

204 THE MAKING OF THE WORKING CLASS

according to such a philosophy. The need for industrial peace, for a stable labour-force, and for a body of skilled and experienced workers, necessitated the modification of managerial techniques—and, indeed, the growth of new forms of paternalism—in the cotton-mills by the 1830s. But in the overstocked outwork industries, where there was always a sufficiency of unorganised "hands" competing for employment, these considerations did not operate. Here, as old customs were eroded, and old paternalism was set aside, the exploitive relationship emerged supreme.

This does not mean that we can lay all the "blame" for each hardship of the Industrial Revolution upon "the masters" or upon *laissez faire*. The process of industrialisation must, in any conceivable social context, entail suffering and the destruction of older and valued ways of life. Much recent research has thrown light upon the particular difficulties of the British experience; the hazards of markets; the manifold commercial and financial consequences of the Wars; the post-war deflation; movements in the terms of trade; and the exceptional stresses resulting from the population "explosion". Moreover, 20th-century preoccupations have made us aware of the overarching problems of economic growth. It can be argued that Britain in the Industrial Revolution was encountering the problems of "take-off"; heavy long-term investment—canals, mills, railways, foundries, mines, utilities—was at the expense of current consumption; the generations of workers between 1790 and 1840 sacrificed some, or all, of their prospects of increased consumption to the future.[1]

These arguments all deserve close attention. For example, studies of the fluctuations in the demand of the South American market, or of the crisis in country banking, may tell us much about the reasons for the growth or retardation of particular industries. The objection to the reigning academic orthodoxy is not to empirical studies *per se*, but to the fragmentation of our comprehension of the full historical process. First, the empiricist segregates certain events from this process and examines them in isolation. Since the conditions which gave rise to these events are assumed, they appear not only as explicable in their own terms but as inevitable. The Wars had to be paid for out of heavy taxation; they accelerated growth in this way and

---

[1] See S. Pollard, "Investment, Consumption, and the Industrial Revolution," *Econ. Hist. Review*, 2nd Series, XI (1958), pp. 215-26.

EXPLOITATION 205

retarded it in that. Since this can be shown, it is also implied that this was *necessarily* so. But thousands of Englishmen at the time agreed with Thomas Bewick's condemnation of "this superlatively wicked war".[1] The unequal burden of taxation, fund-holders who profited from the National Debt, paper-money—these were not accepted as given data by many contemporaries, but were the staple of intensive Radical agitation.

But there is a second stage, where the empiricist may put these fragmentary studies back together again, constructing a model of the historical process made up from a multiplicity of interlocking inevitabilities, a piecemeal processional. In the scrutiny of credit facilities or of the terms of trade, where each event is explicable and appears also as a self-sufficient cause of other events, we arrive at a *post facto* determinism. The dimension of human agency is lost, and the context of class relations is forgotten.

It is perfectly true that what the empiricist points to was there. The Orders in Council had in 1811 brought certain trades almost to a standstill; rising timber prices after the Wars inflated the costs of building; a passing change of fashion (lace for ribbon) might silence the looms of Coventry; the power-loom competed with the hand-loom. But even these open-faced facts, with their frank credentials, deserve to be questioned. Whose Council, why the Orders? Who profited most from corners in scarce timber? Why should looms remain idle when tens of thousands of country girls fancied ribbons but could not afford to buy. By what social alchemy did inventions for saving labour become engines of immiseration? The raw fact—a bad harvest—may seem to be beyond human election. But the way that fact worked its way out was in terms of a particular complex of human relationships: law, ownership, power. When we encounter some sonorous phrase such as "the strong ebb and flow of the trade cycle" we must be put on our guard. For behind this trade cycle there is a structure of social relations, fostering some sorts of expropriation (rent, interest, and profit) and outlawing others (theft, feudal dues), legitimising some types of conflict (competition, armed warfare) and inhibiting others (trades unionism, bread riots, popular political organisation)—a structure which may appear, in the eyes of the future, to be both barbarous and ephemeral.

It might be unnecessary to raise these large questions, since

[1] T. Bewick, *Memoir* (1961 edn.), p. 151.

206   THE MAKING OF THE WORKING CLASS

the historian cannot always be questioning the credentials of the society which he studies. But all these questions were, in fact, raised by contemporaries: not only by men of the upper classes (Shelley, Cobbett, Owen, Peacock, Thompson, Hodgskin, Carlyle) but by thousands of articulate working men. Not the political institutions alone, but the social and economic structure of industrial capitalism, were brought into question by their spokesmen. To the facts of orthodox political economy they opposed their own facts and their own arithmetic. Thus as early as 1817 the Leicester framework-knitters put forward, in a series of resolutions, an under-consumption theory of capitalist crisis:

> That in proportion as the Reduction of Wages makes the great Body of the People poor and wretched, in the same proportion must the consumption of our manufactures be lessened.

> That if liberal Wages were given to the Mechanics in general throughout the Country, the Home Consumption of our Manufactures would be immediately more than doubled, and consequently every hand would soon find full employment.

> That to Reduce the Wage of the Mechanic of this Country so low that he cannot live by his labour, in order to undersell Foreign Manufacturers in a Foreign Market, is to gain one customer abroad, and lose two at home. . . .[1]

If those in employment worked shorter hours, and if child labour were to be restricted, there would be more work for hand-workers and the unemployed could employ themselves and exchange the products of their labour directly—short-circuiting the vagaries of the capitalist market—goods would be cheaper and labour better-rewarded. To the rhetoric of the free market they opposed the language of the "new moral order". It is because alternative and irreconcilable views of human order—one based on mutuality, the other on competition—confronted each other between 1815 and 1850 that the historian today still feels the need to take sides.

It is scarcely possible to write the history of popular agitations in these years unless we make at least the imaginative effort to understand how such a man as the "Journeyman Cotton Spinner" read the evidence. He spoke of the "masters", not as an aggregate of individuals, but as a class. As such,

---

[1] H.O. 42.160. See also Hammonds, *The Town Labourer*, p. 303, and Oastler's evidence on the hand-loom weavers, below, p. 298.

EXPLOITATION

"they" denied him political rights. If there was a trade recession, "they" cut his wages. If trade improved, he had to fight "them" and their state to obtain any share in the improvement. If food was plentiful, "they" profited from it. If it was scarce, some of "them" profited more. "They" conspired, not in this or that fact alone, but in the essential exploitive relationship within which all the facts were validated. Certainly there were market fluctuations, bad harvests, and the rest; but the experience of intensified exploitation was constant, whereas these other causes of hardship were variable. The latter bore upon working people, not directly, but through the refraction of a particular system of ownership and power which distributed the gains and losses with gross partiality.

These larger considerations have been, for some years, overlaid by the academic exercise (through which all students must march and counter-march) known as the "standard-of-living controversy". Did the living standards of the bulk of the people rise or fall between 1780 and 1830—or 1800 and 1850?[1] To understand the significance of the argument, we must look briefly at its development.

The debate on values is as old as the Industrial Revolution. The controversy on the standard-of-living is more recent. The ideological *muddle* is more recent still. We may start at one of the more lucid points of the controversy. Sir John Clapham, in his Preface to the first edition of his *Economic History of Modern Britain* (1926) wrote:

The legend that everything was getting worse for the working man, down to some unspecified date between the drafting of the People's Charter and the Great Exhibition [1837 and 1851: E.P.T.], dies hard. The fact that, after the price fall of 1820-1, the purchasing power of wages in general—not, of course, of everyone's wages— was definitely greater than it had been just before the revolutionary and Napoleonic wars, fits so ill with the tradition that it is very seldom mentioned, the work of statisticians on wages and prices being constantly ignored by social historians.

To this, J. L. Hammond offered a reply in the *Economic History Review* (1930) of two kinds: first, he criticised Clapham's statistics of agricultural earnings. These had been based on totting up the country averages, and then dividing them

[1] The futility of one part of this discussion is shown by the fact that if different datum-lines are taken, different answers may come up. 1780-1830 favours the "pessimists"; 1800-1850 favours the "optimists".

208 THE MAKING OF THE WORKING CLASS

by the number of counties in order to reach a national average; whereas the population in the low wage-earning counties of the south was more numerous than that of the high wage-earning counties (where agricultural earnings were inflated by the proximity of industry) so that Hammond was able to show that the "national average" concealed the fact that 60% of the labouring population was in counties where wages were below the "average" figure. The second part of his reply consisted in a switch to discussions of value (happiness) in his most cloudy and unsatisfactory manner. The first part of this reply Clapham, in his Preface to his second edition (1930), accepted; the second part he met with dry caution ("a curve in words", "higher matters") but nevertheless acknowledged: "I agree most profoundly . . . that statistics of material well-being can never measure a people's happiness." Moreover, he asserted that when he had criticised the view that "everything was getting worse"—"I did not mean that everything was getting better. I only meant that recent historians have too often . . . stressed the worsenings and slurred over or ignored the betterings." The Hammonds, for their part, in a late revision of *The Bleak Age* (1947 edition), made their own peace: "statisticians tell us that . . . they are satisfied that earnings increased and that most men and women were less poor when this discontent was loud and active than they were when the eighteenth century was beginning to grow old in a silence like that of autumn. The evidence, of course, is scanty, and its interpretation not too simple, but this general view is probably more or less correct." The explanation for discontent "must be sought outside the sphere of strictly economic conditions".

So far, so good. The most fertile—but loose—social historians of the period had encountered the astringent criticism of a notable empiricist; and in the result both sides had given ground. And, despite the heat which has subsequently been generated, the actual divergence between the hard economic conclusions of the protagonists is slight. If no serious scholar is now willing to argue that everything was getting worse, no serious scholar will argue that everything was getting better. Both Dr. Hobsbawm (a "pessimist") and Professor Ashton (an "optimist") agree that real wages declined during the Napoleonic Wars and in their immediate aftermath. Dr. Hobsbawm will not vouch for any marked general rise in the

EXPLOITATION 209

standard-of-living until the mid-1840s; whereas Professor Ashton notes a "more genial" economic climate after 1821—a "marked upward movement broken only by the slumps of 1825-6 and 1831"; and in view of increasing imports of tea, coffee, sugar, etc., "it is difficult to believe that the workers had no share in the gain". On the other hand his own table of prices in the Oldham and Manchester districts show that "in 1831 the standard diet of the poor can hardly have cost much less than in 1791", while he offers no corresponding wage-tables. His conclusion is to suggest two main groups within the working class—"a large class raised well above the level of mere subsistence" and "masses of unskilled or poorly skilled workers—seasonally employed agricultural workers and hand-loom weavers in particular—whose incomes were almost wholly absorbed in paying for the bare necessaries of life". "My *guess* would be that the number of those who were able to share in the benefits of economic progress was larger than the number of those who were shut out from these benefits and that it was steadily growing."[1]

In fact, so far as the period 1790-1830 goes, there is very little in it. The condition of the majority was bad in 1790: it remained bad in 1830 (and forty years is a long time) but there is some disagreement as to the size of the relative groups within the working class. And matters are little clearer in the next decade. There were undoubted increases in real wages among organised workers during the burst of trade union activity between 1832-4: but the period of good trade between 1833 and 1837 was accompanied by the smashing of the trade unions by the concerted efforts of Government, magistrates, and employers; while 1837-42 are depression years. So that it is indeed at "some unspecified date between the drafting of the People's Charter and the Great Exhibition" that the tide begins to turn; let us say, with the railway boom in 1843. Moreover, even in the mid-40s the plight of very large groups of workers remains desperate, while the railway crash led to the depression years of 1847-8. This does not look very much like a "success story"; in half a century of the fullest development of industrialism, the standard-of-living still remained—for very large but indeterminate groups—at the point of subsistence.

[1] My italics. T. S. Ashton, "The Standard of Life of the Workers in England, 1790-1830", in *Capitalism and the Historians* (ed. F. A. Hayek), pp. 127 ff.; E. J. Hobsbawm, "The British Standard of Living, 1790-1850", *Economic History Review*, X, August 1957.

210 THE MAKING OF THE WORKING CLASS

This is not, however, the impression given in much contemporary writing. For, just as an earlier generation of historians who were also social reformers (Thorold Rogers, Arnold Toynbee, the Hammonds) allowed their sympathy with the poor to lead on occasions to a confusion of history with ideology, so we find that the sympathies of some economic historians today for the capitalist entrepreneur have led to a confusion of history and apologetics.[1] The point of transition was marked by the publication, in 1954, of a symposium on *Capitalism and the Historians*, edited by Professor F. A. Hayek, itself the work of a group of specialists "who for some years have been meeting regularly to discuss the problems of the preservation of a free society against the totalitarian threat". Since this group of international specialists regarded "a free society" as by definition a capitalist society, the effects of such an admixture of economic theory and special pleading were deplorable; and not least in the work of one of the contributors, Professor Ashton, whose cautious findings of 1949 are now transmuted —without further evidence—into the flat statement that "generally it is now agreed that for the majority the gain in real wages was substantial".[2] It is at this stage that the controversy degenerated into a muddle. And despite more recent attempts to rescue it for scholarship,[3] in many respects it is as a muddle of assertion and special pleading that the controversy remains.

The controversy falls into two parts. There is, first, the very real difficulty of constructing wage-series, price-series, and statistical indices from the abundant but patchy evidence. We shall examine some of the difficulties in interpreting such evidence when we come to the artisans. But at this point a further series of difficulties begins, since the term "standard"

---

[1] Lest the reader should judge the historian too harshly, we may record Sir John Clapham's explanation as to the way in which this selective principle may order the evidence. "It is very easy to do this unawares. Thirty years ago I read and marked Arthur Young's *Travels in France*, and taught from the marked passages. Five years ago I went through it again, to find that whenever Young spoke of a wretched Frenchman I had marked him, but that many of his references to happy or prosperous Frenchmen remained unmarked." One suspects that for ten or fifteen years most economic historians have been busy marking up the happy and prosperous evidence in the text.

[2] T. S. Ashton, "The Treatment of Capitalism by Historians", in *Capitalism and the Historians*, p. 41. Professor Ashton's essay on "The Standard of Life of the Workers in England", reprinted in this volume, originally appeared in the *Journal of Economic History*, 1949.

[3] The most constructive appraisal of the controversy is in A. J. Taylor's "Progress and Poverty in Britain, 1780-1850", *History*, February 1960.

EXPLOITATION 211

leads us from data amenable to statistical measurement (wages or articles of consumption) to those satisfactions which are sometimes described by statisticans as "imponderables". From food we are led to homes, from homes to health, from health to family life, and thence to leisure, work-discipline, education and play, intensity of labour, and so on. From standard-of-life we pass to way-of-life. But the two are not the same. The first is a measurement of quantities: the second a description (and sometimes an evaluation) of qualities. Where statistical evidence is appropriate to the first, we must rely largely upon "literary evidence" as to the second. A major source of confusion arises from the drawing of conclusions as to one from evidence appropriate only to the other. It is at times as if statisticians have been arguing: "the indices reveal an increased *per capita* consumption of tea, sugar, meat and soap, *therefore* the working class was happier", while social historians have replied: "the literary sources show that people were unhappy, *therefore* their standard-of-living must have deteriorated".

This is to simplify. But simple points must be made. It is quite possible for statistical averages and human experiences to run in opposite directions. A *per capita* increase in quantitative factors may take place at the same time as a great qualitative disturbance in people's way of life, traditional relationships, and sanctions. People may consume more goods and become less happy or less free at the same time. Next to the agricultural workers the largest single group of working people during the whole period of the Industrial Revolution were the domestic servants. Very many of them were household servants, living-in with the employing family, sharing cramped quarters, working excessive hours, for a few shillings' reward. Nevertheless, we may confidently list them among the more favoured groups whose standards (or consumption of food and dress) improved on average slightly during the Industrial Revolution. But the hand-loom weaver and his wife, on the edge of starvation, still regarded their status as being superior to that of a "flunkey". Or again, we might cite those trades, such as coal-mining, in which real wages advanced between 1790 and 1840, but at the cost of longer hours and a greater intensity of labour, so that the breadwinner was "worn out" before the age of forty. In statistical terms, this reveals an upward curve. To the families concerned it might feel like immiseration.

212 THE MAKING OF THE WORKING CLASS

Thus it is perfectly possible to maintain two propositions which, on a casual view, appear to be contradictory. Over the period 1790-1840 there was a slight improvement in average material standards. Over the same period there was intensified exploitation, greater insecurity, and increasing human misery. By 1840 most people were "better off" than their forerunners had been fifty years before, but they had suffered and continued to suffer this slight improvement as a catastrophic experience. In order to explore this experience, out of which the political and cultural expression of working-class consciousness arose, we shall do these things. First, we shall examine the changing life-experience of three groups of workers: the field labourers, the urban artisans, and the hand-loom weavers.[1] Second, we shall discuss some of the less "ponderable" elements in the people's standard-of-life. Third, we shall discuss the inner compulsions of the industrial way of life, and the bearing upon them of Methodism. Finally, we shall examine some of the elements in the new working-class communities.

[1] These groups have been selected because their experience seems most to colour the social consciousness of the working class in the first half of the century. The miners and metal-workers do not make their influence fully felt until later in the century. The other key group—the cotton-spinners—are the subject of an admirable study in the Hammonds, *The Skilled Labourer*.

[27]

The Feudal Mode of Production

Perry Anderson

The feudal mode of production that emerged in Western Europe was characterized by a complex unity. Traditional definitions of it have often rendered this partially, with the result that it has become difficult to construct any account of the dynamic of feudal development It was a mode of production dominated by the land and a natural economy, in which neither labour nor the products of labour were commodities. The immediate producer – the peasant – was united to the means of production – the soil – by a specific social relationship. The literal formula of this relationship was provided by the legal definition of serfdom – *glebae adscripti* or bound to the earth: serfs had juridically restricted mobility.[1] The peasants who occupied and tilled the land were not its owners. Agrarian property was privately controlled by a class of feudal lords, who extracted a surplus from the peasants by politico-legal relations of compulsion. This extra-economic coercion, taking the form of labour services, rents in kind or customary dues owed to the individual lord by the peasant, was exercised both on the manorial demesne attached directly to the person of the lord, and on the strip tenancies or virgates cultivated by the peasant. Its necessary result was a juridical amalgamation of economic exploitation with political authority. The peasant was subject to the jurisdiction of his lord. At the same time, the property rights of the lord over his land were typically of degree only: he was invested in them by a superior

---

1. Chronologically, this legal definition emerged much later than the factual phenomenon it designated. It was a definition invented by Roman-law jurists in the 11–12th centuries, and popularized in the 14th century. See Marc Bloch, *Les Caractères Originaux de l'Histoire Rurale Française*, Paris 1952, pp. 89–90. We shall repeatedly encounter examples of this lag in the juridical codification of economic and social relationships.

148 Western Europe

noble (or nobles), to whom he would owe knight-service – provision of a military effective in time of war. His estates were, in other words, held as a fief. The liege lord in his turn would often be the vassal of a feudal superior,[2] and the chain of such dependent tenures linked to military service would extend upwards to the highest peak of the system – in most cases, a monarch – of whom all land could in the ultimate instance be in principle the eminent domain. Typical intermediary links of such a feudal hierarchy in the early mediaeval epoch, between simple lordship and suzerain monarchy, were the castellany, barony, county or principality. The consequence of such a system was that political sovereignty was never focused in a single centre. The functions of the State were disintegrated in a vertical allocation downwards, at each level of which political and economic relations were, on the other hand, integrated. This parcellization of sovereignty was constitutive of the whole feudal mode of production.

Three structural specificities of Western feudalism followed, all of fundamental importance for its dynamic. Firstly, the survival of communal village lands and peasant allods from pre-feudal modes of production, although not generated by the latter, was not incompatible with it either. For the feudal division of sovereignties into particularist zones with overlapping boundaries, and no universal centre of competence, always permitted the existence of 'allogenous' corporate entities in its interstices. Thus although the feudal class tried on occasion to enforce the rule of *nulle terre sans seigneur*, in practice this was never achieved in any feudal social formation: communal lands – pastures, meadows and forests – and scattered allods always remained a significant sector of peasant autonomy and resistance, with important consequences for total agrarian productivity.[3] Moreover,

2. Liegeancy was technically a form of homage taking precedence over all other homages, in cases where a vassal owed loyalty to multiple lords. In practice, however, liege lords soon became synonymous with any feudal superior, and liegeancy lost its original and specific distinction. Marc Bloch, *Feudal Society*, London 1962, pp. 214–18.

3. Engels always justly emphasized the social consequences of village communities, integrated by common lands and the three-field system, for the condition of the mediaeval peasantry. It was they, he remarked in *The Origin of the Family, Private Property and the State*, that gave 'to the oppressed class, the peasants, even under the harshest conditions of mediaeval serfdom, local cohesion and the means of resistance which neither the slaves of antiquity nor the modern

The Feudal Mode of Production 149

even within the manorial system itself, the scalar structure of property was expressed in the characteristic division of estates into the lord's demesne, directly organized by his stewards and tilled by his villeins, and the peasant virgates, from which he received a complementary surplus but in which the organization and control of production was in the hands of the villeins themselves.[4] There was thus no simple, horizontal concentration of the two basic classes of the rural economy within a single, homogeneous property form. Relations of production were mediated through a dual agrarian statute within the manor. Moreover, there was often a further disjuncture between the justice to which serfs were subject in the manorial courts of their lord, and the seigneurial jurisdictions of territorial lordship. Manors did not normally coincide with single hamlets, but were distributed across a number of them; hence conversely in any given village a multiplicity of manorial holdings of different lords would be interwoven. Above this tangled juridical maze would typically lie the *haute justice* of territorial seigneuries, whose area of competence was geographical, not domainial.[5] The peasant class from which the surplus was extracted in this system thus inhabited a social world of overlapping claims and powers, the very plurality of whose 'instances' of exploitation created latent interstices and discrepancies impossible in a more unified juridical

---

proletarians found ready to hand.' Marx-Engels, *Selected Works*, London 1968, p. 575. Basing himself on the work of the German historian Maurer, Engels wrongly believed these communities, which dated back to the earliest Dark Ages, to be 'mark associations'; in fact, the latter were an innovation of the late Middle Ages, which first appeared in the 14th century. But this error does not affect his essential argument.

4. Mediaeval manors varied in structure according to the relative balance between these two components within it. At one extreme, there were (a few) estates entirely devoted to demesne-farming, such as the Cistercian 'granges' tilled by lay brethren; while at the other, there were some estates entirely leased out to peasant tenants. But the modal type was always a combination of home-farm and tenancies, in varying proportions: 'this bilateral composition of the manor and of its revenues was the true hallmark of the typical manor.' M. M. Postan, *The Mediaeval Economy and Society*, London 1972, pp. 89–94.

5. There is an excellent account of the basic traits of this system in B. H. Slicher Van Bath, *The Agrarian History of Western Europe*, London 1963, pp. 46–51. Where territorial lordships were absent, as in most of England, plural manors within a single village gave the peasant community considerable leeway for self-regulation: see Postan, *The Mediaeval Economy and Society*, p. 117.

150 Western Europe

and economic system. The coexistence of communal lands, allods and virgates with the demesne itself was constitutive of the feudal mode of production in Western Europe, and had critical implications for its development.

Secondly, however, and even more importantly, the feudal parcellization of sovereignties produced the phenomenon of the mediaeval town in Western Europe. Here again, the genesis of urban commodity production is not to be located within feudalism as such: it of course predates it. But the feudal mode of production nevertheless was the *first* to permit it an *autonomous development* within a natural-agrarian economy. The fact that the largest mediaeval towns never rivalled in scale those of either Antiquity or Asian Empires has often obscured the truth that their function within the social formation was a much more advanced one. In the Roman Empire, with its highly sophisticated urban civilization, the towns were subordinated to the rule of noble landowners who lived in them, but not from them; in China, vast provincial agglomerations were controlled by mandarin bureaucrats resident in a special district segregated from all commercial activity. By contrast, the paradigmatic mediaeval towns of Europe which practised trade and manufactures were self-governing communes, enjoying corporate political and military autonomy from the nobility and the Church. Marx saw this difference very clearly, and gave memorable expression to it: 'Ancient classical history is the history of cities, but cities based on landownership and agriculture; Asian history is a kind of undifferentiated unity of town and country (the large city, properly speaking, must be regarded merely as a princely camp, superimposed on the real economic structure); the Middle Ages (germanic period) starts with the countryside as the locus of history, whose further development then proceeds through the opposition of town and country; modern history is the urbanization of the countryside, not, as among the ancients, the ruralization of the city.'[6] Thus a *dynamic opposition* of town and country was alone possible in the feudal mode of production: opposition between an urban economy of increasing commodity exchange, controlled by merchants and organized in guilds and corporations, and a rural economy of natural exchange, controlled by nobles and organized in manors and strips, with communal and

6. Karl Marx, *Pre-Capitalist Formations*, London 1964, pp. 77–78.

The Feudal Mode of Production 151

individual peasant enclaves. It goes without saying that the preponderance of the latter was enormous: the feudal mode of production was overwhelmingly agrarian. But its laws of motion, as will be seen, were governed by the complex unity of its different regions, not by any simple predominance of the manor.

Thirdly, there was an inherent ambiguity or oscillation at the vertex of the whole hierarchy of feudal dependencies. The 'summit' of the chain was in certain important respects its weakest link. In principle, the highest superordinate level of the feudal hierarchy in any given territory of Western Europe was necessarily different not in kind, but only in degree, from the subordinate levels of lordship beneath it. The monarch, in other words, was a feudal suzerain of his vassals, to whom he was bound by reciprocal ties of fealty, not a supreme sovereign set above his subjects. His economic resources would lie virtually exclusively in his personal domains as a lord, while his calls on his vassals would be essentially military in nature. He would have no direct political access to the population as a whole, for jurisdiction over it would be mediatized through innumerable layers of subinfeudation. He would, in effect, be master only on his own estates, otherwise to great extent a ceremonial figurehead. The pure model of such a polity, in which political power was stratified downwards in such a way that its apex retained no qualitatively separate or plenipotentiary authority at all, never existed anywhere within mediaeval Europe.[7] For the lack of any real integrating mechanism at the top of a feudal system implied by this type of polity posed a permanent threat to its stability and survival. A complete fragmentation of sovereignty was incompatible with the class unity of the nobility itself, for the potential

7. The Crusader State in the Levant has often been considered the closest approximation to a perfect feudal constitution. The overseas constructs of European feudalism were created *ex nihilo* in an alien environment, and thus assumed an exceptionally systematic juridical form. Engels, among others, remarked on this singularity: 'Did feudalism ever correspond to its concept? Founded in the kingdom of the West Franks, further developed in Normandy by the Norwegian conquerors, its formation continued by the French Norsemen in England and Southern Italy, it came nearest to its concept – in the ephemeral kingdom of Jerusalem, which in the *Assize of Jerusalem* left behind it the most classic expression of the feudal order.' Marx-Engels, *Selected Correspondence*, Moscow, 1965, p. 484. But the practical realities of even the Crusader realm never corresponded to the legal codification of its baronial jurists.

152   Western Europe

anarchy implied by it was necessarily disruptive of the whole mode of production on which their privileges rested. There was thus an inbuilt contradiction within feudalism, between its own rigorous tendency to a decomposition of sovereignty and the absolute exigencies of a final centre of authority in which a practical recomposition could occur. The feudal mode of production in the West thus originally specified suzerainty: it always existed to some extent in an ideological and juridical realm beyond that of those vassal relationships whose summit could otherwise be ducal or comital potentates, and possessed rights to which the latter could not aspire. At the same time, actual royal power always had to be asserted and extended against the spontaneous grain of the feudal polity as a whole, in a constant struggle to establish a 'public' authority outside the compact web of private jurisdictions. The feudal mode of production in the West thus originally specified in its very structure a dynamic tension and contradiction within the centrifugal State which it organically produced and reproduced.

Such a political system necessarily precluded any extensive bureaucracy, and functionally divided class rule in a novel fashion. For on the one hand, the parcellization of sovereignty in early mediaeval Europe led to the constitution of a separate ideological order altogether. The Church, which in Late Antiquity had always been directly integrated into the machinery of the imperial State, and subordinated to it, now became an eminently autonomous institution within the feudal polity. Sole source of religious authority, its command over the beliefs and values of the masses was immense; but its ecclesiastical organization was distinct from that of any secular nobility or monarchy. Because of the dispersal of coercion inherent in emergent Western feudalism, the Church could defend its own corporate interests, if necessary, from a territorial redoubt and by armed force. Institutional conflicts between lay and religious lordship were thus endemic in the mediaeval epoch: their result was a scission in the structure of feudal legitimacy, whose cultural consequences for later intellectual development were to be considerable. On the other hand, secular government itself was characteristically narrowed into a new mould. It became essentially the exercise of 'justice', which under feudalism occupied a functional position wholly distinct from that under capitalism today. Justice was the *central* modality of political power – specified as such by the very

The Feudal Mode of Production   153

nature of the feudal polity. For the pure feudal hierarchy, as we have
seen, excluded any 'executive' at all, in the modern sense of a permanent administrative apparatus of the State for the enforcement of
the law: the parcellization of sovereignty rendered one unnecessary and
impossible. At the same time, there was no room for an orthodox
'legislature' of the later type either, since the feudal order possessed no
general concept of political innovation by the creation of *new* laws.
Royal rulers fulfilled their station by preserving traditional laws, not
by inventing novel ones. Thus political power came for a period to be
virtually identified with the single 'judiciary' function of interpreting
and applying the existing laws. Moreover, in the absence of any public
bureaucracy, local coercion and administration – policing, fining,
tolling and enforcing powers – inevitably accrued to it. It is thus
necessary always to remember that mediaeval 'justice' factually included
a much wider range of activities than modern justice, because it
structurally occupied a far more pivotal position within the total
political system. It was the ordinary name of power.

Typology of Social Formations

We have so far discussed the genesis of feudalism in Western Europe
as a synthesis of elements released by the concurrent dissolution of
primitive-communal and slave modes of production; and then outlined
the constitutive structure of the developed feudal mode of production
in the West as such. It now remains to show briefly how the inherent
nature of this synthesis produced a variegated typology of social
formations in the mediaeval epoch. For the mode of production just
sketched never existed in a 'pure state' anywhere in Europe, any more
than the capitalist mode of production was to do later. The concrete
social formations of mediaeval Europe were always composite systems,
in which other modes of production survived and intertwined with
feudalism proper: slaves, for example, existed throughout the Middle
Ages, and free peasants were never wholly wiped out anywhere by the
Dark Ages.

[28]

The Decline and Fall of Rome

G.E.M. de Ste. Croix

In this last chapter I shall again show how a Marxist analysis on class lines can help to *explain*, and not merely to *describe*, a historical process: in this case the disintegration of large portions of the Roman empire, part of a process which seemed to Gibbon 'the greatest, perhaps, and most awful scene in the history of mankind' (*DFRE* VII.325).

It was, I suggest, the combination of unlimited economic power and political power in the hands of the propertied class, their emperor and his administration which ultimately brought about the disintegration of the Roman empire. There was nothing to restrain the greed and ambition of the rich, except in so far as the emperor himself might feel it necessary to put a curb on certain excesses in order to prevent a general or local collapse, or simply in order that the population of the empire, under a just regime, might be prosperous enough to be able to pay their taxes promptly – a motive which can be seen clearly in numerous imperial constitutions (cf. below).

For the peasant, it was the tax collector who was the cause of the greatest dread.

498 *The Class Struggle in the Ancient Greek World*

What a terrifying individual he could be is nicely illustrated in one of those Lives of Saints from which so much of our information about the lives and outlook of the poor in the Later Roman Empire is derived: the *Life of St. John the Almsgiver*, from which I have quoted above. If we want to characterise a cruel and merciless person, we sometimes say, 'He's like a wild beast'. Well, the Saint is represented as thinking about the dreadful monsters he may meet after death, and the only way he can adequately express the appalling ferocity of these wild beasts is to say that they will be 'like tax–collectors'![39] Certainly, tax collection from the poor in Roman times was not a matter of polite letters and, as a last resort, a legal action: beating–up defaulters was a matter of routine, if they were humble people. A casual remark of the fifth–century ecclesiastical writer Theodoret shows us what the procedure of tax–collection was likely to be in a Syrian village: 'At this time,' he says, 'collectors (*praktores*) arrived, who compelled them to pay their taxes and began to imprison some and maltreat others' (*Hist. relig.* 17; cf. Eunapius, fr. 87). In Egypt the same brutal procedure can be seen at work: local officials would seize taxpayers whom they alleged (rightly or wrongly) to be in default, imprison and ill–treat them, and, with the aid of soldiers and local levies, burn down their houses. After quoting a particular example of such a procedure, from the reign of Justinian, Sir Harold Bell (a leading papyrologist and historian of Graeco–Roman Egypt) remarked, 'Such, to judge by other evidence, were regular accompaniments to the process of collecting arrears of taxes from an Egyptian village in the sixth century' (EVAJ 34). According to Ammianus, an Egyptian in the late fourth century would blush for shame if he could not show on his back scars inflicted by the tax–collector's whip (*erubescit apud eos, si quis non infitiando tributa plurimas in corpore vibices ostendat*: XXII.xvi.23). And it is worth repeating here the statement of Ammianus which I quoted near the end of V.iii above, that the Emperor Julian realised it was no good granting remissions of tax arrears in Gaul in the 350s, because this would only benefit the rich; the poor would have been made to pay immediately and in full (XVI.v.15). There must have been many occasions, too, on which hapless peasants were forced to pay their taxes twice over, whether because the tax had first been extracted from them by the agents of a 'usurper' (cf. VI.vi above), or because their landlord, after collecting the tax, became insolvent before paying it over to the authorities (or the persons to whom he was responsible). There is an example of the latter situation in a letter of Pope Gregory the Great, written in 591, from which we learn that the *rustici* on an estate of the Roman Church in Sicily had been compelled to pay their *burdatio* twice to the head lessee, Theodosius, now almost insolvent. Gregory, an exceptionally conscientious landlord, orders that the 57 solidi concerned are to be repaid to the peasants as a prior claim against Theodosius' estate (*Ep.* I.42).

It will be objected that the appalling situation I have been describing is characteristic only of the Later Empire, and that things were surely very different under the Principate, especially in the first two centuries of the Christian era. Certainly, taxation became much heavier in the fourth century onwards (cf. above, and Section iii of this chapter). But there is no reason to think that defaulting taxpayers who were poor men, especially peasants, would be much better treated in the first century than in the fourth, although, until certain of the privileges of the Roman citizenship became in practice limited to the upper

The 'decline and fall': an explanation 499

classes, during the second century (see Section i of this chapter), the Roman citizen who was a person of no consequence might occasionally be able to assert his legal rights. (St. Paul did so, as we have seen – but of course he was far from being an uneducated peasant.) The native villager, especially if he was not a Roman citizen (as very few villagers were in the Greek-speaking part of the empire before 212), would have had little chance of escaping any brutal treatment which soldiers or officials cared to inflict upon him. There is a certain amount of evidence pointing in this direction, of which I will single out one text, quoted by several modern writers.[40] Philo of Alexandria writes of events which he represents as having taken place 'recently' (and therefore presumably during the reign of Tiberius, 14–37), apparently in Lower Egypt,[41] as a result of the activity of a rapacious and cruel tax-collector:

> When some who appeared to be defaulting merely through sheer poverty took to flight, in dread of severe punishment, he forcibly carried off their women and children and parents and other relatives, beat them, and subjected them to every kind of outrage. Although they were unable either to reveal the fugitive's whereabouts or (because of their own destitution) to pay what was due from him, he persisted, torturing them and putting them to death in a cruel manner. Others committed suicide to avoid such a fate. When there were no relatives left, he extended his outrages to neighbours and sometimes even to villages and towns, which were rapidly deserted by the flight of their inhabitants to places where they hoped to escape detection (*De spec. leg.* III.158–63).

Even if we make the necessary allowance for Philo's characteristic exaggeration, a grim picture emerges; and, as Bell has said, 'records found in Egypt have brought us proof that there is substantial truth in Philo's statements' (*EAGAC* 77–8). We must admit, with Philo, that such outrages, not only against the property but against the bodies and even the lives of those unfortunates who are seized in substitution for the actual debtors are only too likely when the annual collection of taxes is in the hands of 'men of barbarous nature, who have never tasted of human culture and are obeying tyrannical orders' (ibid.).

Some of the numerous complaints about taxation in the literary sources for the Later Roman Empire are of course over-coloured; their exaggerations are often traceable to political or religious spite, or to a desire to flatter the current emperor by damning his predecessors. However, anyone who is inclined to discount the admittedly very rhetorical evidence of the literary sources should read some of the imperial legislation. A particularly interesting specimen is the *Second Novel* (issued on 11 March 458) of the last great Western emperor, the young Majorian, of whom Stein said that we could 'admire in him without reserve the last figure possessing a real grandeur in the history of the Roman West' (*HBE* I².i.375). Although this Novel was issued only in the West, the situation it depicts, *mutatis mutandis*, prevailed also in the Greek East, where the oppression of the vast majority was effected in ways that were basically similar, even if it did not reach quite the same degree of intensity. The Novel is well worth reading as a whole; but it is long, and I can do no more than summarise parts of it. (There is a full translation in Pharr, *TC* 551–3.) The Novel is entitled 'On the remission of arrears [of tax]', *De indulgentiis reliquorum*. It begins by stressing the woes of the provincials, whose fortunes are said to have been enfeebled and worn down, not only by the exaction of the various forms of

500   *The Class Struggle in the Ancient Greek World*

regular tribute but also by extraordinary fiscal burdens (*extraordinaria onera, superindictitii tituli*), and the necessity of purchasing deferments – by bribing officials. A nice abstract phrase, *sub impossibili devotione*, characterises the plight of the landowner (*possessor*), drained of resources (*exhaustus*) and unable to discharge his arrears of tax, when confronted with yet another demand that 'dutiful as he is, he cannot fulfil'. With the exception of one minor tax in kind, a general remission of arrears is granted (§ 1), explicitly for the benefit of the landowners (*possessores*), who are conceived as responsible for all taxes. Even if payment has been undertaken by someone else (no doubt at a high rate of interest), perhaps on the faith of a solemn promise by *stipulatio* by the taxpayer, the latter is still to have relief (cf. *Nov. Marc.* II.2). The Novel goes on to boast (§ 2) that the emperor has 'put an end to the harshness of the ferocious tax collectors'. There is a bitter complaint that the staffs of the highest officials of the state (those of the praetorian prefects are singled out) range around the provinces, and 'by enormous exactions terrorise the landowner and the decurion', accounting for only a small proportion of the taxes they collect and, greedy and swollen with power as they are, extorting twice as much or more by way of commission (*sportulae*) for themselves (cf. Jones, *LRE* I.468). In the good old days, Majorian adds, tax collection had been carried out, through the local councils, by the office staff of the provincial governor, who were fairly humble men and whom the governor could keep in order. But now the collection was in the hands of emissaries of the central 'palatine' administration, described by the emperor as 'terrible with the prestige of their exalted official rank, raging against the vitals of the provincials, to their ruin', and able to snap their fingers at a mere provincial governor. (Majorian was not by any means the first emperor, or the last, to complain about the intervention of central government officials in provincial taxation procedures.) Because of the oppression of these high officials, the emperor goes on, the cities have been despoiled of their councillors and can provide no qualified decurion; and the landowners, terrified by the atrocious behaviour of the financial officials, are deserting their country estates, as they are faced not merely with the loss of their fortunes but with 'severe imprisonment and cruel tortures' inflicted upon them by the merciless officials for their own profit, with military aid. The collection of taxes must be entrusted once more to the provincial governors, and there must be no more interventions by palatine officials and the military, except to encourage governors to do their duty. The emperor stresses again (§ 3) that he is making this ordinance as a remedy for the landowner (*pro remedio possessoris*). He proceeds to complain also (§ 4) of 'the men of power' (*potentes personae*), whose agents throughout the provinces neglect to pay their taxes, and who remain contumaciously on their estates, secure against any summons in the fear inspired by their arrogance. The agents and overseers of those families which are 'senatorial or powerful' must submit themselves to the jurisdiction of the provincial governors (as they had not been doing), and so must the local agents in charge of estates belonging to the imperial household. Moreover (§ 5), provincial govenors must not be subjected to molestation by false accusations from the staffs of the great officers of state, who will be furious at having enormously profitable spoils wrested from their own fraudulent grasp.

Some other laws of the fifth and sixth centuries unloose similar streams of

The 'decline and fall': an explanation

righteous indignation at much the same objectives: see, for example, Valentinian III's *Novel* I.3 § 2 (of 450), followed in § 3 by an ingenuous remark which reveals the main reason for the emperor's solicitude for the *possessores*: 'A landowner who has been made poor is lost to us; one who is not overburdened is useful to us'! There are several similarly revealing laws, notably, for the East, the long *Eighth Novel* of Justinian, of A.D. 535, on which I have remarked elsewhere (SVP 47-8). Justinian too is concerned lest excessive exploitation by the great men, and their imposition of extraordinary burdens, should impair the ability of his subjects to pay their regular taxation, which he calls not only 'accustomed and legal' but also 'pious' (*eusebeis phoroi, Nov.J.* VIII. *Praef., pr.*). Similarly, the anxiety shown by Justinian in a series of three *Novels* in 535 to protect the free peasants of the praetorian prefecture of Illyricum and the provinces of Thracian Haemimontus and Moesia Secunda against money-lenders (*Nov.J.* XXXII-IV) is very likely to have been due in large part to anxiety to preserve them as an important source of recruitment for the army, as we know they were in his reign.[42]

The laws I have been describing nicely illustrate the most fundamental reason why it was necessary to have an emperor in the first place – a subject I have briefly discussed in VI.v-vi above. The Principate was accepted (if at first with some grumbling) by the Roman (and Greek) propertied classes because on the whole they realised that their own privileged position might be imperilled if too many individuals among their number were allowed, as in the Late Republic, to plunder the empire too freely. If that happened, civil wars (accompanied, as they could well be, by proscriptions and confiscations) and even perhaps revolutions from below might destroy many of them. The situation could hardly be put better than in Machiavelli's statement, which I have quoted, about the necessity for having, 'where the material is so corrupt, . . . besides laws, a superior force, such as appertains to a monarch, who has such absolute and overwhelming power that he can restrain excesses due to ambition and the corrupt practices of the powerful' (see VI.vi above, referring to the *Discourses on the First Decade of Livy* I.55; and cf. Machiavelli's diatribe against landed *gentiluomini*, quoted in III.iii above, *ad init.*). In the Later Empire, the *potentes, potentiores* or *dynatoi*, the men of power, became harder to control and often defied or circumvented the emperors with impunity.[43] Senators, at once the richest and the most influential group in the empire, were more easily able than anyone to delay or avoid payment of their taxes and the fulfilment of their other liabilities. This was true even in the Eastern part of the empire. In 397, for example, an edict of the Emperor Arcadius, addressed to the praetorian prefect of the East, complained that in some provinces half of the taxes due from senators were in arrear (*CTh* VI.iii.4). In the West, where the senators were even richer and more powerful, this situation was worse. In the very same year, 397, when the revolt of Gildo in Africa had imperilled the corn supply of Rome itself, three very significant laws were issued in the West, where the young Emperor Honorius was dominated by his able *magister militum* Stilicho. The first, in June, ordered that not even imperial estates should be exempted from the obligation to supply recruits in person (*CTh* VII.xiii.12). The second and third, in September and November, weakly conceded, in response to senatorial objections, that senators alone (even if head lessees of imperial estates) should have the right to commute their liability to

502   The Class Struggle in the Ancient Greek World

supply recruits and pay in gold instead (ibid. 13-14).[44] And as late as the early sixth century we find an edict drafted by Cassiodorus for Theodoric the Ostrogoth, then king of Italy, deploring the fact that Roman senators, who 'ought to be setting an example', had paid virtually none of the taxes due from them, thus leaving the poor (the *tenues*) to bear an intolerable burden (Cassiod., *Var.* II.24-25).

The texts I have been quoting illustrate very well how the 'government' was continually frustrated in such attempts as it did make (for whatever reasons) to protect the peasantry by the fact that the more important of the officials on whom it was obliged to rely to carry out its orders were themselves members of the upper class, and of course felt an instinctive sympathy with its other members and often connived at their malpractices, and indeed were guilty of much extortion themselves. The rulers of the empire rarely if ever had any real concern for the poor and unprivileged as such; but they sometimes realised the necessity to give some of them some protection (as we have just seen), either to prevent them from being utterly ruined and thus become useless as taxpayers, or to preserve them as potential recruits for the army. Try as they would, however, the emperors had no choice but to act through the officials I have just characterised as members of the exploiting class. No text that I know speaks more eloquently of the defects of this system than a Novel of the Emperor Romanus II issued between 959 and 963: 'We must beware lest we send upon the unfortunate poor the calamity of law-officers, more merciless than famine itself.'[45]

Over all, no one I think will doubt that the position of humble folk in the Graeco-Roman world became distinctly worse after the early Principate. I have described in Section i of this chapter how their *Rechtsstellung* deteriorated during the first two centuries; and in Section ii I have shown how even the lower ranges of the curial order (falling only just inside, and sometimes perhaps even a little below, my 'propertied class') were subjected to increasing fiscal oppression from the second half of the second century onwards, and during the latter part of the fourth century lost at least one of their most valuable privileges: exemption from flogging. It need not surprise us when we are told that in the numerous papyri of the Later Roman Empire from the Oxyrhynchus area the use of the Greek word *doulos*, once the standard technical term for 'slave', is almost confined to occasions on which humble members of the free population are referring to themselves when addressing people of higher standing (see IV.ii n.41 below).

I hope it is now clear how I would explain, through a class analysis, the ultimate disintegration of a large part of the Roman empire – although of course a Greek core, centred above all in Asia Minor, did survive for centuries. I would keep firmly in view the process of exploitation which is what I mean primarily when I speak of a 'class struggle'. As I see it, the Roman political system (especially when Greek democracy had been wiped out: see V.iii above and Appendix IV below) facilitated a most intense and ultimately destructive economic exploitation of the great mass of the people, whether slave or free, and it made radical reform impossible. The result was that the propertied class, the men of real wealth, who had deliberately created this system for their own benefit, drained the life-blood from their world and thus destroyed Graeco-Roman civilisation over a large part of the empire – Britain, Gaul, Spain and north Africa in the fifth century; much of Italy and the Balkans in the sixth; and

The 'decline and fall': an explanation   503

in the seventh, Egypt, Syria and Mesopotamia, and again north Africa, which had been reconquered by Justinian's generals in the sixth century.[46] That, I believe, was the principal reason for the decline of Classical civilisation. I would suggest that the causes of the decline were above all economic and social. The very hierarchical political structure of the Roman empire, of course, played an important part; but it was precisely the propertied class as such which in the long run monopolised political power, with the definite purpose of maintaining and increasing its share of the comparatively small surplus which could be extracted from the primary producers. By non-Marxist historians this process has normally been described as if it were a more or less automatic one, something that 'just happened'. If one wants to find a terse, vivid, epigrammatic characterisation of something that happened in the Roman world, one naturally turns first to Gibbon. And indeed, in the excursus at the end of his 38th chapter, entitled 'General observations on the Fall of the Roman empire in the West', there occurs the expressive sentence, 'The stupendous fabric yielded to the pressure of its own weight.' In Peter Brown's sometimes brilliant little book, *The World of Late Antiquity* (1971), there is a metaphor of a rather different kind, which equally expresses the basic idea of something that was essentially either inevitable or else fortuitous: 'Altogether, the prosperity of the Mediterranean world seems to have *drained to the top*' (34, my italics) – Brown is speaking of the fourth century, and he has just mentioned that in the western part of the empire, in that century, the senatorial aristocracy was 'five times richer, on the average, than the senators of the first century'. (In the Greek East, things were not so very different, although the senatorial class was not quite so extravagantly opulent as in the West.) If I were in search of a metaphor to describe the great and growing concentration of wealth in the hands of the upper classes, I would not incline towards anything so innocent and so automatic as drainage: I should want to think in terms of something much more purposive and deliberate – perhaps the vampire bat. The burden of maintaining the imperial military and bureaucratic machine, and the Church, in addition to a leisured class consisting mainly of absentee landowners, fell primarily upon the peasantry, who formed the great bulk of the population; and, ironically enough (as I have already explained), the remarkable military and administrative reorganisation effected by a series of very able emperors from the late third century to the end of the fourth (from Diocletian and Constantine to Theodosius I) succeeded in creating an even greater number of economically 'idle mouths' and thus increased the burdens upon an already overburdened peasantry. The peasants were seldom able to revolt at all, and never successfully: the imperial military machine saw to that. Only in Gaul and Spain did the Bacaudae cause serious if intermittent trouble over several generations (see Section iii of this chapter). But the merciless exploitation of the peasants made many of them receive, if not with enthusiasm at least with indifference, the barbarian invaders who might at least be expected – vainly, as it usually turned out[47] – to shatter the oppressive imperial financial machine. Those who have been chastised with scorpions may hope for something better if they think they will be chastised only with whips.[48]

658 Notes

39. *Vita S. Ioann. Eleemos.* 41: see Dawes and Baynes, op. cit. (in n.30 above) 248, 249.
40. E.g. Naphtali Lewis, 'Μερισμὸς ἀνακεχωρηκότων', in *JEA* 23 (1937) 63–75, at 64–5 and n.6; Bell, *EAGAC* 77–8; MacMullen, *RSR* 36–7.
41. Philo's words are πρώην τις ἐκλογεὺς φόρων ταχθεὶς παρ' ἡμῖν (§ 159). The last two words should mean 'in our area'. MacMullen (see the preceding note) takes this to be Judaea. Certainly the text seems to exclude Alexandria (see § 162). But I think we must take it that Philo is speaking of some area in Lower Egypt.
42. See Jones, *LRE* II.781, with 667–8. It seems to me obvious that most if not all these peasants were freeholders, for otherwise they would not have been driven out of their lands, as each of the three laws says they were.
43. A valuable (and, I think, rather neglected) work on 'the over-powerful' can be found among the 'Études de droit byzantin' (the sub-title of which makes them a 'méditation' on *CJ* IV.lxv.34) published by H. Monnier in *Nouvelle revue historique de droit français et étranger* 24 (1900) in three parts, the relevant section for our purposes being pp.62–107 (Ch.vi: 'Généralités sur les Puissants'; vii: 'Des Puissants à l'époque classique'; viii: 'Quelques exemples des entreprises des Puissants au Bas-Empire'; and ix: 'Le *patrocinium potentiorum*'). This is the richest collection of material on the subject that I have found.
44. Cf. Symm., *Ep.* VI.58, 62, 64, on which see Jones, *LRE* I.365.
45. For the Novel in question see J. and P. Zepos, *Jus Graecoromanum* (8 vols, Athens, 1931; repr. Aalen, 1962) I.240–2, at 242. The translation is that of G. Ostrogorsky, 'The peasant's pre-emption right: an abortive reform of the Macedonian emperors', in *JRS* 37 (1947) 117–26, at 122. The Greek is καὶ χρὴ διευλαβεῖσθαι ἡμᾶς, μὴ λιμοῦ βιαιότεραν ἀνάγκην κριτοῦ τοῖς ἀθλίοις ἐπιστήσομεν πένησι (§ 2).
46. The conquest of Syria, Mesopotamia, Egypt and north Africa by the Arabs was extraordinarily rapid. Particularly striking is the virtual disappearance of Christianity from large parts of that area, especially the lands west of Syria and Egypt. This is all the more remarkable in that, as Mommsen said (if with some exaggeration), 'In the development of Christianity Africa plays the very first part; if it arose in Syria, it was in and through Africa that it became the religion for the world' (*Provinces of the Roman Empire* [1886] II.343).
47. In the case of the Arab conquest of Egypt, this situation existed also in the great city of Alexandria. See e.g. Butler, *ACE*² 337–8, for the view that in the submission of the Alexandrians to the Arabs in 641 the expectation of lighter taxation may have been an important element. He continues, 'This promise of reduced taxation may count for a great deal in all the Muslim conquests. In the case of Alexandria it may have been the determining factor, although it is known that the hope of financial relief was bitterly disappointed.' (Cf. also ibid. 349, 365, 451–6; but see lxxxiii.) For the forced labour which was also exacted by the Arabs later, see ibid. 347–8, 363. I may add that I know of no scholarly treatment of the problems of Arab taxation in the Roman provinces they conquered more recent than D. C. Dennett, *Conversion and the Poll-Tax in Early Islam* (= *Harvard Historical Monographs* 22, 1950); and Frede Løkkegaard, *Islamic Taxation in the Classic Period* (Copenhagen, 1950). Dennett is particularly successful in bringing out the differences in the treatment by the Arabs of the various areas.
48. See IV.i above and its n.1.

Bibliography (and Abbreviations)

Abbreviations of *modern works* (including periodicals) not included here are either obvious or can be easily identified with the aid of such lists of abbreviations as those in *LSJ*⁹ I.xli–xlviii, *OCD*² ix–xxii, *ODCC*² xix–xxv, or any recent number of *L'Année philologique*.

The identification of *ancient sources* will usually be obvious enough to those able to profit by consulting them. In case of doubt, reference can be made to *LSJ*⁹ I.xvi–xli or (for Latin authors) to Lewis and Short's *Latin Dictionary* vii–xi. The best available editions are used. Those less acquainted with Early Christian sources (cited wherever possible from *GCS*, *CSEL* or *SC* editions, otherwise commonly from *MPG* or *MPL*), or with Later Roman ones, will find particularly helpful the lists in Jones, *LRE* III.392–406; Stein, *HBE* I².ii.607–20 and II.847–61; and of course the Patrologies, by B. Altaner, J. Quasten, and O. Bardenhewer, given in Part II below.

662 Bibliography

Bell, Harold Idris, *EAGAC* = *Egypt from Alexander the Great to the Arab Conquest* (1948)

Brown, Peter, *The World of Late Antiquity* (1971)

Butler, A. J., *ACE²* = *The Arab Conquest of Egypt and the Last Thirty Years of the Roman Dominion*, 2nd edn by P. M. Fraser (1978) [See p.652 n.37 above]

Dawes, Elizabeth, and N. H. Baynes, *Three Byzantine Saints* (1948: Eng. trans. of the lives of Daniel the Stylite, Theodore of Sykeon, and John the Almsgiver, of Alexandria, with Notes)

Dennett, D. C., *Conversion and the Poll-Tax in Early Islam* (= *Harvard Historical Monographs* 22, 1950)

Gibbon, Edward, *DFRE* = *The Decline and Fall of the Roman Empire* (1776–88), cited from the standard edn in 7 vols by J. B. Bury (1896–1900 & repr.)

Jones, A. H. M., *LRE* = *The Later Roman Empire 284-602*, 3 vols, plus a vol. of maps (1964)

Lewis, Naphtali, 'Merismos anakechōrhēkotōn', in *JEA* 23 (1937) 63–75

Løkkegaard, Frede, *Islamic Taxation in the Classic Period* (Copenhagen, 1950)

MacMullen, Ramsay, *RSR* = *Roman Social Relations 50 B.C. to A.D. 284* (1974)

Monnier, H., 'Études de droit byzantin', in *NRHDFE* 24 (1900), esp. 62–107 [see p.658 n.43 above]

Ostrogorsky, Georg, 'The peasant's pre-emption right', in *JRS* 37 (1947) 117–26

Pharr, Clyde, *TC* = *The Theodosian Code and Novels and the Sirmondian Constitutions*, Eng. trans., with commentary etc. (Princeton, 1952)

Ste. Croix, G. E. M. de, *SVP* = 'Suffragium: from vote to patronage', in *British Jnl of Sociology* 5 (1954) 33–48

Zepos, J. and P., *Ius Graecoromanum*, 8 vols (Athens, 1931; repr. Aalen, 1962)

Part VII
Colonialism, Race and Gender

[29]

Negroes in the Civil War
Their Role in the Second American Revolution

C.L.R. James
(writing under the name *J.R. Johnson*)

An indispensable contribution to the understanding of the role of the Negro in American history is a study of the period between 1830 and 1865. In this article we treat the subject up to 1860.

The basic economic and social antagonisms of the period embraced the whole life of the country and were fairly clear then, far less today. The system of chattel slavery needed territorial expansion because of the soil exhaustion caused by the crude method of slave production. But as the North developed industrially and in population, the South found it ever more difficult to maintain its political domination. Finally the struggle centered, economically, around who would control the newly-opened territories, and, politically, around the regional domination of Congress.

The regime in the South was by 1830 a dreadful tyranny, in startling contrast to the vigorous political democracy of the North. The need to suppress the slaves, who rebelled continuously, necessitated a regime of naked violence. The need to suppress the hostility to slavery of the free laborers and independent farmers led to the gradual abrogation of all popular democracy in the Southern states.

Previous to 1830 there had been anti-slavery societies in the South itself, but by 1830 cotton was king and, instead of arguing for and against slavery, the Southern oligarchy gradually developed a theory of Negro slavery as a heaven-ordained dispensation. Of necessity they sought to impose it upon the whole country. Such a propaganda can be opposed only actively. Not to oppose it is to succumb to it.

The impending revolution is to be led by the Northern bourgeoisie. But that is the last thing that it wants to do. In 1776 the revolutionary struggle was between the rising American bourgeoisie and a foreign enemy. The bourgeoisie needs little prodding to undertake its task. By 1830 the conflict was between two sections of the ruling class based on different economies but tied together by powerful economic links. Therefore, one outstanding feature of the new conflict is the determination of the Northern bourgeois to make every concession and every sacrifice to prevent the precipitation of the break. They will not lead. *They will have to be forced to lead.* The first standard-bearers of the struggle are the petty bourgeois democracy, organized in the Abolition movement, stimulated and sustained by the independent mass action of the Negro people.

The Petty Bourgeoisie and the Negroes

The petty bourgeoisie, having the rights of universal suffrage, had entered upon a period of agitation which has been well summarized in the title of a modern volume, *The Rise of the Common Man.* Lacking the economic demands of an organized proletariat, this agitation found vent in ever-increasing waves of humanitarianism and enthusiasm for social progress. Women's rights, temperance reform, public education, abolition of privilege, universal peace, the brotherhood of man – middle class intellectual America was in ferment. And to this pulsating movement the rebellious Negroes brought the struggle for the abolition of slavery. The agreement among historians is general that all these diverse trends were finally dominated by the Abolition movement.

The Negro struggle for Abolition follows a pattern not dissimilar to the movement for emancipation before 1776. There are, first of all, the same continuous revolts among the masses of the slaves themselves which marked the pre-1776 period. In the decade 1820-30 devoted white men begin the publication of periodicals which preach Abolition on principles grounds. The chief of these was Benjamin Lundy. No sooner does Lundy give the signal than the free Negroes take it up and become the driving force of the movement.

Garrison, directly inspired by Lundy, began early, in 1831. But before that, Negro Abolitionists, not only in speeches and meetings, but in books, periodicals and pamphlets, posed the question squarely before the crusading petty bourgeois democracy. *Freedom's Journal* was published in New York City by two Negroes as early as 1827. David Walker's *Appeal,* published in 1829, created a sensation. It was a direct call for revolution. Free Negroes organized conventions and mass meetings. And before the movement was taken over by such figures as Wendell Phillips and other distinguished men of the time, the free Negroes remained the great supporters of the *Liberator.* In 1831, out of four hundred and fifty subscribers, fully four hundred were Negroes. In 1834, of 2,300 sub-scribers, nearly two thousand were Negroes.

After the free Negroes came the masses. When Garrison published the *Liberator* in 1831, the new Abolition movement, as contrasted with the old anti-slavery societies, amount to little. Within less than a year its fame was nation-wide. What caused this was the rebellion of Nat Turner in 1831. It is useless to speculate whether Walker's *Appeal* or the *Liberator* directly inspired Turner. What is decisive is the effect on the Abolition movement of this, the greatest Negro revolt in the history of the United States.

The Turner revolt not only lifted Garrison's paper and stimulated the organization of his movement. The South responded with such terror that the Negroes, discouraged by the failures of the revolts between 1800 and 1831, began to take another road to freedom. Slowly but steadily grew that steady flight out of the South which lasted for thirty years and injected the struggle against slavery into the North itself. As early as 1827 the escaping Negroes had already achieved some rudimentary form of organization. It was during the eventful year of 1831 that the Underground Railroad took more definite shape. In time thousands of whites and Negroes risked life, liberty and often wealth to assist the rebel slaves.

The great body of escaping slaves, of course, had no political aims in mind. For years rebellious slaves had formed bands of maroons, living a free life in inaccessible spots. Thousands had joined the Indians. Now they sought freedom in civilization and they set forth on that heroic journey of many hundreds of miles, forced to travel mainly by night, through forest and across rivers, often with nothing to guide them but the North Star and the fact that moss grows only on the north side of trees.

The industrial bourgeoisie in America wanted none of this Abolition. It organized mobs who were not unwilling to break up meetings and to lynch agitators. Many ordinary citizens were hostile to Negroes because of competition in industry and the traditional racial prejudice. At one period in the early 'forties, the Abolition movement slumped and Negro historians assert that it was the escaping slaves who kept the problem alive and revived the movement. But we do not need the deductions of modern historians. What the escaping slaves meant to the movement leaps to the eye of the Marxian investigator from every contemporary page.

By degrees the leadership of the movement passed into the hands of and was supported by some of the most gifted white poets, writers and publicists of their time. The free Negroes, in collaboration with the Abolitionist movement, sometimes by themselves, carried on a powerful agitation. But a very special role was played by the ablest and most energetic of the escaping slaves themselves. These men could write and speak from first-hand experience. They were a dramatic witness of the falseness and iniquity of the whole thesis upon which the Southern case was built. Greatest of them all and one of the greatest men of his time was Frederick Douglass, a figure today strangely neglected. In profundity and brilliance, Douglass, the orator, was not the equal of Wendell Phillips. As a political agitator, he did not attain the fire and scope of Garrison nor the latter's dynamic power in organization. But he was their equal in courage, devotion and tenacity of purpose, and in sheer political skill and sagacity he was definitely their superior. He broke with them early, evolving his own policy of maintenance of the Union as opposed to their policy of disunion. He advocated the use of all means, including the political, to attain Abolition. It was only after many years that the Garrisonians followed his example. Greatest of the activists was another escaped slave, Harriet Tubman. Very close to these ex-slaves was John Brown. These three were the nearest to what we would call today the revolutionary propagandists and agitators.

They drove the South to infuriation. Toward the middle of the century the Abolitionists and the escaping slaves had created a situation that made compromise impossible.

The Anti-Fugitive Slave Law

In 1848 there occurred an extraordinary incident, a harbinger of the great international movement which was to play so great a part in the Civil War itself. When the news of the 1848 revolution in France reached Washington, the capital, from the White House to the crowds in the streets, broke out into illuminations and uproarious celebration. Three nights afterward, seventy-eight slaves, taking this enthusiasm for liberty literally, boarded a ship that was waiting for them and tried to escape down the Potomac. They were recaptured and were led back to jail, with a crowd of several thousands waiting in the streets to see them, and members of Congress in the House almost coming to blows in the excitement. The patience of the South and of the Northern bourgeoisie was becoming exhausted. Two years later, the ruling classes, South and North, tried one more compromise. One of the elements of this compromise was a strong Anti-Fugitive Slave Law. The Southerners were determine to stop this continual drain upon their property and the continuous excitation of the North by fugitive slaves.

It was the impossibility of enforcing the Anti-Fugitive Slave Law which wrecked the scheme. Not only did the slaves continue to leave. Many insurrectionary tremors shook the Southern structure in 1850 and again in 1854. The South now feared a genuine slave insurrection. They had either to secede or force their political demands upon the federal government.

The Northern bourgeoisie was willing to discipline the petty bourgeois democracy. But before long, in addition to their humanitarian drive, the petty bourgeois democrats began to understand that not only the liberty of the slaves but their own precious democratic liberties were at stake. To break the desire of the slaves to escape, and to stifle the nation-wide agitation, the South tried to impose restrictions upon public meetings in the North and upon the use of the mails. They demanded the right to use the civil authorities of the North to capture escaping slaves. Under their pressure, Congress even reached so far as to side-track the right of petition. The Declaration of Independence, when presented as a petition in favor of Abolition, was laid upon the table. Negroes who had lived peaceably in the North for years were now threatened, and thousands fled to Canada. Douglass and Harriet Tubman, people of nation-wide fame (Douglass was an international figure) were in danger. There was no settling this question at all. The petty bourgeois democrats defied the South. The escaping slaves continued to come. There were arrests and there were spectacular rescues by pro-Abolition crowds. Pro-slavery and anti-slavery crowds fought in the streets and with the Northern police. Scarcely a month passed but some escaping slave or ex-slave, avoiding arrest, created a local and sometimes a national agitation.

Slaves on ships revolted against slave-traders and took their ships into port, creating international incidents. Congress was powerless. Ten Northern states legalized their rebelliousness by passing Personal Liberty Laws which protected state officers from arresting fugitive slaves, gave arrested Negroes the right of *habeas corpus* and of trial by jury, and prohibited the use of the jails for runaway Negroes. Long before the basic forces of the nation moved into action for the inevitable show-down the petty bourgeois democrats and revolting slaves had plowed up the ground and made the nation irrevocably conscious of the great issues at stake.

The Free Farmers and the Proletariat

Yet neither Negroes nor petty bourgeois democracy were the main force of the second American revolution, and a more extended treatment of American history would make that abundantly clear if that were needed by any serious intelligence. The great battle was over the control of the public doman! Who was to get the land — free farmers or slave-owners? The Republican Party, as Commons has said, was not an anti-slavery party. It was a Homestead party. The bloody struggle over Kansas accelerated the strictly political development. Yet it was out of the Abolition movement that flowered the broader political organizations of the Liberty Party and the Free Soil Party, which in the middle of the decade finally coalesced into the Republican Party.

It was Marx who pointed out very early (*The Civil War in the United States,* page 226. Letter to Engels, July 1, 1861) that what finally broke down the bourgeois timidity was the great development of the population of free farmers in the Northwest Territory in the decade 1850-60. These free farmers were not prepared to stand any nonsense from the South because they were not going to have the mouth of the Mississippi in the hands of any hostile power. By 1860 the great forces which were finally allied were the democratic petty bourgeoisie, the free farmers in the Northwest, and certain sections of the proletariat. These were the classes that, contrary to 1776, compelled the unwilling bourgeois to lead them. They were the basic forces in the period which led to the revolution. They had to come into action before the battle could be joined. They were the backbone of the struggle.

In all this agitation the proletariat did not play a very prominent rôle. In New England the working masses were staunch supporters of the movement and the writer has little doubt that when the proletariat comes into its own, further research will reveal, as it *always does,* that the workers played a greater role than is accredited to them. Yet the old question of unemployment, rivalry between the Negroes in the North and the Irish, the latest of the immigrant groups, disrupted one wing of the proletariat. Furthermore, organized labor, while endorsing the Abolitionist movement, was often in conflict with Garrison, who, like Wilberforce in England, was no lover of the labor movement. Organized labor insisted that there was wage slavery as well as Negro slavery, and at times was apt to treat both of them as being on the same level — a monumental and crippling error.

Nevertheless, on the whole, the evidence seems to point to the fact that in many areas the organized proletarian movement, though not in the vanguard, supported the movement for Abolition. Finally, we must guard against one illusion. The Abolition movement dominated the political consciousness of the time. Most Northerners were in sympathy. But few wanted war or a revolution. When people *want* a revolution, they make one. They usually want anything else except a revolution. It was only when the war began that the abolitionists reaped their full reward. Despite all this Abolition sentiment in the North, and particularly in the Northwest areas, the masses of the people on the whole were not anxious to fraternize with the free Negroes, and over large areas there was distinct hostility. But the free Negroes in the North never allowed this to demoralize them, and the masses of the revolting slaves kept on coming. Between 1830 and 1860, sixty to a hundred thousand slaves came to the North. When they could find no welcome or resting place in the North, some of them went on to Canada. But they never ceased to come. With the Civil War they will come in tens and then in hundreds of thousands.

Abolition and the International Proletariat

From its very beginning at the end of the eighteenth century, the Negro struggle for freedom and equality has been an international question. More than that, it seems to be able to exercise an effect, out of all proportion to reasonable expectation, upon people not directly connected with it. In this respect, the Abolition movement in America has curious affinities with the Abolition movement a generation earlier in Britain.

In Britain, before the emancipation in 1832, the industrial bourgeoisie was actively in favor of abolition. It was industrially more mature than the American bourgeoisie in 1850; the West Indian planters were weak, and the slaves were thousands of miles away. But there, too, the earlier Abolition movement assumed a magnitude and importance out of all proportion to the direct interests of the masses who supported it. Earlier, during the French Revolution, the mass revolts of the Negroes brought home to the French people the reality of the conditions which had existed for over a hundred and fifty years. A kind of collective "madness" on the Negro question seemed to seize the population all over France, and no aristocrats were so much hated as the "aristocrats of the skin."

The Abolitionist movement in America found not only a ready audience at home but an overwhelming welcome abroad. Not only did Garrison, Wendell Phillips and others lecture in

Britain. Frederick Douglass and other Negro Abolitionists traveled over Europe and enrolled many hundreds of thousands in Abolitionist societies. One inspired Negro won seventy thousand signed adherents to the cause in Germany alone. In the decade preceding the Civil War, *Uncle Tom's Cabin* was read by millions in Britain and on the continent, and even as far afield as Italy. And masses of workers and radicals in France, Spain and Germany took an active interest in the question. Their sentiments will bear wonderful fruit during the Civil War itself.

It is not enough to say merely that these workers loved the great American Republic and looked forward to the possibility of emigrating there themselves one day. There are aspects to this question which would repay modern investigation and analysis by Marxists. Beard, who has some insight into social movements in America, is baffled by certain aspects of the Abolition movement.[1] Thoroughly superficial are the self-satisfied pratings of English historians about the "idealism" of the English as an explanation of the equally baffling Abolition movement in Britain. It would seem that the irrationality of the prejudice against Negroes breeds in revolutionary periods a corresponding intensity of loathing for its practitioners among the great masses of the people.[2]

"The Signal Has Now Been Given"

The slaves played their part to the end. After Lincoln's election and the violent reaction of the South, the North, not for the first time, drew back from Civil War. Congress and the political leaders frantically sought compromise. Frederick Douglass in his autobiography gives an account of the shameful attempts on the part of the North to appease the South. Most of the Northern Legislatures repealed their Personal Liberty Laws. And Douglass concludes his bitter chapter by saying: "Those who may wish to see to what depths of humility and self-abasement a noble people can be brought under the sentiment of fear, will find no chapter of history more instructive than that which treats of the events in official circles in Washington during the space between the months of November, 1859, and March, 1860." (*Life and Times of Frederick Douglass,* Pathway Press, 1941, pages 362-366.)

For a long time even Lincoln's stand was doubtful. On December 20, 1860, the very day on which South Carolina seceded, Lincoln made a statement which seemed to exclude compromise. However, in a series of speeches which he delivered on his eleven-day journey to Washington, he confused the nation and demoralized his supporters. Even after the inaugural, on March 4, the North as a whole did not know what to expect from him. Marx, as we have seen, had no doubt that the decisive influence was played by the North-west farmers, who supplied sixty-six votes or 36.6 per cent of the votes in the college which elected Lincoln.

---

[1]   Rise of American Civilization (page 898). "The sources of this remarkable movement are difficult to discover." Much the same can be said of the movement in Britain, which embraced literally millions of people.

[2]   It is something for revolutionists to observe in the past and to count on in the future. Already in England, a country where race prejudice is still very strong, the presence of American Negro soldiers, the prejudice against them of white American soldiers, and the reports of Negro upheaval in America have awakened a strong interest among the English masses.

But there was *refusal to compromise from the South also.* Says Douglass: "Happily for the cause of human freedom, and for the final unity of the American nation, the South was mad and would listen to no concessions. It would neither accept the terms offered, nor offer others to be accepted."

Why wouldn't they? One reason we can now give with confidence. Wherever the masses moved, there Marx and Engels had their eyes glued like hawks and pens quick to record. On January 11, 1860, in the midst of the critical period described by Douglass, Marx wrote to Engels: "In my opinion, the biggest things that are happening in the world today are, on the one hand, the movement of the slaves in America started by the death of John Brown, and, on the other, the movement of the serfs in Russia .... I have just seen in the *Tribune* there has been a fresh rising of slaves in Missouri, naturally suppressed. But the signal has now been given."

Fifteen days later, Engels replied: "Your opinion of the significance of the slave movement in America and Russia is now confirmed. The Harper's Ferry affair with its aftermath in Missouri bears its fruits .... the planters have hurried their cotton on to the ports in order to guard against any probable consequence arising out of the Harper's Ferry affair." A year later Engels writes to Marx: "Things in North America are also becoming exciting. Matters must be going very badly for them with the slaves if the Southerners dare to play so risky a game."

Eighty years after Marx, a modern student has given details which testify to that unfailing insight into the fundamental processes of historical development, so characteristic of our great predecessors. In Arkansas, in Mississippi, in Virginia, in Kentucky, in Illinois, in Texas, in Alabama, in Northwest Georgia, North Carolina, South Carolina — rebellion and conspiracy swept the South between 1859 and 1860. Writes a contemporary after the John Brown raid: "A most terrible panic, in the meantime, seizes not only the village, the vicinity and all parts of the state, but every slave state in the Union ... rumors of insurrection, apprehensions of invasions, whether well founded or ill founded, alter not the proof of the inherent and incurable weakness and insecurity of society, organized upon a slave-holding basis" (*Ibid.,* page 352).

The struggle of the Negro masses derives its peculiar intensity from the simple fact that what they are struggling for is not abstract but is always perfectly visible around them. In their instinctive revolutionary efforts for freedom, the escaping slaves had helped powerfully to begin and now those who remained behind had helped powerfully to conclude, the self-destructive course of the slave power.

J.R. JOHNSON.

[30]

Race Relations—Its Meaning, Beginning, and Progress

Oliver C. Cox

A Definition

IN A DISCUSSION OF "THE ORIGIN" OF RACE RELATIONS IT SHOULD be well to determine at the outset exactly what we are looking for. We shall proceed, therefore, by first eliminating certain concepts that are commonly confused with that of race relations. These are: ethnocentrism, intolerance, and "racism."

Ethnocentrism, as the sociologists conceive of it, is a social attitude which expresses a community of feeling in any group—the "we" feeling as over against the "others." This attitude seems to be a function of group solidarity, which is not necessarily a racial phenomenon. Neither is social intolerance (which we shall consider in more detail in a subsequent chapter) racial antagonism, for social intolerance is social displeasure or resentment against that group which refuses to conform to the established practices and beliefs of the society. Finally, the term "racism" as it has been recently employed in the literature seems to refer to a philosophy of racial antipathy. Studies on the origin of racism involve the study of the development of an ideology, an approach which usually results in the substitution of the history of a system of rationalization for that of a material social fact.[1] Indeed, it is likely to be an accumulation of an erratic pattern of verbalizations cut free from any on-going social system.

What then is the phenomenon, the beginnings of which we seek to determine? It is the phenomenon of the capitalist exploitation of peoples and its complementary social attitude. Again, one should miss the point entirely if one were to think of racial antagonism as having

---

[1] See Hannah Arendt, "Race-Thinking Before Racism," *The Review of Politics,* Vol. 6, January 1944, pp. 36–73; and Fredrick G. Detweiler, "The Rise of Modern Race Antagonisms," *The American Journal of Sociology,* Vol. 37, March 1932, pp. 738–47.

322   *Caste, Class, and Race*

its genesis in some "social instinct" of antipathy between peoples. Such
an approach ordinarily leads to no end of confusion.[2]

The Beginning of Racial Antagonism

Probably a realization of no single fact is of such crucial significance
for an understanding of racial antagonism as that the phenomenon had
its rise only in modern times.[3] In a previous chapter on "the origin of
caste" we have attempted to show that race conflict did not exist among
the early Aryans in India, and we do not find it in other ancient civilizations. Our hypothesis is that racial exploitation and race prejudice developed among Europeans with the rise of capitalism and nationalism,
and that because of the world-wide ramifications of capitalism, all
racial antagonisms can be traced to the policies and attitudes of the
leading capitalist people, the white people of Europe and North
America.

By way of demonstrating this hypothesis we shall review briefly some
well-known historical situations. In tracing the rise of the Anglo-Saxons
to their position as the master race of the world[4] we shall omit consideration of the great Eastern civilizations from which Greece took a
significant cultural heritage. There seems to be no basis for imputing
racial antagonism to the Egyptians, Babylonians, or Persians. At any

---

[2]Consider, for instance, the following definitive statement by Professor Robert E.
Park: "This [prejudice against the Japanese] is due to the existence in the human
mind of a mechanism by which we inevitably and automatically classify every individual human being we meet. When a race bears an external mark by which every
individual member of it can infallibly be identified, that race is by that fact set apart
and segregated. Japanese, Chinese, and Negroes cannot move among us with the
same freedom as members of other races because they bear marks which identify
them as members of their race. This fact isolates them. . . . Isolation is at once a
cause and an effect of race prejudice. It is a vicious circle—isolation, prejudice;
prejudice, isolation." In Jesse F. Steiner, *The Japanese Invasion*, p. xvi.

Since, however, we may assume that all races "bear marks which identify them
as members of their race," it must follow, according to Park, that a certain human
capacity for classification makes it impossible for races to come together without
racial antagonism and prejudice. We shall attempt to show that this instinct hypothesis is too simple.

[3]Cf. Ina Corine Brown, *National Survey of the Higher Education of Negroes*,
U.S. Office of Education, Misc. No. 6, Vol. I, pp. 4–8.

[4]Professor G. A. Borgese makes an observation pertinent to this remark: "The
English-speaking mind is not fully alive to the gravity of this issue. Unlike their
German cousins and foes, the Anglo-Saxon stocks did not strive to *become* the
master race or *Herrenvolk* holding sway over the world and mankind. . . . Yet,
unlike their German cousins and rivals, they have succeeded in *being* a *Herrenvolk*,
a race of masters." "Europe Wants Freedom from Shame," *Life*, March 12, 1945,
pp. 41–42. (Italics Borgese's.)

"The Germans needed all of Hitler's ranting and daily doses from the Goebbels
propaganda machine to persuade them that they were better than other people.
Englishmen simply take it for granted and rarely waste a syllable discussing it." See
John Scott, *Europe in Revolution*, p. 216.

Race Relations 323

rate, the Greeks were the first European people to enter the stream of eastern Mediterranean civilization, and the possibility of racial exploitation did not really occur until the Macedonian conquest. Our point here is, however, that we do not find race prejudice even in the great Hellenistic empire which extended deeper into the territories of colored people than any other European empire up to the end of the fifteenth century.

The Hellenic Greeks had a cultural, not a racial, standard of belonging, so that their basic division of the peoples of the world were Greeks and barbarians—the barbarians having been all those persons who did not possess the Greek culture, especially its language. This is not surprising, for the culture of peoples is always a matter of great moment to them. But the people of the Greek city-states, who founded colonies among the barbarians on the shores of the Black Sea and of the Mediterranean, welcomed those barbarians to the extent that they were able to participate in Greek culture, and intermarried freely with them. The Greeks knew that they had a superior culture to those of the barbarians, but they included Europeans, Africans, and Asiatics in the concept Hellas as these peoples acquired a working knowledge of the Greek culture.

The experience of the later Hellenistic empire of Alexander tended to be the direct contrary of modern racial antagonism. The narrow patriotism of the city-states was given up for a new cosmopolitanism. Every effort was made to assimilate the barbarians to Greek culture, and in the process a new Greco-Oriental culture with a Greco-Oriental ruling class came into being. Alexander himself took a Persian princess for his wife and encouraged his men to intermarry with the native population.[5] In this empire there was an estate, not a racial, distinction between the rulers and the un-Hellenized natives.

Moreover, the inclination of Alexander to disregard even cultural differences in his policy toward the peoples of his empire seemed to have stimulated one of the most remarkable philosophies of all time: that of the fundamental equality of all human beings. In Athens, in about 300 B.C., Zeno developed a system of thought called stoicism

---

[5] In describing the composition of Alexander's army invading India, E. R. Bevan says: ". . . mingled with Europeans were men of many nations. Here were troops of horsemen, representing the chivalry of Iran, which had followed Alexander from Bactria and beyond, Pashtus and men of the Hindu Kush with their highland-bred horses, Central-Asiatics who ride and shoot at the same time; and among the camp-followers one could find groups representing the older civilizations of the world, Phoenicians inheriting an immemorial tradition of shipcraft and trade, bronzed Egyptians able to confront the Indians with an antiquity still longer than their own." *The Cambridge History of India,* Vol. I, p. 351.

324   *Caste, Class, and Race*

which held in part that "all men should be fellow citizens; and there should be one life and order, as of a flock pasturing together, which feeds together by a common law." This doctrine was not a reaction to race prejudice but rather to certain invidious cultural distinctions among the peoples of the time; and the idea has come down to us by way of the Roman law, the preaching of St. Paul, and the writings of the philosophers of the Enlightenment. It has been given a democratic emphasis in the American Declaration of Independence and in amendments to the Constitution of the United States.

The next great organization of peoples about the Mediterranean Sea —and in so far as European civilization is concerned this may be thought of as constituting the whole world—was the Roman Empire. In this civilization also we do not find racial antagonism, for the norm of superiority in the Roman system remained a cultural-class attribute. The basic distinction was Roman citizenship, and gradually this was extended to all freeborn persons in the municipalities of the empire. Slaves came from every province, and there was no racial distinction among them. Sometimes the slaves, especially the Greeks, were the teachers of their masters; indeed, very much of the cultural enlightenment of the Romans came through slaves from the East. Because slavery was not a racial stigma, educated freedmen, who were granted citizenship upon emancipation, might rise to high positions in government or industry. There were no interracial laws governing the relationship of the great mass of obscure common people of different origin. Moreover, the aristocracy of the empire, the senators and *equites,* was constituted largely from responsible provincials in the imperial administration.

One should not mistake the social relationship among the various social estates of the Greek and Roman world for race relations. The Spartiates, *Perioikoi,* and Helots of Laconia, for instance, were not races but social estates; neither did the *Metics,*[6] the alien residents of Periclean Athens, constitute a race. In early republican Rome intermarriage was forbidden between the privileged patrician class and the plebeian mass, but this was a social-estate partition rather than a racial accommodation.

If we have not discovered interracial antagonism in ancient Greece

---

[6]The Metics may probably be better thought of as presenting a multinationality situation. On this point Gustave Glotz, referring to the Metics of various national origins, concludes: ". . . there was formed in Greece in the fifth and sixth centuries a kind of international nation which was preparing, chiefly in economic interests but also in the domain of ideas and in the very framework of society, for the cosmopolitanism of the Hellenistic period." *Ancient Greece at Work,* p. 191.

Race Relations 325

and Rome, the chances of discovering it in the system which succeeded the fall of the Roman Empire are even more remote. With the rise of the politico-religious system of Christianity, Western culture may be thought of as having entered its long period of gestation. Its first signs of parturition were the Crusades. But during all this time and even after the Renaissance the nature of the movement and of the social contact of peoples in this area precluded the possibility of the development of race prejudice.

The general pattern of barbarian invasions was that of a succession of peoples of increasing cultural inferiority moving into areas of higher culture. Thus, the German nations which invaded the Roman Empire had a smaller capacity for maintaining a complex culture than the Romans had when they conquered the Greeks; and probably the Celtic people of Britain had still fewer resources to continue their Roman cultural heritage. In the movement of barbarian peoples from the East and North toward the general area of the Mediterranean no nationalistic sentiments stood in the way to limit their amalgamation with the native populations.

One aspect of this era of barbarian invasion, the movement of Asiatics into Europe, is of especial significance. The Asiatics were better warriors than rulers. We may say rather conclusively that the white man's rise to superiority over the colored peoples of the other continents is based pivotally on his superiority as a fighter. This is, however, a rather recent achievement. In the Middle Ages the Asiatics outfought him. The Huns, Saracens, Moors, Seljuk Turks, Ottoman Turks, Tartars—all went deep into Europe, subjugated and sometimes enslaved white peoples who today are highly race-prejudiced. At any rate, we shall not find racial antagonism among these invaders. The most powerful of them were Moslems, and both the economic base and religious sanctions of Mohammedanism are opposed to race prejudice. Under Mohammedanism—at least in so far as it has not been recently corrupted by capitalist ideals—the criterion of belonging is a cultural one; furthermore, Islam is a proselyting culture.

In Europe itself the policies of the Roman Catholic Church presented a bar to the development of racial antagonism. The Church, which gradually attained more or less religious, economic, and ideological dominance, had a folk and personal—not a territorial or racial—norm of belonging. The fundamental division of human beings was Christian and non-Christian. Among the non-Christians the heathen, the infidel, and the heretic were recognized by differential negative attitudes; however, as a means of entering the Christian community, conversion or

326

Caste, Class, and Race

recantation was freely allowed and even sought after. There was in medieval Europe—indeed in the Christian world—an effective basis for the brotherhood of peoples. Although a man's economic, contractual relationship in his community determined his livelihood, to be excommunicated by the Church almost had the effect of putting him beyond the purview of society itself. In the Middle Ages, then, we find no racial antagonism in Europe; in fact, Europeans were, at this time, more isolated and ignorant about foreign peoples and world geography than the Romans and Greeks were.

But gradually, under a commercial and religious impulse, Europe began to awaken and to journey toward strange lands. The First Crusade may be taken as the starting point which finally led to world dominance by Europeans. When after their travels in the last quarter of the thirteenth century the Polos returned from the court of the great Kublai Khan in China to tell Europeans a story of fabulous wealth and luxury, the astonished people could hardly believe what they heard. Yet Marco Polo's memoirs were a great stimulant to traders. It was not until the discovery of America and the circumnavigation of the globe, however, that the movement assumed a decidedly irreversible trend. The period between the First Crusade and the discovery of America continued to be characterized by the religious view of world order; but it set a pattern of dealing with non-Christian peoples which was to be continued, minus only its religious characteristics, to this day. To the extent that the religious controls remained effective, racial antagonism did not develop; what really developed was a Jew-heathen-infidel antagonistic complex which was to color European thought for some centuries.

Up to the eleventh century Christian Europe was hemmed in from the North, East, and South by heathens and infidels; the Mediterranean was almost encircled by the Arabian Mohammedans, a people whose culture was superior to that of the northern Europeans. In the eleventh century, however, under the organizing influence of the popes, the holy warriors of Christendom began to carry conquering crusades into the territory of the heathen Slavic and infidel Asiatic peoples. As a general rule the Church made the lands and even the peoples of the non-Christian world the property of the Crusaders, and the trader ordinarily followed the cross.

In fact, it was this need for trade with the East, especially by the Italian, Spanish, and Portuguese merchants, and its obstruction by the Mohammedans whose country lay across their path in the Near East, which induced the Portuguese, in the fifteenth century, to feel their way

Race Relations 327

down the African coast in the hope of sailing around this continent to the East Indies. Here began the great drama that was, in a few hundred years, to turn over the destiny of the world to the decisions of businessmen. But our concern at this point is to indicate that racial antagonism had not yet developed among the Europeans.

In the first place, the geography of the world was still a mystery, and some of the most fantastic tales about its peoples were believed. Stories of the splendor, luxury, and wisdom of the peoples of the East held all Europe in constant wonderment. No one would have been surprised if some traveler had returned from the heart of Africa to break the news that he had found a black monarch ruling over a kingdom surpassing in grandeur and power any that had then existed in Europe. In short, the white man had no conception of himself as a being capable of developing *the* superior culture of the world—the concept "white man" had not yet its significant social definition—the Anglo-Saxon, the modern master race, was then not even in the picture.

But when the Portuguese began to inch their way down the African coast they knew that the Moors and heathens whom they encountered were inferior to them both as fighters and as culture builders.[7] This, however, led to no conclusions about racial superiority. Henry the Navigator, himself, sought in those parts a Christian prince, Prester John, with whom he planned to form an alliance "against the enemies of the faith." All through the latter half of the fifteenth century the Portuguese sailors and explorers kept up this search for the kingdom of the lost black prince.

Of more significance still is the fact that there was as yet no belief in any cultural incapacity of these colored people. Their conversion to Christianity was sought with enthusiasm, and this transformation was supposed to make the Africans the human equals of all other Christians. The Portuguese historian, Gomes Eannes de Azurara, writing in the middle of the fifteenth century, gives us some idea of the religious motives for Prince Henry's exploits among the peoples on the West African coast. One reason for the Navigator's slave raids:

. . . was his great desire to make increase in the faith of our lord Jesus Christ and to bring to him all souls that should be saved,—understanding

---

[7] It should be noted that the Portuguese felt they were superior because they were Christians, not because they were white. In an address to his men just before they attacked an unsuspecting west-coast community, the captain of a caravel declared: ". . . although they are more in number than we by a third yet they are but Moors, and we are Christians one of whom ought to suffice for two of them. For God is He in whose power lieth victory, and He knoweth our good wills in His holy service." Azurara, *The Discovery and Conquest of Guinea*, p. 138.

328   *Caste, Class, and Race*

that all the mystery of the Incarnation, Death, and Passion of our Lord Jesus Christ was for this sole end—namely the salvation of lost souls, whom the said Lord Infant [Henry] by his travail and spending would fain bring into the true faith. For he perceived that no better offering could be made unto the Lord than this. For if God promised to return one hundred goods for one, we may justly believe that for such great benefits, that is to say, for so many souls as were saved by the efforts of this Lord, he will have so many hundreds of guerdons in the Kingdom of God, by which his spirit may be glorified after this life in the celestial realm. For I that wrote this history saw so many men and women of those parts turned to the holy faith, that even if the Infant had been a heathen, their prayers would have been enough to have obtained his salvation. And not only did I see the first captives, but their children and grandchildren as true Christians as if the Divine grace breathed in them and imparted to them a clear knowledge of itself.[8]

This matter of cultural conversion is crucial for our understanding of the development of racial antagonism. For the full profitable exploitation of a people, the dominant group must devise ways and means of limiting that people's cultural assimilation. So long as the Portuguese and Spaniards continued to accept the religious definition of human equality, so long also the development of race prejudice was inhibited. Although it is true that the forays on the African coast were exceedingly ruthless, the Portuguese did not rationalize the fact with a racial argument. To kill or to take into slavery the heathen or infidel was to serve the highest purpose of God. As Azurara pointed out: ". . . though their bodies were now brought into subjection, that was a small matter in comparison to their souls, which would now possess true freedom for evermore."[8a] In granting to Prince Henry a "plenary indulgence," Pope Eugenius IV gave "to each and all those who shall be engaged in the said war [slave raids], complete forgiveness of all their sins."[8b]

The Portuguese people themselves had developed no racial hatred for the captives. Azurara relates how the townspeople at Lagos wept in sympathy for the suffering of the Moors as families were broken to be distributed among different masters. And, it seems, the captives were quite readily assimilated into the population.

. . . from this time forth [after their partition] they began to acquire some knowledge of our country, in which they found great abundance; and our men began to treat them with great favour. For as our people did not find them hardened in the belief [i.e., Islam] of the Moors, and saw how they came unto the law of Christ with a good will, they made no

---

[8]Op. cit., p. 29. See also C. Raymond Beazley, *Prince Henry the Navigator.*
[8a]Op. cit., p. 51.
[8b]Ibid., p. 53.

Race Relations 329

difference between them and their free [Portuguese] servants, born in our own country. But those whom they took [captured] while still young, they caused to be instructed in mechanical arts. And those whom they saw fitted for managing property, they set free and married to women who were natives of the land [of Portugal], making with them a division of their property as if it had been bestowed on those who married them by the will of their own fathers. . . . Yea, and some widows of good family who bought some of these female slaves, either adopted them or left them a portion of their estate by will, so that in the future they married right well, treating them as entirely free. Suffice it that I never saw one of these slaves put in irons like other captives, and scarcely any one who did not turn Christian and was not gently treated.

And I have been asked by their lords to the baptisms and marriages of such; at which they, whose slaves they were before, made no less solemnity than if they had been their children or relations.[9]

The Portuguese had no clear sense of racial antagonism, because its economic and rationalistic basis had not yet developed among them. Indeed the Portuguese and Spaniards never became fully freed of the crusading spirit, which constantly held in check their attainment of a clear appreciation of the values of competitive labor exploitation.[10] The Church received its share of African servants; as yet, however, it had no idea of the economic uses of segregation and "cultural parallelism"—of the techniques for perpetuating the servile status of the black workers. It had developed no rationalizations of inborn human inferiority in support of a basic need for labor exploitation. On the contrary, its obsession with the spiritual values of conversion left the Negroes free to be integrated into the general population. It is reported that before the returning captains of one commission of caravels "did anything else [in the distribution of captured Moors] they took as an offering the best of those Moors to the Church of that place; and another little Moor, who afterwards became a friar of St. Francis, they sent to St. Vincent do Cabo, where he lived ever after as a Catholic Christian, without having understanding or perception of any other law than that true and holy law in which all the Christians hope for salvation."[11]

---

[9]Op. cit., p. 84.

[10]Speaking of the activities of the Portuguese at Goa, India, soon after 1498, L. S. S. O'Malley says: "The Portuguese territories were intended to be outposts of their empire and their religion. . . . Colonization was effected not so much by immigration as by marriage with Indian women. There was no color bar, and the children of mixed marriages were under no stigma of inferiority. . . . Proselytization began soon after the capture of Goa. . . . At the same time the spread of Christianity was assisted by an appeal to material interests. Converts were to be provided with posts in the customs, exempted from impressment in the navy, and supported by the distribution of rice." *Modern India and the West*, pp. 44–45.

[11]Azurara, op. cit., p. 80.

330   *Caste, Class, and Race*

The next era in the history of race relations commenced with the discovery of America. If we see that race prejudice is an attitudinal instrument of modern human, economic exploitation, the question as to whether race prejudice was found among the primitive peoples of the world will not arise. It would be, for instance, a ridiculous inversion of thought to expect the native peoples of America to have had race prejudice for the white invaders.[12] But modern society—Western civilization—began to take on its characteristic attributes when Columbus turned the eyes and interests of the world away from the Mediterranean toward the Atlantic. The mysticism of the East soon lost its grip on human thought, and the bourgeois world got under way. The socioeconomic matrix of racial antagonism involved the commercialization of human labor in the West Indies, the East Indies, and in America, the intense competition among businessmen of different western European cities for the capitalist exploitation of the resources of this area, the development of nationalism and the consolidation of European nations, and the decline of the influence of the Roman Catholic Church with its mystical inhibitions to the free exploitation of economic resources. Racial antagonism attained full maturity during the latter half of the nineteenth century, when the sun no longer set on British soil and the great nationalistic powers of Europe began to justify their economic designs upon weaker European peoples with subtle theories of racial superiority and masterhood.

It should be observed that this view is not generally agreed upon. A popular belief among writers on modern race relations is that the phenomenon has always been known among most, if not all, peoples. This approach apparently tends to give theories of race relations a "scientific" aspect, but it contributes little to an understanding of the problem.

For instance, Jacques Barzun may be misleading in his saying that "if anyone deserves burning in effigy for starting the powerful race-dogma of Nordic superiority" it is Tacitus. This is supposed to be so

---

[12]Although Columbus participated in the enslavement of the Indians of the West Indies, which finally led to their extermination, his first impression of them is well known: "They are a loving uncovitous people, so docile in all things that I do assure your Highness I believe in all the world there is not a better people or a better country; they love their neighbours as themselves, and they have the sweetest and gentlest way of speaking in the world and always with a smile." Again, "As they showed us such friendship and as I recognized they were people who would yield themselves better to the Christian faith and be converted more through love than by force, I gave them some coloured buttons and some glass beads . . . and [they] became so attached to us that it was a marvel to behold." See Francis A. MacNutt, *Bartholomew De Las Casas*, pp. 18, 19.

Race Relations 331

because Tacitus, in his admiration of the primitive "Germans," made assertions "embodying the germ of present-day Nordicism."[13] Yet it seems evident that neither Tacitus, St. Paul, Noah, nor the Rig-Vedic Aryans are responsible for the racial practices and ideologies developed among modern Europeans. Moreover, the use of the metaphor "germ" is likely to convey the idea that this excursus of Tacitus, his "noble-savage" description of the virtues of the tribal Germans, was continually built upon by them over the centuries, until at last it blossomed into nazism.

We might just as well rely upon that notable charge of Cicero to Atticus in the first century B.C., "Do not obtain your slaves from Britain because they are so stupid and so utterly incapable of being taught that they are not fit to form a part of the household of Athens," as a basis for the explanation of modern race prejudice against the British—the only difficulty being that there has never been any such prejudice.

When white scholars began their almost desperate search of the ancient archives for good reasons to explain the wonderful cultural accomplishments among the whites, European economic and military world dominance was already an actuality. Most of the discoveries which explain the racial superiority of the tall, long-headed blond may be called Hamite rationalizations; they are drawn from bits of isolated verbalizations or deductions from cultural situations which cannot be identified with those of modern race relations. Probably the most widely accepted of these has been the biblical story of the descendants of Ham as a people cursed forever to do the menial work of others.

When English, French, and German scholars discovered the Aryans in the Sanskrit literature of the Hindus, the Hindus themselves were unaware of the Aryans' racial potentialities. The concept "Arya" meant practically nothing to them. It remained for the nationalistic Germans to recognize that the term "Aryan" designated Germans particularly and that, because of this, the right of Germans to exploit all other peoples of the world, not excluding the Hindus, was confirmed.

In the study of race relations it is of major importance to realize that their significant manifestations could not possibly have been known among the ancients. If we had to put our finger upon the year which marked the beginning of modern race relations we should select 1493–94. This is the time when total disregard for the human rights and physical power of the non-Christian peoples of the world, the colored peoples, was officially assumed by the first two great colonizing

---

[13]*Race, A Study of Modern Superstition*, pp. 11, 28.

332   *Caste, Class, and Race*

European nations. Pope Alexander VI's bull of demarcation issued under Spanish pressure on May 3, 1493, and its revision by the Treaty of Tordesillas (June 7, 1494), arrived at through diplomatic negotiations between Spain and Portugal, put all the heathen peoples and their resources—that is to say, especially the colored peoples of the world—at the disposal of Spain and Portugal.[14]

Sometimes, probably because of its very obviousness, it is not realized that the slave trade was simply a way of recruiting labor for the purpose of exploiting the great natural resources of America.[15] This trade did not develop because Indians and Negroes were red and black, or because their cranial capacity averaged a certain number of cubic centimeters; but simply because they were the best workers to be found for the heavy labor in the mines and plantations across the Atlantic.[16] If white workers were available in sufficient numbers they would have been substituted. As a matter of fact, part of the early demand for labor in the West Indies and on the mainland was filled by white servants, who were sometimes defined in exactly the same terms as those used to characterize the Africans. Although the recruitment of involuntary labor finally settled down to the African coasts, the earlier kidnapers did a brisk business in some of the most enlightened European cities. Moreover, in the process of exploiting the natural resources of the West Indies, the Spanish conquistadors literally consumed the native Indian population.

This, then, is the beginning of modern race relations. It was not an abstract, natural, immemorial feeling of mutual antipathy between groups, but rather a practical exploitative relationship with its socio-attitudinal facilitation—at that time only nascent race prejudice. Although this peculiar kind of exploitation was then in its incipiency, it

---

[14]As early as 1455 Pope Nicholas V had granted the Portuguese exclusive right to their discoveries on the African coast, but the commercial purpose here was still very much involved with the crusading spirit.

[15]In a discussion of the arguments over slavery during the Constitutional Convention, Charles A. Beard observes: "South Carolina was particularly determined, and gave northern representatives to understand that if they wished to secure their commercial privileges, they must make concessions to the slave trade. And they were met half way. Ellsworth said: 'As slaves multiply so fast in Virginia and Maryland that it is cheaper to raise than import them, whilst in the sickly rice swamps foreign supplies are necessary, if we go no farther than is urged, we shall be unjust towards South Carolina and Georgia. Let us not intermeddle. As population increases, poor laborers will be so plenty as to render slaves useless.' " *An Economic Interpretation of the Constitution*, p. 177. Quote from Max Farrand, *Records*, Vol. II, p. 371.

[16]In a discussion of the labor situation among the early Spanish colonists in America, Professor Bailey W. Diffie observes: "One Negro was reckoned as worth two, four, or even more Indians at work production." *Latin American Civilization*, p. 206.

Race Relations 333

had already achieved its significant characteristics.[17] As it developed and took definite capitalistic form, we could follow the white man around the world and see him repeat the process among practically every people of color. Earl Grey was directly in point when he described, in 1880, the motives and purpose of the British in one racial situation:

> Throughout this part of the British Dominions the colored people are generally looked upon by the whites as an inferior race, whose interest ought to be systematically disregarded when they come into competition with their own, and who ought to be governed mainly with a view of the advantage of the superior race. And for this advantage two things are considered to be especially necessary: first, that facilities should be afforded to the white colonists for obtaining possession of land heretofore occupied by the native tribes; and secondly, that the Kaffir population should be made to furnish as large and as cheap a supply of labor as possible.[18]

But the fact of crucial significance is that racial exploitation is merely one aspect of the problem of the proletarianization of labor, regardless of the color of the laborer. Hence racial antagonism is essentially political-class conflict. The capitalist exploiter, being opportunistic and practical, will utilize any convenience to keep his labor and other resources freely exploitable. He will devise and employ race prejudice when that becomes convenient.[19] As a matter of fact, the white proletariat of early capitalism had to endure burdens of exploitation quite similar to those which many colored peoples must bear today.

However, the capitalist spirit, the profit-making motive, among the sixteenth-century Spaniards and Portuguese, was constantly inhibited by the philosophy and purpose of the Roman Catholic Church. A social

---

[17] Francis Augustus MacNutt describes the relationship in Hispaniola: "Columbus laid tribute upon the entire population of the island which required that each Indian above fourteen years of age who lived in the mining provinces was to pay a little bell filled with gold every three months; the natives of all other provinces were to pay one *arroba* of cotton. These amounts were so excessive that in 1496 it was found necessary to change the nature of the payments, and, instead of the gold and cotton required from the villages, labour was substituted, the Indians being required to lay out and work the plantations of the colonists in their vicinity." *Bartholomew De Las Casas*, p. 25.

[18] Quoted by E. D. Morel, *The Black Man's Burden*, p. 30.

[19] In our description of the uses of race prejudice in this essay we are likely to give the impression that race prejudice was always "manufactured" in full awareness by individuals or groups of entrepreneurs. This, however, is not quite the case. Race prejudice, from its inception, became part of the social heritage, and as such both exploiters and exploited for the most part are born heirs to it. It is possible that most of those who propagate and defend race prejudice are not conscious of its fundamental motivation. To paraphrase Adam Smith: They who teach and finance race prejudice are by no means such fools as the majority of those who believe and practice it.

334   *Caste, Class, and Race*

theory supporting the capitalist drive for the impersonal exploitation of the workers never completely emerged. Conversion to Christianity and slavery among the Indians stood at cross-purposes; therefore, the vital problem presented to the exploiters of labor was that of circumventing the assimilative effects of conversion to Christianity. In the West Indies the celebrated priest, Las Casas, was touched by the destructive consequences of the ruthless enslavement of the Indians, and he opposed it on religious grounds. But work had to be done, and if not voluntarily, then some ideology had to be found to justify involuntary servitude. "The Indians were represented as lazy, filthy pagans, of bestial morals, no better than dogs, and fit only for slavery, in which state alone there might be some hope of instructing and converting them to Christianity."[20]

The capitalist exploitation of the colored workers, it should be observed, consigns them to employments and treatment that is humanly degrading. In order to justify this treatment the exploiters must argue that the workers are innately degraded and degenerate, consequently they naturally merit their condition. It may be mentioned incidentally that the ruling-class conception of degradation will tend to be that of all persons in the society, even that of the exploited person himself; and the work done by degraded persons will tend to degrade superior persons who attempt to do it.

In 1550, finally, the great capitalist interests produced a champion, Gaines de Sepulveda, brilliant theologian and debater, to confront Las Casas in open debate at Valladolid on the right of Spaniards to wage wars of conquest against the Indians. Sepulveda held that it was lawful to make war against (enslave) the Indians:

1. Because of the gravity of their sins. . . .
2. Because of the rudeness of their heathen and barbarous natures, which oblige them to serve those of more elevated natures, such as the Spaniards possess.
3. For the spread of the faith; for their subjection renders its preaching easier and more persuasive [and so on].[21]

It is not surprising that Sepulveda won the debate. His approach was consistent with the exploitative rationalizations of the time. He con-

---

[20]Francis Augustus MacNutt, op. cit., p. 83.

It should be kept clearly in view that this colonial movement was not a transference of the feudal manorial economy to America. It was the beginning of an entirely different economic enterprise—the dawn of colonial capitalism, the moving out of "white" capital into the lands of colored peoples who had to be exploited unsentimentally and with any degree of ruthlessness in the interest of profits.

[21]MacNutt, op. cit., p. 288.

Race Relations 335

trived a reasonably logical justification for the irrepressibly exploitative situation. This clearly was in answer to an urgent necessity for such an authoritative explanation; the whole world, so to speak, was calling for it. As a characteristic, it should be observed that no explanation at all need have been made to the exploited people themselves. The group sentiment and feeling of the exploited peoples were disregarded entirely.

Sepulveda, then, may be thought of as among the first great racists;[22] his argument was, in effect, that the Indians were inferior to the Spaniards, therefore they should be exploited. Yet the powerful religious interest among the Spaniards limited the establishment of a clear philosophy of racial exploitation. Some years earlier an attempt was made to show "that the Indians were incapable of conversion," but this was finally squelched by a threat to bring the advocate before the tribunal of the Inquisition.[23] It remained for later thinkers, mainly from northern European countries, to produce the evidence that "native peoples" have an inferior, animal-like capacity for culture.[24]

---

[22]Among the Spanish writers of the time (about 1535 onward) who were in rather complete accord with the drastic methods of human exploitation in the New World was Gonzolo Fernandez de Oviedo, whose prolific works have been collected in the commentary, *Historia General y Natural de las Indias,* 4 vols. It was Oviedo's opinion, even after visiting America on a royal commission, that the Indians were not far removed from the state of wild animals, and that coercive measures were necessary if they were to be Christianized and taught the uses of systematic labor.

[23]MacNutt, op. cit., pp. 94–95.

[24]Beasts of burden do not have rights which human beings are bound to respect; they may be exploited at will. The latter convenience is a desideratum in the capitalist exploitation of labor, regardless of the color of the laborer. However, the fact of difference in color and culture makes available to the exploiters of colored workers a valuable means of securing their dehumanization in the eyes of a certain public, that is to say, the public of the exploiting class. When a philosophy for the dehumanizing of the exploited people has been developed with sufficient cogency, the ruling class is ready to make its grand statement, sometimes implicitly, and to act in accordance with it: The colored people have no rights which the master race is bound to respect. The exploiting class has an economic investment in this conviction and it will defend it with the same vigor as it would an attack upon private property in land and capital.

Bibliography

AZURARA, GOMES EANNES DE. *The Discovery and Conquest of Guinea,* trans. by C. R. Beazley and E. Prestage, London, 1896–99.

BEARD, CHARLES A. *An Economic Interpretation of the Constitution of the United States,* New York, 1943.

DIFFIE, BAILEY W. *Latin American Civilization,* Harrisburg, 1945.

GLOTZ, GUSTAVE. *Ancient Greeks at Work,* New York, 1926.

MACNUTT, FRANCIS AUGUSTUS. *Bartholomew De Las Casas,* New York & London, 1909.

MOREL, E. D. *The Black Man's Burden,* New York, 1920.

O'MALLEY, L. S. S. *Modern India and the West,* London, 1941.

OVIEDO, GONZALO FERNANDEZ DE. *Historia General y Natural de las Indias,* Madrid, 1885.

SCOTT, JOHN. *Europe in Revolution,* Boston, 1945.

STEINER, JESSE FREDERICK. *The Japanese Invasion,* Chicago, 1917.

[31]

THE FEMINIST STANDPOINT: DEVELOPING THE GROUND FOR A SPECIFICALLY FEMINIST HISTORICAL MATERIALISM*

NANCY C. M. HARTSOCK

The power of the Marxian critique of class domination stands as an implicit suggestion that feminists should consider the advantages of adopting a historical materialist approach to understanding phallocratic domination. A specifically feminist historical materialism might enable us to lay bare the laws of tendency which constitute the structure of patriarchy over time and to follow its development in and through the Western class societies on which Marx's interest centered. A feminist materialism might in addition enable us to expand the Marxian account to include all human activity rather than focussing on activity more characteristic of males in capitalism. The development of such a historical and materialist account is a very large task, one which requires the political and theoretical contributions of many feminists. Here I will address only the question of the epistemological underpinnings such a materialism would require. Most specifically, I will attempt to develop, on the methodological base provided by Marxian theory, an important epistemological tool for understanding and opposing all forms of domination – a feminist standpoint.

Despite the difficulties feminists have correctly pointed to in Marxian theory, there are several reasons to take over much of Marx's approach. First, I have argued elsewhere that Marx's method and the method developed by the contemporary women's movement recapitulate each other in important ways.[1] This makes it possible for feminists to take over a number of aspects of Marx's method. Here, I will adopt his distinction between appearance and essence, circulation and production, abstract and concrete, and use these distinctions between dual levels of reality to work out the theoretical forms appropriate to each level when viewed not from the standpoint of the proletariat but from a specifically feminist standpoint. In this process I will explore and expand the Marxian argument that socially mediated interaction with nature in the process of production shapes both human beings and theories of knowledge. The Marxian category of labor, including as it does both interaction with other humans and with the natural world can help to cut through the dichotomy of nature and culture, and, for feminists, can help to avoid the false choice of characterizing the situation of women as either "purely natural" or "purely social". As embodied humans we are of course

NANCY C. M. HARTSOCK

inextricably both natural and social, though feminist theory to date has, for important strategic reasons, concentrated attention on the social aspect.

I set off from Marx's proposal that a correct vision of class society is available from only one of the two major class positions in capitalist society. On the basis of this meta-theoretical claim, he was able to develop a powerful critique of class domination. The power of Marx's critique depended on the epistemology and ontology supporting this meta-theoretical claim. Feminist Marxists and materialist feminists more generally have argued that the position of women is structurally different from that of men, and that the lived realities of women's lives are profoundly different from those of men.[2] They have not yet, however, given sustained attention to the epistemological consequences of such a claim. Faced with the depth of Marx's critique of capitalism, feminist analysis, as Iris Young has correctly pointed out, often

accepts the traditional Marxian theory of production relations, historical change, and analysis of the structure of capitalism in basically unchanged form. It rightly criticizes that theory for being essentially gender-blind, and hence seeks to supplement Marxist theory of capitalism with feminist theory of a system of male domination. Taking this route, however, tacitly endorses the traditional Marxian position that 'the woman question' is auxiliary to the central questions of a Marxian theory of society.[3]

By setting off from the Marxian meta-theory I am implicitly suggesting that this, rather than his critique of capitalism, can be most helpful to feminists. I will explore some of the epistemological consequences of claiming that women's lives differ structurally from those of men. In particular, I will suggest that like the lives of proletarians according to Marxian theory, women's lives make available a particular and privileged vantage point on male supremacy, a vantage point which can ground a powerful critique of the phallocratic institutions and ideology which constitute the capitalist form of patriarchy. After a summary of the nature of a standpoint as an epistemological device, I will address the question of whether one can discover a feminist standpoint on which to ground a specifically feminist historical materialism. I will suggest that the sexual division of labor forms the basis for such a standpoint and will argue that on the basis of the structures which define women's activity as contributors to subsistence and as mothers one could begin, though not complete, the construction of such an epistemological tool. I hope to show how just as Marx's understanding of the world from the standpoint of the proletariat enabled him to go beneath bourgeois ideology, so a feminist standpoint can allow us to understand patriarchal institutions and ideologies as perverse inversions of more humane social relations.

THE FEMINIST STANDPOINT

285

THE NATURE OF A STANDPOINT

A standpoint is not simply an interested position (interpreted as bias) but is interested in the sense of being engaged. It is true that a desire to conceal real social relations can contribute to an obscurantist account, and it is also true that the ruling gender and class have material interests in deception. A standpoint, however, carries with it the contention that there are some perspectives on society from which, however well-intentioned one may be, the real relations of humans with each other and with the natural world are not visible. This contention should be sorted into a number of distinct epistemological and political claims: (1) Material life (class position in Marxist theory) not only structures but sets limits on the understanding of social relations. (2) If material life is structured in fundamentally opposing ways for two different groups, one can expect that the vision of each will represent an inversion of the other, and in systems of domination the vision available to the rulers will be both partial and perverse. (3) The vision of the ruling class (or gender) structures the material relations in which all parties are forced to participate, and therefore cannot be dismissed as simply false. (4) In consequence, the vision available to the oppressed group must be struggled for and represents an achievement which requires both science to see beneath the surface of the social relations in which all are forced to participate, and the education which can only grow from struggle to change those relations. (5) As an engaged vision, the understanding of the oppressed, the adoption of a standpoint exposes the real relations among human bengs as inhuman, points beyond the present, and carries a historically liberatory role.

The concept of a standpoint structures epistemology in a particular way. Rather than a simple dualism, it posits a duality of levels of reality, of which the deeper level or essence both includes and explains the "surface" or appearance, and indicates the logic by means of which the appearance inverts and distorts the deeper reality. In addition, the concept of a standpoint depends on the assumption that epistemology grows in a complex and contradictory way from material life. Any effort to develop a standpoint must take seriously Marx's injunction that "all mysteries which lead theory to mysticism find their rational solution in human practice and in the comprehension of this practice."[4] Marx held that the source both for the proletarian standpoint and the critique of capitalism it makes possible is to be found in practical activity itself. The epistemological (and even ontological) significance of human activity is made clear in Marx's argument not only that persons are active but that reality itself consists of "sensuous human activity, practice."[5]

286   NANCY C. M. HARTSOCK

Thus Marx can speak of products as crystallized or congealed human activity or work, of products as conscious human activity in another form. He can state that even plants, animals, light, etc. constitute theoretically a part of human consciousness, and a part of human life and activity.[6] As Marx and Engels summarize their position.

> As individuals express their life, so they are. What they are, therefore, coincides with their production, both with *what* they produce and with *how* they produce. The nature of individuals thus depends on the material conditions determining their production.[7]

This starting point has definite consequences for Marx's theory of knowledge. If humans are not what they eat but what they do, especially what they do in the course of production of subsistence, each means of producing subsistence should be expected to carry with it *both* social relations *and* relations to the world of nature which express the social understanding contained in that mode of production. And in any society with systematically divergent practical activities, one should expect the growth of logically divergent world views. That is, each division of labor, whether by gender or class, can be expected to have consequences for knowledge. Class society, according to Marx, does produce this dual vision in the form of the ruling class vision and the understanding available to the ruled.

On the basis of Marx's description of the activity of commodity exchange in capitalism, the ways in which the dominant categories of thought simply express the mystery of the commodity form have been pointed out. These include a dependence on quantity, duality and opposition of nature to culture, a rigid separation of mind and body, intention and behavior.[8] From the perspective of exchange, where commodities differ from each other only quantitatively, it seems absurd to suggest that labor power differs from all other commodities. The sale and purchase of labor power from the perspective of capital is simply a contract between free agents, in which "the agreement [the parties] come to is but the form in which they give legal expression of their common will." It is a relation of equality,

> because each enters into relation with the other, as with a simple owner of commodities, and they exchange equivalent for equivalent. ... The only force that brings them together and puts them in relation with each other, is the selfishness, the gain and the private interests of each. Each looks to himself only, and no one troubles himself about the rest, and just because they do so, do they all, in accordance with the pre-established harmony of things, or under the auspices of an all shrewd providence, work together to their mutual advantage, for the common weal and in the interest of all.

This is the only description available within the sphere of circulation or

THE FEMINIST STANDPOINT 287

exchange of commodities, or as Marx might put it, at the level of appearance. But at the level of production, the world looks far different. As Marx puts it,

On leaving this sphere of simple circulation or of exchange of commodities . . . we can perceive a change in the physiognomy of our *dramatis personae*. He who before was the money-owner, now strides in front as capitalist; the possessor of labor-power follows as his laborer. The one with an air of importance, smirking, intent on business; the other timid and holding back, like one who is bringing his own hide to market and has nothing to expect but – a hiding.

This is a vastly different account of the social relations of the buyer and seller of labor power.[9] Only by following the two into the realm of production and adopting the point of view available to the worker could Marx uncover what is really involved in the purchase and sale of labor power, i.e. – uncover the process by which surplus value is produced and appropriated by the capitalist, and the means by which the worker is systematically disadvantaged.[10]

If one examines Marx's account of the production and extraction of surplus value, one can see in it the elaboration of each of the claims contained in the concept of a standpoint. First, the contention that material life structures understanding points to the importance of the epistemological consequences of the opposed models of exchange and production. It is apparent that the former results in a dualism based on both the separation of exchange from use, and on the positing of exchange as the only important side of the dichotomy. The epistemological result if one follows through the implications of exchange is a series of opposed and hierarchical dualities – mind/body, ideal/material, social/natural, self/other – even a kind of solipsism – replicating the devaluation of use relative to exchange. The proletarian and Marxian valuation of use over exchange on the basis of involvement in production, in labor, results in a dialectical rather than dualist epistemology: the dialectical and interactive unity (distinction within a unity) of human and natural worlds, mind and body, ideal and material, and the cooperation of self and other (community).

As to the second claim of a standpoint, a Marxian account of exchange vs. production indicates that the epistemology growing from exchange not only inverts that present in the process of production but in addition is both partial and fundamentally perverse. The real point of the production of goods and services is, after all, the continuation of the species, a possibility dependent on their use. The epistemology embodied in exchange then, along with the social relations it expresses, not only occupies only one side of the

NANCY C. M. HARTSOCK

dualities it constructs, but also reverses the proper ordering of any hierarchy in the dualisms: use is primary, not exchange.

The third claim for a standpoint indicates a recognition of the power realities operative in a community, and points to the ways the ruling group's vision may be *both* perverse *and* made real by means of that group's power to define the terms for the community as a whole. In the Marxian analysis, this power is exercised in both control of ideological production, and in the real participation of the worker in exchange. The dichotomous epistemology which grows from exchange cannot be dismissed either as simply false or as an epistemology relevant to only a few: the worker as well as the capitalist engages in the purchase and sale of commodities, and if material life structures consciousness, this cannot fail to have an effect. This leads into the fourth claim for a standpoint — that it is achieved rather than obvious, a mediated rather than immediate understanding. Because the ruling group controls the means of mental as well as physical production, the production of ideals as well as goods, the standpoint of the oppressed represents an achievement both of science (analysis) and of political struggle on the basis of which this analysis can be conducted.

Finally, because it provides the basis for revealing the perversion of both life and thought, the inhumanity of human relations, a standpoint can be the basis for moving beyond these relations. In the historical context of Marx's theory, the engaged vision available to the producers, by drawing out the potentiality available in the actuality, that is, by following up the possibility of abundance capitalism creates, leads towards transcendence. Thus, the proletariat is the only class which has the possibility of creating a classless society. It can do this simply (!) by generalizing its own condition, that is, by making society itself a propertyless producer.[11]

These are the general characteristics of the standpoint of the proletariat. What guidance can feminists take from this discussion? I hold that the powerful vision of both the perverseness and reality of class domination made possible by Marx's adoption of the standpoint of the proletariat suggests that a specifically feminist standpoint could allow for a much more profound critique of phallocratic ideologies and institutions than has yet been achieved. The effectiveness of Marx's critique grew from its uncompromising focus on material life activity, and I propose here to set out from the Marxian contention that not only are persons active, but that reality itself consists of "sensuous human activity, practice". But rather than beginning with men's labor, I will focus on women's life activity and on the institutions which structure that activity in order to raise the question of whether this activity

THE FEMINIST STANDPOINT

can form the ground for a distinctive standpoint, that is, to determine whether it meets the requirements for a feminist standpoint. (I use the term, "feminist" rather than "female" here to indicate both the achieved character of a standpoint and that a standpoint by definition carries a liberatory potential.)

Women's work in every society differs systematically from men's. I intend to pursue the suggestion that this division of labor is the first and in some societies the only division of labor, and moreover, that it is central to the organization of social labor more generally. On the basis of an account of the sexual division of labor, one should be able to begin to explore the oppositions and differences between women's and men's activity and their consequences for epistemology. While I cannot attempt a complete account, I will put forward a schematic and simplified account of the sexual division of labor and its consequences for epistemology. I will sketch out a kind of ideal type of the social relations and world view characteristic of male and female activity in order to explore the epistemology contained in the institutionalized sexual division of labor. In so doing, I do not mean to attribute this vision to individual women or men any more than Marx (or Lukacs) meant their theory of class consciousness to apply to any particular worker or group of workers. My focus is instead on institutionalized social practices and on the specific epistemology and ontology manifested by the institutionalized sexual division of labor. Individuals, as individuals, may change their activity in ways which move them outside the outlook embodied in these institutions, but such a move can be significant only when it occurs at the level of society as a whole.

I will discuss the "sexual division of labor" rather than the "gender division of labor" to stress, first my belief that the division of labor between women and men cannot be reduced to purely social dimensions. One must distinguish between what Sara Ruddick has termed "invariant and *nearly* unchangeable" features of human life, and those which despite being "*nearly* universal" are "certainly changeable." [12] Thus, the fact that women and not men *bear* children is not (yet) a social choice, but that women and not men rear children in a society structured by compulsory heterosexuality and male dominance is clearly a societal choice. A second reason to use the term "sexual division of labor" is to keep hold of the bodily aspect of existence — perhaps to grasp it over-firmly in an effort to keep it from evaporating altogether. There is some biological, bodily component to human existence. But its size and substantive content will remain unknown until at least the certainly changeable aspects of the sexual division of labor are altered.

290 NANCY C. M. HARTSOCK

On a strict reading of Marx, of course, my enterprise here is illegitimate. While on the one hand, Marx remarked that the very first division of labor occurred in sexual intercourse, he argues that the division of labor only becomes "truly such" when the division of mental and manual labor appears. Thus, he dismisses the sexual division of labor as of no analytic importance. At the same time, a reading of other remarks — such as his claim that the mental/manual division of labor is based on the "natural" division of labor in the family — would seem to support the legitimacy of my attention to the sexual division of labor and even add weight to the radical feminist argument that capitalism is an outgrowth of male dominance, rather than vice versa.

On the basis of a schematic account of the sexual division of labor, I will begin to fill in the specific content of the feminist standpoint and begin to specify how women's lives structure an understanding of social relations, that is, begin to follow out the epistemological consequences of the sexual division of labor. In addressing the institutionalized sexual division of labor, I propose to lay aside the important differences among women across race and class boundaries and instead search for central commonalities. I take some justification from the fruitfulness of Marx's similar strategy in constructing a simplified, two class, two man model in which everything was exchanged at its value. Marx's schematic account in Volume I of *Capital* left out of account such factors as imperialism, the differential wages, work, and working conditions of the Irish, the differences between women, men, and children, and so on. While all of these factors are important to the analysis of contemporary capitalism, none changes either Marx's theories of surplus value or alienation, two of the most fundamental features of the Marxian analysis of capitalism. My effort here takes a similar form in an attempt to move toward a theory of the extraction and appropriation of women's activity and women themselves. Still, I adopt this strategy with some reluctance, since it contains the danger of making invisible the experience of lesbians or women of color.[13] At the same time, I recognize that the effort to uncover a feminist standpoint assumes that there are some things common to all women's lives in Western class societies.

The feminist standpoint which emerges through an examination of women's activities is related to the proletarian standpoint, but deeper going. Women and workers inhabit a world in which the emphasis is on change rather than stasis, a world characterized by interaction with natural substances rather than separation from nature, a world in which quality is more important than quantity, a world in which the unification of mind and body is inherent in the activities performed. Yet, there are some important

THE FEMINIST STANDPOINT

differences, differences marked by the fact that the proletarian (if male) is immersed in this world only during the time his labor power is being used by the capitalist. If, to paraphrase Marx, we follow the worker home from the factory, we can once again perceive a change in the *dramatis personae*. He who before followed behind as the worker, timid and holding back, with nothing to expect but a hiding, now strides in front while a third person, not specifically present in Marx's account of the transaction between capitalist and worker (both of whom are male) follows timidly behind, carrying groceries, baby and diapers.

THE SEXUAL DIVISION OF LABOR

Women's activity as institutionalized has a double aspect — their contribution to subsistence, and their contribution to childrearing. Whether or not all of us do both, women as a sex are institutionally responsible for producing both goods and human beings and all women are forced to become the kinds of people who can do both. Although the nature of women's contribution to subsistence varies immensely over time and space, my primary focus here is on capitalism, with a secondary focus on the Western class societies which preceded it.[14] In capitalism, women contribute both production for wages and production of goods in the home, that is, they like men sell their labor power and produce both commodities and surplus value, and produce use-values in the home. Unlike men, however, women's lives are institutionally defined by their production of use-values in the home.[15] And here we begin to encounter the narrowness of the Marxian concept of production. Women's production of use-values in the home has not been well understood by socialists. It is no surprise to feminists that Engels, for example, simply asks how women can continue to do the work in the home and also work in production outside the home. Marx too takes for granted women's responsibility for household labor. He repeats, as if it were his own, the question of a Belgian factory inspector: If a mother works for wages, "how will [the household's] internal economy be cared for; who will look after the young children; who will get ready the meals, do the washing and mending?"[16]

Let us trace both the outlines and the consequences of woman's dual contribution to subsistence in capitalism. Women's labor, like that of the male worker, is contact with material necessity. Their contribution to subsistence, like that of the male worker, involves them in a world in which the relation to nature and to concrete human requirements is central, both in the form of interaction with natural substances whose quality, rather than quantity is

NANCY C. M. HARTSOCK

important to the production of meals, clothing, etc., and in the form of close attention to the natural changes in these substances. Women's labor both for wages and even more in household production involves a unification of mind and body for the purpose of transforming natural substances into socially defined goods. This too is true of the labor of the male worker.

There are, however, important differences. First, women as a group work more than men. We are all familiar with the phenomenon of the "double day," and with indications that women work many more hours per week than men.[17] Second, a larger proportion of women's labor time is devoted to the production of use-values than men's. Only some of the goods women produce are commodities (however much they live in a society structured by commodity production and exchange). Third, women's production is structured by repetition in a different way than men's. While repetition for both the woman and the male worker may take the form of production of the same object, over and over — whether apple pies or brake linings — women's work in housekeeping involves a repetitious cleaning.[18]

Thus, the male worker in the process of production, is involved in contact with necessity, and interchange with nature as well as with other human beings but the process of production or work does not consume his whole life. The activity of a woman in the home as well as the work she does for wages keeps her continually in contact with a world of qualities and change. Her immersion in the world of use — in concrete, many-qualitied, changing material processes — is more complete than his. And if life itself consists of sensuous activity, the vantage point available to women on the basis of their contribution to subsistence represents an intensification and deepening of the materialist world view and consciousness available to the producers of commodities in capitalism, an intensification of class consciousness. The availability of this outlook to even non-working-class women has been strikingly formulated by Marilyn French in *The Women's Room*.

Washing the toilet used by three males, and the floor and walls around it, is, Mira thought, coming face to face with necessity. And that is why women were saner than men, did not come up with the mad, absurd schemes men developed; they were in touch with necessity, they had to wash the toilet bowl and floor.[19]

The focus on women's subsistence activity rather than men's leads to a model in which the capitalist (male) lives a life structured completely by commodity exchange and not at all by production, and at the furthest distance from contact with concrete material life. The male worker marks a way station on the path to the other extreme of the constant contact with material necessity in women's contribution to subsistence. There are of course important differences along the lines of race and class. For example, working class men seem to do more domestic labor than men higher up in the class structure — car repairs, carpentry, etc. And until very recently, the wage work done by most women of color replicated the housework required by their own households. Still, there are commonalities present in the institutionalized sexual division of labor which make women responsible for both housework and wage work.

The female contribution to subsistence, however, represents only a part of women's labor. Women also produce/reproduce men (and other women) on both a daily and a long-term basis. This aspect of women's "production" exposes the deep inadequacies of the concept of production as a description of women's activity. One does not (cannot) produce another human being in anything like the way one produces an object such as a chair. Much more is involved, activity which cannot easily be dichotomized into play or work. Helping another to develop, the gradual relinquishing of control, the experience of the human limits of one's action — all these are important features of women's activity as mothers. Women as mothers even more than as workers, are institutionally involved in processes of change and growth, and more than workers, must understand the importance of avoiding excessive control in order to help others grow.[20] The activity involved is far more complex than the instrumental working with others to transform objects. (Interestingly, much of women's wage work — nursing, social work, and some secretarial jobs in particular — requires and depends on the relational and interpersonal skills women learned by being mothered by someone of the same sex.)

This aspect of women's activity too is not without consequences. Indeed, it is in the production of men by women and the appropriation of this labor and women themselves by men that the opposition between feminist and masculinist experience and outlook is rooted, and it is here that features of the proletarian vision are enhanced and modified for the woman and diluted for the man. The female experience in reproduction represents a unity with nature which goes beyond the proletarian experience of interchange with nature. As another theorist has put it," reproductive labor might be said to combine the functions of the arthitect and the bee: like the architect, parturitive woman knows what she is doing; like the bee, she cannot help what she is doing." And just as the worker's acting on the external world changes both the world and the worker's nature, so too "a new life changes the world and the consciousness of the woman."[21] In addition, in the process of producing human beings, relations with others may take a variety of forms

NANCY C. M. HARTSOCK

with deeper significance than simple cooperation with others for common goals — forms which range from a deep unity with another through the many-leveled and changing connections mothers experience with growing children. Finally, the female experience in bearing and rearing children involves a unity of mind and body more profound than is possible in the worker's instrumental activity.

Motherhood in the large sense, i.e., motherhood as an institution rather than experience, including pregnancy and the preparation for motherhood almost all female children receive as socialization, results in the construction of female existence as centered with a complex relational nexus.[22] One aspect of this relational existence is centered on the experience of living in a female rather than male body. There are a series of boundary challenges inherent in the female physiology — challenges which make it impossible to maintain rigid separation from the object world. Menstruation, coitus, pregnancy, childbirth, lactation — all represent challenges to bodily boundaries.[23] Adrienne Rich has described the experience of pregnancy as one in which the embryo was both inside and

> daily more separate, on its way to becoming separate from me and of-itself. In early pregnancy the stirring of the fetus felt like ghostly tremors of my own body, later like the movements of a being imprisoned in me; but both sensations were *my* sensations, contributing to my own sense of physical and psychic space.[24]

In turn, the fact that women but not men are primarily responsible for young children means that the infant first experiences itself as not fully differentiated from the mother, and then as an I in relation to an It that it later comes to know as female.[25]

Jane Flax and Nancy Chodorow have argued that the object relations school of psychoanalytic theory puts forward a materialist psychology, one which I propose to treat as a kind of empirical hypothesis. If the account of human development provided by object relations is correct, one ought to expect to find consequences — both psychic, and social. According to object relations theory, the process of differentiation from a woman by both male and female children reinforces boundary confusion in female egos and boundary strengthening in males. Individuation is far more conflictual for male than for female children, in part because both mother and son experience the other as a definite "other." The experience of oneness on the part of both mother and infant seems to last longer with girls.[26]

The complex relational world inhabited by women has its start in the experience and resolution of the oedipal crisis, cleanly resolved for the boy,

THE FEMINIST STANDPOINT

whereas the girl is much more likely to retain both parents as love objects. The nature of the crisis itself differs by sex: the boy's love for the mother is an extension of mother-infant unity and thus essentially threatening to his ego and independence. Male ego-formation necessarily requires repressing this first relation and negating the mother.[27] In contrast, the girls' love for the father is less threatening both because it occurs outside this unity and because it occurs at a later stage of development. For boys, the central issue to be resolved concerns gender identification; for girls the issue is psycho-sexual development.[28] Chodorow concludes that girls' gradual emergence from the oedipal period takes place in such a way that empathy is built into their primary definition of self, and they have a variety of capacities for experiencing another's needs or feelings as their own. Put another way girls, because of female parenting, are less differentiated from others than boys, more continuous with and related to the external object world. They are differently oriented to their inner object world as well.[29]

The more complex female relational world is reinforced by the process of socialization. Girls learn roles from watching their mothers; boys must learn roles from rules which structure the life of an absent male figure. Girls can identify with a concrete example present in daily life; boys must identify with an abstract set of maxims only occasionally concretely present in the form of the father. Thus, not only do girls learn roles with more interpersonal and relational skills, but the process of role learning itself is embodied in the concrete relation with the mother. The male, in contrast, must identify with an abstract, cultural stereotype and learn abstract behaviors not attached to a well-known person. Masculinity is idealized by boys whereas femininity is concrete for girls.[30]

Women and men, then, grow up with personalities affected by different boundary experiences, differently constructed and experienced inner and outer worlds, and preoccupations with different relational issues. This early experience forms an important ground for the female sense of self as connected to the world and the male sense of self as separate, distinct, and even disconnected. By retaining the preoedipal attachment to the mother, girls come to define and experience themselves as continuous with others. In sum, girls enter adulthood with a more complex layering of affective ties and a rich, ongoing inner set of object relations. Boys, with a simpler oedipal situation and a clear and early resolution, have repressed ties to another. As a result, women define and experience themselves relationally and men do not.[31]

296 NANCY C. M. HARTSOCK

ABSTRACT MASCULINITY AND THE FEMINIST STANDPOINT

This excursion into psychoanalytic theory has served to point to the differences in the male and female experience of self due to the sexual division of labor in childrearing. These different (psychic) experiences both structure and are reinforced by the differing patterns of male and female activity required by the sexual division of labor, and are thereby replicated as epistemology and ontology. The differential male and female life activity in class society leads on the one hand toward a feminist standpoint and on the other toward an abstract masculinity.

Because the problem for the boy is to distinguish himself from the mother and to protect himself against the real threat she poses for his identity, his conflictual and oppositional efforts lead to the formation of rigid ego boundaries. The way Freud takes for granted the rigid distinction between the "me and not-me" makes the point well: "Normally, there is nothing of which we are more certain than the feeling of ourself, of our own ego. This ego appears to us as something autonomous and unitary, marked off distinctly from everything else." At least toward the outside, "the ego seems to maintain clear and sharp lines of demarcation."[32] Thus, the boy's construction of self in opposition to unity with the mother, his construction of identity as differentiation from the other, sets a hostile and combative dualism at the heart of both the community men construct and the masculinist world view by means of which they understand their lives.

I do not mean to suggest that the totality of human relations can be explained by psychoanalysis. Rather I want to point to the ways male rather than female experience and activity replicates itself in both the hierarchical and dualist institutions of class society and in the frameworks of thought generated by this experience. It is interesting to read Hegel's account of the relation of self and other as a statement of male experience: the relation of the two consciousness takes the form of a trial by death. As Hegel describes it, "each seeks the death of the other."

Thus, the relation of the two self-conscious individuals is such that they provide themselves and each other through a life-and-death struggle. They must engage in this struggle, for they must raise their certainty *for themselves* to truth, both in the case of the other and in their own case.[33]

The construction of the self in opposition to another who threatens one's very being reverberates throughout the construction of both class society and the masculinist world view and results in a deepgoing and hierarchical

THE FEMINIST STANDPOINT

dualism. First, the male experience is characterized by the duality of concrete versus abstract. Material reality as experienced by the boy in the family provides no model, and is unimportant in the attainment of masculinity. Nothing of value to the boy occurs with the family, and masculinity becomes an abstract ideal to be achieved over the opposition of daily life.[34] Masculinity must be attained by means of opposition to the concrete world of daily life, by escaping from contact with the female world of the household into the masculine world of public life. This experience of two worlds, one valuable, if abstract and deeply unattainable, the other useless and demeaning, if concrete and necessary, lies at the heart of a series of dualisms — abstract/concrete, mind/body, culture/nature, ideal/real, stasis/change. And these dualisms are overlaid by gender: only the first of each pair is associated with the male.

Dualism, along with the dominance of one side of the dichotomy over the other, marks phallocentric society and social theory. These dualisms appear in a variety of forms — in philosophy, technology, political theory, and the organization of class society itself. One can, for example, see them very clearly worked out in Plato, although they appear in many other forms.[35] There, the concrete/abstract duality takes the form of an opposition of material to ideal, and a denial of the relevance of the material world to the attainment of what is of fundamental importance: love of knowledge, or philosophy (masculinity). The duality between nature and culture takes the form of a devaluation of work or necessity, and the primacy instead of purely social interaction for the attainment of undying fame. Philosophy itself is separate from nature, and indeed, exists only on the basis of the domination of (at least some) of the philosopher's own nature.[36] Abstract masculinity, then, can be seen to have structured Western social relations and the modes of thought to which these relations give rise at least since the founding of the *polis*.

The oedipal roots of these hierarchical dualisms are memorialized in the overlay of female and male connotations: it is not accidental that women are associated with quasi-human and non-human nature, that the female is associated with the body and material life, that the lives of women are systematically used as examples to characterize the lives of those ruled by their bodies rather than their minds.[37]

Both the fragility and fundamental falseness of the masculinist ideology and the deeply problematic nature of the social relations from which it grows are apparent in its reliance on a series of counterfactual assumptions and contentions. Consider how the following contentions are contrary to lived experience: the body is both irrelevant and in opposition to the (real) self, an impediment to be overcome by the mind; the female mind either does not exist (Do women have souls?) or works in such incomprehensible ways as to be unintelligible (the "enigma of woman"); what is real and primary is imperceptible to the senses and impervious to nature and natural change. What is remarkable is not only that these contentions have absorbed a great deal of philosophical energy, but, along with a series of other counterfactuals, have structured social relations for centuries.

Interestingly enough the epistemology and society constructed by men suffering from the effects of abstract masculinity have a great deal in common with that imposed by commodity exchange. The separation and opposition of social and natural worlds, of abstract and concrete, of permanence and change, the effort to define only the former of each pair as important, the reliance on a series of counter factual assumptions — all this is shared with the exchange abstraction. Abstract masculinity shares still another of its aspects with the exchange abstraction: it forms the basis for an even more problematic social synthesis. Hegel's analysis makes clear the problematic social relations available to the self which maintains itself by opposition: each of the two subjects struggling for recognition risks its own death in the struggle to kill the other, but if the other is killed the subject is once again alone.[38] In sum, then, the male experience when replicated as epistemology leads to a world conceived as, and (in fact) inhabited by, a number of fundamentally hostile others whom one comes to know by means of opposition (even death struggle) and yet with whom one must construct a social relation in order to survive.

The female construction of self in relation to others leads in an opposite direction — toward opposition to dualisms of any sort, valuation of concrete, everyday life, sense of a variety of connectednesses and continuities both with other persons and with the natural world. If material life structures consciousness, women's relationally defined existence, bodily experience of boundary challenges, and activity of transforming both physical objects and human beings must be expected to result in a world view to which dichotomies are foreign. Women experience others and themselves along a continuum whose dimensions are evidenced in Adrienne Rich's argument that the child carried for nine months can be defined "*neither* as me or as not-me," and she argues that inner and outer are not polar opposites but a continuum.[39] What the sexual division of labor defines as women's work turns on issues of change rather than stasis, the changes involved in producing both use-values and commodities, but more profoundly in the activity of

THE FEMINIST STANDPOINT 299

rearing human beings who change in both more subtle and more autonomous ways than any inanimate object. Not only the qualities of things but also the qualities of people are important in women's work: quantity becomes peripheral. In addition, far more than the instrumental cooperation of the workplace is required; the mother-child relation and the maintenance of the family, while it has instrumental aspects, is not defined by them. Finally, the unity of mental and manual labor, and the directly sensuous nature of much of women's work leads to a more profound unity of mental and manual labor, social and natural worlds, than is experienced by the male worker in capitalism. The unity grows from the fact that women's bodies, unlike men's, can be themselves instruments of production: in pregnancy, giving birth or lactation, arguments about a division of mental from manual labor are fundamentally foreign.

That this is indeed women's experience is documented in both the theory and practice of the contemporary women's movement and needs no further development here.[40] The more important question here is whether female experience and the world view constructed by female activity can meet the criteria for a standpoint. If we return to the five claims carried by the concept of a standpoint, it seems clear that women's material life activity has important epistemological and ontological consequences for both the understanding and construction of social relations. Women's activity, then, does satisfy the first requirement of a standpoint.

I can now take up the second claim made by a standpoint: that the female experience not only inverts that of the male, but forms a basis on which to expose abstract masculinity as both partial and fundamentally perverse, as not only occupying only one side of the dualities it has constructed, but reversing the proper valuation of human activity. The partiality of the masculinist vision and of the societies which support this understanding is evidenced by its confinement of activity proper to the male to only one side of the dualisms. Its perverseness, however, lies elsewhere. Perhaps the most dramatic (though not the only) reversal of the proper order of things characteristic of the male experience is the substitution of death for life.

The substitution of death for life results at least in part from the sexual division of labor in childrearing. The self-surrounded by rigid ego-boundaries, certain of what is inner and what is outer, the self experienced as walled city, is discontinuous with others. Georges Bataille has made brilliantly clear the ways in which death emerges as the only possible solution to this discontinuity and has followed the logic through to argue that reproduction itself must be understood not as the creation of life, but as death. The core experience to

300 NANCY C. M. HARTSOCK

be understood is that of discontinuity and its consequences. As a consequence of this experience of discontinuity and aloneness, penetration of
ego-boundaries, or fusion with another is experienced as violent. Thus, the
desire for fusion with another can take the form of domination of the other.
In this form, it leads to the only possible fusion with a threatening other:
when the other ceases to exist as a separate, and for that reason, threatening
being. Insisting that another submit to one's will is simply a milder form of
the destruction of discontinuity in the death of the other since in this case
one is no longer confronting a discontinuous and opposed will, despite its
discontinuous embodiment. This is perhaps one source of the links between
sexual activity, domination, and death.

Bataille suggests that killing and sexual activity share both prohibitions
and religious significance. Their unity is demonstrated by religious sacrifice
since the latter:

is intentional like the act of the man who lays bare, desires and wants to penetrate his
victim. The lover strips the beloved of her identity no less than the bloodstained priest
his human or animal victim. The woman in the hands of her assailant is despoiled of her
being . . . loses the firm barrier that once separated her from others . . . is brusquely laid
open to the violence of the sexual urges set loose in the organs of reproduction; she is
laid open to the impersonal violence that overwhelms her from without.[41]

Note the use of the term "lover" and "assailant" as synonyms and the presence of the female as victim.

The importance of Bataille's analysis lies in the fact that it can help to
make clear the links between violence, death, and sexual fusion with another,
links which are not simply theoretical but actualized in rape and pornography.
Images of women in chains, being beaten, or threatened with attack carry
clear social messages, among them that "the normal male is sexually aggressive
in a brutal and demeaning way."[42] Bataille's analysis can help to understand
why "men advertise, even brag, that their movie is the 'bloodiest thing that
ever happened in front of a camera'."[43] The analysis is supported by the
psychoanalyst who suggested that although one of the important dynamics of
pornography is hostility, "one can raise the possibly controversial question
whether in humans (especially males) powerful sexual excitement can ever
exist without brutality also being present."[44]

Bataille's analysis can help to explain what is erotic about "snuff" films,
which not only depict the torture and dismemberment of a woman, but claim
that the actress is *in fact* killed. His analysis suggests that perhaps she is a
sacrificial victim whose discontinuous existence has been succeeded in her

THE FEMINIST STANDPOINT

301

death by "the organic continuity of life drawn into the common life of the beholders."[45] Thus, the pair "lover-assailant" is not accidental. Nor is the connection of reproduction and death.

"Reproduction," Bataille argues, "implies the existence of *discontinuous* beings." This is so because, "Beings which reproduce themselves are distinct from one another, and those reproduced are likewise distinct from each other, just as they are distinct from their parents. Each being is distinct from all others. His birth, his death, the events of his life may have an interest for others, but he alone is directly concerned in them. He is born alone. He dies alone. Between one being and another, there is a *gulf*, a discontinuity."[46] (Clearly it is not just a gulf, but is better understood as a chasm.) In reproduction sperm and ovum unite to form a new entity, but they do so from the death and disappearance of two separate beings. Thus, the new entity bears within itself "the transition to continuity, the fusion, fatal to both, of two separate beings."[47] Thus, death and reproduction are intimately linked, yet Bataille stresses that "it is only death which is to be identified with continuity." Thus, despite the unity of birth and death in this analysis, Bataille gives greater weight to a "tormenting fact: the urge towards love, pushed to its limit, is an urge toward death."[48] Bataille holds to this position despite his recognition that reproduction is a form of growth. The growth, however, he dismisses as not being "ours," as being only "impersonal."[49] This is not the female experience, in which reproduction is hardly impersonal, nor experienced as death. It is, of course, in a literal sense, the sperm which is cut off from its source, and lost. No wonder, then, at the masculinist occupation with death, and the feeling that growth is "impersonal," not of fundamental concern to oneself. But this complete dismissal of the experience of another bespeaks a profound lack of empathy and refusal to recognize the very being of another. It is a manifestation of the chasm which separates each man from every other being and from the natural world, the chasm which both marks and defines the problem of community.

The preoccupation with death instead of life appears as well in the argument that it is the ability to kill (and for centuries, the practice) which sets humans above animals. Even Simone de Beauvoir has accepted that "it is not in giving life but in risking life that man is raised above the animal: that is why superiority has been accorded in humanity not to the sex that brings forth but to that which kills."[50] That superiority has been accorded to the sex which kills is beyond doubt. But what kind of experience and vision can take reproduction, the creation of new life, and the force of life in sexuality, and turn it into death — not just in theory but in the practice of rape,

NANCY C. M. HARTSOCK

pornography, and sexual murder? Any why give pride of place to killing? This is not only an inversion of the proper order of things, but also a refusal to recognize the real activities in which men as well as women are engaged. The producing of goods and the reproducing of human beings are certainly life-sustaining activities. And even the deaths of the ancient heroes in search of undying fame were pursuits of life, and represented the attempt to avoid death by attaining immortality. The search for life, then, represents the deeper reality which lies beneath the glorification of death and destruction.

Yet one cannot dismiss the substitution of death for life as simply false. Men's power to structure social relations in their own image means that women too must participate in social relations which manifest and express abstract masculinity. The most important life activities have consistently been held by the powers that be to be unworthy of those who are fully human most centrally because of their close connections with necessity and life: motherwork (the rearing of children), housework, and until the rise of capitalism in the West, any work necessary to subsistence. In addition, these activities in contemporary capitalism are all constructed in ways which systematically degrade and destroy the minds and bodies of those who perform them.[51] The organization of motherhood as an institution in which a woman is alone with her children, the isolation of women from each other in domestic labor, the female pathology of loss of self in service to others — all mark the transformation of life into death, the distortion of what could have been creative and communal activity into oppressive toil, and the destruction of the possibility of community present in women's relational self-definition. The ruling gender's and class's interest in maintaining social relations such as these is evidenced by the fact that when women set up other structures in which the mother is not alone with her children, isolated from others — as is frequently the case in working class communities or communities of people of color — these arrangements are categorized as pathological deviations.

The real destructiveness of the social relations characteristic of abstract masculinity, however, is now concealed beneath layers of ideology. Marxian theory needed to go beneath the surface to discover the different levels of determination which defined the relation of capitalist and (male) worker. These levels of determination and laws of motion or tendency of phallocratic society must be worked out on the basis of female experience. This brings me to the fourth claim for a standpoint — its character as an achievement of both analysis and political struggle occurring in a particular historical space. The fact that class divisions should have proven so resistant to analysis and

THE FEMINIST STANDPOINT

required such a prolonged political struggle before Marx was able to formulate the theory of surplus value indicates the difficulty of this accomplishment. And the rational control of production has certainly not been achieved.

Feminists have only begun the process of revaluing female experience, searching for common threads which connect the diverse experiences of women, and searching for the structural determinants of the experiences. The difficulty of the problem faced by feminist theory can be illustrated by the fact that it required a struggle even to define household labor, if not done for wages, as work, to argue that what are held to be acts of love instead must be recognized as work whether or not wages are paid.[52] Both the valuation of women's experience, and the use of this experience as a ground for critique are required. A feminist standpoint may be present on the basis of the common threads of female experience, but it is neither self-evident nor obvious.

Finally, because it provides a way to reveal the perverseness and inhumanity of human relations, a standpoint forms the basis for moving beyond these relations. Just as the proletarian standpoint emerges out of the contradiction between appearance and essence in capitalism, understood as essentially historical and constituted by the relation of capitalist and worker, the feminist standpoint emerges both out of the contradiction between the systematically differing structure of male and female life activity in Western cultures. It expresses female experience at a particular time and place, located within a particular set of social relations. Capitalism, Marx noted, could not develop fully until the notion of human equality achieved the status of universal truth.[53] Despite women's exploitation both as unpaid reproducers of the labor force and as a sex-segregated labor force available for low wages, then, capitalism poses problems for the continued oppression of women. Just as capitalism enables the proletariat to raise the possibility of a society free from class domination, so too, it provides space to raise the possibility of a society free from all forms of domination. The articulation of a feminist standpoint based on women's relational self-definition and activity exposes the world men have constructed and the self-understanding which manifests these relations as partial and perverse. More importantly, by drawing out the potentiality available in the actuality and thereby exposing the inhumanity of human relations, it embodies a distress which requires a solution. The experience of continuity and relation – with others, with the natural world, of mind with body – provides an ontological base for developing a non-problematic social synthesis, a social synthesis which need not operate through the denial of the body, the attack on nature, or the death struggle

304 NANCY C. M. HARTSOCK

between the self and other, a social synthesis which does not depend on any of the forms taken by abstract masculinity.

What is necessary is the generalization of the potentiality made available by the activity of women — the defining of society as a whole as propertyless producer both of use-values and of human beings. To understand what such a transformation would require we should consider what is involved in the partial transformation represented by making the whole of society into propertyless producers of use-values — i.e. socialist revolution. The abolition of the division between mental and manual labor cannot take place simply by means of adopting worker-self-management techniques, but instead requires the abolition of provate property, the seizure of state power, and lengthy post-revolutionary class struggle. Thus, I am not suggesting that shared parenting arrangements can abolish the sexual division of labor. Doing away with this division of labor would of course require institutionalizing the participation of both women and men in childrearing; but just as the rational and conscious control of the production of goods and services requires a vast and far-reaching social transformation, so the rational and conscious organization of reproduction would entail the transformation both of *every* human relation, and of human relations to the natural world. The magnitude of the task is apparent if one asks what a society without institutionalized gender differences might look like.

CONCLUSION

An analysis which begins from the sexual division of labor — understood not as taboo, but as the real, material activity of concrete human beings — could form the basis for an analysis of the real structures of women's oppression, an analysis which would not require that one sever biology from society, nature from culture, an analysis which would expose the ways women both partici-pate in and oppose their own subordination. The elaboration of such an analysis cannot but be difficult. Women's lives, like men's, are structured by social relations which manifest the experience of the dominant gender and class. The ability to go beneath the surface of appearances to reveal the real but concealed social relations requires both theoretical and political activity. Feminist theorists must demand that feminist theorizing be grounded in women's material activity and must as well be a part of the political struggle necessary to develop areas of social life modeled on this activity. The outcome could be the development of a political economy which included women's activity as well as men's, and could as well be a step toward the redefining and restructuring of society as a whole on the basis of women's activity.

THE FEMINIST STANDPOINT

Generalizing the activity of women to the social system as a whole would raise, for the first time in human history, the possibility of a fully human community, a community structured by connection rather than separation and opposition. One can conclude then that women's life activity does form the basis of a specifically feminist materialism, a materialism which can provide a point from which both to critique and to work against phallocratic ideology and institutions.

My argument here opens a number of avenues for future work. Clearly, a systematic critique of Marx on the basis of a more fully developed understanding of the sexual division of labor is in order. And this is indeed being undertaken by a number of feminists. A second avenue for further investigation is the relation between exchange and abstract masculinity. An exploration of Mauss's *The Gift* would play an important part in this project, since he presents the solipsism of exchange as an overlay on and substitution for a deeper going hostility, the exchange of gifts as an alternative to war. We have seen that the necessity for recognizing and receiving recognition from another to take the form of a death struggle memorializes the male rather than female experience of emerging as a person in opposition to a woman in the context of a deeply phallocratic world. If the community of exchangers (capitalists) rests on the more overtly and directly hostile death struggle of self and other, one might be able to argue that what underlies the exchange abstraction is abstract masculinity. One might then turn to the question of whether capitalism rests on and is a consequence of patriarchy. Perhaps then feminists can produce the analysis which could amend Marx to read: "Though class society appears to be the source, the cause of the oppression of women, it is rather its consequence." Thus, it is "only at the last culmination of the development of class society [that] this, its secret, appear[s] again, namely, that on the one hand it is the *product* of the oppression of women, and that on the other it is the *means* by which women participate in and create their own oppression".[55]

The Johns Hopkins University

NOTES

* I take my title from Iris Young's call for the development of a specifically feminist historical materialism. See 'Socialist Feminism and the Limits of Dual Systems Theory,' in *Socialist Review* 10, 2/3 (March-June, 1980). My work on this paper is deeply indebted to a number of women whose ideas are incorporated here, although not always

NANCY C. M. HARTSOCK

used in the ways they might wish. My discussions with Donna Haraway and Sandra Harding have been intense and ongoing over a period of years. I have also had a number of important and useful conversations with Jane Flax, and my project here has benefitted both from these contacts, and from the opportunity to read her paper, 'Political Philosophy and the Patriarchal Unconscious: A Psychoanalytic Perspective on Epistemology and Metaphysics'. In addition I have been helped immensely by collective discussions with Annette Bickel, Sarah Begus, and Alexa Freeman. All of these people (along with Iris Young and Irene Diamond) have read and commented on drafts of this paper. I would also like to thank Alison Jaggar for continuing to question me about the basis on which one could claim the superiority of a feminist standpoint and for giving me the opportunity to deliver the paper at the University of Cincinnati Philosophy Department Colloquium; and Stephen Rose for taking the time to read and comment on a rough draft of the paper at a critical point in its development.

[1] See my 'Feminist Theory and the Development of Revolutionary Strategy,' in Zillah Eisenstein, ed., *Capitalist Patriarchy and the Case for Socialist Feminism* (New York: Monthly Review, 1978).

[2] The recent literature on mothering is perhaps the most detailed on this point. See Dorothy Dinnerstein, *The Mermaid and the Minotaur* (New York: Harper and Row, 1976); Nancy Chodorow, The *Reproduction of Mothering* (Berkeley: University of California Press, 1978).

[3] Iris Young, 'Socialist Feminism and the Limits of Dual Systems Theory,' in *Socialist Review* 10, 2/3 (March-June, 1980), p. 180.

[4] Eighth Thesis on Feuerbach, in Karl Marx, 'Theses on Feuerbach,' in *The German Ideology*, C. J. Arthur, ed. (New York: International Publishers, 1970), p. 121.

[5] *Ibid.* Conscious human practice, then, is at once both an epistemological category and the basis for Marx's conception of the nature of humanity itself. To put the case even more strongly, Marx argues that human activity has both an ontological and epistemological status, that human feelings are not "merely anthropological phenomena," but are "truly ontological affirmations of being." See Karl Marx, *Economic and Philosophic Manuscripts of 1844*, Dirk Struik, ed. (New York: International Publishers, 1964), pp. 113, 165, 188.

[6] Marx, *1844*, p. 112. Nature itself, for Marx, appears as a form of human work, since he argues that humans duplicate themselves actively and come to contemplate themselves in a world of their own making. (*Ibid.*, p. 114). On the more general issue of the relation of natural to human worlds see the very interesting account by Alfred Schmidt, *The Concept of Nature in Marx*, tr. Ben Foukes (London: New Left Books, 1971).

[7] Marx and Engels, *The German Ideology*, pp. 42.

[8] See Alfred Sohn-Rethel, *Intellectual and Manual Labor: A Critique of Epistemology* (London: MacMillan, 1978). I should note that my analysis both depends on and is in tension with Sohn-Rethel's. Sohn-Rethel argues that commodity exchange is a characteristic of all class societies — one which comes to a head in capitalism or takes its most advanced form in capitalism. His project, which is not mine, is to argue that (a) commodity exchange, a characteristic of all class societies, is an original source of abstraction, (b) that this abstraction contains the formal element essential for the cognitive faculty of conceptual thinking and (c) that the abstraction operating in exchange, an abstraction in practice, is the source of the ideal abstraction basic to Greek philosophy and to modern science. (See *Ibid.*, p. 28).In addition to a different purpose,

THE FEMINIST STANDPOINT

307

I should indicate several major differences with Sohn-Rethel. First, he treats the productive forces as separate from the productive relations of society and ascribes far too much autonomy to them. (See, for example, his discussions on pp. 84–86, 95.) I take the position that the distinction between the two is simply a device used for purposes of analysis rather than a feature of the real world. Second, Sohn-Rethel characterizes the period preceding generalized commodity production as primitive communism. (See p. 98.) This is however an inadequate characterization of tribal societies.

[9] Karl Marx, *Capital*, I (New York: International Publishers, 1967), p. 176.

[10] I have done this elsewhere in a systematic way. For the analysis, see my discussion of the exchange abstraction in *Money, Sex, and Power: An Essay on Domination and Community* (New York: Longman, Inc., 1983).

[11] This is Iris Young's point. I am indebted to her persuasive arguments for taking what she terms the "gender differentiation of labor" as a central category of analysis (Young, 'Dual Systems Theory,' p. 185). My use of this category, however, differs to some extent from hers. Young's analysis of women in capitalism does not seem to include marriage as a part of the division of labor. She is more concerned with the division of labor in the productive sector.

[12] See Sara Ruddick, 'Maternal Thinking,' *Feminist Studies* 6, 2 (Summer, 1980), p. 364.

[13] See, for discussions of this danger, Adrienne Rich, 'Disloyal to Civilization: Feminism, Racism, Gynephobia,' in *On Lies, Secrets, and Silence* (New York: W. W. Norton & Co., 1979), pp. 275–310; Elly Bulkin, 'Racism and Writing: Some Implications for White Lesbian Critics,' in *Sinister Wisdom*, No. 6 (Spring, 1980).

[14] Some cross-cultural evidence indicates that the status of women varies with the work they do. To the extent that women and men contribute equally to subsistence, women's status is higher than it would be if their subsistence-work differed profoundly from that of men; that is, if they do none or almost all of the work of subsistence, their status remains low. See Peggy Sanday, 'Female Status in the Public Domain,' in Michelle Rosaldo and Louise Lamphere, eds., *Women, Culture, and Society* (Stanford: Stanford University Press, 1974), p. 199. See also Iris Young's account of the sexual division of labor in capitalism, mentioned above.

[15] It is irrelevant to my argument here that women's wage labor takes place under different circumstances than men's — that is, their lower wages, their confinement to only a few occupational categories, etc. I am concentrating instead on the formal, structural features of women's work. There has been much effort to argue that women's domestic labor is a source of surplus value, that is, to inclue it within the scope of Marx's value theory as productive labor, or to argue that since it does not produce surplus value it belongs to an entirely different mode of production, variously characterized as domestic or patriarchal. My strategy here is quite different from this. See, for the British debate, Mariarosa Dalla Costa and Selma James, *The Power of Women and the Subversion of the Community* (Falling Wall Press, Bristol, 1975); Wally Secombe, 'The Housewife and Her Labor Under Capitalism,' *New Left Review* 83 (January-February, 1974); Jean Gardiner, 'Women's Domestic Labour,' *New Left Review* 89 (March, 1975); and Paul Smith, 'Domestic Labour and Marx's Theory of Value,' in Annette Kuhn and Ann Marie Wolpe, eds., *Feminism and Materialism* (Boston: Routledge and Kegal Paul, 1978). A portion of the American debate can be found in Ira Gerstein, 'Domestic Work and Capitalism,' and Lisa Vogel, 'The Earthly Family,' *Radical America* 7, 4/5

308 NANCY C. M. HARTSOCK

(July-October, 1973); Ann Ferguson, 'Women as a New Revolutionary Class,' in Pat Walker, ed., *Between Labor and Capital* (Boston: South End Press, 1979).

[16] Frederick Engels, *Origins of the Family, Private Property and the State* (New York: International Publishers, 1942); Karl Marx, *Capital*, Vol. I, p. 671. Marx and Engels have also described the sexual division of labor as natural or spontaneous. See Mary O'Brien, 'Reproducing Marxist Man,' in Lorenne Clark and Lynda Lange, eds., *The Sexism of Social and Political Theory: Women and Reproduction from Plato to Nietzsche* (Toronto: University of Toronto Press, 1979).

[17] For a discussion of women's work, see Elise Boulding, 'Familial Constraints on Women's Work Roles,' in Martha Blaxall and B. Reagan, eds., *Women and the Workplace* (Chicago, University of Chicago Press, 1976), esp. the charts on pp. 111, 113.

An interesting historical note is provided by the fact that even Nausicaa, the daughter of a Homeric king, did the household laundry. (See M. I. Finley, *The World of Odysseus* (Middlesex, England: Penguin, 1979), p. 73.) While aristocratic women were less involved in actual labor, the difference was one of degree. And as Aristotle remarked in *The Politics*, supervising slaves is not a particularly uplifting activity. The life of leisure and philosophy, so much the goal for aristocratic Athenian men, ten, was almost unthinkable for any woman.

[18] Simone de Beauvoir holds that repetition has a deeper significance and that women's biological destiny itself is repetition. (See *The Second Sex*, tr. H. M. Parshley (New York: Knopf, 1953), p. 59.) But see also her discussion of housework in *Ibid.*, pp. 434ff. There her treatment of housework is strikingly negative. For de Beauvoir, transcendence is provided in the hstorical struggle of self with other and with the natural world. The oppositions she sees are not really stasis vs. change, but rather transcendence, escape from the muddy concreteness of daily life, from the static, biological, concrete repetition of "placid femininity."

[19] Marilyn French, *The Women's Room* (New York: Jove, 1978), p. 214.

[20] Sara Ruddick, 'Maternal Thinking,' presents an interesting discussion of these and other aspects of the thought which emerges from the activity of mothering. Although I find it difficult to speak the language of interests and demands she uses, she brings out several valuable points. Her distinction between maternal and scientific thought is very intriguing and potentially useful (see esp. pp. 350–353).

[21] O'Brien, 'Reproducing Marxist Man,' p. 115, n. 11.

[22] It should be understood that I am concentrating here on the experience of women in Western culture. There are a number of cross-cultural differences which can be expected to have some effect. See, for example, the differences which emerge from a comparison of childrearing in ancient Greek society with that of the contemporary Mbuti in central Africa. See Phillip Slater, *The Glory of Hera* (Boston: Beacon, 1968) and Colin Turnbull, 'The Politics of Non-Aggression,' in Ashley Montagu, ed., *Learning Non-Aggression* (New York: Oxford University Press, 1978).

[23] See Nancy Chodorow, 'Family Structure and Feminine Personality,' in Michelle Rosaldo and Louise Lamphere, *Woman, Culture, and Society* (Stanford: Stanford University Press, 1974), p. 59.

[24] *Of Woman Born* (New York: Norton, 1976), p. 63.

[25] See Chodorow, *The Reproduction of Mothering*, and Flax, 'The Conflict Between Nurturance and Autonomy in Mother-Daughter Relations and in Feminism,' *Feminist Studies* **4**, 2 (June, 1978). I rely on the analyses of Dinnerstein and Chodorow but there are difficulties in that they are attempting to explain why humans, both male and

THE FEMINIST STANDPOINT   309

female, fear and hate the female. My purpose here is to invert their arguments and to attempt to put forward a positive account of the epistemological consequences of this situation. What follows is a summary of Chodorow, *The Reproduction of Mothering*.

[26] Chodorow, *Reproduction*, pp. 105–109.

[27] This is Jane Flax's point.

[28] Chodorow, *Reproduction*, pp. 127–131, 163.

[29] *Ibid.*, p. 166.

[30] *Ibid.*, pp. 174–178. Chodorow suggest a correlation between father absence and fear of women (p. 213), and one should, treating this as an empirical hypotheses, expect a series of cultural differences based on the degree of father absence. Here the ancient Greeks and the Mbuti provide a fascinating contrast. (See above, note 22.)

[31] *Ibid.*, p. 198. The flexible and diffuse female ego boundaries can of course result in the pathology of loss of self in responsibility for and dependence on others. (The obverse of the male pathology of experiencing the self as walled city.)

[32] Sigmund Freud, *Civilization and Its Discontents* (New York: Norton, 1961), pp. 12–13.

[33] Hegel, *Phenomenology of Spirit* (New York: Oxford University Press, 1979), trans. A. V. Miller, p. 114. See also Jessica Benjamin's very interesting use of this discussion in 'The Bonds of Love: Rational Violence and Erotic Domination,' *Feminist Studies* 6, 1 (June, 1980).

[34] Alvin Gouldner has made a similar argument in his contention that the Platonic stress on hierarchy and order resulted from a similarly learned opposition to daily life which was rooted in the young aristocrat's experience of being taught proper behavior by slaves who could not themselves engage in this behavior. See *Enter Plato* (New York: Basic Books, 1965), pp. 351–355.

[35] One can argue, as Chodorow's analysis suggests, that their extreme form in his philosophy represents an extreme father-absent (father-deprived?) situation. A more general critique of phallocentric dualism occurs in Susan Griffin, *Woman and Nature* (New York: Harper & Row, 1978).

[36] More recently, of course, the opposition to the natural world has taken the form of destructive technology. See Evelyn Fox Keller, 'Gender and Science,' *Psychoanalysis and Contemporary Thought* 1, 3 (1978), reprinted in this volume.

[37] See Elizabeth Spelman, 'Metaphysics and Misogyny: The Soul and Body in Plato's Dialogues,' mimeo. One analyst has argued that its basis lies in the fact that "the early mother, monolithic representative of nature, is a source, like nature, of ultimate distress as well as ultimate joy. Like nature, she is both nourishing and disappointing, both alluring and threatening . . . The infant loves her . . . and it hates her because, like nature, she does not perfectly protect and provide for it . . . The mother, then – like nature, which sends blizzards and locusts as well as sunshine and strawberries – is perceived as capricious, sometimes actively malevolent." Dinnerstein, p. 95.

[38] See Benjamin, p. 152. The rest of her analysis goes in a different direction than mine, though her account of *The Story of O* can be read as making clear the problems for any social synthesis based on the Hegelian model.

[39] *Of Woman Born*, p. 64, p. 167. For a similar descriptive account, but a dissimilar analysis, see David Bakan, *The Duality of Human Existence* (Boston: Beacon, 1966).

[40] My arguments are supported with remarkable force by both the theory and practice of the contemporary women's movement. In theory, this appears in different forms in the work of Dorothy Riddle, 'New Visions of Spiritual Power,' *Quest: a Feminist*

310   NANCY C. M. HARTSOCK

Quarterly 1, 3 (Spring, 1975); Susan Griffin, *Woman and Nature*, esp. Book IV: 'The Separate Rejoined'; Adrienne Rich, *Of Woman Born*, esp. pp. 62–68; Linda Thurston, 'On Male and Female Principle,' *The Second Wave* 1, 2 (Summer, 1971). In feminist political organizing, this vision has been expressed as an opposition of leadership and hierarchy, as an effort to prevent the development of organizations divided into leaders and followers. It has also taken the form of an insistence on the unity of the personal and the political, a stress on the concrete rather than on abstract principles (an opposition to theory), and a stress on the politics of everyday life. For a fascinating and early example, see Pat Mainardi, 'The Politics of Housework,' in Leslie Tanner, ed., *Voices of Women's Liberation* (New York: New American Library, 1970).

[41] George Bataille, *Death and Sensuality* (New York: Arno Press, 1977), p. 90.

[42] Women Against Violence Against Women Newsletter, June, 1976, p. 1.

[43] *Aegis: A Magazine on Ending Violence Against Women*, November/December, 1978, p. 3.

[44] Robert Stoller, *Perversion: The Erotic Form of Hatred* (New York: Pantheon, 1975), p. 88.

[45] Bataille, p. 91. See pp. 91ff for a more complete account of the commonalities of sexual activity and ritual sacrifice.

[46] *Death and Sensuality*, p. 12 (italics mine). See also de Beauvoir's discussion in *The Second Sex*, pp. 135, 151.

[47] Bataille, p. 14.

[48] *Ibid.*, p. 42. While Adrienne Rich acknowledges the violent feelings between mothers and children, she quite clearly does not put these at the heart of the relation (*Of Woman Born*).

[49] Bataille, pp. 95–96.

[50] *The Second Sex*, p. 58. It should be noted that killing and risking life are ways of indicating one's contempt for one's body, and as such are of a piece with the Platonic search for disembodiment.

[51] Consider, for example, Rich's discussion of pregnancy and childbirth, Ch. VI and VII, *Of Woman Born*. And see also Charlotte Perkins Gilman's discussion of domestic labor in *The Home* (Urbana, Ill.: The University of Illinois Press, 1972).

[52] The Marxist-feminist efforts to determine whether housework produces surplus value and the feminist political strategy of demanding wages for housework represent two (mistaken) efforts to recognize women's non-wage activity at work. Perhaps domestic labor's non-status as work is one of the reasons why its wages – disproportionately paid to women of color – are so low, and working conditions so poor.

[53] *Capital*, Vol. I, p. 60.

[54] The phrase is O'Brien's, p. 113.

[55] See Marx, *1844*, p. 117.

[32]

Marx's Late Writings on Non-Western and Precapitalist Societies and Gender

Kevin B. Anderson

Marx's 1850s writings on non-Western societies, especially those on India, are far better known than his post-1872 ones. The later writings, some of them still unpublished, lend support to the notion that Marx moved away from the unilinear and often Eurocentric perspectives that are frequently cited in critiques of his work. Unfortunately, some of these late writings are still unpublished, although there are plans to issue them as part of the new *Marx-Engels Gesamtausgabe* (MEGA²).

Unilinearism, Eurocentrism, and Beyond: The 1848–59 Writings on China, India, and Russia

Although Marx's chief preoccupation was Western capitalism, there were two periods when he wrote extensively on non-Western and pre-capitalist societies. Not coincidentally, these periods were also ones when the European labor movement was quiescent. Shortly before the first of them,1853–9, Marx had moved to London, the cosmopolitan center of a world empire. In the library of the British Museum, he began reading widely on India, China, the Ottoman Empire, and Russia. He wrote thousands of pages on those societies in his analytical journalism in the *New York Tribune*. These writings have often been described as Eurocentric. In his introduction to the best-known collection of them, Shlomo Avineri wrote, "The general tone of Marx's views on the non-European world is set in the *Communist Manifesto* (1848)" (1968, 1). In a brief treatment of colonialism in the *Manifesto* (1848), Marx had spoken in modernist fashion of the backwardness of Asia and the progressiveness of Western capitalism.

> The bourgeoisie, by the rapid improvement of all instruments of production, by the immensely facilitated means of communication, draws all, even the most barbarian nations into civilization. The cheap prices of its commodities are the heavy artillery with which it batters down all Chinese walls, with which it forces the barbarians' intensely obstinate hatred of the foreigners to capitulate. It compels all nations, on pain of extinction, to adopt the bourgeois mode of production; it compels them to introduce what it calls civilization into their midst, i.e. to become bourgeois themselves. In one word, it creates a world after its own image. (MECW 6: 488)

In this passage, Marx seemed to support the First Opium War of 1842 by the British against China.

Marx adopted a similar perspective in his 1853 *Tribune* articles on India, a society he declared so static that it lacked any real history. In "The Future Results of British Rule in India," he began by arguing that India was "the predestined prey of conquest" because it was so disunited. India was "not only divided between Mahommedan and Hindoo, but between tribe and tribe, between caste and caste." Therefore, India's history "is the history of the successive conquests she has undergone." Then, with some strong Eurocentric overtones, Marx added that "Indian society has no history at all, at least no known history," calling it an "unresisting and unchanging society" (MECW 12: 217). Writing a decade after Avineri, Edward Said (1978) focused on Marx's Eurocentrism and ethnocentrism in these writings.

Up to now, most scholars have tended to agree with Robert Tucker's suggestion that it was Marx's "assumption that it was the fate of non-Western societies like that of India to go the way of bourgeois development as seen in modern Europe" (1978, 653). Putting a postmodernist touch on this older debate over what was frequently seen as Marx's unilinear perspective, Jean-François Lyotard (1984) held that Marx was trapped in a grand narrative of modernization that subsumed all particularity and difference.

However, some specialist scholars such as Erica Benner (1995) have argued recently that Marx's writings on nationalism, ethnicity, and colonialism are far more nuanced than is generally supposed. A balanced reading of the whole of his much-criticized 1853 India articles suggests that, even in 1853, his perspective was not as one-sided as is commonly assumed. For example, in the same *Tribune* article cited above, he also wrote: "The Indians will not reap the fruits of the new elements of society scattered among them by the British bourgeoisie, till in Great Britain itself the now ruling classes shall have been supplanted by the industrial proletariat, or till the Hindoos themselves shall have grown strong enough to throw off the English yoke altogether. At all events, we may safely expect to see, at a more or less remote period, the regeneration of that great and interesting country" (MECW 12: 221). In this sense his view of India was dialectical: the British overturned precapitalist Indian society and brought progress but this progress, itself marked by "the inherent barbarism of bourgeois civilization" (MECW 12: 221), would have to be overcome in its turn by the Indians. Nonetheless, while the ethnocentric 1848 dichotomy between a "barbaric" East and a "civilized" West has been attenuated, Marx is still operating within a unilinear perspective. India will, he wrote, still have to be swept into capitalist development as a precondition for eventual social emancipation.

Few have noted that Marx came to support strongly Chinese and Indian resistance to Britain during the years 1856–9, a topic on which he wrote extensively. In an 1857 *Tribune* article, Marx seemed to reverse the thrust of his earlier description, in the *Communist Manifesto*, of the Chinese as barbarians and the British as civilized during the 1842 Opium War. Referring again to that conflict, he wrote: "The English soldiery then committed abominations for the mere fun of it; their passions being neither sanctified by religious fanaticism nor exacerbated by hatred against an overbearing and conquering race, nor provoked by the stern resistance of a heroic enemy. The violations of women, the spittings of children, the roastings of whole villages, were then mere wanton sports, not recorded by Mandarins, but by British officers themselves" (MECW 15: 353–4). There was a similar transformation in his perspectives on India as he wrote in the *Tribune* of the Sepoy Rebellion of 1857. By now, references to colonialism as a source of civilization and progress had largely disappeared.

During this period, Marx also began to alter his perspectives on Russia, the large agrarian empire at the edge of European civilization. From the 1840s through the mid-1850s, in writings such as "The Secret Diplomatic History of the Eighteenth Century," Marx had described Russia as an utterly reactionary society incapable of revolution from within, one that also threatened to suppress any revolutionary outbreak in Europe, as it had in 1848. By the late 1850s, however, with the agrarian unrest that accompanied the Tsar's emancipation of the serfs, Marx began to look at Russia in a different light. In an 1858 *Tribune* article on emancipation, he wrote that if a social revolution broke out in Russia, it would be "the second turning point in Russian history, and finally place real and general civilization in the place of that sham and show introduced by Peter the Great" (MECW 16: 147). Significantly, all the writings on India, China, and Russia cited above, except for the *Communist Manifesto*, were composed not in German, but in English. This was not unrelated to the greater awareness that Marx seemed to have developed of the multiplicity of world cultures and civilizations since his move to London in 1849.

At an explicitly theoretical level, as Lawrence Krader (1975) and others have shown, the much discussed passages on precapitalist modes of production in Marx's *Grundrisse* (1857–8) constitute the beginning of a move away from unilinear models. However, Marx did not follow up at that time his brief but suggestive remarks

Toward Multilinearity and a New Focus: Three Strands in Marx's Last Decade, 1872–83

With the collapse of the Western labor movement after the defeat of the Paris Commune, Marx began to concentrate once again on non-Western societies. In his last decade, 1872–83, three strands in his writings illustrate this turn in his thought: (1) changes introduced into the 1872–5 French edition of *Capital*, volume 1, in order to remove suggestions of unilinearism; (2) new writings on Russia that suggested that its communal villages could be a starting point for a socialist development; and (3) his extensive 1879–82 notebooks, many of them still unpublished in any language, and all of which are to appear in MEGA^2, volume IV/27. These notebooks cover a far wider range of societies and historical periods, including Indian history and village culture, Dutch colonialism and the village economy in Indonesia, gender and kinship patterns among Native Americans and in ancient Greece and Rome, and communal and private property in precolonial and colonial Algeria and Latin America.

The first of these strands was the French edition of *Capital*, volume 1. The last version of this work that Marx personally prepared for the printer, it appeared in installment form from 1872 to 1875. In this edition and the second German one of 1872, he had made extensive changes from the 1867 first edition. Some of Marx's changes for the French edition have yet to make their way into standard English or even German editions. Other important changes, such as the development of a separate section on commodity fetishism, became standard.[1] Here I confine myself to two passages that bear on the issue of multilinearism and which cannot be found in standard English or German editions.

First, in a well-known passage on the relationship of capitalist to noncapitalist societies, the English edition reads: "The country that is more developed industrially only shows, *to the less developed*, the image of its own future" (Marx 1976, 91; emphasis added). Some of those who criticize volume one of *Capital* as a deterministic work have interpreted this passage to suggest that Marx thought *all* human societies would be forced to follow a single pathway of development, that of nineteenth-century capitalist England (Shanin 1983). But note how this same passage reads in the French edition, where Marx clarified his argument: "The country that is more

---

1. For more discussion of these various editions, see Anderson (1983, 1997), Rubel in Marx (1963), and Dunayevskaya (1958, 1982). MEGA^2 vols. III/7, III/8, and III/10, published in 1989 and 1991, document many of the extensive differences between the French edition and the earlier German ones, as well as Engels's failure to follow Marx's suggestions on preparing the supposedly definitive fourth German edition of volume 1, which appeared in 1890. This remains the basis for most editions to this day, including the most recent English one (Marx 1976).

developed industrially only shows, *to those which follow it on the industrial path* [*échelle*], the image of its own future" (Marx 1963, 549; emphasis added). Here the notion of one country following the pathway of another is *explicitly* limited to those that are moving toward industrialization. Nonindustrial societies of Marx's time such as Russia and India are now seemingly bracketed out, leaving open the notion of alternative pathways for them.

Marx did something similar with another passage, this one from the section on primitive accumulation, where he discussed the origin of capitalism in the expropriation of the peasantry. In the standard English and German editions, Marx wrote: "The expropriation of the agricultural producer, of the peasant, from the soil, is the basis of the whole process . . . *Only in England, which we therefore take as our example, has it the classic form*" (Marx 1976, 876; emphasis added). However, in the later French edition, this passage reads: "But the basis of this whole development is the expropriation of the peasants. *England is so far the only country where this has been carried through completely . . . but all the countries of Western Europe are going through the same development*" (Marx 1963, 1170–1; emphasis added). Once again, he left room for a possibly alternative development for Russia and other non-Western societies.

The second strand in Marx's late writings on non-Western and precapitalist societies concerns Russia. His renewal of interest in that country was no doubt stimulated by the 1872 translation of *Capital* into Russian, its first non-German edition. Furthermore, to his surprise, the book was being discussed widely there (Resis 1970). In several texts, Marx examined anew the issue of whether Russia and the agrarian societies of Asia were destined to modernize in the Western manner. Teodor Shanin and his colleagues have contextualized these writings for Russia (Shanin 1983). In an 1877 letter responding to a critique of *Capital* by the Russian writer N. K. Mikhailovsky, Marx defended himself against the charge of unilinearism. Quoting from the second example from the French edition of *Capital* cited above, he also argued: "The chapter on primitive accumulation claims no more than to trace the path by which, in Western Europe, the capitalist economic order emerged from the womb of the feudal economic order" (Shanin 1983, 135). As to the charge of unilinearism, Marx also denied strongly that he had developed "a historico-philosophical theory of the general course fatally imposed on all peoples" (136). This letter was apparently never sent.

In his well-known 1881 letter to the Russian revolutionary Vera Zasulich, the topic is once again whether Russia is destined to be swept into the pathway of capitalist development that was already taking place in Western Europe. Marx again cited the same passage from the French edition of *Capital* before stating: "The 'historical inevitability' of this course is therefore expressly limited to *the countries of Western Europe*" (Shanin 1983, 124; emphasis in original). Again, he concluded that alternative pathways of development might be possible.[2] He based his judgment in large

---

2. An unfortunate curiosity resulting from the fact that these alternative passages from the French edition have yet to appear in English is that one of the most widely used collections of Marx's writings offers, without comment, the two very different versions of this text from *Capital*, first in its section on *Capital*, and second, in its material from the late Marx on Russia (McLellan 2000, 523, 617, 623).

part upon the marked differences between the social structure of the Russian village, with its communal property, and the medieval village in Western Europe. He added that his recent studies of Russian society had "convinced me that the commune is the fulcrum for a social regeneration in Russia" (124). In his far lengthier drafts for the letter to Zasulich, Marx indicated that the type of communal social relations he is discussing were also found in other non-Western societies such as India.

Finally, in his last published text, the preface to the 1882 Russian edition of the *Communist Manifesto*, coauthored with Engels, he returned to the issue of the communal form of the Russian village, with its *obschina or mir*.

> Can the Russian obschina, a form, albeit heavily eroded, of the primitive communal ownership of the land, pass directly into the higher, communist form of communal ownership? Or must it first go through the same process of dissolution which marks the West's historical development? Today there is only one possible answer. If the Russian revolution becomes the signal for a proletarian revolution in the West, so that the two complement each other, then Russia's peasant communal land-ownership may serve as the point of departure for a communist development. (139)

While the correspondence with Zasulich is well known, few are aware of either the French edition of *Capital* or Marx's 1879–82 private notebooks, composed just before his death in 1883. These notebooks, the third strand of his writings on non-Western societies from his last decade, are much rougher in form than other posthumously published Marx writings such as the *Grundrisse* or the *1844 Manuscripts*. Their unpolished, often ungrammatical structure, plus the mixture of languages Marx used, means that transcribing them from his minuscule and almost illegible handwriting is quite challenging. Rather than draft manuscripts, they are notebooks in which Marx recorded or summarized passages from books he is studying. However, they are far more than summaries; they show us Marx's own thinking in several ways. First, they include occasional important comments in which Marx was speaking in his own voice. Second, they show Marx as a "reader." Not only do they contain his direct or indirect critique of the assumptions or conclusions of the authors he is studying, but they also show how he connected or took apart themes and issues in the texts he was reading. Third, they indicate which themes and data he found compelling in connection with these studies of non-Western and precapitalist societies. In short, they offer a unique window into his thinking at a time when he was moving in new directions. It is to this third and most substantial strand of Marx's new thinking on non-Western societies in his last decade, and the plans to publish these notebooks, that I turn in the next section.

An Overview of Marx's 1879–82 Notebooks on Non-Western and Precapitalist Societies and Gender

In 1972, Lawrence Krader published his transcription of the *Ethnological Notebooks*, a multilingual volume containing several hundred pages of Marx's 1880–2 notes on anthropological works by Lewis Henry Morgan, Henry Sumner Maine, John Budd Phear, and John Lubbock. An all-English edition with a far more extensive editorial apparatus will be published soon (Smith, forthcoming). However, the *Ethnological Notebooks* contains only about half of Marx's 1879–82 notes on non-Western and precapitalist societies. Working with a group of Marx scholars and editors in Russia, the United States, the Netherlands, and Germany as part of the MEGA² project, we plan to produce an annotated edition of them in their entirety. For MEGA², vol. IV/27, we intend to develop a volume of these writings in their original multilingual form, usually a mixture of German and English.[3] We also intend to publish as much as possible of the material that Krader did not include in his *Ethnological Notebooks* in an all-English edition (see table 1).

During his last years, 1879–83, Marx published little. For example, he did not complete volumes 2 and 3 of *Capital*, which Engels edited posthumously. Many early studies of Marx's life and thought suggested that these were years of ill health during which Marx lost the capacity for serious intellectual work. Since the 1960s, new publications and discussions of Marx's late writings have begun to challenge this view, although it remains the dominant one. In the *Ethnological Notebooks*, Marx engaged in a systematic effort to acquaint himself with diverse non-European or early peoples such as the Iroquois of North America, the Aztecs of pre-Columbian Mexico, the Australian aborigines, the villagers of northern India, and the Celts of ancient Ireland. This led him to a sustained emphasis on clan and village culture across a variety of precapitalist societies. Marx's interest was organic to his wish to understand what was then the periphery of an expanding global capitalist system. In these writings, he pursued the core theoretical issues of (1) multilinear versus unilinear models of social development, (2) family and gender relations across a wide variety of societies, (3) the rise of social classes within tribal societies, and (4) the history of communal and private property. These issues did not arise, except briefly, during any other period of Marx's work.

In the *Ethnological Notebooks*, Marx did not simply record the findings of others. Often he ruminated about their assumptions and conclusions. For example, in his notes on the American anthropologist Lewis Henry Morgan, he distanced himself from the latter's romantic portrait of Native American society. In addition, he frequently inserted scathing attacks on colonialism or patriarchal family structures not found in the originals of the authors he was studying. For example, in his notes on the English legal historian Henry Sumner Maine, Marx writes in a mixture of German and English: "According to the Ancient Irish Law women had some power of

---

3. At present, the editing group includes Kevin B. Anderson (United States), David Norman Smith (United States), Norair Ter-Akopian (Russia), Georgi Bagaturia (Russia), Jürgen Rojahn (The Netherlands), Heinz Osterle, Charles Reitz, Gerhard Schütte, and Annette Kuhlmann (all United States). Our Russian colleagues have been responsible for transcribing Marx's notoriously difficult handwriting, while others have done most of the translation from the German and the Latin. Thus, the account developed in this and the concluding section of this article is a product of this collective effort. However, I am of course solely responsible for the interpretive comments below.

Table 1
Provisional Contents of MEGA Volume IV/27

Karl Marx: Excerpts and Notes, 1879–82
Key themes: Anthropology, non-Western societies, gender, history of landed property

Part 1: London Notebook, 1879–80
(139 manuscript pages, 140,000 words)

1. Chronological History of India, based on Sewell (47 manuscript pages, 50,000 words)
2. Notes on Central and South America, India, and Algeria from Kovalevsky (47 manuscript pages, 50,000 words)
*3. Notes on Roman Slave Revolts from Bücher (4 manuscript pages, 4000 words)
*4. Notes on Roman Culture, Economy, and Class Structure from Friedländer (9 manuscript pages, 9000 words)
*5. Notes on Gender, Family, and Class in Rome from Jhering (8 manuscript pages, 7000 words)
*6. Notes on Gender and the Family in Early Rome from Lange (24 manuscript pages, 20,000 words)

Part 2: London Notebook, 1880–1
(198 manuscript pages, 154,000 words)

7. Notes on Native Americans and Other Tribal Societies from Morgan (98 manuscript pages, 68,000 words)
*8. Notes on Dutch Colonialism in Indonesia from J. W. B. Money (29 manuscript pages, 20,000 words)
9. Notes on Village Life in India and Ceylon from Phear (28 manuscript pages, 20,000 words)
*10. Notes on Roman and Frankish Law from Sohm (5 manuscript pages, 5000 words)
11. Notes on Early Institutions from Maine (38 manuscript pages, 26,000 words)

Part 3: London Notebook, 1881–2
(16 manuscript pages, 10,000 words)

12. Notes on Tribal Societies from Lubbock (8 manuscript pages, 5000 words)
*13. Notes on Egyptian Finances (8 manuscript pages, 5000 words)

Part 4: London Notebook, 1876–81
(69 manuscript pages, 54,000 words)

*14. Notes on Cave Dwellers in Britain from Dawkins, 43 manuscript pages, 27,000 words
*15. Notes on Prehistoric Europe from Geikie, 26 manuscript pages, 17,000 words

*Texts that have never been published in any language.

dealing with their own property without the consent of their husbands, and this was one of the institutions expressly declared by the English blockheaded judges to be illegal at the beginning of the 17th century" (Krader 1972, 323). Elsewhere, in notes on Morgan, Marx again addressed gender, this time in ancient Greece. He quoted Morgan's statement that the Greeks exhibited a "principle of studied selfishness among the males, tending to lessen the appreciation of women." However, Marx, now speaking in his own voice, immediately added his own more nuanced view: "But the situation of the goddesses on Olympus demonstrates nostalgia for the former free and more influential position of the women" (121).

Besides Krader (1972, 1975), only a few scholars have discussed these notebooks. The German historian Hans-Peter Harstick, who published Marx's 1879 notes on the Russian anthropologist Maxim Kovalevsky's book on communal property in Algeria, India, and Pre-Columbian America, wrote that "Marx's gaze turned from the European scene . . . toward Asia, Latin America, and North Africa" (1977, 2). The Marxist humanist philosopher Raya Dunayevskaya ([1982] 1991, 1985) brought the *Ethnological Notebooks* and other late writings of Marx on noncapitalist societies to the attention of a wider public, emphasizing their focus on gender. Other feminist thinkers, such as Adrienne Rich (1991) and Danga Vileisis (1996), have also entered this discussion, as has the economist Paresh Chattopadhyay (1999). Earlier, Peter Hudis (1983) related the notebooks to Marx's writings on the Third World and Franklin Rosemont (1989) commented on their relevance to Native Americans, while David Norman Smith (1995) connected them to Rosa Luxemburg's work (see also Levine 1973; Ito 1996).

As mentioned above, in addition to what Krader published in the *Ethnological Notebooks*, there are an equivalent number of notes that Marx wrote between 1879 and 1882 on non-Western and precapitalist societies, the vast majority of them never published. Occasionally, these texts contain some direct statements of Marx's own views. For example, in his 1879 notes on Kovalevsky's book on Algeria, India, and Latin America, Marx took issue with Kovalevsky's attempt to impose European-based categories of feudalism and private property on pre-Columbian South America. Similarly, in his notes on the classicist Ludwig Lange's discussion of the Roman family, Marx critiqued Lange for having "distorted" things by taking "individual property as the starting point," thus downplaying the importance of communal property (cited in Harstick 1977, 10).

Such comments do not exhaust the importance of these texts, however. In addition, they show not only the topics Marx concentrated on in his last years, but also the ways in which he sifts, takes apart, and then reconstitutes themes in the works he is reading. For example, his notes on Lange show a focus on the varying forms of the marital power of the Roman *paterfamilias*, across not only class and ethnic lines, but also historically, as it gradually weakened. In his notes on the economic historian Karl Bücher's book on Roman slave uprisings, Marx took up the Roman family in a wider sense, in the relation of the master to his slave, also considered part of the patriarchal household. This was in keeping with Marx's statement elsewhere in his notebooks that the "family contains in embryo not only slavery but also serfdom" (Krader 1972, 120). In his notes on Bücher, he looked at slave revolts during the second century B.C., noting year by year the simultaneous development of class conflict within the free population of Rome during the period of the Gracchi. In his notes on Indian history, Marx concentrated on anticolonial revolts, as against his focus in 1853 on what he considered to be the lack of resistance by Indians to foreign conquest. In his notes on Java, he concentrated on the village social structure, just as he did in his notes on India and Russia during the same period.

Marx's Unpublished 1879–81 Notes on Indonesia and Rome

To conclude, I will look in more detail at two of the texts that will be published in MEGA², volume IV/27 for the first time in any language.

Marx's 20,000 word notes on Dutch colonialism in Indonesia, written in 1880–1, indicate a considerable interest in that society and its early integration into the world market. He concentrated on the social organization of the traditional Javanese village. Marx's notes were based on the 1861 book, *Java; or, How to Manage a Colony, Showing a Practical Solution of the Questions Now Affecting British India*, by James William Bayley Money, a British barrister born in India. Money's book, the product of a visit to Java during 1858, at the height of the Sepoy Rebellion in India, was an unabashed panegyric to Dutch colonial rule. In Java, the Dutch had retained more of the precolonial system than had the British in India, where market forces had severely disrupted the traditional communal village. The Dutch extracted a surplus from above while allowing many aspects of traditional land tenure patterns, political organization, and communal village culture to persist.

Marx had made an earlier set of notes on Java at the time of his 1853 writings on India, these based on Henry Stamford Raffles's classic historical and ethnographic study, *The History of Java* (1817). His notes on Raffles[4] stressed indigenous village life and culture, including gender relations, especially in Bali. In his 1880–1 notes on Money's book, Marx almost completely ignored Money's central theme, the comparison to British rule in India. Instead, he concentrated on the empirical data Money presented on Javanese economic and village life (for a more detailed analysis, see Tichelman 1983). He made no directly critical comments on the vantage point of this rather superficial chronicler of life in Java. But with a careful sense of objectivity, Marx left aside the most dubious parts of Money's account, while still managing to turn to his own use a book which was at that time one of the few detailed accounts of life in colonial Java by an outside observer. Marx skipped some parts of Money's text and quoted isolated lines within others, sifting out of Money's book those data he seemed to find relevant and reasonably accurate, while paring away Money's naive praise of Dutch rule.

---

4. These will eventually be published in MEGA², in a volume containing Marx's notebooks from the early 1850s.

94   Anderson

After Marx's death, Engels appeared to have read Money's book and likely Marx's notes as well. In a letter to Karl Kautsky of 16 February 1884, Engels viewed the solidity of Dutch rule as an example of a conservative "state socialism" that, "as in India and Russia" at the time, was grounded in "primitive communism" at the village level (MECW 47: 102–3). This would seem to contrast with Marx's stress in his late writings, especially those on Russia, on the notion that primitive communism could become a jumping off point for revolutionary developments. Here Engels appeared to have ignored the 1882 preface to the Russian edition of the *Communist Manifesto*, which he had coauthored with Marx.

Marx's 45,000-word notes on Rome from 1879–80 are virtually unknown even to Marx specialists and have never been published in any language. They center on the family and on relations between the social classes. As mentioned earlier, to Marx, these were not entirely separate issues. The notes on Rome are mainly in German, but with many passages in Latin and occasional phrases in English. Marx took the longest of his notes on Rome, some twenty-four handwritten pages, on *Römische Alterthümer* [Roman Antiquities] (1856), a three-volume history by Ludwig Lange of Roman social customs during the archaic, pre-Republican period. Lange was an important historian of early Rome. In these notes, made in 1879, Marx focuses on variations within the patriarchal family, marriage and tribal law, the social role of women, and the development of property law. Some of these notes dealt with the Roman husband's power over his wife. Other parts deal with the power of the Roman *paterfamilias* in other spheres: over his children and grandchildren, his free laborers, his bondsmen, his slaves, and his livestock and land. Still other parts of Marx's notes on Lange dealt with clan and tribal relationships. Marx noted that as Roman civilization developed, marriage came increasingly under the jurisdiction of state-based secular law rather than traditional law. This led to a weakening of the power of the *paterfamilias* and a concomitant rise in the power of the wife, at least within the aristocracy.

Again, this part of Marx's notes suggests a different perspective from the more one-sided position of Engels, who wrote more schematically in the *Origin of the Family, Private Property and the State* (1884) of a prehistoric period of supposed matriarchy followed by a "world-historical defeat of the female sex" (MECW 26: 165). Overall, Marx's notebooks of 1879–82 seem to offer a more nuanced, dialectical perspective on gender. Dunayevskaya, who drew a sharp contrast between Marx and Engels on gender, wrote that Engels tended toward a "unilateral instead of a multilateral attitude" to gender. She added with respect to *Origin of the Family*, "it was great, in 1884, to stress the manner in which woman had always been oppressed," ever since the rise of patriarchy. She concluded, however, that on these issues Engels "is neither very dialectical nor comprehensive" ([1982] 1991, 106).

In summation, these and other Marx texts that are to be published in MEGA², volume IV/27 will reveal in a new way his thinking during his last years, 1879–82, on non-Western and precapitalist societies such as India, Indonesia, Algeria, Latin America, and ancient Rome. They also will show his preoccupation with gender during these years. As a whole, Marx's writings in his last decade suggest a turn away from the modernist models of social development espoused in the *Communist Manifesto* and other earlier writings, where he saw Western capitalism as a stage through which all of humanity was destined inevitably to pass.

I would like to thank David Norman Smith, Jürgen Rojahn, Janet Afary, Albert Resis, John Rhoads, Heinz Osterle, Linda Schwarz, Pamela Brown, and Joel Schwartz for helpful comments on earlier versions of this paper.

References

Anderson, K. B. 1983. The "Unknown" Marx's *Capital*, vol. I: The French edition of 1872–75, 100 years later. *Review of Radical Political Economics* 15 (4): 71–80.
———. 1997. On the MEGA and the French edition of *Capital*, vol. I: An appreciation and a critique. *Beiträge zur Marx-Engels Forschung*, N.S. 1997: 131–6.
Avineri, S. 1968. *Karl Marx on colonialism and modernization.* New York: Doubleday.
Benner, E. 1995. *Really existing nationalisms: A post-communist view from Marx and Engels.* New York: Oxford University Press.
Chattopadhyay, P. 1999. Review essay: Women's labor under capitalism and Marx. *Bulletin of Concerned Asian Scholars* 31 (4): 67–75.
Dunayevskaya, R. 1958. *Marxism and freedom: From 1776 until today.* New York: Bookman.
———. 1985. *Women's liberation and the dialectics of revolution: Reaching for the future.* Atlantic Highlands, N.J.: Humanities Press.
———. [1982] 1991. *Rosa Luxemburg, women's liberation, and Marx's philosophy of revolution.* Urbana: University of Illinois Press.
Harstick, H.-P., ed. 1977. *Karl Marx über Formen vorkapitalistischer Produktion.* Frankfurt: Campus Verlag.
Hudis, P. 1983. *Marx and the Third World.* Detroit: News & Letters.
Ito, N. 1996. Überlegungen zu einem Gedanken beim späten Marx. In *Materialien zum Historisch-Kritischen Wörterbuch des Marxismus*, ed. F. Haug and M. Krätke, 38–44. Berlin: Argument Verlag.
Krader, Lawrence, ed. 1972. *The ethnological notebooks of Karl Marx.* Assen: Van Gorcum.
———. 1975. *The Asiatic mode of production.* Assen: Van Gorcum.
Levine, N. 1973. Anthropology in the thought of Marx and Engels. *Studies in Comparative Communism* 6 (1&2): 7–26.
Lyotard, J.-F. 1984. *The postmodern condition.* Minneapolis: University of Minnesota Press.
Marx, K. 1963. *Oeuvres. Economie. I.* Ed. M. Rubel. Paris: Gallimard.
———. 1976. *Capital.* Vol. I. Trans. B. Fowkes. London: Pelican.
McLellan, D., ed. 2000. *Karl Marx: Selected Writings.* 2d ed. New York: Oxford.
MECW: Marx, K., and F. Engels. 1975–2001. *Collected works.* Vols. 1–48. New York: International Publishers.
Resis, A. 1970. *Das Kapital* comes to Russia. *Slavic Review* 29 (2): 219–37.
Rich, A. 1991. Introduction to Dunayevskaya [1982] 1991.
Rosemont, F. 1989. Karl Marx and the Iroquois. In idem, *Arsenal: Surrealist Subversion*, 201–13. Chicago: Black Swan Press.
Rubel, M., ed. 1963. *Karl Marx. Oeuvres. Economie. I.* Paris: Éditions Gallimard.
Said, E. 1978. *Orientalism.* New York: Pantheon.
Shanin, T. et al. 1983. *Marx and the Russian road.* New York: Monthly Review Press.

96   *Anderson*

Smith, D. N., ed. 1995. The ethnological imagination. In *Ethnohistorische Wege und Lehrjahre eines Philosophen*, ed. D. Schorkowitz, 102–19. New York: Peter Lang.

———. Forthcoming. *Patriarchy and property: The ethnological notebooks of Karl Marx.* New Haven: Yale University Press.

Tichelman, F. 1983. Marx and Indonesia: Preliminary Notes. In *Marx on Indonesia and India*, 9–28. Trier: Karl-Marx-Haus.

Tucker, R., ed. 1978. *The Marx-Engels reader.* 2d ed. New York: Norton.

Vileisis, D. 1996. Engels Rolle im "unglucklichen Verhältnis" zwischen Marxismus und Feminismus. *Beiträge zur Marx-Engels Forschung*, N.S., 1996: 149–79.

Part VIII
Ecology

[33]

Marx's Ecology in Historical Perspective

John Bellamy Foster

'For the early Marx the only nature relevant to the understanding of history is human nature...
Marx wisely left nature (other than human nature) alone.' These words are from George
Lichtheim's influential book *Marxism: An Historical and Critical Study*, first published in
1961.[1]

Though he was not a Marxist, Lichtheim's view here did not differ from the general outlook
of Western Marxism at the time he was writing. Yet this same outlook would be regarded by
most socialists today as laughable. After decades of explorations of Marx's contributions to
ecological discussions and publication of his scientific-technical notebooks, it is no longer a
question of whether Marx addressed nature, and did so throughout his life, but whether he can
be said to have developed an understanding of the nature-society dialectic that constitutes a
crucial starting point for understanding the ecological crisis of capitalist society.[2]

A great many analysts, including some self styled eco-socialists, are prepared to acknowledge
that Marx had profound insights into the environmental problem, but nonetheless argue that
these insights were marginal to his work, that he never freed himself from 'Prometheanism' (a
term usually meant to refer to an extreme commitment to industrialisation at any cost), and that
he did not leave a significant ecological legacy that carried forward into later socialist thought
or that had any relation to the subsequent development of ecology.[3] In a recent discussion
in the journal *Capitalism, Nature, Socialism* a number of authors argued that Marx could
not have contributed anything of fundamental relevance to the development of ecological
thought, since he wrote in the 19th century, before the nuclear age and before the appearance
of PCBs, CFCs and DDT--and because he never used the word 'ecology' in his writings.
Any discussion of his work in terms of ecology was therefore a case of taking 120 years of
ecological thinking since Marx's death and laying it 'at Marx's feet'.[4]

My own view of the history of ecological thought and its relation to socialism is different.
In this, as in other areas, I think we need to beware of falling into what Edward Thompson
called 'the enormous condescension of posterity'.5 More specifically, we need to recognise
that Marx and Engels, along with other early socialist thinkers, like Proudhon (in *What
is Property?*) and Morris, had the advantage of living in a time when the transition from
feudalism to capitalism was still taking place or had occurred in recent memory. Hence
the questions that they raised about capitalist society and even about the relation between
society and nature were often more fundamental than what characterises social and ecological
thought, even on the left, today. It is true that technology has changed, introducing massive
new threats to the biosphere, undreamed of in earlier times. But, paradoxically, capitalism's
antagonistic relation to the environment, which lies at the core of our current crisis, was in
some ways more apparent to 19th and early 20th century socialists than it is to the majority of
today's green thinkers. This reflects the fact that it is not technology that is the primary issue,
but rather the nature and logic of capitalism as a specific mode of production. Socialists have

contributed in fundamental ways at all stages in the development of the modern ecological critique. Uncovering this unknown legacy is a vital part of the overall endeavour to develop an ecological materialist analysis capable of addressing the devastating environmental conditions that face us today.

I first became acutely aware of the singular depth of Marx's ecological insights through a study of the Liebig-Marx connection. In 1862 the great German chemist Justus von Liebig published the seventh edition of his pioneering scientific work, *Organic Chemistry in its Application to Agriculture and Physiology* (first published in 1840). The 1862 edition contained a new, lengthy and, to the British, scandalous introduction. Building upon arguments that he had been developing in the late 1850s, Liebig declared the intensive, or 'high farming', methods of British agriculture to be a 'robbery system', opposed to rational agriculture.[6] They necessitated the transportation over long distances of food and fibre from the country to the city--with no provision for the recirculation of social nutrients, such as nitrogen, phosphorus and potassium, which ended up contributing to urban waste and pollution in the form of human and animal wastes. Whole countries were robbed in this way of the nutrients of their soil. For Liebig this was part of a larger British imperial policy of robbing the soil resources (including bones) of other countries. 'Great Britain', he declared:

> ...deprives all countries of the conditions of their fertility. It has raked up the battlefields of Leipsic, Waterloo and the Crimea; it has consumed the bones of many generations accumulated in the catacombs of Sicily; and now annually destroys the food for a future generation of three millions and a half of people. Like a vampire it hangs on the breast of Europe, and even the world, sucking its lifeblood without any real necessity or permanent gain for itself.[7]

The population in Britain was able to maintain healthy bones and greater physical proportions, he argued, by robbing the rest of Europe of their soil nutrients, including skeletal remains, which would otherwise have gone into nurturing their own soils, allowing their populations to reach the same physical stature as the English.

'Robbery', Liebig suggested, 'improves the art of robbery.' The degradation of the soil led to a greater concentration of agriculture among a small number of proprietors who adopted intensive methods. But none of this altered the long term decline in soil productivity. England was able to maintain its industrialised capitalist agriculture, by importing guano (bird droppings) from Peru as well as bones from Europe. Guano imports increased from 1,700 tons in 1841 to 220,000 tons only six years later.

What was needed in order to keep this spoliation system going, Liebig declared, was the discovery of 'beds of manure or guano...of about the extent of English coalfields'. But existing sources were drying up without additional sources being found. By the early 1860s North America was importing more guano than all of Europe put together. 'In the last ten years,' he wrote, 'British and American ships have searched through all the seas, and there is no small island, no coast, which has escaped their enquiries after guano. To live in the hope of the discovery of new beds of guano would be absolute folly.'

In essence, rural areas and whole nations were exporting the fertility of their land: 'Every country must become impoverished by the continual exportation of corn, and also by the needless waste of the accumulated products of the transformation of matter by the town populations.'

All of this pointed to 'the law of restitution' as the main principle of a rational agriculture. The minerals taken from the earth had to be returned to the earth. 'The farmer' had to 'restore to his land as much as he had taken from it', if not more.

The British agricultural establishment, needless to say, did not take kindly to Liebig's message, with its denunciation of British high farming. Liebig's British publisher, rather than immediately translating the 1862 German edition as in the case of previous editions, destroyed the only copy in its possession. When this final edition of Liebig's great work was finally translated into English it was in an abridged form under a different title (*The Natural Laws of Husbandry*) and without Liebig's lengthy introduction. Hence, the English-speaking world was left in ignorance of the extent of Liebig's critique of industrialised capitalist agriculture.

Nevertheless, the importance of Liebig's critique did not escape the attention of one major figure residing in London at the time. Karl Marx, who was then completing the first volume of *Capital*, was deeply affected by Liebig's critique. In 1866 he wrote to Engels, 'I had to plough through the new agricultural chemistry in Germany, in particular Liebig and Schönbein, which is more important for this matter than all of the economists put together.' Indeed, 'To have developed from the point of view of natural science the negative, ie destructive side of modern agriculture,' Marx noted in volume one of *Capital*, 'is one of Liebig's immortal merits'.[8]

Marx's two main discussions of modern agriculture both end with an analysis of 'the destructive side of modern agriculture'. In these passages Marx makes a number of crucial points: (1) capitalism has created an 'irreparable rift' in the 'metabolic interaction' between human beings and the earth, the everlasting nature-imposed conditions of production; (2) this demanded the 'systematic restoration' of that necessary metabolic relation as 'a regulative law of social production'; (3) nevertheless the growth under capitalism of large-scale agriculture and long distance trade only intensifies and extends the metabolic rift; (4) the wastage of soil nutrients is mirrored in the pollution and waste in the towns--'In London,' he wrote, 'they can find no better use for the excretion of four and a half million human beings than to contaminate the Thames with it at heavy expense'; (5) large-scale industry and large-scale mechanised agriculture work together in this destructive process, with 'industry and commerce supplying agriculture with the means of exhausting the soil'; (6) all of this is an expression of the antagonistic relation between town and country under capitalism; (7) a rational agriculture, which needs either small independent farmers producing on their own, or the action of the associated producers, is impossible under modern capitalist conditions; and (8) existing conditions demand a rational regulation of the metabolic relation between human beings and the earth, pointing beyond capitalist society to socialism and communism.[9]

Marx's concept of the metabolic rift is the core element of this ecological critique. The human labour process itself is defined in *Capital* as 'the universal condition for the metabolic interaction between man and nature, the everlasting nature-imposed condition of human existence'.[10] It follows that the rift in this metabolism means nothing less than the undermining of the 'everlasting nature-imposed condition of human existence'. Further there is the question of the sustainability of the earth--ie the extent to which it is to be passed on to future generations in a condition equal or better than in the present. As Marx wrote:

From the standpoint of a higher socio-economic formation, the private property of particular individuals in the earth will appear just as absurd as private property of one man in other men. Even an entire society, a nation, or all simultaneously existing societies taken together, are not owners of *the earth. They are simply its possessors, its beneficiaries, and have to bequeath it in an improved state to succeeding generations as **boni patres familias** [good heads of the household].*[11]

The issue of sustainability, for Marx, went beyond what capitalist society, with its constant intensification and enlargement of the metabolic rift between human beings and the earth, could address. Capitalism, he observed, 'creates the material conditions for a new and higher synthesis, a union of agriculture and industry on the basis of the forms that have developed during the period of their antagonistic isolation'. Yet in order to achieve this 'higher synthesis', he argued, it would be necessary for the associated producers in the new society to 'govern the human metabolism with nature in a rational way'--a requirement that raised fundamental and continuing challenges for post-revolutionary society.[12]

In analysing the metabolic rift Marx and Engels did not stop with the soil nutrient cycle, or the town-country relation. They addressed at various points in their work such issues as deforestation, desertification, climate change, the elimination of deer from the forests, the commodification of species, pollution, industrial wastes, toxic contamination, recycling, the exhaustion of coal mines, disease, overpopulation and the evolution (and co-evolution) of species.

After having the power and coherence of Marx's analysis of the metabolic rift impressed on me in this way, I began to wonder how deeply embedded such ecological conceptions were in Marx's thought as a whole. What was there in Marx's background that could explain how he was able to incorporate natural-scientific observations into his analysis so effectively? How did this relate to the concept of the alienation of nature, which along with the alienation of labour was such a pronounced feature of his early work? Most of all, I began to wonder whether the secret to Marx's ecology was to be found in his materialism. Could it be that this materialism was not adequately viewed simply in terms of a materialist conception of *human* history, but also had to be seen in terms of *natural* history and the dialectical relation between the two? Or to put it somewhat differently, was Marx's materialist conception of history inseparable from what Engels had termed the 'materialist conception of nature'?[13] Had Marx employed his dialectical method in the analysis of both?

The search for an answer to these questions took me on a long intellectual journey through Marx's works, and the historical-intellectual context in which they were written, which eventually became *Marx's Ecology*. Let me mention just a few highlights of the story I uncovered--since I do not have the time to explore it all in detail here, and because part of my purpose here is to add additional strands to the story. My account differs from most present-day accounts of Marx's development in that it highlights the formative significance of Marx's doctoral thesis on Epicurus, the greatest of the ancient materialists, and goes on to situate Marx and Engels' lifelong engagement with developments in the natural sciences. This includes Marx and Engels' opposition to the natural theology tradition, particularly as manifested by Malthus, their treatment of Liebig's work on nutrient cycling and its relation to the metabolic rift, and finally their creative encounter with Darwin, co-evolution, and what has been called 'the revolution in ethnological time' following the discovery of the first prehistoric human remains.[14]

In most interpretations of Marx's development his early thought is seen as largely a response to Hegel, mediated by Feuerbach. Without denying Hegel's significance I argue that Marx's formative phase is much more complex than is usually pictured. Along with German idealism

Marx was struggling early on with ancient materialist natural philosophy and its relation to the 17th century scientific revolution, and the 18th century Enlightenment. In all of this Epicurus loomed very large. For Kant, 'Epicurus can be called the foremost philosopher of sensibility,' just as Plato was the foremost philosopher 'of the intellectual'. Epicurus, Hegel claimed, was 'the inventor of empiric natural science'. For Marx himself Epicurus was the 'the greatest figure of the Greek Enlightenment'.[15]

For Marx, Epicurus represented, most importantly, a non-reductionist, non-deterministic materialism, and articulated a philosophy of human freedom. In Epicurus could be found a materialist conception of nature that rejected all teleology and all religious conceptions of natural and social existence. In studying Epicurus's natural philosophy Marx was addressing a view that had had a powerful influence on the development of European science and modern naturalist-materialist philosophies, and one that had at the same time profoundly influenced the development of European social thought. In the Epicurean materialist worldview knowledge of the world started with the senses. The two primary theses of Epicurus's natural philosophy make up what we today call the principle of conservation: nothing comes from nothing, and nothing being destroyed is reduced to nothing. For Epicureans there was no scale of nature, no sharp, unbridgeable gaps between human beings and other animals. Knowledge of Epicurus provides a way of understanding Marx's deep materialism in the area of natural philosophy. His study of ancient and early modern materialism brought Marx inside the struggle over the scientific understanding of the natural world in ways that influenced all of his thought and was deeply ecological in its significance, since it focused on evolution and emergence, and made nature not god the starting point. Moreover, Marx's dialectical encounter with Hegel has to be understood in terms of the struggle that Marx was carrying on simultaneously regarding the nature of materialist philosophy and science.

Darwin had similar roots in natural philosophy, linked to the anti-teleological tradition extending back to Epicurus, which had found its modern exponent in Bacon. We now know, as a result of the publication of Darwin's notebooks, that the reason that he waited so long--20 years--before making public his theory on species transmutation was due to the fact that his theory had strong materialist roots, and thus raised the issue of heresy in Victorian England. Darwin's view went against all teleological explanations, such as those of the natural theology tradition. He presented an account of the evolution of species that was dependent on no supernatural forces, no miraculous agencies of any kind, but simply on nature's own workings.

Marx and Engels greeted Darwin's theory immediately as 'the death of teleology', and Marx described it as 'the basis in natural science for our views'.[16] Not only did they study Darwin intensely, they were also drawn into the debates concerning human evolution that followed immediately on Darwin's work, as a result of the discovery of the first prehistoric human remains. Neanderthal remains had been found in France in 1856, but it was the discovery of prehistoric remains that were quickly accepted as such in England in Brixham Cave in 1859, the same year that Darwin published his *The Origin of Species*, that generated the revolution in ethnological time, erasing forever within science the biblical chronology for human history/prehistory. Suddenly it became clear that the human species (or hominid species) had existed in all probability for a million years or longer, not simply a few thousand. (Today it is believed that hominid species have existed for around 7 million years.)

Many major works, mostly by Darwinians, emerged in just a few years to address this new reality, and Marx and Engels studied them with great intensity. Among the works that they scrutinised were Charles Lyell's *Geological Evidences of the Antiquity of Man* (1863), Thomas Huxley's *Evidence as to Man's Place in Nature* (1863), John Lubbock's *Prehistoric Times* (1865), Darwin's *Descent of Man* (1871), along with a host of other works in the ethnological realm, including Lewis Henry Morgan's *Ancient Society* (1881).

Out of their studies came a thesis on the role of labour in human evolution that was to prove fundamental. Inspired by the ancient Greek meaning for organ (*organon*)--or tool, which expressed the idea that organs were essentially the 'grown-on' tools of animals, Marx referred to such organs as 'natural technology', which could be compared in certain respects to human technology. A similar approach was evident in Darwin, and Marx was thus able to use Darwin's comparison of the development of specialised organs in plants and animals to that of specialised tools (in chapter 5 of *The Origin of Species* on 'Laws of Variation') to help explain his own conception of the development of natural and human technology. The evolution of natural technology, Marx argued, rooting his analysis in *The Origin of Species*, was a reflection of the fact that animals and plants were able to pass on through inheritance organs that had been developed through natural selection in a process that might be called '"accumulation" through inheritance'. Indeed, the driving force of evolution for Darwin, in Marx's interpretation, was 'the gradually accumulated [naturally selected] inventions of living things'.[17]

In this conception, human beings were to be distinguished from animals in that they more effectively utilised tools, which became extensions of their bodies. Tools, and through them the wider realm of nature, as Marx said early on in his *Economic and Philosophic Manuscripts*, became the 'inorganic body of man'. Or as he was to observe in Capital, 'thus nature becomes one of the organs of his [man's] activity, which he annexes to his own bodily organs, adding stature to himself in spite of the Bible'.[18]

Engels was to develop this argument further in his pathbreaking work, 'The Part Played by Labour in the Transition from Ape to Man' (written in 1876, published posthumously in 1896). According to Engels' analysis--which derived from his materialist philosophy, but which was also influenced by views voiced by Ernst Haeckel a few years before--when the primates, who constituted the ancestors of human beings, descended from the trees, erect posture developed first (prior to the evolution of the human brain), freeing the hands for tool-making. In this way:

> ...**the hand became free** and could henceforth attain ever greater dexterity and skill, and the greater flexibility thus acquired was inherited and increased from generation to generation. Thus the hand is not only the organ of labour, **it is also the product of labour**.[19]

As a result early humans (hominids) were able to alter their relation to their local environment, radically improving their adaptability. Those who were most ingenious in making and using tools were most likely to survive, which means that the evolutionary process exerted selective pressures toward the enlargement of the brain and the development of language (necessary for the social processes of labour and tool-making), leading eventually to the rise of modern humans. Thus the human brain, like the hand, in Engels' view, evolved through a complex, interactive set of relations, now referred to by evolutionary biologists as 'gene-culture co-evolution'. All scientific explanations of the evolution of the human brain, Stephen Jay Gould has argued, have thus far been theories of gene-culture co-evolution, and 'the best 19th century case for gene-culture co-evolution was made by Frederick Engels'.[20]

All of this points to the fact that Marx and Engels had a profound grasp of ecological and evolutionary problems, as manifested in the natural science of their day, and were able to make important contributions to our understanding of how society and nature interact. If orthodoxy in Marxism, as Lukács taught, relates primarily to method, then we can attribute these insights to a very powerful method, but one which, insofar as it encompasses *both* a materialist conception of natural history and of human (ie social) history, has not been fully investigated by subsequent commentators. Behind Marx and Engels' insights in this area lay an uncompromising materialism, which embraced such concepts as emergence and contingency, and which was dialectical to the core.

Engels' *Dialectics of Nature* is known to incorporate numerous ecological insights. But it is frequently contended that Marxism after Marx and Engels either missed out on the development of ecological thought altogether or was anti-ecological and that there were no important Marxian contributions to the study of nature after Engels until the Frankfurt School and Alfred Schmidt's *The Concept of Nature in Marx*, first published in 1962.[21] This position, however, is wrong. There were in fact numerous Marxist contributions to the analysis of the nature-society relation, and socialists played a very large role in the development of ecology, particularly in its formative stages. The influence of Marx and Engels' ideas in this respect was not confined to the 19th century.

But it is not just a question of the direct inheritance of certain propositions with respect to nature-ecology. Marx and also Engels employed a materialist conception of nature, which was not at all foreign to the major revolutions in science of their day (as evident in Darwin's theory), and which they combined with a dialectic of emergence and contingency. A very large part of this was reflected in both socialist and scientific thought in the immediately succeeding generations. Among the socialists who incorporated naturalistic and ecological conceptions into their thinking, after Marx and up through the 1940s, we can include such figures as William Morris, Henry Salt, August Bebel, Karl Kautsky, Rosa Luxemburg, V I Lenin, Nikolai Bukharin, V I Vernadsky, N I Vavilov, Alexander Oparin, Christopher Caudwell, Hyman Levy, Lancelot Hogben, J D Bernal, Benjamin Farrington, J B S Haldane and Joseph Needham--and in the more Fabian tradition, but not unconnected to Marx and Marxism, Ray Lankester and Arthur Tansley. Bukharin employed Marx's concept of the metabolism of nature and society in his writings, and situated human beings in the biosphere. 'Human beings,' he wrote:

> ...are both products of nature and part of it; they have a biological basis when their social existence is excluded from account (it cannot be abolished!); if they are themselves the summits of nature and its products, and if they live within nature (however much they may be divided off from it by particular social and historical conditions of life and by the so called 'artistic environment'), then what is surprising in the fact that human beings share in the rhythm of nature and its cycles?[22]

Kautsky in his *The Agrarian Question*, following Liebig and Marx, addressed the problem of the soil nutrient cycle, raised the question of the fertiliser treadmill, and even referred to the dangers of the intensive application of pesticides--all in 1899! Luxemburg addressed ecological problems in her letters, discussing the disappearance of songbirds through the destruction of their habitat. Lenin promoted both conservation and ecology in the Soviet Union, and demonstrated an awareness of the degradation of soil fertility and the breaking of the soil nutrient cycle under capitalist agriculture--the Liebig-Marx problem. The Soviet

Union in the 1920s had the most developed ecological science in the world. Vernadsky had introduced the concept of the biosphere in a dialectical framework of analysis that reaches down to the most advanced ecology of our day. Vavilov used the historical materialist method to map out the centres of the origin of agriculture and the banks of germ plasm throughout the globe, now known as the Vavilov areas. Oparin, simultaneously with Haldane in Britain, developed the first and still to this day most influential explanation for the origin of life on earth based on Vernadsky's biosphere concept--a theory that was to have an important impact on Rachel Carson's concept of ecology.[23]

Yet this early Marxist ecological thought, or rather the traditions that sustained it, largely died out. Ecology within Marxism suffered something of a double death. In the East in the 1930s Stalinism literally purged the more ecological elements within the Soviet leadership and scientific community--not arbitrarily so since it was in these circles that some of the resistance to primitive socialist accumulation was to be found. Bukharin was executed. Vavilov died of malnutrition in a prison cell in 1943. At the same time in the West, Marxism took an often extreme, avidly anti-positivistic form. The dialectic was seen as inapplicable to nature--a view often associated with Lukács, though we now know that Lukács's position was somewhat more ambiguous. This affected most of Western Marxism, which tended to see Marxism increasingly in terms of a human history severed for the most part from nature. Nature was relegated to the province of natural science, which was seen as properly positivistic within its own realm. In Lukács, Gramsci and Korsch, marking the Western Marxist revolt of the 1920s, nature was increasingly conspicuous in its absence. Nature entered into the Frankfurt School's critique of the Enlightenment, but the nature under consideration was almost always human nature (reflecting the concern with psychology), and rarely so called 'external nature'. There was no materialist conception of nature. Hence genuine ecological insights were rare.

If an unbroken continuity is to be found in the development of socialist nature-science discussions and ecological thought, its path has to be traced primarily in Britain, where a continuous commitment to a materialist dialectic in the analysis of natural history was maintained. A strong tradition in Britain linked science, Darwin, Marx and dialectics. Although some of the negative features of this tradition, which has been referred to as a 'Baconian strand in Marxism', are well known, its more positive ecological insights have never been fully grasped.[24]

Any account of the ecology of British Marxism in this period has to highlight Caudwell, who, though he died at the age of 29 behind a machine-gun on a hill in Spain, left an indelible intellectual legacy. His *Heredity and Development*, perhaps the most important of his science-related works, was suppressed by the Communist Party in Britain due to the Lysenkoist controversy (he was anti-Lysenkoist) and so was not published until 1986.[25] But it contains an impressive attempt to develop an ecological dialectic. Haldane, Levy, Hogben, Needham, Bernal and Farrington--as previously noted--all developed ecological notions (though Bernal's legacy is the most contradictory in this respect). All indicated profound respect not only for Marx and Darwin but also for Epicurus, who was seen as the original source of the materialist conception of nature. The influence of these thinkers carries down to the present day in the work of later biological and ecological scientists, such as Steven Rose in Britain, and Richard Lewontin, Richard Levins and the late Stephen Jay Gould in the US.

I want to concentrate here on two figures who are less well known, more Fabian than Marxist, but clearly socialists--namely Ray Lankester and Arthur Tansley. Ray Lankester taught at University College, London, and Tansley was his student there. Lankester was Huxley's protégé and was considered the greatest Darwinian scientist of his generation. He was the most famous adamantly materialist biologist of his day in Britain. When he was a boy, Darwin and Huxley, who were friends of his father, both played with him, Darwin entertaining him with stories of giant sea turtles, and Huxley carrying him on his back. Lankester was also a young friend of Karl Marx and a socialist, though not himself a Marxist. He was a frequent guest at Marx's household in the last few years of Marx's life. Marx and his daughter Eleanor also visited Lankester at his residence in London. Marx and Lankester had in common, above all, their materialism. Marx was interested in Lankester's research into degeneration--the notion that evolution did not necessarily simply go forward--and made an attempt to get Lankester's work published in Russian. Lankester wrote to Marx that he was absorbing 'your great work on Capital...with the greatest pleasure and profit'. Lankester was to become one of the most ecologically concerned thinkers of his time. He wrote some of the most powerful essays that have ever been written on species extinction due to human causes, and discussed the pollution of London and other ecological issues with an urgency that is not found again until the late 20th century.[26]

Arthur Tansley was the foremost plant ecologist in Britain of his generation, one of the greatest ecologists of all time, and the originator of the concept of ecosystem. He was to become the first president of the British Ecological Society. Tansley was deeply influenced by Lankester, along with the botanist Francis Wall Oliver, in his years at University College, London. Like Lankester, Tansley was a Fabian socialist and an uncompromising materialist. And like Lankester, who wrote a scathing criticism of Henri Bergson's concept of vitalism or the *élan vital*, Tansley was to directly challenge attempts to conceive evolutionary ecology in anti-materialist, teleological terms.[27]

In the 1920s and 1930s a major split occurred in ecology. In the US Frederic Clements and others developed the important concept of ecological succession (successive stages in the development of plant 'communities' in a particular region culminating in a 'climax' or mature stage linked to certain dominant species). But in a much more controversial move, Clements and his followers extended this analysis to a concept of super-organism meant to account for the process of succession. This ecological approach inspired other innovations in ecological theory in Edinburgh and South Africa. South African ecological thinkers, led by Jan Christian Smuts, introduced a concept of 'holism' in the ecological realm, most notably in Smuts' book *Holism and Evolution* (1926), which was to lead to modern conceptions of deep ecology. Smuts, who was usually referred to as General Smuts because of his military role in the Boer War (he fought on the side of the Boers), was one of the principal figures in the construction of the apartheid system. How much Smuts himself contributed directly to the development of apartheid may be disputed. But he was a strong advocate of the territorial segregation of the races and what he called 'the grand white racial aristocracy'. He is perhaps best remembered worldwide as the South African general who arrested Gandhi. Smuts was South African minister of defence from 1910 to 1919, and prime minister and minister of native affairs from 1919 to 1924. He was sometimes seen as a figure soaked in blood. When the Native Labour Union demanded political power and freedom of speech Smuts crushed it with violence, killing 68 people in Port Elizabeth alone. When black Jews refused to work on Passover Smuts sent in the police, and 200 were killed on his orders. When certain black tribal populations in Bondelwaart refused to pay their dog tax Smuts sent in planes and bombed them into submission. Not surprisingly, Smuts' ecological holism was also a form of ecological racism, since it was a holism that contained natural-ecological divisions along racial lines.

The legendary opponent of Smuts' holistic philosophy, in the great 'Nature of Life' debate that took place at the British Association for the Advancement of Science meetings in South Africa in 1929, was the British Marxist biologist Lancelot Hogben (who had a position at the University of Cape Town at that time). Hogben not only debated Smuts--opposing his materialism to Smuts' holism, and attacking Smuts for his racist eugenics--but also hid black rebels fleeing the racist state in a secret compartment in his basement. Another major opponent of Smuts was the British Marxist mathematician Hyman Levy, who, in his *The Universe of Science*, developed a critique of Smuts' holism along similar lines to those of Hogben.[28]

In 1935 Tansley found himself increasingly at odds with anti-materialist conceptions of ecology that were then gaining influence, and entered the lists against ecological idealism. Tansley wrote an article for the journal *Ecology* entitled 'The Use and Abuse of Vegetational Concepts and Terms' that declared war on Clements, Smuts and Smuts' leading follower in South African ecology, John Phillips. In one fell swoop Tansley attacked the teleological notions that ecological succession was always progressive and developmental, always leading to a climax; that vegetation could be seen as constituting a super-organism; that there was such a thing as a biotic 'community' (with members), encompassing both plants and animals; that 'organismic philosophy', which saw the whole universe as an organism, was a useful way to understand ecological relations; and that holism could be seen as both cause and effect of everything in nature. Smuts' holistic view, Tansley claimed, was 'at least partly motivated by an imagined future "whole" to be realised in an ideal human society whose reflected glamour falls on less exalted wholes, illuminating with a false light the image of the "complex organism".' This was quite possibly a polite way of referring to the system of racial stratification that was built into Smutsian holistic ecology.

In combating this type of mystical holism and super-organicism, and introducing the concept of ecosystem in response, Tansley turned to the systems theory utilised in Levy's *The Universe of Science* and at the same time referred to materialist conceptions of dynamic equilibrium in natural systems going back to Lucretius (Epicurus's Roman follower and author of the great philosophical poem *The Nature of Things*). 'The fundamental conception,' represented by his new ecosystem concept, Tansley argued, was that of:

> ...the whole system (in the sense of physics), including not only the organism-complex, but also the whole complex of physical factors forming what we call the environment of the biome-the habitat factors in the widest sense. Though the organisms may claim our primary interest, when we are trying to think fundamentally we cannot separate them from their special environment, with which they form one physical system... These **ecosystems**, as we may call them, are of the most various kinds and sizes. They form one category of the multitudinous physical systems of the universe, which range from the universe as a whole down to the atom.

Following Levy, Tansley emphasised a dialectical conception:

> The systems we isolate mentally are not only included as part of larger ones, but they also overlap, interlock, and interact with one another. The isolation is partly artificial, but it is the only possible way in which we can proceed.

Rather than seeing ecology in terms of natural, teleological order, Tansley emphasised disruptions to that order, referring to 'the destructive human activities of the modern world', and presenting human beings as an 'exceptionally powerful biotic factor which increasingly upsets the equilibrium of pre-existing ecosystems and eventually destroys them, at the same time forming new ones of very different nature'. 'Ecology,' he argued, 'must be applied to conditions brought about by human activity,' and for this purpose the ecosystem concept, which situated life within its larger material environment, and penetrated 'beneath the forms of the "natural" entities', was the most practical form for analysis. Tansley's ecosystem concept was, paradoxically, more genuinely holistic and more dialectical than the super-organicism and 'holism' that preceded it, because it brought both the organic and inorganic world within a more complex materialist synthesis.[29]

At this point you may think that I have deviated from my path in addressing Tansley so extensively. But an analysis that is materialist and at the same time dialectical is bound to provide a more powerful set of insights into both ecology and society, natural history and human history. The Marxian materialist perspective was bound to such an approach. Figures like Bukharin, Vernadsky, Vavilov, Oparin, Caudwell, Haldane, Hogben, Needham and Levy- -but also Lankester and Tansley--shared, albeit with considerable variance among them, both a materialist conception of nature and history and a commitment to dialectical readings of human and natural relations. The fact that these thinkers to varying degrees also sometimes lapsed into mechanicalism should warn us to approach their work cautiously, but it should not blind us to their genuine insights.

Some environmental commentators of course continue to claim that Marx believed one-sidedly in the struggle of human beings against nature, and was thus anthropocentric and unecological, and that Marxism as a whole carried forth this original ecological sin. But the evidence, as I have suggested, strongly contradicts this. In *The German Ideology* Marx assailed Bruno Bauer for referring to 'the antitheses in nature and history as though they were two separate things'. In fact, 'the celebrated "unity of man with nature",' Marx argued, 'has always existed in industry...and so has the "struggle" of man with nature.' A materialist approach will deny neither reality--neither unity nor struggle in the human relation to nature. Instead it will concentrate on 'the sensuous world', as Marx said, 'as consisting of the total living sensuous *activity* of those living in it'.[30] From this standpoint, human beings make their own environments, but not under conditions entirely of their choosing, but rather based on conditions handed down from the earth and from earlier generations in the course of history, both natural and human.

Notes

John Bellamy Foster is co-editor of *Monthly Review* (New York). He is Professor of Sociology at the University of Oregon in Eugene, Oregon. His most recent books are *The Vulnerable Planet* (1994, 1999), *Marx's Ecology* (2000), *Hungry for Profit* (2000, co-edited with Fred Magdoff and Frederick Buttel), and *Ecology Against Capitalism* (2002)--all published by Monthly Review Press. This is a slightly revised version of a talk delivered at the Marxism 2002 conference, London, 6 July 2002.

1. G Lichtheim, *Marxism: An Historical and Critical Study* (New York, 1964), p245.

2. On the strengths of Marx's ecological analysis see J B Foster, *Marx's Ecology* (New York, 2000), and P Burkett, *Marx and Nature* (New York, 1999).
3. For a detailed breakdown of the various criticisms of Marx on the environment see J B Foster, 'Marx's Theory of Metabolic Rift', *American Journal of Sociology*, vol 105, no 2 (September 1999), pp366-405.
4. M de Kadt and S Engel-Di Mauro, 'Failed Promise', *Capitalism, Nature, Socialism*, vol 12, no 2 (June 2001), pp52-55.
5. E P Thompson, *The Essential E P Thompson* (New York, 2001), p6.
6. J Liebig, *Die Chemie in ihrer Anwendung auf Agricultur und Physiologie*, vol 1 (Brunswick, 1862). Except where otherwise indicated all of the brief quotes from Liebig in the text below are taken from an unpublished English translation of the 1862 German edition by Lady Gilbert contained in the archives of the Rothamsted Experimental Station (now IACR-Rothamsted) outside London.
7. The translation of this passage from the introduction to the 1862 edition of Liebig's work follows Erland Mårold in 'Everything Circulates: Agricultural Chemistry and Recycling Theories in the Second Half of the Nineteenth Century', *Environment and History* 8 (2002), p74.
8. K Marx, *Capital*, vol 1 (New York, 1976), p638.
9. Ibid, pp636-639; K Marx, *Capital*, vol 3 (New York, 1981), pp948-950, 959.
10. Ibid, vol 1, pp283, 290.
11. Ibid, vol 3, p911.
12. Ibid, vol 1, p637; Ibid, vol 3, p959.
13. F Engels, *Ludwig Feuerbach and the Outcome of Classical German Philosophy* (New York, 1941), p67.
14. The phrase 'the revolution in ethnological time' is taken from T R Trautmann, *Lewis Henry Morgan and the Invention of Kinship* (Berkeley, 1987), pp35, 220.
15. See J B Foster, *Marx's Ecology*, op cit, pp49-51.
16. See the discussion ibid, pp196-207, 212-221.
17. K Marx, *Theories of Surplus Value*, vol 3 (Moscow, 1971), pp294-295.
18. K Marx, *Early Writings* (New York, 1974), p328; K Marx, *Capital*, vol 1, op cit, pp285-286. See also J B Foster and P Burkett, 'The Dialectic of Organic/Inorganic Relations: Marx and the Hegelian Philosophy of Nature', *Organization and Environment*, vol 13, no 4 (December 2000), pp403-425.
19. F Engels, *The Dialectics of Nature* (New York, 1940), p281.
20. S J Gould, *An Urchin in the Storm* (New York, 1987), pp111-112.
21. See N Castree, 'Marxism and the Production of Nature', *Capital and Class* 72 (Autumn 2000), p14; J B Foster, 'Review of Special Issue of Capital and Class', *Historical Materialism* 8 (Summer 2001), pp465-467.
22. N Bukharin, *Philosophical Arabesques* (written in 1937-1938), ch 8. Quotations from draft of forthcoming English translation.
23. See the discussion in J B Foster, *Marx's Ecology*, op cit, p241-244; R Carson, *Lost Woods* (Boston, 1998), pp229-230.
24. N Wood, *Communism and British Intellectuals* (New York, 1959), p145.
25. Lysenkoism was an erroneous doctrine associated with the work of the Russian agronomist Trofim Denisovich Lysenko that de-emphasised genetic inheritance in favour of a notion

of the plasticity of the life cycle. For a balanced discussion of Lysenkoism see R Levins and R Lewontin, *The Dialectical Biologist* (Cambridge, Mass, 1985), pp163-196.

26. See the more detailed discussions of Lankester in J B Foster, *Marx's Ecology*, op cit, pp221-225; and J B Foster, 'E Ray Lankester, Ecological Materialist: An Introduction to Lankester's "Effacement of Nature by Man"', *Organization and Environment*, vol 13, no 2 (June 2000), pp233-235.

27. For biographical information on Tansley see P Anker, *Imperial Ecology: Environmental Order in the British Empire* (Cambridge, Mass, 2001), pp7-40.

28. Ibid, pp41-75, 118-149; J C Smuts, *Holism and Evolution* (London, 1926); L Hogben, *The Nature of Living Matter* (London, 1931); H Levy, *The Universe of Science* (New York, 1933). For Smuts' racial views see J Smuts, *Africa and Some World Problems* (Oxford, 1930), pp92-94.

29. Ibid, pp152-156; A G Tansley, 'The Use and Abuse of Vegetational Concepts and Terms', *Ecology*, vol 16, no 3 (July 1935), pp284-307.

30. K Marx and F Engels, *Collected Works*, vol 5 (New York, 1975), pp39-41.

[34]

Marx's Vision of Sustainable Human Development

PAUL BURKETT

In developed capitalist countries, debates over the economics of socialism have mostly concentrated on questions of information, incentives, and efficiency in resource allocation. This focus on "socialist calculation" reflects the mainly academic context of these discussions. By contrast, for anti-capitalist movements and post-revolutionary regimes on the capitalist periphery, socialism as a form of human development has been a prime concern. A notable example is Ernesto "Che" Guevara's work on "Man and Socialism in Cuba," which rebutted the argument that "the period of building socialism...is characterized by the extinction of the individual for the sake of the state." For Che, socialist revolution is a process in which "large numbers of people are developing themselves," and "the material possibilities of the integral development of each and every one of its members make the task ever more fruitful."[1]

With global capitalism's worsening poverty and environmental crises, sustainable human development comes to the fore as the primary question that must be engaged by all twenty-first century socialists in core and periphery alike. It is in this human developmental connection, I will argue, that Marx's vision of communism or socialism (two terms that he used interchangeably) can be most helpful.[2]

The suggestion that Marx's communism can inform the struggle for more healthy, sustainable, and liberating forms of human development may seem paradoxical in light of various ecological criticisms of Marx that have become so fashionable over the last several decades. Marx's vision has been deemed ecologically unsustainable and undesirable due to its purported treatment of natural conditions as effectively limitless, and its supposed embrace, both practically and ethically, of technological optimism and human domination over nature.

The well known ecological economist Herman Daly, for example, argues that for Marx, the "materialistic determinist, economic growth is crucial in

---

Paul Burkett teaches economics at Indiana State University, Terre Haute. With Martin Hart-Landsberg, he co-authored *China and Socialism: Market Reforms and Class Struggle* (Monthly Review Press, 2005).

An earlier version of this article was presented at the Conference on the Work of Karl Marx and Challenges for the 21st Century, Havana, Cuba, May 6, 2003.

order to provide the overwhelming material abundance that is the objective condition for the emergence of the new socialist man. Environmental limits on growth would contradict 'historical necessity'...." The problem, says environmental political theorist Robyn Eckersley, is that "Marx fully endorsed the 'civilizing' and technical accomplishments of the capitalist forces of production and thoroughly absorbed the Victorian faith in scientific and technological progress as the means by which humans could outsmart and conquer nature." Evidently Marx "consistently saw human freedom as inversely related to humanity's dependence on nature." Environmental culturalist Victor Ferkiss asserts that "Marx and Engels and their modern followers" shared a "virtual worship of modern technology," which explains why "they joined liberals in refusing to criticize the basic technological constitution of modern society." Another environmental political scientist, K. J. Walker, claims that Marx's vision of communist production does not recognize any actual or potential "shortage of natural resources," the "implicit assumption" being "that natural resources are effectively limitless." Environmental philosopher Val Routley describes Marx's vision of communism as an anti-ecological "automated paradise" of energy-intensive and "environmentally damaging" production and consumption, one which "appears to derive from [Marx's] nature-domination assumption."[3]

An engagement with these views is important not least because they have become influential even among ecologically minded Marxists, many of whom have looked to non-Marxist paradigms, especially that of Karl Polanyi, for the ecological guidance supposedly lacking in Marxism. The under-utilization of the human developmental and ecological elements of Marx's communist vision is also reflected in the decision by some Marxists to place their bets on a "greening" of capitalism as a practical alternative to the struggle for socialism.[4]

Accordingly, I will interpret Marx's various outlines of post-capitalist economy and society as a vision of sustainable human development. Since there are no important disagreements between Marx and Engels in this area, I will also refer to the writings of Engels, and works co-authored by Marx and Engels, as appropriate. After sketching the human developmental dimensions of communal property and associated (non-market) production in Marx's view, I draw out the sustainability aspect of these principles by responding to the most common ecological criticisms of Marx's projection. I conclude by briefly reconsidering the connections between Marx's vision of communism and his analysis of capitalism, focusing on that all important form of human development: the class struggle.

1. Basic Organizing Principles of Marx's Communism

There is a conventional wisdom that Marx and Engels, eschewing all "speculation about...socialist utopias," thought very little about the system to follow capitalism, and that their entire body of writing on this subject is represented by "the *Critique of the Gotha Program*, a few pages long, and not much else."[5]

In reality, post-capitalist economic and political relationships are a recurring thematic in all the major, and many of the minor, works of the founders of Marxism, and despite the scattered nature of these discussions, one can easily glean from them a coherent vision based on a clear set of organizing principles. The most basic feature of communism in Marx's projection is its overcoming of capitalism's social separation of the producers from necessary conditions of production. This new social union entails a complete decommodification of labor power plus a new set of communal property rights. Communist or "associated" production is planned and carried out by the producers and communities themselves, without the class-based intermediaries of wage-labor, market, and state. Marx often motivates and illustrates these basic features in terms of the primary means and end of associated production: free human development.

A. The New Union and Communal Property

For Marx, capitalism involves the "decomposition of the original union existing between the labouring man and his means of labour," while communism will "restore the original union in a new historical form." Communism is the "historical reversal" of "the separation of labour and the worker from the conditions of labour, which confront him as independent forces." Under capitalism's wage system, "the means of production employ *the workers*"; under communism, "the workers, as subjects, employ the means of production...in order to produce wealth for themselves."[6]

This new union of the producers and the conditions of production "will," as Engels phrases it, "emancipate human labour power from its position as a *commodity*." Naturally, such an emancipation, in which the laborers undertake production as "united workers" (see below), "is only possible where the workers are the owners of their means of production." This worker ownership does not entail the individual rights to possession and alienability characterizing capitalist property, however. Rather, workers' communal property codifies and enforces the new union of the *collective* producers and their communities with the conditions of production. Accordingly, Marx describes communism as "replacing capitalist production with cooperative production, and capitalist property with a *higher form*

MARX'S VISION OF SUSTAINABLE HUMAN DEVELOPMENT 37

of the archaic type of property, i.e. communist property."[7]

One reason why communist property in the conditions of production cannot be individual private property is that the latter form "excludes co-operation, division of labour within each separate process of production, the control over, and the productive application of the forces of Nature by society, and the free development of the social productive powers." In other words, "the individual worker could only be restored as *an individual* to property in the conditions of production by divorcing productive power from the development of [alienated] labour on a large scale." As stated in *The German Ideology*, "the appropriation by the proletarians" is such that "a mass of instruments of production must be made subject to each individual, and property to all. Modern universal intercourse cannot be controlled by individuals, unless it is controlled by all....With the appropriation of the total productive forces by the united individuals, private property comes to an end."[8]

Besides, given capitalism's prior socialization of production, "private" property in the means of production is already a kind of social property, even though its social character is class-exploitative. From capital's character as "not a personal, [but] a social power" it follows that when "capital is converted into common property, into the property of all members of society, personal property is not thereby transformed into social property. It is only the social character of the property that is changed. It loses its class-character."[9]

Marx's vision thus involves a "reconversion of capital into the property of producers, although no longer as the private property of the individual producers, but rather as the property of associated producers, as outright social property." Communist property is collective precisely insofar as "the material conditions of production are the co-operative property of the workers" as a whole, not of particular individuals or sub-groups of individuals. As Engels puts it: "The 'working people' remain the collective owners of the houses, factories and instruments of labour, and will hardly permit their use... by individuals or associations without compensation for the cost." The collective planning and administration of social production requires that not only the means of production but also the distribution of the total product be subject to explicit social control. With associated production, "it is possible to assure each person 'the full proceeds of his labour'...only if [this phrase] is extended to purport not that each individual worker becomes the possessor of 'the full proceeds of his labour,' but that the whole of society, consisting entirely of workers, becomes the possessor of the total product of their labour, which product it partly distributes among its members for consumption, partly uses for replacing and increasing its means of production, and partly stores up as a reserve fund for production and consumption." The latter two "deductions from the...proceeds of labour are an economic necessity"; they represent "forms of surplus-labour and surplus-product...which are common to all social modes of production." Further deductions are required for "general costs of administration," for "the communal satisfaction of needs, such as schools, health services, etc.," and for "funds for those unable to work." Only then "do we come to...that part of the means of consumption which is divided among the individual producers of the co-operative society."[10]

Communism's explicit socialization of the conditions and results of production should not be mistaken for a complete absence of individual property rights, however. Although communal property "does not re-establish private property for the producer," it nonetheless "gives him individual property based on the acquisitions of the capitalist era: i.e., on co-operation and the possession in common of the land and of the means of production." Marx posits that "the *alien property* of the capitalist...can only be abolished by converting his property into the property...of the *associated, social individual*." He even suggests that communism will "make individual property a truth by transforming the means of production...now chiefly the means of enslaving and exploiting labor, into mere instruments of free and associated labour."[11]

Such statements are often interpreted as mere rhetorical flourishes, but they become more explicable when viewed in the context of communism's overriding imperative: the free development of individual human beings as social individuals. Marx and Engels describe "the community of revolutionary proletarians" as an "association of individuals...which puts the conditions of the free development and movement of individuals under their control—conditions which were previously left to chance and had acquired an independent existence over against the separate individuals." Stated differently, "the all-round realisation of the individual will only cease to be conceived as an ideal...when the impact of the world which stimulates the real development of the abilities of the individual is under the control of the individuals themselves, as the communists desire." In class-exploitative societies, "personal freedom has existed only for the individuals who developed under the conditions of the ruling class"; but under the "real community" of communism, "individuals obtain their freedom in and through their association." Instead of opportunities for individual development being obtained mainly at the expense of others, as in class societies, the future "community" will provide "each individual [with] the means of cultivating his gifts in all directions; hence personal freedom becomes possible only within the community."[12]

In short, communal property is individual insofar as it affirms each person's claim, as a member of society, for access to the conditions and results of production as a conduit to her or his development as an individual "to whom the different social functions he performs are but so many modes of giving free scope to his own natural and acquired powers." Only in this way can communism replace "the old bourgeois society, with its classes and class antagonisms," with "an association, in which the free development of each is a condition for the free development of all."[13]

The most basic way in which Marx's communism promotes individual human development is by protecting the individual's right to a share in the total product (net of the above-mentioned deductions) for her or his private consumption. The *Manifesto* is unambiguous on this point: "Communism deprives no man of the power to appropriate the products of society; all that it does is to deprive him of the power to subjugate the labour of others by means of such appropriation." In this sense, Engels observes, "social ownership extends to the land and the other means of production, and private ownership to the products, that is, the articles of production." An equivalent description of the "community of free individuals" is given in volume 1 of *Capital*: "The total product of our community is a social product. One portion serves as fresh means of production and remains social. But another portion is consumed by the members of society as means of subsistence."[14]

All of this, of course, raises the question as to how the distribution of individual workers' consumption claims will be determined. In *Capital*, Marx envisions that "the mode of this distribution will vary with the productive organisation of the community, and the degree of historical development attained by the producers." He then suggests ("merely for the sake of a parallel with the production of commodities") that one possibility would be for "the share of each individual producer in the means of subsistence" to be "determined by his labour-time." In the *Critique of the Gotha Programme*, the conception of labor time as the determinant of individual consumption rights is less ambiguous, at least for "the first phase of communist society as it is when it has just emerged after prolonged birth pangs from capitalist society." Here, Marx forthrightly projects that

> the individual producer receives back from society—after the deductions have been made—exactly what he gives to it. What he has given to it is his individual amount of labour....The individual labour time of the individual producer is the part of the social labour day contributed by him, his share in it. He receives a certificate from society that he has furnished such and such an amount of labour (after deducting his labour for the common fund), and with this certificate he draws from the social stock of means of consumption as much as the same amount of labour costs. The same amount of labour which he has given to society in one form, he receives back in another.

The basic rationale behind labor-based consumption claims is that "the distribution of the means of consumption at any time is only a consequence of the distribution of the conditions of production themselves."[15] Given that the conditions of production are the property of the producers, it stands to reason that the distribution of consumption claims will be more closely tied to labor time than under capitalism, where it is money that rules. This labor-time standard raises important social and technical issues that cannot be addressed here—especially whether and how differentials in labor intensity, work conditions, and skills would be measured and compensated.[16]

However, what Marx emphasizes is that insofar as the individual labor-time standard merely codifies the ethic of equal exchange regardless of the connotations for individual development, it is still infected by "the narrow horizon of bourgeois right." Marx therefore goes on to suggest that "in a higher phase of communist society," labor-based individual consumption claims can and should "be fully left behind and society inscribe on its banners: from each according to his ability, to each according to his needs!" It is in this higher phase that communism's "mode of distribution…allows *all* members of society to develop, maintain and exert their capacities in all possible directions." Here, "the individual consumption of the labourer" becomes that which "the full development of the individuality requires."[17]

Even in communism's lower phase, the means of individual development assured by communal property are not limited to individuals' private consumption claims. Human development will also benefit from the expanded social services (education, health services, utilities, and old-age pensions) that are financed by deductions from the total product prior to its distribution among individuals. Hence, "what the producer is deprived of in his capacity as a private individual benefits him directly or indirectly in his capacity as a member of society." Such social consumption will, in Marx's view, be "considerably increased in comparison with present-day society and it increases in proportion as the new society develops."[18]

For example, Marx envisions an expansion of "technical schools (theoretical and practical) in combination with the elementary school." He projects that "when the working-class comes into power, as inevitably it must, technical instruction, both theoretical and practical, will take its proper place in the working-class schools." Marx even suggests that the younger members of communist society will experience "an early combination of productive labour with education"—presuming, of course, "a strict regulation of the working time according to the different age groups and other safety measures for the protection of children." The basic idea here is that "the fact of the collective working group being composed of individuals of both sexes and ages, must "necessarily, under suitable conditions, become a source of humane development." Another, related function of theoretical and practical education "in the Republic of Labour" will be to "convert science from an instrument of class rule into a popular force," and thereby "convert the men of science themselves from panderers to class prejudice, place-hunting state parasites, and allies of capital into free agents of thought."[19]

Along with expanded social consumption, communism's "shortening of the working-day" will facilitate human development by giving individuals more free time in which to enjoy the "material and intellectual advantages...of social development." Free time is "time...for the free development, intellectual and social, of the individual." As such, "free time, *disposable time*, is wealth itself, partly for the enjoyment of the product, partly for free activity which—unlike labour—is not dominated by the pressure of an extraneous purpose which must be fulfilled, and the fulfillment of which is regarded as a natural necessity or a social duty." Accordingly, with communism "the measure of wealth is...not any longer, in any way, labour time, but rather disposable time." Nonetheless, since labor is always, together with nature, a fundamental "substance of wealth," labor time is an important "measure of the *cost* of [wealth's] production...even if exchange-value is eliminated."[20]

Naturally, communist society will place certain responsibilities on individuals. Even though free time will expand, individuals will still have a responsibility to engage in productive labor (including child-rearing and other care-giving activities) insofar as they are physically and mentally able to do so. Under capitalism and other class societies, "a particular class" has "the power to shift the natural burden of labour from its own shoulders to those of another layer of society." But under communism, "with labour emancipated, every-man becomes a working man, and productive labour ceases to be a class attribute." Individual self-development is also not only a right but a responsibility under communism. Hence, "the workers assert in their communist propaganda that the vocation, designation, task of every person is to achieve all-round development of his abilities, including, for example, the ability to think."[21]

It is important to recognize the two-way connection between human development and the productive forces in Marx's vision. This connection is unsurprising seeing as how Marx always treated "the human being himself" as "the main force of production." And he always saw "forces of production and social relations" as "two different sides of the development of the social individual." Accordingly, communism can represent a real union of all the individual producers with the conditions of production only if it ensures each individual's right to participate to the fullest of her or his ability in the cooperative utilization and development of these conditions. The highly socialized character of production means that "individuals must appropriate the existing totality of productive forces, not only to achieve self-activity, but, also, merely to safeguard their very existence." In order to be an effective vehicle of human development, this appropriation must not reduce individuals to minuscule, interchangeable cogs in a giant collective production machine operating outside their control in an alienated pursuit of "production for the sake of production." Instead, it must enhance "the development of human productive forces" capable of grasping and controlling social production at the human level in line with "the *development of the richness of human nature as an end in itself.*" Although communist "appropriation [has] a universal character corresponding to...the productive forces," it also promotes "the development of the individual capacities corresponding to the material instruments of production." Because these instruments "have been developed to a totality and...only exist within a universal intercourse," their effective appropriation requires "the development of a totality of capacities in the individuals themselves." In short, "the genuine and free development of individuals" under communism is both enabled by and contributes to "the universal character of the activity of individuals on the basis of the existing productive forces."[22]

B. Planned, Non-Market Production

In Marx's view, a system run by freely associated producers and their communities, socially unified with necessary conditions of production, by definition excludes commodity exchange and money as primary forms of social reproduction. Along with the decommodification of labor power comes an explicitly "socialised production," in which "society"—not capitalists and wage-laborers responding to market signals—"distributes labour-power and means of production to the different branches of production." As a result, "the money-capital" (including the payment of wages) "is eliminated." During communism's lower phase, "the producers may...receive paper vouchers entitling them to withdraw from the social supplies of consumer goods a quantity corresponding to their labour-time"; but "these vouchers are not money. They do not circulate." In other words, "the future distribution of the necessaries of life" cannot be treated "as a kind of more exalted wages."[23]

For Marx, the domination of social production by the market is specific to a situation in which production is carried out in independently organized production units on the basis of the producers' social separation from necessary conditions of production. Here, the labors expended in the mutually autonomous enterprises (competing capitals, as Marx calls them) can only be validated as part of society's reproductive division of labor *ex post*, according to the prices their products fetch in the market. In short, "commodities are the direct products of isolated independent individual kinds of labour," and they cannot be directly "compared with one another as products of social labour"; hence "through their alienation in the course of individual exchange they must prove that they are general social labour."[24]

By contrast, "communal labour-time or labour-time of directly associated individuals...is *immediately social* labour-time." And "where labour is communal, the relations of men in their social production do not manifest themselves as 'values' of 'things'":

> Within the co-operative society based on common ownership of the means of production, the producers do not exchange their products; just as little does the labour employed on the products appear here *as the value* of these products, as a material quality possessed by them, since now, in contrast to capitalist society, individual labour no longer exists in an indirect fashion but directly as a component part of the total labour.[25]

The *Grundrisse* draws a more extended contrast between the indirect, *ex post* establishment of labor as social labor under capitalism and the direct, *ex ante* socialization of labor "on the basis of common appropriation and control of the means of production":

> The communal character of production would make the product into a communal, general product from the outset. The exchange which originally takes place in production—which would not be an exchange of exchange values but of activities, determined by the communal needs and communal purposes— would from the outset include the participation of the individual in the communal world of products. On the basis of exchange values, labour is *posited* as general only through *exchange*. But on this foundation it would be *posited* as such before exchange; i.e. the exchange of products would in no way be the *medium* by which the participation of the individual in general production is mediated. Mediation must, of course, take place. In the first case, which proceeds from the independent production of individuals...mediations take place through the exchange of commodities, through exchange values and through money....In the second case, the *presupposition is itself mediated*; i.e. a communal production, communality, is presupposed as the basis of production. The labour of the individual is posited from the outset as social labour....The product does not first have to be transposed into a particular form in order to attain a general character for the individual. Instead of a division of labour, such as is necessarily created with the exchange of exchange values, there would take place an organization of labour whose consequence would be the participation of the individual in communal consumption.[26]

The immediately social character of labor and products is thus a logical outgrowth of the new communal union between the producers and necessary conditions of production. This de-alienation of production negates the necessity for the producers to engage in monetary exchanges as a means of establishing a reproductive allocation of their labor:

> The very necessity of first transforming individual products or activities into *exchange value*, into *money*, so that they obtain and demonstrate their social *power* in this *objective* form, proves two things: (1) That individuals now produce only for society and in society; (2) that production is not *directly* social, is not "the offspring of association," which distributes labour internally. Individuals are subsumed under social production; social production exists outside them as their fate; but social production is not subsumed under individuals, manageable by them as their common wealth.[27]

That the bypassing of market exchange and the overcoming of workers' alienation from production are two aspects of the same phenomenon explains why, in at least one instance, Marx defines communism simply as "dissolution of the mode of production and form of society based on exchange value. Real positing of individual labour as social and vice versa." Communism's "directly associated labour...is entirely inconsistent with the production of commodities."[28]

As noted earlier, academic debates over the "economics of socialism" have tended to focus on technical issues of allocative efficiency ("socialist calculation"). Marx and Engels themselves often argued that the post-capitalist economy would enjoy superior planning and allocative capabilities compared to capitalism. In *Capital*, Marx describes "freely associated" production as "consciously regulated...in accordance with a settled plan." With "the means of production in common,...the labour-power of all the different individuals is consciously applied as the combined labour-power of the community...in accordance with a definite social plan [which] maintains the proper proportion between the different kinds of work to be done and the various wants of the community." In *The Civil War in France*, Marx projects that "united cooperative societies" will "regulate national production upon a common plan, thus taking it under their own control, and putting an end to the constant anarchy and periodic convulsions which are the fatality of capitalist production."[29]

Nonetheless, Marx and Engels did not treat planned resource allocation as the most fundamental factor distinguishing communism from capitalism. For them, the more basic characteristic of communism is its de-alienation of the conditions of production *vis-à-vis* the producers, and the enabling effect this new union would have on free human development. Stated differently, they treated communism's planning and allocative capacities as symptoms and instruments of the human developmental impulses unleashed by the new communality of the producers and their conditions of existence. Communism's decommodification of production is, as discussed above, the flip side of the de-alienation of production conditions. The planning of production is just the allocative form of this reduced stunting of humans' capabilities by their material and social conditions of existence. As Marx says, commodity exchange is only "the bond natural to individuals within specific limited relations of production"; and the "alien and independent character" in which this bond "exists *vis-à-vis* individuals proves only that the latter are still engaged in the creation of the conditions of their social life, and that they have not yet begun, on the basis of these conditions, to live it." Hence, the reason communism is "a society organised for co-operative working on a planned basis" is not in order to pursue productive efficiency for its own sake, but rather "to ensure all members of society the means of existence and the full development of their capacities." This human developmental dimension also helps explain why communism's "cooperative labor...developed to national dimensions" is not, in Marx's projection, governed by any centralized state power; rather, "the system starts with the self-government of the communities." In this sense, communism can be defined as "the people acting for itself by itself," or "the reabsorption of the state power by society as its own living forces instead of as forces controlling and subduing it."[30]

2. Marx's Communism, Ecology, and Sustainability

Many have questioned the economic practicality of communism as projected by Marx. Fewer have addressed the human development dimension of Marx's vision, one major exception being those critics who argue that it anchors free human development in human technological domination and abuse of nature, with natural resources viewed as effectively limitless. It is useful to address this environmental dimension on three levels: (1) the responsibility of communism to manage its use of natural conditions; (2) the ecological significance of expanded free time; (3) the growth of wealth and the use of labor time as a measure of the cost of production.

A. Managing the Commons Communally

That communist society might have a strong commitment to protect and improve natural conditions appears surprising, given the conventional wisdom that Marx presumed "natural resources" to be "inexhaustible," and thus saw no need for "an environment-preserving, ecologically conscious, employment-sharing socialism." Marx evidently assumed that "scarce resources (oil, fish, iron ore, stockings, or whatever)...would not be scarce" under communism. The conventional wisdom further argues that Marx's "faith in the ability of an improved mode of production to eradicate scarcity indefinitely" means that his communist vision provides "no basis for recognizing any interest in the liberation of nature" from anti-ecological "human domination." Marx's technological optimism—his "faith in the creative dialectic"—is said to rule out any concern about the possibility that "modern technology interacting with the earth's physical environment might imbalance the whole basis of modern industrial civilization."[31]

In reality, Marx was deeply concerned with capitalism's tendency toward "sapping the original sources of all wealth, the soil and the labourer." And he repeatedly emphasized the imperative for post-capitalist society to manage its use of natural conditions responsibly. This helps explain his insistence on the extension of communal property to the land and other "sources of life." Indeed, Marx strongly criticized the Gotha Programme for not making it "sufficiently clear that land is included in the instruments of labour" in this connection. In Marx's view, the "Association, applied to land,...reestablishes, now on a rational basis, no longer mediated by serfdom, overlordship and the silly mysticism of [private] property, the intimate ties of man with the earth, since the earth ceases to be an object of huckstering." As with other means of production, this "common property" in land "does not mean the restoration of the old original common ownership, but the institution of a far higher and more developed form of possession in common."[32]

Marx does not see this communal property as conferring a right to overexploit land and other natural conditions in order to serve the production and consumption needs of the associated producers. Instead, he foresees an eclipse of capitalist notions of land *ownership* by a communal system of *user rights and responsibilities*:

> From the standpoint of a higher economic form of society, private ownership of the globe by single individuals will appear quite as absurd as private ownership of one man by another. Even a whole society, a nation, or even all simultaneously existing societies taken together, are not the owners of the globe. They are only its possessors, its usufructuaries, and, like *boni patres familias*, they must hand it down to succeeding generations in an improved condition.[33]

Marx's projection of communal landed property clearly does not connote a right of "owners" (either individuals or society as a whole) to unrestricted use based on "possession." Rather, like all communal property in the new union,

MARX'S VISION OF SUSTAINABLE HUMAN DEVELOPMENT 47

it confers the right to *responsibly utilize* the land as a condition of free human development, and indeed as a basic source (together with labor) of "the entire range of permanent necessities of life required by the chain of successive generations." As Marx says, the association treats "the soil as *eternal* communal property, an *inalienable* condition for the existence and reproduction of a chain of successive generations of the human race."[34]

Why have the ecological critics missed this crucial element of Marx's vision? The answer may lie in the ongoing influence of so-called "tragedy of the commons" models, which (mis)identify common property with uncontrolled "open access" to natural resources by independent users. In reality, the dynamics posited by these models have more in common with the anarchy of capitalist competition than with Marx's vision of communal rights and responsibilities regarding the use of natural conditions. Indeed, the ability of traditional communal property systems to sustainably utilize common pool resources has been the subject of a growing body of research in recent years. This research arguably supports the potential for ecological management through a communalization of natural conditions in post-capitalist society.[35]

Marx's emphasis on the future society's responsibility toward the land follows from his projection of the inherent unity of humanity and nature being realized both consciously and socially under communism. For Marx and Engels, people and nature are not "two separate 'things'"; hence they speak of humanity having "an historical nature and a natural history." They observe how extra-human nature has been greatly altered by human production and development, so that "the nature that preceded human history...today no longer exists"; but they also recognize the ongoing importance of "natural instruments of production" in the use of which "individuals are subservient to nature." Communism, far from rupturing or trying to overcome the necessary unity of people and nature, makes this unity more transparent and places it at the service of a sustainable development of people as natural and social beings. Engels thus envisions the future society as one in which people will "not only feel but also know their oneness with nature." Marx goes so far as to define communism as "the unity of being of man with nature."[36]

Naturally, it will still be necessary for communist society to "wrestle with Nature to satisfy [its] wants, to maintain and reproduce life." Marx thus refers to "the associated producers rationally regulating their interchange with nature, bringing it under their common control." Such a rational regulation or "real conscious mastery of Nature" presumes that the producers have "become masters of their own social organisation."[37] But it does not presume that humanity has overcome all natural limits; nor does it presume that the producers have attained complete technological control over natural forces.

For instance, Marx sees the associated producers setting aside a portion of the surplus product as a "reserve or insurance fund to provide against misadventures, disturbances through natural events, etc." especially in agriculture. Uncertainties connected with the natural conditions of production ("destruction caused by extraordinary phenomena of nature, fire, flood, etc.") are to be dealt with through "a continuous relative over-production," that is, "production on a larger scale than is necessary for the simple replacement and reproduction of the existing wealth." More specifically, "There must be on the one hand a certain quantity of fixed capital produced in excess of that which is directly required; on the other hand, and particularly, there must be a supply of raw materials, etc., in excess of the direct annual requirements (this applies especially to means of subsistence)." Marx also envisions a "calculation of probabilities" to help ensure that society is "in possession of the means of production required to compensate for the extraordinary destruction caused by accidents and natural forces."[38]

Obviously, "this sort of over-production is tantamount to control by society over the material means of its own reproduction" only in the sense of a far-sighted regulation of the productive interchanges between society and uncontrollable natural conditions. It is in this prudential sense that Marx foresees the associated producers "direct[ing] production from the outset so that the yearly grain supply depends only to a very minimum on the variations in the weather; the sphere of production—the supply- and the use-aspects thereof—is rationally regulated." It is simply judicious for "the producers themselves…to spend a part of their labour, or of the products of their labour in order to insure their products, their wealth, or the elements of their wealth, against accidents, etc." "Within capitalist society," by contrast, uncontrollable natural conditions impart a needless "element of anarchy" to social reproduction.[39]

Contradicting their ecological critics, Marx and Engels simply do not identify free human development with a one-sided human domination or control of nature. According to Engels,

> Freedom does not consist in the dream of independence of natural laws, but in the knowledge of these laws, and in the possibility this gives of systematically making them work towards definite ends. This holds good in relation both to the laws of external nature and to those which govern the bodily and mental existence of men themselves—two classes of laws which we can separate from each other at most only in thought but not in reality. . . . Freedom therefore consists in the control over ourselves and over external nature which is founded on natural necessity.

B. Expanded Free Time and Sustainable Human Development

In short, Marx and Engels envision a "real human freedom" based on "an existence in harmony with the established laws of nature."[40]

B. Expanded Free Time and Sustainable Human Development

Marx's ecological critics often argue that his vision of expanded free time under communism is anti-ecological because it embodies an ethic of human self-realization through the overcoming of natural constraints. Routley, for example, suggests that Marx adopts "the view of bread labor as necessarily alienated, and hence as something to be reduced to an absolute minimum through automation. The result must be highly energy-intensive and thus given any foreseeable, realistic energy scenario, environmentally damaging." For Marx, evidently, "it is the fact that bread labor ties man to nature which makes it impossible for it to be expressive of what is truly and fully human; thus, it is only when man has overcome the necessity to spend time on bread labour that he or she can be thought of as mastering nature and becoming fully human." Less dramatically, Walker points to a tension between Marx's vision of expanding free time, which "clearly implies that there must be resources over and above those needed for a bare minimum of survival," and Marx's purported failure to "mention...limitations on available natural resources."[41]

The preceding discussion has already done much to dispel the notions that Marx and Engels were unconcerned about natural resource management under communism, and that they foresaw a progressive *separation* of human development from nature as such. However, it must also be pointed out that the ecological critics have mischaracterized the relation between free time and work time under communism. It is true that, for Marx, the "development of human energy which is an end in itself...lies beyond the actual sphere of material production," that is, beyond that "labour which is determined by necessity and mundane considerations." But for Marx, this "true realm of freedom...can blossom forth only with [the] realm of necessity as its basis," and the relationship between the two realms is by no means one of simple *opposition* as claimed by the ecological critics. As Marx says, the "quite different...free character" of directly associated labor, where "labour-time is reduced to a normal length and, furthermore, labour is no longer [from the standpoint of the producers as a whole] performed for someone else," means that "labour time itself cannot remain in the abstract antithesis to free time in which it appears from the perspective of bourgeois economy":

> Free time—which is both idle time and time for higher activity—has naturally transformed its possessor into a different subject, and he then enters into the direct production process as this different subject. This process is then both discipline, as regards the human being in the process of becoming; and, at the

same time, practice, experimental science, materially creative and objectifying science, as regards the human being who has become, in whose head exists the accumulated knowledge of society.[42]

In Marx's vision, the enhancement of free human development through reductions in work time resonates positively with the development of human capabilities in the realm of production which still appears as a "metabolism" of society and nature. Marx's emphases on "theoretical and practical" education, and on the de-alienation of science *vis-à-vis* the producers, are quite relevant in this connection. Marx sees communism's diffusion and development of scientific knowledge taking the form of new combinations of natural and social science, projecting that

> natural science...will become the basis of *human* science, as it has already become the basis of actual human life, albeit in an estranged form. One basis for life and another basis for science is *a priori* a lie.... Natural science will in time incorporate into itself the science of man, just as the science of man will incorporate into itself natural science: there will be *one* science.[43]

This intrinsic unity of social and natural science is, of course, a logical corollary of the intrinsic unity of humanity and nature. Accordingly, Marx and Engels "know only a single science, the science of history. One can look at history from two sides and divide it into the history of nature and the history of men. The two sides are, however, inseparable; the history of nature and the history of men are dependent on each other so long as men exist."[44]

In short, the founders of Marxism did not envision communism's reduced work time in terms of a progressive separation of human development from nature. Nor did they see expanded free time being filled by orgies of consumption for consumption's sake. Rather, reduced work time is viewed as a necessary condition for the intellectual development of social individuals capable of mastering the scientifically developed forces of nature and social labor in environmentally *and* humanly rational fashion. The "increase of free time" appears here as "time for the full development of the individual" capable of "the grasping of his own history as a *process*, and the recognition of nature (equally present as practical power over nature) as his real body." The intellectual development of the producers during free time *and* work time is clearly central to the process by which communist labor's "social character is posited...in the production process not in a merely natural, spontaneous form, but as an activity regulating all the forces of nature."[45] Far from anti-ecological, this process is such that the producers and their communities become more theoretically and practically aware of natural wealth as an eternal condition of production, free time, and human life itself.

MARX'S VISION OF SUSTAINABLE HUMAN DEVELOPMENT 51

The ecological critics also seem to have missed the potential for increased free time as a means of *reducing* the pressure of production on the natural environment. Specifically, rising productivity of social labor need not increase material and energy throughput insofar as the producers are compensated by reductions in work time instead of greater material consumption. However, this aspect of free time as a measure of wealth is best located in the context of communism's transformation of human needs.

C. Wealth, Human Needs, and Labor Cost

Some would argue that insofar as Marx envisions communism encouraging a shared sense of responsibility toward nature, this responsibility remains wedded to an anti-ecological conception of nature as primarily an instrument or material of human labor. Alfred Schmidt, for example, suggests that "when Marx and Engels complain about the unholy plundering of nature, they are not concerned with nature itself but with considerations of economic utility." Routley asserts that for Marx, "Nature is apparently to be respected to the extent, and *only* to the extent, that it becomes man's handiwork, his or her artifact and self-expression, and is thus a reflection of man and part of man's identity."[46]

It should be clear from our previous discussion that any dichotomy between "economic utility" and "nature itself" is completely alien to Marx's materialism. A related point is that Marx's conception of wealth or use value encompasses "the manifold variety of human needs," whether these needs be physical, cultural, or aesthetic. In this broad human developmental sense, "use value...can quite generally be characterised as the *means of life*." David Pepper rightly concludes that "Marx did see nature's role as 'instrumental' to humans, but to him instrumental value...included nature as a source of aesthetic, scientific and moral value."[47]

As per "man's handiwork," Marx does not employ an oppositional conception of labor and nature in which the former merely subsumes the latter. He insists that the human capacity to work, or labor power, is itself "a natural object, a thing, although a living conscious thing"; hence labor is a process in which the worker "opposes himself to Nature *as one of her own forces*" and "appropriates *Nature's productions* in a form *adapted to* his own wants." Marx views labor as "a process in which both man and Nature participate...the necessary condition for effecting exchange of matter between man and Nature" in production. As a "universal condition for the metabolic interaction between nature and man," labor is "a natural condition of human life...independent of, equally common to, all particular social forms of human life." Labor is, of course, only part of "the universal metabolism of nature" and

as a materialist Marx insists that "the earth...exists independently of man."
In this ontological sense, "the priority of external nature remains unassailed,"
even though Marx does insist on the importance of social relations in the
structuring of the productive "metabolism" between humanity and nature.[48]

But what of Marx and Engels's notorious references to continued growth
in the production of wealth under communism? Are these not immanently
anti-ecological? Here it must be emphasized that these growth projections are
always made in close connection with Marx's vision of free and well-rounded
human development, not with growth of material production and consumption for their own sake. Accordingly, they always refer to growth of wealth in
a general sense, encompassing the satisfaction of needs other than those
requiring the industrial processing of natural resources (matter and energy
throughput). In discussing the "higher phase of communist society," for example, Marx makes the "to each according to his needs" criterion conditional
upon a situation where "the enslaving sub-ordination of individuals under
division of labour, and therewith also the antithesis between mental and
physical labour, has vanished; after labour, from a mere means of life, has itself
become the prime necessity of life; after the productive forces have also
increased with the all-round development of the individual." Similarly, Engels
does refer to "a practically limitless growth of production," but then fills out
his conception of "practical" in terms of the priority "of securing for every
member of society...an existence which is not only fully sufficient from a
material standpoint...but also guarantees to them the completely unrestricted development of their physical and mental faculties."[49] Such human development need not involve a limitless growth of material consumption.

For Marx, communism's "progressive expansion of the process of reproduction" encompasses the entire "living process of the *society* of producers"
and, as discussed earlier, he specifies the "material and intellectual advantages" of this "social development" in holistic human developmental terms.
When Marx and Engels envision communism as "an organisation of production and intercourse which will make possible the normal satisfaction of
needs...limited only by the needs themselves," they do not mean a complete
satiation of limitlessly expanding needs of all kinds:

> Communist organisation has a twofold effect on the desires produced in the
> individual by present-day relations; some of these desires—namely desires
> which exist under all relations, and only change their form and direction under
> different social relations—are merely altered by the communist social system,
> for they are given the opportunity to develop normally; but others—namely
> those originating solely in a particular society, under particular conditions of
> production and intercourse—are totally deprived of their conditions of exis-

MARX'S VISION OF SUSTAINABLE HUMAN DEVELOPMENT 53

tence. Which will be merely changed and which eliminated in a communist society can only be determined in a practical way.[50]

As Ernest Mandel points out, this social and human developmental approach to need satisfaction is quite different from the "absurd notion" of unqualified "abundance" often ascribed to Marx, that is, "a regime of unlimited access to a boundless supply of all goods and services." Although communist need satisfaction is consistent with a "definition of abundance [as] *saturation of demand*," this has to be located in the context of a hierarchy of "basic needs, secondary needs that become indispensable with the growth of civilization, and luxury, inessential or even harmful needs." Marx's human developmental vision basically foresees a satiation of basic needs and a gradual extension of this satiation to secondary needs as they develop socially through expanded free time and cooperative worker-community control over production—*not* a full satiation of all conceivable needs.[51]

Here, one begins to see the full ecological significance of free time as a measure of communist wealth. Specifically, if the secondary needs developed and satisfied during free time are less material and energy intensive, their increasing weight in total needs should reduce the pressure of production on limited natural conditions. This is crucial insofar as Marx's vision has the producers using their newfound material security and expanded free time to engage in a variety of intellectual and aesthetic forms of self-development.[52] Such a development of secondary needs is to be enhanced by the greater opportunities that real worker-community control provides for people to become informed participants in economic, political, and cultural life.

Of course, labor (along with nature) remains a fundamental source of wealth under communism. This, together with the priority of expanded free time, means that the amounts of social labor expended in the production of different goods and services will still be an important measure of their *cost*. As Marx explains in the *Grundrisse:*

> On the basis of communal production, the determination of time remains, of course, essential. The less time the society requires to produce wheat, cattle etc., the more time it wins for other production, material or mental. Just as in the case of an individual, the multiplicity of its development, its enjoyment and its activity depends on economization of time. Economy of time, to this all economy ultimately reduces itself. Society likewise has to distribute its time in a purposeful way, in order to achieve a production adequate to its overall needs; just as the individual has to distribute his time correctly in order to achieve knowledge in proper proportions or in order to satisfy the various demands on his activity. Thus, economy of time, along with the planned distribution of labour time among the various branches of production, remains the first economic law on the basis of communal production. It becomes law, there, to an even higher degree.

Marx immediately adds, however, that communism's economy of time "is essentially different from a measurement of exchange values (labour or products) by labour time." For one thing, communism's use of labor time as a measure of cost "is accomplished...by the direct and conscious control of society over its working time—which is possible only with common ownership," unlike the situation under capitalism, where the "regulation" of social labor time is only accomplished indirectly, "by the movement of commodity prices." More importantly, communism's economy of labor time serves use value, especially the expansion of free time, whereas capitalism's economy of time is geared toward increasing the surplus labor time expended by the producers.[53]

Marx and Engels do not, moreover, project labor time as the sole guide to resource-allocation decisions under communism: they only indicate that it is to be one important measure of the social costs of different kinds of production. That "production...under the actual, predetermining control of society...establishes a relation between the volume of social labour-time applied in producing definite articles, and the volume of the social want to be satisfied by these articles" in no way implies that environmental costs are left out of account. Equivalently, it does not preclude the maintenance and improvement of natural conditions from being included under the "social wants to be satisfied" by production and consumption.[54]

For strong evidence that Marx and Engels did not see communism prioritizing minimum labor cost over ecological goals, one need only point to their insistence on the "abolition of the antithesis between town and country" as "a direct necessity of...production and, moreover, of public health." Observing capitalism's ecologically disruptive urban concentrations of industry and population, industrialized agriculture, and failure to recycle human and livestock wastes, Marx and Engels early on pointed to the "abolition of the contradiction between town and country" as "one of the first conditions of communal life." As Engels later put it: "The present poisoning of the air, water and land can only be put an end to by the fusion of town and country" under "one single vast plan." Despite its potential cost to society in terms of increased labor time, he viewed this fusion as "no more and no less utopian than the abolition of the antithesis between capitalist and wage-workers." It was even "a practical demand of both industrial and agricultural production." In his *magnum opus*, Marx foresaw communism forging a "higher synthesis" of "the old bond of union which held together agriculture and manufacture in their infancy." This new union would work toward a "restoration" of "the naturally grown conditions for the maintenance of [the] circulation of matter...under a form appropriate to the full development of the human race." Accordingly, Engels ridiculed Dühring's projection "that the union between

3. Capitalism, Communism, and the Struggle Over Human Development

agriculture and industry will nevertheless be carried through even *against* economic considerations, as if this would be some economic sacrifice!"[55] It is obvious that Marx and Engels would gladly accept increases in social labor time in return for an ecologically more sound production.

Still, one need not accept the notion, repeated *ad nauseam* by Marx's ecological critics, of an inherent opposition between labor cost reductions and environmental friendliness. Marx's communism would dispense with the waste of natural resources *and* labor associated with capitalism's "anarchical system of competition" and "vast number of employments...in themselves superfluous." Many anti-ecological use values could be eliminated or greatly reduced under a planned system of labor allocation and land use, among them advertising, the excessive processing and packaging of food and other goods, planned obsolescence of products, and the automobile. All these destructive use values are "indispensable" for capitalism; but from the standpoint of environmental sustainability they represent "the most outrageous squandering of labour-power and of the social means of production."[56]

3. Capitalism, Communism, and the Struggle Over Human Development

Marx argues that "if we did not find concealed in society as it is the material conditions of production and the corresponding relations of exchange prerequisite for a classless society, then all attempts to explode it would be quixotic." He refers to "development of the productive forces of social labour" as capitalism's "historical task and justification...the way in which it unconsciously creates the material requirements of a higher mode of production." In short, the "original unity between the worker and the conditions of production...can be re-established only on the material foundation which capital creates."[57]

Time and again, Marx's ecological critics have found in such pronouncements evidence that he uncritically endorsed capitalism's anti-ecological subjugation of nature to human purposes, and that he saw this subjugation continuing and even deepening under communism. Ted Benton, for example, asserts that in seeing capitalism as "preparing the conditions for future human emancipation," Marx shared "the blindness to natural limits already present in...the spontaneous ideology of 19th-century industrialism." This critique may be viewed as an ecological variation on Nove's theme that Marx thought "the problem of production had been 'solved' by capitalism," so that communism would not be required "to take seriously the problem of the allocation of scarce resources."[58]

In addition to bypassing Marx and Engels's deep concern with natural resource management and, more fundamentally, with the de-alienation of nature and the producers, under communism, these ecological critics have also misinterpreted Marx's conceptions of capitalist development and the transition from capitalism to communism.

What, exactly, is the historical potential capitalism creates in Marx's view? Does it lie in the development of mass production and consumption to the point where all scarcity disappears? Not really. It is, first, that by developing the productive forces, capitalism creates the possibility of a system "in which coercion and monopolisation of social development (including its material and intellectual advantages) by one portion of society at the expense of another are eliminated," partly through a "greater reduction of time devoted to material labour in general." In short, insofar as it develops human productive capabilities, capitalism negates, not scarcity as such (in the sense of a non-satisfaction of all conceivable material needs), but rather the scarcity rationale for class inequalities in human developmental opportunities. As Marx indicates, "Although at first the development of the capacities of the human species takes place at the cost of the majority of human individuals and even classes, in the end it breaks through this contradiction and coincides with the development of the individual."[59]

Secondly, capitalism potentiates less restricted forms of human development insofar as it makes production an increasingly broad social process, "a system of general social metabolism, of universal relations, of all-round needs and universal capacities." Only with this socialized production can one foresee "free individuality, based on the universal development of individuals and on their subordination of their communal, social productivity as their social wealth." For Marx, capitalism's development of "the universality of intercourse, hence the world market" connotes "the possibility of the universal development of the individual." As always, it is with all-round human development in mind (not growth of production and consumption for their own sake) that Marx praises "the universality of individual needs, capacities, pleasures, productive forces etc., created through universal exchange" under capitalism.

The same goes for people-nature relations. The potential Marx sees in capitalism does not involve a one-sided human subordination of, or separation from, nature, but rather the possibility of less restricted relations between humanity and nature. It is only by comparison with these richer, more universal human-nature relations that "all earlier ones appear as mere *local developments* of humanity and as *nature-idolatry*." In earlier modes of production, "the restricted attitude of men to nature determines their restricted relation to one another, and their restricted attitude to one another deter-

MARX'S VISION OF SUSTAINABLE HUMAN DEVELOPMENT   57

mines men's restricted relation to nature."[60]

Marx's analysis would only be anti-ecological if it had *uncritically* endorsed capitalism's appropriation of natural conditions. In fact, Marx emphasizes "the alienated form" of "the objective conditions of labour," including nature, in capitalist society. He insists that capitalism's alienation of "the general social powers of labour" encompasses "natural forces and scientific knowledge." As a result, in his view, "the forces of nature and science...confront the labourers as *powers* of capital." Under capitalism, "science, natural forces and products of labour on a large scale" are utilized mainly "as *means for the exploitation* of labour, as means of appropriating surplus-labour." Nor is Marx's critique of capital's use of natural resources limited to the exploitation directly suffered by workers in production and the limits it places on workers' consumption. As shown by John Bellamy Foster, Marx had a profound grasp of the broader "metabolic rift" between humanity and nature produced by capitalism, one symptom of which is the anti-ecological division of labor between town and country with its "irreparable break in the coherence of social interchange prescribed by the natural laws of life." Marx used this framework to explain how capitalism both "violates the conditions necessary to lasting fertility of the soil" and "destroys the health of the town labourer." According to Engels, the system's alienation of nature is manifested in the narrow viewpoint on nature's utility necessarily adopted by "individual capitalists," who "are able to concern themselves only with the most immediate useful effect of their actions" in terms of "the profit to be made"—ignoring "the natural effects of the same actions."[61]

For Marx, the "alienated, independent, social power" attained by nature and other "conditions of production" under capitalism poses a challenge to workers and their communities: to convert these conditions "into general, communal, social, conditions" serving "the requirements of socially developed human beings...the living process of the *society* of producers." Such a conversion requires a prolonged struggle to qualitatively transform the system of production, both materially and socially. Communist production is not simply inherited from capitalism, needing only to be signed into law by a newly elected socialist government. It requires "long struggles, through a series of historic processes, transforming circumstances and men." Among these transformed circumstances will be "not only a change of distribution, but a new organization of production, or rather the delivery (setting free) of the social forms of production...of their present class character, and their harmonious national and international co-ordination." This "long struggle" scenario for post-revolutionary society is a far cry from the interpretation put forth by the ecological critics, which has Marx endorsing capitalist industry as a qualitatively appropriate basis for communist development. Indeed, Marx's vision corresponds more accurately to Roy Morrison's view that the "struggle for the creation of an ecological commons is the struggle for the building of an ecological democracy—community by community, neighborhood by neighborhood, region by region...the struggle and work of fundamental social transformation from below."[62]

In Marx's view, the struggle for "the conditions of free and associated labour...will be again and again relented and impeded by the resistance of vested interests and class egotisms." This is precisely why communism's human developmental conditions will be generated in large part by the revolutionary struggle itself—both in the taking of political power by the working class and in the subsequent struggle to transform material and social conditions. As Marx and Engels put it, communist "appropriation...can only be effected through a union, which by the character of the proletariat itself can again only be a universal one, and through a revolution, in which, on the one hand, the power of the earlier mode of production and intercourse and social organisation is overthrown, and, on the other hand, there develops the universal character and the energy of the proletariat, which are required to accomplish the appropriation, and the proletariat moreover rids itself of everything that still clings to it from its previous position in society."[63]

By now it should be clear why Marx argued that "the emancipation of the working classes must be conquered by the working classes themselves." The struggle for human development ultimately requires "the abolition of all class rule," and the working class is the only group capable of undertaking such a project. The self-emancipatory nature of communism also explains why Marx's vision does not take the form of a detailed blueprint à la the utopian socialists. As Alan Shandro observes, any such blueprint would only foreclose political debates, conflicts, and strategies developed by the working class itself "understood as a unity in diversity, as a political community." Marx and Engels's attempts to envision communism's basic principles should be seen not as a "master plan" but "as means of organising the workers' movement and structuring and guiding debate in and around it." Although their projections need to be constantly updated in light of developments in capitalist and post-revolutionary societies, their basic approach is still relevant today.[64]

The demand for more equitable and sustainable forms of human development is central to the growing worldwide rebellion against elite economic institutions—transnational corporations, the IMF, World Bank, NAFTA, WTO, and so on. But this movement needs a vision that conceives the various institutions and policies under protest as elements of one class-exploitative system: capitalism. And it needs a framework for the debate, reconciliation,

MARX'S VISION OF SUSTAINABLE HUMAN DEVELOPMENT   59

and realization of alternative pathways and strategies for negating the power of capital over the conditions of human development: that framework is communism. The classical Marxist vision of communism as de-alienation of production in service of human development still has much to contribute to this needed framework.

Notes

1. Oskar Lange and Fred M. Taylor, *On the Economic Theory of Socialism* (New York: McGraw-Hill, 1964); "Socialism: Alternative Views and Models," symposium in *Science & Society* 56, no. 4 (Spring 1992); "Building Socialism Theoretically: Alternatives to Capitalism and the Invisible Hand," symposium in *Science & Society* 66, no. 1 (Spring 2002); Ernesto Che Guevara, "Man and Socialism in Cuba," in *Man and Socialism in Cuba: The Great Debate*, ed. Bertram Silverman (New York: Atheneum, 1973), 337, 350.

2. For prior discussions of Marx's vision of communism, see Paresh Chattopadhyay, "Socialism: Utopian and Feasible," *Monthly Review* 37, no. 10 (March 1986); Bertell Ollman, "Marx's Vision of Communism," in *Social and Sexual Revolution: Essays on Marx and Reich* (Boston: South End Press, 1979).

3. Herman E. Daly, *Steady-State Economics*, 2nd ed. (London: Earthscan, 1992), 196; Robyn Eckersley, *Environmentalism and Political Theory* (Albany: State University of New York Press, 1992), 80; Victor Ferkiss, *Nature, Technology, and Society* (New York: New York University Press, 1993), 110; K. J. Walker, "Ecological Limits and Marxian Thought," *Politics* 14, no. 1 (May 1979), 35–6; Val Routley, "On Karl Marx as an Environmental Hero," *Environmental Ethics* 3, no. 3 (Fall 1981), 242. For additional references to ecological criticisms of Marx's communism, see John Bellamy Foster, "Marx and the Environment," *Monthly Review* 47, no. 3 (July–August 1995), 108–9; Paul Burkett, *Marx and Nature: A Red and Green Perspective* (New York: St. Martin's Press, 1999), 147–8, 223.

4. Karl Polanyi, *The Great Transformation* (New York: Farrar & Rinehart, 1944); Thomas E. Weisskopf, "Marxian Crisis Theory and the Contradictions of Late Twentieth-Century Capitalism," *Rethinking Marxism* 4, no. 4 (Winter 1991); Blair Sandler, "Grow or Die: Marxist Theories of Capitalism and the Environment," *Rethinking Marxism* 7, no. 2 (Summer 1994); Andriana Vlachou, "Nature and Value Theory," *Science & Society* 66, no. 2 (Summer 2002).

5. Paul Auerbach and Peter Skott, "Capitalist Trends and Socialist Priorities," *Science & Society* 57, no. 2 (Summer 1993), 195.

6. Karl Marx, *Value, Price and Profit* (New York: International Publishers, 1976), 39; *Theories of Surplus Value*, part 3 (Moscow: Progress Publishers, 1971), 271–2; *Theories of Surplus Value*, part 2 (Moscow: Progress Publishers, 1968), 580 (emphasis in original).

7. Frederick Engels, *Anti-Dühring* (New York: International Publishers, 1939), 221 (emphasis in original); Marx, *Theories of Surplus Value*, part 3, 525; "Drafts of the Letter to Vera Zasulich, March 8, 1881," in *Collected Works*, Karl Marx and Frederick Engels, vol. 24 (New York: International Publishers, 1989), 362 (emphasis in original).

8. Marx, *Capital*, vol. I (New York: International Publishers, 1967), 762; "Economic Manuscript of 1861–63, Conclusion," in *Collected Works*, Karl Marx and Frederick Engels, vol. 34 (New York: International Publishers, 1994), 109 (emphasis in original); Karl Marx and Frederick Engels, *The German Ideology* (Moscow: Progress Publishers, 1976), 97.

9. Karl Marx and Frederick Engels, "Manifesto of the Communist Party,' in *Selected Works* (London: Lawrence & Wishart, 1968), 47. See also Marx, *Capital*, 3:437–40; "Economic Manuscript of 1861–63, Conclusion," 108.

10. Marx, *Capital*, 3:437, 876; *Critique of the Gotha Programme* (New York: International Publishers, 1966), 7–8, 11; Frederick Engels, *The Housing Question* (Moscow: Progress Publishers, 1979), 28, 94. See also Marx, *Theories of Surplus Value*, part 1 (Moscow: Progress Publishers, 1963), 107; *Capital*, 1:530 and 2:819, 847.

11. Marx, *Capital*, 1:763; "Economic Manuscript of 1861–63, Conclusion," 109 (emphases in original); "The Civil War in France," in *On the Paris Commune*, by Karl Marx and Frederick Engels (Moscow: Progress Publishers, 1985), 75.

12. Marx and Engels, *The German Ideology*, 86–9, 309.

13. Marx, *Capital*, 1:488; Marx and Engels, "Manifesto of the Communist Party," 53.

14. Marx and Engels, "Manifesto of the Communist Party," 49; Engels, *Anti-Dühring*, 144; Marx, *Capital*, 1:78.

15. Marx, *Capital*, 1:78; *Critique of the Gotha Programme*, 8, 10.

16. Engels, *Anti-Dühring*, 220–2.

17. Marx, *Critique of the Gotha Programme*, 10; Engels, *Anti-Dühring*, 221 (emphasis in original); Marx, *Capital*, 3:876. See also Marx and Engels, *The German Ideology*, 566.

18. Marx, *Critique of the Gotha Programme*, 7–8.

19. Marx, *Critique of the Gotha Programme*, 20, 22; *Capital*, 1:488, 490; "The Civil War in France," 162.

20. Marx, *Capital*, 1:530 and 2:819–20; *Theories of Surplus Value*, part 3, 257 (emphases in original); *Grundrisse* (New York: Vintage, 1973), 708.

21. Marx, *Capital*, 1:530; "The Civil War in France," 75; Marx and Engels, *The German Ideology*, 309.

22. Marx, *Grundrisse*, 190, 706; *Theories of Surplus Value*, part 2, 117–8 (emphasis in original); Marx and Engels, *The German Ideology*, 96, 465.

23. Marx, *Capital*, 2:358; Engels, *Anti-Dühring*, 221.

24. Marx, *A Contribution to the Critique of Political Economy* (New York: International Publishers, 1970), 84–5.

25. Marx, *A Contribution to the Critique of Political Economy*, 85 (emphasis in original); *Theories of Surplus Value*, part 3, 129; *Critique of the Gotha Programme*, 8 (emphasis in original).

26. Marx, *Grundrisse*, 159, 171–2 (emphases in original).

27. Marx, *Grundrisse*, 158 (emphases in original).

28. Marx, *Grundrisse*,, 264; *Capital*, 1:94. See also Engels, *Anti-Dühring*, 337–8.

29. Marx, *Capital*, 1:78–80; "The Civil War in France," 76.

30. Marx, *Grundrisse*, 162; Engels, *Anti-Dühring*, 167; Marx, "Inaugural Address of the International Working Men's Association," in *The First International and After*, ed. David Fernbach (New York: Random House, 1974), 80; "Notes on Bakunin's Book *Statehood and Anarchy*," in *Collected Works*, Karl Marx and Frederick Engels, 24:519; "The Civil War in France," 130, 153.

31. Alec Nove, "Socialism," in *The New Palgrave: Problems of the Planned Economy*, ed. John Eatwell, Murray Milgate, and Peter Newman (New York: Norton, 1990), 230, 237; Alec Nove, *The Economics of Feasible Socialism* (London: Allen & Unwin, 1983), 15–6; Geoffrey Carpenter, "Redefining Scarcity: Marxism and Ecology Reconciled," *Democracy & Nature* 3, no. 3 (1997), 140; Andrew McLaughlin, "Ecology, Capitalism, and Socialism," *Socialism and Democracy*, no. 10 (Spring–Summer 1990), 95; Lewis S. Feuer, "Introduction," in *Karl Marx and Frederick Engels: Basic Writings on Politics and Philosophy*, ed. Lewis Feuer (Garden City, N.Y.: Anchor Books, 1989), xii.

32. Marx, *Capital*, 1:507; *Critique of the Gotha Programme*, 5–6; *Economic and Philosophical Manuscripts of 1844* (New York: International Publishers, 1964), 103; Engels, *Anti-Dühring*, 151.

MARX'S VISION OF SUSTAINABLE HUMAN DEVELOPMENT 61

33. Marx, *Capital*, 3:776.

34. Marx, *Capital*, 617, 812 (emphases added).

35. H. Scott Gordon, "The Economic Theory of a Common Property Resource: The Fishery," *Journal of Political Economy* 62, no. 2 (April 1954); Garrett Hardin, "The Tragedy of the Commons," *Science* 162 (December 1968); S. V. Ciriacy-Wantrup and Richard C. Bishop, "'Common Property' as a Concept in Natural Resource Policy," *Natural Resources Journal* 15, no. 4 (October 1975); James A. Swaney, "Common Property, Reciprocity, and Community," *Journal of Economic Issues* 24, no. 2 (June 1990); Elinor Ostrom, *Governing the Commons* (Cambridge: Cambridge University Press, 1990); Peter Usher, "Aboriginal Property Systems in Land and Resources," in *Green On Red: Evolving Ecological Socialism*, ed. Jesse Vorst, Ross Dobson, and Ron Fletcher (Winnipeg: Fernwood Publishing, 1993); Burkett, *Marx and Nature*, 246–8; Robert Biel, *The New Imperialism* (London: Zed Books, 2000), 15–8, 98–101.

36. Marx and Engels, *The German Ideology*, 45–6, 71; Frederick Engels, *Dialectics of Nature* (Moscow: Progress Publishers, 1964), 183; Marx, *Economic and Philosophical Manuscripts of 1844*, 137.

37. Marx, *Capital*, 3:820; Engels, *Anti-Dühring*, 309.

38. Marx, *Critique of the Gotha Programme*, 7; *Capital*, 2:177, 469.

39. Marx, *Capital*, 2:469; "Notes on Wagner," in *Texts on Method*, ed. Terrell Carver (Oxford, UK: Blackwell, 1975), 188; *Theories of Surplus Value*, part 3, 357–8.

40. Engels, *Anti-Dühring*, pp. 125–6.

41. Routley, "On Karl Marx as an Environmental Hero," 242; Walker, "Ecological Limits and Marxian Thought," 242–3.

42. Marx, *Capital*, 3:820; *Theories of Surplus Value*, part 3, 257; *Grundrisse*, 712.

43. Marx, *Economic and Philosophical Manuscripts of 1844*, 143 (emphasis in original).

44. Marx and Engels, *The German Ideology*, 34. See also Ollman, "Marx's Vision of Communism," 76.

45. Marx, *Grundrisse*, 542 , 612 (emphasis in original).

46. Alfred Schmidt, *The Concept of Nature in Marx* (London: New Left Books, 1971), 155; Routley, "On Karl Marx as an Environmental Hero," 243 (emphasis in original).

47. Marx, *Grundrisse*, 527; "Economic Manuscript of 1861-63, Third Chapter," in *Collected Works*, Karl Marx and Frederick Engels, vol. 30 (New York: International Publishers, 1988), 40 (emphasis in original); David Pepper, *Eco-Socialism* (London: Routledge, 1993), 64.

48. Marx, *Capital*, 1:177, 183–4, 202 (emphases added); "Economic Manuscript of 1861-63, Third Chapter," 63; Marx and Engels, *The German Ideology*, 46. For details on Marx's dialectical conception of human labor and nature, see Burkett, chapters 2–4 in *Marx and Nature*; John Bellamy Foster, *Marx's Ecology: Materialism and Nature* (New York: Monthly Review Press, 2000); John Bellamy Foster and Paul Burkett, "The Dialectic of Organic/Inorganic Relations: Marx and the Hegelian Philosophy of Nature," *Organization & Environment* 13, no. 4 (December 2000).

49. Marx, *Critique of the Gotha Programme*, 10; Engels, *Anti-Dühring*, 309.

50. *Capital*, 3:250, 819 (emphasis in original); Marx and Engels, *The German Ideology*, 273.

51. Ernest Mandel, *Power and Money: A Marxist Theory of Bureaucracy* (London: Verso, 1992), 205–7 (emphasis in original); Howard J. Sherman, "The Economics of Pure Communism," *Review of Radical Political Economics* 2, no. 4 (Winter 1970).

52. Marx, *Grundrisse*, 287; Marx and Engels, *The German Ideology*, 53.

53. Marx, *Grundrisse*, 172–3, 708; Marx to Engels, January 8, 1868, in *Selected Correspondence*, Karl Marx and Frederick Engels (Moscow: Progress Publishers, 1975), 187; Marx, *Capital*, 1:71 and 3:264.

54. Marx, *Capital*, 3:187.

55. Engels, *Anti-Dühring*, 323–4 (emphasis in original); *The Housing Question*, 92; Marx and Engels, *The German Ideology*, 72; Marx, *Capital*, 1:505–6.

56. Marx, *Capital*, 1:530. For further discussion of socialist planning, technology, and ecological efficiency, see Victor Wallis, "Socialism, Ecology, and Democracy: Toward A Strategy of Conversion," *Monthly Review* 44, no. 2 (June 1992); "Technology, Ecology, and Socialist Renewal," *Capitalism, Nature, Socialism* 12, no. 1 (March 2004).

57. Marx, *Grundrisse*, 159; *Capital*, 3:259; *Theories of Surplus Value*, part 3, 422–3.

58. Ted Benton, "Marxism and Natural Limits," *New Left Review*, no. 178 (November/December 1989), 74, 77; Nove, "Socialism," 230.

59. Marx, *Capital*, 3:819; *Theories of Surplus Value*, part 2, 118.

60. Marx, *Grundrisse*, 158, 409–10, 488, 542 (emphases in original); Marx and Engels, *The German Ideology*, 50. Toward the end of his life Marx reconsidered his earlier stance on the relative backwardness of pre-capitalist *communal* relations as supporters of human development, and argued that the traditional Russian commune could—if assisted by a European socialist revolution—make a direct transition to socialism. See *The Ethnological Notebooks of Karl Marx*, ed. Lawrence Krader (Assen, The Netherlands: Van Gorcum, 1974); "Drafts of the Letter to Vera Zasulich"; Teodor Shanin, *Late Marx and the Russian Road* (New York: Monthly Review Press, 1983); Franklin Rosemont, "Karl Marx and the Iroquois," http://www.geocities.com/cordobakaf/marx_iroquois.html.

61. Marx, "Economic Manuscript of 1861–63, Conclusion," 29; *Theories of Surplus Value*, part 1, 391–2 (emphases in original); *Capital*, 1:505 and 3:813; Engels, *Dialectics of Nature*, 185; Foster, *Marx's Ecology*, 141–77. See also Paul Burkett and John Bellamy Foster, "Metabolism, Energy and Entropy in Marx's Critique of Political Economy: Beyond the Podolinsky Myth," *Theory and Society*, forthcoming, 2006.

62. Marx, *Capital*, 3:250, 258, 264 (emphasis in original); "The Civil War in France," 76, 157; Roy Morrison, *Ecological Democracy* (Boston: South End Press, 1995), 188.

63. Marx, "The Civil War in France," 157; Marx and Engels, *The German Ideology*, 97.

64. Marx, "Provisional Rules," in *The First International and After*, 82; Alan Shandro, "Karl Marx as a Conservative Thinker," *Historical Materialism*, no. 6 (Summer 2000), 21–3; Bertell Ollman, "The Utopian Vision of the Future (Then and Now)," *Monthly Review* 57, no. 3 (July–August 2005); Michael A. Lebowitz, "Building Socialism in the 21st Century," http://mrzine. monthlyreview.org/lebowitz280705.html.

The top fifth of earners in Manhattan now make 52 times what the lowest fifth make—$365,826 compared with $7,047—which is roughly comparable to the income disparity in Namibia....Put another way, for every dollar made by households in the top fifth of Manhattan earners, households in the bottom fifth made about 2 cents.

This represents a substantial widening of the income gap from previous years. In 1980, the top fifth of earners made 21 times what the bottom fifth made in Manhattan.

—*New York Times*, September 4, 2005

Name Index

Acton, H.B. 61
Adorno, Theodor W. xxiii, 405–23, 438
Agee, James 446
Alexander the Great 551
Alexander VI, Pope 560
Allen, George 399
Allende, Salvador 280
Althusser, Louis 71, 85, 309, 457
Ammianus 530
Anderson, Kevin B. xv–xxv, 593–605
Anderson, Perry xxiv, 521–7
Arcadius, Emperor 533
Arendt, Hannah 219, 226, 232, 427
Aristotle 35, 361, 426
Arkwright, Richard 500
Aron, Raymond 194, 300
Arrighi, Giovanni 229, 230, 232
Ash, Timothy Garto 333–4
Ashton, T.S. 503, 516–17, 518
Atticus 559
Audiganne, Armand 119, 121
Avineri, Shlomo 594
Aznar, José María 281
Azurara, Gomes Eannes de 555–6

Bacon, Francis 33, 613
Baker, Dean 277
Balbus, Ike 396
Balzac, Honoré de 412
Baraka, Amiri 58
Baran, Paul A. 85, 310
Barnes, Harry Elmer 375
Barzun, Jacques 558
Bataille, Georges 581–3 *passim*
Bauer, Bruno 619
Beard, Charles A. 251, 546
Beauvoir, Simone de 583
Bebel, August 615
Bédarida, François 467–8
Beecher, J.J. 382
Beethoven, Ludwig van 407, 412, 418
Bell, Daniel 439
Bell, Sir Harold 530, 531

Benjamin, Walter 431, 432
Benner, Erica 594
Benton, Ted 643
Bergson, Henri 617
Bernal, J.D. 615, 616
Bernstein, Eduard 325
Bettelheim, Charles 197, 300
Bewick, Thomas 513
Bhagwati, Jagdish Natwarlal 221
Bibo, Istvan 358
bin Laden, Osama 231
Bismark, Otto von 224
Blair, Tony 231, 281
Bonald, Louis Gabriel Ambroise de 270, 475
Boorstein, Daniel 434
Borg, Bjorn 399
Bottomore, Tom 297
Bourdieu, Pierre 426, 430, 431
Braudel, Fernand 184, 224, 229
Bremer, Paul 285
Brenner, Robert 85, 214, 215, 229
Brougham, Lord Henry 510
Brown, John 543, 547
Brown, Peter 535
Bücher, Karl 601, 602
Bukharin, Nikolai 615, 616, 619
Bunyan, John 502
Burke, Edmund 475
Burkett, Paul xxv, 623–51
Burrin, Philippe 468
Burroughs, William S. 437
Bush, George H.W. Senior 276, 283, 398
Bush, George W. Junior 144, 276, 281, 283, 284
Butler, Bishop 52

Cage, John 437
Carlile, Richard 499
Carlyle, Thomas 459, 484, 485–8 *passim*, 514
Carson, Rachel 616
Carter, Jimmy 275
Cassiodorus 534
Caudwell, Christopher 615, 616, 619
Ceserani, Remo 446

Karl Marx

Chamberlain, Joseph 218, 230
Chandler, Raymond 448
Chaplin, Charlie 420
Charles V, King of Spain 203, 208
Chattopadhyay, Paresh 601
Chávez, Hugo Rafael 231, 288
Chodorow, Nancy 576, 577
Cicero 559
Clapham, Sir John 515–16, 503
Clements, Frederic 617, 618
Clinton, Bill 276, 283, 425
Cobbett, William 514
Cole, G.D.H. 71
Coleman, James 47
Comte, Auguste 183
Constantine, Emperor 535
Cooper, Robert 231
Cox, Oliver C. xxiv, 549–64
Crispi, Francesco 219
Crittenden, Ann 282

Daly, Herman 623
Dante (Dante Alighieri) 210
Darwin, Charles 456, 458, 460, 612, 613–14
     passim, 615, 616
Davis, Bette 420
Derrida, Jacques 444
Descartes, René 33
Dinwiddie, Gerda 375–84
Diocletian, Emperor 535
Disraeli, Benjamin 380
Dobb, Maurice 189, 195
Donoso Cortes, Juan 270
Douglass, Frederick xxiv, 543, 544, 546, 547
Dryden, Ken 399
Duchamp, Marcel 440
Dühring, Eugen Karl 643
Dunayevskaya, Raya xx, 27–39, 44, 601, 603
Durkheim, Émile 183

Eakin, Emily 274
Eaton, Daniel 499
Ebert, Friedrich 321
Emmanuel, Arghiri 197
Engels, Friedrich xv, xix, 21, 23, 35, 47, 52,
     58, 59, 61, 62, 63, 72, 74, 75, 81, 119,
     190, 301, 322, 349, 428, 430, 456, 457,
     458, 459, 462, 480–81 passim, 484–5,
     486–8 passim, 499, 500, 544, 547, 568,
     573, 598, 599, 603, 609, 611, 612, 613,

     614–15 passim, 624–5, 626, 627, 628,
     633, 636, 637–8, 639, 640, 641, 643–4,
     646, 647
Epicurus 612–13, 616, 618
Euclid 107
Eugenius IV, Pope 556
Eunapius 530
Evans, Walker 446

Farahmandpur, Ramin 386
Farrington, Benjamin 615, 616
Faux, Jeff 285
Ferkiss, Victor 623
Ferry, Jules 219
Feuerbach, Ludwig von 109, 458, 464, 612
Fielden, John 500
Flax, Jane 576
Foster, John Bellamy xxv, 609–21, 646
Foucault, Michel 441, 448, 455
Frank, André Gunder 185, 187–8 passim, 189,
     190, 193
Freire, Paulo 434
French, Marilyn 574
Freud, Sigmund xxii, 347, 450, 455, 578
Fromm, Erich xxii, 345–7

Gandhi, Mahatma 617
Garbo, Greta 417
Garrison, William Lloyd 542, 543, 545
Garson, Greer 420
Gaskell, Peter 498, 500
Gehry, Frank xxiii
George, Dorothy 503
George, Susan 274
Gerry, Elbridge 245
Gibbon, Edward 529, 535
Gildo 533
Gill, Michael Gates 388
Gimenez, Martha E. xxi, 155–9
Gindin, Sam 394
Glass, Phil 437
Godard, Jean-Luc 437
Goethe, Johann Wolfgang von 486
Goldwin, Robert A. 241
Goodman, Benny 419
Goodman, Matthew 396
Gorbachev, Mikhail 332, 333, 337, 338
Gorham, Nathaniel 244
Gorz, André 111
Gould, Carol 71

Gould, Stephen Jay 614, 616
Gowan, Peter 214, 220, 229
Graham, Laurie 390
Gramsci, Antonio xxii, 295, 304, 305, 349,
    351–2, 401, 425, 616
Greenspan, Alan 135, 142, 148, 149
Gregory the Great, Pope 530
Grey, Lord Albert 561
Guérin, Daniel 28, 29
Guevara, Ernesto 'Che' 623

Habermas, Jürgen 111 *passim*, 427
Haeckel, Ernst 614
Haldane, J.B.S. 615, 616, 619
Hamilton, Alexander 244, 245, 252, 255
Hammond, Barbara 503, 504, 516, 518
Hammond, J.L. 503, 504, 515–16, 518
Hamper, Ben 390
Hardt, Michael 274
Harstick, Hans-Peter 601
Hartsock, Nancy C.M. xxiv–xxv, 565–92
Harvey, David xxi, 213–37
Hayek, F.A. 518
Hegel, Georg Wilhelm Friedrich xx, 3, 28, 33–7
    passim, 41, 44, 52, 53, 78, 92, 93, 94, 95,
    96, 97, 98 *passim*, 101–2, 103–4 *passim*,
    106, 109, 111–12 *passim*, 183, 218, 266,
    349, 351, 578, 580, 612, 613
Heidegger, Martin 443–4, 446
Henderson, Jeffrey 220
Henry the Navigator 555, 556
Heraclitus 46–7
Hilferding, Rudolf 224
Hitler, Adolf 468
Hobbes, Thomas 319
Hobsbawn, Eric 274, 516–17
Hoch, Paul 396
Hodgskin, Thomas 514
Hogben, Lancelot 615, 616, 618, 619
Holmes, Oliver Wendell 251
Honorius, Emperor 533
Horkheimer, Max xxiii, 405–23
Hudis, Peter 601
Hugo, Victor 412
Hume, David 52, 416
Hussein, Saddam 231
Huxley, Thomas 614, 617

James, C.L.R. (writing as J.R. Johnson) xxiv,
    541–7

James, William 41
Jameson, Fredric xxiii, 437–53, 469
Jaurès, Jean 325
Jefferson, Thomas 258
Jephcott, Edmund 405–23
Jhally, Sut xxiii, 395–401
Jintao, Hu 144
Jones, Arnold Hugh Martin 532
Joyce, James 439, 440
Julian, Emperor 530
Justinian, Emperor 530, 533, 535

Kant, Immanuel xx, 20, 33, 97, 98, 103, 111, 112,
    416, 430, 613
Kautsky, Karl xv, 86, 228, 290, 325, 603, 615
Keane, John 354–5
Khan, Kublai 554
Khrushchev, Nikita 333
Kimmelman, Michael 429, 430, 433
Kirchheimer, Otto 375, 376
Korsch, Karl 86, 431, 616
Kovalevsky, Maxim 601
Krader, Lawrence 595, 598, 599, 601, 602
Kraus, Karl 419
Krens, Tom 425, 426, 428, 429, 430, 431, 432–3
Kubrick, Stanley 449

Lacan, Jacques 442
Laclau, Ernesto 188, 189
Landa, Ishay xxiii–xxiv, 455–93
Lange, Ludwig 601, 603
Lankester, Ray 615, 616–17 *passim*, 619
Las Casas, Bartolomé de 562
Le Corbusier 438
Le Play, Frédéric 118–19
Leavis, F.R. 438
Leclerc, Theophile 31
Lederer, Emil 268–70
Lefebvre, Georges 28
Leibniz, Gottfried Wilhelm 53
Lenin, Vladimir Ilyich 213, 218, 219, 220, 224,
    226, 228, 296, 301, 318, 325, 426, 615
Levine, Norman 601
Levins, Richard 616
Levy, Hyman 615, 616, 618, 619
Lewontin, Richard 616
Lichtheim, George 609
Liebig, Justus von 610–11 *passim*, 612, 615
Lincoln, Abraham 316, 546
Livant, Bill xxiii, 395–401

Livingston, William 252
Lombardo, Guy 419
Louis XVIII, King of France 320
Lubbock, John 599, 614
Lucretius 618
Lukács, Georg xix–xx, 3–25, 41, 44, 183, 571,
    615, 616
Lula (Luiz Inácio Lula da Silva) 221
Lundy, Benjamin 542
Luxemburg, Rosa 154, 188, 213, 223, 224, 225,
    229, 325, 326–7, 601, 615
Lyell, Charles 614
Lynd, Staughton 252
Lyotard, Jean-François 452, 594

Machiavelli, Niccolò 533
Madison, James 245, 247–51 *passim*, 257, 258
Magritte, René 446
Mahler, Gustav 439
Maine, Henry Sumner 599
Maistre, Joseph de 270, 475
Majorian, Emperor 531, 532
Malon, Benoît 117
Malthus, Thomas 612
Mandel, Ernest xxii, 315–42, 439, 642
Mannheim, Karl 76–7
Mao, Tse Tung (Mao Zedong) 44, 190, 191–3
    passim, 209, 210, 211
Marat, Jean-Paul 29
Marcuse, Herbert 85, 110
Marmot, Michael 287
Marx Brothers 420
Marx, Eleanor 617
Marx, Karl xv–xxv *passim*, 3, 4, 5, 6, 7, 9–10, 11,
    12, 13, 19, 21, 32, 33, 34, 35, 37, 41–86
    passim, 91–112 *passim*, 117–23 *passim*,
    145, 148, 150, 163, 167, 175, 183, 184,
    188–9, 190, 194, 195, 213, 223–4, 226,
    242, 274, 289–93 *passim*, 296, 298, 299,
    300, 301, 302, 308, 309, 312, 314, 347,
    349, 351, 354, 358, 425, 426, 428, 429,
    430, 431, 440, 455–9 *passim*, 462, 467,
    469–72 *passim*, 476, 480–84 *passim*,
    489, 497, 503, 507, 511, 524, 544, 546,
    547, 565–73 *passim*, 585, 587, 593–604
    passim, 609–19 *passim*, 623–48 *passim*
Mason, George 254
Mattick, Paul 85
Mauss, Marcel 587
McCullough, John Ramsay 78,

McEnroe, John 399
McHenry, James 257
McLaren, Peter 386
McNally, David xx, 133–54
Meikle, Scott 45
Melossi, Dario 376
Mepham, John 85
Mercer, John 250
Merrill, John O. 449
Meyer, Sigfried 105
Michels, Robert 206
Mies, Ludwig van der Rohe 438
Mikhailovsky, N.K. 597
Milanovic, Branco 278
Miliband, Ralph xxii, 84–5, 295–314, 356
Mill, James 94
Mill, John Stuart 99, 231
Mills, C. Wright 308
Money, James William Bayley 602–3
Monroe, Marilyn 447, 450
Montebello, Philippe de 426, 430, 431–2
Moore, Barrington 316
Moore, G.E. 52
Morales, Juan Evo 148
Morgan, Lewis Henry 599, 601, 614
Morris, Gouverneur 244, 250
Morris, William 609, 615
Morrison, Roy 647
Moseley, Fred 136
Mozart, Wolfgang Amadeus 412, 414
Munch, Edvard 447–8, 450, 451

Napoleon 320, 351
Napoleon III 71
Navarro, Vincent xxi–xxii, 273–88
Needham, Joseph 615, 616, 619
Negri, Antonio 274
Neumann, Franz xxi, 263–72
Newman, John Henry (Cardinal) 460
Newton, Isaac 107
Nietzsche, Friedrich xxiii–xxiv, 455–7 *passim*,
    458, 459, 461–3 *passim*, 465, 466–8
    passim, 469, 471–80 *passim*, 482, 483,
    484, 485, 486, 487, 488–9
Nisbet, Robert 184
Nixon, Richard 208, 220, 398
Noah 559
Noske, Gustav 321

Oliver, Francis Wall 617

Ollman, Bertell xv–xxv, 41–89
Oparin, Alexander 615, 616, 619
Owen, Robert 498, 500, 514
Owings, Nathaniel 450

Paine, Thomas 499, 502
Palestrina, Giovanni Pierluigi da 412
Palmerston, Lord 71
Panofsky, Erwin 426
Parenti, Michael xxi, 241–62
Pater, Walter 425, 426, 431, 435
Paul, Saint 531, 552, 559
Peacock, Thomas Love 514
Pepper, David 640
Perlman, Fredy xxi, 161–82
Peter the Great 595
Petty, William 99
Phear, John Budd 599
Phillips, John 618
Phillips, Wendell 542, 543, 545
Philo of Alexandria 531
Picasso, Pablo 414, 440
Pinckney, Charles 244
Pinochet, General Augusto 280
Pitt, William the Younger 505
Place, Francis 501–2
Plato 35, 108, 418, 578
Polanyi, Karl 186, 187, 624
Polo, Marco 554
Popper, Karl 41
Poulantzas, Nicos xxii, 84–5, 295–314, 356
Prester John 555
Proudhon, Pierre-Joseph 101, 609
Pynchon, Thomas 437

Quincy, Josiah 243

Rader, Melvin 53
Raffles, Henry Stamford 602
Rakowski, Mieczyslaw 333, 334
Rancière, Jacques 430–31
Rand, Ayn 435
Rato, Rodrigo 281
Rawls, John 286
Reagan, Ronald 275, 276, 361, 398
Reed, Ishmael 437
Reich, Robert 391
Reich, William 394
Renner, Karl xxii, 289–93
Resis, Albert 597

Rhodes, Cecil 218
Ricardo, David 41, 58, 78, 92, 93, 94, 95, 106
Rich, Adrienne 576, 580, 601
Riley, Terry 437
Rilke, Rainer Maria 446
Rimbaud, Arthur 446
Robespierre, Maximilien 28, 29, 31–2
Robinson, Joan 41
Rogers, Thorold 518
Romanus II, Emperor 534
Rooney, Mickey 417
Roosevelt, Theodore 219
Rose, Steven 616
Rosemont, Franklin 601
Rosnick, David 277
Rostow, Walt Whitman 184
Rousseau, Jean-Jacques 33, 319, 431
Roussel, Raymond 440
Routley, Val 624, 638, 640
Roux, Jean 31
Rubin, Isaak Illich 103
Rubin, Robert 228
Ruddick, Sara 571
Ruge, Arnold 95, 102
Rusche, Georg xxii–xxiii, 375–84

Sachs, Jeffrey 285
Said, Edward 594
Saint-Simon, Henri de 183
Salt, Henry 615
Sartre, Jean-Paul 85
Schambra, William A. 241
Schiller, Friedrich 427, 428, 431
Schmidt, Alfred 615, 640
Schmoller, Gustav von 381
Schönbein, Christian Friedrich 611
Schönberg, Arnold 414, 419
Sedgewick, Edie 450
Sellin, Thorsten 375–6
Senior, Nassau William 92, 99
Sepulveda, Gaines de 562–3
Shandro, Alan 647
Shanin, Teodor 596, 597
Shank, Greg 376
Shao-Chi, Liu 190, 192, 209
Shaw, George Bernard 378
Shays, Daniel 245
Shelley, Percy Bysshe 319, 514
Sherman, Roger 245
Simmel, Georg 15

Skidmore, Louis 449
Smedley, Agnes 379
Smith, Adam 27, 93, 94, 95, 242, 265, 351, 427
Smith, David Norman 599, 601
Smuts, Jan Christian 617–18 *passim*
Socrates 108
Sorel, George 41
Sorge, Friedrich Adolf 117
Spinoza, Baruch 53, 319
Stalin, Joseph 190
Stammler, Rudolf 290
Ste. Croix, G.E.M. de xxiv, 529–37
Stein, Ernst 531
Stein, Gertrude 440
Steuart, James 351
Stevens, Wallace 437
Stilicho 533
Stillman, Peter xx, G. 91–115
Stirner, Max 58
Sue, Eugène 481
Sulzberger, Arthur Ochs 432
Summers, Lawrence 285
Sutherland, Edwin 375
Sweezy, Paul 85, 189, 193, 310
Szücs, Jeno 358, 359–60 *passim*

Tacitus 558–9
Tansley, Arthur 615, 616–19 *passim*
Taylor, Cooke 498, 500
Teeters, Negley King 375
Thatcher, Margaret 361
Thelwall, John 497
Theodoret 530
Theodoric the Ostrogoth 534
Theodosius 530
Theodosius I, Emperor 535
Thompson, Edward P. xxiv, 497–520, 609
Thompson, William 514
Tiberius, Emperor 531
Tichelman, Fritjof 602
Tocqueville, Alexis de 416
Toynbee, Arnold 503, 507, 518
Trotsky, Leon 317, 325, 328, 332, 333, 407
Tubman, Harriet 543, 544
Tucker, Robert 594
Turner, Frederic Jackson 219
Turner, Nat 542

Ure, Andrew 500

Valentinian III, Emperor 533

Van Gogh, Vincent 442–5 *passim*, 446, 450
Varlet, Jean 31
Vavilov, N.I. 615, 616, 619
Veneroso, Frank 225
Venturi, Robert 438
Vernadsky, V.I. 615, 616, 619
Vico, Giovanni Battista 319
Vileisis, Danga 601
Villeneuve-Bargement, Alban de 118
Vincent, J.M. 304
Voltaire, François-Marie Arouet de 319

Wade, Robert 225
Wagner, Richard 408
Walker, David 542
Walker, K.J. 624, 638
Wallerstein, Immanuel xxi, 85, 183–211
Warhol, Andy xxiii, 437, 444–5, 446, 447, 450
Washington, George 244
Webb, Beatrice 503
Webb, Sidney James 503
Weber, Max 15, 183, 299
Weinberger, Caspar 275
Weisbrot, Mark 277
Weiss, Hilde xx, 117–29
Welles, Orson 413
Wellmer, Albrecht 111
Werner, Paul xxiii, 424–35
Weydemeyer, Joseph 108
Whannel, Gary 396
Wilberforce, Samuel (Bishop) 460
Wilberforce, William 545
Wilkes, John 505
Williams, Raymond 442
Williamson, John 276
Wilson, James 253
Wood, Ellen Meiksins xxii, 349–73
Wordsworth, William 319
Wright, Frank Lloyd 438
Wyvill, Christopher 505

Yates, Michael D. xxiii, 385–94
Young, Iris 566

Zanuck, Darryl F. 413
Zapatero, Jose Luis Rodriguez 284
Zasulich, Vera 597, 598
Zeno 551
Zinn, Howard xvii
Zoellick, Robert 221